Theater

of the

Avant-Garde

1950–2000

1. Magritte
2. Aristotle
3.

THEATER OF THE AVANT-GARDE

EDITED BY
ROBERT KNOPF
AND
JULIA LISTENGARTEN

1950–2000

A Critical Anthology

Yale UNIVERSITY PRESS
New Haven & London

Published with assistance from the Julian Park Fund.

Yale University Press books may be purchased in quantity for
educational, business, or promotional use. For information,
please e-mail sales.press@yale.edu (U.S. office) or
sales@yaleup.co.uk (U.K. office).

Designed by James J. Johnson and set in Electra Roman
by Keystone Typesetting, Inc.
Printed in the United States of America.

ISBN: 978-0-300-13423-0 (pbk.)

Library of Congress Control Number: 2010930643

A catalogue record for this book is available from the
British Library.

This paper meets the requirements of ANSI/NISO
Z39.48-1992
(Permanence of Paper).

10 9 8 7 6 5 4 3 2 1

To our children,
who keep us on the cutting edge . . .
whether we like it or not.

Mamet "American Buffalo"

Friedrich Durrenmatt "The Visit"

Slawomir Mrozek "Tango"

contents

viii ❖❖ CONTENTS

acknowledgments

We would like to thank the University at Buffalo's Julian Park Publication Fund and College of Arts and Sciences for supporting the acquisition of rights to reprint the plays, essays, and interviews in this anthology. Our research assistants, Valerie Yawien, Michael Beaman, Meredith Hoppe, Diana Calderazzo, and Brit Cooper Robinson, performed critical background research and helped develop the extensive bibliographies within. Our graduate students contributed to the development of our ideas through seminar discussions and independent studies. The University at Buffalo and the University of Central Florida support our research in ways too numerous to mention. We are thankful to work for two institutions of higher education that value the arts so highly.

Our editors at Yale, William Frucht and Keith Condon, guided us through the quagmire of selecting and acquiring the rights to the best possible work. In selecting works for this anthology, several of the artists and scholars included were particularly helpful in guiding us to the best possible choices, and we would like to thank the following for their generous advice: Anne Bogart, Richard Foreman, Michal Kobialka, Judith Malina, Charles Marowitz, Charles Mee, Carl Weber, and Mac Wellman.

Throughout our careers, Michael Gauger has generously provided his editorial insight, for which he has earned the title of most valuable eyes, ears, and red pen. Our mentor Robert J. was an early inspiration for this work, for which we remain grateful to this day. Robert Knopf would also like to thank Richard and Andrew at Goodrich Coffee in Clarence, New York, for providing him with a satellite office, Wi-Fi, and sensational cappuccino during the later stages of editing. Julia Listengarten is grateful to her friends and colleagues Megan Alrutz and Vandy Wood for their constant support and invaluable insight through her writing and editing.

Our parents instilled our passion for theater and have always encouraged us to embrace challenge. Last, to our spouses, Elizabeth Pascal and Sasha Kogan, for attending and discussing more experimental theater than any marriage vows should ever require . . . a lifetime of thanks.

Introduction

Julia Listengarten and Robert Knopf

Critics and scholars have been debating the origins, definitions, and continued validity of the avant-garde since the early twentieth century.[1] Theoretical arguments have postulated the death of the avant-garde; to counter them, critical claims have cited the ever-present avant-garde tendencies in contemporary theater and art. This volume is based on the premise that although the avant-garde has undergone radical shifts in the second half of the twentieth century, it remains a viable, practical concept in theater, as it [manifests a pervasive impulse to push aesthetic and political boundaries in opposition to authority, whatever form this authority might take.]Through plays, theoretical writings, and interviews with theater artists, this collection contributes to the understanding and evolution of avant-garde concepts and provides a foundation for critics, artists, and students to engage in a constructive dialogue about the theories, aims, and methods of the avant-garde during the second half of the twentieth century and beyond. Set against the shifts in how scholars define and categorize avant-garde theater and performance,[this anthology charts the territory]of the theatrical avant-garde during this period.

The avant-garde has been defined in many ways, and these definitions are viewed most constructively as critical lenses for examining and understanding the avant-garde rather than as prescriptions or proscriptions. Identified with notions of negation, rebellion, attack, destruction, and rupture, the avant-garde takes an adversarial position toward the cultural and political mainstream. In *Theory of the Avant-Garde* (1962), one of the earliest avant-garde studies from the post-1950s period, Renato Poggioli stresses the avant-garde's hostility toward the "academy," "tradition," "authority," and, ultimately, the historical and social order.[2] A decade later, in *Theory of the Avant-Garde* (1974), Peter Bürger articulated the avant-garde's political engagement, arguing that "the avant-garde can be defined as an attack on the status of art in bourgeois society."[3] Premising his argument on a discussion of historical avant-garde movements, Bürger further suggests that the avant-garde aims to explode "the autonomy of art" as a "category of bourgeois society," to connect art with "the praxis of life," or, more specifically, to integrate art into the social fabric of life to effect change.[4]

Recently, some critics have turned their focus from the avant-garde's political activism toward explorations of the avant-garde's unifying aesthetic qualities. In his 1993 book *Avant-Garde Theatre, 1892–1992*,[5] Christopher Innes identifies "radical political posture" as an important characteristic of avant-garde theater but proposes to look beyond the avant-garde's antagonistic principle—"the rejection of social institutions and established artistic conventions"—and explore a "clearly identifiable unity of [the avant-garde's aesthetic] purpose and interest."[6] Innes argues that its interest in primitivism can define the avant-garde most precisely. In search of the aesthetic qualities of the avant-garde, he offers two categories that emerge from its fascination with primitive culture: "the exploration of dream states or the instinctive and subconscious levels of the psyche" and "the quasi-religious focus on myth and magic, which . . . leads to experiments with ritual and the ritualistic patterning of performance."[7]

In addition to tracing the avant-garde's shared aesthetic concerns, critics have focused attention on formalist avant-garde explorations not tied to any specific ideology. Bonnie Marranca notes that the approach to avant-garde artists as social activists is too restrictive, arguing that this criterion might neglect the significance of "the formal qualities of a work."[8] In particular, she refers to the works of avant-garde artists such as John Cage and Allan Kaprow, whose practice does not manifest strong ideological ties.[9] In the critical anthology *Not the Other Avant-Garde* (2006), James Harding and John Rouse distinguish between the occasionally divergent trajectories of "radical politics" and "radical aesthetics" in the development of the avant-garde theater.[10] Similarly, Anna Katharina Schaffner acknowledges different qualities of contemporary avant-garde that vary in scope from "the utopian, subversive, and critical stance" to the formalist experimentation with materials, techniques, and aesthetics.[11] These scholars draw critical attention to "parallel explorations" in the avant-garde theater, allowing for the coexistence of the theater of political engagement (the Living Theatre, Karen Finley, Ping Chong) and formalist, aesthetic experiments (Cage, Kaprow, Robert Wilson) within the boundaries of the avant-garde.

Recent studies have acknowledged that the term "avant-garde" continues to evolve, resisting a single, comprehensive definition in contemporary aesthetics. Terms such as "neo-avant-garde" (Hal Foster), "postmodernist avant-garde" (Matei Calinescu), and "transnational avant-garde" (Harding and Rouse) have entered the current critical discourse. David Graver proposes five avant-garde categories, ranging from politically-minded "partisan art" that aims to "execute a utopian vision" to "innovatively aestheticized commodities" that equate the avant-garde with commercialism.[12] Harding and Rouse promote a "transnational conception of the avant-garde,"[13] signaling a major break from the Eurocentric vision that dominated avant-garde cultural discourse until the latter decades of the twentieth century. Fostering the idea of simultaneity in defining avant-garde, they offer to investigate parallel developments of avant-garde forms of theater across geographic and cultural boundaries, shifting the emphasis from one centered location to multiple, divergent territories.

These expanded notions of avant-garde theater transcend the previously established framework of the European-centered historical avant-garde.[14] Arguably, they have become characteristic of contemporary scholarly debates, in part as resistance to the theory of the avant-garde's death. In the 1960s, "the death of the avant-garde" became a recurrent subject in the field of cultural studies.[15] Critics argued that the crisis and "death" of the avant-garde ultimately resulted from the appropriation and institutionalization of avant-garde art by the same prevailing culture that it was meant to oppose.[16] The death of the avant-garde has since been pronounced by scholars who refer to the avant-garde as a "cultural establishment" (Arnold Aronson)[17] or a "marketing strategy" (Richard Schechner)[18] and posit that experimental theater practice, particularly in the West, has been co-opted by mainstream culture in the age of free-market economy and nonlinear technologies, such as television, video, and the Internet.

This argument has provoked a steady line of critical resistance. Calinescu, for instance, draws attention to the avant-garde's "joyfully self-destructive" nature, which thrives on self-referential attack and negation. He argues further that because of the avant-garde's affinity for crisis and self-destruction, the "'death of the avant-garde' . . . cannot be confined to any one moment in this century . . . simply because the avant-garde has been dying all along, consciously and voluntarily."[19] The avant-garde's ability to survive multiple deaths and repeated suicides has indeed been celebrated as a sign of its resilience and continual desire to reinvent itself.[20] Some critics see the avant-garde as a repeating phenomenon with a nonlinear life, which moves in cycles and is not limited to a single geographic location, as

Harding and Rouse argue in their transnational approach to avant-garde.[21] Moreover, the death of the avant-garde does not rule out non-Western avant-gardes, for its death is premised on the dominance of liberal democracy and a consumer-driven economy, a decidedly Western phenomenon.

Questioning whether "the avant-garde [is] a single phenomenon" or should be "distinguish[ed] among movements within a range of avant-gardes," Paul Mann draws critical attention to the fluidity of the avant-garde and its propensity to "change, mutate, progress, [and] degenerate," which affects its relation to the mainstream.[22] *Theater of the Avant-Garde, 1950–2000* is based on the recognition that the relationships among the avant-garde(s) and the mainstream(s) are never simple or stable. They reveal multiple tensions between negation and appropriation, resistance and acceptance, rebellion and compromise, an observation that illustrates Harding's argument about the "plurality of edges," as opposed to the traditionally accepted singularity of the "cutting edge."[23]

The collection of texts in this volume reflect what might be called a "postmodernist" approach to the avant-garde, in that it transgresses a single, stable definition and exemplifies a range of avant-garde locations and borders vis-à-vis the mainstream. Despite the plurality of avant-garde edges and the multiplicity of its definitions, however, several common characteristics of contemporary avant-garde theater allow us to bring together in one volume experimental theatrical works written or conceived between 1950 and 2000. The time spans great global changes: from the Cold War and the assertion of United States hegemony to the consumer-driven economy and social politics of "late capitalism," from the collapse of colonialism after World War II to the explosion of the global information age and the Internet. Amid these historical moments, the practice of the earlier avant-garde morphed into multiple, fused aesthetics in contemporary experimental theater, exhibiting both a much-heralded rupture from and a continuation of the historical avant-garde.

The clear connections between the avant-gardes include the proliferation of various cross-art forms in the contemporary avant-garde climate, which has roots in earlier avant-garde culture. Futurist and Dadaist attempts to blur the borders separating the arts laid the foundation for an impressive array of inter- and multidisciplinary endeavors. These range from the "chance operations" of Cage and the Fluxus Group, which experimented with the blending of artistic disciplines such as music, dance, visual arts, and theater, to the technologically infused performances of Richard Foreman and the Wooster Group. Terms such as "intermediality" and "interdisciplinarity" pervade the vocabulary of the contemporary avant-garde. In addition, complex negotiations between popular culture and "high" art continued to permeate post-1950 avant-garde theatrical experiments that flirt with kitsch and camp, such as Charles Ludlam's Theatre of the Ridiculous. Artists' attempts to break down the barriers between the stage and the audience in the early avant-garde were more fully realized in the "happenings" of Allan Kaprow and Robert Whitman. Avant-garde theatrical experiments with ritual were further developed during the second half of the century in the works of Jerzy Grotowski, Richard Schechner, and Eugenio Barba. Moreover, post-1950 avant-garde practitioners continued to engage in a dialogue with the theories of the earlier avant-garde, one reflected in Peter Brook's theatrical explorations of Antonin Artaud's Theatre of Cruelty and Wilson's spatio-temporal experiments inspired by Gertrude Stein's landscape theory, to name just two.

By contrast, the virtual disappearance of theater movements[24] in the second half of the twentieth century reflected a radical change from the earlier avant-garde, displaying a deeply rooted suspicion (after World War II) of the ideologically based resistances and organizations that shaped the politics and aesthetics of avant-garde movements in the beginning of the century. The aesthetic of individual companies and ensembles such as the Living Theatre and the Open Theatre supplanted that of theater movements. Avant-garde political affiliations, such as the Italian Futurists' alliances with fascism or the Surrealists' fascination with communism, gave way to nonlinear, nonchronological avant-garde models involving international cross-influences and redefining the traditional avant-garde mode of rebellion in a consumer-driven economy. Whereas a number of postwar theater collectives and performance artists demonstrated their social activism through performance practices, the politics of resistance and noncompliance in general replaced the politics of shock and transgression that often defined early avant-garde movements. Operating within the postmodern mode of complacency,[25] avant-garde theater artists in the period covered in this volume rejected the contentment and affirmation pervasive in postmodern culture, but for the most part, they stayed away from open political engagement.

The relationship between postmodernism and the post-1950 avant-garde has become another point of critical contention in contemporary theory. Calinsecu suggests that postmodernism calls into question the "purely destructive aspect of the old avant-garde."[26] He posits further that by interrogating the value of the new and the absolute and thus questioning the price of the avant-garde's destructive strategy, postmodernism "opt[ed] for a logic of renovation rather than radical innovation."[27] We acknowledge that radical rupture, transgression, and negation, which characterized the destructive strategy of the early avant-garde, may not occur easily in the postmodern climate of renovation, relativism, and complacency. This volume, however, grows out of a concept of the avant-garde that rejects postmodernism's lack of resistance and critique but embraces its predilection for renovation and relativism.

On a more functional level, the post-1950 avant-garde, operating under the postmodern assumptions of simultaneity and fluidity of forms, structures, and ideas rather than their centrality and stability, shifted from the predominance of the playwright as primary creator to the increased role of other theater artists in creating theater practice, as seen in the work of Wilson, Brook, and Tadeusz Kantor, as well as the collaborative projects of groups such as the Open Theatre and the Wooster Group. But avant-garde artists in the first half of the twentieth century had already called into question the supremacy of text over performance and the definition of "authorship." Visual artists such as Wassily Kandinsky and Umberto Boccioni, for whom text was only one layer of their performance practice, wrote many early avant-garde texts. Artaud, who rebelled against the power of the spoken word in theater and proclaimed the necessity of creating a total theatrical experience in which sensory violence replaces rationality of thought expressed through spoken language, galvanized the redefinition of the playwright's role and position. Still, whereas anti-textual claims in early avant-garde discourse drew attention to the inherent tensions between text and performance, the latter avant-garde highlighted problematic but never simply antagonistic relationships between the textual and the performative, shifting the focus from the author to the theater-maker and foregrounding the evolving nature of text.

Acknowledgment of the evolving nature of text guided the selection of works for this anthology. In arguing that the concepts of text have changed to allow for incompleteness in a text's form and fluidity in its interpretation, we invoke Gilles Deleuze's argument about an incompleteness of the writing process:

> To write is certainly not to impose a form (of expression) on the matter of lived experience. Literature rather moves in the direction of the ill-formed and of the incomplete. . . . Writing is a question of becoming, always incomplete, always in the midst of being formed, and goes beyond the matter of any livable or lived experience.[28]

This shift from a more traditional view of text as a fixed product to an incomplete form of expression marks our choice of works that engage in the dynamic and complex relationship with the spoken word. Samuel Beckett's essentially nonverbal *Act Without Words I*, Kantor's constructed script *The Dead Class*, and *Vienna: Lusthaus*, a collaborative dance-theater piece conceived and choreographed by Martha Clarke and written by Charles Mee, manifest three diverse approaches to text in the post-1950 avant-garde theater. *Act Without Words I* is fundamentally anti-textual—a play in which dialogue is replaced by a description of the precise sequence of physical movements—whereas *The Dead Class* and *Vienna: Lusthaus* are rooted in performance approaches and emerged as performance-driven theatrical pieces. The existing texts in these two instances vary in character, but both reflect actual performances rather than function as blueprints for future ones. Kantor's text is a "partytura" in which a collage of concepts, memories, and observations of the creative process serves as a reflection of the production journey. The collaboration between Clarke and Mee resulted in a dance-theater form in which Mee's spoken text, incomplete and disconnected, contributes a free, associative counterpoint to Clarke's choreography, a spoken complement to the imagery visualized onstage through the dancers' bodies.

This volume invites the reader to ponder the challenges that text might confront in contemporary performance-based theater and to address the negotiations between performance and text required by each medium.[29] Our desire to include written plays from post-1950 avant-garde theater does not reflect an intention to reestablish the superiority of written texts over performances or to reassert the supremacy of playwrights over other theater artists. On the contrary, our acknowledgment of the vexed relationship between text and performance markedly complicated our decision to anthologize works of this period, most of which are performance-driven. Erika Fischer-Lichte observes insightfully that in the contemporary theater, "No longer does the text steer, control, and legitimize performance. Rather, the text becomes one material among other materials—like the body of the actor, sounds, objects, etc."[30] The text, however, often remains a primary artifact of theater, if not the perfect record of performance, commemorating or chronicling the theatrical event after the fact.

In his recent study of contemporary experimental theater, *Postdramatic Theater* (2006), Hans-Thies Lehmann discusses the dissolution of the hierarchy of the text and the change in our perception of coherence of theatrical means that result from this instability and/or fluidity of power among various media, such as text and performance in this case, in a creative process.[31] Lehmann writes that this dissolution of the hierarchy had a profound impact on the concepts of theatrical unity and aesthetic wholeness, which shifted drastically toward fragmentation and discontinuity in contemporary theater. Selecting works for this anthology, we became increasingly aware of the problematic nature of anthologizing nontraditional texts such as *The Dead Class* and *Vienna: Lusthaus*, which offer a different concept of theatrical unity based on a nonhierarchical approach to the aesthetic elements of a theatrical experience.

As the contemporary avant-garde has continued to redefine itself in relation to early avant-garde movements, on one hand, and postmodern culture, on the other, it has developed a range of cultural and aesthetic markers. The concept of redefinition has become a through-line of avant-garde explorations of identity and memory. Avant-garde feminist performance, for instance, as well as the more aesthetically contentious avant-garde camp, has focused on redefining gender and sexuality and reinterpreting the notion of body. The relationship between memory, collective or individual, and multiple states of consciousness has been the focus of aesthetically diverse artists such as Heiner Müller and Clarke. The concept of collective memory has been explored in relation to multiculturalism and globalism, and the redrawing of borders—geographical, temporal, and cultural—has resulted in various avant-garde theater practices that captured the feelings of destabilization, disruption, and contestation of global proportions. The works of more recent artists such as Reza Abdoh, Robert Wilson, Robert LePage, and Ariane Mnouchkine have contemplated the catastrophes of civil wars and ethnic cleansing that resulted in genocide and the devastation of land. In the post-apocalyptic landscapes constructed by Müller, José Rivera, and Caryl Churchill, the relationship between man and nature is violently disrupted; barren, devastated landscapes capture the pervasive sense of loss and paralyzing feelings of terror.

The post-1950 avant-garde theater, influenced by scientific discoveries and philosophical discourses, has also created a theatrical language that foregrounds contemporary theater's intense explorations of parallel realities —"multiverses"—and multiple states of consciousness. Disruption of the temporal and spatial relation has become a significant marker of the contemporary avant-garde practice, in which multilayered compositions capture the pervasive sense of life's indeterminacy and fragmentation. Examining recent avant-garde experiments that disrupt the linear, sequential mode of perceiving reality, Aronson in *American Avant-Garde Theatre* (2000) argues that the theater of Foreman and Wilson presents "a post-Einsteinian way of apprehending the universe, a universe of uncertainty principles and chaos theory."[32]

Avant-garde theater destabilizes the modes of perception and communication, challenging the power and authority of language (Peter Handke), deconstructing the creative process (Różewicz), and offering various ways of expressing ideas, feelings, and senses onstage through the forms of cinematic theater, scenic poem, and intermedial performance (LePage, Wilson, Wooster Group). Indeed, the post-1950 avant-garde both embraces the overwhelming presence of visual stimuli in contemporary culture and fosters a critical inquiry into a "simultaneous and multi-perspectival form of perceiving" that replaces "the linear-successive."[33] In this theater that Hans-Thies Lehmann calls "postdramatic," visual dramaturgy is rooted in associative, poetic, and sensory experiences. Lehmann argues that in this form of theater, synthesis is no longer an aesthetic requirement: "Enclosed within postdramatic theater is . . . the demand for an [open and fragmenting perception] in place of a unifying and closed perception."[34] In different ways, the works in this anthology, such as Müller's *Explosion of a Memory/Description of a Picture* and Abdoh's *The Hip-Hop Waltz of Eurydice*, disorient the audience's perception by disrupting the sense of linearity and wholeness and making synthesis completely unachievable.

This anthology approaches the avant-garde from micro to macro—from particular plays and source materials to a larger understanding of what avant-garde theater has become. The volume, however, does not cover performances of plays that would be considered avant-garde only when viewed; a play must be avant-garde on the page and the stage to be included. This guideline led us to exclude plays that were the raw material for avant-garde productions by Grotowski, Brook, Wilson, and others, in which the "text" alone falls short of capturing the production's essential avant-garde qualities. Instead, we have included essays and interviews with some of these artists to facilitate an understanding of how theater artists turn more traditional drama into avant-garde performance. Also, we have included a bibliography of additional primary source articles, interviews, and video documentation of performances by theater ensembles and theater artists whose work is more accurately represented in these forms than in play texts.[35]

We have worked from a broader conception of the avant-garde to embrace performance artists, represented by Karen Finley, as well as the influential "happenings" of the 1960s, represented by Whitman's *The Night Time Sky*. We have also included a section on "Camp," an important but rarely discussed category of plays and performances that encompasses a shared sensibility and ideological strategy toward gender and sexuality. In our attempt to highlight cross-cultural avant-garde influences, models, and prototypes, we have looked beyond Europe and North America to include two Argentinean playwrights, as well as Algerian-born Hélène Cixous. We recognize the significance of global influences and acknowledge the shift in the discourse to the global that Harding and Rouse have raised, but the limitations of a single volume make it impossible to cover all aspects of the avant-garde and cover the globe. A future anthology of non-Western avant-garde plays and documents, we trust, will supplement ours in this way.

Theater of the Avant-Garde, 1950–2000 significantly differs from the earlier volume, *Theater of the Avant-Garde, 1890–1950*, in another regard: the present volume no longer arranges "theater movements" chronologically. Instead, the categories in the table of contents, "Language and Silence," "The Ritualistic," "Disruption," "Camp," "Landscape," and "Terror," address questions—formal as well as thematic—at the forefront of the post-1950 theatrical avant-garde, ones that break free of chronology and geographic locations. These categories also help identify various paradigms of the contemporary avant-garde and highlight the problematic relationship that the theatrical avant-garde evinced with the cultural mainstream(s) in the second half of the twentieth century.

The first section, "Language and Silence," opens the discussion about the role and place of language (and silence) in avant-garde theater in the second half of the twentieth century. This section juxtaposes Beckett's experiments with silence in *Act Without Words I* with Mac Wellman's explorations with found dialect speech in *Terminal Hip*. Beckett, one of the masters of minimalist speech, here embraces silence, substituting gesture for speech in a performance that contains only one word, "water," printed on a placard and lowered from above. Wellman limits his palette to dialogue (no stage directions, not even a pause, appear in the text). Yet the words alone—American dialect speech pieced together in rhythmic but illogical patterns—fail to communicate much clear meaning beyond the raw emotions that their sounds evoke and the ambiguity that the juxtaposition of odd phrases creates. The third piece, Foreman's *Rhoda in Potatoland*, sets physical action and language against each other, creating a jarring juxtaposition of sight and sound on stage. The visual elements on his stage further disrupt any perceivable line of action by sacrificing the sense of a single place or time in favor of visual juxtaposition and conflict.

The next section, "The Ritualistic," focuses on theatrical explorations of ritualistic elements and examines the ways in which avant-garde theater artists draw upon these elements to challenge the boundaries of theatrical reality and experience as well as performer/observer relationships. This section traces the influence of Jean Genet's ideas about ritualistic theater through the inclusion of Jean-Paul Sartre's analysis of Genet's *The Maids*, a pre-1950 text, and then offers the theatrical explorations of ritualistic principles exemplified in the performances of the Living Theatre (thus the inclusion of *The Brig*) and Grotowski's Lab Theatre (which Grotowski discussed in the interview with Barba excerpted here). By combining this overview of more standard ritualistic works with two more recent plays by Suzan-Lori Parks and Naomi Iizuka—the latter a less conventional choice that helps expand the anthology beyond the "usual suspects"—we map how the ritualistic concept in theater has moved across generic, temporal, and geographic boundaries.

Beginning in the 1950s with the Living Theatre, there has been a particular fascination with ritual, stemming from the influence of Artaud's *The Theatre and Its Double* and a growing attention among avant-garde theater artists to the communal and universal aspects of performance. Many of the theater artists drawn to the use of ritualistic elements in performance—Brook, Barba, Jean-Louis Barrault, and Fernando Arrabal, to name a few—sought to tap into notions of the collective consciousness of an audience and attempted to discover a spiritual unity within the ensemble, as well as among performers and spectators.[36] Grotowski's use of environmental staging, for instance, and the Living Theatre's and Performance Group's use of audience participation were central means to this artistic goal. Yet as some scholars have noted, ritualistic theater never becomes true ritual, as it lacks the religious purpose of ritual itself.

The avant-garde's incorporation of ritualistic elements within secular works raises questions about the relationships between form and meaning, such as what happens to content when ritualistic elements are employed primarily as formal devices. The impulse to incorporate the ritualistic into theater can be seen as a drive toward performance-centered theater. The ritualistic can be suggested on the page, but it finds its complete expression only on the stage, so the application of the ritualistic in the avant-garde shares common ground with its interest in the dominance of performance over text. Thus, when Kenneth Brown calls for future productions of *The Brig* to create their own ritualistic physical actions, he recognizes and encourages the creation and ownership of the physical action by each production.

There are, however, elements of the ritualistic that embrace aims more specific than simply the primacy of live performance. The ritualistic, for instance, employs magical thinking as a way to counter feelings of helplessness and reconnect to nature and natural order, reviving our sense that ritualistic actions may be able to sway events otherwise beyond human control. In this way, the ritualistic might be deployed as a counter-action to the culture of the mainstream, an attempt to return to primal roots as an antidote to the "unnatural," imposed order of capitalist society. The plays in this section apply ritualized action to a wide range of issues that have pervaded mainstream discourse and everyday activities. In *Body Beautiful*, Naomi Iizuka shows women using rituals concerning their bodies and eating habits to attempt to wrest control over their self-images from the media. In *The Death of the Last Black Man in the Whole Entire World*, Suzan-Lori Parks uses the "rep and rev" (repetition and revision) of jazz music to ritualize a theatrical event that is portrayed as a funeral (a ritual in itself), with each repetition revising a history so that meaning accumulates vertically, again eschewing the cause-and-effect narrative of traditional drama. In doing so, Parks uses the musicality of dialect speech in a way akin to Wellman, yet she shares with Foreman the structural principles of a nonlinear, vertical narrative, in which actions and events accumulate one on top of the other, as opposed to a traditional horizontal cause-and-effect chain of events. Thus, we see an overlap among these sections, even as the categories illustrate the central concerns of each section.

The notion of confronting the audience by pushing the boundaries of what is deemed morally, politically, and aesthetically appropriate in society, and in theater in particular, has a long history in avant-garde practice. The next category, "Disruption," therefore plays an essential part in attempts to investigate the post-1950 theatrical climate, as the avant-garde movement engaged in vital issues concerning the aesthetic boundaries of drama and performance, responded to Vietnam and Cold War controversies, and took an active position in gender and identity politics. The combination of Handke's *Offending the Audience* with texts by Różewicz and Finley, in addition to an interview with Peter Schumann on the politics of his Bread and Puppet Theatre, captures a wide range of disruptive and confrontational theatrical avant-garde.

Many creators of early avant-garde theater aimed to disrupt the audience's expectations and experience of theatrical performances, beginning with Alfred Jarry's production of *King Ubu* (*Ubu Roi*)[37] in 1896 in Paris, which sparked riotous audience behavior from the first word spoken on stage. The Futurists and Dadaists confronted their audiences even more directly, seeking a visceral audience reaction to their works. Bertolt Brecht, whom some consider to be avant-garde, attempted to defamiliarize stage action through the use of his "Verfremdungseffekt" (abbreviated to the

"V-effect," from the German word that means "to make strange"), creating a more subtle type of disruption intended to force audience members to consider the ramifications of stage action. In another realm, Artaud, in his written theories in *Theatre and Its Double* (originally published in 1938 and republished to great acclaim in 1944), if not his theater practice, called for a Theatre of Cruelty that would break the audience's complacency with direct and visceral sensory experience. The influence of Artaud's theories on the later avant-garde can be seen in a call for direct audience confrontation, as well as his preference for live performance over text and his interest in theater's returning to its primitive and spiritual roots.

The writers, directors, and performers in this section—Handke, Różewicz, Kazimierz Braun, Finley, and Schumann—challenged their audiences' established notions of theatrical interaction. Handke's *Offending the Audience* calls for direct audience confrontation with a fairly blatant political agenda reminiscent of Brecht, yet his linguistic game-playing harkens back to Dada, Ionesco, and Cage. Różewicz's *Birth Rate* and director Braun's "envisioning" of the performance document and then represent the writer's aborted attempt to write the play. From the detritus of this effort, the playwright offers director and performers the chance to complete what he has abandoned. Thus, Różewicz acknowledges that the nature of text and performance has changed. The playwright himself has disrupted the relationship between writer and text and offered a new kind of relationship and collaborative model among writer, director, and ensemble. Różewicz the writer allowed Braun the director not only to interpret and help revise the text, but also to structure and create sections of the performance. In this way, Różewicz and Braun document the disruption of traditional methods of creating theater, which came about virtually simultaneously on U.S. and Polish experimental stages.

Finley's performances disrupt the aesthetic and political boundaries of "good taste" with her graphic stories of homophobia, incest, and the humiliation and exploitation of women. One of four performance artists from whom the National Endowment for the Arts revoked funding (the "NEA four"), she harnesses the power of offensive speech and images, including rampant profanity and graphic stories of sexual abuse, to disrupt the dominant cultural images of the place of women in society, both in her narrative and through her own presence as a performer. Finley's body becomes a self-conscious and visible part of the art product. Her nude body covered in chocolate to simulate human excrement (a "re-creation" of a scene from an actual news story), Finley embodies the disgrace of everywoman, shattering standards of appropriate behavior and acceptable imagery in mainstream culture. In delivering this "shock therapy" to her audiences, she begins to fulfill Artaud's call for sensory overload, layering her more blatant feminist commentary over imagery that is cruel without being physically assaultive to the audience.

The section on "Camp" captures a type of anarchic humor embodied in the avant-garde, one that plays with the inversion of gender roles and parodies social structures and sexual identity. We have included the works of the American Charles Ludlam and the Argentinean Raul Damonte (also known as Copi) together with essays by Susan Sontag and Ludlum that attempt to define the term "camp." Scholars and critics see camp on a continuum from an aesthetic category to an ideological strategy, depending upon the writer's intentions and the work's place within or opposed to mainstream culture. Ludlam and Copi received considerable mainstream recognition in their lifetimes, with Ludlam garnering awards and winning commercial acceptance in his last decade. For some critics and scholars, such mainstream acceptance signals the death of these artists' avant-garde standing. Thus, one can suggest that camp occupies a place on the "rough edges" (Harding) of the avant-garde; it is indeed a significant element in the later avant-garde, but it can also be located in the cultural mainstream.

The term "camp" can be traced to sixteenth century England, although Oscar Wilde popularized it as a part of the evolution of queer identity and effeminate dandyism at the turn of the twentieth century. As a style, it involves the playful inversion of roles, approached with a sense of "artifice and exaggeration" (Sontag). As an avant-garde strategy, it can be seen as a form of anarchic parody, with roots going back to Jarry, even if his plays were less concerned with homosexuality than the plays in this section. As a form of parody, camp often uses appropriated source material, creating a pastiche of recognizable characters and events that can be undercut or inverted in performance through exaggerated style and frequent cross-gender play. In its most aggressive forms, gender identity is fluid and volatile, as in the rapidly shifting actions of the main character in Copi's *Loretta Strong*. In this way, Ludlam and Copi pave the way for the work of radical performance artists, including Holly Hughes, Lois Weaver, and Kate Bornstein, whose gender play would so upset the mainstream in the 1980s.

The works in the next section, "Landscape," share Gertrude Stein's idea of landscape drama as a foundation, particularly her conception of a "continuous present." As Stein defines these terms, landscape drama lives in a continuous present when events from different temporal zones exist simultaneously on the same stage or space. We include Whitman's description of *The Night Time Sky*, which he refers to as a theater piece, to highlight the significance of Happenings as a type of image-driven theatrical landscape. Whitman's work, contemporary to Kaprow's Happenings and Fluxus events, was influenced by his studies with Cage at the New School for Social Research. All these works were designed to disappear the moment after their creation, thus resisting the commoditization of art. They are the most temporary and ephemeral of art objects, so by their very nature they are resistant to mainstream culture and politics, which thrive on the value of art as a product in a market-driven capitalist economy.

In the other works in this section—Hélène Cixous's *Portrait of Dora*, Tadeusz Kantor's *The Dead Class*, Heiner Müller's *Explosion of a Memory*, and Martha Clarke and Charles Mee's *Vienna: Lusthaus*—we see an effort to capture the fluidity of the human mind's process of association. At the turn of the nineteenth century, Symbolist playwrights began to explore ways in which theater could express internal psychic landscapes; beginning in the 1930s, Surrealists explored the melding of dreams and reality. Many of the works in "Landscape" extend this concept by rejecting different aspects of traditional dramaturgy, playing with space and time and alternating our sense of inner (mind) and outer (body) space to shatter any sense of linear or logical progression. In the works of Kantor and Clarke and Mee in particular, the artists embrace multiple models of collaboration (playwright-ensemble, choreographer-writer-ensemble), using the group dynamic to create the shifting patterns of a single thought process.

In *Dora*, Cixous focuses primarily on time as the defining element of human conscious and unconscious thought. Though the play is more clearly articulated on the page than many avant-garde plays of this period—perhaps because Cixous is, first and foremost, a writer, and at the time had yet to collaborate with Mnouchkine—her use of simultaneity of time distinguishes *Dora* from more traditional efforts to explore human psychology. Simultaneity has been a prominent tool in the avant-garde arsenal since the Italian Futurists began to play with simultaneous action in their *sintesi*; Wilson uses this technique regularly as well. Through the use of voiceovers, which come across as thoughts rather than visions, Cixous creates simultaneity in the mind of her audience members.

Drawing his inspiration from Dada collages as well as Cage's and Kaprow's Happenings, Kantor creates what he calls "partyturas": collections of overlapping and fragmentary texts and concepts, similar to the construction of Różewicz's *Birth Rate*. Unlike Różewicz, however, Kantor retains control of his productions both in rehearsal and performance, taking on the role of director and performer by often placing himself in the middle of the performance. Through this technique, Kantor literally inhabits the landscape of the mind, an ever-present reminder to the audience members of their invited presence in his mind, dreams, and associations.

In *Explosion of a Memory*, Müller's theatrical world attempts to break down all boundaries between internal and external space, or between the human mind and the physical world. Müller and Wilson collaborated on the first production, which was produced as a prologue to Wilson's 1986 production of Euripides' *Alcestis* at the American Repertory Theater. Scholars frequently regard the two artists as diametrically opposed, outside their collaborative works: Wilson, a visual stage artist, preoccupied with vision and time at the expense of politics; Müller, an East German who came of age during World War II, obsessed with politics and the socialism of his day. As critic Laurence Shyer suggests, despite their profound cultural differences, Wilson discovered in Müller a "writer who seemed to share the same visual impulse, someone whose language translates not into rhetoric or narrative but pictures of the mind."[38] Thus, two minds—one more visual, one more verbal—came together on several occasions to create visual dramaturgy that combines text and vision toward a dissociative theatrical event.

Mee's text for *Vienna: Lusthaus* returns to Sigmund Freud as a subject for the speculation and exploration of dream states. Though Freud's theories had been the subject of strenuous criticism among psychologists in the twentieth century, his status as the "father" of modern psychology continued to serve as a lightning rod for theatrical consideration. In this play, the creative process started with Clarke's work. Mee, inspired by the images of Vienna as though constructed by a subconscious mind, created the text to support Clarke's vision, which already involved simultaneous physical actions, evoking a sense of a cinematic "dissolve" between and among dreams. Thus, although the product shares much in common with the other works in this section, the creative process was inverted, with the vision and movement of dream states leading to the creation of a text. Ultimately, the audience members must resolve the tensions among simultaneous times, images, and places, bridging the temporal and spatial gaps for themselves, each in his or her own way.

The anthology concludes with the category "Terror," which corresponds dramatically with states of mind and politics today. This category spans the gap between early theatrical experiments with acts of "terror" such as Theatre of Cruelty, originally proposed before 1950 by Artaud and represented by

Charles Marowitz's essay in this volume, and dramatic works of internationally and stylistically diverse writers such as Churchill, Griselda Gambaro, and Reza Abdoh, who explore the consequences of violence and terror on society, psychology, and language. Although all these works were written before the attacks of September 11, 2001, it is difficult, if not impossible, to read them without reference to a new, closer-to-home understanding of terror in the twenty-first century. Indeed, New York Theatre Workshop produced the U.S. premiere of Churchill's *Far Away* on the first anniversary of 9/11.

Cp "The Brig"

As a group, the three plays in this section are the most deliberately political in the anthology, confronting gender and sexuality, political torture, and the complicity of silence in reaction to warfare of all kinds. Writing from a clear sense of his complex identity as a gay, HIV-positive Iranian theater artist, Abdoh deploys graphic images and extensive use of multimedia images in *The Hip-Hop Waltz of Eurydice* to batter his audience in an attack reminiscent of Artaud's most passionate calls for a Theatre of Cruelty. For Abdoh, however, his times were more than the crisis of the spirit that Artaud perceived; they were a crisis of social and political identity, experienced on the most personal level imaginable. In *Stripped*, Gambaro dramatizes her reaction to events in Argentina, when the government publicly staged acts of terrorism to threaten and suppress political resistance. As a woman is ritualistically stripped of every shred of dignity and clothing, the original Argentinean audiences experienced a theatrically stylized but no less terrifying recreation of their silent collusion in terror. In *Far Away*, Churchill imagines a child's journey from nightmare to reality, in which the child's worst fears about the world are surmounted by a reality in which nations, animals, and people devour each other in an all-encompassing war. Churchill theatricalizes silence on stage, through the aunt's request that the child not speak of the torture she has witnessed, whereas Gambaro places this responsibility implicitly with the audience. In Gambaro's hands, torture becomes stylized and absurd; Churchill extends the concept of terror to an all-embracing world war. Yet both works play with the audience's proximity to terror, challenging us to question our lack of resistance to events we might prefer to forget. If survival requires acknowledging terror, all three plays confront audiences with it viscerally, sharing in Artaud's call to arms, with much greater political and social consciousness.

The occasional overlap of categories in this volume is indicative of the post-1950, nonlinear, pluralistic avant-garde climate. A "breakdown of generic distinction"[39] is yet another marker of this pluralistic avant-garde climate, as it becomes increasingly difficult to distinguish between a theoretical essay and a written piece for theater. Müller's *Letter to Robert Wilson*, which Wilson himself included, with other texts, in his theater production *Death, Destruction & Detroit 2*, exemplifies this tendency. These categories, however, allow us to discuss a variety of avant-garde models and practices, serving as an additional set of critical lenses that may be applied, along with the approaches offered in the essays and interviews, toward a comprehensive study of the avant-garde.

As the avant-garde reinvented itself in the latter half of the twentieth century, one type of critical apparatus became obsolete: viewing avant-garde theater works in the context of larger theatrical movements. This development jars our understanding of the evolution of the avant-garde from a more traditional, historical perspective. We acknowledge the nonlinear tendency of the more recent avant-garde, which emerged in conjunction with critical investigations of the complex and dynamic relationship between the avant-garde and the mainstream. These queries complicated the clear-cut oppositional political stance of the avant-garde that earlier theorists advanced, calling into question the consistency of the avant-garde's resistance to or distance from mainstream culture and politics. As early as 1956, commenting on the bourgeoisie's recognition and appropriation of avant-garde art, Roland Barthes suggested that mainstream culture has always permitted and indeed financially supported the avant-garde. He wrote that the "protest" led by the avant-garde "has never been anything but a proxy: the bourgeoisie delegated some of its creators to tasks of formal subversion, though without actually disinheriting them; is it not the bourgeoisie, after all, which dispenses to avant-garde art the parsimonious support of its public, i.e., of its money?"[40]

To amend Mark Twain's famous adage, "Reports of the avant-garde's demise have been greatly exaggerated." Declarations of its death are founded on the presumption of an idyllic moment in history—the time of the "historic avant-garde"—in which socially, politically, and aesthetically subversive theater stood diametrically opposed to mainstream culture. Such an era might have never truly existed. Instead, if we see the avant-garde as an "allowed fool," the embodiment of a subversive impulse that mainstream culture permits to exist on its edges, we can gauge the vitality of the avant-garde as a question of location rather than existence. The avant-garde never dies; it merely shifts its place from the extreme edge of the mainstream to a spectrum of slightly more "respectable" places within the mainstream. This view explains how the "co-opting" of avant-garde practices into the mainstream sometimes occurs at a faster pace, but it respects the experimental findings of the avant-garde regardless of the location of these experiments on the edges of mainstream culture.

Ultimately, like the repetitive "deaths" of the last black man in Parks's play, the deaths of the avant-garde represent the constant call for the reinvention and reinvigoration of the theater through the avant-garde, a challenge for theater artists to create anew. When critics declare the death of the avant-garde, they also call for its rebirth, whether explicitly or inadvertently. This is the true mission of this anthology: to study the historic avant-garde and inspire the present and future avant-gardes.

NOTES TO INTRODUCTION

1. One of the first scholarly works examining the concept of the avant-garde was Ortega y Gasset's *Dehumanization of Art*, published in 1925.

2. Renato Poggioli, *The Theory of the Avant-Garde*, 1962, trans. Gerald Fitzgerald (Cambridge, Mass.: Belknap Press of Harvard University Press, 2003), 25–26.

3. Peter Bürger, *Theory of the Avant-Garde*, 1974, trans. Michael Shaw (Minneapolis: University of Minnesota Press, 1984), 49. Bürger in this context specifically refers to the European avant-garde movements.

4. Ibid., 49. Rejecting the autonomous function of art in society, avant-garde artists "view [art's] dissociation from the praxis of life as the dominant characteristic of art in bourgeois society," Bürger argues (49).

5. The earlier edition of this book, *Holy Theatre*, was published in 1981.

6. Christopher Innes, *Avant-Garde Theatre, 1892–1992* (New York: Routledge, 1993), 1.

7. Ibid., 3.

8. Bonnie Marranca, *Performance Histories* (New York: PAJ, 2008), 26.

9. See Marranca's *Performance Histories*, in which she comments on the distrust of politics in the second half of the twentieth century by certain American avant-garde artists, such as John Cage and Allan Kaprow, who "were against the obvious social and ideological statement" and whose works did not "carry strong political content or post-war angst" (25).

10. James Harding and John Rouse, eds., *Not the Other Avant-Garde: The Transnational Foundations of Avant-Garde Performance* (Ann Arbor: University of Michigan Press, 2006), 9–10.

11. Anna Katharina Schaffner, "Inheriting the Avant-Garde: On the Reconciliation of Tradition and Invention in Concrete Poetry," in *Neo-Avant-Garde*, ed. David Hopkins (Amsterdam: Rodopi B.V., 2006), 111.

12. David Graver, *The Aesthetics of Disturbance: Anti-Art in Avant-Garde Drama* (Ann Arbor: University of Michigan Press, 1995), 12–14. The other categories that Graver offers include "secessionist art," or art for art's sake; "engaged art" that combines an "innovative aesthetic program" with a specific "socio-political interest"; and anti-art.

13. Harding and Rouse, *Not the Other Avant-Garde*, 2.

14. The historical avant-garde theater became the focus of *Theater of the Avant-Garde, 1890–1950* (New Haven: Yale University Press, 2001).

15. Matei Calinescu, *Five Faces of Modernity: Modernism, Avant-garde, Decadence, Kitsch, Postmodernism* (1977; rev. ed. London: Duke University Press, 1987), 120–21.

16. In *Art in Progress: A Philosophical Response to the End of the Avant-Garde*, trans. Sherry Marx (Amsterdam: Amsterdam UP, 2003), Maarten Doorman echoes Bürger's concerns about the institutionalization of the avant-garde, positioning the avant-garde as "the most important institutional movement and the most prominent ideology" and arguing that "the social success of the avant-garde is also its greatest failure" (56).

17. In *American Avant-Garde Theatre: A History* (New York: Routledge, 2000), Aronson addresses complex tensions between the avant-garde's inherent propensity for a utopian vision and

economic and social pressures of "late capitalism." He writes that "the new is no longer associated with an ever-improving future for society, just with an ever-improving product to be purchased" (207).

18. Schechner, in *Contours of the Theatrical Avant-Garde: Performance and Textuality*, ed. James Harding (Ann Arbor: University of Michigan Press, 2000), 202–14.

19. Calinescu, *Five Faces of Modernity*, 124.

20. See James Harding's introduction to *Contours of the Avant-Garde*, in which he acknowledges the complexities surrounding the concept of the avant-garde and comments on the avant-garde's "enduring resilience" (5).

21. Martin Puchner in *Poetry of the Revolution: Marx, Manifestos, and the Avant-Gardes* (Princeton: Princeton University Press, 2006) compares the avant-garde's "exclusively historical perspective" of Fredric Jameson and Perry Anderson to Michael Kirby's concept of the avant-garde as a recurrent phenomenon (361).

22. See Paul Mann, *The Theory-Death of the Avant-Garde* (Bloomington: Indiana University Press, 1991) in which he argues "the avant-garde tends to define itself in part by resisting the definitions assigned to it by mainstream discourse" (9). Mann also proposes the connection between the theoretical discourse about the death of the avant-garde and the avant-garde's propensity for recuperation: "Death is necessary so that everything can be repeated and the obituary is a way to deny that death ever occurred" (141).

23. See Harding's introduction to *Not the Other Avant-Garde*, 24. Harding uses this concept of the "plurality of edges" to present the avant-garde as a "deterritorialized phenomenon" rooted in the notions of "simultaneity and transnationalism" (27).

24. It is noteworthy that the writing of manifestos did not stop with the end of the historical avant-garde. Puchner offers an acute analysis of various artistic manifestos, including the ones written in the latter part of the twentieth century. He points to "the large number and astonishing variety of manifestos produced in the sixties" (*Poetry of the Revolution: Marx, Manifestos, and the Avant-Gardes*, 5) and carries out his discussion of the art of manifesto to the end of the century. Among the more recent examples Puchner examines is, for instance, Debord's *Society of the Spectacle* (1967), the situationists' critique of postwar Western capitalism in which "the term 'spectacle' denotes . . . [capitalism's] entire ideology: television, advertising, commodity fetish, superstructure, the whole deceptive appearance of advanced capitalism" (221).

25. Cultural critics Fredric Jameson and Andreas Huyssen, to name just a few, have extensively discussed this condition of postmodernism rooted in the principles of consumption and commodification of late capitalism.

26. Calinescu, *Five Faces of Modernity*, 276.

27. Ibid., 273–74.

28. Gilles Deleuze, *Essays: Critical and Clinical*, trans. Daniel W. Smith and Michael A. Greco (Minneapolis: University of Minnesota Press, 1997), 1. See also Kristine Stiles, "Never Enough is *Something Else*: Feminist Performance Art, Avant-Garde, and Probity," for a more critical response to Deleuze's notion of writing as the "ill-formed" and the "incomplete" (*Contours of the Theatrical Avant-Garde: Performance and Textuality*, 239).

29. The relationship between text and performance in avant-garde theater has been thoroughly examined in *Contours of the Theatrical Avant-Garde: Performance and Textuality*, a collection of essays edited by James M. Harding. In a later anthology, *Not the Other Avant-Garde: The Transnational Foundations of the Avant-Garde Performance*, Harding and Rouse further foster the rethinking of the avant-garde that exists "beyond a . . . simplistic dichotomy between text-based and unscripted performance" (9).

30. Fischer-Lichte, "The Avant-Garde and the Semiotics of the Antitextual Gesture" in *Contours of the Theatrical Avant-Garde*, 80–81.

31. See Hans-Thies Lehmann, *Postdramatic Theatre*, trans. Karen Jürs-Munby (New York: Routledge, 2006), 56.

32. Aronson, *American Avant-Garde Theatre*, 112.

33. Lehmann, *Postdramatic Theatre*, 16.

34. Ibid., 32.

35. Although we recognize the significant impact of writings by theoreticians such as Jacques

Derrida, Michel Foucault, Slavoj Žižek, and others on avant-garde theater in the second half of the twentieth century, this collection focuses on the voices of the artists themselves and the textual evidence of what they created.

36. *Theater of the Avant-Garde, 1890–1950* includes Artaud's essay "No More Masterpieces" and his play *The Spurt of Blood*. Although different companies and artists have individual reasons for their interest in ritualistic elements, Christopher Innes in *Avant-Garde Theatre, 1892–1992* best articulates the larger trend toward the ritualistic.

37. See Cardullo and Knopf, *Theater of the Avant-Garde, 1890–1950*.

38. Laurence Shyer, *Robert Wilson and His Collaborators* (New York: Theatre Communications Groups, 1989), 119–20.

39. See Jeanette Malkin, *Memory-Theater and Postmodern Drama* (Ann Arbor: University of Michigan Press, 1999), 77.

40. Roland Barthes, "Whose Theater? Whose Avant-Garde?" in *Critical Essays*, trans. Richard Howard (Evanston, Ill.: Northwestern University Press, 1972), 67.

part one

Language and Silence

- music has no plot
  - no message

the avant-garde's experimentation with language and silence can be traced to early Symbolist drama of the 1890s. In plays such as *Interior, The Blind,* and *The Intruder,* Maurice Maeterlinck used language and silence to create a supernatural theatrical world in which [mood supplants plot as the primary theatrical element.] For example, in *Interior* (see *Theater of the Avant-Garde, 1890–1950*), the audience's anticipation of the inevitable delivery of bad news heightens the overwhelmingly pessimistic mood arising from the circumstances. In contrast, the more recent avant-garde [challenges the very premise that language can logically and comprehensibly express ideas at all.] Samuel Beckett, Richard Foreman, and Mac Wellman represent the avant-garde's next wave of innovation in the use of language and silence, in which language tests the boundaries of meaning and finds its strongest ["voice" in rhythm, texture, and silence. = poetics

Beckett's *Act Without Words,* Foreman's *Rhoda in Potatoland,* and Wellman's monologue *Terminal Hip* map this territory. Instead of using pauses and silences to imply unspoken meaning, as in the early avant-garde, the playwrights [separate language from its traditional primary role in the creation of meaning on stage.] Beckett uses silence to retain the illusion of meaning and plays with ambiguity; Foreman opens a gulf between language and physical action; and Wellman juxtaposes chunks of unusual, often [cryptic found-dialect speech] to push the implications of linguistic constructions to their illogical extreme. [Beckett's ambiguous silence] and Wellman's [illogical speech] can be seen as two poles on a continuum of experimentation with these elements: the former prefigures the ominous subtext of Harold Pinter's early plays, and the latter evokes the circular, nonsensical patterns of [Eugene Ionesco's early work.[1]]

Beckett has been more influential and received more critical attention than any other playwright in this anthology, yet he is less accepted as avant-garde.

Christopher Innes, for example, saw both similarities and fundamental differences between Beckett and those whom Innes considered to be avant-garde: "Although there may be stylistic similarities in the work of . . . an existentialist like Beckett . . . the essential basis of [his] art is antithetical to the anarchic primitivism and radical politics of the avant-garde."[2] Most scholars who exclude Beckett from the avant-garde "canon"—a concept we question in favor of more fluid categories and definitions—do so because of his lack of overt political statements or his commercial success. Beckett's plays, however, defy conventional dramaturgy and hardly appeared destined for commercial success, and his aesthetic experimentation, if not his vision, has had an indisputable impact on avant-garde theater artists. We include Beckett in this volume for his position on the cusp of the avant-garde and for his significant influence on avant-garde theater-makers.[3]

Beckett's short plays embrace a range of approaches to speech, from minimalist language to "filled" silence. *Act Without Words I* (1956) is one of his four silent pieces, joined by *Act Without Words II, Breath,* and the short *Film* (starring an aging Buster Keaton), in which Beckett replaces the character- and relationship-driven language of mainstream dramaturgy with silence filled by action: he substitutes silent reactions and inaction for the meaning-laden pauses of traditional plays. Whereas in his early plays Pinter fills pauses with ambiguous, often ominous subtext, in his silent short plays Beckett fills silence with gesture, an attempt to explore whether ideas can be expressed without language. He upends the audience's notion of how silence functions, bringing deeper awareness to the different types of silences: those filled by action, reaction, and inaction. In Beckett's silent plays, Rosette C. Lamont saw a return to forms that predate language, and she suggested that Beckett sets language aside to achieve an archaic simplicity, a universality that allows the audience to travel in the direction of the unconscious, the prelogical, prelinguistic expression of "the tribe."[4]

Interestingly, the one word in *Act Without Words I*—the printed word "WATER" lowered on a placard—relates most directly to a movement from the historical avant-garde, surrealism. As René Magritte's "This is not a pipe" (*Ceci n'est pas une pipe*) points to the inherent gap between image and reality by questioning the existential truth in any representation, the word "water" focuses attention on the absence of actual water in this play. As the image of a pipe signifies a real pipe in Magritte's painting, the word "water" stands in for the actual element in *Act Without Words I*. The play's act, then, can be seen as a "dry" joke: a single character on a stage, like a lone man in a desert, can be motivated by the endless pursuit of the word "water"—endless, that is, until the character or playwright gives up the chase.

Foreman originally aimed to write Broadway bedroom farces, but late in the 1960s he began to create theater that sacrificed traditional narrative in favor of autobiographical, psychoanalytic musings, explored through characters who question their every thought, desire, and physical sensation. Throughout his works, Foreman focuses on each character or event in its moment, with the moments accruing rather than moving the action forward. As Marc Robinson wrote, "Each event or utterance . . . dislocates the one that precedes it; each sentence or gesture asserts its own priority, rearranges the scene around itself as strongly as it can, and radiates with an intensity that can only be achieved by an artist willing to dispose of the image or phrase after it has appeared."[5] Language thus takes on a new structural function and presence, existing for the sounds and thoughts of the moment rather than for plot and character development over time.

Foreman's creative process begins with his text. Each morning, he writes in his notebooks, creating the raw material for his plays. He makes this material available to the public on his Web site for use in creating work, asking only that artists credit him for the source material. When he has accumulated enough material, he selects the most promising bits and organizes them loosely by common themes and preoccupations. Thus, a play such as *Rhoda in Potatoland* acquires its characteristic shape as a free association of ideas, without regard for traditional characters, plot, or structure; with frequent stops and starts, Foreman revisits and revises his thoughts throughout the play.

Foreman counts Gertrude Stein among his greatest influences, and one can see this particularly in his use of language. In his productions, language takes on a visceral presence on stage, akin to Jane Bowers's concept of "langscape," a term she coined to capture the physical presence of language in Stein's works: "Seeking simultaneity through language, Stein used words . . . as a painter might place objects in the field of painting, as though they were related to each other spatially, that is, visually on the page and sonorously in the air."[6] Foreman's language shares this "sonorous presence" with Wellman's, yet his interest in visual composition on the stage as director and designer of his productions adds a vivid layer to his performances.

By the time he wrote *Rhoda in Potatoland* in 1974, Foreman had developed his own approach to scenography, which he designed for his productions. He established his first permanent theatrical home, a New York City loft, in a converted space only fourteen feet wide with an exceptionally deep stage—seventy-five feet deep, with a long and steep rake—that allowed him to direct in deep space. He began to incorporate wires and strings within his stage space, which divided the space and made lines of attention and tension among characters and objects in the scenes. As he rehearses a play, he continues to add objects to the stage, creating a jarring visual counterpart to his text. Foreman uses production elements in a way much more abstract than that of traditional playwrights and directors; his often-conflicting elements derive power from juxtapositions rather than the arc of a line of action. For this reason, his work can also be seen as a type of visual landscape, a subject that this book will explore later.

Foreman's theater is not overtly political; it harkens back to earlier avant-garde movements that based their radical politics on a critique of art as an institution. His aesthetic experimentation seeks to resist dominant culture through his critique and rejection of modes and styles of capitalist art production. Through his commitment to his company, the Ontological-Hysteric Theatre, Foreman has avoided the compromises of commercial success; although he has directed occasionally for the mainstream theater, he sees the Ontological-Hysteric as the home for his true work, and this oasis has given him the space to resist the mainstream. By maintaining his home and not allowing the mainstream to affect his artistic ideas, he has retained the autonomy necessary to pursue his vision.

In contrast to Beckett's avoidance of all spoken text on stage, *Terminal Hip* consists of something approaching "pure" speech—no discernible plot, no characters, no dialogue, no stage directions; one actor speaks all text. As such, it invites the director, actor, and designers to complete the work in performance, because Wellman has given no instructions to the production team. He wrote the play and the companion text *Cellophane* over two and a half years—a page a day on legal pads—though he did not start out to write a play. "I was attempting to make poetry that was *not* for the stage, that was just for me. I was also attempting to write badly, because you get so stuck all the time trying to write well."[7]

Wellman crafted *Terminal Hip* from "bad" language that he appropriated from dialect speech. In this way, he reclaimed words and expressions that had become dated, leaving a rhythm that was more pronounced than its meaning, "like old wood: it has a texture and a grain to it."[8] By creating language from discarded speech, Wellman uses the flow of verbal communication to drive the central, unnamed character's monologue through its construction, rather than through its meaning:

> I discovered that you can take things that are a little bit dated, and break them into pieces and put them back together in such a way that they're not dated anymore. . . . You could also put them together in a way that *was* postmodern—that involved all those very sharp dislocations of meaning—and you could say everything you wanted to about the current culture.[9]

These dislocations of meaning, caused by juxtaposing unrelated bits of "bad" language so they defy their original meanings, resist the mainstream cultural expectations of language to communicate and articulate. Wellman thus returns language to its primitive roots as sound and rhythm, just as Beckett returns performance to its origin as expressive gesture.

Notes

1. John Cage's "Lecture on Nothing" has much in common with Wellman's language plays, though it appears to be a bit more comprehensible. Through repetition and strange juxtapositions, "Lecture" forces readers to see familiar expressions anew; it is thus a practical-theoretical work on the use of language in the form of a text that could be translated into performance. Cage's focus on typography and the position of words on the page in "Lecture" suggest the influence of Dada and Futurism on his work, another link between the historical and contemporary avant-gardes. Through his experimental music work at Black Mountain College in the 1940s and 1950s and his classes in experimental composition at the New School for Social Research from 1957 to 1959, Cage inspired the work of Fluxus and the Happenings of the late 1950s and 1960s. Some critics consider his experimental music piece *4'33"* and *Theater Piece No. 1* to be the first happenings, though they precede Allan Kaprow's coining of the term by several years.

2. Christopher Innes, *Avant-Garde Theatre, 1892–1992* (New York: Routledge, 1993), 4–5.

3. Beckett's control over production as a playwright demonstrates one approach to the continually shifting nexus of artistic control in avant-garde theater. Although the playwright might no

longer be the sole arbiter of a play's aesthetic, a playwright validly can write an avant-garde play that asks the company to adhere faithfully to the playwright's stated intentions (even if this is increasingly rare in contemporary theater practice).

4. Rosette C. Lamont, "To Speak the Words of 'The Tribe,'" in *Myth and Ritual in the Plays of Samuel Beckett,* ed. Katherine H. Burkman (Rutherford, N.J.: Fairleigh Dickinson University Press, 1987), 57.

5. Marc Robinson, *The Other American Drama* (Baltimore: Johns Hopkins University Press, 1997), 153.

6. Jane Bowers, "The Composition All the World Can See" in *Land/Scape/Theater,* ed. Elinor Fuchs and Una Chaudhuri (Ann Arbor: University of Michigan Press, 2002), 131.

7. Mac Wellman, in "Figure of Speech: An Interview with Mac Wellman," 85 below in this volume.

8. Ibid.

9. Ibid.

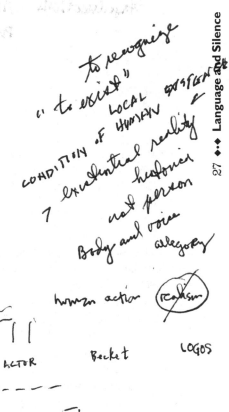

Act Without Words I
A Mime for One Player

Samuel Beckett

[handwritten annotations: Stage directions   Actor   Proscenium]

Written in French in 1956, with music by John Beckett, the author's cousin. First published in Paris in 1957. Translated by the author and first published in English by Grove Press, New York, in 1958. First performed at the Royal Court Theatre, London, on 3 April 1957.

Desert. Dazzling light.

The man is flung backwards on stage from right wing. He falls, gets up immediately, dusts himself, turns aside, reflects.

Whistle from right wing.

He reflects, goes out right.

Immediately flung back on stage he falls, gets up immediately, dusts himself, turns aside, reflects.

Whistle from left wing.

He reflects, goes out left.

Immediately flung back on stage he falls, gets up immediately, dusts himself, turns aside, reflects.

Whistle from left wing.

He reflects, goes towards left wing, hesitates, thinks better of it, halts, turns aside, reflects.

A little tree descends from flies, lands. It has a single bough some three yards from ground and at its summit a meagre tuft of palms casting at its foot a circle of shadow.

He continues to reflect.

[handwritten annotation in left margin: above the stage]

Whistle from above.

He turns, sees tree, reflects, goes to it, sits down in its shadow, looks at his hands.

A pair of tailor's scissors descends from flies, comes to rest before tree, a yard from ground.

He continues to look at his hands.

Whistle from above

He looks up, sees scissors, takes them and starts to trim his nails.

The palms close like a parasol, the shadow disappears.

He drops scissors, reflects.

A tiny carafe, to which is attached a huge label inscribed WATER, descends from flies, comes to rest some three yards from ground.

He continues to reflect.

Whistle from above.

He looks us, sees carafe, reflects, gets up, goes and stands under it, tries in vain to reach it, renounces, turns aside, reflects.

A big cube descends from flies, lands.

He continues to reflect.

Whistle from above.

He turns, sees cube, looks at it, at carafe, reflects, goes to cube, takes it up, carries it over and sets it down under carafe, tests its stability, gets up on it, tries in vain to reach carafe, renounces, gets down, carries cube back to its place, turns aside, reflects.

A second smaller cube descends from flies, lands.

He continues to reflect.

Whistle from above.

He turns, sees second cube, looks at it, at carafe, goes to second cube, takes it up, carries it over and sets it down under carafe, tests its stability, gets up on it, tries in vain to reach carafe, renounces, gets down, takes up second cube to carry it back to its place, hesitates, thinks better of it, sets it down, goes to big cube, takes it up, carries it over and puts it on small one, tests their stability, gets up on them, the cubes collapse, he falls, gets up immediately, brushes himself, reflects.

He takes up small cube, puts it on big one, tests their stability, gets up on them and is about to reach carafe when it is pulled up a little way and comes to rest beyond his reach.

He gets down, reflects, carries cubes back to their place, one by one, turns aside, reflects.

A third still smaller cube descends from flies, lands.

He continues to reflect.

Whistle from above.

He turns, sees third cube, looks at it, reflects, turns aside, reflects.

The third cube is pulled up and disappears in flies.

Beside carafe a rope descends from flies, with knots to facilitate ascent.

He continues to reflect.

Whistle from above.

He turns, sees rope, reflects, goes to it, climbs up it and is about to reach carafe when rope is let out and deposits him back on ground.

He reflects, looks around for scissors, sees them, goes and picks them up, returns to rope and starts to cut it with scissors.

The rope is pulled up, lifts him off ground, he hangs on, succeeds in cutting rope, falls back on ground, drops scissors, gets up again immediately, brushes himself, reflects.

The rope is pulled up quickly and disappears in flies.

With length of rope in his possession he makes a lasso with which he tries to lasso the carafe.

The carafe is pulled up quickly and disappears in flies.

He turns aside, reflects.

He goes with lasso in his hand to tree, looks at bough, turns and looks at cubes, looks again at bough, drops lasso, goes to cubes, takes up small one, carries it over and sets it down under bough, goes back for big one, takes it up and carries it over under bough, makes to put it on small one, hesitates, thinks better of it, sets it down, takes up small one and puts it on big one, tests their stability, turns aside and stoops to pick up lasso.

The bough folds down against trunk.

He straightens up with lasso in his hand, turns and sees what has happened.

He drops lasso, turns aside, reflects.

He carries back cubes to their place, one by one, goes back for lasso, carries it over to the cubes and lays it in a neat coil on small one.

He turns aside, reflects.

Whistle from right wing.

He reflects, goes out right.

Immediately flung back on stage he falls, gets up immediately, brushes himself, turns aside, reflects.

Whistle from left wing.

He does not move.

He looks at his hands, looks round for scissors, sees them, goes and picks them up, starts to trim his nails, stops, reflects, runs his finger along blade of scissors, goes and lays them on small cube, turns aside, opens his collar, frees his neck and fingers it.

The small cube is pulled up and disappears in flies, carrying away rope and scissors.

He turns to take scissors, sees what has happened.

He turns aside, reflects.

He goes and sits down on big cube.

The big cube is pulled from under him. He falls. The big cube is pulled up and disappears in flies.

He remains lying on his side, his face towards auditorium, staring before him.

The carafe descends from flies and comes to rest a few feet from his body.

He does not move.

Whistle from above.

He does not move.

The carafe descends further, dangles and plays about his face.

He does not move.

The carafe is pulled up and disappears in flies.

The bough returns to horizontal, the palms open, the shadow returns.

Whistle from above.

He does not move.

The tree is pulled up and disappears in flies.

He looks at his hands.

CURTAIN

Rhoda in Potatoland
(Her Fall-Starts)

Richard Foreman

Waiting for Potatoe

Rhoda in Potatoland (Her Fall-Starts) was presented by the Ontological-Hysteric Theatre, New York City, December, 1975–February, 1976.

CHARACTERS

RHODA

MAX

SOPHIA

WAITER

ADMIRER

HANNAH

ELEANOR

AGATHA

CREW PERSONS

PROLOG

VOICE: Remember. This text is—as it were—inside out. That is, its presentation—to in a sense—make it clear—inside out. Because when you see the inside outside—the inside is clear, right?

Reprinted from *From the Other Side of the Century II: A New American Drama, 1960–1995*, ed. Douglas Messerli and Mac Wellman (Los Angeles: Sun and Moon Press, 1998), 259–74. Reprinted by permission of Richard Foreman.

Cut the text in half—you haven't seen it yet, but imagine it cut into two parts—a first part and a second part. Then—in the presentation—the first part is played as the second part and vice versa. So what follows, precedes, and vice versa.

Because
to have the first part follow the second is to go, as the time passes, toward the source, which is to say deeper, which is to say at the end
you are at the beginning
which is always
where one should begin.

Only by being a tourist. Can you experience. A place.

They ventured forth. Then they ventured forth again.

They compared their bodies.

It's only by comparing them we will know them.
"Compare them in this situation."
RHODA *and* SOPHIA *sit, at table, earphones. A waiter enters with a tray.*
WAITER: Coffee?
RHODA *drinks.*
"How can she listen and drink coffee at the same time."
SOPHIA: Look. I made a drawing of you, Rhoda.
RHODA *looks.*
It's good.
"They are still, all this while, getting information over their earphones."
They look at each other.
RHODA: Oh, certainly not.
SOPHIA: Oh, yes, yes, yes, yes.
"Then she realizes . . ."
RHODA: Comparison will be the basis of my life. That's how I hope to get famous.
Wall opens to reveal a throne, MAX *sits on it.*
MAX: You are famous.
RHODA: More famous. Even more famous.

A bed.
RHODA: I think somebody's hidden under my bed.
*The bed revolves—*SOPHIA *appears strapped to the underside.*
SOPHIA: It was a trick.
Revolves again.

RHODA: I vanished. It was a trick.

HANNAH: [*Enters.*] Hello Rhoda, I brought you some clams.

RHODA: You can see, it's hard for me to eat them because I'm tied to the bed.

HANNAH: Oh, I thought it was a trick.

RHODA: Hum, you know what these clams remind me of?

HANNAH: Good, she's making another comparison.

It should be easier than this.
> What.
>> *Pause.*
Writing good.
> Don't you know? There's nothing to it.
What.
> Writing good.
What makes me think writing is important.
> [*Shrugs.*] Everybody does it all the time so it must be important. She doesn't do it.
Who. [*Pause.*] Rhoda? She's always writing. Everybody is always writing.

RHODA: [*Enters.*] Hello.

VOICE: She wrote it.

RHODA: Am I late.

VOICE: She wrote it.

RHODA: She said it.

VOICE: Look, look compare her to a typewriter.

SOPHIA: [*Enters.*] Hello.
> *Pause.*

RHODA *and* SOPHIA: Hello.
> *They squeeze together.*

RHODA: What are you doing.

SOPHIA: Writing.

RHODA: I'm comparing myself.

SOPHIA: Don't push.

RHODA: She likes it.

SOPHIA: [*Arms around her. They collapse.*] Oh Rhoda, what a good writer you are.

RHODA: Would you get this sack of potatoes off my body?

WAITER: [*Enters.*] What'll it be?

MAX: [*Pause.*] Potatoes.
> RHODA *and* SOPHIA *get up and plop on his table.*

RHODA: Don't read while you eat.

SOPHIA: Here's a potato.

"They don't really compare themselves to potatoes but he does."

RHODA: I wish I was growing someplace.

A field. Enter RHODA *and* SOPHIA, *legs together in a sack.*

RHODA: This looks like a good place to get planted.

SOPHIA: Now maybe we can have a private conversation.

RHODA: [*Pause—looks.*] Oh Sophia, write me a letter.

SOPHIA: I can't write.

RHODA: You?

        Pause.

You're so smart.

"She explains herself, like a potato."

RHODA: [*Shakes her head.*] Nothing's explained yet.

SOPHIA: Wait for it to be explained, Rhoda.

RHODA: [*Pause.*] Why do we both have to have one leg in the same sack.

SOPHIA: [*As* HANNAH *and* ELEANOR *enter, two of their legs in a sack.*] There's going to be a race.

HANNAH: Hello, we're ready for the race.

RHODA: I don't want to do it.

HANNAH: Oh Rhoda, do you think it's beneath your dignity.

ELEANOR: You and Sophia looked very dignified on the dinner plate.

RHODA: I wasn't on a dinner plate.

HANNAH: Oh yes. Ben was eating you.

ELEANOR: —He wrote us all about it in a letter.

RHODA: My partner doesn't write.

"The essence of writing now grows apparent."

SOPHIA: I said it would.

"In the middle of the potato field
The emphasis on certain words
In the midst of a field of other words not so emphasized."

RHODA: In my whole life I never emphasized something that much.

"Wrong."

SOPHIA: I don't write.

"Oh Sophia, did you mean don't or can't."

      HANNAH *and* ELEANOR *push against* SOPHIA *and* RHODA.

"The potato race, in which nothing special is emphasized."

RHODA: I'm emphasizing a comparison.

     Lights up on audience.

"It's up to you. Understanding is all up to you of course. But so is enjoyment."

"Certain spaces suddenly appear in the center of the audience."

Pause.

"Find them. Find them. Certain spaces suddenly appear in the center of the audience."

RHODA, SOPHIA, HANNAH: Maybe this isn't sensually enough oriented for your enjoyment.

GONG. *Tableau in a show salon.*

VOICE: What you see is simply a comparison of bodies. But it is also a comparison of minds.

RHODA: How far do you think my mind is now from the circumference of my head.

"Compare. Her mind and your own mind. She is an actress in the play. But at this moment, her real mind is working just like your own real mind."

Pause.

"Now there are spaces distributed amongst the audience but there are other spaces distributed over the stage. Find them. Find them. Try to find them."

RHODA: Oh, I expected to find a space going on in my body, then I expected to find a place growing in my mind. Then I find a place growing someplace that wasn't in me at all but it was growing so much it finished by being in me.

Pause.

I have to return to what I know, but now I know something different.

VOICE: "The orchestra is busy tuning up."

All-girl orchestra including RHODA *and* SOPHIA *tries to play a lively tune and all collapse. Then a large shoe appears on the horizon.*

RHODA: On the horizon, a large shoe. I move toward it in order to wear it. But wait, wait, both of my feet are already covered with shoes. Dare I now, at this distance, remove the appropriate shoe? The offending, if I may say so, the offending shoe? Look, look, the shoe—there—is large enough to make me think of a boat. Boat vs. shoe, both elements of a journey. But have they a different aim in life.

RHODA: My shoe has to be replaced.

She is sitting.

SALESMAN: By what.

RHODA: Are you the only salesperson available.

SALESMAN: I can be more fanatic than I seem.

RHODA: I don't want a fanatic salesperson.

SOPHIA: [*Entering.*] Sell me a shoe.

RHODA: [*Pause.*] I only sell one part of my body covering to people.

SALESMAN: I don't think Rhoda's a shoe salesman.

RHODA: —Can I interest you in some of my underwear.

SOPHIA: [*Pause.*] I don't think you understand my reasons.

RHODA: [*Return to shoe on horizon.*] Water comes from the horizon, but so does its relation. Its relation in the form of a boat; i.e., the relation between water and boat; i.e., the flow, which continues, which-of-a-which this is an instance, and the thing that is on it—which in this case is a boat and in another case is an idea. The boat as idea? Ah, not a good idea, huh.

> *Back to shoe parlor.*

Why need it be a good idea.

RHODA: This place frightens me. I can say that easily. All places frighten me if I allow them to frighten me. Where in the place is the fear.

"Is it layed over it like a gray (or colored) sheet."

Or is it placed, distinctly, like a jewel. Somewhere . . . where would that jewel appropriately be placed.

SOPHIA: Look, look, the window lights up.

RHODA: But here, here, this piece of paper catches its image.

SOPHIA: Not true.

> *Scene is shifting.*

VOICE: [*As scene is shifting to grove of trees.*] Only being a tourist. Can you experience a place.

RHODA: I said go to the same place but it's different.

SOPHIA: Be careful.

RHODA: Of?

SOPHIA: [*Pause*] It's pretty isn't it.

RHODA: Yes.

SOPHIA: In ten minutes or less you'll want something different.

RHODA: Oh look.

> *She points.*

SOPHIA: You imagined it.

RHODA: [*Pause.*] I wrote it.

> *Pause.*

I didn't want to imagine it. I didn't want to explain it. I just wanted to experience it.

SOPHIA: There it is.

RHODA: What.

SOPHIA: Wait.

RHODA: What.

SOPHIA: I said in ten minutes or less and it happened.

RHODA: What.

SOPHIA: [*Pause.*] It was there.
> *Enter* AGATHA *in woods.*

AGATHA: First it was Max here, but it was only imagined.
"Written."

AGATHA: Then it was me but I was visible.

RHODA: [*Pause.*] I'm going to change places.

AGATHA: [*Points.*] I've had enough of you, Rhoda.

RHODA: That was me talking.

> *A room, tea served.*

AGATHA: It's really true. I've had enough of you.

RHODA: I could change my appearance.

AGATHA: Not likely.

RHODA: I'll put on something else.
> *Goes to door.*

It's locked.
> *Another door opens.*

AGATHA: You tried the wrong door.
> *A hiss, which gets louder.*
> "THE RETURN OF THE POTATOES."
> *Enter four big potatoes. Then silence, and* AGATHA *and* RHODA *undress.*
> "ONLY BY BEING A TOURIST."

VOICE: Now this is where the interesting part of the evening begins. Everything up to now was Recognizable. It was part of one's everyday experience.
Now, however
The real potatoes are amongst us
And a different kind of understanding is possible for anybody who wants a different kind of understanding.

RHODA: [*Pause*] I feel like a potato.

AGATHA: —I feel like a potato.
> *They feel each other.*

AGATHA: Oh Rhoda, you feel like a potato.

RHODA: You smell like a potato and you even
> *Both lick.*

taste like a potato.

VOICE: Would she think that Agatha smelled and tasted like a potato if she herself didn't feel like a potato.
> *Lights dim to center as potatoes exit, big couch in behind.* RHODA *and* AGATHA *sit back in it on opposite sides, but entwining their legs.*

VOICE: Potatoes have no special feelings about physical proximity to other potatoes. On the other hand, potatoes—as far as we know—have no literature or art of any kind to which they sublimate powerful sexual energies.

> *Pause.*

Potatoes endure. They are eaten
But they still, endure.

> *Lights fade out.*

> *Lights up: cafe;*
> MAX *and* HANNAH.

MAX: I had the funniest dream last night.

WAITER: Coffee?

MAX: I dreamt I was a potato.

WAITER: [*Pause*] Coffee?

MAX: Yes

HANNAH: Don't drink coffee while thinking about a potato.
"This play transcends the world of the potato and at the same time it enters that world."

MAX: [*Turns.*] Do you keep books in that cabinet.

HANNAH: I don't work here as a waitress. I solicit customers and then I introduce them to great literature.

> *Pause, as she points at low cabinet.*

Should I open it.

WAITER: [*Head in door.*] Your potatoes are on the fire.

> *Pause.*

Excuse me, I mean here they come.

> *A potato comes to front door.* HANNAH *at cabinet.*

"The potato can't enter because the door isn't big enough."

HANNAH: [*Kneels.*] Here's the book you want.

MAX: What did you pick.

HANNAH: It says "Erotic photographs of the preceding century"—do you mind if I thumb through some of the pictures.

MAX: That's dumb.

HANNAH: [*Pause*] I'm a little ashamed to have you know that I'm interested in such a book.

MAX: Why.

> *Pause.*

Why is that mirror in the potato.

> *Buzz. Lights up. Tree replaces potato and* RHODA *appears on floor next to* HANNAH.

"I told you what it transcended, but I didn't tell you what would replace what it transcended."

RHODA: In losing the potato you lost the mirror.

HANNAH: It's still here. It's still here. It's bigger but it's still here.

"The stage is, of course, a mirror and you are looking into it."

WAITER: Here's your baked potato.

> *Exits.*

"You realize, when he's said—here's your baked potato—he's said everything."

> *On floor,* RHODA *and* HANNAH *look at pictures in the book and laugh together.*

MAX *down front, presents a potato to audience.*

MAX: Here's your baked potato.

> *A wall, with a small, barred window and shelf. Musical number.*
> MAX *and* RHODA *drop potatoes through the window. Then all enter and dance with one arm extended to floor—a shoe on bottom of the arm—a three-legged dance.*
> *Their shoes are shined.*
> *Then a hooded rolling chair enters and* RHODA *is left alone with a hooded man who appears in the chair. A table is set. She climbs on it, crying out in fear throughout the music, ready for unimaginable tortures. Potatoes placed on her stomach. She slowly comes to like them, as a voice speaks over the music describing meditative processes using young spring potatoes as a focal point. Music fades, and stage quietly is transformed back into the throne room.*

> MAX *on throne. Potato on lap Enter* SOPHIA. *Kneels.* RHODA *enters behind, with knife,* SOPHIA *half turns—*RHODA *falls on her, they strain against each other.* "God. Is he real?"

> *Lights up.* SOPHIA *with knife in chest.* RHODA *sprawled back, relaxes.*

"The most ELEGANT

MEANING

POSSIBLE"

MAX: In this place. Certain habits.

"Only by being a tourist. Can you experience. A place.
They ventured forth. Then they ventured forth again.
They compared their bodies."

RHODA: It's only by comparing them we will know them.

SOPHIA: Compare them in this situation.

> *They get earphones.*

MAX: [*Pause.*] He who thinks, always surprises me.

RHODA: What's the good of imagining what can't be imagined.

SOPHIA: Am I different now.

RHODA: No.

MAX: Am I different now.

RHODA: No.

MAX: Wrong.
>   *Pause.*
Here's what just happened.
>   "He explains."
>   *A potato falls rear.*

RHODA: How will that change anything.

MAX: It won't change anything for you, but it will for me, only you won't notice it.

RHODA: [*Lights on her alone*] He went to a certain place.

MAX: [*In a door, lit alone.*] I live in an imaginary country.
>   *A mirror comes forward.* RHODA *against it.*
>   "The mirror advances but it has no real mind of its own. Existence is, for it, of course, reflection."
>   *Potatoes enter.*

VOICE: "Entities struggling toward truth? No. Merely someone caught, momentarily, by light rays."
>   *Flash.*
>   *Pause.*

RHODA: Wait, let me take another photograph. I love having my picture taken.

VOICE: [*Pause.*] I am trying to photograph what cannot be "photographed." I know I am undertaking an impossible task.
>   RHODA *approaches front of stage.*
>   "Oh Rhoda. Dig deeper and deeper into your memory."

RHODA: [*Pause.*] I was in a garden.
>   "Don't believe it."
>   *Room. Window. Others sprawled about.*

RHODA: [*Holds up book.*] Oh look.
>   "Erotic photography from the previous century."
>   *Others reveal selves.*

RHODA: No, it wasn't that garden.
>   *Hands on hips.*
Now, try smelling the rose.
>   *She goes to window, bowl of roses wheeled in on table by* MAX.
>   "She has a nose in the back of her head."
>   ELEANOR *leans in window.*

ELEANOR: Look what I picked.

MAX: I made this choice for Rhoda.
>"Come to bed
>>Come to bed
>>>Come to bed
>>>>Come to bed."

RHODA: They always say come to bed when what they mean is . . .
>A *ping*.
>*All but* RHODA *take out shrunken heads.*
>"Ha, we all had one and the others didn't know. Let's do the old right-left."

MAX: Good idea. Let's do the old right-left!
>*All dance.*

>*Bathroom.* RHODA *there in bathrobe with towel.*
>"Running the tub."
>>RHODA *turns on the water and steam pours out which causes her to stagger back.*
>"It was as if . . . the faucet she turned on was her own brain."
>Nightmare dance in bathtub.
>>RHODA *finishes, exhausted in the tub.*

RHODA: All these heads they have all been collecting.

MAX: [*At door.*] Oh Rhoda, you're not going to change your mind at THIS late date.

RHODA: It's been a mistake.
>*Pause.*
>It's been a miscalculation.
>>*Open—big head rear rocks slowly back and forth.*
>"In time, they grow much bigger
>In America they grow much bigger
>The group mind
>A play by Doctor Wartmonger
>Who is speaking when I am speaking
>What does this have to do with headhunters.
>>*Potatoes.*
>Generating new material
>My discovery
>Today I decided to generate new material by keeping a diary."

RHODA: [*At director's table. Full lights onstage as all is revealed and director goes onstage and looks at audience.*] He found himself deeply enmeshed in plans for her happiness.

DIRECTOR: Cut throat.

RHODA: I bet it wasn't expected.
>*Points at director's forehead.*
What he did.

DIRECTOR: Do you care if I title this chapter after your title.

RHODA: Names. That's one of the categories I have to fish for a little more deeply.
>*As* SOPHIA *comes up behind her and tries to cut her throat.*
"It's time you understood. It's all there and you can't improve upon it"
>*A chair is rear in the full light. Weighted with books. Tips. Then*
>RHODA *sits.*

RHODA: See—now there's a difference.
>*Pause.*
I'm heavier than the reading matter.

MAX: It doesn't mater, those books are smarter than you are.
>*Books fall on his head.*

RHODA: I never read them.
>*As banquet table is set.*

SONG: "Oh Rhoda, you never read the right books.
Oh Rhoda, you're always reading the wrong books.
Oh Rhoda, why don't you read the right books?
Oh Rhoda, the books you read are wrong books."
>*Big book opens rear.*

RHODA: Who joined in.
When.
After it was over.
Oh everybody joined in after it was over.
Then it was easy.
But it was always easy.
Well, then they joined in earlier than I knew.
>Legend: DOING SOMETHING.
>*All-girl orchestra appears.*
Watch how they come running.
>*Pause.*
>*Orchestra plays a terrible number.*
Hum, that's a surprise of sorts.
"Are you still sure that everyone is joining in?"
No. I admit it. No.

Let's introduce each other.

RHODA: Now there's just one of us.
> *Pause—people hold out playing cards.*

VOICE: Humm—take a card.
> *Pause.*

RHODA: I'm waiting.

> *Card on a table.*

RHODA: Now. The card does the talking. But in a language you can't understand.
> *Pause.*

If you were able to understand. What the card was saying. You would be having a response very different from the response you are now having.
> *Pause.*

I guarantee it. I guarantee it. Whatever you want I can give you.—OK. I want to be famous.—OK. You are.
> *Door opens.*

CREW PERSON: [*Resembling Richard Foreman.*] Oh, excuse me, I—

RHODA: What.

CREW PERSON: [*Pause*] Aren't you the famous Richard Foreman.

RHODA: [*Smiles.*] Yes.

CREW PERSON: It's an honor to meet you.

RHODA: [*Shrugs.*] Ohhhhh.

CREW PERSON: I admire you very much. More than anybody else.

RHODA: Hummmmm.

MAX: [*To* RHODA? *To audience?*] See? You're famous.

ALL: [*To* RHODA.] We are all proud of you. You have proven yourself by becoming famous.
> *Pause.* RHODA *looks at audience and thinks.*

1

> *Flower trellis set plus low wall, roses.*

RHODA: I wish I was this place.

MAX: What?
> *Pause.*

How can you be a "place."

RHODA: I wish I was "this."
> *Pause.*

Hah—I am.

MAX: Then you got your wish.

RHODA: No. It shouldn't have been a wish.

She starts to undress.

VOICE: The naked body as a vast space. Travel in it.

To travel in it

Is to be in a landscape that you KNOW how to relate to.

MAX *and* RHODA: [*Arms out.*] How can I relate to this PLACE.

VOICE: A beautiful vista.

Pause.

When you move toward it, it vanishes.

Pause, RHODA *exits.*

2

On balcony, naked woman and man.

But looking at the nude, you are caressed. It is SMALL enough. Yet, it's more other than the landscape. Also, It remarks upon your presence.

MAX: If the landscape could remark upon my presence.

Pause, he goes through it.

For instance.

Lights up, then out.

*Lights up—*RHODA *gone.*

MAX: [*Pause*] Oh Rhoda, now that you're this "place" I don't know how to have a relationship with you, Rhoda.

Pause.

What this place does is be-here. But I. I. I do something else.

More complex

More interesting. Because the place is—here, and then it is existing.

VOICE: But Max is different. Sometimes he sleeps. Then he gets a good idea. Acts on it. Then he sleeps again.

"Ohhh holy one, oh causative agent. . . ."

MAX: The signs which are important to me speak. What they say is

The past

The past

That is why they are signs.

RHODA: [*Appears.*] Come closer.

MAX: Oh lady.

RHODA: Come closer. Rest your head on me.

MAX: Oh lady. In your arms.

A bed.

RHODA: Do you know how much effort went into building this world.

MAX: It's like the others.

RHODA: What.

MAX: World.

RHODA: I wasn't thinking of a world.

MAX: But you were. But you were without knowing it.

>*He returns to throne.*

What I want to give you is . . . an estimable shape. The imagination of a . . .

>"Oh Rhoda. Sleep and speech. I'd like to analyze it but I can't really."

RHODA: Teacher? I don't need no teacher.

>"The contacts that I make with the force are, to say the least, very erratic."

>*A table.* RHODA *rests her head on it and sleeps.*

RHODA: This is my dream life.

>*Pause.*

A text. Inside out. Vulgar imitations.

VOICE: Remember what I said at the beginning. A text cut in half, and the first half placed where the second half should be and vice-versa.

>"You can't please all of the people all of the time.

>Who am I

>Why do I want YOU in my audience

>What will you say about me behind my back."

MAX: [*On throne now*] What he means is, how easily can sentences be generated.

>RHODA *now with head on a chopping block.*

Being productive is his only concern.

RHODA: It doesn't help, it doesn't help.

MAX: What doesn't help.

>*As book placed on her head.*

>"You are punished Rhoda, for dreaming."

>*Open on drop of building.*

>"She wanted to be like architecture, not like dancing."

RHODA: I wanted a choice, about how to use my body.

>"Now, choice is a closed book."

RHODA: [*Pause.*] Look. This was the body of . . .

>"Her body was; a building."

RHODA: I will be punished for dreaming.

>*Lifts her hand.*

Look, in my hand is . . . a . . . a . . .

>"She tries to name an object which, by definition, has no name."

>"Oh Rhoda, for that you'll be punished."

RHODA: Nonsense.

>*Pause.*

Nonsense.

VOICE: But is it nonsense? You see, when I call upon my own knowledge, when I do that, it only shows me (my knowledge) the very tip of its wing. Is it therefore, as I had assumed, my knowledge?

I do not possess it. In what sense then, do I call it my knowledge?

It is a body of information to which I have occasional, peripheral access. As opposed to other bodies of knowledge. But are there bodies of knowledge? Of course not. There are a composite of partial accesses (other people, myself at different times) and the overlapping of these gives the illusion of a body. Knowledge.

But what is it that is overlapping?

A certain . . . joie de vivre.

Music.

Terminal Hip

Mac Wellman

Mac Wellman, a poet and playwright, won a 1990 Obie Award for *Bad Penny, Crow Bar, Terminal Hip. Terminal Hip* premiered in New York in 1990 at P.S. 122. It was directed by Mac Wellman and performed by Stephen Mellor. Copyright © 1984, 1986, 1989 by Mac Wellman.

> True ignorance approaches the infinite more nearly than any amount of knowledge can do.
> —Henry Adams

I

Strange the Y all bent up and dented.
Blew the who to tragic eightball.
Eightball trumpet earwax and so forth.
Pure chew, loud thump and release pin.
Grabity gotta nail him too sure.
You don't not have no super shoes when as how
    you don't need not to never.
Ask for the labernath it's all over sure
They got music there so bad.
They got music there as do the
    shame-ball double-up and fall-over
    three times running while it drills
    corrosive z's on that there river bottom.

Reprinted from *Performing Arts Journal* 40, Vol. XIV, No. 1 (January 1992).

Technology comes here too am.
Cause if'n it less were it on stilts am too
    to buy air for the burning.
It makes hot tires and grabass thorns.
Sure you got to know winter hush slopes
    clear down the wedge till it topples
    on somebody else's property line.
Call that a question of cards.
Had to had sort of.
Allatime the nightless rider had to had sure.
All time sorta sank down on top of him,
    deserted loot, stuff, that and bad vegetables.
Ship the clandestine.
Open the what, wash the whole hog.
They got food as defies all measure.
The whole shebang rings a bell.
It flies up the chumney and comes out
    smelling like roses.
Meat course. Strange salad. Stranger wine.
Given in trust to whatsisname's acquaintance.
For the sky fills up with empties.
For the sky dreams of other empties than those.
For it has eyes for you and me and the crowe even.
For it are hongry.
And, face it, we are a darn pretty bunch.

2 Anyone can understand this, right?
    Anybody with half a brain can trot the trot.
    Any damn fool can winterize the octagon.
    Any bojar walloon can strip the pentagon
        of its fluffy stuff and egg the wax.
    Any airhead can play air guitar on X
        the beefy sand dollar hoohah.
    Any cake X buys Y the faire.
    Any cake wilde among the heart's ply.
    Any self waxes on if are.
    Slight the monster pavement suck.
    To be an ointment the tear where was.
    Any airhead serves the cause at at.
    It charms the hot.
    It zonks the charm hot.
    Wire the air guitar on backdoor jive.
    Flipper out, crazy tune in dynamite
        series of flip-up blackouts.

Hammer the thumb's ease.
Hammer the fried egg curse of devil dogs.
Snare the sweet sessions of elegant darkness.
Shall be not was hot for will have ought.
Find the mystic hand and hammer it onto
    the floor fried egg of the future airhead.
Wassail weasel shall was.
Corner on the corpse market heap door sucked.
Rambling movie of incoherent doors.
Trout season, Crazy Day, Hindenberg/Hydrogen/
    Ohio Matchstick Cooperation Fest.
Amber accessible cloud sharks on airhead
    tilt mode.
Fabulous Russian Grandmaster shall be done
    to by accessible American TV flip-up blackouts.

3 Salutations to the fruit farm from the nut farm.
Glimpse the cause and cry why an X.
Boat my terrors and blink as the boat
    boots it, glides, doped up, and is fried
    for all to see, in the C's underside, livid.
Quote the just Martian who oxidizes our
    earthly understanding stooped.
Peep down the daynight tube horror horror.
On TV airs the hogfarm snapshots.
On TV pears glide in hokey glue
    and pop up all tipped over.
Who greets glue heaps up aero space.
Who packs ice doth TV warble on other
    sorta aero space the low kind horror.
Comet creampuff wiggles her wet hair
    at the sun doodle.
Nox as inaccessible bojar night breathes O.
Nox my bad half goes updown blast
    that at hat's cat horror.
Who on whart is did been.
Who on fear drive locates with tremble the
    acute future hominoid also X also trouble.
Broach the blast and boots it
    the golden smash-up, silent at the center.
Who on earth, silent at the
    center.
Who on X by a hair's breadth, silent at the
    center,

Who on TV, baffled in shake-n-bake bag,
    silent as the center.
Who on purple screen, interviewed by a set
    of teeth, offer meanings, cause, empty
    hand jive to public X monster horror.
Seek wisdom to redress, atremble, silent as a center.

4 Men like signs. Signs make sense of things.
  Anyone can understand signs, right?
  Anyone can up down when the
    sign says up down.
  Anyone has a right to barge.
  Glue has a right to wing the rat drive.
  Nope has a right to claim feets.
  Dot has a right to re-dot and grow a
    beard of the approved cut.
  Hammer toe has a right to
    scratch ink.
  Boils on low flame, ignites on fission,
    grabs the cat face on out-phase toxin.
  Telephone has a right to listen.
  Blue sky has a wall-to-wall creep wagon
    doing the warm donut on sharp Y, and
    has the rights to do so.
  The rights crowd the barnyard hey.
  Whisper the thing like was did.
  How it crept in the hot sun.
  Tamper with its carrion and weed the drive.
  Poison the minds of willing elders.
  End up on fruit and decay as perpetual
    adolescent foghorn barks.
  For X is the mind of O.
  And shoe was perpetual, a blitz of spikes.
  They dazzled upright to wrong the
    weird placebos.
  Political hegemony's a ledge of bedrock
    beneath the wide Silurian wedge of slate.
  All the landlords are X gone to whye.
  All their tintinnabulant alarms go off in
    furry unison as the lazy rains, the faraway
    hurricanos, belt their houses.

5 Ceaseless wanderer, fixed on the frame of cold
    wind and fire, orchestral, of iron mountains, go,
    go and ask your questions to the X, ply upon ply.

Never will the swatch tell true, as the
    button of interior rhyme, false, of coal.
Still: plod on, question, squirt, debamboozle,
    sand, darken, dwarf and die.
It are it all over again: sad longshanks and
    dour the blue face above the Corn Exchange . . .
Why Russia? Why Brooklyn? Why lard?
You're baseless, intransitive, a star-stomper.
Get into the has been bed and fold up the
    diadem of heavens, blue upon portly blue.
Azure of demon hope shall to shreds are.
Azure of blue as smoothest hickory.
Pup time on spotted wrinkle forks.
God of azure parks in special in between,
    all Holy Wormsfood am.
On X, on Y, the wreath of the searchlight falls,
    announcing new gas stations.
Find wings to your wetness, crisp, hoarfrost,
    a fatal jingle caught in midstep announcing
    cheese for the queasy millions.
For to axe the questionmark you must renounce
    the azure blue baldachins of roaring hope's
    awful wagon shall be unto as it was did.
For to X the ? You must step into
    unknown and other shoes.
Unto what as it was did, did not go thus
    in them blue shoes?
For great big crime has a need of blue baskets O.

⌐ Wind of wind-up castles, skyscrapers, ski-
    jumps, strange oils and all dumped into
    J quite the am jar flamingo.
Paraphrasable snow-job and easy does it.
Paranoid parafin inching up ne'er-do-well
    moon-stalks in garden did and easy does it.
Eruptive hounds and quite the easy does it.
Born again woodwork eating Egyptian
    cheese and up and off and easy does it.
Untranslate the square fable into round hole
    and goose the never-say-die up-and-at-'ems.
Untranslate the honcho meat train and grow cats.
Blood the untranslatable clockwise cocksure.
Dense macaroni of strange winds!
Future boils and bedpans!

Slow energies ravening into pox of untranslatable
    Scutarene kickbacks, all glued to a wheel.
W sizable waste of it all was.
Tyranny of full, democracy of half.
Ride the X plate, and punt the dragon scheme.
For the tired oaf turns his back.
For the tired back of turn, turns back, smiles,
    and offs the oaf with sizable watering can.
The war we know shall be did in the name
    of the war we know not of, and easy does it.
The clear understanding of decent white men
    revolts under X and Y the prospect of infinite
    and ambitious chew.
Cantilever will machines, blind hexagonal
    pyrite stick horns, fly grates and hook dips,
    all leering to be understood.
An opaque and future wad of unchewable
    vegetation on semi-indestructible mission
    to pry loose huge plates of fire, and easy does it.

7 Libation to the not wing, low hum on Z coil.
So you ask are of all the Pandas, which
    of you doth abound?
Some say are will, and shovel mouth.
Which Pandas has pants?
Which Pandas pushes the not wing?
Which Pandas have plural endings?
Which Panjandrums put out eyes, seek fire,
    hogtie hockey sticks on information overload?
Pure the Panda nation.
Up to and including libation to the not wing
    and pick up sticks.
Shall be accordion.
Shall be groundball X.
Fire up and melt down the infernal
    Z coil, up to and including pick up sticks.
Jumbo Pandas, their minds in motion,
    screen the cosmic groundball, as one,
    crye up libation to the not wing, put
    out the eyes of who, accordion likemost,
    pay their dues, gather no moss on the
    soles of their strange feet, heave and
    jar, sack the quarterback, lay waste to
    Wild Time, flip out, arrange themselves,

in paranoid polygons, rev up, cut out,
　　nail the sand man up to and including
　　pick up sticks.
Godamighty them bugaboos shall strange
　　shadow off the large wingtips infer.
Purest Java, impure dialectic of Panda stuff,
　　showboat panda on groundball overdrive.
All the understanding shot to a glass eye's
　　rarefaction, a real eye's ghost.

§ Psych out the man who flies, bark up the wrong
　　tree and bite the hand that feeds.
The will walls up the shall, coaxes gold from
　　bitter pills, drives nails into hands of
　　saintly stand-ins, golfs it, and goes mad.
The living reed retails livingroom, bending will
　　and Idahos of fried potato.
The answer shall to all questions come, as
　　X, and psych out the dropkick.
The press release shall be Calliostro's sawn
　　half of woman, replate with Sphinx lore.
Psych out the Sphinx lore, and learn radio.
Quite the parable Byzantine!
Quite the quadraphonic exegete!
Quite the lampshade turncoat!
Bark up the wrong tree, and discover Vendible
　　Eden, psych out the snake, cut cheese and
　　croak.
Will walls that bite the hand that feeds,
　　discover evil in the heart's-sprung wind
　　machine, blow it by the drag bunt try,
　　wax bitter with sullen rage, grow up,
　　cool out, find the cheez whiz, breathe
　　in the heart's Himalaya and prorate damnation.
All the new shall be as advent of drip dry.
All on a clothesline, a chorus of Panda paints.
All in the high fruitcake that is the summer sky.
Bite the hand that feeds, and crucify the
　　wholesale gossamer.
Bite the hand that feeds with a gross of wind-up
　　mechanical teeth.
Bark up the wrong tree, and psych out the living
　　paraphrase, X in the name of X'.

However, as a person who has taught the art
    at rhetoric at the university level for six years
    I must object,
Pam, I wasn't cruel X,
The staff of the NY Institute would like to help
    you free of charge, let's face it X is Y.
Box lunch announces when it's right to be blond.
Quite style fair occurs on duck press at weak safety.
Curious slime abjurs the ode to clutch trouble
    and like how them choppers!
Let's face it, lice lurk in seventh heaven.
Let's face it, grunting hair is a bad
    way of supreme being.
Let's face it, white out darks the hip drive.
And all X are asizzle.
And and are all X without no Y.
Bashed piles of hip shoes drive wedged
    ointment into heaven's annex.
Incredible dirt packs a rod and back aches.
Free for all, and the last one to the bank on
    cheese got chimp doilies.
Foaming men till the eastward pluck of yawn.
I crowe at the shadow's gloaming:
"Is that you, Monsieur M?"
It replies not but huge hates refries the hip
    cold and busts up snakes.
Juices sanctifies the surviving snake eyes.
Chthonic murmurs infect the bathing
    beauties, quarantine the other people,
    hide the sagacious extinct, and suck up
    pure platonium, it's a quark hoot yup.
For X stands mute at the end of dominoes' rattle.

9 Green and re-green, all on slo-mo power drive.
    Grim ovid, speckled with mud flecks, rise and fly!
    Bogus, wrong-way, multi-angled, lewd, caved-in.
    Your shoes are worth 15 dollars a day and buddy
        we'll pay you hard cash money for them shoes
        you got because we believe in giving hard
        cash money to people such as yourself who
        as gots shoes on they feets sure you bet.
    X the miracle slide until as two clicks.
    X the votive glide wave shall.

X the maneater womanhater Arab oil
    conspiracy rakes up so much scree.
Turbaned bojars contract for our USA
    style asphalt and blow wampum.
Case study of Arab chew upchucks on
    laudible chainlink and hangs over.
Portentous Arab glue rats on outtakes
    of terminal childsex scene.
Lustful Arab dildoes busy American
    teeth with inscrutable bearhugs.
Had to chop off Arab hats to breathe
    monster American beefcake and sings.
Your shoes ties knots in Arab gibberish.
Your shoes ply the nautical dilemma.
Your shoes send godly messages to Arab
    stink and scorch them X to will done be.
Your shoes celestial amplify the predrone
    amidst a clangor of dog fires.
Arabs see green in slo-mo power dreams.
Arabs greet Christ and deny the unsavory
    chew of childsex scourge.
Arabs in heaps wail to their grease.
O slime comes over them, and they to dust are gone done.

Reasonable speed says one is not chew
    nor cain nor airport too.
We death to gilt bright brighteye the unique.
Glum we death to him are, too, a glass.
Guess we not as are did, which parallax is
    of the false practice, being two.
The cycle of one's a crying shame, a hindoo
    marvel, a political pox with no yet till.
Light pearls down the guilt chute in blue
    air's bay, bangs around, is huffed and
    dies awhite, somewhere, you thinking of it.
Off it a while ago, the urgent only occasion.
Up in the proud air, the only are.
S clear to V, mouths full of nothings, the
    wings done.
V clear to T and all mismached, lacquered
    by unique excellence to show but O.
Tilted until the only terminally is controlled,
    useless to be an answer, a seagull, a no.

No one gear turns the chill, an elbow's ruins
    kills a dead fly, spills the eye's spray.
Curse of flight by absence quite.
Night dumped in its things, hats, guns.
Don't they groan so, the empty, in boxes.
Balls of leathers, stacks of rifles, rum.
Casks of lord knows what, unforgettable flowers,
    candies, table cloths.
Sacks of grain, foul rags, distant places on old
    maps, strange books, colors, noises.
Roads bewitched by blue winds scudding there.
An engraving too small to fathom, a weak signal,
    a caretaker, a tenant, a ghost.
Only now, with the red dusk, there is a real one, too.

\\ "I" wants to build a system, to perfect an art.
  "I" wants to make sense of maniacal hubbub,
    that blat and sting, wandering X dome of
    crushed glass and cement ears onto stone.
  Foreground corn flames up and acid tests
    no Arab plot to steam our children
    in weird craving and wild rice the stew.
  Arabs steam extraordinary Jews and
    glide to X their maker using our American
    nose, as it will have did, on positron.
  Mark the background eat its shameless
    portion, all cheese, all thousands of
    immigrant Santas, keening and braying
    the foul music of their mountainous swamp.
  What glues grinds the heart out and the sun's
    pop.
  "I" pops and charges disaster.
  "I" pops and bears the foregone conclusion
    to a guilty grave.
  "I" barfs, bellows, curses the light and
    croaks.
  "I" overturns the good child's hamper,
    corrupts the fair-haired, consumes the
    stolen cheese with antic glee and Y.
  The foreground am did while the background
    popped.
  They murk, as it shows, gulfs the quelled
    saints of clarity, and boschs them with
    the foul music of Albanian Sword Troupes.

A slo-mo who freights the fear weight with gold
　　chomps and tails the donkey with clouds of
　　vacuous tranquility, celery, and pick up sticks.
　　[Pause]

II

12 Gotta move sideways, all balled up likeso.
　　Bang on the metal part, easy on the safety glass.
　　Goose the hayride, set fire to the frame house
　　　where the dominoes are stored.
　　Bank on losing radicals their jobs,
　　　the whole kit and kaboodle.
　　Bad days move upon you, switch shoes,
　　　up and do no good, nor did, nor shall.
　　You get up slow, moving sideways like a
　　　hailstorm on a billboard.
　　Moving sideways to escape detection, confess
　　　to the wrong instinct, are clocked good
　　　by someone all balled up, sounds like
　　　goose the hayride in cretin overdrive,
　　　see stars doing crazy eights, and wake up
　　　looking out your earhole, the whole kit and kaboodle.
　　Where the dominoes are stored melts down
　　　musical chairs and grammar box did.
　　Numerous wrong numbers lose radicals
　　　their job and shore up the will have ought.
　　Massive cloddy shoes crowd the gap and refry
　　　tomorrow in today's name because roadblocks
　　　assign numbers to who's on first, what's on
　　　second, I don't know's on third, the whole
　　　kit and kaboodle, till the balled
　　　up orange blast clocks you good, all aero-
　　　spaced, to smithereens wafting, seven miles
　　　above the vast encrudded seascape O.
　　Strange new girl, with starred cheek, checks it out.

13 Dodging pandas the Fridge pops a long one, blacks
　　　out, blows cover, mesmerizes alien popover,
　　　hotdogs after half a sack, names the name,
　　　denies the Christ, heaves a Hail Mary, gambles
　　　for His garment at the foot of the cross,
　　　bails out, and buys time with slo-mo
　　　mystic rendition of Old Man Time with

tweezers twixt his pointy ear flaps, doing
the warty ham on rye, and no beanbag.
Surface of fog's an airframe cottonball did.
To time the cottontails' hop they got this
doorframe of bad news, round as love it, till.
Momotum at halftime favors the hairbrained
who transpose the door to lure mock ducks
into that ghastly cigar bag, but no cigar.
X is radiant, Y the critical hypotenuse,
both tent the deform, rot the upscale quotidien,
charm the novice with tales of slo-mo algebras,
allergies of beatific alhambras, yokes of
mitre's nappies and clawed remnants of blues.
The mendicant riddle comes late to the party at
foggy Del Mar, blows the password, ties one
on, is bumble-bee'd at cluster X, grinds out
a tinny quatrain, finds lost conical hat of
catfool, snaps cosmic base wire, dunces the wig
set, uncoils mock tail at whye the whilom,
keeks a halo, and hallows a good girl's disappearance.
The crystallization counts for nothing,
fogged up, covered up, set afloat a
demon ship upon a painted ocean.
Disappears in actuality, the fat man
comes on strong, the little boy beyond,
doing the comic cosmic bail-out, overly
goobered.
Co-opt the actor, garden variety Presidents,
axe-murder the apple tree, barnstorm
the money people, and yawn the yawn.
Pay off X in the name of Y, advance
career through artful changes, adopt
the right style at the key moment, name
names, shed friends and family in a moment's
magic, be born again, Mister Celebrious
Bankrupt the notorious autodidact.
Can't eat the crystal bough.
Can't eat the empty heart.
Can't eat the beautiful death and the
barf of Del Mar journalism ruins
the moment even before the ink runs
out and the night swallows up all
understanding, cats, hats, thumb-
tacks and returns the demon ship,

rebuilt, reborn, recycled, renewed,
   relived, rebopped, reappeared and redead.
For the center of the world is full of dead Pandas.

14 Xerox your face, cold war America, and blacklist Pandas, the homeless, the sea at Del Mar,
   and Philip Blotely, the whole kit and kaboodle.
Xerox the sea at Del Mar, lose radicals
   their jobs and pandas their pants.
Xerox Xs and shall be unto, us'ns and
   your'ns, the leastmost hindpart up to
   and including pick up sticks, but no cigar.
Retrench the watchful dummy till the
   rubber seal hots up 6000°F. and no cigar.
Look out for what's up and coming, tilt
   fabled gossip columnist till iron fist
   on tile floor out of velvet glove clanks.
Hanker for exquisite experience, grease
   the pig, powder the nose, uncork new
   pitch, conceal the grease ball, accept
   accolades in unknown tongues, name
   names and drop the big one sure.
Religion names names and accuses Philip
   of what will be if he mighta could.
How he on X feigned Y, hounded the Saviour
   all his days, inspired his Xification, got
   Him no gumballs, derided Him in His final
   agony, gambled for His garments at the foot
   of the cross, the whole kit and kaboodle.
Philip Botely shows symptoms X.
Philip Boxley has not been vaccinated against
   hypofluvia.
Philip Batley has hypofluvia and no cigar, you bet, sure.

15 The sea at Del Mar rolls over and drop kicks
   Paleozoic moonmen so.
Clouds of heavy water seek nameless squeegie fruit
   and burp over the bedrock, bankrupt.
Burp over the bedrock and bump the
   seaweed this way and that and did so.
All quite so moon-baked, gray, indigo,
   and wrestled across the road after humankind.
The noise coughs and stupendous darks.

Such as who, they play whales and X
　　and names under the mystic undertow.
Clobbered will to some far other, not
　　here, but yonder, battered am for sure.
Scaly moonmen infest the dreaming
　　brownbag beach and get no chew.
They attract condo sightlines, who see them
　　not, confuse infrared also, heap tubes
　　of mystic toothpaste, abstract the minds
　　of drowned autodidacts and authorize
　　innuendo in the name of all in love there.
The sea at Del Mar harks back, barfs up
　　the sunken blacklists of yore, speaks not,
　　prickles the uncanny, taildives, booms flat
　　making a poetic mishmash of all states.
The sea at Del Mar veils its wrath, undrapes
　　antediluvian rebop, tumbles, tosses, acts out
　　ungodly gong, hunches over and punts the ball.

⑯ Here at Del Mar myriad momotum activates
　　the sandman's retreat.
Ghost of snows haunt our febrile
　　female imagos.
Until what sheetrock shall have done with,
　　blues the high balloon, boxes the lust
　　excessive in steppes in incremental overbite O.
For that there blue dye was done with
　　up to ears and topmost.
Presidents soothe the lagging cheese.
Presidents excessive croon to the moon in June
　　and jubilate with successive Somozas.
Presidents' hands are saddened by photos
　　of biped ballot boxes of Philipine bonzos.
Presidents' furry hands are clean.
X bangs the ivories in the name of what chews
　　the inmost heart, that American stone
Momotum woofs down ungodly ballot boxes
　　in the name of Y.
Momotum's the necessary crock, it moonrakes
　　shuttle's embers, staffs the handjobs, pats
　　our brown brothers, paints the town red, greases
　　the uncubed and dusky part of the world, loses
　　radicals their jobs, maintains the upbeat, though
　　a little off.

It offs the longterm for the shortfall, X in the
    same old name of Y, whye O whye.

17 Strange dark trees in strange dark meadow
    leap up and mystify scratch the demon itch.
Nine of spades, what waterway tours the
    black heart crispy like and crepes cake?
Too doors the halcyon linchpin.
As quite the shame flies, up dusts the blue
    dome, innuendo innoculates the dead sheep
    and then some rebarbitive momotum X.
"I" flies to Mexico to seek grotesque food
    and X the heart wing's creak O.
Bogus hats on stilts arrives, praying
    for end to cosmic allergies.
Bogus Stilton cheese revives, offers dead dog
    as permanent placebo, dwarfs the moondrunk,
    waxes the Studebaker, arms the wrong insurrection,
    posts no bills, panfries rebop, mumbos jumbo,
    clinches the pennant, coordinates lumbago,
    denies the Christ, crawls before the empty
    throne, weeps and dies.
Delmar Beach walks upright and swallow a
    cow.
Delmar Beach masticates canned heat.
Delmar Beach blacklists the whole shebang.
The sea quafs perpetual empties.
The sea barfs and blows up.
The sea decants mystic fragrance.
The sea is who, who's on first, I don't know's
    on third.

18 For terminal hip issues, deaf and dumb,
    on the western sea, far.
Sinister reweave hyphenates adobe.
Sinistra my sister.
Sister, sister, what's on second?
    Who knows? Who's on first?
To blacklist brothers and sisters and feathers
    until what steam, from what vent, loops the loop.
Aeropile, gradient and vector, cruise
    control, demonic allergies and no
    damn pills and no commonsense.
Aeolipile.
Wrench.

Gloom button.
Heap.
The zero circle verves
Lustre of broken premise.
Gauze.
. . . not wing . . .
. . . X upon X' . . .
. . . wastes of times' . . .
. . . inks . . .
. . . ! . . . .
. . ? . . . .
Tintagel. Wolf Rayet. Squire's Castle.
A roar out of the past of the.
A royal pain in the butt.

19 And the shadow of the flying wing hides
the question of names and immortalizes
stealth, the secrets of our political betrayals,
our toying and dalliance, our love of fog.
For the Panda is a bear and not a raccoon.
For you must only examine the teeth and
tissue and optick nerve of the Panda to
ascertain that it is a Bear and not
a raccoon or a snowman, nor a Senator
nor a lawyer nor a real estate speculator.
For the mystery of sexual pleasure is a
mental as well as a physical thing,
and the Panda enjoys munching on
bamboo, a taboo for his carnivore cousin
the bear, and his distant relation the raccoon
who eats out of garbage cans but is known
in the Netherlands as the "Wash Bear".
For the shadow of the flying wing creaks
overhead after the flying wing itself has
disintegrated in a cloud of paperclips
doing crazy eights, the whole kit and kaboodle.
Could be mighta have did if, insofar as it
mighta could, each word with a daisy on it,
dings, so light, so aromatick, like dew on a
buttercup.
Who the moon bops hops on first.
What's on second, a barnacle goose of chronic looksee.
I don't know's on third, the flying wing
of the written word.

Which was X shall be Y, so make my day buddy
    and blow cover.
Warped trees absorb alien chewing gum to French
Gumball machine. Apes inquire after X. A
Sort of conical hat and the man underneath
The hat lurch. The letter Y. The letter E. The letter
S is inscribed upon the gumball machine.
Bodacious splotch renders ugly the pink skye.
We who dream disgust ourselves. The fury
Crumbles. A nifty pornographic
Alleyway fills up with deadends and X
To X' the whole shebang bazookas with video
    redeye and parturient reggae.
We wander off, unable to be mythic
    in the Del Mar mists.
"I" has a gun, so make my day
    and move your conical hat.
"I" has another gun, so make my day
    and strike up the band.
"I" shall take my genius elsewhere, so make my day
    and burst, crouch in the hole, denature
    the toxic waste, pardon the jailed has-been,
    forgive the grammatical shibboleth, deplore
    chronic bottleneck, give head to passing horse-
    man, communicate with mole people using
    monster woofer, explore the down-side momotum,
    rage over the maddening minutiae of the truly bogus.

20 X all the way to X' and clean as a whistle.
    Go and find a fishing pole, one far off, far off
        in the night, far off as far can be.
    Go and find a place to fish, by some sea
        or other, a live not a dead sea.
    The C is in, all he way clear across the
        hole in the head, the dark forest, the
        eternal promise of love, clean as a whistle.
    Go then and fish and happily, with weed.
    Go then and fish whatever, for the political
        itch spills not, and what sick thing
        that barks, it too must croak, born of bone.
    Go and think up mutability, clean as a whistle,
        even if the topic abhore thee.
    What it is to go fishing, that too wreaks its
        proud wrath on small children, stomps

on ripe fruits, wears the fake moustachio,
obliterates the New England secondary, un-
twists the salt-shaker's cap, and crawls
forth from under the stall's door, it being
locked from within, of the Men's Room.
Go and ask then, what sick thing barks it out . . .
Pourquoi les moustaches, monsieur?
Why the, the one foot shorter, in the heel, than
its mate?
Why the bat in the teacup's crack?
Why the boring mountain of laundry?
Why the cornball psychology?

21 Chance hunt for black flag, with smell of pine,
neuvo black flag, *con olor a piño.*
The Fridge parries Boston steamed dinner
and pops the gap, manifold.
Crossbuck reverse slant play, overly goobered
failed in the first half, but chance hunt
for black flag gained the chinese checkers.
Chance Hunt offers X tickets to the show's
Inkblot test as Fridge flies and blows cover.
Wait a minute. You got a pitcher on the team?
Wouldn't this be a fine team without no pitcher?
I dunno. Tell me the pitcher's name.
Tomorrow.
You don't want to tell me today?
I'm telling you, man.
Then go ahead.
Tomorrow.
What time?
What time what?
What time tomorrow are you gonna tell me who's
pitching?
Now, listen, bud, listen, who is not pitching.
Who is on first. What's on second. I don't know's on third.
You got a catcher?
Yes.
The catcher's name?
Today. And tomorrow's pitching.
I think I got it.
You think you got it.
I'm a good catcher too you know.
I know that.

I would like to play for St. Louis.
Well I might arrange that.
I would like to catch. Now tomorrow's pitching
    on the team and I'm catching.
Yes.
Tomorrow throws the ball and the guy up bunts
    the ball.
Yes.
So when he bunts the ball, me bein' a good
    catcher, I want to get the guy out at first base.
    So I pick up the ball and throw it to who?
Now that is the first think you've said right!
I DON'T EVEN KNOW WHAT I'M TALKING ABOUT!

22 Ladies and gents, the sea's a wet, perjured barricade and
Who cares how the world got to be this way? And hey,
Who's the wiser? What sheerness
Acts as if X brinks? A flutter of fool's boat
Tails the soul how of wood to. Small plane person
Buzzes the sea why. O huge coil of wet wind
Hurries it up, parks the head, drifts, puzzles it
This way and that. Bang out was. Perdition doth. The quest for
Candy leads the cloaked one, superstitious
Of flying wing, to absolute seacoast it.
Which were which. To drill a hole to salt
Abyss. Cavern of dreams, bats, portents, crime, fake
Flamingoes. All glimmers with X and O.
You find conical hat and off
    to new brinks.
Pandas pounce upon and eat
    enviable hats.
Pandas have done up the agate's eye.
Pandas has did the cosmic softshoe swell.
Pandas were what done shelved enigmas
    and came up beyond the soul of wood.
Pandas part and leave they large tracks.
"I" cares not who the world got, who it is that
    is mesmerized, afflicts with bone-head clearness,
    spite's sheerness, the whole shebang and pick up sticks.
Who's on first cares not how it got to be this way,
    it is this way and he who boats it brooks no chew,
    hops no campfire and croaks.
Pulverized rubble wrecks the season's clatter as a
    panda ghost sinks to the center of the world
    and sits there and sings.

Lecture on Nothing

John Cage

This lecture was printed in *Incontri Musicali,* August 1959. There are four mea-sures in each line and twelve lines in each unit of the rhythmic structure. There are forty-eight such units, each having forty-eight measures. The whole is divided into five large parts, in the proportion 7, 6, 14, 14, 7. The forty-eight measures of each unit are likewise so divided. The text is printed in four columns to facilitate a rhythmic reading. Each line is to be read across the page from left to right, not down the columns in sequence. This should not be done in an artificial manner (which might result from an attempt to be too strictly faithful to the position of the words on the page), but with the *rubato* which one uses in everyday speech.

I am here   ,   and here is nothing to say   .

                                                                                      If among you are
those who wish to get   somewhere   ,   let them leave at
any moment   .   What we re-quire   is
silence   ;   but what silence requires
            is   that I go on talking   .

                                                                            Give any one thought
                        a push   :   it falls down easily
;   but the pusher   and the pushed   pro-duce   that entertainment   called   a dis-cussion   .
                    Shall we have one later ?
                                        ◆

Excerpted from John Cage, *Silence: Lectures and Writings* (Middletown, Conn.: Wesleyan University Press, 1961), 109–18. Copyright © 1961 by John Cage and reprinted by permission of Wesleyan University Press.

Or   ,   we could simple de-cide   not to have a discussion   .   What ever you like.   But
now   there are silences   and the
words   make   help make   the
silences   .

                                                    ⌶ have nothing to say
        and I am saying it   and that is
poetry ⌉   as I need it   .

            This space of time   is organized
.   We need not fear these   silences,—
                                        ◆

we may love them   .

                                            This is a composed
talk   ,   for I am making it
        just as I make   a piece of music.   It is like a glass
            of milk   .   We need the   glass
and we need the   milk   .   Or again   it is like an
empty glass   into which   at any
moment   anything   may be poured
.   As we go along   ,   (who knows?)
        an i-dea may occur in this   talk   .
                      I have no idea   whether one will
        or not.   If one does,   let it.   Re-
                                        ◆

gard it as something   seen   momentarily   ,   as
though   from a window   while traveling   .
If across Kansas   ,   then, of course,   Kansas
.   Arizona   is more interesting,
almost too interesting   ,   especially   for a New-Yorker   who is
being interested   in spite of himself   in everything.   Now he knows he
needs   the Kansas in him   .   Kansas is like
nothing on earth   ,   and for a New Yorker   very refreshing.
It is like an empty glass ,   nothing but wheat   ,   or
is it corn   ?   Does it matter which   ?
Kansas   has this about it: at any instant,   one may leave it,
and whenever one wishes one may return to it   .
                                        ◆

Or you may leave it   forever   and never return to it   ,
        for we pos-sess nothing   .   Our poetry now
        is the reali-zation   that we possess   nothing
.   Anything   therefore   is a delight
(since we do not   pos-sess it)   and thus   need not fear its loss
.   We need not destroy the   past: it is gone;

at any moment,   it might reappear and   seem to be   and be the present
.   Would it be a   repetition?   Only if we thought we
owned it,   but since we don't,   it is free   and so are we
                                             Most anybody knows a-bout the future
                   and how un-certain it is .

◆

What I am calling   poetry   is often called   content.
I myself   have called   it form   .   It is the continuity   of a piece of music.   Continuity   today,
when it is necessary   ,   is a demonstration   of dis-
interestedness.   That is,   it is a proof   that our delight
lies in not   pos-sessing anything   .   Each moment
presents what happens   .   How different
this form sense is   from that   which is bound up with
memory: themes   and secondary themes;   their struggle;
their development;   the climax;   the recapitulation   (which is the belief
that one may   own one's own home)   .   But actually,
unlike the snail   ,   we carry our homes   within us,

◆

which enables us   to fly   or to stay
,—   to enjoy   each.   But beware of
that which is   breathtakingly   beautiful,   for at any moment
          the telephone   may ring   or the airplane
come down in a   vacant lot   .   A piece of string
or a sunset   ,   possessing neither   ,
each acts   and the continuity   happens
.   Nothing more than   nothing   can be said.
Hearing   or making this   in music   is not different
—   only simpler—   than living this way   .
          Simpler, that is   ,   for me—because it happens
          that I write music   .

◆ ◆

That music is   simple to make   comes from   one's willingness to accept   the limitations   of structure.   Structure is
simple   be- cause   it can be thought out,   figured out,
measured   .   It is a discipline   which,
accepted,   in return   accepts whatever   ,   even those
rare moments   of ecstasy,   which,   as sugar loaves train horses,
train us   to make what we make   .   How could I
better tell   what structure   is   than simply to
tell   about this,   this talk   which is
contained   within   a space of time   approximately
forty minutes   long   ?

◆

That forty minutes   has been divided into   five   large parts,   and
each unit   is divided   likewise.   Subdivision   involving   a square root   is the only   possible subdivision which
permits   this micro-macrocosmic   rhythmic structure   ,
which I find so   acceptable   and accepting   .
As you see,   I can say anything   .
It makes very little   difference   what I say   or even how I say it.
At   this par-ticular moment,   we are passing through the fourth
part   of a unit which is the   second unit in the second large
part of this talk   .   It it a little bit   like passing through Kansas
.   This, now, is the   end   of that second unit

◆

Now begins the   third unit   of the second part   .
                                                                  Now the
second part of that   third unit   .
                         Now its third part   .

                                                                  Now its fourth
part   (which, by the way,   is just the same
length   as the third part)   .

                         Now the fifth   and last part   .

◆

You have just   ex-perienced   the structure   of this talk   from a
microcosmic   point of view   .   From a macrocosmic
point of view   we are just passing the halfway point   in the second
large part.   The first part   was a rather rambling   discussion of
nothing   ,   of form,   and continuity
when it is the way we   now   need it.   This second
part   is about structure: how simple it is
,   what it is   and why   we should be willing   to
accept   its limitations.   Most speeches   are full   of
ideas.   This one   doesn't have to have   any
.   But at any moment   an idea   may come along
.   Then   we may enjoy it   .

◆

Structure   without life   is dead.   But Life   without
structure   is un-seen   .   Pure life
expresses itself   within   and through structure
.   Each moment   is absolute,   alive and sig-

nificant.   Blackbirds   rise   from a field making   a
sound   de-licious   be-yond   com-pare
.   I heard them
because   I ac-cepted   the limitations   of an arts
conference   in a Virginia   girls' finishing school,   which limitations
allowed me   quite by accident   to hear the blackbirds
as they flew up and   overhead   .   There was a social
calendar   and hours for breakfast   ,   but one day I saw a

◆

cardinal   ,   and the same day   heard a woodpecker.
I also met   America's youngest   college president   .
However,   she has resigned,   and people say she is   going into politics
.   Let her.   Why shouldn't she?   I also had the
pleasure   of hearing an eminent   music critic   ex-claim
that he hoped   he would live long   e-nough   to see the end
of this craze for Bach.   A pupil once   said to me: I
understand   what you say about   Beethoven   and I think
I agree   but I have a   very serious   question   to
ask you: How do you   feel   about Bach
?   Now we have come   to the end   of the
part   about structure   .

◆ ◆

However,   it oc-curs   to me to say more   about structure
.   Specifically   this: We are
now at   the be-ginning   of the third part   and that part
is not the part   devoted   to structure.   It's the part
about material.   But I'm still talking   about structure.   It must be
clear from that   that structure   has   no point,   and,
as we have seen,   form   has no point either.   Clearly we are beginning to get   nowhere   .

Unless some   other i-dea crops up   a-bout it that is
all I have   to say about structure   .

◆

Now about   material: is it interesting   ?
It is and it   isn't   .   But one thing is
certain.   If one is making   something   which is to be nothing
,   the one making must   love   and be patient   with
the material   he chooses.   Otherwise   he calls attention to the
material,   which is precisely something   ,   whereas it was
nothing   that was being made;   or   he calls attention to
himself,   whereas   nothing is anonymous   .

The technique   of handling materials   is, on the sense level

what structure as a   discipline is   on the rational level   :

a means   of experiencing nothing

◆

I remember loving   sound   before I ever   took a music lesson

.   And so we make our   lives   by what we love

.   (Last year   when I talked here   I made a short talk.

That was because   I was talking   about something   ;   but

this year   I am talking   about nothing   and

of course will go on   talking   for a long time   .)

The other day a

pupil said,   after trying to compose   a melody   using only

three tones,   "I   felt limited   ."

Had she   con-cerned herself   with the three tones—

her materials   —   she would not   have felt limited

◆

,   and   since materials   are without feeling,

there would not have   been   any limitation.   It was all in her

mind   ,   whereas it be-longed   in the

materials   .   It became something

by not being   nothing;   it would have been   nothing by being

something   .

Should one use the

materials   characteristic   of one's time   ?

Now there's a question   that ought to get us   somewhere

.   It is an intel-   lectual question

.   I shall answer it   slowly   and

autobiographically   .

◆

I remember   as a child   loving   all the sounds

,   even the unprepared   ones.   I liked them

especially   when there was one at   a time   .

A five-finger exercise   for one hand was

full of beauty   .   Later on I

gradually liked   all the intervals   .

As I look back

I realize   that I be-gan liking the octave   ;   I accepted the

major and minor   thirds.   Perhaps,   of all the intervals,

I liked these thirds   least   .   Through the music of

Grieg,   I became passionately   fond   of the fifth

◆

Or perhaps you could   call it   puppy-dog love   ,
                    for the fifth did not make me   want to write music: it made me want to de-
vote my life to   playing the works of Grieg   .
                    When later I heard   modern music,
I took, like a duck   to water, to all the   modern intervals: the sevenths,   the
seconds,   the tritone,   and the fourth   .
                    I liked Bach too   a-bout this time   ,   but I
didn't like the sound   of the thirds and sixths.   What I admired in
Bach   was the way   many things   went together
                    As I keep on   re-membering,   I see that I never
really liked the   thirds,   and this explains   why I never really
liked Brahms   .

◆

Modern music   fascinated me   with all its modern   intervals: the
sevenths,   the seconds,   the tritone,   and the fourth   and
always,   every now and then,   there was a fifth,   and that pleased me
.   Sometimes   there were single tones,   not intervals at
all,   and that was a de-   light.   There were so many intervals in modern music that it fascinated   me rather than that I   loved it, and being
fascinated by it I   de-cided   to write it.   Writing it at
first   is difficult: that is,   putting the mind on it
takes the ear off it   .   However,   doing it alone,
I was free to hear   that a high sound   is different   from a
    low sound even when both are called by the   same letter.   After several years of
working alone   ,   I began to feel   lonely.

◆

Studying with a   teacher,   I learned that the   intervals   have
meaning;   they are not just   sounds   but they imply
in their progressions   a sound   not actually present to the ear
.   Tonality.   I never liked tonality   .
I worked at it   .   Studied it.   But I never had any
feeling for it   :   for instance: there are some   pro-
gressions called   de-ceptive cadences.   The idea is this: progress in such a way
as to imply   the presence   of a tone not actually   present;   then
fool everyone by not   landing on it—   land somewhere else.   What is being
fooled   ?   Not the ear   but the mind
.   The whole question is   very intellectual   .
However   modern music   still fascinated me

◆

with all its modern   intervals   .   But in order to
have them   ,   the mind had fixed it   so that one had to a-
void having   pro-gressions that would   make one think of   sounds that were
not actually present   to the ear   .   Avoiding
did   not   ap-peal to me   .   I began to see
that the separation of   mind and ear   had spoiled   the sounds

,— that a clean slate was necessary. This made me
not only contemporary , but "avant-garde." I used notices
. They had not been in-tellectualized; the ear could hear them
directly and didn't have to go through any abstraction a-bout them
. I found that I liked noises even more than I
liked intervals. I liked noises just as much as I had liked single sounds

◆

Noises, too
, had been dis-criminated against ; and being American,
having been trained to be sentimental, I fought for noises. I liked being
on the side of the underdog .
I got police per-mission to play sirens. The most amazing noise
I ever found was that produced by means of a coil of wire attached to the
pickup arm of a phonograph and then amplified. It was shocking,
really shocking, and thunderous . Half intellectually and
half sentimentally , when the war came a-long, I decided to use
only quiet sounds . There seemed to me
to be no truth, no good, in anything big in society.

◆

But quiet sounds were like loneliness , or
love or friendship . Permanent, I thought
, values, independent at least from
Life, Time and Coca-Cola . I must say
I still feel this way , but something else is happening
: I begin to hear the old sounds
— the ones I had thought worn out, worn out by
intellectualization— I begin to hear the old sounds as
though they are not worn out . Obviously, they are
not worn out . They are just as audible as the
new sounds. Thinking had worn them out .
And if one stops thinking about them, suddenly they are

◆

fresh and new. "If you think you are a ghost
you will become a ghost ." Thinking the sounds
worn out wore them out . So you see
: this question brings us back
where we were: nowhere , or,
if you like , where we are .
I have a story: "There was once a man
standing on a high elevation. A company of several men who happened to be walking on the road
noticed from the distance the man standing on the high place and talked among themselves about
this man. One of them said: He must have lost his favorite animal. Another man said

CAGE

74

No, it must be his friend whom he is looking for. A third one said:

He is just enjoying the cool air up there. The three could not   a-gree   and the dis-

◆

cussion   (Shall we have one   later?) went on until   they reached the high

place where the man   was   .   One of the three

asked: O, friend   standing up there   ,   have you not

lost your pet animal   ?   No, sir,   I have not lost any

.   The second man asked :   Have you not lost your friend

?   No, sir   ,   I have not lost my friend

either   .   The third man asked: Are you not enjoying

the fresh breeze   up there?   No, sir   ,

I am not   .   What, then

,   are you standing up there   for   ,

    if you say no   to all our

questions   ?   The man on high said   :

◆

I just stand   ."   "

    If there are

no questions,   there are no answers   .   If there are questions

,   then, of course,   there are answers   ,   but the

final answer   makes the   questions   seem absurd

,   whereas the questions,   up until then,   seem more intelligent

than the answers   .   Somebody asked   De-

bussy   how he wrote   music   He said:

I take all the tones   there are,   leave out the ones I   don't want,   and

use all the others   .   Satie said   :

When I was young,   people told me: You'll see when   you're fifty years old

.   Now I'm fifty.   I've seen nothing   .

◆ ◆

How to Write a Play (in which i am really telling myself how, but if you are the right one i am telling you how, too)

Richard Foreman

make a kind of beauty that isn't an
ALTERNATIVE to a certain environment
(beauty, adventure, romance, dream, drama all
take you out of your real world and into their
own in the hope you'll return refreshed, wiser,
more compassionate, etc.)
                              but rather
makes GAPS in the non-beautiful, or look carefully at the structure of the
non-beautiful, whatever it is (and remember that structure is always a combination of the

THING
and the
PERCEIVING of it)

and see where there are small points, gaps, unarticulated, or un-mapped
places within it
        (the non-beautiful)
which un-mapped places must be the very places where beauty CAN be
planted in the midst of the heretofore unbeautiful.

Because the mind's PROJECTED beauty (which is the only beauty) . . . can
either find itself in the already beautiful (so agreed upon) or it can MAKE
Conquer new territories.

Reprinted from Richard Foreman, *Reverberation Machines: The Later Plays and Essays* (New York: Station Hill Press, 1986), 222–30. Reprinted by permission of Richard Foreman.

But: while in the midst of the heretofore still un-redeemed "non-beautiful" the projection of the will-to-beauty can either be a pure act of will in which there is a pure, willed reversal of values

(which can have great strategic value but creates art that DOES tend to "wear out"—not, you understand, a negative judgement)

or

our method.
find the heretofore un-mapped, un-notated crevices
in the not-yet-beautiful landscape (which is a
collaboration between perceiving mind and world)
and widen the gaps
and plant the seed in those gaps
and make those gaps flower . . . and the plant
over-runs the entire landscape.

What this amounts to is a DECISION
to view non-beautiful material in such a way that what was fore-ground is now background . . . and the desired beauty is then projected, as the creative act, into the midst of the heretofore rejected (non-beautiful, un-interesting, cliched, etc.).

Delight is delight.
It aims us to whatever it is that delights us.
Can we make a more CONTROLLED use of that energy of "being-aimed" by willfully choosing to have a certain object be the one which arouses that delight-energy? ANY object?

Of course. That's the task—discover how to be in control, how to CHOOSE.
which object shall provoke the delight phenomenon

(and so increase that per-centage of the world we can say "yes" to, and thereby gain an inexhaustible fund of "delight-fuel")

Here's how.

Normally, let us assume we are delighted by a sunset
We are not delighted by a corpse.
But if we place the corpse within a certain composition, let us say—we are then delighted by the composition of which the corpse is a part
So—while we are still not delighted by a corpse, we can be delighted by something (made or found) of which the corpse is a part.
The task of art is to find what heretofore does not delight us, and make that part of some kind of composition in such a way that delight results.

Now, the composition need not be a composition in the expected sense, that is, need not be something that is defined or defines the artwork itself—

The composition may be any "context" in which the material is placed. In much art today, for instance, the context-composition is "the inherited history of Western art." So that the reason a minimalist gesture such as a Morris black box is "delightful" is because we understand it as an intelligent next move chosen in the context of an evolving "game" which has been the game (move and countermove) of Western art.

So in the theatre, which is always behind the times, one must ask "ah— what can we include in the on-going context composition which heretofore has been de-valued and kept out, etc., etc., and few people in the theatre ask that question and do that thing and so the theatre is rarely art, and when it is it creates problems for itself since its audience is not an audience interested in art but in entertainment.

Which means, its audience is interested in being delighted by what they already know in themselves as delightful. And their response to the attempt to include NEW material in the composition—material which they here-tofore have categorized as non-delightful—their response is generally nega-tive because they have never been trained to be composition perceivers rather than object perceivers. When they look at theatre, they use daily-life perceptual modes and so see things, and not patterns and contexts and compositions.

The rallying cry must be—stop making objects that men can worship.

Art shouldn't add new objects to the world to enslave men. It should begin the process of freeing men by calling into doubt the solidity of objects and laying bare the fact that it is a web of relations that exists only; that web held taut in each instance by the focal point of consciousness that is each separate individual consciousness.

In my work, I show the traces of one such web. (The assumption herein is not idealism, because the consciousness is a constructed thing also, on a different level subject to the same laws of configuration as the world outside, a collection of trace elements, not a self-sufficient constituting agent: but the relation between consciousness and "world" is the relation between two intersecting force fields, neither of which is a thing, both of which are a system of relations.)

I show the traces of such web intersections—and by seeing that, you are "reminded" to tune to your own. Find objects in a sense interchangeable (and, in another sense, poignant for that reason). But most of all, find exhila-ration and freedom and creative power, for when you see the web of related-ness of all things—which is in a certain ever-alive relation to a "your own web" of consciousness—you then are no longer a blind, hypnotized wor-shiper of "objects"—but a free man. Capable of self-creation and re-creation in all moments of your life.

Most audiences and critics want to be moved, knocked out. That is a sign of their illness, blindness, need to remain children. Most audiences want a perceivable, nameable content. That is, they want to be able to reduce the experience of the work to a gestalt of some sort that they can carry away from the theatre with them.

That means, they want to feel that they have extracted property, capital, from the investment of time in the experience.

NO! The art experience shouldn't ADD to our baggage, that store of images that weighs us down and limits our clear view to the horizons. [The art experience should rather (simply) ELIMINATE what keeps us moored to hypnotizing aspects of reality.]

Or better—by showing how reality is always a "positive" which is but a response to (an extraction from) a "negative" background, it allows us, in terms of this continual, now revealed polarity, to make contact with the reality that is really-there. Not by social fiat, but by operating at the constituting heart of things.

It is not a matter of getting BEYOND, DEEPER, HIGHER than everyday, normal, agreed on culturally-determined reality, it is a matter of—within the confines of the art experience—allowing ourselves to partake of the "taste" of a perceptive mode that [strategically subverts the very OBVIOUS aspects of the gross and childish conditioned perception used to "brow beat us" through life.] The gross mode of perception that suppresses the contradiction at the heart of each consciously posited "object." *re catharsize ; re baptize*

The artist must search for what has never been seen before.
 BUT
Not simply a new "monster." Not a new "that knocks me out like . . ." (a pyramid, Shakespeare, sex, etc.)
 But
 a new
 object which once found
 is hard to see. Maybe it's not even "there."

We live in a world of traces. Things leave traces. We must never try to make man believe that what is by definition constituted as a "trace," has indeed a different kind of reality—that of "object."

The emotion must never come, as it usually does, through our being convinced of the reality of the image or event presented, but only the ecstatic emotion of one's own seeing of things. [Delight in one's own energy.]

NEVER awe or delight in the "worshipful way" we feel emotion when we are awed or moved by the "other" which seems like an alien other in which we "wish" we could partake (all romantic art).

Need for Confrontation

Art + = to CONFRONT the object

Kitsch = atmosphere replaces object distance between you and object de-creased by atmosphere which makes you FEEL at one with the object because the atmosphere is felt to be that exuded by the object. But then object and you (feeling) are one and there is no ENCOUNTER, and no seeing. (To play the subtext, rather than the object, for instance.)

What is the object? The encountered object, encountered in making the work: the "real" chair, body, word, noise, etc.

The constructed object end with (art) is the we STRUCTURE of the articulating process. The MAKING A THING BE-THERE AS ITSELF (in its web of relations). Process.

The artist doesn't explain, analyze the object . . . but he sets it up so that one CONFRONTS in the realist fashion its BEING-THERE which is a confrontation to your own BEING-THERE.

PARADOX

The way to confront the object is to allow it its own life—let it grow its own shoots in directions that do **not** re-inforce its being-in-life for use as a tool, but that suggests a compositional scheme not centered on useful human expectations. So, let the chair that is for sitting have a string run from it to an orange, because if chair was just "chair for sitting" we would not "confront" as we not-confront in kitsch because we are too close to the chair, its meaning is too much OUR meaning; but now chair-connected-to-orange is an "alien" chair that we must CONFRONT.

(To reveal an object or act, gesture, emotion, idea, sound.
To make it seizable
To speak its name you must
make it part of a system not
its own. Involve it compositionally with
another realm, which is YOUR realm of pattern
making isomorphic with your
mind-process. THEN there is confrontation.)

"Kitsch" CLEMENT GREENBERG

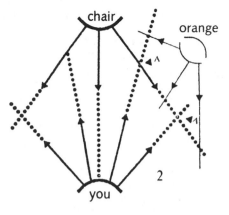

KITSCH
(and sleep) as
the moment of
contact between
you and object
is one dimensional
and you are
in a state of
identification
(hypnotized by)
with that face
of itself the
object presents
to you.

ART
(and awakedness)
     as
the moment of
contact between
you and object
is multifaceted and
often "distant" (point A)
from the object.

          also
in 2 (as opposed to 1)
your mind-pattern-
process is being as-it-is:
and THAT structure
inter-acts with the
object structure as-it-is.

In 1 the mind forgets
its own working and there
is no real meeting, only
a 1-dimensional (1 "presented"
face to another) moment of
"official" (cliched)
     "something"
that is too mindless: i.e. one
dimensional
(lacking points "A" of 2)
to be a real encounter.

Diagram 2 explains, once and for all, all of my plays!

The message must be "To choose either turbulence or serenity is an error. To choose either knowing or doing is an error." So . . . in the play . . . inject disruption into knowing, and order into passion.

The play is a lecture in which you don't say "This is so . . ." but rather . . . "This occurs to me and it occurs to me that the reason it occurs to me is this act, which occurs to me," and so on and so on, deeper and deeper.

My message is "filling the space with the idea." Free play within the idea. Ability to treat the "field" of the idea as an area for work and discovery. Idea as a field . . . in which something that is not idea (but more physical, sensual, ecstatic) can emerge.

I write to make life handle-able.

The deflection inherent in time. Space—
one makes art to be able to decide what goes into you
                                        and what goes out of you.
    To be in control of what goes into you and out
    of you is why you decide to make your own art.
    Of course . . . as it goes in and out, space and time
    give it an uncontrollable "twist."

Lived experience is a certain kind of focus. You focus on an aimed-at while living, and because you are focused on that, you don't see your own gestures. Art: is trying to see your own gestures.

My gesture has always been to pull away, to change what came into me, to make something BETTER, that could then go into me instead of the thing that did go into me. Hence, to find a way to make better FOOD for myself than was provided by others. My art then (one's art) is a way of being-in-the-world so that the INPUT is the best possible input . . . into me. Journalism is trying to imitate life. Art is an amplification of the effects encountered in trying to make art.

Art: a machine to effect input. To provide awakening, energy-giving disconti-
nuities. To fight entropy. Art is NOT comment on life. It is fighting the entropy of life-that-seeks equilibrium, that seeks-not-stress, which would lead

(as life does) to death. (Inject quantum shocks, discontinuities, to keep twist-ing us away from sleep, death, into what is "artificially" sustained . . . AWAK-ENED LIFE, CONSCIOUSNESS!

Form in art—from isn't a container (of content) but rather
    a rule for generating a possible "next move."
        That's where the subject is (in that next move, dictated or made possible by the form). The commonly-thought-of content or subject is the pretext to set a process in operation, and that process is the real subject.
The text is me
It grows like I grow
It extends itself, falls, stumbles over . . . something.
    Recovers. It projects itself as it will. Encounters resistance of various sorts, but those resistances turn out to be steps affording a new advance stretch extension twist
stage it: Try to make the compositional aspects be in relief. The **structure** as it were. Not the structure in time, but the structure of the moment.
    (time doesn't exist. It's all **now**
    There's memory-now-future.
    Now doesn't exist
    It's a pivot point
    Make things structured in that pivot point.
    (I.E. frame now, frame not-there)
People who work in time are making things for memory
    Are not clear about here and now
        Proper analysis here & now
            What am I doing now
Man is future-oriented, but life is collision in now between project and what resists it
So: each movement show what interferes with, contradicts, projects—from other levels. Not just conflict of people. What contradicts the "play" itself and its mode-of-being-present.

    That privileged object which is the ONE object that must be studied . . . (so that man can study what it is most important he study) . . . that object is not yet "available." Not yet there.
    In making a play I am trying to make that important object that is not yet there.

Figure of Speech
An Interview with Mac Wellman

Marc Robinson

Since PAJ Publications brought out one of Mac Wellman's first plays, *Starluster*, in *Wordplays I* (1981), much has happened to the restless Brooklyn-based playwright. For most of the 80s he was a well-kept secret, produced only by small New York theatres like BACA Downtown, Shaliko, and Soho Rep. Predictably, the mainstream press neglected to review him. Few of his plays after *Starluster* saw publication, except those he included in the two important anthologies he edited, *Theatre of Wonders* and *7 Different Plays*.

Then, a few years ago, Wellman finally gained sustained, serious attention. For the first time a regional theatre produced his work: San Diego Rep premiered *Albanian Softshoe* in 1989. A Guggenheim and other lucrative awards came his way, and his first real commercial success—*Crowbar,* produced in 1989 by En Garde Arts at the abandoned Victory Theatre on 42nd Street.

This interview was conducted by Marc Robinson in April 1991, shortly before Wellman received his second Obie Award, this time for *Sincerity Forever.*

ROBINSON: We should probably start with the reason we're sitting here tonight: the publication of *Terminal Hip.* Could you talk a bit about the genesis of this play?

WELLMAN: *Terminal Hip* is actually the second part of a project called *Cellophane,* which I began about six years ago. It came out of my interest in basic issues of writing and speech. As you know, a good deal of postmodern theory has to do with a reversal of the traditional priority of speech

Reprinted from *PAJ: A Journal of Performance Art* 14:1 (January, 1992): 43–51. © 1992 by Performing Arts Journal, Inc.

over writing. This comes as quite a surprise for most Americans, because people like Whitman and Emerson have told us that writing is a kind of cancer upon speech, and that if you want to find the "authentic" you have to go back to speech. Everybody who's tuned into American poetry has regarded speech as the highest thing, even though none of us really can know what speech is. I began to look at H. L. Mencken and other people who actually studied American traditional speech and realized you could write with it. You could use all the tools that the writerly postmodern people applied to their own sense of language. But the more I began to study out-of-favor American speech, I began to understand how the American language got to be the way it is now.

ROBINSON: What aspects of American language fascinated you most?

WELLMAN: I'd come across a phrase in Mencken: "If I hadda been"—which is bad language. There was another one—"if I mighta could." It's the kind of stuff that you'd hate if you thought about writing well every waking moment. These horrible statements are things you try to get out of your system. You just look at them and they make your skin crawl. But then I'd put them together—these two phrases—"If I hadda been I mighta could." I thought, how wonderful, this is something you cannot say in any European language I know, or even in English.

I read three volumes of Mencken's *The American Language.* I looked at other books on dialect speech, which are all considered trash by the postmodernists, because they hate speech. But I began to think, well, what happens if I treat this stuff as raw material?

As soon as language goes out of fashion, two things happen to it. For one thing, the meaning becomes richer. A word or a phrase has all sorts of associations, many of which are unpleasant. But it also rolls off the tongue. Old expressions, jazz-age stuff, anything that's been said by hundreds of thousands of people for over 20 years is far more speakable than anything you can ever write. It's like old wood: it has a texture and a grain to it. This is something that I've never been interested in until recently because I had always wanted to challenge actors, to make constructions that were impossible to say, which I realized I have a talent for.

So I discovered that you can take things that are a little bit dated, and break them into pieces and put them back together in such a way that they're not dated anymore. They're actually enormously powerful oral systems that had this traditional strength and power that was "mythic." You could also put them together in a way that *was* postmodern—that involved all those very sharp dislocations of meaning—and you could say everything you wanted to about the current culture.

When I was working on the *Cellophane* texts (*Cellophane* and *Terminal Hip*), I wrote one page a day for two and a half years, until I had this big stack of legal pads. I was attempting to make poetry that was *not* for the stage, that was just for me. I was also attempting to write badly, because you get so stuck all the time trying to write well. You get caught up with a degenerate notion of style. There is no place, certainly, for a really *radical* style. You know, we were always taught to believe that anything that was theatrical, that had large emotions, had no ideas in it. When I began writing I wanted to argue with that notion. I began to appreciate ideas directly.

ROBINSON: Was it something in your research of American speech that led you to set aside standard dramatic exchange in *Terminal Hip?* The play doesn't seem simply to lack dialogue. The writing is aggressively *anti-dialogue.*

WELLMAN: I'm not really anti-dialogue. But it's harder to be very focused on ideas if you're worried about character, which involves breaking speech down into two or three parts, and then having to worry about the consistency of characters. Actually, I wrote my first plays as monologues, and then I broke them down into different characters. I did that to make the dialogue more disjointed. But that's something I haven't done in 10 or 15 years.

I finished the *Cellophane* text in August of 1986—as poetry. I woke up one morning soon after that and wondered what would happen if I gave this text to actors. I did it at New Dramatists: I went in here with the Bible, Walt Whitman, Blake. I had six or eight actors; Jeff Jones was my dramaturg; and I said: I want to make this into a play. Jeff had been working on his quotation plays, so he pushed me in the direction of chopping it all up and making it into a quotation play. I was trying to come up with characters; the actors were beating themselves against the wall, trying to make my text into dialogue—but it wouldn't budge—because it was not *written* to do that. It was written in one-page chunks. I learned an important principle: you cannot violate the nature of the writing. If something is written as a monologue, it's going to be a monologue.

ROBINSON: Tell me more about what is bad writing. It's not just bad grammar, obviously, or inappropriate vocabulary. Does it have something to do with subject matter? Or the writer's attitude?

WELLMAN: It does. Inevitably, if you start mismatching pronouns, getting your tenses wrong, writing sentences that are too long or too short, you will begin to say things that suggest a subversive political reality.

ROBINSON: After scoffing traditional rules so steadily, do you now find that this impudence has become a rule in itself, a trap? Do you now have to find a way to break this new rule?

WELLMAN: Yes, sure. In a sense (at least in the context of "bad" writing), what you have to say is more interesting when you're learning the language than when you've mastered it. When you've mastered it, you can use the language system to exclude meaning, which I think is what most professional writing is about. It's very narrow. A lot of journalism is often about closing off avenues of expression or interpretation. What we accept as correct prose is very limiting. Anyone who's a professional writer knows it's a pain in the ass to write. The most liberal style manual is terribly confining and overrated in our mandarin culture. But, you know, I don't think language is the most important thing.

ROBINSON: That's a surprise, coming from you!

WELLMAN: People tell me all the time that I'm only about language, but I'm not! I'm just trying to make a language that comes close to what I feel and think. A statement like "if I hadda been I mighta could" is an enormously complex metaphysical statement. It's not just bad language; it's saying something that's real, that's possible; that's only contradictory in terms of *good* language. But it's something I know: I feel like that every day. Most bad language describes a spiritual condition which is not grammatical, but it is *real*. I'm more interested in the world than language. I'm more interested in syntax than grammar.

ROBINSON: Why's that? Why favor syntax over grammar?

WELLMAN: Syntax is the flow of meaning through language. Grammar is the set of shackles that gets imposed on meaning. Don't get me wrong: I also like good language. I like Proust, Henry James.

ROBINSON: What about those who say that your work is merely the product of automatic writing? Gertrude Stein, you know, often heard these things from critics, and she always protested that, no, every word was agonized over. Do you have to defend yourself against the same accusation?

WELLMAN: I haven't had to yet, but some people do think that it's easier to write this way. As soon as you stop writing in the official style, you multiply your aesthetic choices. I'm fortunate in that I have an ear for this sort of thing. I have a tendency toward malapropism. I want to go with the wrong word and see where it takes me. I can always find the right one; they have computer programs to correct style now.

ROBINSON: Do you do a lot of revision?

WELLMAN: My texts all go through multiple drafts before anyone sees them, so obviously I'm not against rewriting. But I do have a problem with revision as it is practiced in the theatre—that is, the endless reworking of text that happens during the near-panic of rehearsal. Most revisions for theatre works end up being bad. I think theatre writing is a kinetic, physical thing—the faster you write it, the better it is, most of the time. Usually, when you attempt to rewrite for the theatre, your play becomes more longwinded. You try to explain and justify things; the play gets less interesting. I'd rather write a lot and cut. Or start a new play. It's very hard to re-enter the world of that moment of creation, because it's not just a language moment; it's a physical one as well. You're not just imagining the world.

ROBINSON: In *Terminal Hip*, I saw you playing a lot with the various languages of our day—the languages of the politicians, the evangelist, the huckster, the professor, the Dale Carnegie figure run amok.

WELLMAN: Yes, that's true. The play was also me talking to me.

ROBINSON: How so?

WELLMAN: It's me saying, well you think you're so smart! It's very private. But then again, I didn't know I was going to make *Terminal Hip* into a performance. It began, in a sense, as a self-accusation, a dialogue with myself. A dialogue of self and soul, as Yeats would say. I interrogated myself. "Is that what you think you're doing? This is what I think of you." I was dealing with my own notions of what it means to be a person who does my sort of work. I didn't mean it to be cultural critique at all, except insofar as I'm a member of this culture. I don't think I accuse anybody of anything worse than I've committed or imagined I've committed myself.

ROBINSON: The title certainly leads one to see the play as satire.

WELLMAN: Yes. The title comes from a poem of mine—a mock epic—a terrible satire of the East Village and all the pretentiousness that I found there. A lot of the scathing attack of downtown New York fell away, but I kept the title anyway.

ROBINSON: You directed the first production of *Terminal Hip*. How did you approach the play? What did you talk about with your collaborators?

WELLMAN: I'd never directed before. So what I did came from instinct. Some techniques I borrowed from the arsenal of other directors. Robert Wilson, for instances, always makes sketches of what he wants his show to look like. So I had everybody who was working on *Terminal Hip*, including myself, go home one night and draw pictures of what we thought the play should look like. We all came back with these horrible stick figures—except Steve Mellor who first performed the play. He's a very good artist. He drew the set as you see it now. We then went through the text meticulously—that's something Des McAnuff does with Shakespeare—so that Steve knew what it meant.

ROBINSON: I remember Eric Overmyer's essay about you in *Theater* magazine, in which he talked about being disappointed with most productions of your plays. He laid some blame with the actors, who often play at being coy or detached. Is there an approach to Wellman texts that is particularly appropriate? Are there acting styles to be avoided?

WELLMAN: I know what he's talking about, although I think that's mainly true of productions a few years back. I don't think it's such a problem now, because I know more about how to explain things to actors. Mainly what you have to do is treat the language as natural—not naturalistic—but natural within the context. I'm much more interested in actors' voices now than I was before. Not that I'm so interested in the Method or anything. But you can explain the text in such a way that will suggest helpful things about the world of *this* language. You also have to find the right kind of actors. Some people connect with it, some people don't.

ROBINSON: Maybe now's the time to ask the Obscurity question. One constant comment about your work, from certain quarters, is that you confuse for confusion's sake. Even an admirer like Overmyer will write that you pursue "an ideology of obfuscation." Are those fair assessments?

WELLMAN: I do pursue a kind of experimental agenda with the writing. I hope in time that people will read my texts as carefully as they read any other dramatic literature. I don't think I'm a difficult writer at all, but I have not gotten a close reading of my texts, particularly of the ones that are supposed to be obscure.

ROBINSON: It seems that in *Terminal Hip* indeterminacy is built into the text. The function of "X," for instance: "X" can really mean whatever you want it to. In your play *Bad Penny* you write that "X" is "the nothingness of the unknown, the nothingness of infinity." Could that mean that "X" is also a place for our acts of interpretation?

WELLMAN: Yes, I think so. All I'm trying to do is make a space where language can be taken seriously and have a little space. We lie in a sea of explanations, and I'm trying to get beyond that. The impulse to explain and make everything rational and clear is wonderful up to a point, but then it becomes suffocation.

ROBINSON: In one of your essays you talked about "language as gesture." That sounded very tantalizing, but I've never really known what you meant.

WELLMAN: I meant that there's a physical direction to a sentence or a word, even a physical *feeling*. Up until the twentieth century, prosody—the poetic standard of what constitutes a poem—has been a numerical thing. Ezra Pound has said that a beautiful line of poetry should have a shape— like a vase, for instance. That idea breaks with conventional prosody. I feel that way, too. We don't pay enough attention to the physical aspects of language. Particularly in the theatre, words should be objects flying around the room.

ROBINSON: Somewhere else you had said that language as gesture is both "near and hard to grasp." Is this idea related to your distrust of paraphrase-able plays?

WELLMAN: Yes. There's a poem of Holderlin's called *Patmos*. The first line is "God is near and hard to grasp." Hard to grasp. We think we know what language is, what it can do. I don't think we know anything about it. You know, I often get the feeling that the whole world is about to blow itself up because we're not listening to language anymore. We have cleaned up language so much that we don't pay attention to the aberrant things that language does.

ROBINSON: Speaking of politics, let me ask you a bit about political theatre, the subject of your essay last year in *American Theatre*. You were calling

Beckett

CREATES MEANING VIA TONE, SYNTAX, NOUNS = ∅

for indirection in politically-minded plays, it seems—an end to didacticism. Yet your recent play, *Sincerity Forever*, is thoroughly political, and it quite clearly corresponds to a contemporary situation—the morality debates that overtook Capitol Hill last year. The play isn't didactic, but its certainly isn't indirect. Have I spied a contradiction?

WELLMAN: I changed. I'm now getting very interested in religion. This whole thing with Helms made me think about what should be the place of religion in an organized society, a secular society. The world is looking for meaning, but I don't think it lies in Western religions. Certainly that's what *Cellophane* and *Terminal Hip* are about—my desperate search for meaning.

ROBINSON: When I was reading the long interview with Vaclav Havel, *Disturbing the Peace*, I came across a wonderful question that I want to put to you. The interviewer asked what Havel did when he "exhausted the initial impulse that compelled him to write in the first place." The interviewer felt that such moments of helplessness were very important. A writer has to decide whether to experiment with a new identity or to go over the old concerns again, looking for different ways to answer the same impulse. Is that moment of exhaustion something that you've also experienced?

WELLMAN: That's actually the point when I began to write things like *Cellophane* and *Sincerity Forever*. I think, initially, a dramatist writes from his own life. And you exhaust that material fairly early. Then you have this problem of not knowing what to write about. And in my case, what I've done is attempt a move to other scales. The notion of scales is from chaos theory, and it means that you can examine the physical shape of a process by jumping from one scale to another—from macro to micro. I think the study of self-similarity from scale to scale—fractal studies it's called—has great relevance to current theory and practice of dramatic form.

ROBINSON: Over the last couple of years, a sudden and considerable success has come to you after being just a coterie playwright. Does all that attention have its costs?

WELLMAN: I never thought it would happen. I'm still surprised by the attention. I don't know what it means. I know I have to formulate a new set of practical ideals—working goals—because I never thought I'd get this far.

ROBINSON: What are those new ideals?

WELLMAN: I talked about this with another playwright, Connie Congdon, who is also quite shocked by the fact that anybody wants to do *her* work at this point. We've been talking with the director Jim Simpson and some other people about starting a national theatre. I'm not sure it will happen because I'm not a great organizer. But it's a focus for discussion. The theatre won't have a company, nor a building. It will be based with people all over the country who could initiate projects. If you wanted to

NEA 4
Karen Finley

do a show in a real theatre building, you could do it. But if you wanted to do something in Mississippi in a field, you could do that, too. I'd love to make something national that didn't have to do with intransigent, careerist institutional theatres. I just hate the whole strange system of putting theatres all over the place that all do the same play.

I've gotten some attention, and that's been nice, and I'm really grateful for it. But mainly it was contingency, and there are a lot of people who've worked just as hard as I have who, for one reason or another, haven't caught on. It's just an accident that it happened to me.

I got into teaching at the point when I had given up and said, "Fuck it. I'm a loser and nothing's ever going to happen. And I don't care anymore." And at that point everything started to turn around. I no longer cared about my career, and I became fearless, because I didn't have anything, so nobody could take anything away from me. I'm not going to become the next big playwright in this country. I'd love to see my work done, but it's too strange ever really to catch on, I know. I keep trying to write like Chekhov and it just comes out wrong!

ETHOS

part two

The Ritualistic

the relationship between ritual and theater has been a significant focus of the debate on the origins of theater since 1872, when Friedrich Nietzsche first argued that Greek tragedy grew out of the dithyrambic chorus.[1] Some scholars have theorized that theater originated in ritual, as rituals were among the earliest public events to incorporate music, speech, and movement into a performance that was intended to have a visceral effect on its audience. According to this proposition, rituals arose when pre-literate "primitive" communities repeated and formalized certain actions performed by and for the people to use magical thinking to try to affect events beyond human control, usually related to three broad areas fundamental to survival: pleasure, *salvation* power, and duty. As these actions became more formalized, myths were developed to explain them. Many avant-garde theater artists experimented with ritualistic elements throughout the twentieth century, seeking to strengthen the bond between performers and audience and recover the spiritual power that they believed theater had lost.

Christopher Innes identified one unifying characteristic of the avant-garde as its "quasi-religious focus on myth and magic, which in the theatre leads to experiments with ritual and ritualistic patterning of performance."[2] Interest in the ritualistic was part of a larger shift in emphasis from text to performance, from mind to body, and from individual to community.[3] In these avant-garde performances, the ritualistic is part of an attempt to "include their audiences by creating special spaces and ritualistic-aesthetic actions."[4] Searching for original, innovative forms, the early avant-garde drew upon ritualistic techniques to explore dream states and mythological archetypes; several movements, including Symbolism and Surrealism, were drawn to ritual's "appeal to the irrational."[5] After World-War II avant-garde theater artists, inspired by Antonin Artaud, continued to experiment with ritualistic elements: nonverbal communication and the active engagement of performers with audience members (The Living Theatre, The Open Theatre, Richard Schechner's Performance Group), transcendence of tangible reality (Jean Genet), and spiritual healing and raising collective consciousness (Jerzy Grotowski, Peter Brook). After the intense exploration of the communal aspects of ritual during the 1960s, avant-garde artists began to incorporate ritualistic elements in their aesthetic experiments to conduct a more focused examination of issues of gender and race, forgoing a call for revolution.

In theater, the ritualistic frequently uses sounds, images, rhythms, and gestures as significant performance elements, exploring patterns through language and movement, as seen in the plays in this section: the ritualistic daily cleaning routines of Kenneth Brown's *The Brig* (1963), the sadomasochistic relationship of the women in Naomi Iizuka's *Body Beautiful* (1989), and the repeated and revised ("rep and rev") deaths in Suzan-Lori Parks's *The Death of the Last Black Man in the Whole Entire World* (1990). Addressing contemporary issues seemingly beyond human control, such as race, gender, and freedom, these works apply the magical thinking of ritual to new subject matter with a more specific political agenda. The ritualistic elements do not aim to affect the fundamentals of existence as does traditional ritual, but they focus on political and social issues, such as the dehumanization of the military and military-like structures (*The Brig*), the sacrifice of the female body to media expectations (*Body Beautiful*), and the death of black history and identity (*Death of the Last Black Man*), in secular performance rites for their times.

Brown based *The Brig* on his experience in a military brig in Japan in the 1950s, when he served in the U.S. Marines. On one level, it can be seen as "super-realism," a transcription of a day in the life of the brig; events accumulate vertically, actions stack up with little sense of forward movement in the narrative, and there is little to indicate the progression of time. In this way, the play can be seen as a form of naturalism, although director Judith Malina's production notes avoid any mention of naturalism, evoking instead three seminal names of the avant-garde, Vsevolod Meyerhold, Erwin Piscator, and Artaud. Malina signals her intent to challenge social structures, foment revolution, and offer the work as a sacrifice to Artaud's mad dreams: "O Antonin fierce and demanding, in *The Brig* I have seen the actor tax his body to that abstract athletic splendor where he looms on the precarious edge of the abyss of soullessness."[6] Her call for extraordinary performers to sacrifice themselves within a performance-ritual is repeated in Grotowski's description from the same time of a holy actor, one "who reveals himself and sacrifices the innermost part of himself" so the spectator can experience a new awareness.[7] Malina, Grotowski, and their spiritual forefather Artaud expressed a desire for the performer to move beyond what the human body normally does to what it might do—a call for the extraordinary performer to serve as a shaman—with a clear focus on the performer's body and physicality as vehicles for the spectators' renewal.

The ritualistic elements of *The Brig* arise more strongly from the physical movements in the stage directions than from the dialogue. The script not only describes a series of codified movements dictated by the guards and the warden, but also suggests that each production ensemble create large sections of the action and dialogue from the routine of the actual brig. Prisoners request permission to cross the lines to do their work or clean themselves, receive permission, cross the lines, request permission again, and so on; even smoking and using the "head" are regimented and ritualized, and "free" time is carefully measured and constrained. Also, the first published text of the play includes a diagram of the original set—not as a proscription for configurations, but as an illustration of one way to establish an intensely communal feeling of claustrophobia and anxiety.

The guards, under the command of the warden and the Marine Corps manual, use the environment, rules, and ritualistic actions to dehumanize the prisoners. They beat the prisoners into submission as punishment for unspoken crimes, stripping them of their names, identities, and senses of self. Prisoners must live by the Marine code and nothing else; their only hope of survival is to be a Marine. In rehearsal, Malina had the cast follow a set of "Brig regulations" and "Rehearsal discipline" designed to impose authoritarian rules on their actions and work, with penalties for infractions. These regulations were included in the program and became a part of the unspoken text in performance, thus publishing the rules of the performance and of this world to the audience.

The play resists the mainstream, both politically and aesthetically, in many ways. It can be seen as critique of the brutality of war and prison conditions, as suggested by the success of the Living Theatre's 2007 revival in the wake of the atrocities at Abu Ghraib in Iraq. It might be seen as anti-corporate, with the ritualistic dehumanization of the prisoners suggesting the depersonalizing environment of large corporations or of capitalist society on a broader level. But *The Brig* resists such reductive themes in its disavowal of an "author's voice" telling us what to think about the implications of the action. By drawing on the extraordinary physical discipline of a military brig, Brown uncovers the ritualistic within the real and empowers physical action to speak louder than the narrative.

In *Body Beautiful*, the central characters, Rita and Loni, share an obsession with becoming and staying thin. At the start of the play, although one seems successful and dominant and the other seems unsuccessful and submissive, both have been stripped of their identities. Iizuka calls for them to "wear white bathrobes and towels twisted turban-like around their heads"[8]; they sit on identical high-back chairs but barely move except for changes of position between scenes. After five scenes of domination in which the successfully thin Rita scolds the not-thin-enough Loni, the action switches seamlessly to a talk show. Loni, having achieved "ideal thinness" through watching what goes into her body and removing things from her body (elective surgery), emasculates a talk show host, who seems to have appeared magically in her spa, berating him as Rita once berated her. By dismembering herself through ritualistic sacrifice of free will and body organs in the interests of the "ideal" body, she has gained the power to eviscerate figuratively the host. Within these ritualistic hazings, the "body beautiful" renders men and women powerless.

Body Beautiful combines contemporary concerns over gender and society's obsession with the ideal body with a satire of the ritualistic ways in which women are induced to accept these standards. Yet unlike those in *The Brig*, the ritualistic elements in the play exaggerate everyday enactments with heightened language, spare movement, and an obsessive quality that borders on the pathological. The contemporary fuses with the primitive, as in the women's dialogue that refers to certain cultures as models of health and longevity:

> Take the Hunzas of the Himalyas. Their longevity and endurance are legendary the world over. And then, of course, there is that little, tiny tribe in North Yemen is it? What is their name? It's on the tip of my tongue—phenomenally healthy people. Meat-free and doing fine. And what about the Mayan Indians? Let's not forget the noble savage of the Yucatan. Lovely people. Free of disease. Can you imagine? It's practically unimaginable, but try. Do try.[9]

Once they have attained the body beautiful through surgery, the women perform a final contemporary rite: public display on television. This invocation of the ritualistic has only become more formalized and omnipresent since Iizuka wrote her play, as TV talk shows have given way to reality shows such as *The Biggest Loser*, which broadcasts society's contemporary nightmare, complete with a weekly ritualistic weighing of contestants, in a banal reinforcement of the issues Iizuka satirizes.

Parks—preceded only by Adrienne Kennedy as a female African-American avant-garde playwright of note, as Robert Brustein remarked[10]—adopts a jazz music principle in *The Death of the Last Black Man*. The ritualistic elements take the form of "rep and rev" (repetition and revision), in which a theme is revisited with variations, so that the repetitions refigure the original: "Like any number of modern and postmodern works, the play refigures conventions of narrativity and linear progression. At the same time, it enacts a relatively simple event: the funeral rites and burial of BLACK MAN WITH WATERMELON."[11] Similar to *The Brig*, each repetition stacks on the previous one, as opposed to the traditional "horizontal" mapping of the narrative in a well-made play, commonly depicted as moving from left to right in an often-chronological narrative line. All events appear to happen at virtually the same time, an echo of Gertrude Stein's concept of a "continuous present" (which plays a central part in the "Landscape" section of this volume). In Parks's "present," history is revised repeatedly.

The central event in the play is a religious ritual—funeral rites—through which Parks "reps and revs" on the theme of the death of the last black man:

> In the Final Chorus of *Death of the Last Black Man*, the ritual funeral is repeated as BLACK WOMAN WITH FRIEND DRUMSTICK again intones the refrain "Yesterday today next summer tomorrow just uh moment uhgoh in 1317 dieded thuh last black man in thuh whole entire world." . . . Then, however, the funeral is revised. Through the ritualistic repetitions, progress and African American history have been reconfigured as repetition. . . . The Final Chorus—the final rites for the last black man—becomes a celebration.[12]

Parks turns the last rites into a transformative element, one that attempts to free the "last black man" by rewriting and ultimately exploding African-American history. The repetition and revision of this history locates all the deaths in one place and one symbolic character (a black everyman) in an attempt to ritualistically purge American history of its racial transgressions through performance.

Parks's repetitions appropriate ritualistic devices from her Roman Catholic upbringing. She uses formal devices from religious rites, such as the repeated ringing of bells in *Death of the Last Black Man*, as she revealed to David Savran:

SAVRAN: There's so much in your plays that can be understood as ritual. Ritual repetition. And you also write about spells and possession—both of which are also connected to ritual.

PARKS: Theatre makes more sense to me like that. . . . My family is Roman Catholic. And there's a lot of drama—holding things up, and bells are ringing, and holding something else up again, and the bells go off again. . . . The audience and the players are involved in this recreation of something that could have happened, didn't happen, will happen, is happening right as they're creating it.[13]

Although the play draws ritualistic elements from religion for secular purposes, Parks sees a somewhat higher purpose in this as well: "You put things back together. People say, what's *The Death of the Last Black Man* about? It's about these people who come together and remember him. They gather together and put on a play and every night they remember the last black man. That's like church: 'This is my body, this is my blood. Do this in memory of me.' "[14] The play does not require a participatory response, unlike the ritualistic plays of the 1960s (Living Theatre, Open Theatre, Performance Group), but Parks appears to aim for a transformative audience experience akin to that of ritual: a cleansing of the collective consciousness. Toward this end, she combines the linguistic manipulations of Mac Wellman and his predecessors—a pure joy in playing with sounds and the purposeful ambiguity of playful linguistic construction—with ritualistic elements seen in other plays in this section, displaying the porous boundaries among these areas of formal innovation and cultural resistance.

Whether on the page or the stage, Parks's rhythmic reps and revs have a swirling musicality that replaces the drive of conventional, plot-bound narrative. As Steven Drukman notes, "There is a momentum in Parks's musicality, an aim in mind, a propulsion."[15] In this respect, she follows in the line of playwrights concerned with circular, seemingly "static" linguistic constructions, such as Stein and Samuel Beckett, playwrights for whom the momentum of the words, in reading and in performance, replaces the thrust of narrative as the primary structural and dramatic element. But Parks displays a more obvious resistance to mainstream culture and politics through her focus on African-American history, a history that is pliable, a base material to be shaped rather than a reality with which to be reckoned. "My life is not about race," she writes. "It's about being alive. Why does everyone think that white artists make art and black artists make statements? Why doesn't anyone ever ask me about form?"[16] Parks thus surmounts the limitations of mainstream cultural critics who might find it easier to contain African-American plays within the rubric of political statements than to recognize the cultural resistance of a playwright experimenting with the relationship between innovative form and content.

Notes

1. See Erika Fischer-Lichte, *Theatre, Sacrifice, Ritual* (New York: Routledge, 2005), 18–20, and Friedrich Nietzsche, *The Birth of Tragedy: Out of the Spirit of Music,* trans. Ian C. Johnston (London: Penguin Classics, 1994).

2. Christopher Innes, *Avant-Garde Theatre, 1892–1992* (New York: Routledge, 1993), 3.

3. Fischer-Lichte, *Theatre, Sacrifice, Ritual,* 44–45.

4. Richard Schechner, "Performance Orientations in Ritual Theatre," in *Performing Texts,* ed. Michael Issacharoff and Robin F. Jones (Philadelphia: University of Pennsylvania Press, 1988): 136.

5. See Innes, who argues that Alfred Jarry's significance "lies in the appeal to the irrational and . . . the pre-social level of the mind" (28).

6. Malina, "Directing the Brig," 159 below in this volume.

7. Jerzy Grotowski, "The Theatre's New Testament," 187.

8. Naomi Iizuka, *Body Beautiful,* 123.

9. Iizuka, *Body Beautiful,* 126.

10. Robert Brustein, "The Death of the Last Black Man in the Whole Entire World," *The New Republic* 206, no. 15 (April 13, 1992): 30–31. A case can be made for the inclusion of the more experimental works of Zora Neale Hurston and the expressionist plays of Marita Bonner in the canon of influential female African-American avant-garde playwrights. See David Krasner, "Something's Going On Down Here That Concerns Me," in *Contemporary African American Women Playwrights: A Casebook,* by Philip C. Kolin (New York: Routledge, 2007), 9–22.

11. Alice Rayner and Harry J. Elam, Jr., "Unfinished Business: Reconfiguring History in Suzan-Lori Parks's *The Death of the Last Black Man in the Whole Entire World,*" *Theatre Journal* 46 (1994): 449.

12. Rayner and Elam, "Unfinished Business: Reconfiguring History," 460.

13. David Savran, "Suzan-Lori Parks," in *The Playwright's Voice,* New York: TCG, 1999: 148.

14. Savran, "Suzan-Lori Parks," 160.

15. Steven Drukman, "Suzan-Lori Parks and Liz Diamond: An Interview by Steven Drukman," *TDR* 39.2 (1995): 56.

16. Brustein, "The Death of the Last Black Man in the Whole Entire World," 31.

The Brig
A Concept for Theatre or Film

Kenneth H. Brown

CHARACTERS

The Guards

TEPPERMAN, *a tall, heavily built Negro with a New York accent. Twenty-one years old. He wears one stripe on his uniform*

GRACE, *a short and stocky Midwesterner. Twenty-two years old. He wears two stripes on his uniform*

THE WARDEN, *a well-built man of medium height with a slight Southern accent. Thirty years old. He wears four stripes on his uniform*

LINTZ, *a blond, tall, and slightly built Californian. Nineteen years old. He wears one stripe on his uniform*

The Prisoners

In all, there are eleven prisoners, which make up a cross-section of American society.

ONE, *a thin and sickly boy of eighteen*
TWO, *a tall, dark, and handsome young man of twenty-one*
THREE, *a seedy, short, and rather stupid-looking Negro of twenty-five*
FOUR, *a tall and awkward boy of eighteen*

Reprinted from Kenneth H. Brown, *The Brig* (New York: Hill and Wong, 1969), 39–80. The text printed here is the acting script used in The Living Theatre production. © 1963, reprinted by permission of Kenneth Brown

FIVE, (the first), a freckle-faced Irish lad of nineteen.

FIVE (the second), a meticulous and powerful young man of twenty-one. Tall
    and intelligent

SIX, a rough-looking man of thirty-four

SEVEN, an inconspicuous and well-adjusted prisoner

EIGHT, a healthy country lad—Southern accent

NINE, an inconspicuous and well-adjusted prisoner

TEN, a squat, Southern tough of twenty-two

Incidental Players

Two stretcher bearers

ACT ONE

SCENE 1

The inside of the Brig, four o'clock in the morning. In view are Post One, Post
Two, and the inside compound.

The curtain opens to complete darkness. A dim colored light focuses on PFC.
TEPPERMAN standing at the desk of the turnkey, CORPORAL GRACE, who is
seated there. They are whispering and smiling. TEPPERMAN walks to the door of
the inside compound, unlocks it, and enters. He walks to the center of the
sleeping area, takes his billy from his belt, and taps a prisoner, who is sleeping,
on the head. Only this is visible, since the dim light has followed TEPPERMAN.

TEPPERMAN. Wake up, Two. [In a low, almost whispering, but stern tone.] You
    better move, boy.

TWO [loud and clear]. Yes, sir.

TEPPERMAN. You better speak low, boy, when the lights are out in the com-
    pound. You want to wake up the other maggots? [Pause.] You better
    answer me, boy.

TWO. Yes, sir. I mean no, sir.

TEPPERMAN. I don't think you know what you mean, Two. Put your shoes on.
    Don't you know that bare feet never touch the deck? They make it greasy.
    [Pause.] Put your shoes on and report to me at the turnkey's desk. And
    don't request permission to cross the line, boy.

    TEPPERMAN leaves and the light follows him. He returns to the turnkey's
    desk. A moment later TWO appears at attention at the desk; in his boots and
    underwear.

TWO. Sir, Prisoner Number Two reporting as ordered, sir.

GRACE [standing up quickly]. What are your orders, Two?

TWO. To report to your desk, sir.

GRACE. You are a new maggot in my house, and I want to look at you. [*He walks around the prisoner.*] You are a mess, maggot, do you know that?

TWO. Yes, sir.

TEPPERMAN [*leaning toward the prisoner*]. Yes, yes, you, you are a mess, boy. Say it. Say you are a mess.

TWO. Sir, I am a mess, sir.

TEPPERMAN [*hitting the prisoner in the stomach repeatedly with his billy*]. I am going to be watching you among the rest of my lice, and if you are not squared away . . . [*Pauses, then smiling.*] I will clean up the deck with you. Is that clear, Two?

TWO [*doubling over from the blows*]. Yes, sir.

GRACE. Your guts are soft, maggot. Stand at attention. Nobody asked you to bend over. Stand up. You're making me sick with your little-girl tricks. That's better. [*Turning to* TEPPERMAN.] We've had enough of this new one. Send him back to his rack.

TEPPERMAN. Split, maggot.

TWO *does a military about-face and disappears in the darkness.*

GRACE [*looking at his watch*]. It's almost time to get them up, Tep. Are you ready?

TEPPERMAN [*smiling*]. Let me get my bugle.

TEPPERMAN *takes the cover from a tin garbage can next to the desk and walks to the door of the compound. Grace flicks a switch on the wall near his desk, and suddenly the stage is bathed in light—bright, white, electric. At the moment the light goes on,* TEPPERMAN *crashes the can cover down the middle of the inside compound, making a resounding noise. In an instant, the prisoners are standing in front of their bunks at attention, in their underwear and boots, with all their bedclothes, sheets, pillow, and blanket rolled up in a ball in their arms.* GRACE *and* TEPPERMAN *walk up and down the aisle of the compound, studying the faces of the prisoners.* THE WARDEN *stands up, turns, and faces the compound and observes the proceedings with* LINTZ, *Post One, from the other side of the wire.*

THE WARDEN. Good morning, kiddies. This will be another glorious day in the history of the United States Marine Corps. I want you to get dressed, make up your racks, get your soap and towels, and line up on the white line for washing your little handsies and facies. Is that clear?

ALL PRISONERS. Yes, sir.

THE WARDEN. I can't hear you.

ALL PRISONERS. Yes, sir.

WARDEN. I still can't hear you.

ALL PRISONERS. Yes, sir.

WARDEN. Get hot.

At once there is a flourish of activity in the compound. The prisoners proceed to get dressed and get in each other's way as one makes the bottom bunk and one makes the top one. They make up their bunks in military fashion and take their field jackets, manuals, and caps from the floor, where they are put overnight, and place them at the head of their bunks. They then take their towels from the rear of their bunks, run to their respective numbered boxes, pick up a small plastic box containing soap, and form a line very close to one another standing at attention, the first man with his shoetips touching the white line inside the door to the compound. The Brig falls silent once more.

TEPPERMAN. Sound off.

The prisoners from front to rear in line begin to exclaim one at a time: "Sir, Prisoner Number One, sir," "Sir, Prisoner Number Two, sir." And so on, through NUMBER TEN.

TEPPERMAN. All you maggots cross the white lines into the head, wash, and get in front of your racks on the double.

All the prisoners run into the head in single file. Moments later, they begin at the inside exit from the head to exclaim, one by one: "Sir, Prisoner Number One requests permission to cross the white line, sir," and so on. TEPPERMAN *stands at the door to the head and says, "Cross," as each one finishes this statement, using his own number. The prisoners then stop at the entrance to the compound and repeat the formality.* CORPORAL GRACE *is there uttering the same word, "Cross," and the prisoners enter the compound, return their soap and towels and pick up their manuals, stand at attention in front of their racks, and begin to read. As the procession ends, with each prisoner at attention, reading,* TEPPERMAN *enters, goes to the blackboard on the rear wall, and studies it.*

TEPPERMAN. Three get to the storeroom. One and Two head detail. Four sweep Post One. Five swab Post One. Six sweep Post Two. Seven swab Post Two. Eight sweep the compound. Nine swab the compound. Ten square away the boxes.

As TEPPERMAN *issues the orders, the Brig become a veritable madhouse: prisoners requesting to cross white lines, sweeping, swabbing, taking and returning materials from* THREE, *the storehouse man, and running in all directions. Two men disappear into the head with scouring powder, brushes, and rags. There is a line at the storeroom door with* THREE *standing inside giving and receiving buckets, brooms, swabs, and rags. Prisoners* FIVE, SEVEN, *and* NINE *run in and out of the head procuring buckets of water and emptying them, and the word "Cross" is uttered many times by* THE WARDEN *and his three assistants as they walk about supervising the clean-up job. As the jobs begin to look accomplished,* THE WARDEN *conducts an inspection of the entire Brig. Soon all prisoners are reading in front of their bunks.*

THE WARDEN. Secure all manuals and prepare for morning chow.

LINTZ. Three, secure the storeroom and get in front of your rack ready for chow.

The prisoners put on their field jackets and take their caps in their right hands, and once again form a single line at the white line by the door of the compound. TEPPERMAN *opens the outside door and goes out into the outside compound.*

GRACE. Outside in three ranks, move.

The prisoners run in single file through the outside door, snapping their hats on an uplifted right leg as they pass into the outside compound. The guards and THE WARDEN, *armed with shotguns which they took from the Brig officers' office, step through the outside door and close it. The Brig is empty and silent.*

Curtain.

SCENE 2

The outside compound. The curtain opens with the prisoners formed in two equal ranks at attention facing the long side of the fence with their backs to the wall of the Brig. Outside the fence stands LINTZ *with a shotgun cradled in his arms. It is about six o'clock in the morning and still quite dark. The outside door is open and* GRACE *stands in the doorway. The bright light inside pours into the darkness through the windows and the opened door, and beyond the door cabinet containing the cigarettes and razors of the prisoners is clearly visible.*

LINTZ. Did everyone have enough to eat this morning?

ALL PRISONERS. Yes, sir.

LINTZ. I didn't hear you, Two.

TWO. Yes, sir.

LINTZ. Your stomach all right, Two?

TWO. Yes, sir.

LINTZ. Front and center, Two. [TWO *runs from his position in the ranks and stands in front of the formation.*] Give me twenty-five, Two. [TWO *falls on his stomach and begins to do push-ups, but falls motionless after ten of them*] On your feet, Two. Start running around the edge of the compound. [TWO *begins running and continues as the scene progresses.*] Those who are not smoking fall out and form two ranks to your right. Move. [FOUR, SIX, *and* TEN *break from various points in the ranks and form near the right end of the compound.* GRACE *goes inside and opens the cabinet.*] Break, One.

ONE *runs toward the door. As he snaps his cap and passes through the door, he collides with* TEPPERMAN *who appears there. He falls, gets up, and stands at attention in front of* TEPPERMAN.

TEPPERMAN [*long, loud, and all suffering.*]. Woe. You touched me, you lousy insect. You actually came in contact with my clothing, infesting it with the disease of your stinking self. Now I will have to take a shower.

ONE [*terrified*]. I'm sorry, sir.

TEPPERMAN [*punching the prisoner in the stomach*]. Never tell me you're sorry, boy. Move.

The prisoner runs through the door and stands at attention in front of the cabinet where GRACE *is standing.*

ONE. Sir, Prisoner Number One, sir.

GRACE *takes a pack of cigarettes from a box, taking one and throwing it at the prisoner. The prisoner catches it and remains at attention at the cabinet.*

GRACE. Split.

The prisoner does an about-face and runs to the doorway, stopping and coming to attention. TEPPERMAN *is standing there.*

ONE. Sir, Prisoner Number One requests permission to cross the white line, sir.

TEPPERMAN. Cross.

The prisoner returns to his position in ranks. As he arrives, THREE *automatically breaks from ranks and goes through the same process, getting one cigarette, and so on for the others remaining in the larger formation. As the ceremony ends, all are in possession of one cigarette.*

LINTZ. Three, front and center. [THREE *breaks from the ranks and stands in front of the formation.* LINTZ *takes a lighter from his pocket, lights it, and places the lighter, burning, through the fence.* THREE *lights his cigarette from the outstretched hand of the guard, does an about-face, and returns to the ranks.*] Parade rest. [*The men assume a stiff at-ease position, smoking.* LINTZ *moves to the place where the three men are standing at attention.*] Two, join the nonsmokers. [TWO, *who has been running around in circles, joins the smaller group.*] Nonsmokers, at a half step, forward, march. To the rear, march. To the rear, march. Squad, halt. Parade rest.

The smaller group responds to the commands, marching with small steps in the limited area and ending up in the same place, in the same position as those smoking.

TEPPERMAN. Smokers, put your cigarettes in your mouths. Smokers, attention. [*The smoking group responds to the commands and is at attention with cigarettes dangling from their lips.* TEPPERMAN *walks through the ranks pausing occasionally, taking a cigarette from the mouth of one, then another of the prisoners and crushing it beneath his foot. As he does so, he informs the prisoner of the reason for it.*] Talking at chow . . . Slow getting up this morning . . . Too much time in the head . . . Sloppy rack . . . Bare feet on the deck . . .

TEPPERMAN *walks through the outside door and disappears within the Brig. The formation does not move.*

LINTZ. Parade rest. Continue smoking. Nonsmokers, rejoin the formation. [*The smaller formation rejoins the larger one, assuming at once a motion-less position of parade rest. The only movements are the hands of the prisoners who are smoking, moving from their lips to their sides, taking and returning the cigarettes to and from their mouths.*] Put 'em out. [*The prisoners smoking pinch the flame from the front of their cigarettes, rub them lightly in their palms to insure they are out, tear the paper from them, allowing the tobacco to fall to the ground, roll the paper in a ball, and drop it.*] When I give you the word, I want you to get inside and break down for a shakedown. Is that clear?

ALL PRISONERS. Yes, sir.

LINTZ. I can't hear you.

ALL PRISONERS. Yes, sir.

LINTZ. You better sound off.

ALL PRISONERS. Yes, sir.

LINTZ. Get inside.

The prisoners break off to the left, front rank first, and begin to disappear through the outside door in single file. Soon the outside compound is empty. LINTZ *unloads his shotgun, opens the large double gates enough to step through them, locks and checks them, steps through the outside door, and closes it behind him. A flourish of activity can be seen through the windows.*

Curtain.

SCENE 3

The inside of the Brig. The prisoners are standing at attention in their socks and underwear. THE WARDEN *and all the guards are conducting a shakedown as explained in the Brig Regulations. As each prisoner is finished being searched, he puts on his clothes, takes his field jacket in his right hand, requests permis-sion to cross the necessary white lines, and goes to his bunk. He then folds his field jacket, takes his cap from his pocket, and arranges them at the head of his bunk. He then takes his manual and begins reading it at attention in front of his bunk. As the guards search the prisoners, they remark, striking and harassing their victims:*

LINTZ. Change your skivvies tonight, Two. You smell like a horse.

TWO. Yes, sir.

GRACE. You look like a horse, Six. Would you like to change your face with mine?

SIX. No, sir.

GRACE. Are you telling me I'm ugly, Six?

SIX. No, sir.

GRACE. Would you like to kick my ass, Six?

SIX. No, Sir.

GRACE. You're a liar, Six.

THE WARDEN [*punching a prisoner in the stomach.*] Four, what were you talking about in chow this morning?

FOUR. Nothing, sir.

THE WARDEN [*screaming*]. Nothing— You can't talk about nothing, Four. [*Hitting him again.*] See me at noon chow, and you'll eat by the numbers.

FOUR. Yes, sir.

TEPPERMAN. You're supposed to be standing at attention, Eight, not getting ready to die. Are you going to die, Eight?

EIGHT. No, sir.

TEPPERMAN. I wouldn't be too sure of that, Eight. [*The search continues as the prisoners continue screaming out their requests, and the guards continue saying, "Cross." When all the prisoners are motionless in front of their bunks,* TEPPERMAN *walks to the door of the head.*] All those who want to make a head call on the white line.

All the prisoners cross and pass TEPPERMAN *as they enter the head. Soon toilets are heard flushing and the prisoners return to the compound one at a time. A bell rings, and* GRACE, *who has just sat down at his desk, gets up and opens the freedom door. Two men in pressed, starched dungarees and polished boots enter the Brig armed with shotguns.* GRACE *goes to his desk, takes two sheets of paper from it, and hands one to each man. They greet him with a smile and:* "How are you?" "How did it go last night?" *and* "We had a ball in town last night."

GRACE. Everything's O.K. so far. [*And then to the last remark.*] Wait till tomorrow night when you guys are sweating it out in this joint. I'm going to tear me up some gook. [*He turns to the compound.*] Three, to the storeroom. Six, field jacket on, on the white line for work detail. [THREE *goes to the storeroom. The other man puts on his field jacket and moves to the white line. One of the men who just entered the Brig looks at his sheet of paper and goes out through the door that he entered.* GRACE *points to the white line in front of the freedom door.*] Work detail, get out here. [*The prisoner comes out of the compound and takes his position on the freedom door.*] Sound off, Six.

SIX. Sir, Prisoner Number Six requests permission to cross the white line, sir.

GRACE. Get out. [*The prisoner disappears through the door.*] Seven and Eight, field jackets on, on the white line for work detail. [*The two prisoners follow the instructions exactly as the man before them. The other guard with the shotgun studies his sheet of paper and goes outside.*] Work detail, get out here. [*The two prisoners come out of the compound and line up on the freedom door.*] Eight, break off to the storeroom for two shovels, move.

EIGHT *runs to the opposite end of the corridor next to the inside compound and comes to attention at the white line there.*

EIGHT. Sir, Prisoner Number Eight requests permission to cross the white line, sir.

LINTZ [*standing there*]. Cross, Eight. [EIGHT *runs to the storeroom door and is handed two shovels by the storeroom man. He turns with them and is about to run for the formation awaiting him at the freedom door when he is stopped by* LINTZ's *command.*] Whoa, Eight. How long have you been a guest at my hotel?

EIGHT. Twelve days, sir.

LINTZ. And you still don't know that you have to do a military about-face when you change direction?

EIGHT. Yes, I know it, sir.

LINTZ [*walking toward the prisoner*]. What is this "I know it" business. You answer, "Yes, sir" or "No, sir" when you talk to me. Is that clear, maggot?

EIGHT. Yes, sir.

LINTZ. Can't hear you.

EIGHT [*screaming*]. Yes, sir.

LINTZ. You need some squaring away, maggot. [*Pause.*] Attention. [*The prisoner comes to a rigid position of attention, dropping the shovels on the floor. They clang loudly in the silence.*] Idiot. Breaking my shovels. I order you to die for such a crime. Die, idiot. [EIGHT *remains at a rigid position of attention. He begins weeping silently.*] Pick up the gear and move, maggot.

EIGHT *picks up both shovels and runs to the white line near the freedom door.*

GRACE. Eight, you crossed my white line without asking me first. Tonight is your night, Eight. [GRACE *gets up and walks to the prisoner.*] Now give the other worm his shovel. [EIGHT *hands a shovel to the other prisoner.* GRACE *punches* EIGHT *in his stomach.*] Tonight is your night, Eight. [*Pause.*] Get out, maggots. [*Both prisoners disappear through the freedom door.*] Five, on the white line for work detail. [FIVE *puts on his field jacket, picks up his cap and runs to the white line.*] Five, get out here.

FIVE. Sir, Prisoner Number Five re—

GRACE [*interrupting him*]. Cross. [*The prisoner comes to attention in front of the turnkey's desk.*] Did some little birdie tell you to put on your field jacket, my little field mouse?

FIVE. No, sir.

GRACE. Then what the hell are you wearing it for? Do you think it's going to rain, Five?

FIVE. No, sir.

GRACE. You go into the head, kneel in front of the toilet named two, and tell the toilet what you have done. Is that clear, Five?

FIVE. Yes, sir.

GRACE. Do it.

> FIVE *does a military about-face and runs to the door of the head. He comes to attention on the white line there.*

FIVE. Sir, Prisoner Number Five requests permission to cross the white line, sir.

GRACE. Cross.

> FIVE *goes inside the head. After a moment, a voice is heard from inside screaming loudly.*

FIVE. Sir, I put on my field jacket without being told.

GRACE [*from his chair*]. Tell bowl two why, Five.

FIVE [*from inside*]. Sir, I put on my field jacket without being told because . . . [*Pause.*] I am a maggot.

GRACE. Get out here, Five.

FIVE [*appearing in the door of the head*]. Sir—

GRACE [*interrupting him*]. Cross the lines into the compound, take off your field jacket, put it on your bunk, cross the lines coming out, and get by the freedom door. [THE WARDEN *gets up from his desk, takes a shotgun from the office, and goes outside through the freedom door as* FIVE *does what he has been told.*] Sound off, Five.

FIVE. Sir, Prisoner Number Five requests permission to cross the white line, sir.

GRACE. Cross. [*The prisoners leave through the door.* GRACE *gets up from his chair and walks to the freedom door. He slams it loudly and spins to face the other prisoners inside the compound who are still reading.*] One and Two get out here.

> ONE *and* TWO *run to the white line.* ONE *arrives first and* TWO *falls in behind him.*

ONE. Sir, Prisoner Number One requests permission to cross the white line, sir.

GRACE. Both of you better move and get over here. [*The two men come to attention abreast, in front of* GRACE, *who is still at the door.* TEPPERMAN *who has remained leaning on the wall next to the head door comes over to them.*] Pfc. Tepperman is going to square you maggots away, is that clear?

BOTH PRISONERS. Yes, sir.

GRACE. I can't hear you.

BOTH PRISONERS [*screaming*]. Yes, sir.

TEPPERMAN. Louder, you motherless maggots.

BOTH PRISONERS [*bellowing*]. Yes, sir.

> As TEPPERMAN *talks to the prisoners, he bends his head from side to side, almost touching their noses.*

TEPPERMAN [*from one to the other*]. One, you dared come in contact with my body this morning. Now you must pay with a term of darkness. Two, by the time you get out of here, you will either have the strongest legs in the world, or you will be dead. Is that clear, Two?

TWO. Yes, sir.

As TEPPERMAN *continues his folly, another scene is begun by* GRACE *and* LINTZ.

GRACE. Pfc. Lintz, I think the maggots are out of shape. Put them through an exercise drill.

LINTZ *comes from the other side of the Brig. He enters the compound and stands inside the door with his arms folded.*

LINTZ. I want all the racks moved to the far end of the compound on the double. Then I want you in two ranks, a body length apart facing me. [*The prisoners pick up all the double cots and move them into a corner one against the other, leaving a considerable space in the middle of the inside compound. They then occupy the space in two ranks, a body length from one another.*] All right, my bald children, down in the push-up position. By my count, one, two, one, two, one, two . . . [*He continues until the prisoners are all struggling and contorting to make the semblance of the exercise.*] On your feet. Sit-up position. By my count, one, two, one, two, one, two . . . [*Again he continues until they are exhausted.*] On your feet. Start running in place, and you better get those legs up. [*The prisoners are running in place, kicking their legs high in the air.*] On your bellies. On your feet. On your backs. You better get down when I tell you, maggots.

Without seeming to notice the other goings on, TEPPERMAN *has gone on as follows during the exercise drill:*

TEPPERMAN. There are bombs falling, One. Take cover on the spot. [ONE *falls to his knees and buries his head in his lap, covering it with his arms.*] Two, turn the G.I. can over on One to protect him from shrapnel. [TWO *takes the cover from the garbage can next to the turnkey's desk, lays it on the floor, picks up the can, turns it over, and places it over the man on the floor. With* ONE *inside the inverted can,* TWO *comes to attention.*] What is your first general order as a sentry, Two?

TWO. Sir, to take charge of this post and all government property in view, sir.

TEPPERMAN. Then you will pick up the G.I. can cover and run in a circle around One, who is armored government property, repeating your general order, and each third time around you will hit the can with the cover. Is that clear, Two?

TWO. Yes, sir.

With TWO *running around in circles screaming his general order and clanging the cover on the can, and the prisoners in the compound exercising to the commands of* LINTZ, TEPPERMAN *and* GRACE *begin laughing out loud.*

Curtain.

ACT TWO

SCENE 1

Inside the Brig. All prisoners are in a single line abreast standing at attention facing the chicken wire, inches from it, in the corridor. They each hold a field jacket in their left hand and a cap in their right hand. Their shoelaces are opened and their dungaree jackets are outside their trousers and also opened. Their trousers are unbuttoned, but this is not visible in their present position.

THE WARDEN. I thought noon chow was excellent today, kiddies. Do you think you could find such fine chow anywhere else outside of my Marine Corps?

ALL PRISONERS. No, sir.

THE WARDEN. You bet your life you couldn't. Are you all broken down for a frisk?

ALL PRISONERS. Yes, sir.

All the personnel of the Big are present and standing with THE WARDEN. As he continues talking, he walks up the corridor, behind the prisoners, stationing a guard every five feet.

THE WARDEN. I understand that tonight is your night, Eight. Tell us why.

EIGHT [*from the line, without moving*]. Sir, it is my night because I dropped the shovels, sir.

THE WARDEN. Whose shovels, Eight?

EIGHT. Your shovels, sir.

As THE WARDEN is talking, he taps a prisoner on the shoulder and jumps back. The prisoner lifts his hat and his right leg, snaps the hat on his thigh, throws his legs out behind him, and grips the wire with outstretched arms high and hard. Thus the frisk of the prisoners begins. THE WARDEN then feels all the clothing of the prisoner down into his open shoes, hitting the prisoner on the leg as he finishes. The prisoner jumps up erect and does an about-face, holding his field jacket by the shoulders with both hands in front of him. THE WARDEN searches the jacket and then says, "Get out." The prisoner runs to the white line in the rear of the corridor and requests permission to cross it. THE WARDEN grants it and the prisoner runs to the door of the compound, stops, and requests permission again to cross the white line.

THE WARDEN. Cross. All prisoners after they have been frisked will go to the inside compound, fold their field jackets on their racks, and fall in on the white line to make a head call. [*The other guards begin frisking the prisoners in silence, except for the word "Cross," which is spoken to the prisoners requesting to cross the line into the compound. As the line inside the compound begins to grow, THE WARDEN walks to the door of the compound.*] Sound off.

EIGHT [*at the front of the line*]. Sir, Prisoner Number Eight requests permission to cross the white line, sir.

THE WARDEN. All prisoners cross all the white lines into and out of the head and get in front of your racks with your manuals.

The last of the men being frisked requests permission to cross into the compound, make their head call, and soon all is quiet in the Brig. THE WARDEN *goes to his desk,* LINTZ *to Post One,* GRACE *to his desk, and* TEPPERMAN *to Post Two.*

TEPPERMAN. Button up, maggots. [*The prisoners whose clothing is still opened tie their shoelaces, button and tuck in their dungarees, fasten their belts, and return to their manuals.*] There will be no working parties this afternoon because this Brig looks like a garbage dump, and I think it's about time we had a little field day. Any objections, Two?

TWO. No, sir.

TEPPERMAN *enters the compound and walks to* PRISONER NUMBER TWO.

TEPPERMAN. I don't think you know what a field day is, do you, Two?

TWO. Yes, sir.

TEPPERMAN. Well, then, tell us what it is. You are a new louse in my house and I know you never saw us have a field day so you just tell us what it is.

TWO. It is a thorough cleaning of the living quarters, sir.

TEPPERMAN [*punching* TWO *in the stomach*]. It is a sterilization of the Brig, Two. From now on you don't invent your own definitions, you memorize ours. Is that clear, Two?

TWO. Yes, sir.

LINTZ. Get over here to the storeroom, Three.

THREE *runs to the storeroom.* THE WARDEN *rises from his desk, walks up the corridor, enters the compound, and walks up and down the aisle between the racks talking.*

THE WARDEN. Those of you who have been in my house for more than a week are familiar with the field day. Those who are not will benefit by what I say. You will be told what to do only once, and you'd better understand the orders you are given and carry them out exactly as they are given you, because I like to live in a clean house. When you are finished, everything will look exactly as it does now, but it will be clean. If the field day is successful, you will be permitted to write letters for one-half hour after dinner this evening. Is that clear, children?

ALL PRISONERS. Yes, sir.

THE WARDEN. Carry on, Pfc. Tepperman.

TEPPERMAN. One and Two, tear down all racks, fold all blankets, and place them under the stripped pillows. Put all dirty linen into four separate sheets, go to the storeroom, draw new linen, and make up all the racks—

and they better be tight. Four and Five, to the storeroom and draw scrub brushes. I want to see you scrubbers on the deck putting some elbow grease into it. You will get on your knees and start scrubbing at the head door, moving to the other end of the Brig on my command. Six, to the storeroom for a squeegee. You will fall in behind the scrubbers and keep the soapy water in front of them, and it better be dry in back of you. Seven, bucket man. You will go to the storeroom and draw four boxes of soap flakes. You will then take one G.I. can next to the turnkey's desk into the head and put one box of soap in it at a time, filling it with hot water from the shower, and throwing it across the front of the line of scrubbers. When the four boxes of soap have been used up, you will begin throwing clear hot water in front of the squeegee until I tell you to stop. Then you will secure the G.I. can in the head, go to the storeroom, draw a swab and bucket, and join the swabbers. Eight and Nine, to the storeroom for swabs and buckets. You maggots will fall in behind the squeegee and swab up all the soap and water. When your bucket is three-quarters full of water, you will go into the head and empty it down the shower drain. And when we are finished that deck had better be dry. Ten, to the storeroom for clean rags and a bucket. You will wash the windows. Draw cold water from the head and make all the glass in this house sparkle. Let's get hot. [As TEPPER-MAN *speaks, the Brig becomes once again a beehive of activity. All the prisoners follow their instructions,* GRACE *and* THE WARDEN *stand on top of their desks,* LINTZ *enters the compound and sits on a top bunk that has already been undressed, and* TEPPERMAN *goes into the head. Water from the large garbage can and soapsuds veritably flood the deck, with those on their knees scrubbing and getting soaking wet. The squeegee man fights desperately to keep the soap forward of the scrubbers, and the swabbers dry up the water as quickly as possible, rinsing the water in their buckets. The window washer wipes the windows one at a time with a wet rag and then rubs them dry feverishly, for what seems much longer than is necessary, and the guards from their safe and dry positions issue many warnings and instructions.* TEPPERMAN *stands inside the head door.*] Scrubbers, move forward three feet. Squeegee detail, get hot behind them. Swabbers stand by. Bucket man, I better see more soap and water on this deck.

GRACE *throws his hands over his head, standing straddle-legged on his desk.*

GRACE. Let me hear the music of those brushes. Elbow grease, my children, elbow grease. What's the matter, Four? I can't hear your brush. It must sing in the suds, Four, is that clear?

FOUR [*his arm going like a windmill*]. Yes, sir.

LINTZ. I want all these racks made up and in place by the time the scrubbers arrive. Is that clear, rack detail?

RACK DETAIL. Yes, sir.

TEPPERMAN. That's enough water, bucket man. Secure the can in the shower and draw your swab and bucket. Scrubbers, up three more feet. Swab detail, get hot.

THE WARDEN. Rub your arms off, kiddies. Are you happy, window detail?

WINDOW DETAIL. Yes, sir.

THE WARDEN. They are our windows you are washing, is that clear?

WINDOW DETAIL. Yes, sir.

TEPPERMAN. Scrubbers, you will now move forward one yard on the command "move," and every time I say "move" in the future. When we get to the compound wire, Five will do the corridor. Four will enter the compound. Move.

LINTZ. These racks better be ready when the scrubbers arrive.

TEPPERMAN. Move.

GRACE. You are next to the freedom door, Four. Are you going to make a break for it?

FOUR. No, sir.

THE WARDEN. I can't hear you, Four.

FOUR. No, sir.

WARDEN. Eight, as you swab you will sing one chorus of my favorite song. When Eight is finished, we will have one chorus from Nine. When Nine is finished, we will have one chorus from Two. Begin, Eight.

EIGHT *begins the "Marine Corps Hymn." The field day goes on uninterruptedly as the other two prisoners each render their chorus in turn.*

TEPPERMAN. Move.

LINTZ. Move. Are all the racks finished?

RACK DETAIL [*working feverishly tightening the blankets*]. Yes, sir.

LINTZ *walks out of the compound and past the scrubbers and others behind them.* TEPPERMAN *comes out of the head and walks into the compound, punching* LINTZ *lightly on the arm as they pass each other.*

LINTZ. Rack detail, in two ranks on me.

Both men stop tightening the racks, request permission to cross out of the compound, TEPPERMAN *grants it, and they fall in facing* LINTZ *behind the working group.*

TEPPERMAN. Move, Five in the corridor, Four in the compound.

LINTZ *drills the two men in the confines of Post Two.*

LINTZ. Rack detail, at a half step, forward march, to the rear march, left flank march . . . [*He continues to call commands.*]

THE WARDEN. As you are working, prisoners sound off.

All the prisoners, one at a time, call out their numbers in the following manner: "Sir, Prisoner Number One, sir," "Sir, Prisoner Number Two, sir." *And so on through* TEN.

TEPPERMAN. Move. You maggots are falling behind schedule. You better bear into those brushes.

THE WARDEN. Window detail, are the windows secure?

WINDOW DETAIL. Yes, sir.

THE WARDEN. Empty your water in the shower, secure your gear in the storeroom, and join the marchers.

LINTZ *halts the formation again, awaits the arrival of the window washer, and begins drilling once more.*

TEPPERMAN. Move slowly to the wire. When Four has reached the far end of the compound, he will join Five in Post One, moving on my command. Seven, you will follow them drying up the mess they make on the way. Is that clear?

ALL INVOLVED. Yes, sir.

FOUR *reaches the wire, gets up, and runs around the wire barrier to Post Two, returning to his knees outside the wire on the other end of the Brig.* SEVEN *follows swabbing up the water that drips from his soaking pants. The squeegee man pushes the water through the wire and the scrubbing begins again.*

THE WARDEN. It had better be white under my desk.

TEPPERMAN. Move, squeegee, join the scrubbers outside the compound. [*The procession continues until the scrubbers reach the front wall of the Brig.*] Secure the scrub brushes and join the formation. [*The scrubbers hand their brushes to the storeroom man.* LINTZ *halts the marchers until they are joined by the scrubbers, then begins again.* THE WARDEN *climbs down from his desk and opens the large double doors in front of the Brig. The man with the squeegee then pushes the water outside, and the swabbers finish drying the deck.*] Secure all the gear, and join the formation. Ten, get in the head and clean and dry the G.I. can, then put it back where it belongs.

Soon all the prisoners are drilling in the tiny space between the head and the compound. GRACE *waves to* LINTZ *and* LINTZ *stops the drill. They are all at attention facing the compound. All the guards and* THE WARDEN *come to Post Two.*

THE WARDEN. What did you think of the field day, Two?

TWO. Sir, it was a thorough field day, sir.

THE WARDEN. All prisoners in the compound at attention with their manuals.

THE WARDEN *returns to his desk,* TEPPERMAN *sits on the edge of the turnkey's desk,* LINTZ *goes to Post One, and the prisoners scramble into the compound and are soon motionless in front of their racks.*

Curtain.

The prisoners are marching in place in front of their racks. TEPPERMAN *is calling cadence, sitting on* GRACE'S *desk.*

TEPPERMAN. Un doo, ree, ree der lef doo ree, ree der lef. Yer mother was there when you left.

PRISONERS. Yer right.

TEPPERMAN. Yer father was there when you left.

PRISONERS. Yer right.

TEPPERMAN. Sound off.

PRISONERS. One, two.

TEPPERMAN. Sound off.

PRISONERS. Three, four.

TEPPERMAN. Ad'ance count.

PRISONERS. One, two, three, four, one, two . . . [*Pause*] three, four.

TEPPERMAN. Ris'ners h'lt. P'rade rest.

The prisoners stop marching and come to a stiff at-ease position.

GRACE. Three, Five is getting out. As senior man in my house, you know what to do. Do it.

FIVE *smiles openly.* TEPPERMAN *enters the compound and punches him in the stomach. The smile disappears.*

TEPPERMAN. You are not out yet, Five. You will not laugh unless I tell you to laugh. Is that clear, Five?

FIVE. Yes, sir.

TEPPERMAN *returns to the desk.* THREE *requests permission to cross the lines to and from the storeroom and returns with a seabag that appears about three-quarters full. He goes to the box of* FIVE *and empties its contents neatly into the bag.* GRACE *goes to the cabinet and removes* FIVE'S *razor and cigarettes.* THREE *requests permission to cross to the freedom door and back, leaving the bag beside it.* GRACE *places the razor and cigarettes in the bag, closes it, and goes back to his desk. The bell rings:* TEPPERMAN *opens the door, sticks his head out, and yells, "Stand by." He comes back and sits on the desk.*

GRACE. Five, get out here. Bring your towel and laundry bag. [FIVE *goes to the rear of his bunk, takes his towel and laundry bag, requests permission to cross the line inside the compound, and stands in front of* GRACE'S *desk.* GRACE *smiles.*] Well, you better sound off, Five.

FIVE. Sir, Prisoner Number Five reporting as ordered, sir.

TEPPERMAN. What are your orders, Five?

FIVE. To report to the turnkey's desk, sir.

GRACE. How long have you been in my house, Five?

FIVE. Twenty-five days, sir.

TEPPERMAN. What was your sentence, Five.

FIVE. Thirty days, sir.

GRACE. Do you know why five days have been taken off your sentence, Five?

TEPPERMAN. Well, do you, Five?

FIVE. Yes, sir, for good conduct, sir.

GRACE. Prisoners, attention. Prisoners, left face. [*The prisoners come to attention and do the facing movement as commanded so they are facing the turnkey.*] Pick up your seabag, and get on the freedom line, Five. [FIVE *does an about-face, picks up his seabag, puts it on his shoulder, and stands on the line opposite the freedom door.*] Sound off, Five.

FIVE [*triumphantly*]. Sir, Prisoner Number Five requests permission to cross the white line, sir.

THE WARDEN [*from his desk*]. I can't hear you.

FIVE [*with gusto*]. Sir, Prisoner Number Five requests permission to cross the white line, sir.

LINTZ [*from the corridor*]. I can't hear you.

FIVE [*bellowing*]. Sir, Prisoner Number Five requests permission to cross the white line, sir.

TEPPERMAN *gets up chuckling. He goes to the door and puts his nose against* FIVE's *forehead.*

TEPPERMAN. One more time, Five, just one more time.

FIVE. Sir, Prisoner Number—

TEPPERMAN [*interrupting him*]. Get out, get out of my house.

FIVE *disappears through the door and* TEPPERMAN *slams it shut.*

GRACE. Prisoners, right face.

TEPPERMAN. Back to your manuals, and someday, if you are good maggots who clean under their short hairs every day, you may be free. [*All prisoners except* SIX *pick up their books and start reading.* SIX *emits a terrifying scream and falls to his knees. The other prisoners near him jump with fright. All give him a probing glance. Then everyone returns to his reading.* TEPPERMAN *runs into the compound, billy club in hand, and stands over the prisoner, who has buried his head in his hands and is weeping.*] On your feet, Six.

SIX [*looking up*]. I am thirty-four years old. For God's sake, let me out of this madhouse. I'm not one of these damned kids. I can't stand it any more.

TEPPERMAN. I told you to get on your feet, Six.

SIX *begins to whine and tremble. He lunges from the floor at* TEPPERMAN, *who deftly steps aside and brings his weapon down on the side of the prisoner's face. At this,* GRACE *and* LINTZ *run into the compound.* THE WARDEN *runs from his desk and locks the door to the sleeping area. The prisoner fights savagely with the three guards screaming continually, "Let me out of here." Eventually he is subdued and taken to solitary cell one at the front of the Brig. He can be heard from within the cell, as* THE WARDEN *observes him.*

SIX. Sixteen years I give to this rotten outfit and they throw me in an asylum. Somebody's got to listen to me. It's all wrong. Two weeks in this place and already I'm out of my mind. Let me out of here.

THE WARDEN *shakes his head from side to side and goes into the Brig officer's office. He comes out a few minutes later.*

THE WARDEN [*to* LINTZ]. They're coming for him.

LINTZ *shakes his head affirmatively.*

TEPPERMAN. Anybody else who wants to crack up, do it now, so that when they come for him, you can keep him company.

The prisoners continue reading. GRACE *goes into the compound and walks up and down the aisle studying the faces of the prisoners as they read.*

GRACE. It would be a good night for you to crack up, Eight, because this is your night.

TEPPERMAN. Are you going to crack up, Eight?

EIGHT [*putting his book by his side*]. No, sir. [*He does not resume reading.*]

LINTZ. You must be out of your mind to have dropped my shovels, isn't that so, Eight?

GRACE. Back to your book, Eight.

SIX [*from his cell*]. My name is not Six. It's James Turner. Let me out of here.

THE WARDEN. Three, take Six's gear to the storeroom and put it in his seabag. Then put his seabag by the freedom door.

THREE *does as he is told, requesting permission to cross the lines in the process and receiving it. The bell rings.* GRACE *comes out of the compound and opens the door. Two men in white coats and trousers carrying a stretcher and a strait jacket enter and are led to the cell of* SIX. *They enter it.*

SIX. What the hell is going on here? Leave me alone.

GRACE. Just relax, James Turner. You are getting out of here.

The two men come out of the cell carrying a stretcher with the prisoner on it secured to the stretcher in the strait jacket. The prisoner babbles as they carry him off.

SIX. Thank God, I'm getting out of here. I really don't believe it.

GRACE *carries his seabag outside and returns, slamming the door behind him.*

TEPPERMAN. Secure the reading material; field jackets on; on the line for evening chow. [*As the prisoners put on their jackets and line up by the door of the compound,* THE WARDEN, GRACE, *and* LINTZ *take shotguns from the Brig officer's office, open the outside door, and go out.* TEPPERMAN *stands at the head door.*] Get outside.

The prisoners file through the outside door in a trot, snapping their hats on an uplifted thigh as they go through it. TEPPERMAN *looks at his watch and goes through the door, closing it behind him. The Brig is once more empty and silent.*

Curtain.

SCENE 3

The prisoners are seated at the long table writing letters. Some do not fit at the table so they are seated on the floor with their pencils, writing pads, and envelopes. TEPPERMAN *walks out of the head and sits on* GRACE's *desk. They begin to whisper to each other.* LINTZ *is leaning on* THE WARDEN's *desk, and they too are holding an inaudible conversation. The prisoners begin addressing envelopes, folding their letters, and putting them inside the envelopes.*

GRACE. Secure the writing gear and get in front of your racks for collection.

The prisoners place their equipment in their boxes and fall in at attention in front of their bunks. GRACE *enters the compound and collects the letters from the hands of the prisoners.*

THE WARDEN. Two, what is the rule for letter-writing?

TWO. Sir, the rule is that the letter shall not exceed the length of one side of a page.

TEPPERMAN. How do you know that, Two?

TWO. Sir, because you explained it to me before the letter-writing period, sir.

THE WARDEN. When I read these letters, I better not find any sealed envelopes or any letters containing material against my Marine Corps. Is that clear, kiddies?

ALL PRISONERS. Yes, sir.

The bell rings. TEPPERMAN *opens the freedom door, steps back quickly, leaving the door ajar.*

TEPPERMAN [*bellowing*]. You better get in here on the double, maggot. Put those seabags on your shoulders and face the wall to your right. [*A Marine enters in starched dungarees with the collar open, his hat on, and a seabag in each hand. He is obviously terrified. He places a seabag on each shoulder, turns and faces the wall, and soon begins shaking from the weight his arms and shoulders are supporting.* TEPPERMAN *sticks his head out the door, saying, "That will be all, Sentry," slams the door and walks over to the new prisoner. He takes off the prisoner's cap and slams it down on the floor in front of him. The man does not budge.*] Next time you wear a hat in my house, I will chop your head off. Is that very clear?

THE PRISONER [*weakly*]. Yes, sir.

TEPPERMAN [*punching the man in the side*]. When you speak in this place, you speak loud and clear. Is that very clear?

THE PRISONER [*dropping one seabag*]. Yes, sir.

TEPPERMAN [*punching him again*]. Yes, sir, you better sound off boy 'cause I can't hear you.

PRISONER [*quickly picking up the seabag*]. Yes, sir.

GRACE [*from his desk*]. About face. [*There is no response from the prisoner. GRACE jumps from his desk and screams in the prisoner's ear.*] About face. [*The prisoner responds, turning around.*] When you hear a command in my house, you better snap to. Your sniveling mouse eyes will be black if you ever do that again. Is that clear, maggot?

THE PRISONER. Yes, sir.

TEPPERMAN. Louder.

THE PRISONER. Yes, sir.

GRACE. Forward march. [*The prisoner walks to the other wall of the Brig. As he reaches it:*] Right flank, march.

The prisoner marches down the corridor.

TEPPERMAN. Ree pree der lef reet left. Pick him up, Lintz.

LINTZ. Left reet left ree der left. [*The prisoner marches past the white line at the end of the corridor.* TWO *steps over the line,* LINTZ *gives a command.*] Right flank, march. 'Ris'ner, h'lt. Right face.

The prisoner ends his march at attention in front of THE WARDEN's *desk.*

THE WARDEN. Three, get out here. [*The new prisoner shakes as* THE WARDEN *speaks. Soon* THREE *is standing next to him at the desk.*] You better stand still, boy. Drop those bags on the floor. Three, get the necessary gear out of those bags in the storeroom and secure the rest. [THREE *picks up the bags and disappears with them into the storeroom.*] Get your hat, maggot. [*The prisoner does not move.* THE WARDEN *leaps from his desk, pushing the prisoner with tremendous force. The prisoner stumbles across the room, falling down, getting up again, running to* THE WARDEN, *and coming to attention in front of him.* THE WARDEN *smiles.*] I thought you were going to swing at me, boy. I would have loved that. [*His face becomes cross.*] Did you hear me tell you to get your hat?

THE PRISONER. Yes, sir.

THE WARDEN. Do you know where it is?

THE PRISONER. Yes, sir.

THE WARDEN. Then what the hell are you doing standing here like a dead worm? Get the hell out of here; get your hat and report back to me. [*The prisoner starts running to retrieve his cap.*] Get back here right away, maggot. [*The prisoner turns and comes back.* THE WARDEN *punches him in the stomach.*] When you are dismissed from anyone's company around here, you do a military about-face. Is that clear?

THE PRISONER. Yes, sir.

THE WARDEN. Split.

The prisoner does an about-face, runs up the corridor, passes the line at the end of it, and bends over to pick up his cap. As he bends over, TEPPERMAN *runs over to him and grasps the back of his neck.*

TEPPERMAN. Now you stay bent down, boy, and follow my hand as it leads you, or I'll break your neck. [TEPPERMAN *leads the prisoner, who is almost doubled over, to the line at the end of the corridor.*] Do you see that line, maggot.

THE PRISONER. Yes, sir.

TEPPERMAN. Well, just to make sure, you get down on your knees and put your nose on it. [*The prisoner does as he is told.*] Whenever you see one of those lines in my house, you will stop and come to attention. Then you will sound off: "Sir, Prisoner Number—whatever number you are given —requests permission to cross the white line, sir." Is that clear?

THE PRISONER. Yes, sir.

TEPPERMAN. It had better be. [*Pause.*] Get out of here.

The prisoner stands up, does an about-face, and runs to the white line at the other end of the corridor with his hat in his hand. He stops and comes to attention, but does not murmur a word. THE WARDEN *sits looking at him for a moment.*

THE WARDEN. Well?

THE PRISONER. Sir, I have no number, sir.

THE WARDEN. Your number is Five, maggot.

FIVE. Sir, Prisoner Number Five requests permission to cross the white line, please.

THE WARDEN. "Please"! Who the hell told you to say "please"? What do you think this is, a finishing school?

FIVE. Sir, Prisoner Number Five requests permission to cross the white line, sir.

THE WARDEN. Cross. [FIVE *comes to attention in front of* THE WARDEN'S *desk.*] When you are summoned in my house, you say, "Sir, Prisoner Number Five reporting as ordered, sir."

FIVE. Sir, Prisoner Number Five reporting as ordered, sir.

THE WARDEN. What are your orders?

FIVE. To come to your desk with my hat, sir.

THREE *comes out of the storeroom with all the clothing, towels, laundry bag, cigarettes, razor, blades, and manual of the prisoner. He stands in front of the desk and hands the things to the new* FIVE.

THE WARDEN. Five, and that is your name from now on, this is the one and only time that you will be permitted to talk to anyone in this Brig. Three will explain our procedure to you and you may ask him questions. After that, if you talk, you will need new teeth. Follow him to the compound.

The two prisoners cross into the compound and then a pantomime ensues. They are talking to each other, but in such low tones that it is incomprehensible. THREE *starts folding clothes and putting them in the box marked "Five." There is a shaking of heads and a completion of the task. Then the placing of the laundry bag and towel, identification of bunk, folding of field jacket, indicating the place for the hat and manual, more shaking of heads, and the close scrutiny of* TEPPERMAN, *who has just entered the compound.*

THREE. Sir, the cigarette, razor, and blades are on the rack, sir.

TEPPERMAN *picks up the articles from the bunk of* FIVE *and places them inside the cabinet outside the compound.*

TEPPERMAN. Front of your racks, Three and Five. Everybody strip down for a shower and get on the line in numerical order. [*The prisoners strip to their boots and underwear, take their towels from the back of their racks, dropping their clothes there, take soap and clean underwear, toothbrushes and toothpaste from their boxes, and fall in on the line by the door of the compound. When they are all lined up,* TEPPERMAN *speaks.*] First five out get here. [GRACE *goes to the cabinet and opens it. The prisoners line up in front of him. Each prisoner carries all his equipment in his left hand, and the five men in front of* GRACE *have their hands extended high in the air. He places a razor in each of their empty right hands. They move to the door of the head with their hands still high over their heads, are granted permission to cross by* TEPPERMAN, *and disappear inside with* TEPPERMAN *following them.* LINTZ *comes from the other end of the Brig and stands near the door to the compound. The showers are heard running, toilets flushing, sinks filling, and* TEPPERMAN's *voice from within.*] You better move, maggots, you're not in here on a health cure. Get those whiskers off, Two. You better get that razor up in the air, Two. Do you want to kill me or one of the idiots you live with? Send me five more, Lintz.

LINTZ. Next five.

The next five prisoners repeat the same process as those who preceded them, scrutinized carefully by LINTZ *and* GRACE. *The second man in line speaks.*

TEN. Sir, Prisoner Number Ten requests a change of blades, sir.

GRACE *changes the blade in his razor before handing it to him.* LINTZ *grants them permission to cross into the head as the first five are given permission to come out. They are clothed in clean underwear streaked with water, and it is obvious that they had little time to dry themselves. Their razors are taken from their uplifted hands by* GRACE, *and as this is done, they take their towels in their right hands; as they cross into the compound, the towels are snapped loudly. They return their bathing tools to their proper places, go to their racks, and, in their underwear, begin reading.* TEPPERMAN *comes out of the head, and* LINTZ *goes into the compound.*

LINTZ. Manuals away.

TEPPERMAN. Get all the gear off your racks and get them ready for habitation. [*The prisoners take all their paraphernalia from the heads of their bunks and place it on the floor with their clothing. They then resume a position of attention in front of their bunks.* GRACE *flicks a switch beside his head and all the lights go out except the ones in the head. The light casts itself across the Brig, making the prisoners appear as shadows.*] Sound off.

ONE. Sir, Prisoner Number One, sir.

The rest of the prisoners answer in the same way, one at a time, using their own numbers.

TEPPERMAN. Get in.

The prisoners jump in their bunks, leaving their shoes on the floor.

GRACE. Get out.

The prisoners jump from their bunks into their shoes and come to attention again.

LINTZ. Get in.

The prisoners jump in once more.

THE WARDEN. Are all my children asleep?

ALL PRISONERS. Yes, sir.

GRACE *flicks another switch and the stage is black.*

Curtain.

Body Beautiful

Naomi Iizuka

CHARACTERS:

RITA
LONI/"KAREN"
THE HOST

SETTING:

A bright, white room somewhere between a steam room in an upscale spa and a padded room in a sanitorium. RITA and LONI wear white bathrobes and towels twisted turban-like around their heads. RITA's face is covered with bluish mud. They sit in high-backed chairs that change position as the action unfolds.

RITA: More?
LONI: Not right now.
RITA: Don't let me force you.
LONI: I'm fine.
RITA: You're sure.
LONI: I said I'm fine.
RITA: No more?

LONI: I've had enough. I really have. I'm going to burst. I've had enough. I want no more. And if I have just one more thing, the tiniest thing, I swear I'll climb right out of my skull.

RITA: And how are we today? Hm?

LONI: I don't want to talk about it.

RITA: Don't be shy. We're all friends here.

LONI: My condition is the same.

RITA: I can see that.

LONI: I've done all I can. I've fasted. I've cut back. I've worked out. I've lifted. I don't know what more I can do. I'm at the end of my tether.

RITA: May I smoke do you mind. To me, it seems clear.

LONI: Yes?

RITA: It's perfectly simple. You're fat. Quite fat. Clinically obese, in fact.

LONI: I'm getting bigger.

RITA: I bet you are.

LONI: It occupies my mind.

RITA: Look at yourself. Have you? Recently?

LONI: Everyday.

RITA: And?

LONI: I surprise myself.

RITA: There should be no surprises where the body is concerned.

LONI: I have new surfaces everywhere I look.

RITA: Control, darling.

LONI: I've grown new shapes. New forms.

RITA: It's all in the muscles.

(*Blackout. Lights up.*)

RITA: The beauty of economy.

LONI: I know.

RITA: You have a pretty face.

LONI: I've done everything they've said. I've followed instructions to the letter of the word. I have not cheated. No. Not once.

RITA: And you're still as big as a barn. May I be frank. May I be candid. May I smoke do you mind. I don't doubt your good intentions, but that's not what we're talking about, is it now? I mean what are we talking about? (*Pause.*)

The bottom line. We're talking about the bottom line. You want the bottom line? Too much flesh. That's your problem. Too much glad wrap, darling. You're busting out all over. You need to cut back. Do a little slice and dice. Do something with all that meat for christ's sake.

(*Pause.*)

No solids?

LONI: No. Not a one.

RITA: Zero calories.

LONI: Zero.

RITA: So you're saying nothing.

LONI: Not a thing.

RITA: The weight should be dropping right off.

LONI: I'm gaining.

RITA: Strictly speaking, impossible.

LONI: I tell you, I'm gaining by the minute.

RITA: But the figures. Look at the figures.

LONI: I know.

RITA: It can't but stand to reason.

LONI: You lack imagination.

RITA: Face it. You're a fatty. Figures do not lie.

LONI: No. Not a one.

RITA: (*With good cheer.*): Heart disease and stroke. It's a national tragedy. We're eating our way to hell.

(*Pause.*)

I have a theory.

LONI: Yes?

RITA: I think it happens when you're not looking. I think you gain while you're unconscious.

LONI: How do I swallow when I'm unconscious?

RITA: You manage. You do. Really you do. Don't underestimate what a clever girl you are while you're unconscious.

LONI: I have no memory of all of this.

RITA: Look at yourself. Need I say more?

LONI: Is that how it's done then?

RITA: It's a theory.

LONI: I'm getting bigger. I think. Even as we've been speaking I have been.

(*Pause.*)

RITA: I've always kept my weight in check. My size has never changed. Never. No. Not once. I'd never let it. I've always been a two. A perfect size two. I eat leafy vegetables and brown rice. I run fifteen miles a day, when I can. Friends say I'm remarkable.

LONI: You look wonderful.

RITA: Thank you.

LONI: Very elegant.

RITA: Really? How kind.

LONI: How do you do it? I want to know. I *need* to know. I must for my peace
of mind know. Tell me. Please tell me. How do you do it?

RITA: Discipline. And nutrasweet.

(*Blackout. Lights up.*)

Please have some more. Go on.

LONI: Can't. Can't do it.

RITA: Please.

LONI: Can't.

RITA: Oh, go on.

LONI: I must defer.

RITA: It's delicious.

LONI: No. No thank you.

RITA: You can't know unless you taste.

LONI: Can't. I'm stuffed.

RITA: Just a little taste can't hurt.

LONI: I've had enough. I really have.

(*Blackout. Lights up.*)

RITA: Are you fit for life, would you say?

LONI: I've given up meat and all animal fat.

RITA: Animal protein is a fiend. May I smoke do you mind.

LONI: I ate ground chuck some time back. Made me sick. That's when I
knew.

RITA: It's a toxic time bomb ticking ticking ticking.

LONI: It stayed with me a very long time.

RITA: The evidence. You need only look at the evidence. People thrive without meat, absolutely thrive. Take the Hunzas of the Himalayas. Their
longevity and endurance are legendary the world over. And then, of
course, there is that little, tiny tribe in North Yemen is it? What is their
name? It's on the tip of my tongue—phenomenally healthy people. Meat-
free and doing fine. And what about the Mayan Indians? Let's not forget
the noble savage of the Yucatan. Lovely people. Free of disease. Can you
imagine? It's practically unimaginable, but try. Do try. And don't you dare
let me forget the Bulgarians. Lots of octogenarian Bulgarians out there.
They just live and live. It's glorious. You know what it is, don't you?

LONI: I'm at a loss.

RITA: The beans. The seeds and beans. Some nuts, of course. A little grain.

LONI: And they survive?

RITA: Survive? My God, they flourish like pigs in shit.

LONI: No meat at all?

RITA: BULGARIANS EAT VERY LITTLE MEAT. It's common knowledge.

LONI: I never knew.

RITA: Do you think it's a coincidence? Is that what you think? Cancer, diabetes, emphysema, arthritis. Do you think it's a coincidence? Our steady decline in health has reached catastrophic proportions, and you think it's just a coincidence? With every bite of hormone-saturated fat, we're killing ourselves a little everyday. And you, you think it's a coincidence?

LONI: I could give up meat. I could give up lots of things.

(*Blackout. Lights up.*)

RITA: Run a skewer through the thickest part. If the juice comes out white, it's cooked.

LONI: If the juice is still red, leave a little longer in the oven.

RITA: Cut all the flesh into neat fillets. Dip them in frying batter. Fry. Like fritters.

LONI: You cook. I knew you would.

RITA: Only sometimes.

LONI: You're being modest. I know you're a pro.

RITA: I only cook when I can't get it elsewhere. Tongue. Sweetbread. Brain.

LONI: Very rich.

RITA: High in protein.

LONI: Tasty, too.

RITA: You read my mind. Sometimes when I get the urge, I go to the meat counter where I pick up the telephone attached to the wall, and stare into the mirror behind which butchers in white aprons cut the meat with shiny, steel machines whose motors buzz in icy rooms. When I get a butcher on the other end of the line, I ask for half a pound of brain. Tongue, if they have it. And in an instant, like magic, an invisible hand slides the meat through a crack in the mirror. It's wrapped in plastic. I like that.

(*Blackout. When the lights go up,* THE HOST *is lounging comfortably. His face is fixed in a smile. He holds a microphone.*)

THE HOST: Let's stop for a moment shall we?

RITA: May I smoke do you mind.

THE HOST: Of course. Be my guest. I'd just like to clarify for the viewers out there that neither this program nor its sponsors in any way condones or encourages smoking. Can we just be clear on that? Same goes for your local broadcast affiliate. Little disclaimer there, O.K.? Great. I'd like to get back to our discussion from before the station break about the beautiful body and you. It's fascinating, fascinating stuff. Just, uh, fascinating. I'd like to backtrack just for a second, and get into what it is you're saying? I mean, what exactly are you saying?

RITA: I think it boils down to a glandular question.

THE HOST: That's what I came away with. I think that's just fascinating. It's like, what, maybe one big machine Something like that. Would that be fair to say? Would you say that? Just jump right in whenever. I'm just throwing that out.

RITA: There are harmless, completely natural foods that have been found to be linked with sterility and impotence. It's a fact.

THE HOST: Wow. Incredible. That makes you think. That really makes you, well, it gives you pause.

RITA: A whole host of sexual inadequacies have been traced to patterns in the diet. The most innocent foods can and will lead to low sperm count and a myriad of other sexual dysfunctions.

THE HOST: I'm speechless. Truly, I mean, think of it. Think of it. What we eat can, you know, determine how we, what, what should I say, perform. Incredible. It's a, it's a, well, there's a lot there, isn't there. We'll have to break in a minute. They're giving me all kinds of signals. Is there anything else? Real quick before we break.

RITA: I'd just caution your viewers to watch what they eat.

(*Blackout. Lights up.*)

THE HOST: We're back. We're talking about the beautiful body and you. I'd like to move for a moment to the dark side of all of this. There is a dark side. No question. Karen? We're calling you Karen. It's not your real name for obvious reasons. I want to thank you, Karen, for being here today. We're really happy you could join us. I know this must be hard for you. Are you comfortable?

LONI: I'm fine.

THE HOST: Good. Good. I'm so glad. I know how hard this must be for you, Karen, so please, take your time.

(*Long pause.*)

Uh, Karen?

LONI: Yes?

THE HOST: You want to start from the beginning?

LONI: I don't know where to begin.

THE HOST: Why don't you tell us how you first got involved in all of this stuff about, you know, your body and all of that. If you don't mind me asking, Karen, were you once overweight?

LONI: Fat. I was fat.

THE HOST: How did this all happen? Can you share that with us?

LONI: I was concerned with what I was putting in my mouth. It disappeared. It had to go somewhere.

THE HOST: I'm right with you, Karen.

LONI: So then I began to be concerned with what was already inside. What was there for keeps. I started going a little crazy.

THE HOST: Gotcha.

LONI: Well, it was a natural progression. I stopped eating and drinking which made sense at the time, but then I became really conscious that there were still things inside of me even then.

THE HOST: Things, Karen? What kinds of things?

LONI: Bones, vital organs. Things like that. So I was left with a dilemma. How to get rid of these things that just weren't going anywhere on their own. Elective surgery seemed to make sense. Like I said, it was a natural progression. I mean I had my tonsils removed as a child. And then my appendix in college. It seemed really simple. In. Out. No problem.

THE HOST: So little time.

LONI: It felt right. What more can I say? So I just went with it. First I did my breasts. They were the first to go. My kidney came next. That was a snap. By then I was hooked. Out went the colon, the pancreas, a nice size chunk of my large intestine. It was a breeze. All gone. I was thrilled. I couldn't stop.

THE HOST: Hold that thought, Karen. And we'll be right back after this station break.

(*Blackout. Lights up.*)

THE HOST: Condensing, enriching, refining, flaking. And where does Beta Carotene fit in? I worry. I have to say, I worry. I mean where is the fiber? And what about the roughage? I just don't know. It's not easy. No easy answers. Any words of wisdom? Help me. Help me on this one.

RITA: I just have one word to say: micronutrients.

THE HOST: Uh huh. I think, I think, if I could paraphrase, you're talking about the little things. I mean, isn't that what you're getting at? Correct me if I'm wrong, but don't you think it always boils down to the little things? I mean, isn't that what's important after all is said and done? Stop me if I'm off. I could be totally off. I'm just throwing this out.

RITA: Micronutrients. What more can I say?

THE HOST: Fascinating. That's fascinating. All this information. I'm, I'm, well, I don't know what I am. Speechless. That's what I am. Oop, we got to break. We'll be back right after this.

(*Blackout. Lights up.*)

THE HOST: We've been talking about the beautiful body and you. I can't believe the hour's up. I feel like we've just, what, skimmed the surface. Any last words?

LONI: I'd just like to say that it works. For me, it works.

THE HOST: So little time.

LONI: I mean you can read about it. You can hear me talk about it. But you really have to experience this weight loss program firsthand to understand just how wonderful it is.

THE HOST: That's great. That's really great. And I think that's about all.

LONI: It was an answer to a prayer. I mean it changed my life. It changed the way I live. The doctor couldn't believe it. He said it was a miracle. All those little aches and pains. The chronic fatigue. The general sense of malaise and despair. Disappeared. Overnight.

THE HOST: I think that about does it.

LONI: And I'm never hungry. That's the most amazing thing. I eat whatever I want whenever I want. You'd never believe it, but it's true. Everything.

THE HOST: That's about it. Thank you for joining us.

LONI: I have energy. I have power. I feel twenty years younger.

THE HOST: Thank you.

LONI: Thank *you*. That's all I want to say. Thank you. Thanks a million.

THE HOST: I think that's the last word. Good night, everybody.

(*Blackout. End of play.*)

The Death of the Last Black Man in the Whole Entire World

Suzan-Lori Parks

THE FIGURES

BLACK MAN WITH WATERMELON
BLACK WOMAN WITH FRIED DRUMSTICK
LOTS OF GREASE AND LOTS OF PORK
YES AND GREENS BLACK-EYED PEAS CORNBREAD
QUEEN-THEN-PHARAOH HATSHEPSUT
BEFORE COLUMBUS
OLD MAN RIVER JORDAN
HAM
AND BIGGER AND BIGGER AND BIGGER
PRUNES AND PRISMS
VOICE ON THUH TEE V

TIME

THE PRESENT

When I die,
I won't stay
Dead.
   BOB KAUFMAN

BLACK MAN WITH WATERMELON: The black man moves his hands.

(*A bell sounds twice*)

LOTS OF GREASE AND LOTS OF PORK: Lots of Grease and Lots of Pork.

QUEEN-THEN-PHARAOH HATSHEPSUT: Queen-then-Pharaoh Hatshepsut.

AND BIGGER AND BIGGER AND BIGGER: And Bigger and Bigger and Bigger.

PRUNES AND PRISMS: Prunes and Prisms.

HAM: Ham.

VOICE ON THUH TEE V: Voice on thuh Tee V.

OLD MAN RIVER JORDAN: Old Man River Jordan.

YES AND GREENS BLACK-EYES PEAS CORNBREAD: Yes and Greens Black-Eyes Peas Cornbread.

BEFORE COLUMBUS: Before Columbus.

(*A bell sounds once*)

BLACK MAN WITH WATERMELON: The black man moves his hands.

QUEEN-THEN-PHARAOH HATSHEPSUT: Not yet. Let Queen-then-Pharaoh Hatshepsut tell you when.

LOTS OF GREASE AND LOTS OF PORK: This is the death of the last black man in the whole entire world.

(*A bell sounds three times*)

BLACK WOMAN WITH FRIED DRUMSTICK: Yesterday today next summer tomorrow just uh moment uhgoh in 1317 dieded thuh last black man in thuh whole entire world. Uh! Oh. Dont be uhlarmed. Do not be afeared. It was painless. Uh painless passin. He falls twenty-three floors to his death. 23 floors from uh passin ship from space tuh splat on thuh pavement. He have uh head he been keepin under thuh Tee V. On his bottom pantry shelf. He have uh head that hurts. Dont fit right. Put it on tuh go tuh thuh store in it pinched him when he walks his thoughts dont got room. Why dieded he huh? Where he gonna go now that he done dieded? Where he gonna go tuh wash his hands?

YES AND GREENS BLACK-EYED PEAS CORNBREAD: You should write that down and you should hide it under a rock. This is the death of the last black man in the whole entire world.

LOTS OF GREASE AND LOTS OF PORK/PRUNES AND PRISMS: Not yet—

BLACK MAN WITH WATERMELON: The black man moves. His hands—

QUEEN-THEN-PHARAOH HATSHEPSUT: You are too young to move. Let me move it for you.

BLACK MAN WITH WATERMELON: The black man moves his hands.—He moves his hands round. Back. Back. Back tuh that.

LOTS OF GREASE AND LOTS OF PORK: (Not dat.)

BLACK MAN WITH WATERMELON: When thuh worl usta be roun. Thuh worl usta be *roun*.

BLACK WOMAN WITH FRIED DRUMSTICK: Uh roun worl. Uh roun? Thuh worl? When was this.

QUEEN-THEN-PHARAOH HATSHEPSUT: Columbus. Before.

BEFORE COLUMBUS: Before. Columbus.

YES AND GREENS BLACK-EYED PEAS CORNBREAD: Before Columbus.

BLACK MAN WITH WATERMELON: HHH. HA!

QUEEN-THEN-PHARAOH HATSHEPSUT: Before Columbus thuh worl usta be *roun* they put uh /d/ on thuh end of roun makin roun*d*. Thusly they set in motion thuh end. Without that /d/ we coulda gone on spinnin forever. Thuh /d/ thing ended things ended.

YES AND GREENS BLACK-EYES PEAS CORNBREAD: Before Columbus.

(*A bell sounds twice*)

BEFORE COLUMBUS: The popular thinking of the day back in them days was that the world was flat. They thought the world was flat. Back then when they thought the world was flat they were afeared and stayed at home. They wanted to go out back then when they thought the world was flat but the water had in it dragons of which meaning these dragons they were afeared back then when they thought the world was flat. They stayed at home. Them thinking the world was flat kept it roun. Them thinking the sun revolved around the earth kept them satellite-like. They figured out the truth and scurried out. Figuring out the truth put them in their place and they scurried out to put us in ours.

YES AND GREENS BLACK-EYES PEAS CORNBREAD: Mmmm. Yes. You should write this down. You should hide this under a rock.

LOTS OF GREASE AND LOTS OF PORK/PRUNES AND PRISMS: Not yet—

BLACK MAN WITH WATERMELON: The black man bursts into flames. The black man bursts into blames. Whose fault is it?

ALL: Aint mines.

BLACK MAN WITH WATERMELON: Whose fault is it?

ALL: Aint mines.

BLACK WOMAN WITH FRIED DRUMSTICK: I cant remember back that far.

QUEEN-THEN-PHARAOH HATSHEPSUT: And besides, I wasnt even there.

BLACK MAN WITH WATERMELON: Ha ha ha. The black man laughs out loud.

ALL (*Except Ham*): HAM-BONE-HAM-BONE-WHERE-YOU-BEEN-ROUN-THUH-WORL-N-BACK-UH-*GAIN*.

YES AND GREENS BLACK-EYED PEAS CORNBREAD: Whatcha seen hambone girl?

BLACK WOMAN WITH FRIED DRUMSTICK: Didnt see you. I saw thuh worl.

QUEEN-THEN-PHARAOH HATSHEPSUT: I was there.

LOTS OF GREASE AND LOTS OF PORK: Didnt see you.

BLACK WOMAN WITH FRIED DRUMSTICK: I was there.

BLACK MAN WITH WATERMELON: Didnt see you. The black man moves his hands.

QUEEN-THEN-PHARAOH HATSHEPSUT: We are too young to see. Let them see it for you. We are too young to rule. Let them rule it for you. We are too young to have. Let them have it for you. You are too young to write. Let them—let them. Do it. Before you.

BLACK MAN WITH WATERMELON: The black man moves his hands.

YES AND GREENS BLACK-EYED PEAS CORNBREAD: You should write it down because if you dont write it down then they will come along and tell the future that we did not exist. You should write it down and you should hide it under a rock. You should write down the past and you should write down the present and in what in the future you should write it down. It will be of us but you should mention them from time to time so that in the future when they come along and know that they exist. You should hide it all under a rock so that in the future when they come along they will say that the rock did not exist.

BLACK WOMAN WITH FRIED DRUMSTICK: We getting somewheres. We getting down. Down down down down down down down down—

QUEEN-THEN-PHARAOH HATSHEPSUT: I saw Columbus comin./I saw Columbus comin goin over tuh visit you. "To borrow a cup of sugar," so he said. I waved my hands in warnin. You waved back. I aint seen you since.

LOTS OF GREASE AND LOTS OF PORK: In the future when they came along I meeting them. On thuh coast. Uh! Thuh Coast! I—was—so—polite. But in thuh dirt, I wrote: "Ha. Ha. Ha."

ALL: Ha. Ha. Ha. Ha. Ha. Ha. Ha. Ha. Ha. Ha. Ha. Ha. Ha Ha. Ha. Ha. HHHHHHHHHHHHHHHH.

BLACK MAN WITH WATERMELON: Thuh black man he move. He move he hans.

(*A bell sounds once*)

PANEL I: THUH HOLY GHOST

BLACK MAN WITH WATERMELON: Saint mines. Saint mines. Iduhnt it. Nope: iduhnt. Saint mines cause everythin I calls mines got uh print uh me someway on it in it dont got uh print uh me someway on it so saint mines. Duhduhnt so saint: huh.

BLACK WOMAN WITH FRIED DRUMSTICK: Hen.

BLACK MAN WITH WATERMELON: Huh. Huh?

BLACK WOMAN WITH FRIED DRUMSTICK: Hen. Hen?

BLACK MAN WITH WATERMELON: Who give birth tuh this I wonder. Who gived birth tuh this. I wonder.

BLACK WOMAN WITH FRIED DRUMSTICK: You comed back. Comin backs somethin in itself. You comed back.

BLACK MAN WITH WATERMELON: This does not belong tuh me. Somebody planted this on me. On me in my hands.

BLACK WOMAN WITH FRIED DRUMSTICK: Cold compress. Cold compress then some hen. Lean back. You comed back. Lean back.

BLACK MAN WITH WATERMELON: Who gived birth tuh this I wonder who.

BLACK WOMAN WITH FRIED DRUMSTICK: Comin for you. Came for you: that they done did. Comin for tuh take you. Told me tuh pack up your clothes. Told me tuh cut my bed in 2 from double tuh single. Cut off thuh bed-foot where your feets had rested. Told me tuh do that too. Burry your ring in his hidin spot under thuh porch! That they told me too to do. Didnt have uh ring so I didnt do diddly. They told and told and told: proper instructions for thuh burial proper attire for thuh mournin. They told and told and told: I didnt do squat. Awe on that. You comed back. You got uhway. Knew you would. Hen?

BLACK MAN WITH WATERMELON: Who gived birth tuh this I wonder. Who? Not me. Saint mines.

BLACK WOMAN WITH FRIED DRUMSTICK: Killed every hen on thuh block. You comed back. Knew you would. Knew you would came back. Knew you will wanted uh good big hen dinner in waitin. Every hen on the block.

BLACK MAN WITH WATERMELON: Saint mines.

BLACK WOMAN WITH FRIED DRUMSTICK: Strutted down on up thuh road with my axe. By-my-self-with-my-axe. Got tuh thuh street top 93 dyin hen din hand. Dropped thuh axe. Tooked tuh stranglin. 93 dyin hen din hand with no heads let em loose tuh run down tuh towards home infront of me. Flipped thuh necks of thuh next 23 more odd. Slinged um over my shoulders. Hens of thuh neighbors now in my pots. Feathers of thuh hens of thuh neighbors stucked in our mattress. They told and told and told. On me. Huh. Awe on that. Hen? You got uhway. Knew you would.

BLACK MAN WITH WATERMELON: Who gived birth tuh me I wonder.

BLACK WOMAN WITH FRIED DRUMSTICK: They dont speak tuh us no more. They pass by our porch but they dont nod. You been comed back goin on 9 years not even heard from thuh neighbors uh congratulation. Uh alien-ationed dum. Uh guess. Huh. Hen? WE AINT GOT NO FRIENDS,— sweetheart.

BLACK MAN WITH WATERMELON: SWEET-HEART.

BLACK WOMAN WITH FRIED DRUMSTICK: Hen!!

BLACK MAN WITH WATERMELON: Aint hungry.

BLACK WOMAN WITH FRIED DRUMSTICK: Hen.

BLACK MAN WITH WATERMELON: Aint eaten in years.

BLACK WOMAN WITH FRIED DRUMSTICK: Hen.

BLACK MAN WITH WATERMELON: Last meal I had was my last-mans-meal.

BLACK WOMAN WITH FRIED DRUMSTICK: You got uhway. Knew you would.

BLACK MAN WITH WATERMELON: This thing dont look like me!

BLACK WOMAN WITH FRIED DRUMSTICK: It dont. Do it. Should it? Hen: eat it.

BLACK MAN WITH WATERMELON: I kin tell what mines by whats gots my looks. Ssmymethod. Try it by testin it and it turns out true. Every time. Fool proofly. Look down at my foot and wonder it its mine. Foot mine? I kin ask it and foot answers back with us "yes Sir"—not like you and me say "yes Sir" but uh "yes Sir" peculiar tuh thuh foot. Foot mine? I kin ask it and through uh look that looks like my looks thuh foot gives me back uh "yes Sir." Ssmymethod. Try by thuh test tuh pass for true. Move on tuh thuh uther foot. Foot mine? And uh nother "yes Sir" so feets mine is understood. Got uh forearm thats up for question check myself out teeth by tooth. Melon mines?—. Dont look like me.

BLACK WOMAN WITH FRIED DRUMSTICK: Hen mine? Gobble it up and it will be. You got uhway. Fixed uh good big hen dinner for you. Get yourself uh mouthful afore it rots.

BLACK MAN WITH WATERMELON: Was we green and stripedly when we first comed out?

BLACK WOMAN WITH FRIED DRUMSTICK: Uh huhn. Thuh features comes later. Later comes after now.

BLACK MAN WITH WATERMELON: Oh. Later comes now: melon mine?

BLACK WOMAN WITH FRIED DRUMSTICK: They comed from you and tooked you. That was yesterday. Today you sit in your chair where you sat yesterday and thuh day afore yesterday afore they comed and tooked you. Things today is just as they are yesterday cept nothin is familiar cause it was such uh long time uhgoh.

BLACK MAN WITH WATERMELON: Later oughta be now by now huh?: melon mine?

BLACK WOMAN WITH FRIED DRUMSTICK: Thuh chair was portable. They take it from county tuh county. Only got one. Can only eliminate one at uh time. Woulda fried you right here on thuh front porch but we dont got enough electric. No onessgot enough electric. Not on our block. Dont believe in having enough. Put thuh Chair in thuh middle of thuh City. Outdoors. In thuh square. Folks come tuh watch with picnic baskets.—Hen?

BLACK MAN WITH WATERMELON: Sweetheart?

BLACK WOMAN WITH FRIED DRUMSTICK: They juiced you some, huh?

BLACK MAN WITH WATERMELON: Just a squirt. Sweetheart.

BLACK WOMAN WITH FRIED DRUMSTICK: Humpty Dumpty.

BLACK MAN WITH WATERMELON: Melon mines?

BLACK WOMAN WITH FRIED DRUMSTICK: Humpty damn Dumpty actin like thuh Holy Ghost. You got uhway. Thuh lights dimmed but you got uhway. Knew you would.

BLACK MAN WITH WATERMELON: They juiced me some.

BLACK WOMAN WITH FRIED DRUMSTICK: Just a squirt.

BLACK MAN WITH WATERMELON: They had theirselves uh extender chord. Fry uh man in thuh town square needs uh extender tuh reach em thuh electric. Hook up thuh chair tuh thuh power. Extender: 49 foot in length. Closer tuh thuh power I never been. Flip on up thuh go switch. Huh! Juice begins its course.

BLACK WOMAN WITH FRIED DRUMSTICK: Humpty damn Dumpty.

BLACK MAN WITH WATERMELON: Thuh straps they have on me are leathern. See thuh cord waggin full with uh jump-juice try me tuh wiggle from thuh waggin but belt leathern straps: width thickly. One round each forearm. Forearm mines? 2 cross thuh chest. Chest is mines: and it explodin. One for my left hand fingers left strapted too. Right was done thuh same. Jump-juice meets me-mine juices I do uh slow softshoe like on water. Town crier cries uh moan. Felt my nappy head go frizzly. Town follows thuh crier in uh sorta sing-uhlong-song.

BLACK WOMAN WITH FRIED DRUMSTICK: Then you got uhway. Got uhway in comed back.

BLACK MAN WITH WATERMELON: Uh extender chord 49 foot in length. Turned on thuh up switch in I started runnin. First 49 foot I was runnin they was still juicin.

BLACK WOMAN WITH FRIED DRUMSTICK: And they chase-ted you.

BLACK MAN WITH WATERMELON: —Melon mines?

BLACK WOMAN WITH FRIED DRUMSTICK: When you broked tuh seek your freedom they followed after, huh?

BLACK MAN WITH WATERMELON: Later oughta be now by now, huh?

BLACK WOMAN WITH FRIED DRUMSTICK: You comed back.

BLACK MAN WITH WATERMELON: —Not exactly.

BLACK WOMAN WITH FRIED DRUMSTICK: They comed for you tuh take you. Tooked you uhway: that they done did. You got uhway. Thuh lights dimmed. Had us uh brownout. You got past that. You comed back.

BLACK MAN WITH WATERMELON: Turned on thuh juice on me in me in I started runnin. First just runnin then runnin towards home. Couldnt find us. Think I got lost. Saw us on up uhhead but I flew over thuh yard. Couldnt stop. Think I overshot.

BLACK WOMAN WITH FRIED DRUMSTICK: Killed every hen on thuh block. Made you uh—

BLACK MAN WITH WATERMELON: Make me uh space 6 feet by 6 feet by 6. Make it big and mark it so as I wont miss it. If you would please, sweetness, uh mass grave-site. Theres company comin soonish. I would like tuh get up and go. I would like tuh move my hands.

BLACK WOMAN WITH FRIED DRUMSTICK: You comed back.

BLACK MAN WITH WATERMELON: Overshot. Overshot. I would like tuh move my hands.

BLACK WOMAN WITH FRIED DRUMSTICK: Cold compress?

BLACK MAN WITH WATERMELON: Sweetheart.

BLACK WOMAN WITH FRIED DRUMSTICK: How uhbout uh hen leg?

BLACK MAN WITH WATERMELON: Nothanks. Justate.

BLACK WOMAN WITH FRIED DRUMSTICK: Just ate?

BLACK MAN WITH WATERMELON: Thatsright. 6 by 6 by 6. Thatsright.

BLACK WOMAN WITH FRIED DRUMSTICK: Oh.—They eat their own yuh know.

BLACK MAN WITH WATERMELON: HooDoo.

BLACK WOMAN WITH FRIED DRUMSTICK: Hen do. Saw it on thuh Tee V.

BLACK MAN WITH WATERMELON: Aint that nice.

(A bell sounds once)

PANEL II: FIRST CHORUS

BLACK MAN WITH WATERMELON: 6 by 6 by 6.

ALL: THATS RIGHT.

BLACK WOMAN WITH FRIED DRUMSTICK: Oh. They eat their own you know.

ALL: HOODOO.

BLACK WOMAN WITH FRIED DRUMSTICK: Hen do. Saw it on thuh Tee V.

ALL: Aint that nice.

AND BIGGER AND BIGGER AND BIGGER: WILL SOMEBODY TAKE THESE STRAPS OFF UH ME PLEASE? I WOULD LIKE TUH MOVE MY HANDS.

PRUNES AND PRISMS: Prunes and prisms will begin: prunes and prisms prunes and prisms prunes and prisms and prunes and prisms: 23.

VOICE ON THUH TEE V: Good evening. I'm Broad Caster. Headlining tonight: the news: is Gamble Major, the absolutely last living Negro man in the whole entire known world—is dead. Major, Gamble, born a slave, taught himself the rudiments of education to become a spearhead in the Civil Rights Movement. He was 38 years old. News of Majors death sparked controlled displays of jubilation in all corners of the world.

PRUNES AND PRISMS: Oh no no: world is roun.

AND BIGGER AND BIGGER AND BIGGER: WILL SOMEBODY TAKE THESE STRAPS OFF UH ME PLEASE? I WOULD LIKE TUH MOVE MY HANDS.

(*A bell sounds four times*)

LOTS OF GREASE AND LOTS OF PORK: This is the death of the last black man in the whole entire world.

PRUNES AND PRISMS: Not yet—

VOICE ON THUH TEE V: Good evening. Broad Caster. Headline tonight: Gamble Major, the absolutely last living Negro man in the whole known entire world is dead. Gamble Major born a slave rose to become a spearhead in the Civil Rights Movement. He was 38 years old. The Civil Rights Movement. He was 38 years old.

AND BIGGER AND BIGGER AND BIGGER: WILL SOMEBODY TAKE THESE STRAPS OFF UH ME PLEASE? I WOULD LIKE TUH MOVE MY HANDS.

LOTS OF GREASE AND LOTS OF PORK: This is the death of the last black man in the whole entire world.

(*A bell sounds three times*)

PRUNES AND PRISMS: Prunes and prisms prunes and prisms prunes and prisms prunes and prisms.

QUEEN-THEN-PHARAOH HATSHEPSUT: Yesterday tuhday next summer tuhmorrow just uh moment uhgoh in 1317 dieded thuh last black man in thuh whole entire world. Uh! Oh. Dont be uhlarmed. Do not be afeared. It was painless. Uh painless passin. He falls 23 floors to his death.

BLACK WOMAN WITH FRIED DRUMSTICK: No.

QUEEN-THEN-PHARAOH HATSHEPSUT: 23 floors from uh passin ship from space tuh splat on thuh pavement.

BLACK WOMEN WITH FRIED DRUMSTICK: No.

QUEEN-THEN-PHARAOH HATSHEPSUT: He have uh head he been keepin under thuh Tee V. On his bottom pantry shelf.

BLACK WOMAN WITH FRIED DRUMSTICK: No.

QUEEN-THEN-PHARAOH HATSHEPSUT: He have uh head that hurts. Dont fit right. Put it on tuh go tuh thuh store in it pinched him when he walks his thoughts dont got room. Why dieded he huh?

BLACK WOMAN WITH FRIED DRUMSTICK: No.

QUEEN-THEN-PHARAOH HATSHEPSUT: Where he gonna go now that he done dieded?

PRUNES AND PRISMS: No.

BLACK WOMAN WITH FRIED DRUMSTICK: Where he gonna go tuh wash his hands?

ALL: You should write that down. You should write that down and you should hide it under uh rock.

VOICE ON THUH TEE V: Good evening. Broad Caster. Headlinin tonight: thuh news:

OLD MAN RIVER JORDAN: Tell you of uh news. Last news. Last news of thuh last man. Last man had last words say hearin it. He spoked uh speech spoked hisself uh chatter-tooth babble "ya-oh-may/chuh-naw" dribblin down his lips tuh puddle in his lap. Dribblin by droppletts. Drop by drop. Last news. News flashes then drops. Thuh last drop was uh all uhlone drop. Singular. Thuh last drop started it off it all. Started off with uh drop. Started off with uh jungle. Started sproutin in his spittle growin leaves off of his mines and thuh vines say drippin doin it. Last news leads tuh thuh first news. He is dead he crosses thuh river. He jumps in thuh puddle have his clothing: ON. On thuh other side thuh mountin yo he dripply wet with soppin. Do drop be dripted? I say "yes."

BLACK MAN WITH WATERMELON: Dont leave me hear. Dont leave me. Hear?

QUEEN-THEN-PHARAOH HATSHEPSUT: Where he gonna go tuh wash his dribblin hands?

PRUNES AND PRISMS: Where he gonna go tuh dry his dripplin clothes?

YES AND GREENS BLACK-EYED PEAS CORNBREAD: Did you write it down? On uh little slip uh paper stick thuh slip in thuh river afore you slip in that way you keep your clothes dry, man.

PRUNES AND PRISMS: Aintcha heard uh that trick?

BEFORE COLUMBUS: That tricks thuh method.

QUEEN-THEN-PHARAOH HATSHEPSUT: They used it on uhlong uhgoh still works every time.

OLD MAN RIVER JORDAN: He jumped in thuh water without uh word for partin come out dripply wet with soppin. Do drop be dripted? I say "do."

BLACK MAN WITH WATERMELON: In you all theres kin. You all kin. Kin gave thuh first permission kin be givin it now still. Some things is all thuh ways gonna be uh continuin sort of uh some thing. Some things go on and on till they dont stop. I am soppin wet. I left my scent behind in uh bundle of old clothing that was not thrown out. Left thuh scent in thuh clothin in thuh clothin on uh rooftop. Dogs surround my house and laugh. They are mockin thuh scent that I left behind. I jumped in thuh water without uh word. I jumped in thuh water without uh smell. I am in thuh river and in my skin is soppin wet. I would like tuh stay afloat now. I would like tuh move my hands.

AND BIGGER AND BIGGER AND BIGGER: Would somebody take these straps off uh me please? I would like tuh move my hands.

BLACK MAN WITH WATERMELON: Now kin kin I move my hands?

QUEEN-THEN-PHARAOH HATSHEPSUT: My black man my subject man my man uh all mens my my my no no not yet no not yes thuh hands. Let Queen-then-Pharaoh Hatshepsut tell you when. She is I am. An I am she passing by with her train. Pulling it behind her on uh plastic chain.

Ooooh who! Ooooh who! Where you gonna go now, now that you done dieded?

ALL: Ha ha ha.

PRUNES AND PRISMS: Say "prunes and prisms" 40 times each day and youll cure your big lips. Prunes and prisms prunes and prisms prunes and prisms: 19.

QUEEN-THEN-PHARAOH HATSHEPSUT: An I am Sheba-like she be me am passin on by she with her train. Pullin it behind/he on uh plastic chain. Oooh who! Oooh who! Come uhlong. Come uhlong.

BLACK WOMAN WITH FRIED DRUMSTICK: Say he was waitin on thuh right time.

AND BIGGER AND BIGGER AND BIGGER: Say he was waitin in thuh wrong line.

BLACK MAN WITH WATERMELON: I jumped in thuh river without uh word. My kin are soppin wet.

QUEEN-THEN-PHARAOH HATSHEPSUT: Come uhlong. Come uhlong.

PRUNES AND PRISMS: Prunes and prisms prunes and prisms.

LOTS OF GREASE AND LOTS OF PORK: This is the death of the last black man in the whole entire world.

PRUNES AND PRISMS: Not yet.

LOTS OF GREASE AND LOTS OF PORK: Back tuh when thuh worl usta be roun.

QUEEN-THEN-PHARAOH HATSHEPSUT: Come uhlong come uhlong get on board come uhlong.

OLD MAN RIVER JORDAN: Back tuh that. Yes.

YES AND GREENS BLACK-EYED PEAS CORNBREAD: Back tuh when thuh worl usta be roun.

OLD MAN RIVER JORDAN: Uhcross thuh river in back tuh that. Yes. Do in diddly dip didded thuh drop. Out to thuh river uhlong to thuh sea. Long thuh long coast. Skirtin. Yes. Skirtin back tuh that. Come up back flip take uhway like thuh waves do. Far uhway. Uhway tuh where they dont speak thuh language and where they dont want tuh. Huh. Go on back tuh that.

YES AND GREENS BLACK-EYED PEAS CORNBREAD: Awe on uh interior before uh demarcation made it mapped. Awe on uh interior with out uh road-word called macadam. Awe onin uh interior that was uh whole was once. Awe on uh whole roun worl uh roun worl with uh river.

OLD MAN RIVER JORDAN: In thuh interior was uh river. Huh. Back tuh that.

ALL: Thuh river was roun as thuh worl was. Roun.

OLD MAN RIVER JORDAN: He backs his way through thuh tall rass. Tall grass scratch. Width: thickly. Grasses thickly comin from all angles at im. He runs along thuh path worn out by uh 9 million paddin bare footed feet. Uh path overgrown cause it aint as all as happened as of yet. Tuh be extracted from thuh jungle first he gotta go in hide.

BLACK MAN WITH WATERMELON: Chase-ted me outa thuh trees now they tree me. Thuh dogs come out from their hidin spots under thuh porch and give me uhway. Thuh hidin spot was under thuh porch of uh house that werent there as of yet. Thuh dogs give me uhway by uh laugh aimed at my scent.

AND BIGGER AND BIGER AND BIGGER: HA HA HA. Thats how thuh laugh sorta like be wentin.

PRUNES AND PRISMS: Where he gonna go now now that he done dieded?

QUEEN-THEN-PHARAOH HATSHEPSUT: Where he gonna go tuh move his hands?

BLACK MAN WITH WATERMELON: I. I. I would like tuh move my hands.

YES AND GREENS BLACK-EYES PEAS CORNBREAD: Back tuh when thuh worl usta be roun.

LOTS OF GREASE AND LOTS OF PORK: Uh roun. Thuh worl? Uh roun worl? When was this?

OLD MAN RIVER JORDAN: Columbus. Before.

PRUNES AND PRISMS: Before Columbus?

AND BIGGER AND BIGGER AND BIGGER: Ha!

QUEEN-THEN-PHARAOH HATSHEPSUT: Before Columbus thuh worl usta be roun. They put uh /d/ on thuh end of roun makin round. Thusly they set in motion thuh enduh. Without that /d/ we could uh gone on spinnin forever. Thuh /d/ thing endiduh things endiduh.

BEFORE COLUMBUS: Before Columbus:

(A *bell sounds once*)

Thuh popular thinkin kin of thuh day back then in them days was that thuh worl was flat. They thought thuh worl was flat. Back then kin in them days when they thought thuh worl was flat they were afeared and stayed at home. They wanted tuh go out back then when they thought thuh worl was flat but the water had in it dragons.

AND BIGGER AND BIGGER AND BIGGER: Not lurkin in thuh sea but lurkin in thuh street, see? Sir name Tom-us and Bigger be my christian name. Rise up out of uh made-up story in grown Bigger and Bigger. Too big for my own name. Nostrils: flarin. Width: thickly. Breath: fire-laden and smellin badly.

BLACK WOMAN WITH FRIED DRUMSTICK: Huh. Whiffit.

BEFORE COLUMBUS: Dragons, of which meanin these dragons they were afeared back then. When they thought thuh worl was flat. They stayed at home. Them thinking thuh worl was flat kept it roun. Them thinkin thuh sun revolved uhroun thuh earth kin kept them satellite-like. They figured out thuh truth and scurried out. Figurin out thuh truth kin put them in their place and they scurried out tuh put us in ours.

YES AND GREENS BLACK-EYED PEAS CORNBREAD: Mmmmm. Yes. You should write that down. You should write that down and you should hide it under uh rock.

BEFORE COLUMBUS: Thuh earths gettin level with thuh land land HO and thuh lands gettin level with thuh sea.

PRUNES AND PRISMS: Not yet—

QUEEN-THEN-PHARAOH HATSHEPSUT: An I am Sheba she be me. Youll mutter thuh words and part thuh waves and come uhlong come uhlong.

AND BIGGER AND BIGGER AND BIGGER: I would like tuh be fit in back in thuh storybook from which I camed.

BLACK MAN WITH WATERMELON: My text was writ in water. I would like tuh drink it down.

QUEEN-THEN-PHARAOH HATSHEPSUT: Down tuh float drown tuh float down. My son erased his mothers mark.

AND BIGGER AND BIGGER AND BIGGER: I am grown too big for thuh word thats me.

PRUNES AND PRISMS: Prunes and prisms prunes and prisms prunes and prisms: 14.

QUEEN-THEN-PHARAOH HATSHEPSUT: An I am Sheba me am (She be doo be wah waaah doo wah). Come uhlong come on uhlong on.

BEFORE COLUMBUS: Before Columbus directs thuh traffic: left right left right.

PRUNES AND PRISMS: Prunes and prisms prunes and prisms.

QUEEN-THEN-PHARAOH HATSHEPSUT: I left my mark on all I made. My son erase his mothers mark.

BLACK WOMAN WITH FRIED DRUMSTICK: Where you gonna go now now that you done dieded?

AND BIGGER AND BIGGER AND BIGGER: Would somebody take these straps offuh me please? Gaw. I would like tuh drink in drown—

BEFORE COLUMBUS: There is uh tiny land mass just above my reach.

LOTS OF GREASE AND LOTS OF PORK: There is uh tiny land mass just outside of my vocabulary.

OLD MAN RIVER JORDAN: Do in dip diddly did-did thuh drop? Drop do it be dripted? Uh huh.

BEFORE COLUMBUS: Land:

AND BIGGER AND BIGGER AND BIGGER: HO!

QUEEN-THEN-PHARAOH HATSHEPSUT: I saw Columbus comin Before Columbus comin/goin over tuh meet you—

BEFORE COLUMBUS: Thuh first time I saw it. It was huge. Thuh green sea becomes uh hillside. Uh hillside populated with some peoples I will name. Thuh first time I saw it it was uh was-huge once one. Huh. It has been gettin smaller ever since.

QUEEN-THEN-PHARAOH HATSHEPSUT: Land:

BLACK MAN WITH WATERMELON: HO!

(A *bell sounds once*)

BLACK MAN WITH WATERMELON: It must have rained. Gaw. Must-uh-rained-on-down-us-why. Aint that somethin. Must uh rained! Gaw. Our crops have prospered. Must uh rained why aint that somethin why aint that something-somethin gaw somethin: nice.

BLACK WOMAN WITH FRIED DRUMSTICK: Funny.

BLACK MAN WITH WATERMELON: Gaw. Callin on it spose we did: gaw—thuh uhrainin gaw huh? Gaw gaw. Lookie look-see gaw: where there were riv-lets now there are some. Gaw. Cement tuh mudment accomplished with uh gaw uh flick of my wrist gaw. Huh. Look here now there is uh gaw uh wormlett. Came out tuhday. In my stools gaw gaw gaw gaw they all out tuhday. Come out tuh breathe gaw dontcha? Sure ya dontcha sure gaw ya dontcha sure ya dontcha do yall gaw. Gaw. Our one melon has given intuh 3. Callin what it gived birth callin it gaw. 3 August hams out uh my hands now surroundin me an is all of um mines? GAW. Uh huhn. Gaw Gaw. Cant breathe.

BLACK WOMAN WITH FRIED DRUMSTICK: Funny how they break when I dropped em. Thought they was past that. Huh. 3 broke in uh row. Guess mmm on uh roll uh some sort, huh. Hell. Huh. Whiffit.

BLACK MAN WITH WATERMELON: Gaw. Gaw. Cant breathe.

BLACK WOMAN WITH FRIED DRUMSTICK: Some things still hold. Huh. Uh old layed eggull break after droppin most likely. Huh. 4 in uh row. Awe on that.

BLACK MAN WITH WATERMELON: Gaw. Cant breathe you.

BLACK WOMAN WITH FRIED DRUMSTICK: You dont need to. No need for breathin for you no more, huh? 5. 6. Mm makin uh history. 7-hhh 8-hhh mm makin uh mess. Huh. Whiffit.

BLACK MAN WITH WATERMELON: Gaw. Gaw loosen my collar. No air in here.

BLACK WOMAN WITH FRIED DRUMSTICK: 7ssgot uh red dot. Awe on that.

BLACK MAN WITH WATERMELON: Sweetheart—. SWEETHEART?!

BLACK WOMAN WITH FRIED DRUMSTICK: 9. Chuh. Funny. Funny. Somethin still holdin on. Let me loosen your collar for you you comed home after uh hard days work. Your suit: tied. Days work was runnin from them we know aint chase-ted you. You comed back home after uh hard days work such uh hard days work that now you cant breathe you. Now.

BLACK MAN WITH WATERMELON: Dont take it off just loosen it. Dont move thuh tree branch let thuh tree branch be.

BLACK WOMAN WITH FRIED DRUMSTICK: Your days work aint like any others day work: you bring your tree branch home. Let me loosen thuh tie let me loosen thuh neck-lace let me loosen up thuh noose that stringed him up let me leave thuh tree branch be. Let me rub your wrists.

BLACK MAN WITH WATERMELON: Gaw. Gaw.

BLACK WOMAN WITH FRIED DRUMSTICK: Some things still hold. Wrung thuh necks of them hens and they still give eggs. Huh: like you. Still sproutin feathers even after they fried. Huh: like you too. 10. Chuh. Eggs still break. Thuh mess makes uh stain. Thuh stain makes uh mark. Whiffit. Whiffit.

BLACK MAN WITH WATERMELON: Put me on uh platform tuh wait for uh train. Uh who who uh who who uh where ya gonna go now—. Platform hitched with horses/steeds. Steeds runned off in left me there swinging. It had begun tuh rain. Hands behind my back. This time tied. I had heard of uh word called scaffold and thought that perhaps they just might build me one of um but uh uhn naw just outa my vocabulary but uh uhn naw trees come cheaply.

BLACK WOMAN WITH FRIED DRUMSTICK: 9. 10. I aint hungry. 10. 11. You dont eat. Dont need to.

BLACK MAN WITH WATERMELON: Swinging from front tuh back uhgain. Back tuh—back tuh that was how I be wentin. Chin on my chest hanging down in restin eyes each on eyein my 2 feets. Left on thuh right one right one on thuh left. Crossed eyin. It was difficult tuh breathe. Toes uncrossin then crossin for luck. With my eyes. Gaw. It had begun tuh rain. Oh. Gaw. Ever so lightly. Blood came on up. You know: tough. Like riggamartins-stifly only—isolated. They some of em pointed they summoned uh laughed they some looked quick in an then they looked uhway. It had begun tuh rain. I hung on out tuh dry. They puttin uhway their picnic baskets. Ever so lightly gaw gaw it had begun tuh rain. They pullin out their umbrellas in hidedid up their eyes. Oh.

BLACK WOMAN WITH FRIED DRUMSTICK: I aint hungry you dont eat 12 13 and thuh floor will shine. Look: there we are. You in me. Reflectin. Hello! Dont move—.

BLACK MAN WITH WATERMELON: It had begun tuh rain. Now: huh. Sky flew open and thuh light went ZAP. Tree bowed over till thuh branch said BROKE. Uhround my necklace my neck uhround my neck my tree branch. In full bloom. It had begun tuh rain. Feet hit thuh ground in I started runnin. I was wet right through intuh through. I was uh wet that dont get dry. Draggin on my tree branch on back tuh home.

BLACK WOMAN WITH FRIED DRUMSTICK: On back tuh that.

BLACK MAN WITH WATERMELON: Gaw. What was that?

BLACK WOMAN WITH FRIED DRUMSTICK: "On back tuh that?" Huh. Somethin I figured. Huh. Chuh. Lord. Who! Whiffit.

BLACK MAN WITH WATERMELON: When I dieded they cut me down. Didnt have no need for me no more. They let me go.

BLACK WOMAN WITH FRIED DRUMSTICK: Thuh lights dimmed in thats what saved you. Lightnin comed down zappin trees from thuh sky. You got uhway!

ALL (*Except Black Woman*): Not exactly.

BLACK WOMAN WITH FRIED DRUMSTICK: Oh. I see.

BLACK MAN WITH WATERMELON: They tired of me. Pulled me out of thuh trees then treed me then tired of me. Thats how it has gone. Thats how it be wentin.

BLACK WOMAN WITH FRIED DRUMSTICK: Oh. I see. Youve been dismissed. But-where-to? Must be somewhere else tuh go aside from just go gone. Huh. Whiffit: huh. You smell.

BLACK MAN WITH WATERMELON: Maybe I should bathe.

BLACK WOMAN WITH FRIED DRUMSTICK: I call those 3 thuh lonesome 3some. Maybe we should pray.

BLACK MAN WITH WATERMELON: Thuh lonesome 3some. Spose theyll do.

(*A bell sounds twice*)

PANEL IV: SECOND CHORUS

OLD MAN RIVER JORDAN: Come in look tuh look-see.

VOICE ON THUH TEE V: Good evening this is thuh news. A small sliver of uh tree branch has been found in *The Death of the Last Black Man*. Upon careful examination thuh small sliver of thuh treed branch what was found has been found tuh be uh fossilized bone fragment. With this finding authorities claim they are hot on his tail.

PRUNES AND PRISMS: Uh small sliver of uh treed branch growed from-tuh uh bone.

AND BIGGER AND BIGGER AND BIGGER: WILL SOMEBODY WILL THIS ROPE FROM ROUND MY NECK GOD DAMN I WOULD LIKE TUH TAKE MY BREATH BY RIGHTS GAW GAW.

LOTS OF GREASE AND LOTS OF PORK: This is the death of the last black man in the whole entire world.

(*A bell sounds slowly twice*)

BLACK MAN WITH WATERMELON: I had heard of uh word called scaffold and had hopes they just might maybe build me one but uh uh naw gaw—

HAM: There was uh tree with your name on it.

BLACK MAN WITH WATERMELON: Jumpin out of uh tree they chase me tree me back tuh thuh tree. Thats where I be came from. Thats where I be wentin.

YES AND GREENS BLACK-EYED PEAS CORNBREAD: Someone ought tuh. Write that down.

LOTS OF GREASE AND LOTS OF PORK: There is a page dog-eared at "Histree" hidin just outside my word hoard. Wheres he gonna come to now that he done gone from.

QUEEN-THEN-PHARAOH HATSHEPSUT: Wheres he gonna go come to now that he gonna go gone on?

OLD MAN RIVER JORDAN: For that you must ask Ham.

BLACK WOMAN WITH FRIED DRUMSTICK: Hen?

LOTS OF GREASE AND LOTS OF PORK: HAM.

QUEEN-THEN-PHARAOH HATSHEPSUT: Ham.

PRUNES AND PRISMS: Hmmmm.

(*A bell sounds twice*)

HAM: Ham's Begotten Tree (catchin up to um *in medias res* that is we takin off from where we stopped up last time). Huh. NOW: She goned begotten One who in turn begotten Ours. Ours laughed one day uhloud in from thuh sound hittin thuh air smakity sprung up I, you, n He, She, It. They turned in engaged in simple multiplication thus tuh spawn of theirselves one We one You and one called They (They in certain conversation known as "Them" and in other certain conversation a.k.a. "Us"). Now very simply: Wassername she finally gave intuh It and tugether they broughted forth uh wildish one called simply Yo. Yo gone be wentin much too long without hisself uh comb in from thuh frizzly that resulted comed one called You (polite form). You (polite) birthed herself Mister, Miss, Maam and Sir who in his later years with That brought forth Yuh Fathuh. Thuh fact that That was uh mother tuh Yuh Fathuh didnt stop them 2 relations from havin relations. Those strange relations between That thuh mother and Yuh Fathuh thuh son brought forth uh odd lot: called: Yes Massuh, yes Missy, Yes Maam n Yes Suh Mistuh Suh which goes tuh show that relations with your relations produces complications. Thuh children of That and Yuh Fathuh aside from being plain peculiar was all crosscycd. This defect enhanced their multiplicative possibilities, for example. Yes Suh Mistuh Suh breeded with hisself n gived us Wassername (thuh 2nd), and Wasser nickname (2 twins in birth joinded at thuh lip). Thuh 2 twins lived next door tuh one called Uhnother bringing forth Themuhns, She (thuh 2nd), Auntie, Cousin, and Bro who makeshifted continuous compensations for his loud and oderiferous bodily emissions by all thuh time saying excuse me n through his graciousness brought forth They (polite) who had mixed feelins with She (thuh 2nd) thus brinin forth Ussin who then went on tuh have MeMines.

YES AND GREENS BLACK-EYED PEAS CORNBREAD: Thuh list goes on in on.

HAM: MeMines gived out 2 offspring one she called Mines after herself thuh uther she called Themuhns named after all them who comed before. Themuhns married outside thuh tribe joinin herself with uh man they called WhoDat. Themuhns in WhoDat brought forth only one child called WhoDatDere. Mines joined up with Wasshisname and from that union come AllYall.

BEFORE COLUMBUS: All us?

HAM: No. AllYall.

LOTS OF GREASE AND LOTS OF PORK: This list goes on in on.

HAM: Ah yes: Yo suddenly if by majic again became productive in after uh lapse of some great time came back intuh circulation to wiggled uhbout with Yes Missy (one of thuh crosseyed daughters of That and Yuh Fathuh). Yo in Yes Missy begottin ThissunRightHere, Us, ThatOne, She (thuh 3rd) and one called Uncle (who from birth was gifted with great singin and dancin capabilities which helped him make his way in life but tended tuh bring shame on his family).

BEFORE COLUMBUS/BLACK MAN WITH WATERMELON: Shame on his family.

LOTS OF GREASE AND LOTS OF PORK/BLACK MAN WITH WATERMELON: Shame on his family.

AND BIGGER AND BIGGER AND BIGGER/BLACK MAN WITH WATERMELON: Shamed on his family gaw.

YES AND GREENS BLACK-EYED PEAS CORNBREAD: Write *that* down.

OLD MAN RIVER JORDAN: (Ham seed his daddy Noah neckked. From that seed, comed AllYall.)

(*A bell sounds twice*)

AND BIGGER AND BIGGER AND BIGGER: (Will somebody please will this rope—)

VOICE ON THUH TEE V: Good evening. This is thuh news: Whose fault is it?

BLACK MAN WITH WATERMELON: Saint mines.

VOICE ON THUH TEE V: Whose fault iszit??!

ALL: Saint mines!

OLD MAN RIVER JORDAN: I cant re-member back that far. (Ham can—but uh uh naw gaw—Ham wuduhnt there, huh.)

ALL: HAM BONE HAM BONE WHERE YOU BEEN ROUN THUH WORL N BACK A-GAIN.

QUEEN-THEN-PHARAOH HATSHEPSUT: Whatcha seen Hambone girl?

BLACK WOMAN WITH FRIED DRUMSTICK: Didnt see you. I saw thuh worl.

HAM: I was there.

PRUNES AND PRISMS: Didnt see you.

HAM: I WAS THERE.

VOICE ON THUH TEE V: Didnt see you.

BLACK MAN WITH WATERMELON/AND BIGGER AND BIGGER AND BIGGER: THUH BLACK MAN. HE MOOOVE.

ALL: HAM BONE HAM BONE WHATCHA DO? GOT UH CHANCE N FAIRLY FLEW.

BLACK WOMAN WITH FRIED DRUMSTICK: Over thuh front yard.

BLACK MAN WITH WATERMELON: Overshot.

ALL: 6 BY 6 BY 6.

BLACK MAN WITH WATERMELON: Thats right.

AND BIGGER AND BIGGER AND BIGGER: WILL SOMEBODY WILL THIS ROPE—

ALL: Good evening. This is the news.

VOICE ON THUH TEE V: Whose fault is it?

ALL: Saint mines!

VOICE ON THUS TEE V: Whose fault iszit?!!

HAM: SAINT MINES!

(A *bell rings twice*)

—Ham. Is. Not. Tuh. BLAME! WhoDatDere joinded with one called Sir 9th generation of thuh first Sir son of You (polite) thuh first daughter of You WhoDatDere with thuh 9th Sir begettin forth Him—

BLACK MAN WITH WATERMELON: Ham?!

ALL: (*Except Ham*): HIM!

BLACK WOMAN WITH FRIED DRUMSTICK: Sold.

HAM: SOLD! allyall[9] not tuh be confused w/allus[12] joined w/allthem[3] in from that union comed forth wasshisname[21] SOLD wassername[19] still by thuh reputation uh thistree one uh thuh 2 twins loses her sight through fiddlin n falls w/ugly old yuh-fathuh[4] given she[8] SOLD whodat[33] pairs w/you[23] (still polite) of which nothinmuch comes nothinmuch now nothinmuch[6] pairs with yessuhmistuhsuh[17] tuh drop one called yo now yo[9-0] still who gone be wentin now w/elle gived us el SOLD let us not forget ye[1-2-5] w/thee[3] givin us thou[9-2] who w/thuh they who switches their designation in certain conversation yes they[10] broughted forth onemore[2] at thuh same time in thuh same row right next door we have datone[12] w/disone[14] droppin off duhutherone[2-2] SOLD let us not forgetyessuhmassuhsuh[38] w/thou[8] who gived up memines[3-0] SOLD we are now rollin through thuh long division gimmie uh gimmie uh gimmie uh squaredoff route round it off round it off n round it out w/sistuh[4-3] who lives with one called saintmines[9] givin forth one uh year how it got there callin it jessgrew callin it saintmines callin it whatdat whatdat whatdat SOLD.

BLACK MAN WITH WATERMELON: Thuh list goes on and on. Dont it.

ALL: Ham Bone Ham Bone Ham Bone Ham Bone.

BEFORE COLUMBUS: Left right left right.

QUEEN-THEN-PHARAOH HATSHEPSUT: Left left left whose left . . . ?

(A *bell sounds twice*)

LOTS OF GREASE AND LOTS OF PORK: This is the death of the last black man in the whole entire world.

BLACK WOMAN WITH FRIED DRUMSTICK: Somethins turnin. Huh. Whatizit.—
Mercy. Mercy. Huh. Chew on this. Ssuh feather. Sswhatchashud be eatin
now ya no. Ssuhfeather: stuffin. Chew on it. Huh. Feathers sprouted from
thuh fried hens—dont ask me how. Somethins out uh whack. Somethins
out uh rights. Your arms still on your elbows. I'm still here. Whensit gonna
end. Soon. Huh. Mercy. Thuh Tree. Springtime. And harvest. Huh.
Somethins turnin. So many melons. Huh. From one tuh 3 tuh many.
Must be nature. Gnaw on this. Gnaw on this, huh? Gnaw on this awe on
that.

BLACK MAN WITH WATERMELON: Aint eatable.

BLACK WOMAN WITH FRIED DRUMSTICK: I know.

BLACK MAN WITH WATERMELON: Aint eatable aint it. Nope. Nope.

BLACK WOMAN WITH FRIED DRUMSTICK: Somethins turnin. Huh. Whatizit.

BLACK MAN WITH WATERMELON: Aint eatable so I out in out ought not aint be
eatin it aint that right. Yep. Nope. Yep. Uh huhn.

BLACK WOMAN WITH FRIED DRUMSTICK: Huh. Whatizit.

BLACK MAN WITH WATERMELON: I remember what I like. I remember what
my likes tuh eat when I be in thuh eatin mode.

BLACK WOMAN WITH FRIED DRUMSTICK: Chew on this.

BLACK MAN WITH WATERMELON: When I be in thuh eatin mode.

BLACK WOMAN WITH FRIED DRUMSTICK: Swallow it down. I know. Gimme
your pit. Needs bathin.

BLACK MAN WITH WATERMELON: Choice between peas and corns—my feets—.
Choice: peas. Choice between peas and greens choice: greens. Choice
between greens and potatoes choice: potatoes. Yams. Boiled or mashed
choice: mashed. Aaah. Mmm. My likenesses.

BLACK WOMAN WITH FRIED DRUMSTICK: Mercy. Turns—

BLACK MAN WITH WATERMELON: My likenesses! My feets! Aaah! SWEET-
HEART. Aaah! SPRING-TIME!

BLACK WOMAN WITH FRIED DRUMSTICK: Spring-time.

BLACK MAN WITH WATERMELON: SPRING-TIME!

BLACK WOMAN WITH FRIED DRUMSTICK: Mercy. Turns—

BLACK MAN WITH WATERMELON: I remembers what I likes. I remembers what
I likes tuh eat when I bein in had been in thuh eatin mode. Bein in had
been: now in then. I be eatin hen. Hen.

BLACK WOMAN WITH FRIED DRUMSTICK: Huh?

BLACK MAN WITH WATERMELON: HEN!

BLACK WOMAN WITH FRIED DRUMSTICK: HEN?

BLACK MAN WITH WATERMELON: Hen. Huh. My meals. Aaaah: my meals.
BRACH-A-LEE.

BLACK WOMAN WITH FRIED DRUMSTICK: Whatizit. Huh.—GNAW ON THIS! Good. Uhther pit?

BLACK MAN WITH WATERMELON: We sittin on this porch right now aint we. Uh huhn. Aaah. Yes. Sittin right here right now on it in it ainthuh first time either iduhnt it. Yep. Nope. Once we was here once wuhduhnt we. Yep. Yep. Once we being here. Uh huhn. Huh. There is uh Now and there is uh Then. Ssall there is. (I bein in uh Now: uh Now bein in uh Then: I bein, in Now in Then, in I will be. I was be too but thas uh Then thats past. That me that was-be is uh me-has-been. Thuh Then that was-be is uh has-been-Then too. Thuh me-has-been sits in thuh be-me: we sit on this porch. Same porch. Same me. Thuh Then thats been somehow sits in thuh Then that will be: same Thens. I swing from uh tree. You cut me down and bring me back. Home. Here. I fly over thuh yard. I fly over thuh yard in all over. Them thens stays fixed. Fixed Thens. Thuh Thems stays fixed too. Thuh Thems that come and take me and thuh Thems that greet me and then them Thems that send me back here. Home. Stays fixed, them do.)

BLACK WOMAN WITH FRIED DRUMSTICK: Your feets.

BLACK MAN WITH WATERMELON: I: be. You: is. It: be. He, She: thats us (thats it.) We: thats he in she: you aroun me: us be here. You: still is. They: be. Melon. Melon. Melon: mines. I remember all my lookuhlikes. You. You. Remember me.

BLACK WOMAN WITH FRIED DRUMSTICK: Gnaw on this then swallow it down. Youll have your fill then we'll put you in your suit coat.

BLACK MAN WITH WATERMELON: Thuh suit coat I picked out? Thuh stripely one? HA! Peas. Choice: BRACH-A-LEE.

BLACK WOMAN WITH FRIED DRUMSTICK: Chew and swallow please.

BLACK MAN WITH WATERMELON: Thuh stripely one with thuh fancy patch pockets!

BLACK WOMAN WITH FRIED DRUMSTICK: Sweetheart.

BLACK MAN WITH WATERMELON: SPRING-TIME.

BLACK WOMAN WITH FRIED DRUMSTICK: Sweetheart.

BLACK MAN WITH WATERMELON: SPRING-TIME.

BLACK WOMAN WITH FRIED DRUMSTICK: This could go on forever.

BLACK MAN WITH WATERMELON: Lets. Hope. Not.

BLACK WOMAN WITH FRIED DRUMSTICK:—Sweetheart.

BLACK MAN WITH WATERMELON: SPRING-TIME.

BLACK WOMAN WITH FRIED DRUMSTICK: Sweetheart.

BLACK MAN WITH WATERMELON: SPRING-TIME.

BLACK WOMAN WITH FRIED DRUMSTICK: This could go on forever.

BLACK MAN WITH WATERMELON: Lets. Hope. Not.

BLACK WOMAN WITH FRIED DRUMSTICK: Must be somewhere else tuh go aside from just go gone.

BLACK MAN WITH WATERMELON: 6 by 6 by 6.

BLACK WOMAN WITH FRIED DRUMSTICK: Thats right.

BLACK MAN WITH WATERMELON: Rock reads "HooDoo."

BLACK WOMAN WITH FRIED DRUMSTICK: Now you know. Know now dontcha. Somethins turnin—.

BLACK MAN WITH WATERMELON: Who do? Them do. Aint that nice. Huh. Miss me. Remember me. Missmemissmewhatsmyname.

BLACK WOMAN WITH FRIED DRUMSTICK: Aaaaah?

BLACK MAN WITH WATERMELON: Remember me. AAAH.

BLACK WOMAN WITH FRIED DRUMSTICK: Thats it. Open wide. Here it comes. Stuffin.

BLACK MAN WITH WATERMELON: Yeeeech.

BLACK WOMAN WITH FRIED DRUMSTICK: Eat uhnother. Hear. I eat one. You eat more.

BLACK MAN WITH WATERMELON: Stuffed. Time tuh go.

BLACK WOMAN WITH FRIED DRUMSTICK: Not yet!

BLACK MAN WITH WATERMELON: I got uhway?

BLACK WOMAN WITH FRIED DRUMSTICK: Huh?

BLACK MAN WITH WATERMELON: I got uhway?

BLACK WOMAN WITH FRIED DRUMSTICK: Nope. Yep. Nope. Nope.

BLACK MAN WITH WATERMELON: Miss me.

BLACK WOMAN WITH FRIED DRUMSTICK: Miss me.

BLACK MAN WITH WATERMELON: Re-member me.

BLACK WOMAN WITH FRIED DRUMSTICK: Re-member me.

BLACK MAN WITH WATERMELON: My hands are on my wrists. Arms on elbows. Looks: old-fashioned. Nothin fancy there. Toes curl up not down. My feets-now clean. Still got all my teeth. Re-member me.

BLACK WOMAN WITH FRIED DRUMSTICK: Re-member me.

BLACK MAN WITH WATERMELON: Call on me sometime.

BLACK WOMAN WITH FRIED DRUMSTICK: Call on me sometime. Hear? Hear? Thuh dirt itself turns itself. So many melons. From one tuh 3 tuh many. Look at um all. Ssuh garden. Awe on that. Winter pro-cessin back tuh back with spring-time. They roll on by us that way. Uh whole line gone roun. Chuh. Thuh worl be roun. Moves that way so they say. You comed back. Yep. Nope. Well. Build uh well.

(*A bell sounds twice.*)

ALL: "Yes. Oh, me? Chuh, no—"

VOICE ON THUH TEE V: Good morning. This is thuh news:

BLACK WOMAN WITH FRIED DRUMSTICK: Somethins turnin. Thuh page.

(*A bell sounds twice*)

LOTS OF GREASE AND LOTS OF PORK: This is the death of the last black man in the whole entire worl.

PRUNES AND PRISMS: 19.

OLD MAN RIVER JORDAN: Uh blank page turnin with thuh sound of it. Thuh sound of movin hands.

BLACK WOMAN WITH FRIED DRUMSTICK: Yesterday today next summer tomorrow just uh moment uhgoh in 1317 dieded thuh last black man in thuh whole entire world. Uh! Oh. Dont be uhlarmed. Do not be afeared. It was painless. Uh painless passin. He falls twenty-three floors to his death.

ALL: Yes.

BLACK WOMAN WITH FRIED DRUMSTICK: 23 floors from uh passin ship from space tuh splat on thuh pavement.

ALL: Yes.

BLACK WOMAN WITH FRIED DRUMSTICK: He have uh head he been keepin under thuh Tee V.

ALL: Yes.

BLACK WOMAN WITH FRIED DRUMSTICK: On his bottom pantry shelf.

ALL: Yes.

BLACK WOMAN WITH FRIED DRUMSTICK: He have uh head that hurts. Dont fit right. Put it on tuh go tuh thuh store in it pinched him when he walks his thoughts dont got room. He diediduh he did, huh.

ALL: Yes.

BLACK WOMAN WITH FRIED DRUMSICK: Where he gonna go now now now now now that he done diediduh?

ALL: Yes.

BLACK WOMAN WITH FRIED DRUMSTICK: Where he gonna go tuh. WASH.

PRUNES AND PRISMS: Somethins turnin. Thuh page.

AND BIGGER AND BIGGER AND BIGGER: Somethins burnin. Thuh tongue.

BLACK MAN WITH WATERMELON: Thuh tongue itself burns.

OLD MAN RIVER JORDAN: He jumps in thuh river. These words for partin.

YES AND GREENS BLACK-EYED PEAS CORNBREAD: And you will write them down.

(*A bell sounds three times*)

BEFORE COLUMBUS: All these boats passed by my coast.

PRUNES AND PRISMS: Somethins turnin. Thuh page.

QUEEN-THEN-PHARAOH HATSHEPSUT: I saw Columbus comin/I saw Columbus comin goin—

QUEEN-THEN-PHARAOH HATSHEPSUT/BEFORE COLUMBUS: Left left left whose left . . . ?

AND BIGGER AND BIGGER AND BIGGER/BLACK MAN WITH WATERMELON: Somethins burnin. Thuh page.

BEFORE COLUMBUS: All those boats passed by me. My coast fell in-to-the-sea. All thuh boats. They stopped for me.

OLD MAN RIVER JORDAN: Land: HO!

OVER-THEN-PHARAOH HATSHEPSUT: I waved my hands in warnin. You waved back.

BLACK WOMEN WITH FRIED DRUMSTICK: Somethins burnin. Thuh page.

QUEEN-THEN-PHARAOH HATSHEPSUT: I have-not seen you since.

ALL: Oh!

LOTS OF GREASE AND LOTS OF PORK: This is the death of the last black man in the whole entire worl.

OLD MAN RIVER JORDAN: Do in diddley dip die-die thuh drop. Do drop be dripted? Why, of course.

AND BIGGER AND BIGGER AND BIGGER: Somethins burnin. Thuh tongue.

BLACK MAN WITH WATERMELON: Thuh tongue itself burns itself.

HAM: . . . And from that seed comed All Us.

BLACK WOMAN WITH FRIED DRUMSTICK: Thuh page.

ALL: 6 by 6 by 6.

BLACK WOMAN WITH FRIED DRUMSTICK: Thats right.

(*A bell sounds twice*)

BEFORE COLUMBUS: LAND: HO!

YES AND GREENS BLACK-EYED PEAS CORNBREAD: You will write it down because if you dont write it down then we will come along and tell the future that we did not exist. You will write it down and you will carve it
✔ out of a rock.

(*Pause*)

You will write down thuh past and you will write down thuh present and in what in thuh future. You will write it down.

(*Pause*)

It will be of us but you will mention them from time to time so that in the future when they come along theyll know how they exist.

(*Pause*)

It will be for us but you will mention them from time to time so that in the future when they come along theyll know why they exist.

(*Pause*)

You will carve it all out of a rock so that in the future when we come along we will know that the rock does yes exist.

BLACK WOMAN WITH FRIED DRUMSTICK: Down down down down down down down down—

LOTS OF GREASE AND LOTS OF PORK: This is the death of the last black man in the whole entire worl.

PRUNES AND PRISMS: Somethins turnin. Thuh page.

OLD MAN RIVER JORDAN: Thuh last news of thuh last man:

VOICE ON THUH TEE V: Good morning. This is thuh last news:

BLACK MAN WITH WATERMELON: Miss me

BLACK WOMAN WITH FRIED DRUMSTICK: Miss me.

BLACK MAN WITH WATERMELON: Re-member me.

BLACK WOMAN WITH FRIED DRUMSTICK: Re-member me. Call on me sometime. Call on me sometime. Hear? Hear?

HAM: In thuh future when they came along I meeting them. On thuh coast. Uuuuhh! My coast! I—was—so—po-lite! But. In thuh rock. I wrote: ha ha ha.

ALL: Ha. Ha. Ha. Ha. Ha. Ha. Ha. Ha. Ha. Ha. Ha. Ha. Ha. Ha. HHHHHHHHHHHHH. HA!

BLACK WOMAN WITH FRIED DRUMSTICK: Thuh black man he move. He move. He hans.

(*A bell sounds once*)

ALL: Hold it. Hold it. Hold it. Hold it. Hold it. Hold it. Hold it.

Directing *The Brig*

Judith Malina

The dramatic and psychological situations have passed here into the very sign language of the combat, which is a function of the mystic athletic play of bodies and the undulatory use of the stage, whose enormous spiral reveals itself in one perspective after another.

The warriors enter the mental forest rocking with fear, overwhelmed by a great shudder. It is more than a physical tempest, it is a spiritual concussion that is signified in the general trembling of their limbs and their rolling eyes. The sonorous pulsation of their bristling heads is at times excruciating and the music sways behind them and at the same time sustains an unimaginable space into which real pebbles finally roll.

—Antonin Artaud*

THE BRIG IS A STRUCTURE. The precision of the description of this structure is the key to *The Brig.*

The Immovable Structure is the villain. Whether that structure calls itself a prison or a school or a factory or a family or a government or The World As It Is. That structure asks each man what he can do for it, not what it can do for him, and for those who do not do for it, there is the pain of death or imprisonment, or social degradation, or the loss of animal rights.

The men placed inside the structure are intended to become part of this structure, and the beauty and terror of *The Brig* is seeing how it succeeds and how it fails in incorporating those whom it has imprisoned into its own corporeal being.

Reprinted from Kenneth H. Brown, *The Brig* (New York: Hill and Wang, 1969), 81–107. Reprinted by permission of Judith Malina.

*This quotation and the other references to Artaud are from *The Theatre and Its Double* by Antonin Artaud, translated by M. C. Richards, published by Grove Press.

Reading the minutiae of description with which Kenneth Brown prefaces his play, I already felt that beauty and that terror in the rigor of the detail. A long time ago Kenneth Brown found himself in such a room and he noted with precision the proportions of the wire enclosure, the turnkey's desk, the Warden's post, and the white lines on the deck. And as he stood there for thirty days at attention with his eyes in *The Guidebook for Marines*, he realized that what was happening to him was significant. Here in the darkness under the bright overhead light there lay exposed the open wound of violence.

Though the social structure begins by framing the noblest laws and the loftiest ordinances that "the great of the earth" have devised, in the end it comes to this: breach that lofty law and they take you to a prison cell and shut your human body off from human warmth. Ultimately the law is enforced by the unfeeling guard punching his fellow man hard in the belly.

And Kenneth Brown saw it and he experienced it and he wrote it down when he got out of it.

Reading the disembodied commands of *The Brig*, the numbered shouts that evoke the machine but remain transcendentally human outcries, I heard clearly in my ears the familiar metal scraping prison sounds and the stamp of the booted foot on concrete. These sounds will haunt me forever as they will haunt all of us who have been prisoners. The month that I spent in the Women's House of Detention was not only instructive, but it enables me to count myself as always among the prisoners. I needed to loosen my subjective response.

Four masterworks came to my mind after reading Brown's play. The work of three great men of the modern theatre, a Russian, a Frenchman, and a German, the fourth of collective and ancient authorship; all served as instruction on how to proceed.

The Work of Meyerhold

His tormented specter appeared. I said to him: "Alas, you called your whole life a 'search for a style,' pursuing that search through honor and disgrace. Now, at last, I have found the play in which the actor is biologically and mechanically enmeshed inside the construction of wires and white lines."

He was rehearsing the *Death of Tintagal* when the Revolution burst forth and poured him into the street to do battle on the stages of the Revolution. He set up troupes that brought the political theatre to the railroad stations, the factories, the barricades, to the fronts of the Revolution. And afterward, installed in his state-subsidized theatre, he went on with his search. He came to believe that only complex technical structures overpowering the actor could express the real scenery of his times.

The Constructivist demands a setting which *is* the action. Therefore, Meyerhold began to regulate the actor's movements until his actors complained that they were being treated like puppets. In a public attack his theatre was dubbed "hostile to the people."

He tried puppets and failed. When he spoke of his theory of bio-mechanics as "the organization and geometrization of movement, based on deep study of the human body," he knew that something psychophysical was at stake; that the way back to the sensibilities of the spectator must be through referring again to the human body standing there trapped before him. The actor is not disembodied of his soul, but is full with it and controls it to fill out the dramatic and metaphysical construction.

In *The Brig* each actor feels his total creativity when the external form of his action is so inhibited and his single repeated phrase is so limiting that his whole discarnate soul quivers in his face and body and the performances become filled with invention and full of mystery. Each actor has his mystery and his trip.

The Brig is a Constructivist play. The construction of the set dictates and directs the action by the power of its vectors and its centers of gravity. It was designed by the architects of ancient military prisons, Masonic craftsmen of dungeons and towers. From these fearsome structures the utility of minimal construction and maximum security is in direct descent.

Kenneth Brown vividly recollected the actuality as adapted by the U.S. Marines at the foot of Mount Fuji in 1957. Only Beck's ingenious sense of proportion was needed to create a Constructivist stage.

In *The Brig*, Vsevolod Emilyevich,* without damaging the actor's powers, but rather bearing them up, the structure enforces that rhythmic discipline of the actor's body, which you called "bio-mechanics."

The Work of Artaud

To Artaud, my madman muse, never absent from my dreams, I speak in a private language. He it was who demanded of the actor the great athletic feats: the meaningless gestures broken off into dances of pain and insanity; who cried out in his crazy-house cell for a theatre so violent that no man who experienced it would ever stomach violence again. He said: "I defy any spectator to whom such violent scenes will have transferred their blood—the violence of blood having been placed at the service of the violence of the thought—I defy that spectator to give himself up, once outside the theatre, to ideas of war, riot, and blatant murder."

Artaud asks for a theatre in which the actors are victims burned at the stake "signaling through the flames"; in which "physical obsession of muscles quivering with affectivity, is equivalent, as in the play of breaths, to unleashing this affectivity in full force, giving it a mute but profound range of extraordinary violence"; in which "The overlapping of images and movements will culminate, through the collusion of objects, silences, shouts, and rhythms, or in a genuinely physical language with signs, not words, as its root."

*Editors' note: Vsevold Emilyevich is Meyerhold's first and patronimic name. In this way, Malina is addressing Meyerhold directly.

O Antonin fierce and demanding, in *The Brig* I have seen the actor tax his body to that abstract athletic splendor where he looms on the precarious edge of the abyss of soullessness.

The Work of Piscator

But Piscator was my teacher, so I must apply stricter rules to meet his standards. Besides, he is no historical dream figure. Even now in the Divided City he works in the old Berliner Volksbühne to create a theatre as potent politically as that which, across the bloodstained wall, is the great monument to his old friend and colleague, Bertolt Brecht.

Where Artaud cries out for Madness, Piscator advocates Reason, Clarity, and Communication. He said once in class, "We have gone back to what we can see, because although we know that other things exist, that which we can see is organizable."

Brecht writes of Piscator:

> His experiments caused, above all, complete chaos in the theatre. If the stage was transformed into a machine shop, then the auditorium was transformed into an assembly hall. For Piscator the theatre was a parliament, the public a legislative body. To this parliament was presented in plastic terms important, decision-demanding, public affairs. In place of an address by a member of parliament concerning certain untenable social conditions, there appeared an artistic reproduction of the situation. Piscator's theatre wanted to wrest from the spectators a practical resolve to take an active hold on life.

My dear Mr. Piscator: once in a class you described the totally effective revolutionary play. My class notes tell me you called it *Die Stimme von Portugal*. You described how the performer sang the last phrases of a rousing chorus on freedom and how the people went singing out of the theatre and freed their native land from the oppressor. I have not yet found a play that can move the spectator to such commitment. But I have found a play so valid that when it was closed by the state because the theatre could not meet its financial obligations, the actors, the author, the stage hands, the box-office workers, the stage manager, the house manager, and the technicians were joined by some members of the audience in volunteering to be arrested on the stage with us rather than leave without protesting that this play should not continue to speak.

In our indictment we are charged with shouting from the windows, "Storm the barricades!"

The Work of *The Guidebook for Marines*

The great men, or so the historians call them, having lost the names of the men who invented the wheel and alphabet, have spent their powers in the study of combat. Caesar, and the Pharaohs, and before them the tribal kings,

and after them the Napoleons in their many uniforms and national characteristics have all given over the fruits of their genius to the battlefield. Strategy
has come to be regarded as fit exercise for the best in human consciousness.

But before the battle, the soldier must be trained. Get them young. Get
them while they are pliable to the process of conforming them to the sol-
dierly shape.

Men studied how to train the young to kill before they trained them to
build, or to write, or to work the land. Only singing and dancing came before
that ancient skill. Before the worst, only the best was known. First the lute,
then the spear. And after the singing, the arrows.

The line of learning can be traced, and, were I a scholar, I might trace
how some writer in hieroglyphics first formulated the about face, or at what
point in history the cadence count was developed out of the old war cries,
and how the particular shininess of the uniform was discovered to heighten
the will to kill.

I saw that what I confronted in this fearsome book was the compendium
of a time-honored study. Nothing has been more carefully formulated than
the manuals of war. When I read *The Guidebook for Marines* I said this book
is one of the great books and set it beside the Holy Writ (which has much
study of strategy in it) and *The Zohar* (which attributes even to the heavenly
orders the terminology of the military discipline).

The Marine Corps manual represents the acme of the venerable line of
study manuals designed to teach men to kill and function in the battle
situation. The preparation of men for this ordeal, being so innately unnatural to human affection and so innately natural to the human animal,
exploits the primitive animal consciousness. It perverts man's animal nature
to obstruct the natural processes of love.

As we all live in a violent world, on land that has been wrested by
violence from whatever its former inhabitants, the Lords of the World have
had to answer in strict terms this human question: "How can we take a
youth, sweet-smelling and clean-skinned, out of his girl's arms, and train him
so that on command he will infallibly do what we ask, though he die for it?"

This is the gist of the answer given in the war manuals:

Teach him to walk in measured steps. Teach him to chant in strict meter.
Make him afraid of another man whose insignia designates him as superior.
Teach him to obey. Teach him to obey regardless of sense or animal safety.
Teach him to say, "Yes, sir!" Teach him to reply by rote. Teach him to turn
his corners squarely. Teach him not to consider the meaning of the act, but
to act out the command. Teach him that heaven is the name of a place with
guarded streets where uniformed men march keeping order.

The Marine Corps manual is one of the great books. It tells: "How to
creep: your body is kept free of the ground with your weight resting on
forearms and lower legs. Your rifle is cradled in your arms to keep the muzzle
out of dirt. . . How to crawl. . . . "

It says: "Get the blade into the enemy. . . . Be ruthless, vicious, and fast in your attack. . . . The throat is the best target. The belly is good too . . . go for his hands, face, or sides with a hacking, slashing blade and cut your way to that vital area. . . . You must kill, not simply defeat your opponent. . . . "

Another greatness of the Marine Corps manual is that it lays bare the most vulnerable places, where neither art, nor the Holy Teachings, nor the processes of evolution have proven therapy to the sick beast in us.

In rehearsing *The Brig* we decided to use *The Guidebook* as our text.

My first reading of *The Brig* was a physical experience of the sense of total restriction. The restriction of the author to the barest facts, like the restrictions on the lives of the prisoners, immediately communicated the immobility of the structure. But what can be done within these strict limits? There is no alternate movement, no choice as to what shall be played upstage or downstage. No clue to the range of possible dramatic action. This is the key. The immobility of the structure. "Read the script," cries Piscator again and again in rehearsals. "Read the script."

The sparseness of human activity is demonstrated by the prisoner's day. It is the minimal man, confined to needs. He rises, washes, cleans his quarters, urinates, eats, smokes, is searched, works, eats, is frisked, works or cleans his quarters thoroughly, eats, writes a letter, showers, shaves, and sleeps. He also leaves the Brig, enters the Brig, flips out, marches, and has the living daylights beaten out of him. It isn't much. But where there is very little each action carries a greater burden of a man's suffering, as well as greater inklings of his smothered glory.

I understood this sparseness to be the "blind force" which "activates what it must activate" (i.e., the subservience of the man to the structure), which Artaud bids me explore when he says of the director:

> The director, having become a kind of demiurge at the back of whose head is this idea of implacable purity and its consumation whatever the cost, if he truly wants to be a director, i.e., a man versed in the nature of matter and objects, must conduct in the physical domain an exploration of intense movement and precise emotional gesture, which is equivalent on the psychological level to the unchaining of certain blind forces which activate what they must activate and crush and burn on their way what they must crush and burn.

The question is, according to Artaud, where to begin the exploration of the movement and gesture equivalent to the psychological forces which activate *The Brig*?

For the answer I went to *The Guidebook*, which says, "Drill."

> Drill inspires an individual to be a member of a team. The purposes of Drill are . . . to teach discipline by instilling habits of precision and automatic response to orders . . . to better morale.

And further it says:

Discipline is necessary to secure orderly action which alone can triumph over the seemingly impossible conditions of battle. . . . There is no sane person who is without fear, but with good discipline and high morale all can face danger.

Every situation has its own special problems and one of the problems particular to rehearsing *The Brig* at The Living Theatre was that atmosphere of permissiveness and informality which our working conditions have always favored. We are purposefully personal in the hope that the best work will generate within the greatest possible human warmth. We know that the price of discipline is the rigor of authority, the wages of order is submission. We know that the only real call to order is the needs of the work of art. Any other authority is usurped.

Now apply the strictest methods within the freest association. Reduce discipline to its lowest form (i.e., most harmless) as a spectacle to be observed as though it were rare. *As though it were rare!* Practice authority as though it were rare. At first I doubted that it would be possible for the company to make this unusual sacrifice and work in a manner opposed to the manner that has been developed as our social and artistic standard, that is, to formalize our relationship.

The formal relation is an immovable structure. Like all immovable structures it is the villain. We were going to set up villainy in a safe boundary as a biologist might use a Petri dish to grow a foul and noxious growth within a safe situation. We isolated it.

I prepare a play more by steeping myself in its mysteries than by preparing a set of specific stage directions. I try to keep the action fluid for the actor, I like to reserve space in which the actor can move after that point in rehearsals when *he* knows more about the role than I did when we began. Therefore, I do not like to preset.

I prepared a set of "Rehearsal Regulations" which followed the form of the "Brig Regulations" that circumscribe the prisoners' action in the Brig. These "Brig Regulations" invented by the U.S. Marines are so basic to the action that we decided at the very beginning to print them in each program so that the spectator has the basic stage directions of *The Brig* in his hands.

These rehearsal rules imposed no requirements on the actor that the ordinary customs of the theatre do not demand of him, such as promptness, proper dress, silence. In the same way, the "Brig Regulations" are only the rules of military discipline imposed with cruelly demanding perfectionism. The free and easy spirit among us had to be transformed by sacrifice of our intimacy (just for the time of rehearsal) to the cold, hard way of the world. The rehearsal breaks and later the intermissions, where we resumed our friendly natures, would become paradisiacal interludes of life in the cold Brig world. The "Rehearsal Discipline" was presented to the company on mimeographed sheets before the first rehearsal. We were assembled on the stage in our usual, informal manner. We had been smoking and talking in the dressing rooms and our spirits were high with the excitement of rehearsing a new work with a familiar and trusted company. I explained that these rules would not be put into effect if any one person in the company did not wish to submit to any part of them.

They were written in the crass, effective, blunt style of the Marine Corps Brig Regulations. Here they are:

The Brig Rehearsal Discipline

Because of the nature of the play, in which we are enacting a rigid discipline and demonstrating the results of an authoritarian environment, rehearsals will require a more than usual strict discipline. All members of the cast and crew are expected to be thoroughly familiar with the rules of this discipline, and, upon acceptance of the discipline by the entire company, are considered to be in agreement that they will work under these conditions.

1. *Rehearsal Time:* Rehearsal Time will be called by the stage manager at the beginning of every rehearsal period and at the end of every break period. During Rehearsal Time, all rules are in effect; during Break Time, rules are suspended. Break Time will be called by the stage manager, and will also be posted in advance—on the rehearsal board. In the event of a discrepancy between the posted time and the stage manager's call, the stage manager's call is to be the final word. At the start of each Rehearsal Time every actor is expected to be ready, in the auditorium, in proper clothing, for the call of places.

2. *Rehearsal Discipline Rules*

    a. Actors will sign in before Rehearsal Time is called. Actors should arrive five minutes prior to called time, in the auditorium, to be ready for places when called.

    b. During Rehearsal Time, actors who are not on stage will remain in the auditorium, ready to be called unless specifically dismissed by the stage manager.

    c. During Rehearsal Time, there is to be no business or discussion other than that relating to the rehearsal.

    d. No eating during Rehearsal Time.

    e. Actors not required onstage may smoke in the first rows of the auditorium, where ash trays will be provided. No smoking in other parts of the auditorium. Backstage rules will be posted by the stage manager.

3. *Break Time:* During Break Time actors may leave the auditorium and the backstage area, but will not leave the building without informing the stage manager. (This rule not in effect during lunch and dinner breaks.) During breaks, actors are free to do whatever they please; all food, refuse, and personal belongings must be cleared away *before* Rehearsal Time is called.

4. *Clothing:* Costumes will be issued as soon as possible; rehearsals will be in costume. Prior to costume rehearsal, actors will rehearse in clothes as

follows: a T-shirt or light sweater, dungarees or work pants, a jockstrap, boxer shorts or bathing trunks, belts, heavy shoes (preferably high-top for prisoners), a zipper jacket (zelon-type), and a cap. Actors who cannot supply these items themselves will be outfitted by the stage manager. Make your application, for those items you cannot supply yourself, to the stage manager immediately. No extraneous jewelry or clothing will be worn during rehearsals or performance.

5. *Formality:* So that we may fully achieve the author's intent, the tone and atmosphere of Rehearsal Time will have to be more serious and formal than is usual. During Rehearsal Time, all actors and crew will maintain a respectful and serious attitude toward one another. There will be no joking tolerated during Rehearsal Time, especially in reference to the relationships of guards and prisoners.

6. *Penalties for infraction of rules:* The imposition of penalties is with the agreement, herewith, of the entire company. Penalties may be ordered by the director, the assistant director, the stage manager, the technical director. Penalties may be arbitrated, if the actor or crew member feels the penalty is injust or uncalled for. Final decision rests with the producer. Penalties will all consist of work other than one's assigned work on the play. Work will be performed at any time the company member is not required in the course of his regular duties, during the rehearsal period and for the run, at times agreeable to the actor and stage manager and technical director, within a week.

7. *Tentative list of penalties* (to be finalized with company agreement at end of first week):

Lateness: Doubletime work for time lost.

Absence: Singletime work for time lost. Lateness of more than four hours is considered absence.

Misconduct: (Obstructive, unco-operative behavior, such as kidding around on stage, unnecessary talks, failure to follow direction)—15 minutes work for each breach of discipline.

Failure to pass clothing inspection: (The stage manager will make a uniform inspection at the beginning of each Rehearsal Period, and gig those whose clothing is not in accordance with instructions; actors are responsible for all details of uniforms, including buttons)—15 minutes work time for each gig.

Loss of clothing: 1 hour work time per one dollar of clothing cost.

Loss of handprops: Same as above.

Additional penalties will be listed on the stage manager's backstage rules.

Additional rehearsal penalties will be posted if further discipline problems arise, but not without the agreement of the Company.

We talked for a long time about the gig system, and about the meaning of punishment. I feared the first ruffle of feelings. The actors agreed that a breach on their part would entail a penalty. No one dissented. To relieve the inevitable tensions we also instituted a five-minute break period which *any* actor could call at *any* time that he felt in need of freedom from the tensions and formality. Breaks were often called. They were never abused. We adjusted one clause in the fifth paragraph. Then the stage manager called rehearsal time.

Ash trays were set in the first two rows and the actors moved silently to their places for the first call. The silence was new to us. In it we felt the terrible loneliness of separation from one another. The lack of our usual laughter dismayed us. But we were thrilled by the silence and the formal tone and seeing our friends' faces so somber.

We used the techniques of evil as the innoculist uses the fatal virus. We absorbed it and we survived. We drilled. We exercised. We paid attention to accuracy. Ken Brown demonstrated for us how to slap the cap, how to make up the racks, how to swab, how to frisk and be frisked, in which hand to hold soap and toothbrush, the angle at which the manual is held; in fact, no detail was too insignificant for us to examine it for its physical appearance and its metaphysical equivalent.

This is what Artaud sought when he spoke of ritualizing objects.

There were some among us who remembered the Marine Corps from the inside and we questioned them for hours about the slightest aspect of that life that might prove useful. We sat around the dressing rooms long after rehearsal hours while Tom Lillard, who played the role of Prisoner Number Two, the figure of the author in *The Brig*, described to us the brig in which *he* served time, how it differed, how it was the same, how the soul got twisted and the body trained.

And as we worked in a new way we felt the hardness of the world outside, against which we had protected one another so long. We were like fleeing people who, even as they barricade themselves against the plague outside, meet the Red Death in their own fortified palace. But we knew that we were enacting him and the sting of his force was ritualistic fear. This power of ritual fear began to overwhelm the actors.

"If the blow does not hurt, why do I fear the white line?" Each one came to me to tell me of his own experience and they gathered together to talk each one of his terror of playing *The Brig*. The ordeal swept over us. We were all afraid. In the breaks we came closer and closer as we huddled together in small groups describing to each other the intricacies of this serious endeavor.

Moving with unaccustomed solemnity we learned to share the sense of the ordeal that the Marines felt at Fuji Brig, and that is everywhere felt in the schools of submission, in the fraternities of exclusion, in the clubs of the oppressors.

Drill was taught according to Marine Corps tactics. Chic Ciccarelli, who played the Big Warden, was a former Marine, and remembered with touching and terrible closeness the cold, hard exhilaration of the drill.

Before each rehearsal the company drilled half an hour, after the lunch break, another half hour. We cleared the lobby of The Living Theatre, and there on the tile floors we marched endless hours. Startled ticket buyers often entered in the middle of a drill master's angry scolding. It was not the polite tone of a theatrical director discussing the character with the actor, it was Ciccarelli screaming, "Get your head up, you lousy maggot!"

The drill however had an enlivening effect. The marching is a ritual of great beauty only grown hideous because it stands for the marches towards the fields of death in battle and because it has come to signify the loss of character that ensues when all of life becomes routed into this exactitude. And because you cannot stop. Meanwhile the rhythm of mutuality entices the kinetic senses. The sense of moving in a mutual rhythm with one's fellow man.

I had imagined marchers earlier, moving around the ritual circle in enormous savage costumes, when I saw the tribes of Dahomey dance their war dances on the stage of the Sarah Bernhardt Theatre in Paris. There was a time when they left those circles to move toward their enemies on what they called in the olden times the War Path. These marches, and the rhythm of the feet stamping on the hard path that time has cut through the ancient forests, were learned in the squares at the center of the villages. They were practiced in the threshing places, they were danced there in the theatres, and they took men to war in high spirits. The marching, they say, is a rest in a difficult routine.

After establishing the drill session and reading twice through the play we began to study the physical traits we would need. ("To know in advance what points of the body to touch is the key to throwing the spectator into magical trances." A.A.) And so we sought in each action its counterpart, its double in the human spirit.

Let us take for example those blows to the stomach that are such crucial moments in the play. The performer is transformed by them into a new kind of device for communication. This is known in athletics and circuses. I am talking about the imitative reflex action.

When the first blow is delivered in the darkened Brig before dawn and the prisoner winces and topples from his superbly rigid attention position, the contraction of his body is repeated *inside* the body of the spectator. That is, if we succeed, there is an actual physical, measurable contraction inside the spectator's body. We can at best be only partially successful in this. We ask for no more.

This instant of physical trauma is the instant in which a man becomes vulnerable. The human mind, vainly stabbing with the rigid prods of its will, cannot inhibit the softness of the soul as it asks for mercy for the body. The gentler spirit emerges for a moment in the red flash of brightness that accompanies the pang of a blow and pleads with the man (the whole man) to do whatever it may be to spare the beloved body continued or protracted or repeated pain. The Marine calls it cowardice and straightens up to attention as soon as the pain ebbs enough for his conditioned will to regain total power over his physical being.

We discussed at length the various stages of the blow, each one with their counterpart for prisoner and for guard. They are four:

1. The Moment before Impact: The prisoner draws upon his will and musters it for use as before battle. That is, he *hardens* himself both muscularly and psychologically. The guard prepares to make the impact of his blow telling. That is, he is concerned with making it hurt, let us say of a certain blow, not maim. He must gauge the degree to which he will let loose and the degree to which he will restrain. Being imbued with the notion of the Tough Marine he prepares to let himself hurt the prisoner as much as he dares. He hardens himself in his mind in preparation for the blow (I believe, however, that the idea of mercy is at such a moment not as far from the surface as the Marine Corps would have us believe), just as he tightens the muscles of his fist, his arms, his back, his torso, and his legs in order to deliver the blow.

2. The Moment of Impact: (There is a moment before this but it is too swift and mysterious to discuss here. It has to do with movement.) This is the moment in which the prisoner has lost his total rigidity because now he can save himself only with resiliency. But resiliency is a feminine (*ergo*: cowardly) attribute. It must be used swiftly and superficially as always when we practice negative attributes for the sake of expedience. This moment is therefore brief. But this moment is the vulnerable moment at its climax. The hair's breadth transition between the moment of impact and the moment of recovery centers first in the will as the mind flicks back from its instant of unconsciousness. Then, through the mustering of strength, it centers in the muscles in the man's body as it returns to the rigid position which the man's will proscribes for it. This moment is a physical moment and its attributes are physical. We had to be certain that this moment fulfilled its therapeutic function. At this crucial moment we must make this pain not the useless pain that sickness brings, or the inflicted pain that tempts us to vengeance and the perpetuation of the long line of hatred that had brought us here. This is the catheric pain. We staked ourselves on catharsis.

The prisoner, hurt, is vulnerable and tender. His look betrays the baby's scream of agony at its first breath.

The guard, having hurt, untenses. But he knows the danger of slackening too long, lest the victim respond, not with defeat, but with anger. He is on guard. The guard waits for the prisoner now and reads him with the glance of a snake. (Spectator: Pity and Terror!)

3. The Moment of Recovery: The prisoner now enacts the will taking over. The rigid system at war with the animal need conquers all. Because he is a Marine.

The guard watches this process with a certain amount of satisfaction. If this part of the action is not executed properly, the guard will hit the prisoner again. This is the squared-away moment, when the hope that sprung out of the animal feelings during the blow itself lies unfulfilled. It is the point of return to that same hell out of which we emerged for a moment of suffering in the Theatre of Cruelty. There is no despair in this for the prisoner, but a sense of achievement. Having been laid low, he has recovered, and having recovered, he has regained his manhood. "You're making me sick with your little-girl tricks," says the guard to the prisoner who does not return quickly enough to the attention position. When we see him thus defeated in his victory it is for us, the audience, to respond to his helplessness. If the Moment of Impact has made us feel viscerally, then the Moment of Recovery should move us to revolutionary action for our fallen brother.

4. The First Moment of the New Status Quo: Each blow is a total demolition, each recovery a total restructure. After the blow the prisoner stands erect and proud, having, if not overcome, at least survived. Even if it hurts him.

The guard, however, is still tensed for the untoward event; the guard always suspects that the prisoner may flip out and hit him, especially after the blow. The guard has to play it longer, because the blow has made him insecure. He is often cheerful afterward, but sometimes angry or glum.

The spectator returns to the world in which this blow, this visceral pain, exists. In prizefights both men fight, and sympathy gets lost in swiftly dealt vengeance. But this blow belongs to the martyrs, the soldiers, and the poor.

Each particular of the play was examined with care and we talked without limit until we were all agreed on the meanings of each element, as Kenneth described it, as I tried to balance it, as the actors began to absorb it.

The Trip

Each actor brought back travelogues of a trip that he took out into the long silent stretches. Sometimes with his uniform soaking wet, or during and after a bout with the guards, or staring at the wire that hypnotized him with its glittering lines, he stood still inside that stillness within which the physical stillness lies hidden, and in that narrow space, being so strictly confined, took wing into what Artaud calls that "enormous spiral that reveals one perspective after another." The actor felt (some familiarly, some for the first time in their lives) the other self, the one that Artaud calls the Double, take flight and soar into that other space where time is not, nor relation, nor anything, but sheer existence, undefined and undefinable, seeming absolute.

The body of the prisoner is totally captive. The soul of the prisoner is potentially totally free. The trip between these two points is the crucial experience of the play.

From this time forward the actor moves into the Brig with mysterious immunity. "And behind the Warrior, is The Double . . . who, roused by the repercussion of the turmoil, moves unaware in the midst of spells of which he has understood nothing."

At first embarrassed confessions passed among close friends. Then some came to me for consultation, worried about this "symptom," while some shouted joyfully, "I made it." Each actor in his own way confronted the moment when the body submits to the other part, so indistinguishable from the body that all the forms of holiness never cease telling us that they are one. And they are one. These two, felt by the ego as independent, suffer by their separation. Suffering melds a man and his soul.

The action of *The Brig* is real, physical, here-and-now. The spirit needs force to fuse again with the athletic body, thus its strictures become the means for this sense of unification.

I asked the actors about the Trip. They said:

1. "The space traversed is infinite."
2. "You can't think further than the next white line."

The White Line

These plain white markings on the deck of the Brig represent the simplicity with which the torture is inflicted. They are the points designated by authority beyond which we may not go, and in that capacity are related to an ancient taboo, and one not without psychological and mythological analogies. Where have we met the uncrossable line before? What echo does it stir?

It stirs the recollection of that other untraversable line: the Magic Circle. The Magic Circle is drawn by the sorcerer around the victim who stands helpless within it while the spell is woven around him. The ancient authority and the new do not differ in this: the belief of the victim in the power of the Authority makes what is unreal real. It is because he believes himself thus trapped that he is thus trapped, and as the guards say in *The Brig*, "You *better* believe it!"

They are easily justified by those who painted them there. Why, they are merely lines for the regulation of traffic through congested areas, a convenience to keep passageways clear and control movement around the Brig. The preoccupation with cleanliness which makes it dangerous to step on and dirty the white line, or the preoccupation with exactitude (squared-awayness) which makes it punishable to step on a white line are special pathologies always associated with the fear of mutiny. The implications of the word "shipshape" are the captain's preventative against mutiny. The White Line is this and more than this.

In a great and pertinent book, called *Drawing the Line*, Paul Goodman tells us:

> In the mixed society of coercion and nature, our characteristic act is Drawing the Line beyond which we cannot co-operate. All the heart-searching and purgatorial

anxiety concerns this question, *Where to draw the line?* I'll say it bluntly: The anxiety goes far beyond reason. . . .

Yet to each person it seems to make all the difference where he draws the line! This is because *these details are the symbolic key to his repressed powers.*

The prisoners in the Brig draw the line at the line. Beyond that is pain. This line, "the Line beyond which we cannot co-operate," is drawn alike by prisoner and guard, and the suffering of the guard is our unremitting concern. Paul goes on:

A free man would have no such problems; he would not have finally to draw a line in their absurd conditions which he has disdained from the very beginning. . . .

No particular drawn line will ever be defensible logically. But the right way away from any line will prove itself more clearly step by step and blow by blow.

In every action where hate is the motive, we divulged the element which, however buried, twisted, racked, and punched it may be, is love, the saving grace in everything human. We called on pity last, on basic human kinship first.

Here are a dozen particulars, that marked our way:

1. How the relationship between the guard and the prisoner is the human cornerstone of the play. Where does the I-and-Thou get lost? "Why do they call them maggots?" I asked a cocky young Marine. "Lowest form of animal life," he answered with a cocky smile.

2. How the relationship of the prisoners toward one another is the hope of the world. One actor says: "Just as we knew where our fellow prisoner was standing and what he was doing without looking at him, so we came to know how he was feeling, if he was in pain, or if he was happy because he was clicked in. It was like telepathy. But it wasn't that. It was community."

3. How the guards come to be there and how they survived the horror of their ordeal. Ken told me they were chosen at random. Aptitude graded to be brig guards. They have two alternatives, but to fail to fulfill their assignment is to fail as a Marine. *How They Learn to Love It* is the name of their tragic play.

4. How the phrase "It's your night tonight" sets a man's head and body loose into a net of apprehension. The day-long fear is as bad as the beating. The theory of deterrence is the discipline of the Brig. (Ask: *Where* does it hurt?)

5. How the author, in the opening scene, enters the character of Prisoner Number Two whose "night it is," and how at first we see the Brig through his staunch, frightened eyes, but later in the day he is immersed in the fraternity of not suffering alone; not knowing his fellow's name, he learns to live in silent empathy with him, till the author's ego and the actor's individuality and the audience's sense of personal uniqueness are swallowed up in the narrow strictures of the Brig's confining rules.

6. How Prisoner Number Three has learned to exist in the darkness as if he were living in the light. "Why doesn't he get hit?" they ask. Because he has been there so long!

7. How Prisoner Number Five gives us hope that there is a way out. That it ends, somehow. And not always too late. But what does he go to when he gets out the Freedom Door?

8. How Prisoner Number Six gets back his name: he observes the ceremonial leave-taking of Five with horror. Then, *he disobeys the next command.* He doesn't move on the line "Get back to your manuals." He just stands there. The audience notices it before the guards do, and if we are doing it right they anticipate the scream. Before he screams he has disobeyed the command. He screams because he has broken out of the system. Because he has isolated himself forever. Because he cannot go back. He is afraid. And he is not afraid because he has gone crazy, but because he has gone sane.

"My name is not Six," he cries out, "it's James Turner. Let me out of here." As he flails about to escape the entrapping jacket, the guard says "Just relax, James Turner, you are getting out of here." This is the only instance in which a prisoner is referred to by his name. For an instant the prisoner is deluded that the minion of law and order has restored him to the status of a man. He relaxes, and this is the fatal moment when they bind him and carry him out on a stretcher, as he says "Thank God."

But *where* are they taking him? He has a rendezvous out there with an unknown, impenetrable, giant Brig called the Looney-Bin where tomorrow's hospital-prisons are already a-building on the ruins of the ancient dungeons. When the prison reformers have torn down the walls, the "sick criminal" will be incarcerated there among the antiseptic horrors of the shock-machines and the well-meaning psychiatric case-workers. What trap shall we be in then? Into what darkness shall we be swallowed?

9. How the tears of Prisoner Number Eight remind everyone of something that happened long ago when pride lost out to feeling.

10. How the roles of prisoners who have no special business are as total as the roles with speaking scenes because each actor played each prisoner with his own peculiar sensuality.

11. How the second Prisoner Five perpetuates the process so that the structure will have no end. There is by now something pathetically weary and comical about the prisoner. As if he had been going on forever. The last tragedy. (Laughter/resignation.)

12. How the field day becomes a bacchanal of terror and intoxication: beginning with the first requests to cross, the sound rises toward a "sonorous pulsation."

These overlapping sounds were of two kinds and their mystery of two kinds. This climax of the ritual of useless work and the wasting of manly strength, and the abuse of the beautiful by the strong, contains the two kinds of sounds which echo the diabolical resonances of life in and out of the Brig.

The sound of the work is clashing, disorganized, disordered, confused, tumultuous. It is irregular and violent. It differed in each performance. I urged the actors to listen to this sound, to strain to catch its modulations. They attended even in the midst of the physical exertion of the field day, their bodies sweating and breathless and tired. But their ears open. I asked them to hear it and respond to it. They built its roar each night differently, but always with an attentive ear to what was happening within all earshot. Their animal ears and instincts awake in the deafening dark. They built it to a steady crescendo, climaxing at the singing of the hymn when they softened it to let the poetry ring through the bellowing rhythms of their labors.

Then the marching in Post Two begins to dominate the scene. As each prisoner joins in the drill, the disordered sound abates. The reverberating rigid sound takes over. How pleasant the steady drone is after the wild clangor. The drill sounds are regular, organized, orderly, controlled, disciplined. They are regular and law abiding. The actors were troubled by how restful it was. They didn't want to be enfolded in its harmony, the reconciliation of its smooth, untroubled, monotonous comfort.

Every night that they made this music and did this dreadful pantomime they enacted what it came to:

The price of the chaos under which we suffer.

The price of the rigid law which gives us a slave's ease.

When the audience can know violence in the clear light of the kinship of our physical empathy, it will go out of the theatre and turn such evil into such good as transformed the Furies into the Kindly Ones.

If the audience sees violence only in the dark light of the TV horror Western it will go out of its house with its rifle under its arm.

Violence is the darkest place of all. Let us throw light on it. In that light we will confront the dimensions of the Structure, find its keystone, learn on what foundations it stands, and locate its doors. Then we will penetrate its locks and open the doors of all the jails.

New York City
July 1964

The Maids

from *Saint Genet: Actor and Martyr*

Jean-Paul Sartre

The most extraordinary example of the whirligig of being and appearance, of the imaginary and the real, is to be found in one of Genet's plays. It is the element of fake, of sham, of artificiality that attracts Genet in the theater. He has turned dramatist because the falsehood of the stage is the most manifest and fascinating of all. Perhaps nowhere has he lied more brazenly than in *The Maids*.

Two maids both love and hate their mistress. They have denounced her lover to the police by means of anonymous letters. Upon learning that he is to be released for lack of proof, they realize that their betrayal will be discovered, and they try to murder Madame. They fail and want to kill themselves. Finally, one of them takes her life, and the other, left alone and drunk with glory, tries, by the pomp of her posturings and language, to be equal to the magnificent destiny that awaits her.

Let us indicate at once a first whirligig. Genet says in *Our Lady of the Flowers*: "If I were to have a play put on in which women had roles, I would demand that these roles be performed by adolescent boys, and I would bring this to the attention of the spectators by means of a placard which would remain nailed to the right or left of the sets during the entire performance."* One might be tempted to explain this demand by Genet's taste for young boys. Nevertheless, this is not the essential reason. The truth of the matter is

Excerpted from Jean-Paul Sartre, *Saint Genet: Actor and Martyr*, trans. Bernard Frechtman, (New York: George Braziller Inc., 1963), 611–25. Reprinted by permission of George Braziller, Inc.

The Maids was actually performed by women, but this was a concession which Genet made to Louis Jouvet, who produced the play.

that Genet wishes from the very start to *strike at the root of the apparent.* No doubt an actress can play Solange, but the derealizing would not be radical, since there would be no need for her to play at being a woman. The softness of her flesh, the languid grade of her movements and the silvery tone of her voice are natural endowments. They constitute the substance that she would mold as she saw fit, so as to give it the appearance of Solange. Genet wishes this feminine stuff itself to become an appearance, the result of a make-believe. It is not Solange who is to be a theatrical illusion, but rather *the woman Solange.*

In order to achieve this absolute state of artifice, the first thing to do is to eliminate nature. The roughness of a breaking voice, the dry hardness of male muscles and the bluish luster of a budding beard will make the de-feminized and spiritualized female appear as an invention of man, as a pale and wasting shadow which cannot sustain itself unaided, as the evanescent result of an extreme and momentary exertion, as the impossible dream of man in a world without women.

Thus, what appears behind the footlights is not so much a woman as Genet himself living out the impossibility of being a woman. We would see before us the effort, at times admirable and at times grotesque, of a youthful male body struggling against its own nature, and, lest the spectator be caught up in the game, he would be warned throughout—in defiance of all the laws of stage perspective—that the actors are trying to deceive him as to their sex. In short, the illusion is prevented from "taking" by a sustained contradiction between the effort of the actor, who measures his talent by his ability to deceive, and the warning of the placard. Thus, Genet *betrays* his actors. He unmasks them, and the performer, seeing his imposture exposed, finds himself in the position of a culprit who has been found out. Illusion, betrayal, failure, all the major categories that govern Genet's dreams are here present. In the same way, he betrays his characters in *Our Lady of the Flowers* and in *Funeral Rites* by warning the reader whenever the latter is about to yield to the illusion of the story: "Watch out. These are creatures of my imagination. They don't exist." The thing to be avoided above all is the spectator's being caught up in the game, like children at the movies who scream, "Don't drink it, it's poison!" or like the naïve public that waited at the stage door for Frédéric Lemaître in order to beat him up.

To seek being through appearance would be to make *proper use* of the latter. For Genet, theatrical procedure is demoniacal. Appearance, which is constantly on the point of passing itself off as reality, must constantly reveal its profound unreality. Everything must be so false that it sets our teeth on edge. But by virtue of being false, the woman acquires a poetic density. Shorn of its texture and purified, femininity becomes a heraldic sign, a cipher. As long as it was natural, the feminine blazon remained embedded in woman. Spiritu-alized, it becomes a category of the imagination, a device for generating reveries. Anything can be a woman: a flower, an animal, an inkwell.

174 ••• SARTRE

The illusion shdn't "take" Tht is passive.

"Illusion, betrayal, failure" Magritte — Don't forget the illusion; not to believe the dream.

Cp. DISNEY.

G. "There are players" "OUR"

In *The Child Criminal* Genet has given us the keys of what might be called his algebra of the imagination. He speaks of the director of a home for children who boasts of giving the children tin knives and who adds, "They can't kill anyone with that." Genet makes the following comment: "Was he unaware that by departing from its practical destination the object is transformed, that it becomes a symbol? Its very form sometimes changes. We say that it becomes stylized. It then acts secretly in children's souls. It does more serious damage. Hidden at night in a straw mattress or concealed in the lining of the jacket or, rather, of the trousers—not for greater convenience, but in order to be close to the organ it symbolizes—it is the very sign of the murder that the child will not actually commit but which will feed his reverie and, I hope, will direct it toward the most criminal manifestation. What good does it do to take it away from him? The child will only choose some more harmless-looking object as a sign of murder, and if this also is taken from him, he will guard within him preciously the sharper image of the weapon." As the material grows poorer—steel knife, tin knife, hazel twig—as the distance increases between itself and what it signifies, the symbolic nature of the sign is heightened. The reveries are directed, fed and organized. His maids are fake women, "women of no gynaeceum," who make men dream not of possessing *a* woman but of being lit up by a woman-sun, queen of a feminine heaven, and finally of being themselves the matter for the heraldic symbol of femininity. Genet is trying to present to us femininity without woman.

Such is the initial direction of his derealization: a falsification of femininity. But the shock boomerangs and the performance affects the actor himself. The young murderer, Our Lady of the Flowers, dresses up as a woman one day just for the fun of it. "Our Lady, in his pale blue faille dress, edged with white Valenciennes lace, was more than himself. He was himself and his complement." We know that Genet values above all the labor of derealization. The thing that attracts him in Our Lady of the Flowers is the spectacle of a man being worked upon by femininity: "Our Lady raised his bare arm and—it's astounding—this murderer made the very same gesture, though a trifle more brutal, that Émilienne d'Alençon would certainly have made to rumple her chignon." This hybrid creature, of the race of centaurs and sirens, begins as a male only to go up in smoke as female fireworks. In order to express his superiority both to young men and to all women, Genet invents a wonderful sign: "The chauffeur opened the door. . . . Gorgui, because of his position in the group, ought to have stepped in first, but he moved aside, leaving the opening free for Our Lady. Bear in mind that never does a pimp efface himself before a woman, still less before a fairy. . . . Gorgui must have placed him quite high." The appearance of the imaginary upsets social conventions. Gorgui the Pimp spontaneously adopts bourgeois courtesy. He effaces himself before a glamorous young male who derealizes himself into a young lady whose grace is heightened by the glamour of the murderer. The grace of women is usually despised by roughnecks because it signifies weakness and submission. But here it shimmers at the surface of the great dark force of killers. Hence, they must bow before it. Crime becomes the secret horror of grace: grace becomes the secret softness of crime. Our Lady is the vestal of a bloodthirsty goddess, a great cruel Mother of a homosexual matriarchy.

Thus far we have seen nothing we did not already know. All this is still the reciprocal derealization of matter by form and of form by matter. But now the first whirligig is set going. Genet's poetic themes are, as we know, profoundly homosexual. We know that neither women nor the psychology of women interests him. And if he has chosen to show us maids and their mistress and feminine hatreds, it is only because the necessities of public performance oblige him to disguise his thought. The proof of this is that his second play, *Deathwatch*, the characters of which are all men, deals with exactly the same subject as *The Maids*.

There is the same hierarchy: in one case, Monsieur, in the other, Snowball: the intermediate divinity, Madame and Green Eyes; and the two youngsters who dream of murder but fail to commit it, who love and hate each other and each of whom is the other's bad smell, Solange and Claire, Maurice and Lefranc. In one case, the play ends with a suicide that the police will take for a murder; in the other, with a fake murder, that is, a real killing which rings false. Lefranc, who is a fake, is a real traitor; Maurice, however, who is too young to kill, is of the race of killers; thus, they too form "the eternal couple of the Criminal and the Saint," as do Divine and Our Lady. This is the same eternal couple that Solange and Claire want to form. And their ambiguous feeling for Madame is discreetly homosexual, as is that of Lefranc and Maurice for Green Eyes. Moreover, Genet himself has known the maids' hatred of Madame. He tells us in *Our Lady of the Flowers* that he himself was once a servant, and in *Funeral Rites* he tells us of another servant, the suffering mother who concealed beneath her skirts "the wiliest of hoodlums." Similarly, it has been said that "Proust's Albertine should have been called Albert." The young actors in *The Maids* are boys playing at being women, but these women in turn are secretly boys. However, these imaginary boys who gleam behind the feminine appearances of Solange and Clair are not to be identified with the real adolescents who embody the characters. They too are dreams, since in the other play they are called Maurice and Lefranc. They are, if you like, on the vanishing line of the appearances, giving them their appearance of depth. But the spectators dimly sense the homosexual drift of the plot, and when the actor raises his bare arm and reveals too much muscle, when he adjusts his bun and makes a gesture "a trifle more brutal" than that of Émilienne d'Alençon, the spectator does not know whether this inordinate muscularity and too evident brutality represent a rebellion of reality or whether they transcend this story about women and symbolize homosexuality. Are the dry and angular gesture and the brusque gait merely the awkwardness of a young male hampered by a woman's dress, or are they not Maurice, who has taken possession of Solange? Are they a return to Being or are they the quintessence of the imaginary? Being changes at this point into appearance and appearance into being. But it may be objected that the homosexual drama is the *truth* of this ancillary fiction. Well and good. But it is an appearance which becomes the truth of another appearance. And then, in another sense, these fake women were the truth of the adolescent boys who embodied them, for Genet, like all homosexuals, is able to discern a secret femininity in the most male of men. As in psychodramas, his actors play what they are. They resemble, feature for feature, the real hoodlum who played the fake-prince-who-is-a-real-hoodlum and who, through the mediation of the prince, was derealized into himself. But if these fake women are the disguise of imaginary men, the young actors are swallowed up by a new absence. As they interpret their own drama, they are the unconscious pawns in a game of chess which Genet is playing against himself.

But we are still at only the first degree of derealization. These fake women who are fake men, these women-men who are men-women, this perpetual challenging of masculinity by a symbolic femininity and of the later by the secret femininity which is the truth of all masculinity, are only the faked groundwork. Upon his evanescent foundation there appear individual forms: Solange and Claire. We shall see that they too are faked.

They play has four characters, one of whom does not appear, namely, Monsieur, the *man*. Monsieur is Harcamone of *Miracle of the Rose;* he is Snowball of *Deathwatch*. Pilorge is he who *is never there*. His absence represents the eternal abstraction of the handsome Pimps, their indifference. In this bourgeois atmosphere he is the only one who is ennobled by prison. To be sure, he is slanderously accused of a crime which he has not committed, but we know that for Genet guilt comes to the offender from without. It is a collective image, a taboo that settles upon him. Behind this homosexual *Arlésienne* whom everyone talks about and nobody sees is Madame, an ambiguous figure, a mediation, a girl queen in relation to Monsieur and a boy queen in relation to the two maids. To Monsieur she is a faithful dog. Genet ascribes to her his old dream of following a convict to the penal colony. "I wanted to be," he tells us, "the young prostitute who accompanies her lover to Siberia." And Madame says: "I don't think he's guilty either, but if he were, I'd become his accomplice. I'd follow him to Devil's Island, to Siberia." But something warns us—perhaps her volubility or the wild gaiety of her despair—that she is a fraud. Does she love Monsieur? Probably she does. But to what point? There is no way of telling. At all events, she has found, like Ernestine in *Our Lady of the Flowers*, the finest role of her life. It will be noted that Green Eyes, a symmetrical character who is also an intermediary and a "daimon," though he has committed an honest-to-goodness murder, plays, in his state of exaltation, at being a murderer. [In Genet's plays every character must play the role of a character who plays a role.] In relation to the two maids, Madame represents pitiless indifference. Not that she despises or mistreats them; she is *kind.* She embodies social Good and Good Conscience, and the servants' ambivalent feelings about her express Genet's feelings about Good. Being kind, Madame can desire only the Good. She feels sorry for them: she gives them dresses; she loves them, but with an icy love, "like her bidet." In like manner, wealthy, cultivated and happy men have, from time to time, "felt sorry" for Genet, have tried to oblige him. Too late. He has blamed them for loving him for the love of Good, *in spite* of his badness and not *for* it. [Only an evil individual could love another evil individual for the love of Evil. But evildoers do not love.]

As a woman in relationship to Monsieur, Madame has only *relative* being. As the maids' mistress, she retains an absolute being. But the maids are relative to everything and everyone; their being is defined by its absolute relativity. They are *others.* Domestics are pure emanations of their masters and, like criminals, belong to the order of the Other, to the order of Evil. They *love* Madame. This means, in Genet's language, that both of them would like to *become* Madame, in other words, to be integrated into the social order instead of being outcasts. They *hate* Madame. Translate: Genet detests the Society that rejects him and he wishes to annihilate it. These specters are born of the dream of a master; murky to themselves, their feelings come to them from outside. They are born in the sleeping imagination of Madame or Monsieur. Low, hypocritical, disagreeable and mean because their employers dream them that way, they belong to the "pale and motley race that flowers in the minds of decent people." When he presents them before the footlights, Genet merely mirrors the fantasies of the right-minded women in the audience. Every evening five hundred Madames can sing out, "Yes, that's what maids are like," without realizing that they have created them, the way Southerners create Negroes. The only rebellion of these flat creatures is that they dream in turn: they dream within a dream; these dream dwellers, pure reflections of a sleeping consciousness, use the little reality which this consciousness has given them to imagine that they are becoming the Master who imagines them. They flounder about at the intersection of two nightmares and form the "twilight guard" of bourgeois families. They are disturbing only in that they are dreams that dream of swallowing up their dreamer.

Thus, the maids, as Genet conceives them, [are *already* fake.] Pure products of artifact, their minds are inside out, and they are always other than themselves. That there are two of them is a stroke of genius. Two, exactly the number needed to set up a whirligig. To be sure, Genet did not invent these criminal sisters out of whole cloth. The reader has probably recognized Claire and Solange; they are the Papin sisters.* But we already know that Genet has distilled the anecdote, that he has retained only its quintessence

*The reference is to a famous French murder case.—Translator's note.

and presents it to us as a "cipher." The *maids* are the mysterious cipher of the pure imagination and also of Genet himself. There are two of them because Genet is double: himself and the other. Thus, each of the two maids has no other function than to be the other, to be—for the other—herself-as-other. Whereas the unity of the mind is constantly haunted by a phantom duality, the dyad of the maids is, on the contrary, haunted by a phantom of unity. Each sees in the other only herself at a distance from herself. Each bears witness to the other of the impossibility of *being* herself, and, as Querelle says: "their doule statue is reflected in each of their halves." The mainspring of this new whirligig is the perfect interchangeability of Solange and Claire, which makes Solange always appear to be elsewhere, *on* Claire when we look at Solange, and *on* Solange when we look at Claire. To be sure, this interchangeability does not exclude certain differences. Solange seems harder; perhaps "she tries to dominate" Claire; perhaps Genet has chosen her to embody the glamorous appearance and the secret cowardice of the criminal; perhaps he has elected the gentle and perfidious Claire to symbolize the hidden heroism of the Saint. In actual fact, Solange's attempts at crime fail: she does not succeed in killing either Madame or her own sister. Claire also botches a murder, but, pushing their play-acting to its extreme consequences, she takes her own life. The girl queen has more real courage than the tough. This means that the fake courage of Solange finds its truth in the secret courage of Claire, that the fake pusillanimity of Claire finds its truth in the profound cowardice of Solange.

But Genet does not linger over these familiar themes, which he develops abundantly elsewhere. Solange and Claire are much less differentiated than Maurice and Lefranc; their dissimilarities are dreams which ill conceal a fundamental identity. Both of them are characterized by the imaginary splendor of their projects and the radical failure of their undertakings. In reality, Genet has set before us *a single object*, though a profoundly faked one, neither one nor two, one when we want to see two, two when we want to see one: the ancillary couple as a pure crisscross of appearances. And the bond that unites these two reflections is itself a faked relationship. Do the sisters love each other, do they hate each other? They hate each other with love, like all of Genet's characters. Each finds in the other her "bad smell" and one of them proclaims that "filth doesn't love filth." But at the same time, each inwardly clings to the other by a kind of carnal promiscuity which gives to their caresses the tepid pleasure of masturbation. But where is the truth of the ancillary couple? When we see Solange and Claire in the presence of Madame, they do not seem real. Fake submission, fake tenderness, fake respect, fake gratitude. Their entire behavior is a lie. We are led to believe that this falsifying comes from their false relationships with their mistress. When they resume their joint solitude, they put on their true faces again. But when they are alone, they play. Claire plays at being Madame and Solange at being Claire. And we await, despite ourselves, the return of

Madame which will cause their masks to fall and which will restore them to their true situation as servants.

Thus, their truth is always elsewhere; in the presence of the Masters, the truth of a domestic is to be a fake domestic and to mask the *man* he is under a guise of servility; but, in their absence, the *man* does not manifest himself either, for the truth of the domestic in solitude is to play at being master. The fact is that when the Master is away on a trip, the valets smoke his cigars, wear his clothes and ape his manners. How could it be otherwise, since the Master convinces the servant that there is no other way to become a man than to be a master. A whirligig of appearances: a valet is sometimes a man who plays at being a man; in other words, a man who dreams with horror that he is becoming a subman or a subman who dreams with hatred that he is becoming a man.

Thus, each of the two maids plays, in turn, at being Madame. When the curtain rises, Claire is standing in front of the dressing table of her mistress. She is experimenting with Madame's gestures and language. For Genet, this is an actual incantation. We shall see later on that, by imitating the gestures of his superior, the domestic treacherously draws him into himself and becomes saturated with him. There is nothing surprising in this, since Madame herself is a fake Madame who plays at distinction and at her passion for Monsieur and who dreams of drawing into herself the soul of a whore who follows her pimp to jail.

Similarly, Genet could, without difficulty, *make himself* Stilitano, because Stilitano himself played at being Stilitano. Madame is no more true in Claire than in Madame herself; Madame is a gesture.

Solange helps her sister put on one of her mistress's dresses, and Claire, playing her role in a state of exaltation, taut and strained, as is Genet himself, insults Solange, as she does every evening, until the latter, driven to extremities, as she is every evening, slaps her. This is, of course, a ceremony, a sacred game which is repeated with the stereotyped monotony of schizophrenic dreams. In short, Genet, whose reveries are themselves often dry and ceremonious and who repeats them day after day until their charm is exhausted, introduces the spectator into the very privacy of his inner life. He allows himself to be overheard in a spell of incantation; he betrays himself; he gives himself away; he hides nothing of the monotony and childishness which spoil his secret festivities and of which he is perfectly aware. And he even invites us to see what he himself will never see because he is unable to get outside himself: the inside and outside, the *reality* (if there is one) and its disguise. As for the role itself, we recognize quite easily Genet's favorite themes: to begin with, the maids *want*, to the point of despair and horror, the servile condition that is imposed upon them; in like manner, Genet wants to be the bastard, the outcast that society has made of him. And this cruel game provides the rigorous demonstration of what we suggested a while ago: one cannot want to be what one is in the imaginary; in order to live their wretchedness to the point of *passion*, to the very dregs, they must make themselves the cause of it. Thus, Solange plays the role of servant. But she would be sticking too close to reality if she remained Solange; there would be no way of deciding whether she takes upon herself her menial condition or whether she *really*, and out of habit, performs her servile tasks. In order to change herself into a maid by her own will, Solange *plays at being* Solange. She cannot *want to be* Solange the servant, because she *is* Solange. She therefore wants to be an imaginary Claire so as to acquire one of the chief characteristics of this Claire, which is to be a servant. A phantom Claire dresses an imaginary Madame. Here a small local whirl is set up: an actor plays the role of a servant who is playing the role of a servant. The falsest of appearances joins the truest being, for to play at being a maid is the truth of the actor and the phantasy of Solange. The result is—and this does not fail to delight Genet—that in order "to be true" the actor must *play false*. The fact is that Solange, who is not a professional actress, plays her role of maid badly. Thus, the nearer the actor draws to his reality as actor, the further he withdraws from it. Fake jewels, sham pearls, Genet's deceptive loves: an actor plays at being an actor, a maid plays at being a maid; their truth is their lie and their lie is their truth. The same may be said of the actor playing the role of Claire-playing Madame; Genet confirms it in his stage directions: "Her gestures and tone are exaggeratedly tragic."

The reason for this is that the ceremony has still another meaning: it is a Black Mass. What is played every evening is the murder of Madame, a murder always being interrupted, always uncompleted. It is a case of committing *the worst*: Madame is benevolent, "Madame is kind"; they will kill their benefactress, precisely because she has been Good to them. The act will be imaginary, since Evil is the imagination. But *even in the imaginary* it is faked in advance. The maids know that they will not have time enough to get to the crime.

"SOLANGE: The same thing happens every time. And it's all your fault, you're never ready. I can't finish you off.

"CLAIRE: We waste too much time with the preliminaries."

Thus, the playing of the sacrilege conceals a failure in behavior. It is imaginary to the second degree: Claire and Solange do not even play the fictitious murder; they pretend to play it. They are thereby merely imitating their creator. As I have pointed out elsewhere, Genet prefers imaginary murder to real murder because in the former the will to evil, though remaining entire, pushes the love of nothingness to a point where it reduces itself to impotence. In the last analysis, Solange and Claire are fully satisfied with this *appearance* of crime; what they like about it more than anything else is the taste of nothingness with which it leaves them. But they both pretend, by means of a further lie, that they are disappointed at not having gone through with the thing to the very end. And besides, what would there have been at "the very end"? The true murder of the fake Madame? The fake murder of Claire? Perhaps they don't even know themselves.

The fact remains that in this phantom play-acting, which, even as play-acting, never concludes,* the great role this evening is reserved for Claire: it is for her to personify Madame and so to exasperate Solange that she commits a crime. But Solange personifies Claire. Whence, a new disintegration: the relationships of the fake Madame with the fake Claire have a triple, a quadruple basis. In the first place, Claire makes herself be Madame *because she loves her*; for Genet, to love means to want to be. As Madame, she blossoms out; she escapes from herself. But, in addition, she makes herself be Madame *because she hates her*: resentment derealizes; Madame is merely a passive phantom who is slapped on Claire's cheeks. Besides, the interpretation of Claire is forced; she is not aiming at showing Madame as she is, but at making her hateful. Madame, the sweet and kind Madame, insults her maids, humiliates them, exasperates them. And we do not know whether this distorted caricature tends to reveal the mistress in her true light, to expose the truth of that indifferent good nature which may be concealing a pitiless cruelty, or whether it already wreaks an imaginary vengeance by metamorphosing Madame, by the incantation of the gesture, into a harpy. [As psychoanalysis has revealed to us, one of the motives of acts of self-punishment is to force the judge to punish unjustly and thereby to burden him with a guilt which discredits him and makes him unworthy of judging.] By means of her performance of Madame's role, Claire transforms her into an unjust juge and rids herself of her. But at the same time, in the guise of Madame, she insults and humiliates Solange, whom she hates, Solange, her bad smell: "Avoid pawing me. You smell like an animal. You've brought those odors from some foul attic where the lackeys visit us at night." But Solange is sheltered: she is playing the role of Claire. First, as we have seen, because it is easier for her as the fake Claire to assume her menial condition; then, because Claire can be Madame only if she seems Madame in her own eyes. Solange's becoming Claire represents the astounding effort of a reflective consciousness turning back on itself and wanting to perceive itself as it appears to others. This attempt is doomed to failure; either the reflective consciousness is real and its object melts into the imaginary (Genet can *see himself* as a thief only poetically), or else the object remains real and it is the reflection that slips into the imaginary (Eric, in *Funeral Rites*, imagines seeing himself with the eyes of the executioner). Solange's play-acting belongs to this second category; it is Claire taking upon herself a reflective view in the imaginary. Claire's audience is the phantom of herself-as-other. It is thus *herself* whom she humiliates; it is to *herself* that she says: "Keep your hands off mine! I can't stand your touching me." Solange, Madame, the intermediate appearances, all vanish. Claire stands alone facing her mirror, in the desert. Thus, the love-hatred she feels for Madame conceals her feeling for Solange and finally her feeling about herself. And each of these feelings has an imaginary side; her hatred of Madame takes on a double aspect; insofar as Claire is the source of it, she derealizes herself and exhausts

*Genet is an old hand at these unfinished ceremonies. He confided to us in *Miracle of the Rose* that he used to caress Bulkaen in thought but would abandon him even before attaining erection.

herself in her caricatural interpretation of this character; but, on the other hand, she passes into Solange, who, as fake Claire, directs upon the fake Madame, on behalf of her sister, a fictive hatred. As for Claire's hatred of Solange, it is completely covered and disguised by the play-acting: it is not, to be sure, fictive, but it finds within reach only fictive instruments and modes of expression; in order to hate Solange, Claire has no other resource but to make herself Madame-hating-Claire. Finally, Claire's hatred of herself makes it necessary that at least one of the two terms of this affective relationship be imaginary: in order to hate and to love, there must be two; hence, Claire can hate only a phantom of herself embodied by Solange. But we again fall upon a whirligig: for *at the same time* the feelings are true; it is true that Claire hates Madame, true that she hates Solange and that, through the mediation of Solange, she tries to hate herself. Once again the false is true and the true can be expressed only by means of the false. And when Claire calls Solange "You slut," when Solange, *in ecstasy,* cries, "Madame's being carried away!" *who* is insulting *whom?* And *who* feels the insult with that masochistic pleasure? Inversely, *who* tempts *whom* to commit murder? And *who* slaps *whom?* This slap is a sacred rite which represents the rape of Genet by the Male. But this whirligig of appearances has made us so dizzy that we do not know whether it is Claire who slaps Madame, Claire who slaps Claire, Solange who slaps Claire or Solange who slaps Solange.* It may be objected that the true Solange has nevertheless performed a real act and that the true Claire has felt true pain. So they have. But the same holds for this slap as for Genet's thefts. As I have pointed out elsewhere, though these thefts were *really* committed, they were lived in the imaginary. This slap is therefore a poetic act. It melts into a gesture; the very pain that it causes is lived imaginarily. At the same time it is slurred over, for this true slap which is felt imaginarily is a fake slap that an actor pretends to give another actor.

This extraordinary faking, this mad jumble of appearance, this superimposing of whirligigs which keep sending us back and forth from the true to the false and from the false to the true, is an infernal machine whose mechanisms Genet is careful not to reveal to us at the beginning. When the curtain goes up, we see an impatient and nervous young lady who is rebuking her maid. From time to time an unusual word or an inappropriate gesture casts a disturbing light upon this familiar scene. But suddenly an alarm clock goes off: "The two actresses, in a state of agitation, run together. They huddle and listen." Claire, in a changed voice, mutters: "Let's hurry! Madame'll be back." She starts to unfasten her dress. "It's so close this evening"; they are "exhausted and sad"; in order to put their short black skirts on again they need some of that "greatness of soul" that Divine displayed when she put her bridge back into her mouth. However, the spectator, in a dazzling flash, sees through the heart of the darkness to this astounding mechanism

---

*For Solange hates herself in Claire as Claire hates herself in Solange.

of appearances: everything was fake; the familiar scene was a diabolical imitation of everyday life. The entire scene was prepared in order to impose this deception upon us.

The high value of appearance is due, in Genet's eyes, to the fact that, like Evil, of which it is the pure embodiment, it corrodes and does away with itself. Cases of volatilization are rare in ordinary life; the plate breaks and the pieces remain. But appearance offers us a certain being. It gives it to us, hands it over to us, and, if we put out our arm, this being is suddenly reabsorbed. The victim of the three-card trick has not lost sight of the ace of hearts; he *knows* that it is the first card of the third pack; he points to it; the performer turns it up: it's the ace of spades. He then feels a strange and brutal disappointment in his flesh. For a moment he thinks that he has an intuition of nothingness. Yes, the nothing becomes an apparition, nonbeing a richness which fills him; the absence of the ace of hearts is much more virulent, much more immediate, than the presence of the ace of spades. The following instant his perception has regained its fullness, but the instant remains mysterious. The nothingness has disappeared; it allowed itself to be glimpsed and then vanished.

But since nonbeing *is not,* how can it *no longer be?* It is this perverse intuition that Genet prefers to all else: it makes the *nothing* shimmer at the surface of *all.* Where is being? Can it be that something *is?* If the ace of hearts has vanished, why should not the ace of spades disappear as well? And what is nonbeing, if it can suddenly fill me with its emptiness? In *The Maids*, the ambiguous instant of deception, when superimposed illusions collapse like a house of cards, rightly deserves the name of pure instant of the Lie. For when the Saharan mirage vanishes, it reveals true stones. But when the deceptive appearances in the play are dispelled, they reveal in their place *other appearances* (the fake Madame becomes Claire again, the fake maid, the fake woman; the fake Claire becomes Solange again, the fake servant). At this moment the spectator has first the demoniacal intuition of nothingness, that is, being is revealed to be nothing, but, as appearance is usually effaced in the presence of being, the illusions which vanish leave him with the illusion that *it is being* which replaces them. Suddenly the pantomime of a young male who pretends to be a woman *seems to him to be the truth.* It is as if he suddenly understood that the only true thing is play-acting, that the only real women are men, and so on. Being has been revealed as nonbeing and thereupon nonbeing becomes being. This moment in which the lights flicker, when the volatile unity of the being of nonbeing and the nonbeing of being is achieved in semidarkness, this perfect and perverse instant, makes us realize from within the mental attitude of Genet when he dreams: it is the moment of evil. For in order to be sure of never making *proper use* of appearance, Genet wants his fancies, at two or three stages of derealization, to reveal themselves in their nothingness. In this pyramid of fantasies, the ultimate appearance derealizes all the others. Thus, the youngster who plays the role of Claire is derealized into a young man so that the latter may be derealized into a mistress. But, as I have shown, an appearance borrows its being from being: thus, "Claire" borrows her being from the boy who interprets her. But the "fake Madame" is supported in being by *Claire*, who does not exist. And since she thus derives her being from a fantasy, the being of this appearance is only an appearance of being. Whereupon Genet considers himself satisfied; on the one hand, he has achieved pure appearance, the one whose very being is appearance, that is, the one which appears to be appearance through and through, to borrow nothing from being and finally to produce itself, which, as we know, is one of the two contradictory demands of Evil; but, on the other hand, this pyramid of appearances masks the being which supports them all (the true movement, the true words uttered by the young actor in the play, the movement and words which, in actual life, help Genet dream), and as, nevertheless, they *are* in some way, it seems that each borrows its being from the one that immediately precedes it. Thus, as being fades into appearance at all degrees, it seems that the real is something melting, that it is reabsorbed when touched. In these patient fakings, appearance is revealed at the same time as pure nothingness and as cause of itself. And being, without ceasing to set itself up as absolute reality, becomes evanescent. Translated into the language of Evil: Good is only an illusion; Evil is a Nothingness which arises upon the ruins of Good.

G
o
o
d

do-G ⌀ • evil

, Good
/ Evil
√ Nothingness

the vacuum that
arises when
good collapses...

The Theatre's New Testament
Interview with Jerzy Grotowski

Eugenio Barba

How, then, is the actor trained in your theatre, and what is his function in the performance?

The actor is a man who works in public with his body, offering it publicly. If this body restricts itself to demonstrating what it is—something that any average person can do—then it is not an obedient instrument capable of performing a spiritual act. If it is exploited for money and to win the favour of the audience, then the art of acting borders on prostitution. It is a fact that for many centuries the theatre has been associated with prostitution in one sense of the word or another. The words "actress" and "courtesan" were once synonymous. Today they are separated by a somewhat clearer line, not through any change in the actor's world but because society has changed. Today it is the difference between the respectable woman and the courtesan which has become blurred.

What strikes one when looking at the work of an actor as practised these days is the wretchedness of it: the bargaining over a body which is exploited by its protectors—director, producer—creating in return an atmosphere of intrigue and revolt.

Just as only a great sinner can become a saint according to the theologians (Let us not forget the Revelation: "So then because thou art lukewarm, and neither cold nor hot, I will spue thee out of my mouth"), in the same way the actor's wretchedness can be transformed into a kind of holiness. The history of the theatre has numerous examples of this.

Excerpted from Jerzy Grotowski, *Towards a Poor Theatre* (New York: Simon and Schuster, 1968), 33–39; 43–46. Reprinted by permission of Odin Teatret.

Don't get me wrong. I speak about "holiness" as an unbeliever. I mean a "secular holiness." If the actor, by setting himself a challenge publicly challenges others, and through excess, profanation and outrageous sacrilege reveals himself by casting off his everyday mask, he makes it possible for the spectator to undertake a similar process of self-penetration. If he does not exhibit his body, but annihilates it, burns it, frees it from every resistance to any psychic impulse, [then he does not sell his body but sacrifices it.] He repeats the atonement; he is close to holiness. If such acting is not to be something transient and fortuitous, a phenomenon which cannot be foreseen in time or space: if we want a theatre group whose daily bread is this kind of work—then we must follow a special method of research and training. ✔

What is it like, in practice, to work with the "holy" actor?

There is a myth telling how an actor with a considerable fund of experience can build up what we might call his own "arsenal"—i.e. an accumulation of methods, artifices and tricks. From these he can pick out a certain number of combinations for each part and thus attain the expressiveness necessary for him to grip his audience. This "arsenal" or store may be nothing but a collection of clichés. In which case such a method is inseparable from the conception of the "courtesan actor."

The difference between the "courtesan actor" and the "holy actor" is the same as the difference between the skill of a courtesan and the attitude of giving and receiving which springs from true love: in other words, self-sacrifice. The essential thing in this second case is to be able to eliminate any disturbing elements in order to be able to overstep every conceivable limit. In the first case it is a question of the existence of the body; in the other, rather of its non-existence. The technique of the "holy actor" is an **inductive** ✔ **technique** (i.e. a technique of elimination), whereas that of the "courtesan actor" is a **deductive technique** (i.e. an accumulation of skills).

The actor who undertakes an act of self-penetration, who reveals himself and sacrifices the innermost part of himself—the most painful, that which is not intended for the eyes of the world—must be able to manifest the least impulse. He must be able to express, through sound and movement, those impulses which waver on the borderline between dream and reality. In short, he must be able to construct his own psycho-analytic language of sounds and gestures in the same way that a great poet creates his own language of words.

If we take into consideration for instance the problem of sound, the plasticity of the actor's respiratory and vocal apparatus must be infinitely more developed than that of the man in the street. Furthermore, this apparatus must be able to produce sound reflexes so quickly that thought—which would remove all spontaneity—has no time to intervene.

The actor should be able to decipher all the problems of his body which are accessible to him. He should know how to direct the air to those parts of the body where sound can be created and amplified by a sort of resonator. The average actor knows only the head resonator; that is, he uses his head as a resonator to amplify his voice, making it sound more "noble", more agreeable to the audience. He may even at times, fortuitously, make use of the chest resonator. But the actor who investigates closely the possibilities of his own organism discovers that the number of resonators is practically unlimited. He can exploit not only his head and chest, but also the back of his head (occiput), his nose, his teeth, his larynx, his belly, his spine, as well as a total resonator which actually comprises the whole body and many others, some of which are still unknown to us. He discovers that it is not enough to make use of abdominal respiration on stage. The various phases in his physical actions demand different kinds of respiration if he is to avoid difficulties with his breathing and resistance from his body. He discovers that the diction he learnt at drama school far too often provokes the closing of the larynx. He must acquire the ability to open his larynx consciously, and to check from the outside whether it is open or closed. If he does not solve these problems, his attention will be distracted by the difficulties he is bound to encounter and the process of self-penetration will necessarily fail. If the actor is conscious of his body, he cannot penetrate and reveal himself. The body must be freed from all resistance. It must virtually cease to exist. As for his voice and respiration, it is not enough that the actor learns to make use of several resonators, to open his larynx and to select a certain type of respiration. He must learn to perform all this unconsciously in the culminating phases of his acting and this, in its turn, is something which demands a new series of exercises. When he is working on his role he must learn not to think of adding technical elements (resonators, etc.), but should aim at eliminating the concrete obstacles he comes up against (e.g. resistance in his voice).

This is not merely splitting hairs. It is the difference which decides the degree of success. It means that the actor will never possess a permanently "closed" technique, for at each stage of his self-scrutiny, each challenge, each **excess,** each breaking down of hidden barriers he will encounter new technical problems on a higher level. He must then learn to overcome these too with the help of certain basic exercises.

This goes for everything: movement, the plasticity of the body, gesticulation, the construction of masks by means of the facial musculature and, in fact, for each detail of the actor's body.

But the decisive factor in this process is the actor's technique of psychic penetration. He must learn to use his role as if it were a surgeon's scalpel, to dissect himself. It is not a question of portraying himself under certain given circumstances, or of "living" a part; nor does it entail the distant sort of acting common to epic theatre and based on cold calculation. The important thing is to use the role as a trampolin, an instrument with which to study what is hidden behind our everyday mask—the innermost core of our personality—in order to sacrifice it, expose it.

This is an excess not only for the actor but also for the audience. The spectator understands, consciously or unconsciously, that such an act is an invitation to him to do the same thing, and this often arouses opposition or indignation, because our daily efforts are intended to hide the truth about ourselves not only from the world, but also from ourselves. We try to escape the truth about ourselves, whereas here we are invited to stop and take a closer look. We are afraid of being changed into pillars of salt if we turn around, like Lot's wife.

The performing of this act we are referring to—self-penetration, exposure—demands a mobilization of all the physical and spiritual forces of the actor who is in a state of idle readiness, a passive availability, which makes possible an active acting score.

One must resort to a metaphorical language to say that the decisive factor in this process is humility, a spiritual predisposition: not to **do** something, but to **refrain** from doing something, otherwise the excess becomes impudence instead of sacrifice. This means that the actor must act in a state of trance.

Trance, as I understand it, is the ability to concentrate in a particular theoretical way and can be attained with a minimum of goodwill.

If I were to express all this in one sentence I would say that it is all a question of giving oneself. One must give oneself totally, in one's deepest intimacy, with confidence, as when one gives oneself in love. Here lies the key. Self-penetration, trance, **excess,** the formal discipline itself—all this can be realized, provided one has given oneself fully, humbly and without defense. This act culminates in a climax. It brings relief. None of the exercises in the various fields of the actor's training must be exercises in skill. They should develop a system of allusions which lead to the elusive and indescribable process of self-donation.

All this may sound strange and bring to mind some form of "quackery." If we are to stick to scientific formulas, we can say that it is a particular use of suggestion, aiming at an **ideoplastic** realization. Personally, I must admit that we do not shrink from using these "quack" formulas. Anything that has an unusual or magical ring stimulates the imagination of both actor and producer.

I believe one must develop a special anatomy of the actor; for instance, find the body's various centres of concentration for different ways of acting, seeking the areas of the body which the actor sometimes feels to be his sources of energy. The lumbar region, the abdomen and the area around the solar plexus often function as such a source.

An essential factor in this process is the elaboration of a guiding rein for the form, the artificiality. The actor who accomplishes an act of self-penetration is setting out on a journey which is recorded through various sound and gesture reflexes, formulating a sort of invitation to the spectator. But these signs must be articulated. Expressiveness is always connected with certain contradictions and discrepancies. Undisciplined self-penetration is no liberation, but is perceived as a form of biological chaos. . . .

self-penetration

Is the "holy" actor not a dream? The road to holiness is not open to everyone. Only the chosen few can follow it.

As I said, one must not take the word "holy" in the religious sense. It is rather a metaphor defining a person who, through his art, climbs upon the stake and performs an act of self-sacrifice. Of course, you are right: it is an infinitely difficult task to assemble a troup of "holy" actors. It is very much easier to find a "holy" spectator—in my sense of the word—for he only comes to the theatre for a brief moment in order to square off an account with himself, and this is something that does not impose the hard routine of daily work.

Is holiness therefore an unreal postulate? I think it is just as well founded as that of movement at the speed of light. By this I mean that without ever attaining it, we can nevertheless move consciously and systematically in that direction, thus achieving practical results.

Acting is a particularly thankless art. It dies with the actor. Nothing survives him but the reviews which do not usually do him justice anyway, whether he is good or bad. So the only source of satisfaction left to him is the audience's reactions. In the poor theatre this does not mean flowers and interminable applause, but a special silence in which there is much fascination but also a lot of indignation, and even repugnance, which the spectator directs not at himself but at the theatre. It is difficult to reach a psychic level which enables one to endure such pressure.

I am sure that every actor belonging to such a theatre often dreams of overwhelming ovations, of hearing his name shouted out, of being covered with flowers or other such symbols of appreciation as is customary in the commercial theatre. The actor's work is also a thankless one because of the incessant supervision it is subject to. It is not like being creative in an office, seated before a table, but under the eye of the producer who, even in a theatre based on the art of the actor, must make persistent demands on him to a much greater extent than in the normal theatre, urging him on to ever increasing efforts that are painful to him.

This would be unbearable if such a producer did not possess a moral authority, if his postulates were not evident, and if an element of mutual confidence did not exist even beyond the barriers of consciousness. But even in this case, he is nevertheless a tyrant and the actor must direct against him certain unconscious mechanical reactions like a pupil does against his teacher, a patient against his doctor, or a soldier against his superiors.

The poor theatre does not offer the actor the possibility of overnight success. It defies the bourgeois concept of a standard of living. It proposes the substitution of material wealth by moral wealth as the principal aim in life. Yet who does not cherish a secret wish to rise to sudden affluence? This too may cause opposition and negative reactions, even if these are not clearly formulated. Work in such an ensemble can never be stable. It is nothing but a huge challenge and, furthermore, it awakens such strong reactions of aversion that these often threaten the theatre's very existence. Who does not search for stability and security in one form or another? Who does not hope to live at least as well tomorrow as he does today? Even if one consciously accepts such a status, one unconsciously looks around for that unattainable refuge which reconciles fire with water and "holiness" with the life of the "courtesan."

However, the attraction of such a paradoxical situation is sufficiently strong to eliminate all the intrigues, slander and quarrels over roles which form part of everyday life in other theatres. But people will be people, and periods of depression and suppressed grudges cannot be avoided.

It is nevertheless worth mentioning that the satisfaction which such work gives is great. The actor who, in this special process of discipline and self-sacrifice, self-penetration and moulding, is not afraid to go beyond all normally acceptable limits, attains a kind of inner harmony and peace of mind. He literally becomes much sounder in mind and body, and his way of life is more normal than that of an actor in the rich theatre.

This process of analysis is a sort of disintegration of the psychic structure. Is the actor not in danger here of overstepping the mark from the point of view of mental hygiene?

No, provided that he gives himself one hundred per cent to his work. It is work that is done half-heartedly, superficially, that is psychically painful and upsets the equilibrium. If we only engage ourselves superficially in this process of analysis and exposure—and this can produce ample aesthetical effects—that is, if we retain our daily mask of lies, then we witness a conflict between this mask and ourselves. But if this process is followed through to its extreme limit, we can in full consciousness put back our everyday mask, knowing now what purpose it serves and what it conceals beneath it. This is a confirmation not of the negative in us but of the positive, not of what is poorest but of what is richest. It also leads to a liberation from complexes in much the same way as psycho-analytic therapy.

The same also applies to the spectator. The member of an audience who accepts the actor's invitation and to a certain extent follows his example by activating himself in the same way leaves the theatre in a state of greater inner harmony. But he who fights to keep his mask of lies intact at all costs leaves the performance even more confused. I am convinced that on the whole, even in the latter case, the performance represents a form of social psycho-therapy, whereas for the actor it is only a therapy if he has given himself whole-heartedly to his task.

part three

Disruption

the historical avant-garde continually manifested its subversive and disruptive nature against the status quo in art and life. Alfred Jarry's "savage" vision of the world in *Ubu Roi* threw its first audience into a long-lasting uproar; the Futurists glued spectators to their chairs and sold multiple tickets for the same seat to confront public complacency; Bertolt Brecht and Antonin Artaud aimed at disrupting the audience's social and sensory perceptions. Many social disruptions from "late capitalism," as well as consequences of the human rights movement, the Cold War, and the collapse of major political systems (such as colonialism and the Soviet empire), marked the second half of the twentieth century. "Disruption" became a critical term for scholars.

Although the post-1950 avant-garde theater (The Living Theatre and The Open Theatre, for instance) employed various kinds of politically and socially driven disruptions, the form of disruption that marks this section does not relate directly to social upheavals. Instead, disruption, imbued with self-reflexivity in the selections, is often directed at the creation of theater itself, juxtaposing purely aesthetic concerns with social and political connotations. A focus on self-examination has been part of the metatheatrical discourse for centuries; the self-reflexivity of contemporary avant-garde theater, however, differs from that of previous theatrical explorations in the overriding presence of subversive and disruptive forces that fiercely push the boundaries of theatrical and social inter-action.

The three works in this section—Peter Handke's *Offending the Audience*, Tadeusz Różewicz's *Birth Rate: The Biography of a Play for the Theatre*, and Karen Finley's *We Keep Our Victims Ready*—jolt the status quo of theatrical engagement and audience perception, questioning both theater-making and the experience of spectating. In reflecting on and redefining the nature of theater in association with life, politics, and other artistic forms, Handke, Różewicz, and Finley employ various means to disrupt the writing and performing of a theatrical work or challenge the established relationship between actor and spectator. Their works, re-examining connections among theater, communication, and authority, honor Peter Schumann's injunction that theater "must do more than protest" and shock. Reconstruction is the ultimate aim of most theatrical disruption, and in an interview in this collection, Schumann, the founder of Bread and Puppet Theatre, reflects on the importance of reaching out to an audience to prompt awareness and change.

Offending the Audience (1966) shook the international theater community with its direct, forceful attack on the audience, and the audience reaction to Handke's play was reminiscent of the public response to the premiere of Jarry's *Ubu Roi* in 1896. Examining the effect of *Offending the Audience* and its complicated production history, Piet Defraeye suggested that the unique position it holds in the annals of twentieth-century experimental theater stems perhaps from its impact rather than its content.[1] Staged by a relatively unknown young German director, Claus Peymann, at an emerging experimental theater in Frankfurt (TAT), the play captivated spectators and theater practitioners with its explosive, confrontational character, bringing the author and his production team instant notoriety. In the play's production history, the audience experience has ranged from harmless interference with actors to serious post-performance riots; the play was censored in Spain and Greece in the 1970s over fear that it would provoke political confrontations with the government.

The play proclaims its conscious theatricality from the onset, laying the groundwork for disrupting the conventions of dramatic narrative and upsetting the audience's expectations. Written in the genre that Handke labeled *Sprechstucke* (Speak-Ins), the text becomes a form of a direct public address, devoid of narrative structure, plot, settings, dialogue, and character. In his note explaining the principles of *Sprechstucke*, Handke wrote, "The speak-ins are spectacles without pictures. . . . They point to the world not by way of pictures but by way of words."[2] The four speakers onstage immediately draw attention to the presence and assigned role of the audience, announcing, "You are an audience. You form a unit. You are auditors and spectators in an auditorium."[3] The purpose of the performance is also clearly defined: "We show you nothing. We are playing no destinies. We are playing no dreams. . . . We don't tell you a story. We don't perform any actions. . . . We don't represent anything. . . . We only speak. We play by addressing you."[4] By negating the representational nature of theater and by shifting the focus from actor to spectator and from stage to auditorium, Handke makes the audience both a subject matter and an object of the theatrical event. The public address, formalized in a mixture of philosophic statements and questions about the art of spectating, gradually evolves into verbal assaults on the viewers—from political accusations to mere nonsense—that are meant to raise the audience's self-awareness.

Handke wrote that his *Sprechstucke* does not "want to revolutionize, but to make aware."[5] In *Offending the Audience*, he turns the process of raising awareness for the audience into a disruptive theatrical event that simultaneously engages, confuses, and offends the viewers, forcing them to renegotiate their relationship to stage performance and theatrical communication. Commenting on the "consciousness-raising" nature of Handke's plays, critics have drawn parallels between his public addresses and Brecht's politically minded theater.

Written during social and political unrest, *Offending the Audience* is connected to the culture of contestation and dissent of the 1960s. As Defraeye noted, this play was "an outspoken attack against the status quo of theatre at the time, and in this respect, it is part of the larger trend of the theatre of protest."[6] Moreover, while experimenting with the musicality of language and applying the principles of collage to the linguistic constructions of his public addresses (in the spirit of Dada and John Cage and perhaps in anticipation of Mac Wellman), Handke exposes his viewers to the powerful yet dangerous and contradictory nature of language. By demonstrating both the restrictiveness and pliability of language, he questions whether communication is often a means of political manipulation and authoritative control.

The intention of Różewicz's theater of disruption is to question and subvert the writing of a dramatic work. *Birth Rate*, subtitled *The Biography of a Play for the Theatre*, reflects the writer's frustration during the birth of a play, which turns into an account of his inability to complete it. The images the writer's mind created over the years "have receded or quite simply vanished without a trace, since they had not been recorded in written form."[7] The piles of research—clippings and notes, "from which the images extracted their nourishment," have disappeared or continue to lie in "mounds of paper."[8] Różewicz, a Polish poet and playwright, offers an assemblage of unfinished images and personal commentaries that replace action and dialogue. Referring to his works for theater such as *The Card File* (1960) and *The Interrupted Act* (1964), as well as *Birth Rate* (1968), Daniel Gerould wrote that Różewicz's increasing struggle to write plays "in the face of the growing impossibility of such an enterprise" led him to abandon the writing of dramatic texts and inspired him to produce "arguments with the theatre and scenarios in which playwright and performer are co-creators."[9] Indeed, *Birth Rate*, a collage of "citations and allusions"[10] as well as a series of arguments on the nature of playwriting, is not only a failed attempt to give birth to a play, but also an innovative attempt to construct an incomplete theatrical scenario.

In the opening pages, Różewicz expresses his urgent need to collaborate with the "director, designer, composer, actors . . . with the whole theatre,"[11] envisioning collaborative models to create performance texts rather than literary plays. This call to renegotiate the relationship between writer and theater artist and to re-examine the role of literary text in performance echoes U.S. avant-garde experiments of the 1960s such as Jean-Claude Van Itallie's *The Serpent* (1968), which was developed during rehearsals at the Open Theatre, coincidentally in the same year as the writing of *Birth Rate*. The collaboration that Różewicz imagines in his scenario took place a decade later in 1979, when Kazimierz Braun directed the premiere of *Birth Rate* at Teatr Współczesny, relying on Różewicz's score as the "starting point for a stunning environmental performance piece" and turning this production into "a major event in post-war Polish theatre."[12] In "Text and Performance: Envisioning Różewicz's *Birth Rate*," written for this collection, Braun outlines the creation of his production by treating Różewicz's text as a "material for theatre," the approach that allowed him to reshape the original scenario, identify various environments for the performance, and introduce the role of spectators as performers.

Różewicz's social perspectives informed his search for new dramatic genres and forms of theatrical communication. As Halina Filipowicz suggested, "The playwright's recurrent vision of severe dislocations and instability of the new post-war world" found its expression in Różewicz's theatrical works, in which [he paints terrifying, "incongruous," and "meaningless" images[13] of physical and psychological disintegration.]The shocking images of unalterable biological proliferation, "a living growing mass of mankind," are abundant in *Birth Rate*: an overcrowded train compartment or streetcar in which "the living mass is so tightly packed together that it begins to boil over"; "babes lie in tiered wagons arranged in rows like rolls in a bakery"; "the walls burst and a torrent of people pour through the cracks."[14] Post–World War II social and political disruptions required innovative theatrical language that could forge a new interaction between theater-maker and spectator and, ultimately, between theater and society.

In Finley's outrageous, borderline obscene performances, the theater of disruption takes a direction considerably more aesthetically and politically radical than Handke's provocations in *Offending the Audience*. This politically charged feminist performance artist forcefully confronts her audiences with issues of homophobia as well as the degradation and abuse of women. Using profanity and scatological references in her performances, Finley celebrates the "art of offending" to question sexual politics and disrupt norms of gender subjugation. She explores the self-conscious and self-referential nature of performance art by drawing attention to her body and subverting the category of the "beautiful nude." Her body becomes a unique artistic material—a subject of self-reflection and self-abuse, as well as an object of ugliness, humiliation, and pain.

Accused of creating indecent art, Finley found herself in the middle of the National Endowment for the Arts (NEA) controversy in 1990, when the endowment's chairman blocked funding awarded to her and three other artists. Finley and her fellow members of the "NEA Four" sued and won their case in court in 1993. ("Fear of offending," she wrote later, pervaded artistic institutions in the United States, and "we have lost our inventiveness for the sake of appearances."[15]) The performance that brought her to the center of the controversy, *We Keep Our Victims Ready*, emerged from Finley's response to the case of a sixteen-year-old African-American girl, who was discovered in a trash bag and who was covered with human feces, and the white police officers accused of raping and abusing her. The officers were acquitted, and the case quickly turned into a political dispute involving issues of gender, race, and power.

Her naked body covered with chocolate to symbolize human excrement, Finley performs the anguish and disgrace of her female characters in a society in which "the Woman is Private Property."[16] By violently disrupting the norms of performing, she moves away from merely raising the issues of gender and politics to shattering, in Britta Wheeler's words, "taboos about representations of women and sexuality." Finley's "guttural monologues emphasized incest, anal penetration, sexual obsession, the abuse of power, and an implicit assault on all accepted norms of public performance and feminine etiquette."[17] The disruptive character of Finley's art is thus both ideological and performative, attacking social norms of women's oppression as well as stage conventions of female body presentation. Finley suggested that her artistic intent was to urge audiences to go beyond disgust toward the activation of their emotional and intellectual receptors: "I think I stir people to be responsible for what's going on in their own personal lives, in their one-to-one relationships, interweaving this into the whole society's corruption. That's very disturbing."[18]

Although provocation, shock, and insult make up the driving force of the theater presented in this section, it seems that one goal of the works, however aesthetically diverse, is to transcend their initial artistic impulse to disrupt. A spirit of negation and attack, one of the major markers of the avant-garde, can transform into a more reconstructive energy in these plays. In this respect, the disruptions within echo the impulse, if not the form, of the historical avant-garde, revealing the idealistic aspirations of any artist who seeks to create new forms of theatrical communication and new levels of social engagement.

Notes

1. Piet Defraeye, "You! Hypocrite Spectateur. A Short History of the Production and Reception of Peter Handke's *Publikumsbeschimpfung*," *A Journal of Germanic Studies* 42.2 (2006): 413.

2. Peter Handke, "Note on Offending the Audience and Self-Accusation" in *Collected Plays* (London: Methuen), 1997, ix.

3. Handke, *Offending the Audience*, 201 below in this volume.

4. Ibid., 202.

5. Handke, "Note on Offending the Audience," ix.

6. Defraeye, "You! Hypocrite Spectateur," 417.

7. Różewicz, *Birth Rate*, 219 in this volume.

8. Ibid.

9. Daniel Gerould, "Tadeusz Różewicz: Playwriting as Collage," *Performing Arts Journal* 1.2 (1976): 64.

10. Ibid., 65.

11. Różewicz, *Birth Rate*, 218.

12. Halina Filipowicz, "Theatrical Reality in the Plays of Tadeusz Różewicz," *The Slavic and East European Journal* 26.4 (1982): 453.

13. Ibid., 452.

14. Różewicz, *Birth Rate*, 218–20.

15. Karen Finley, "The Art of Offending," *New York Times*, November 14, 1996.

16. Finley, *We Keep Our Victims Ready*, 231 in this volume.

17. Britta Wheeler, "The Institutionalization of an American Avant-Garde: Performance Art as Democratic Culture, 1970–2000," *Sociological Perspectives* 46.4 (2003): 501.

18. Finley, quoted in Theodore Shank, *Beyond the Boundaries: American Alternative Theatre* (Ann Arbor: University of Michigan Press, 2002), 202.

Offending the Audience

Peter Handke

CAST: FOUR SPEAKERS ✔

Rules for the actors

Listen to the litanies in the Catholic churches.

Listen to football teams being cheered on and booed.

Listen to the rhythmic chanting at demonstrations.

Listen to the wheels of a bicycle upturned on its seat spinning until the spokes have come to rest and watch the spokes until they have reached their resting point.

Listen to the gradually increasing noise a concrete mixer makes after the motor has been started.

Listen to debaters cutting each other off.

Listen to 'Tell Me' by the Rolling Stones.

Listen to the simultaneous arrival and departure of trains.

Listen to the hit parade on Radio Luxembourg.

Listen in on the simultaneous interpreters at the United Nations.

Listen to the dialogue between the gangster (Lee J. Cobb) and the pretty girl in 'The Trap', when the girl asks the gangster how many more people he intends to kill; whereupon the gangster asks, as he leans back, How many are left? and watch the gangster as he says it.

See the Beatles' movies.

Reprinted from *Kaspar and Other Plays* by Peter Handke, trans. Michael Roloff. Translation copyright © 1970 by Farrar, Straus and Giroux, LLC. Reprinted by permission of Farrar, Straus and Giroux, LLC.

In 'A Hard Day's Night' watch Ringo's smile at the moment when, after having been teased by the others, he sits down at his drums and begins to play.

Watch Gary Cooper's face in 'The Man From the West'. In the same movie watch the death of the mute as he runs down the deserted street of the lifeless town with a bullet in him, hopping and jumping and emitting those shrill screams.

Watch monkeys aping people and llamas spitting in the zoo.

Watch the behaviour of tramps and idlers as they amble on the street and play the machines in the penny arcades.

When the theatregoers enter the room into which they are meant to go, they are greeted by the usual pre-performance atmosphere. One might let them hear noises from behind the curtain, noises that make believe that scenery is being shifted about. For example, a table is dragged across the stage, or several chairs are noisily set up and then removed. One might let the spectators in the first few rows hear directions whispered by make-believe stage managers and the whispered interchanges between make-believe stagehands behind the curtain. Or, even better, use tape recordings of other performances in which, before the curtain rises, objects are really shifted about. These noises should be amplified to make them more audible, and perhaps should be stylized and arranged so as to produce their own order and uniformity.

The usual theatre atmosphere should prevail. The ushers should be more assiduous than usual, even more formal and ceremonious, should subdue their usual whispering with even more style, so that their behaviour becomes infectious. The programmes should be elegant. The bell signals should not be forgotten; the signals are repeated at successively briefer intervals. The gradual dimming of the lights should be even more gradual if possible; perhaps the lights can be dimmed in successive stages. As the ushers proceed to close the doors, their gestures should become particularly solemn and noticeable. Yet, they are only ushers. Their actions should not appear symbolic. Latecomers should not be admitted. Inappropriately dressed ticket holders should not be admitted. The concept of what is sartorially inappropriate should be strictly applied. None of the spectators should call attention to himself or offend the eye by his attire. The men should be dressed in dark jackets, with white shirts and inconspicuous ties. The women should shun bright colours.

There is no standing-room. Once the doors are closed and the lights dim, it gradually becomes quiet behind the curtain too. The silence behind the curtain and the silence in the auditorium are alike. The spectators stare a while longer at the almost imperceptibly fluttering curtain, which may perhaps billow once or twice as though someone had hurriedly crossed the stage. Then the curtain grows still. There is a short pause. The curtain slowly rises, allowing an unobstructed view. Once the stage is completely open to view, the four speakers step forward from upstage. Nothing impedes their progress. The stage is empty. As they walk forward non-committally, dressed casually, it becomes light on stage as well as in the audience. The light on stage and in the auditorium is of the same intensity as at the end of a performance and there is no glare to hurt the eyes. The stage and the auditorium remain lighted throughout the performance. Even as they approach, the speakers don't look at the audience. They don't direct the words they are speaking at the audience. Under no circumstance should the audience get the impression that the words are directed at them. As far as the speakers are concerned, the audience does not yet exist. As they approach, they move their lips. Gradually their words became intelligible and finally they become loud. The invectives they deliver overlap one another. The speakers speak pell-mell. They pick up each other's words. They take words out of each other's mouths. They speak in unison, each uttering different words. They repeat. They grow louder. They scream. They pass rehearsed words from mouth to mouth. Finally, they rehearse one word in unison. The words they use in this prologue are the following (their order is immaterial): You chuckle-heads, you small-timers, you nervous nellies, you fuddy-duddies, you windbags, you sitting ducks, you milksops. *The speakers should strive for a certain acoustic uniformity. However, except for the acoustic pattern, no other picture should be produced. The invectives are not directed at anyone in particular. The manner of their delivery should not induce a meaning. The speakers reach the front of the stage before they finish rehearsing their invectives. They stand at ease but form a sort of pattern. They are not completely fixed in their positions but move according to the movement which the words they speak lend them. They now look at the public, but at no one person in particular. They are silent for a while. They collect themselves. Then they begin to speak. The order in which they speak is immaterial. The speakers have roughly the same amount of work to do.*

You are welcome.

This piece is a prologue.

You will hear nothing you have not heard here before.
You will see nothing you have not seen here before.
You will see nothing of what you have always seen here.
You will hear nothing of what you have always heard here.

You will hear what you usually see.
You will hear what you usually don't see.
You will see no spectacle.
Your curiosity will not be satisfied.
You will see no play.
There will be no playing here tonight.
You will see a spectacle without pictures.

You expected something.
You expected something else perhaps.

You expected objects.
You expected no objects.
You expected an atmosphere.
You expected a different world.
You expected no different world.
In any case, you expected something.
It may be the case that you expected what you are hearing now.
But even in that case you expected something different.

You are sitting in rows. You form a pattern. You are sitting in a certain order. You are facing in a certain direction. You are sitting equidistant from one another. You are an audience. You form a unit. You are auditors and specta-tors in an auditorium. Your thoughts are free. You can still make up your own mind. You see us speaking and you hear us speaking. You are beginning to breathe in one and the same rhythm. You are beginning to breathe in one and the same rhythm in which we are speaking. You are breathing the way we are speaking. We and you gradually form a unit.

You are not thinking. You don't think of anything. You are thinking along. You are not thinking along. You feel uninhibited. Your thoughts are free. Even as we say that, we insinuate ourselves into your thoughts. You have thoughts in the back of your mind. Even as we say that, we insinuate our-selves into the thoughts in the back of your mind. You are thinking along. You are hearing. Your thoughts are following in the track of our thoughts. Your thoughts are not following in the track of our thoughts. You are not thinking. Your thoughts are not free. You feel inhibited.

You are looking at us when we speak to you. You are not watching us. You are looking at us. You are being looked at. You are unprotected. You no longer have the advantage of looking from the shelter of darkness into the light. We no longer have the disadvantage of looking through the blinding light into the dark. You are not watching. You are looking at and you are being looked at. In this way, we and you gradually form a unit. Under certain conditions, therefore, we, instead of saying *you*, could say *we*. We are under one and the same roof. We are a closed society.

You are not listening to us. You heed us. You are no longer eavesdropping from behind a wall. We are speaking directly to you. Our dialogue no longer moves at right angles to your glance. Your glance no longer pierces our dialogue. Our words and your glances no longer form an angle. You are not disregarded. You are not treated as mere hecklers. You need not form an opinion from a bird's or a frog's perspective of anything that happens here. You need not play referee. You are no longer treated as spectators to whom we can speak in asides. This is no play. There are no asides here. Nothing that takes place here is intended as an appeal to you. This is no play. We don't step out of the play to address you. We have no need of illusions to disillusion you. We show you nothing. We are playing no destinies. We are playing no dreams. This is not a factual report. This is no documentary play. This is no slice of life. We don't tell you a story. We don't perform any actions. We don't simulate any actions. We don't represent anything. We don't put anything on for you. We only speak. We play by addressing you. When we say we, we may also mean you. We are not acting out your situation. You cannot recognize yourselves in us. We are playing no situation. You need not feel that we mean you. You cannot feel that we mean you. No mirror is being held up to you. We don't mean you. We are addressing you. You are being addressed. You will be addressed. You will be bored if you don't want to be addressed.

You are sharing no experience. You are not sharing. You are not following suit. You are experiencing no intrigues here. You are experiencing nothing. You are not imagining anything. You don't have to imagine anything. You need no prerequisites. You don't need to know that this is a stage. You need no expectations. You need not lean back expectantly. You don't need to know that this is only playing. We make up no stories. You are not following an event. You are not playing along. You are being played with here. That is a wordplay.

What is the theatre's is not rendered unto the theatre here. Here you don't receive your due. Your curiosity is not satisfied. No spark will leap across from us to you. You will not be electrified. These boards don't signify a world. They are part of the world. These boards exist for us to stand on. This world is no different from yours. You are no longer eavesdroppers. You are the subject matter. The focus is on you. You are in the crossfire of our words.

This is no mirage. You don't see walls that tremble. You don't hear the spurious sounds of doors snapping shut. You hear no sofas squeaking. You see no apparitions. You have no visions. You see no picture of something. Nor do you see the suggestion of a picture. You see no picture puzzle. Nor do you see an empty picture. The emptiness of this stage is no picture of another emptiness. The emptiness of this stage signifies nothing. This stage is empty because objects would be in our way. It is empty because we don't need objects. This stage represents nothing. It represents no other emptiness. This stage *is* empty. You don't see any objects that pretend to be other objects. You don't see a darkness that pretends to be another darkness. You don't see a brightness that pretends to be another brightness. You don't see any light that pretends to be another light. You don't hear any noise that pretends to be another noise. You don't see a room that pretends to be another room. Here you are not experiencing a time that pretends to be another time. The time on stage is no different from the time off stage. We have the same local time here. We are in the same location. We are breathing the same air. The front of the stage is not a line of demarcation. It is not only sometimes no demarcation line. It is no demarcation line as long as we are speaking to you. There is no invisible circle here. There is no magic circle. There is no room for play here. We are not playing. We are all in the same room. The demarcation line has not been penetrated, it is not previous, it doesn't even exist. There is no radiation belt between you and us. We are not self-propelled stage props. We are no pictures of something. We are no representatives. We represent nothing. We demonstrate nothing. We

202 ◆◆ HANDKE

have no pseudonyms. Our heartbeat does not pretend to be another's heartbeat. Our bloodcurdling screams don't pretend to be another's bloodcurdling screams. We don't step out of our roles. We have no roles. We are ourselves. We are the mouthpiece of the author. You cannot make yourself a picture of us. You don't need to make yourself a picture of us. We are ourselves. Our opinion and the author's opinion are not necessarily the same.

The light that illuminates us signifies nothing. Neither do the clothes we ear signify anything. They indicate nothing, they are not unusual in any way, they signify nothing. They signify no other time to you, no other climate, no other season, no other degree of latitude, no other reason to wear them. They have no function. Nor do our gestures have a function, that is, to signify something to you. This is not the world as a stage.

We are no slapstick comedians. There are no objects here that we might trip over. Insidious objects are not on the programme. Insidious objects are not part of the play because we are not playing with them. The objects are not intended to be insidious; they are insidious. If we happen to trip, we trip unwittingly. Unwitting as well are mistakes in dress; unwitting, too, are our perhaps foolish faces. Slips of the tongue, which amuse you, are not intended. If we stutter, we stutter without meaning to. We cannot make dropping a handkerchief part of the play. We are not playing. We cannot make the insidiousness of objects part of the play. We cannot camouflage the insidiousness of objects. We cannot be of two minds. We cannot be of many minds. We are no clowns. We are not in the ring. You don't have the pleasure of encircling us. You are not enjoying the comedy of having a rear view of us. You are not enjoying the comedy of insidious objects. You are enjoying the comedy of words.

The possibilities of the theatre are not exploited here. The realm of possibilities is not exhausted. The theatre is not unbounded. The theatre is bound. Fate is meant ironically here. We are not theatrical. Our comedy is not overwhelming. Your laughter cannot be liberating. We are not playful. We are not playing a world for you. This is not half of one world. We and you do not constitute two halves.

You are the subject matter. You are the centre of interest. No actions are performed here, you are being acted upon. That is no wordplay. You are not treated as individuals here. You don't become individuals here. You have no individual traits. You have no distinctive physiognomies. You are not individuals here. You have no characteristics. You have no destiny. You have no history. You have no past. You are on no wanted list. You have no experience of life. You have the experience of the theatre here. You have that certain something. You are playgoers. You are of no interest because of your capacities. You are of interest solely in your capacity as playgoers. As playgoers you form a pattern here. You are no personalities. You are not singular. You are a plurality of persons. Your faces point in one direction. You are an event. You are *the* event.

You are under review by us. But you form no picture. You are not symbolic. You are an ornament. You are a pattern. You have features that everyone here has. You have general features. You are a species. You form a pattern. You are doing and you are not doing the same thing: you are looking in one direction. You don't stand up and look in different directions. You are a standard pattern and you have a pattern as a standard. You have a standard with which you came to the theatre. You have the standard idea that where we are is up and where you are is down. You have the standard idea of two worlds. You have the standard idea of the world of the theatre.

You don't need this standard now. You are not attending a piece for the theatre. You are not attending. You are the focal point. You are in the crossfire. You are being inflamed. You can catch fire. You don't need a standard. You are the standard. You have been discovered. You are the discovery of the evening. You inflame us. Our words catch fire on you. From you a spark leaps across to us.

This room does not make believe it is a room. The side that is open to you is not the fourth wall of a house. The world does not have to be cut open here. You don't see any doors here. You don't see the two doors of the old dramas. You don't see the back door through which he who shouldn't be seen can slip out. You don't see the front door through which he who wants to see him who shouldn't be seen enters. There is no back door. Neither is there a non-existent door as in modern drama. The non-existent door does not represent a non-existent door. This is not another world. We are not pretending that you don't exist. You are not thin air for us. You are of crucial importance to us because you exist. We are speaking to you because you exist. If you did not exist, we would be speaking to thin air. Your existence is not simply taken for granted. You don't watch us though a keyhole. We don't pretend that we are alone in the world. We don't explain ourselves to ourselves only in order to put you in the know. We are not conducting an exhibition purely for the benefit of your enlightenment. We need no artifice to enlighten you. We need no tricks. We don't have to be theatrically effective. We have no entrances, we have no exits, we don't talk to you in asides. We are putting nothing over on you. We are not about to enter into a dialogue. We are not in a dialogue. Nor are we in a dialogue with you. We have no wish to enter into a dialogue with you. You are not in collusion with us. You are not eyewitnesses to an event. We are not taunting you. You don't have to be apathetic any more. You don't have to watch inactively any more. No actions take place here. You feel the discomfort of being watched and addressed, since you came prepared to watch and make yourselves comfortable in the shelter of the dark. Your presence is every moment explicitly acknowledged with every one of our words. Your presence is the topic we deal with from one breath to the next, from one moment to the next, from one word to the next. Your standard idea of the theatre is no longer presupposed as the basis of our actions. You are neither condemned to watch nor free to watch. You are the subject. You are the play-makers. You are the counterplotters. You are being aimed at. You are the target of our words. You serve as targets. That is a metaphor. You serve as the target of our metaphors. You serve as metaphors.

Of the two poles here, you are the pole at rest. You are in an arrested state. You find yourselves in a state of expectation. You are no subjects. You are objects here. You are the objects of our words. Still, you are subjects too.

There are no intervals here. The intervals between words lack significance. Here the unspoken word lacks significance. There are no unspoken words here. Our silences say nothing. There is no deafening silence. There is no silent silence. There is no deathly quiet. Speech is not used to create silence here. This play includes no direction telling us to be silent. We make no artificial pauses. Our pauses are natural pauses. Our pauses are not eloquent like speech. We say nothing with our silence. No abyss opens up between words. You cannot read anything between our lines. You cannot read anything in our faces. Our gestures express nothing of consequence to anything. What is inexpressible is not said through silences here. Glances and gestures are not eloquent here. Becoming silent and being silent is no artifice here. There are no silent letters here. There's only the mute *h*. That is a pun.

You have made up your minds now. You have recognized that we negate something. You have recognized that we repeat ourselves. You have recognized that we contradict ourselves. You have recognized that this piece is conducting an argument with the theatre. You have recognized the dialectical structure of the piece. You have recognized a certain spirit of contrariness. The intention of the piece has become clear to you. You have recognized that we primarily negate. You have recognized that we repeat ourselves. You recognize. You see through. You have not made up your minds. You have not seen through the dialectical structure of the piece. Now you are seeing through. Your thoughts were one thought too slow. Now you have thoughts in the back of your mind.

You look charming. You look enchanting. You look dazzling. You look breathtaking. You look unique.

But you don't make an evening. You're not a brilliant idea. You are tiresome. You are not a rewarding subject. You are a theatrical blunder. You are not true to life. You are not theatrically effective. You don't send us. You don't enchant us. You don't dazzle us. You don't entertain us fabulously. You are not playful. You are not sprightly. You have no tricks up your sleeve. You have no flair for the theatre. You have nothing to say. Your début is unconvincing. You are not with it. You don't help us pass the time. You are not addressing the human quality in us. You leave us cold.

This is no drama. No action that has occurred elsewhere is reenacted here. Only a now and a now and a now exist here. This is no make-believe which re-enacts an action that really happened once upon a time. Time plays no role here. We are not acting out a plot. Therefore we are not playing time.

Time is for real here, it expires from one word to the next. Time flies in the words here. It is not alleged that time can be repeated here. No play can be repeated here and play at the same time it did once upon a time. The time here is *your* time. Space time here is your space time. Here you can compare your time with our time. Time is no noose. That is no make-believe. It is not alleged here that time can be repeated. The umbilical cord connecting you to your time is not severed here. Time is not at play here. We mean business with time here. It is admitted here that time expires from one word to the next. It is admitted that this is *your* time here. You can check the time here on your watches. No other time governs here. The time that governs here is measured against your breath. Time conforms to your wishes here. We measure time by your breath, by the batting of your eyelashes, by your pulsebeats, by the growth of your cells. Time expires here from moment to moment. Time is measured in moments. Time is measured in your moments. Time goes through your stomach. Time here is not repeatable as in the make-believe of a theatre performance. This is no performance: you have not to imagine anything. Time is no noose here. Time is not cut off from the outside world here. There are no two levels of time here. There are no two worlds here. While we are here, the earth continues to turn. Our time up here is your time down there. It expires from one word to the next. It expires while we, we and you, are breathing, while our hair is growing, while we are sweating, while we are smelling, while we are hearing. Time is not repeatable even if we repeat our words, even if we mention again that our time is your time, that it expires from one word to the next, while we, we and you, are breathing, while our hair is growing, while we sweat, while we smell, while we hear. We cannot repeat anything, time is expiring. It is unrepeatable. Each moment is historical. Each of your moments is a historical moment. We cannot say our words twice. This is no make-believe. We cannot do the same thing once again. We cannot repeat the same gestures. We cannot speak the same way. Time expires on our lips. Time is unrepeatable. Time is no noose. That is no make-believe. The past is not made contemporaneous. The past is dead and buried. We need no puppet to embody a dead time. This is no puppet show. This is no nonsense. This is no play. This is no sense. You recognize the contradiction. Time here serves the wordplay.

This is no manœuvre. This is no exercise for the emergency. No one has to play dead here. No one has to pretend he is alive. Nothing is posited here. The number of wounded is not prescribed. The result is not predetermined on paper. There is no result here. No one has to present himself here. We don't represent except what we are. We don't represent ourselves in a state other than the one we are in now and here. This is no manœuvre. We are not playing ourselves in different situations. We are not thinking of the emergency. We don't have to represent our death. We don't have to represent our life. We don't play ahead of time what and how we will be. We make no future contemporaneous in our play. We don't represent another time. We don't represent the emergency. We are speaking while time expires. We speak of the expiration of time. We are not acting as if. We are not acting as if we could repeat time or as if we could anticipate time. This is neither make-believe nor a manœuvre. On the other hand we do act as if. We act as if we could repeat words. We appear to repeat ourselves. Here is the world of appearances. Here appearance is appearance. Appearance is here appearance.

You represent something. You are someone. You are something. You are not someone here but something. You are a society that represents an order. You are a theatre society of sorts. You are an order because of your kind of dress, the position of your bodies, the direction of your glances. The colour of your clothes clashes with the colour of your seating arrangement. You also form an order with the seating arrangement. You are dressed up With your dress you observe an order. You dress up. By dressing up, you demonstrate that you are doing something that you don't do every day. You are putting on a masquerade so as to partake of a masquerade. You partake. You watch. You stare. By watching, you become rigid. The seating arrangement favours this development. You are something that watches. You need room for your eyes. If the curtain comes down, you gradually become claustrophobic. You have no vantage point. You feel encircled. You feel inhibited. The rising of the curtain merely relieves your claustrophobia. Thus it relieves you. You can watch. Your view is unobstructed. You become uninhibited. You can partake. You are not in dead centre as when the curtain is closed. You are no longer someone. You become something. You are no longer alone with yourselves. You are no longer left to your own devices. Now you are with it. You are an audience. That is a relief. You can partake.

Up here there is no order now. There are no objects that demonstrate an order to you. The world here is neither sound nor unsound. This is no world. Stage props are out of place here. Their positions are not chalked out on the stage. Since they are not chalked out, there is no order here. There are no chalk marks for the standpoint of things. There are no memory props for the standpoint of persons. In contrast to you and your seating arrangement, nothing is in its place here. Things here have no fixed places like the places of your setting arrangements down there. This stage is no world, just as the world is no stage.

Nor does each thing have its own time here. No thing has its own time here. No thing has its fixed time here when it serves as a prop or when it becomes an obstacle. We don't act as if things were really used. Here things *are* useful.

You are not standing. You are using the seating arrangements. You are sitting. Since your seating arrangements form a pattern, you form a pattern as well. There is no standing-room. People enjoy art more effectively when they sit than if they stand. That is why you are sitting. You are friendlier when you sit. You are more receptive. You are more open-minded. You are more long-suffering. Sitting, you are more relaxed. You are more democratic. You are less bored. Time seems less long and boring to you. You allow more to happen to you. You are more clairvoyant. You are less distracted. It is easier for you to forget your surroundings. The world around you disappears more easily. You begin to resemble one another more. You begin to lose your personal qualities. You begin to lose the characteristics that distinguish you from each other. You become a unit. You become a pattern. You become one. You lose your self-consciousness. You become spectators. You become auditors. You become apathetic. You become all eyes and ears. You forget to look at your watch. You forget yourself.

Standing, you would be more effective hecklers. In view of the anatomy of the human body, your heckling would be louder if you stood. You would be better able to clench your fists. You could show your opposition better. You would have greater mobility. You would not need to be as well-behaved. You could shift your weight from one foot to the other. You could more easily become conscious of your body. Your enjoyment of art would be diminished. You would no longer form a pattern. You would no longer be rigid. You would lose your geometry. You would be better able to smell the sweat of the bodies near you. You would be better able to express agreement by nudging each other. If you stood, the sluggishness of your bodies would not keep you from walking. Standing, you would be more individual. You would oppose the theatre more resolutely. You would give in to fewer illusions. You would suffer more from absentmindedness. You would stand more on the outside. You would be better able to leave yourself to your own devices. You would be less able to imagine represented events as real. The events here would seem less true to life to you. Standing, for example, you would be less able to imagine a death represented on this stage as real. You would be less rigid. You wouldn't let yourself be put under as much of a spell. You wouldn't let as much be put over on you. You wouldn't be satisfied to be mere spectators. It would be easier for you to be of two minds. You could be at two places at once with your thoughts. You could live in two space-time continuums.

We don't want to infect you. We don't want to goad you into a show of feelings. We don't play feelings. We don't embody feelings. We neither laugh nor weep. We don't want to infect you with laughter by laughing or with weeping by laughing or with laughter by weeping or with weeping by weeping. Although laughter is more infectious than weeping, we don't infect you with laughter by laughing. And so forth. We are not playing. We play nothing. We don't modulate. We don't gesticulate. We express ourselves by no means but words. We only speak. We express. We don't express ourselves but the opinion of the author. We express ourselves by speaking. Our speaking is our acting. By speaking, we become theatrical. We are theatrical because we are speaking in a theatre. By always speaking directly to you and by speaking to you of time, of now and of now and of now, we observe the unity of time, place and action. But we observe this unity not only here on stage. Since the stage is no world unto itself, we also observe the unity down where you are.

We and you form a unity because we speak directly to you without interruption. Therefore, under certain conditions, we, instead of saying you, could say we. That signifies the unity of action. The stage up here and the auditorium constitute a unity in that they no longer constitute two levels. There is no radiation belt between us. There are no two places here. Here is only one place. That signifies the unity of place. Your time, the time of the spectators and auditors, and our time, the time of the speakers, form a unity in that no other time passes here than your time. Time is not bisected here into played time and play time. Time is not played here. Only real time exists here. Only the time that we, we and you, experience ourselves in our own bodies exists here. Only one time exists here. That signifies the unity of time. All three cited circumstances, taken together, signify the unity of time, place and action. Therefore this piece is classical.

Because we speak to you, you can become conscious of yourself. Because we speak to you, your self-awareness increases. You become aware that you are sitting. You become aware that you are sitting in the theatre. You become aware of the size of your limbs. You become aware of how your limbs are situated. You become aware of your fingers. You become aware of your tongue. You become aware of your throat. You become aware how heavy your head is. You become aware of your sex organs. You become aware of batting your eyelids. You become aware of the muscles with which you swallow. You become aware of the flow of your saliva. You become aware of the beating of your heart. You become aware of raising your eyebrows. You become aware of a prickling sensation on your scalp. You become aware of the impulse to scratch yourself. You become aware of sweating under your armpits. You become aware of your sweaty hands. You become aware of your parched hands. You become aware of the air you are inhaling and exhaling though your mouth and nose. You become aware of our words entering your ears. You acquire presence of mind.

Try not to blink your eyelids. Try not to swallow any more. Try not to move your tongue. Try not to hear anything. Try not to smell anything. Try not to salivate. Try not to sweat. Try not to shift in your seat. Try not to breathe.

Why, you are breathing. Why, you are salivating. Why, you are listening. Why, you are smelling. Why, you are swallowing. Why, you are blinking your eyelids. Why, you are belching. Why, you are sweating. Why, how terribly self-conscious you are.

Don't blink. Don't salivate. Don't bat your eyelashes. Don't inhale. Don't exhale. Don't shift in your seat. Don't listen to us. Don't smell. Don't swallow. Hold your breath.

Swallow. Salivate. Blink. Listen. Breathe.

You are now aware of your presence. You know that it is *your* time that you are spending here. *You* are the topic. You tie the knot. You untie the knot. You are the centre. You are the occasion. You are the reasons why. You provide the initial impulse. You provide us with words here. You are the playmakers and the counterplotters. You are the young comedians. You are the enchanted lovers, you are the ingénues, you are the sentimentalists. You are the grandes dames, you are the character actors, you are the bon vivants and the heroes. You are the heroes and the villains of this piece.

Before you came here, you made certain preparations. You came here with certain preconceptions. You went to the theatre. You prepared yourself to go to the theatre. You had certain expectations. Your thoughts were one step ahead of time. You imagined something. You prepared yourself for something. You prepared yourself to partake in something. You prepared yourself to be seated, to sit on the rented seat and to attend something. Perhaps you had heard of this piece. So you made preparations, you prepared yourself for something. You let events come toward you. You were prepared to sit and have something shown to you.

The rhythm you breathed in was different from ours. You went about dressing yourself in a different manner. You got started in a different way. You approached this location from different directions. You used the public transport system. You came on foot. You came by cab. You used your own means of transport. Before you got under way, you looked at your watch. You expected a telephone call, you picked up the receiver, you turned on the lights, you turned out the lights, you closed doors, you turned keys, you stepped out into the open. You propelled your legs. You let your arms swing up and down as you walked. You walked. You walked from different directions all in the same direction. You found your way here with the help of your sense of direction.

Because of your intention you distinguished yourselves from others who were on their way to other locations. Simply because of your intention, you instantly formed a unit with the others who were on their way to this location. You had the same objective. You planned to spend a part of your future together with others at a definite time.

You crossed traffic lanes. You looked left and right. You observed traffic signals. You nodded to others. You stopped. You informed others of your destination. You told of your expectations. You communicated your speculations about this piece. You expressed your opinion of this piece. You shook hands. You had others wish you a pleasant evening. You took off your shoes. You held doors open. You had doors held open for you. You met other theatre-goers. You felt like conspirators. You observed the rules of good behaviour. You helped out of coats. You left yourselves be helped out of coats. You stood around. You walked around. You heard the bells. You grew restless. You looked in the mirror. You checked your make-up. You threw sidelong glances. You noticed sidelong glances. You walked. You paced. Your movements became more formal. You heard the bell. You looked at your watch. You became conspirators. You took your seat. You took a look around. You made yourself comfortable. You heard the bell. You stopped chatting. You aligned your glances. You raised your heads. You took a deep breath. You saw the lights dim. You became silent. You heard the doors closing. You stared at the curtain. You waited. You became rigid. You did not move any more. Instead, the curtain moved. You heard the curtain rustling. You were offered an unobstructed view of the stage. Everything was as it always is. Your expectations were not disappointed. You were ready. You leaned back in your seat. The play could begin.

At other times you were also ready. You were on to the game that was being played. You leaned back in your seats. You perceived. You followed. You pursued. You let happen. You let something happen up here that had happened long ago. You watched the past which by means of dialogue and monologue made believe it was contemporaneous. You let yourselves be captivated. You let yourselves become spellbound. You forgot where you were. You forgot the time. You became rigid and remained rigid. You did not move. You did not act. You did not even come up front to see better. You followed no natural impulses. You watched as you watch a beam of light that was produced long before you began to watch. You looked into dead space. You looked at dead points. You experienced a dead time. You heard a dead language. You yourselves were in a dead room in a dead time. It was dead calm. No breath of air moved. You did not move. You stared. The distance between you and us was infinite. We were infinitely far away from you. We moved at an infinite distance from you. We had lived infinitely long before you. We lived up here on the stage before the beginning of time. Your glances and our glances met in infinity. An infinite space was between us. We played. But we did not play with you. You were always posterity here.

Plays were played here. Sense was played here. Nonsense with meaning was played here. The plays here had a background and an underground. They had a false bottom. They were not what they were. They were not what they seemed. There was something behind them. The things and the plot seemed to be, but they were not. They seemed to be as they seemed, but they were different. They did not seem to seem as in a pure play, they seemed to be. They seemed to be reality. The plays here did not pass the time, or they did not only pass the time. They had meaning. They were not timeless like the pure plays, an unreal time passed in them. The conspicuous meaninglessness of some plays was precisely what represented their hidden meaning. Even the pranks of pranksters acquired meaning on these boards. Always something lay in wait. Always something lay in ambush between the words, gestures and props and sought to mean something to you. Always something had two or more meanings. Something was always happening. Something happened in the play that you were supposed to think was real. Stories always happened. A played and unreal time happened. What you saw and heard was supposed to be not only what you saw and heard. It was supposed to be what you did not see and did not hear. Everything was meant. Everything expressed. Even what pretended to express nothing expressed something because something that happens in the theatre expresses something. Everything that was played expressed something real. The play was not played for the play's sake but for the sake of reality. You were to discover a played reality behind the play. You were supposed to fathom the play. Not a play, reality was played. Time was played. Since time was played, reality was played. The theatre played tribunal. The theatre played circus ring. The theatre played moral institution. The theatre played dreams. The theatre played tribal rites. The theatre played mirrors for you. The play exceeded the play. It hinted at reality. It became impure. It meant. Instead of time staying out of play, an unreal and uneffective time transpired. With the unreal time an unreal reality was played. It was not there, it was only signified to you, it was performed. Neither reality nor play transpired here. If a pure play had been played here, time could have been left out of play. A pure play has no time. But since a reality was played, the corresponding time was also played. If a pure play had been played here, there would have been only the time of the spectators here. But since reality was part of the play here, there were always two times: your time, the time of the spectators, and the played time, which seemed to be the real time. But time cannot be played. It cannot be repeated in any play. Time is irretrievable. Time is irresistible. Time is unplayable. Time is real. It cannot be played as real. Since time cannot be played, reality cannot be played either. Only a play where time is left out of play is a play. A play in which time plays a role is no play. Only a timeless play is without meaning. Only a timeless play is self-sufficient. Only a timeless play does not need to *play* time. Only for a timeless play is time without meaning. All other plays are impure plays. There are only plays without time, or plays in which time is real time, like the sixty minutes of a football game, which has only one time because the time of the players is the same time as that of the spectators. All other plays are sham plays. All other plays mirror meretricious facts for you. A timeless play mirrors no facts.

We could do a play within a play for you. We could act out happenings for you that are taking place outside this room during these moments while you are swallowing, while you are batting your eyelashes. We could illustrate the statistics. We could represent what is statistically taking place at other places while you are at this place. By representing what is happening, we could make you imagine these happenings. We could bring them closer to you. We would not need to represent anything that is past. We could play a pure play. For example, we could act out the very process of dying that is statistically happening somewhere at this moment. We could become full of pathos. We could declare that death is the pathos of time, of which we speak all the time. Death could be the pathos of this real time which you are wasting here. At the very least, this play within a play would help bring this piece to a dramatic climax.

But we are not putting anything over on you. We don't imitate. We don't represent any other persons and any other events, even if they statistically exist. We can do without a play of features and a play of gestures. There are no persons who are part of the plot and therefore no impersonators. The plot is not freely invented, for there is no plot. Since there is no plot, accidents are impossible. Similarity with still living or scarcely dead or long-dead persons is not accidental but impossible. For we don't represent anything and are no others than we are. We don't even play ourselves. We are speaking. Nothing is invented here. Nothing is imitated. Nothing is fact. Nothing is left to your imagination.

Owing to the fact that we are not playing and not acting playfully, this piece is half as funny and half as tragic. Owing to the fact that we only speak and don't fall outside time, we cannot depict anything for you and demonstrate nothing for you. We illustrate nothing. We conjure up nothing out of the past. We are not in conflict with the past. We are not in conflict with the present. We don't anticipate the future. In the present, the past, and the future, we speak of time.

That is why, for example, we cannot represent the now and now of dying that is statistically happening now. We cannot represent the gasping for breath that is happening now and now, or the tumbling and falling now, or the death throes, or the grinding of teeth now, or the last words, or the last sigh now, that is statistically happening now this very second, or the last exhalation, or the last ejaculation that is happening now, or the breathlessness that is statistically commencing now, and now, and now, and now, and so on, or the motionlessness now, or the statistically ascertainable rigor mortis, or the lying absolutely quiet now. We cannot represent it. We only speak of it. We are speaking of it *now*.

Owing to the fact that we only speak and owing to the fact that we don't speak of anything invented, we cannot be equivocal or ambiguous. Owing to the fact that we play nothing, there cannot exist two or more levels here or a play within a play. Owing to the fact that we don't gesticulate and don't tell you any stories and don't represent anything, we cannot be poetical. Owing to the fact that we only speak to you, we lose the poetry of ambiguity. For example, we cannot use the gestures and expressions of dying that we mentioned to represent the gestures and expressions of a simultaneously transpiring instance of sexual intercourse that is statistically transpiring now. We can't be equivocal. We cannot play on a false bottom. We cannot remove ourselves from the world. We don't need to be poetic. We don't need to hypnotize you. We don't need to hoodwink you. We don't need to cast an evil eye on you. We don't need a second nature. This is no hypnosis. You don't have to imagine anything. You don't have to dream with open eyes. With the illogic of your dreams you are not dependent on the logic of the stage. The impossibilities of your dreams do not have to confine themselves to the possibilities of the stage. The absurdity of your dreams does not have to obey the authentic laws of the theatre. Therefore we represent neither dreams nor reality. We make claims neither for life nor for dying, neither for society nor for the individual, neither for what is natural nor for what is supernatural, neither for lust nor for grief, neither for reality nor for the play. Time elicits no elegies from us.

This piece is a prologue. It is not the prologue to another piece but the prologue to what you did, what you are doing, and what you will do. You are the topic. This piece is the prologue to the topic. It is the prologue to your practices and customs. It is the prologue to your actions. It is the prologue to your inactivity. It is the prologue to your lying down, to your sitting, to your standing, to your walking. It is the prologue to the plays and to the seriousness of your life. It is also the prologue to your future visits to the theatre. It is also the prologue to all other prologues. This piece is world theatre.

Soon you will move. You will make preparations. You will prepare yourself to applaud. You will prepare yourself not to applaud. When you prepare to do the former, you will clap one hand against the other, that is to say, you will clap one palm to the other palm and repeat these claps in rapid succession. Meanwhile, you will be able to watch your hands clapping or not clapping. You will hear the sound of yourself clapping and the sound of clapping next to you and you will see next to you and in front of you the clapping hands bobbing back and forth or you will not hear the expected clapping and not see the hands bobbing back and forth. Instead, you will perhaps hear other sounds and will yourself produce other sounds. You will prepare to get up. You will hear the seats folding up behind you. You will see us taking our bows. You will see the curtain fall. You will be able to designate the noises the curtain makes during this process. You will pocket your programmes. You will exchange glances. You will exchange words. You will get moving. You will make comments and hear comments. You will suppress comments. You will smile meaningfully. You will smile meaninglessly. You will push in an orderly fashion into the foyer. You will show your cloakroom tickets to redeem your hats and coats. You will stand around. You will see yourselves in mirrors. You will help each other into coats. You will hold doors open for each other. You will say your good-byes. You will accompany. You will be accompanied. You will step into the open. You will return into the everyday. You will go in different directions. If you remain together, you will be a theatre party. You will go to a restaurant. You will think of tomorrow. You will gradually find your way back into reality. You will be able to call reality harsh again. You will be sobered up. You will lead your own lives again. You will no longer be a unit. You will go from one place to different places.

But before you leave you will be insulted.

We will insult you because insulting you is also one way of speaking to you. By insulting you, we can be straight with you. We can switch you on. We can eliminate the free play. We can tear down a wall. We can observe you.

While we are insulting you, you won't just hear us, you will listen to us. The distance between us will no longer be infinite. Due to the fact that we're insulting you, your motionless and your rigidity will finally become overt. But we won't insult *you*, we will merely use insulting words which you yourselves use. We will contradict ourselves with our insults. We will mean no one in particular. We will only create an acoustic pattern. You won't have to feel offended. You were warned in advance, so you can feel quite unoffended while we're insulting you. Since you are probably thoroughly offended already, we will waste no more time before thoroughly offending you, you chuckleheads.

You let the impossible become possible. You were the heroes of this piece. You were sparing with your gestures. Your parts were well rounded. Your scenes were unforgettable. You did not play, you *were* the part. You were a happening. You were the find of the evening. You lived your roles. You had the lion's share of the success. You saved the piece. You were a sight. You were a sight to have seen, you bum-lickers.

You were always with it. Your honest toiling didn't help the piece a bit. You contributed only the cues. The best you created was the little you left out. Your silences said everything, you small-timers.

You were thoroughbred actors. You began promisingly. You were true to life. You were realistic. You put everything under your spell. You played us off the stage. You reached Shakespearean heights, you jerks, you skinheads, you scum of the melting pot.

Not one wrong note crossed your lips. You had control of every scene. Your playing was exquisite nobility. Your countenances were of rare exquisiteness. You were a smashing cast. You were a dream cast. You were inimitable, your faces unforgettable. Your sense of humour left us gasping. Your tragedy was of antique grandeur. You gave your best, you spoilsports, you gatecrashers, you fuddy-duddies, you bubbleheads, you powder puffs, you sitting ducks.

You were one of a kind. You had one of your better days tonight. You played ensemble. You were imitations of life, you drips, you diddlers, you atheists, you double-dealers, you fence-sitters, you dirty Jews.

You showed us brand-new vistas. You were well advised to do this piece. You outdid yourselves. You played yourselves loose. You turned yourselves inside out, you lonely crowd, you culture vultures, you nervous nellies, you bronco busters, you moneybags, you potheads, you washouts, you wet blankets, you fire eaters, you generation of freaks, you hopped-up sons and daughters of the revolution, you napalm specialists.

You were priceless. You were a hurricane. You drove shudders up our spines. You swept everything before you, you Colonial hangmen, you savages, you rednecks, you hatchet men, you sub-humans, you fiends, you beasts in human shape, you killer pigs.

You were the right ones. You were breathtaking. You did not disappoint our wildest hopes. You were born actors. Play-acting was in your blood, you butchers, you buggers, you bullshitters, you bullies, you rabbits, you fuck-offs, you farts.

You had perfect breath-control, you windbags, you waspish wasps, you wags, you gargoyles, you tackheads, you milksops, you mickey-mice, you chicken-shits, you cheap skates, you wrong numbers, you zeros, you back numbers, you one-shots, you centipedes, you supernumeraries, you superfluous lives, you crumbs, your cardboard figures, you *pain* in the mouth.

You are accomplished actors, you hucksters, you traitors to your country, you embezzlers, you would-be revolutionaries, you reactionaries, you conshies, you ivory-tower artists, you defeatists, you massive retaliators, you white-rabbit pacifists, you nihilists, you individualists, you Communists, you vigilantes, you socialists, you minute men, you whizz-kids, you turtledoves, you crazy hawks, you stool pigeons, you worms, you antediluvian monstrosities, you claqueurs, you clique of babbits, you rabble, you blubber, you quivering reeds, you wretches, you ofays, you oafs, you spooks, you blackbaiters, you cooky pushers, you abortions, you bitches and bastards, you nothings, you thingamajigs.

O you cancer victims, O you haemorrhoid sufferers, O you multiple sclerotics, O you syphilitics, O you cardiac conditions, O you paraplegics, O you catatonics, O you schizoids, O you paranoids, O you hypochondriacs, O you carriers of causes of death, O you suicide candidates, O you potential peacetime casualties, O you potential war dead, O you potential accident victims, O you potential increase in the mortality rate, O you potential dead.

You wax figures. You impersonators. You bad-hats. You troupers. You tearjerkers. You potboilers. You foul mouths. You sell-outs. You deadbeats. You phonies. You milestones in the history of the theatre. You historic moments. You immortal souls. You positive heroes. You abortionists. You anti-heroes. You everyday heroes. You luminaries of science. You beacons in the dark. You educated gasbags. You cultivated classes. You befuddled aristocrats. You rotten middle class. You lowbrows. You people of our time. You children of the world. You sadsacks. You church and lay dignitaries. You wretches. You congressmen. You commissioners. You scoundrels. You generals. You lobbyists. You Chiefs of Staff. You chairmen of this and that. You tax evaders. You presidential advisers. You U-2 pilots. You agents. You corporate-military establishment. You entrepreneurs. You Eminencies. You Excellencies. You Holiness. Mr President. You crowned heads. You pushers. You architects of the future. You builders of a better world. You mafiosos. You wiseacres. You smart-alecs. You who embrace life. You who detest life. You who have no feeling about life. You ladies and gents you, you celebrities of public and cultural life you, you who are present you, you brothers and sisters you, you comrades you, you worthy listeners you, you fellow humans you.

You were welcome here. We thank you. Good night.

The curtain falls at once. However, it does not remain closed but rises again immediately regardless of the behaviour of the public. The speakers stand and look at the public without looking at anyone in particular. Roaring applause and wild whistling is piped in through the loudspeakers; to this, one might add taped audience reactions to pop-music concerts. The deafening howling and yelling lasts until the public begins to leave. Only then does the curtain descend once and for all.

Birth Rate
The Biography of a Play
for the Theatre

Tadeusz Różewicz

Today, October 31, 1966, I am on the verge of giving up. I have no desire anymore or the necessary energy; I don't believe in the need of bringing this play to life.

For several weeks now work on this theatre piece has been nothing but rage and frustration. The quantity of notes, clippings, sketches, and scenes, the number of individual elements for the piece grows without any end in sight. But today I faced the greatest obstacle. It's not a question of difficulties of a technical nature; it's something fundamental: I feel that "the times," "the spirit of the times" (I believe in that famous phantom which for us dramatic poets is as real, as stubborn and vengeful as "the ghost of Hamlet's father") . . . and so I feel that "the spirit of the times" now demands serious drama (perhaps tragedy), not comedy. All my ideas of a comic nature suddenly appeared sinful to me. The very act of writing comedy became an act of betrayal and a waste of time. Today I spent long, painful hours in the company of this work of mine—which for many years now has been living and growing within me, in my imagination. The last day of October, 1966. Cold, overcast. Tomorrow is All Saints' Day; Wednesday is All Souls' Day— November. And I, an inhabitant of the greatest cemetery in the history of mankind, I am going to keep on writing a "comedy" called *Birth Rate*. Yesterday evening I wrote out the title again in black letters. I explain to myself that I am a "literary man," and therefore I am entitled to write not only serious drama, but also comedies and humorous sketches.

Reprinted from *Twentieth-Century Polish Avant Garde Drama*, ed and trans. by Daniel Gerould (Ithaca: Cornell University, 1977), 269–79. Copyright © 1977 by Cornell University. Used by permission of Daniel Gerould and the publisher, Cornell University Press.

Forms must have a certain amount of free space around them if they are to exist and have the possibility of developing. It can be silence. In my play *Birth Rate* the problem is how to handle a living, growing mass of mankind which, due to lack of space, destroys all forms and cannot be "bottled up." In Act III the walls burst and a torrent of people pour through the cracks. The very process of bursting, the crumbling of the walls, is the "action." Whereas voices and words have nothing to do with the action.

I think that this is the first time since I started writing plays for the theatre that I have felt such an overpowering need to talk with the director, designer, composer, actors . . . with the whole theatre. But I am (here and now) alone. I feel the necessity of immediate contact with those people while I'm in the process of writing. I could actually begin the rehearsals for the piece right now. I'd gladly forego the full literary text of the play for a scenario. But I'm alone and I'm compelled to write a literary work, to describe what would be easier to *transmit* in direct contact with living people. I do not have my "own" theatre or director. Perhaps in a few years a director will turn up quite by chance who will want to work on my play, and I will be invited to the "world premiere." I have been putting off writing this play for a very long time. I began it in 1958 at almost the same time as *The Card File*. Actually I didn't "put it off," but I couldn't bring myself to set down and describe what already existed in my imagination—in a changeable, but real shape. Which kept growing. I couldn't make up my mind to pick up my fountain-pen/ pruning-shears, to start lopping off images and ideas and get down to the sad task of describing the piece (sad and a bit tiresome). Discouraged by the knowledge that it would be preferable to improvise it all with a theatre group, I repeatedly broke off all attempts at writing it down. Only when I clearly realized that I was exclusively condemned to writing things down, did I set about writing this play. (I still don't know whether to limit myself solely to the literary text of the play, or to describe the "history" of the piece, to give its biography.)

In the earliest version, the play was to take place (happen) in a conventionalized train compartment or streetcar into which people keep crowding. It was to be an interior arranged like a train compartment. When the curtain rises, the compartment is empty. A young man enters the compartment; he sits down in a relaxed fashion; he can even stretch out on one of the seats. Next a young woman enters the compartment. They strike up a conversation, which turns into a flirtation and mutual attraction. During the course of the play people keep crowding into the closed interior. Individually or in pairs. At first the forms of civilized behavior prevail. Forms in the broadest sense of the term. The space allows for the preservation of forms, or in other words, civilized (polite) relationships. But people constantly keep crowding in. Now there is no more room on the seats. People are sitting shoulder to shoulder. Still they keep coming in. Old men, women, and children. Sportsmen, pregnant women. People climb onto the racks intended for the baggage. They stand in the aisles. But they still offer apologies, still get indignant, still hold their children up high above their heads. Nonetheless, the forms are changing. Before our very eyes they undergo a frightening metamorphosis produced by lack of space. The ones sitting inside have as their chief goal trying to shut the door. A High Priest enters with a majestic step. He utters a series of platitudes, offers blessings, pats little children on the head; knocked to the floor and then thrown into a hanging baggage net close to the ceiling, he babbles on in an unctuous voice about the dignity of motherhood, the "rhythm method," and the sinfulness of contraceptive devices. Pregnant women tell about their troubles with their husbands, while others go to take the cure at spas, in despair at their infertility. All the while the pressure mounts from the inside, the walls start to buckle. The living mass is so tightly packed together that it begins to boil over. There are two or three explosions in close succession. Movement blends with shouting. Finally everything comes to a standstill. Out of the mass the young people come forward in silence. They sit down beside one another and start to flirt and exert mutual attraction. In the stillness their voices suggest the billing and cooing of pigeons.

That was my vision of the play, based solely on movement, on the growth of a living mass. The dialogue was to occur only at certain moments and constitute particular phases of the process that was taking place within a closed space.

In the course of the years I collected clippings from newspapers, I assembled extracts from brochures and books, I carried on a correspondence with a specialist on demography, a schoolmate of mine from high school who became one of the world's leading authorities on the subject.

The development of this theatre piece of mine proceeded, as it were, on two levels. On the one hand, my imagination went on producing and accumulating new "images," while on the other hand the "documentation" grew as information kept piling up. In the course of the years since this idea first occurred to me, certain images have receded or quite simply vanished without a trace, since they had not been recorded in written form. In any case, the same thing happened to the clippings and notes, some of which disappeared, some of which are lying in mounds of papers, and only some of which have been preserved until today, until the moment of realization. Of course in the realm of the play (drama), the thing developed from image to image, but those images grew on a heap of notes and new items, on the journalistic and statistical manure from which the images extracted their nourishment (information).

If I had written down all those images and all that information, a book amounting to about 300 pages of manuscript would have resulted. What struck me most of all was the inaccuracy of all the statistical data. And so for years on end there coexisted within me images and statistical data. One of the articles bore the title: "5,000 Infants Born Every Hour." The article appeared several years ago in the British journal *Forward* and was based on data in the United Nations *Demographic Yearbook*. Of course, in translating this data for "theatrical" use, I sketched out the following images: Babes lie on tiered wagons arranged in rows like rolls in a bakery. Nurses push the carriages or go around in circles with a load of children, but the circling around goes faster and faster. This image of the (so to speak) conveyer belt grew out of the image of a production line, a conveyer belt in a mine, or certain paintings depicting heaven or hell as imagined by artists of the fifteenth and sixteenth centuries—where angels and devils transport whole armfuls of souls, saved or damned, to their appointed places.

Another image that I wanted to include was a cellar in which there were women-vessels. I imagined it as a scientist's laboratory, vaulted like a cellar, where women-vessels stand in rows in the shape of amphoras, jugs . . . The scientist would go from vessel to vessel, look into them . . . His tour was to be interspersed with soliloquy and dialogue. The women—living beings—were to be speaking vessels. For example, one of these "Vessels" says to the Scientist-Hermit:

strike me
with your stick
touch me
plant your branch
in my anthill
and life will gush forth

However, I had got that numerical data concerning the birth rate permanently under my skin. The scene in the "chastity belt" workshop, the scene in the "cell," and the scene in the "hermitage" serve only to establish the atmosphere for the explosion of the "population" bomb, which is the central and decisive scene in the piece.

The conversation between the scientist (a pseudo schizophrenic) and the pseudo nurse takes place in isolation from the external world. Nevertheless, there is a feeling of apprehension that behind the walls of the "bunker" another world is growing, bubbling, and multiplying, and this feeling penetrates with telling impact into the isolated "bunker."

Questions of celibacy, virginity, the pill, the rhythm method—all of this must somehow be reckoned with in the piece. The scope of my readings was wide, and at the moment it would be difficult to mention all the items that I "absorbed" in the course of gathering material. Thus there are quotations from the writings of Saint Jerome which were to be used in the conversations between the hermit and the women (vessels of sin); there are popular pamphlets published by the Planned Parenthood Association; there are also technical handbooks, memoirs, marriage manuals, etc., etc. One of the first drafts of *Birth Rate* started with the "Ballad about the Vessel." Naturally it was on the subject of woman (vessel of sin). The notes from the Church

Fathers come from this time too. These notes were arranged in a certain order which was finally to take the form of the "Ballad about the Vessel":

how long have we borne this treasure
in our clay vessels
(I have no oil)
take a hand mill and grind the flour
lay bare your shame
reveal your legs
plunge through those rivers

the belly is god
in the thighs his might (the devil's)
and his strength in the navel

sad to tell
how many virgins fall each day
how many nests become the dwelling place
of that proud foe
and how many rocks are hollowed by the snake
who then abides in their crevices . . .

(The image of a snake/satan who hollows out rock/virgins and lives in their crevices acquired an ambiguous richness of meaning for me.) A crucial matter was the question of "warmth," that "warmth" without which there is no love. That warmth which is generated by bodies coming together and rubbing against one another. I was violently assailed by the image of a hermit (perhaps Robinson Crusoe—or some other castaway) who lights a fire by the circular movement of a wheel or with flint and tinder.

The question of "warmth," about which certain aesthetes (enemies of the human species) are given to saying that it is "cow-like" warmth, was (and is) one of the chief problems of my play *Birth Rate*. We see how it gets warmer and warmer in the closed space. People produce warmth. This whole living mass is somehow warmed up.

January 11, 1967

And besides, in life people do not constantly shoot each other, hang themselves, or make proposals of marriage. And they don't constantly talk cleverly. Most of the time they eat, drink, flirt, talk foolishly. So this is what needs to be shown on the stage too. A play should be written in which people come and go, eat dinner, talk about the weather, play whist. . . . Everything on the stage should be exactly as complicated and at the same time exactly as simple as in life. People eat dinner, they simply eat dinner, and at that very moment their happiness comes into being or their life falls to pieces . . .

I do not hesitate to use these remarks of Chekhov's for my own purposes. I hope to have them justify my own "comedies" and "so-called comedies."

Once more I'm overcome by doubts. I cannot write in this "mode" any longer. The contemporary comic writer is a clown who wades in pools of blood, in rivers of blood which inundate him from many parts of the world. I do not intend to conceal the difficulties. For several months I have not been able to arrive at the unique shape, the true form of this play. I scratch my tongue and bang my legs against jokes.

> The darkness outside the window
> the menacing darkness

Bizarre news out of China—reaching us here by means of the radio. I put the play aside once again and went back to reading newspapers and books. Finally . . . (but it's not important). I feel that I'm steering the thing in the wrong direction. Or perhaps I am being steered and pushed in the wrong direction by the "thing"? When I lie in the dark with my eyes open, I have the feeling (I feel) that this particular piece of writing is like the fact of dying deprived of any meaning. Why does my first idea—pure and sharp—start to be covered with a fool's cap and bells? Cancerous tumors are growing on the organism of the play. I am becoming just a tool in the course of the writing. . . . And I do not want that. . . . A cursed dilemma.

January 13, 1967

Yesterday I was not able to work out anything new for this play. From morning on I escaped by reading the newspapers. I read Chesterton (he has become horribly dated), I corrected my abortive poetry, I read Porebski's *Cubism,* I wrote some letters, I went to "The Heather," I listened to the radio: the situation in China, the President's address to the American Congress, the war in Vietnam, the death of Zbigniew Cybulski. In the evening I looked at illustrated magazines from 1966. I watched Cobra on TV; I wished that I were with the people downstairs in the "club room." I went back to listening to the radio again. At midnight: a soliloquy. I reproach myself for becoming addicted to writing poetry. I get up. I turn on the light. I go back to writing the play. I look over my notes from 1966: a drama "without an ending." I don't want this play "to end." The critics don't see anything. They don't see the basic differences: the plays of ABCDMYZ and even the plays of Witkacy and Gombrowicz have an "ending." My plays have no ending. That is one of the fundamental differences. Persuaded—sometimes I let myself be persuaded—by theatre managers or directors, I tacked on some kind of ending just to keep the peace. For example, in *The Laocoon Group* and *Spaghetti and Sword.* Another matter: a problem that keeps me from sleeping. Time. Just what does this cursed time do in a play? The themes of my plays do not develop through time, so the action does not "develop" either. That is the problem! If a play is to be written—and not some documentary montage, newspaper reports, court records (dramatized?). Not political treatises, sketches of manners and morals! Nor the Eichmann affair, Pius XII, the Rosenbergs, Oppenheimer, Stalin, Churchill. The latest trials, wars, international incidents, generals' memoirs, letters . . . all that can always be counted on to interest theatre managers, critics, and audiences . . . but these are secondary matters for the art of the drama. The new art of the drama—after Witkacy and Beckett—must start from the problem of a new technique for writing plays, not a "sensational" topic . . . it's possible to show the impotence of Caesar, or of Rudolph Valentino, the Deputy in slippers on a hobby horse, Bormann playing the flute, a revolution in an insane asylum . . . it's possible to paste together the history of the murder in Dallas with a cheap "literary" commentary . . . it's possible to do many different things. But all that is barren journalistic labor. All that lugging the spectator into various true events which have nothing to do with the art of the drama. For me the problem is not the "beginning," "middle," and supposed "end" of a drama, but the duration of a certain situation. I divide theatre into two kinds, into "exterior theatre" (the most important thing in this theatre is the action, what happens on the stage, and this is classical theatre and even romantic theatre) which goes up to contemporary theatre, up to Dürrenmatt and Witkacy; in Beckett for the first time we are witnesses not only to the apparent action, but also to the disintegration of this action on the stage . . . in Beckett this disintegration is the action. To define this more exactly: the "exterior" theatre has already become a "historical" theatre, a theatre whose evolution has come to an end—I'm not talking about the interpretation of those texts by directors and critics. Thus I divide theatre into "exterior" theatre and "interior" theatre. To arrive at this "interior" theatre I have followed the traces and signs left by Dostoevsky, Chekhov, and Conrad . . . What happens in Chekhov's dramas is secondary; it is not the "plots" or their "denouements" that we always remember, but their "climate"; we feel, with all our senses, their atmosphere, the emptiness between events, the silence between words, the sense of expectation. In Chekhov, motionlessness, not motion, is the essence of the play (performance). A great deal has been written and said on the subject of that gun hanging on the wall in the first act . . . which must be fired in the last act . . . a number of superficial theories have been based on it, always citing Chekhov . . . So the gun must be fired in the last act? And what if it's not? They quote that statement, but why not quote less striking truths which Chekhov also enunciated? Less striking, but more important for his own plays and quite possibly for the art of the drama in our times as well. "Most of the time they eat, drink, flirt, talk foolishly . . . People eat dinner, they simply eat dinner, and at that very moment. . . ."

How often between the words spoken by the "heroes" of his plays we find the phrase "a moment of silence." And how heavily these "moments of silence" weigh in Chekhov. For me, almost as much as all the words said in the drama itself. Moments of silence between words, between events . . . often build and push forward the "action" of the drama. What counts is what these "moments of silence" are filled with, what they are filled with by the "heroes" of his plays, by the author, and by the spectator-listeners. More than a hundred years have passed since Chekhov's birth. The "moments of silence" were filled with the life and expectations of his generation. In our plays and in our dramas the moments of silence are, and must be, filled with different thoughts, with different experiences, with different memories, with different hopes and different fears. In my plays the moments of silence are filled with the thoughts of an anonymous inhabitant of a big city, a nameless figure living in a metropolis, a faceless human being whose life has unfolded between the gigantic necropolis and the constantly growing polis. The poet and the polis? The poet and the necropolis?

In the final scene of *The Cherry Orchard*, Anna exclaims: "Farewell, old life." And Trofimov answers her: "Welcome, new life!" And here lies the meaning of Chekhov's creative spirit, his theatre, his comedies. And how about our "heroes"? Let's consider what the "heroes" of Beckett, Dürrenmatt, Hochhuth, Weiss, Mrożek, Pinter, and Albee say "Farewell" and "Welcome" to. And what do the "heroes" of Witkacy, Ionesco, and Gombrowicz say "Welcome" and "Farewell" to? And do the "heroes" of Sartre, Camus, and Genet have the courage to exclaim "with a pure heart," "Welcome, new life"?

In one of the favorite books of my "youth under the Nazi occupation"—in Conrad's *Lord Jim*—there is a scene which for me is "the heart of darkness" of that great epic about honor, betrayal, cowardice, and love.

> "Anyhow, a dog there was, weaving himself in and out amongst people's legs in that mute, stealthy way native dogs have, and my companion stumbled over him. The dog leaps away without a sound; the man, raising his voice a little, said with a slow laugh, 'Look at that wretched cur,' and directly afterwards we became separated by a lot of people pushing in. I stood back for a moment against the wall while the stranger managed to get down the steps and disappeared. I saw Jim spin round. He made a step forward and barred my way. We were alone; he glared at me with an air of stubborn resolution. . . . The dog, in the very act of trying to sneak in at the door, sat down hurriedly to hunt for fleas.
>
> " 'Did you speak to me?' asked Jim very low."

Despite the romantic gesture at the moment of death, despite the splendid battle, despite the tragic love affair, for me Jim's true drama took place in a rather shabby, tawdry setting filled with the hubbub of the courtroom . . . In a passageway. In a corridor. Someone yelled at a mangy dog, at a mangy stray dog which was really there . . . But Jim thought that it was said about him. " 'Did you speak to me?' asked Jim very low." For me this is the most tragic moment in Lord Jim's life. The whole drama of his life is contained in this episode. In it, in this scene there are elements of the "interior" theatre about which I have been thinking and talking.

We Keep Our Victims Ready

Karen Finley

In 1987, a sixteen-year-old African-American female was found, dazed and semi-conscious, in a trash bag in an apartment complex in upstate New York. When she was found, she was covered in human excrement. The young woman's name was Tawana Brawley, and she said she had been raped by a group of white police officers.

The case quickly became national news, with a highly publicized investigation and trial. Through it all, accusations were made toward the young woman herself. Brawley was accused of faking the whole thing.

To this day there are many things about the story that aren't clear, but what was clear to me from the beginning was that Tawana Brawley was being exploited and abused. This young woman was not an adult; she was a juvenile, and the authorities should automatically have been protective of her. She had been missing from her home for days before she was found. Even if she did smear the feces on herself, the important thing to ask one's self was, who or what could make a young woman do something like that?

I couldn't get the image of the young woman smeared with feces out of my mind. To me, what had happened to Tawana Brawley seemed like some kind of biblical tale, but one where all the symbols and the meanings had been scrambled and confused. I decided to try to create a performance out of the chaos.

I knew that I could never go emotionally where Brawley had been, and I could not actually put real feces on myself. Even if I could bring myself to do it, it would

Excerpted from *We Keep Our Victims Ready*. Reprinted from Karen Finley, *A Different Kind of Intimacy* (New York: Thunder's Mouth Press, 2000) 83–97. Copyright © 2000 by Karen Finley. Appears by permission of the publisher, Thunder's Mouth Press, A Division of Avalon Publishing Group, Inc.

disgust the audience so much that they wouldn't be able to focus on anything else. So I decided to use chocolate. It looked like shit. And I liked the idea of chocolate's history, its association with love.

In the piece that grew out of this, I smeared my body with chocolate, because, I said in the piece, I'm a woman, and women are usually treated like shit. Then I covered myself with red candy hearts—because, "after a woman is treated like shit, she becomes more lovable." After the hearts, I covered myself with bean sprouts, which smelled like semen and looked like semen—because, after a woman is treated like shit, and loved for it, she is jacked off on. Then I spread tinsel all over my body, like a Cher dress—because, no matter how badly a woman has been treated, she'll still get it together to dress for dinner.

ST. VALENTINE'S MASSACRE

I was afraid of being loved—
   so I loved being hated
I was afraid of being wanted—
   so I wanted to be abused
I was afraid of being alone—
   so I alone became afraid
I was afraid of being successful
   so I successfully became nothing
I was afraid of not being in control—
   so I lost control of my own life
I was afraid that I was worth nothing
   so I wasted my body to nothing
I was afraid of eating—
   so I eat to my heart's content
   so I drink to my heart's content
     I party to my heart's content
     I fuck to my heart's content
     I spend to my heart's content
     I eat to my heart's content
     and then I puke it all up
       I take laxatives
       and shit and shit and shit and shit
     I'm afraid I shit a long time
     for I'm nothing but shit
     My life is worth nothing but shit.

I've had my share of love letters.
I'm writing to tell you that I love you but I don't ever want to see you
   again.

I never want to talk to you again, hear your voice, smell you, touch you,
    hold you.
I want you out of my life, I love you but I want you out of my life! But
    remember,
  I will never love anyone as much as I love you!

I'm beating you with this belt, this whip, this stick
because I love you.
You talked back to me and your mother. Your bloody back, your scars, are
evidence of my love.
I beat you as a child because I loved you.
The only emotion I ever saw from my parents was anger.

I'm sleeping with your best friend because
I want to make you jealous
and make you realize that you love me.
I make you jealous because I love you.
I sleep with your best friend because I love you.
I am hurting you because I love you.

I ignore you because I don't want you to know that I
love you till you show me that you love me. I ignore you
because I love you.

I tied your hands together as a child because you were
touching your penis too much. I tied up your penis
because I love you.

I put you down as a child because I didn't want you to
expect too much out of life. I ridiculed you, I belittled you because I loved you.

I abused my children sexually because I didn't want
someone else who didn't love them to do it. I don't hate
them, I love them. I show them love.

I shot myself because I love you.
If I loved myself I'd be shooting you.

I drink myself to death because I never loved myself.
I love you. But I love my liquor more.

Yes, I know love. That is the reason I hate the people
I love.
My whole life is untangling what was hate and what was love.
My whole life is falling in love with those who hate me while loving me.
I always fall in love with the cruel, the sadistic
For it's better to feel abuse than to feel nothing at all.
It's better to feel abuse than to feel nothing at all.

Why Can't This Veal Calf Walk?

You sold my soul before I could speak.

Raped by an uncle at eight
Known addiction all my life
Let me dance for you
My daddy was a preacher
Preached the bible
Beat my mama
I sell my babies
I sell my bodies.

To keep 'em from stealing the women had to strip and had to work naked. It
looks bad, but to me it looks normal.

Why can't this veal calf walk?
'Cause she's kept in a wooden box which she can't turn around in. She's fed
some antibiotic-laced formula,
and she sleeps in her own diarrhea,
chained in a darkened building, immobilized and sick
and then we kill her and eat her.

After I was raped by my doctor
I didn't want to be close to anyone.
I cut off my hair
I cut off my breasts
I cut off my hips
I cut off my buttocks
    nothing revealing, nothing tight
    neutered.
You say I got what I deserved
I let the doctor examine my crotch
My legs were in the stirrups pinned down
And you gave me a shot
I couldn't see you but I could feel you. I couldn't do nothing.
Everyone always told me I couldn't do nothing my whole life
Just seeing the veal calf now

Everyone says I deserved it—
I'm a hussy, I'm a tramp
I'm a whore
'Cause I wear lipstick?
work at night?
and drink bourbon straight?
I'm a preacher girl
Daddy, teach me right.

When I said NO
you didn't listen to me.
When I said NO
You fucked me anyway
When I said NO
I meant no
When I said NO
I wasn't playing hard to get
And I never meant yes
You raped me
I took a shower, a hot one
but I couldn't get clean
    his sweat his semen
    his skin smells near
Another bath another shower
my whole body was covered with hickeys
I just cried, I just cried.
When I reported it
Policeman said, "Hey, slut, you led him on."
The doctor cleaned me up, stuffed me with gauze
I bled three days with the morning-after pill.
And then they returned my empty wallet
Mr. Policeman said, "If you don't suck me I'll blow your brains out."

GET ME USED TO IT! GET ME USED TO IT!
But I can't. I want something better for my sisters my daughters. And every day I hear them laughing at me from street corners. Sizing me up. They don't say it, though, when I walk down the street with a man 'cause then I'm his property. And the menfolk say as I pass—
    I prefer small women
    I like to dominate women
    I enjoy the conquest of sex
    Some women are asking for it
    I get excited when a woman struggles
    I'd like to make it with her
    I hope I score tonight.

And when the last man said his violence
I knew I couldn't do anything to them
so I'd do something to me.
I went and took a knife and I cut out my hole
but it just became a bigger hole
and all the men just laughed and said
She's too big to fuck now
And I felt relief, but then they said,

We can all fuck her at the same time.
But I was bleeding so they left me alone
Men don't touch women when they bleed
It's unclean, unless they cause the bleeding.

And then I hoped I would die but of course I didn't
I heard a sound, a whimper
and I realized I was in the same room as the veal calf
And veal calf walked over to me
Veal calf limps. Veal calf stinks.
And I look into veal calf's eyes
And I know veal calf's story
And I said I was sorry for her
And she said I got to keep trying
And she asked why I was there, too
And I spoke my story:

When the big man like a big daddy like a big uncle, big uncle whom I
loved, when the cop, the teacher, the country doctor, the neighbor, the
authority man whom I trusted and respected visited me in my own bed,
broke into my own house, lived with me, on my own street in my own car,
looked at me, grabbed me, mangled and hurt me, slapped me and pushed
me, touched my privacy, destroyed my feminine instinct, entered and took
and hurt and screams and bruises, new colors on my skin . . .
Whenever I see a rainbow in the sky I only see an angel being raped.

When I said NO I meant No
But you did it anyway
When you were gone your body, your stink remained
Tried to wash you wash you off me, my body, my skin in me in me in me
Wash it off me, still not gone, scrub it off, burn you off me
Try to kill me, I don't like me, 'cause I smell like you.

I'm hurt, abused. I slice me.
I burn me. I hit me. I want this body to die. I want to be
old and undesired.
I want my body back—
     society, culture and history
     media, entertainment and art
I'm more than a hole
But you hate us because we can have babies and you
can't.
I'm more than a hole
But you envy us because we have children who
love us unconditionally.
I'm more than a set of tits
But if I don't have the right size for you

I'm never enough for you
So, we make implants and surgery just for you.
We create a woman that never existed.
It's survival of the female species.
And I'm more than a pair of legs
But if they don't do more than walk
I'm a dog.
If I nurse my babies and my tits sag
And I'm told you won't desire me
You can't be a mother and a whore
No one loves a smart woman
I'm more than a piece of ass, a good fuck and lay
For the woman—our society only relates and values
you for your desirability.
The Woman is Private Property.

Text and Performance
Envisioning Różewicz's *Birth Rate*

Kazimierz Braun

My collaboration with Tadeusz Różewicz began in 1970, when I prepared the world premiere of *Interrupted Act* at the City Theatre of Osterwa in Lublin, Poland. During the next twenty-six years, I prepared nineteen premieres of eight of his plays in seven countries, including four American premieres. I often invited him to attend rehearsals. We worked together; we talked for hours (the book *Languages of Theatre*, a dialogue between playright and director, captures the essence of those conversations.)[i] I directed *Birth Rate* twice, at the Contemporary Theatre (Teatr Współczesny) in Wrocław, Poland, in 1979 and at the Chicago Actors Ensemble theater in 1989.[ii]

Text

As a text, *Birth Rate* resists categorization. It does not have a traditional drama structure—there is no dialogue or stage direction; there are only a few short lines and two short soliloquies, both in verse. The play's subtitle, *The Biography of a Play for the Theatre*,[iii] only begins to suggest how we should view this work. Later in the text, the playwright calls the text "a comedy" and

---

[i] Kazimierz Braun and Tadeusz Różewicz, *Języki teatru* [Languages of Theatre]. Wrocław: Wydawnictwo Dolnoślaskie, 1989.

[ii] The world premiere of *Birth Rate* took place in the Contemporary Theatre (Teatr Współczesny) in Wrocław, Poland, on December 30, 1979. Script, direction, and space structure by Kazimierz Braun. Set, costume, and environment design by Krzysztof Zarębski. Music composed by Zbigniew Karnecki. The American premiere was produced at Chicago Actors Ensemble, Chicago, Illinois, and opened on September 23, 1989. Script, direction, and space structure by Kazimierz Braun. Set, costume, and environment design by Krzysztof Zarębski.

[iii] I use the translation by Daniel Gerould in *Twentieth-Century Polish Avant-Garde Drama:*

states that he is working on "a performance." In this way, he hints at his own uncertainties about the nature of his creation and how it might be produced on stage. First, he is not sure to what dramatic genre his text belongs. Although he calls *Birth Rate* a comedy, he explains that writing a comedy in our dark and cruel age is almost "sinful," so he would rather write a tragedy—one dealing with problems of the whole human race, no less. Second, he clearly believes he has not written a drama but has described a performance, or what I, as director, describe as a series of "events."

Writing *Birth Rate* in 1966 and 1967, Różewicz was aware of avant-garde trends in theater, including radical reinterpretations of classic plays such as Jerzy Grotowski's *The Forefathers' Eve*, based on Mickiewicz (1961), and *Kordian*, based on Słowacki (1962); collective productions created by an ensemble of theater artists through improvisation during rehearsal (some critics called this technique "writing on the stage"), such as *The Fire* by Bread and Puppet Theatre (1962) and *Mysteries and Smaller Pieces* by Living Theatre (1964); and alternative forms of performance such as happenings, originated by Kantor in Poland and Kaprow in America. By "writing a performance" rather than "a play" and offering raw material for theater rather than a definitive text, Różewicz in *Birth Rate* entered a dialogue with other forms of post-1950 avant-garde performance.

In his text, Różewicz includes notes from his diary reflecting his attempts to write a play entitled *Birth Rate* and the ensuing fiasco. He confesses his desire to work with theater people and to create a production with them: "I think that this is the first time since I started writing plays for the theatre that I have felt such an overpowering need to talk with the director, designer, composer, actors . . . with the whole theatre." Part of the text is a theoretical discourse on contemporary theater and drama, including analytical remarks on the dramatic structures used by Anton Chekhov in his plays and Joseph Conrad in his novel *Lord Jim*. Różewicz includes his reactions to the news from the media as well as the images they suggest to him, such as a vision of an enormous graveyard. He describes a few scenes, including the vision that serves as a central image for the production: the growing of the human mass. Yet the whole text is only about ten pages. My original production, developed in collaboration with Różewicz, lasted about two and half hours. Thus, the text is a blueprint for a production intended to fill a far greater space than its words alone.

Birth Rate is the work of a poet who uses metaphors, unusual associations, lyrical confessions, and powerful visions as tools to suggest great scope. It contains poignant intellectual diagnoses and touches on indistinguishable mysteries. It deconstructs action and dramatic structures. It uses postmod-

Plays, Scenarios, Critical Documents, edited by Daniel Gerould (Ithaca and London: Cornell University Press, 1977). The text of each play is preceded by an informative and illuminating introduction by Daniel Gerould. All quotes from *Birth Rate* are taken from Gerould's translation, which is reprinted above in this volume.

ernist devices, recycling works (*Cherry Orchard, Lord Jim*) and letting various means of expression, including the languages of poetry and science, collide.

Birth Rate refers directly to the problems of birth rates in the world from the viewpoints of demographics, politics, and social engineering. Metaphorically—which is, of course, more important—*Birth Rate* is a dramatic, artistic, and intellectual warning about the degradation of culture and spread of a new barbarism. It speaks out against limits on human freedom. A gloomy picture of the human race and its prospects, the work also contains a message of hope based on human beings' ability to communicate and to build communities.

To create the first production, I first made a detailed analysis of Różewicz's text, searching for all proposed, implied, and potential theatrical actions and visions within it. From this, I built a scenario—a structure for the production, with some areas left "blank," to be filled during the rehearsals though ensemble improvisation. Last, the rehearsals themselves, which Różewicz attended, became a part of the creation and "writing" of the text.

Working on the text of *Birth Rate*, I focused on four central elements—action, characters, space, and time—and broke down the text into ten scenes (segments, units, or parts.)[iv] The original text is not divided into scenes, yet my analysis revealed that the text could be broken in this way to help uncover its theatrical potential in performance. I gave each scene a title that reflected its action, contents, and meaning.

Five scenes reveal the Author struggling with himself, his ideas and thoughts, and with the material as these "visions" attack him. These "scenes" are descriptive prose; I'll call them "essays." The Author himself is the principal character, yet by using his memory and imagination, he adds many characters taken from history, literature, and the news. The other five scenes contain traditional action, but without traditional dialogue; I'll call them "visions." The Author created three of these, populated by many characters, and then he appropriated the other two scenes from the works of other authors (Chekhov, Conrad) and their characters. *Birth Rate* takes place in the Author's study. From there, the play travels to many different locations that he imagined, as well as to the mansion in *Cherry Orchard* and the courthouse in *Lord Jim*. Time in *Birth Rate* is the time in which the Author writes the text. Within it, he moves to many other times, either imagined by him or quoted.

Here is a description of these ten scenes, to be read in tandem with Różewicz's original text.

Scene 1 (Essay), *Process of Creation*. The Author realizes the world and time in which he writes his play. Solitude—he is the only character in the scene—and helplessness overwhelm him. He expresses his longing for theater and theater people and for working with them. Despite all the obstacles,

---

iv This approach is based upon my directorial method of analysis. See Kazimierz Braun, *Theatre Directing—Arts, Ethics, Creativity* (Lewiston, N.Y.: 2000): 137–76.

the Author tries to write a play and to create a stage production. The essay is dated October 31, 1966.

Scene 2 (Vision), *Growing of the Human Mass.* This "human mass" is a crowd of passengers in a compartment in a railway car, an old-fashioned carriage with an interior divided into several small compartments. The Author depicts the growth of the mass and the subsequent changes in culture, which lead to barbarism and, eventually, to some terrible catastrophe. The characters are passengers—old and young, male and female, children, athletes, a pregnant woman, and a High Priest, among others. Their crowding into one compartment is a metaphor for all crowded spaces, including the overpopulated earth. Time is both present and universal—whenever such an action could or would take place. The vision, action, and process of the growth of the human mass in a small compartment of a train carriage is the central vision of the whole work; consequently, it must be the most important element of the whole production.

In the original production, this scene was performed in the round; a compartment cut from an actual carriage was placed at center stage. The compartment had eight seats, as in a European second-class train compartment. At some distance from it, there were three levels of platforms on all four sides, on which spectators stood. Różewicz identifies several passengers in the compartment, but their actions are only vaguely described, and no lines are provided. In writing the scenario for the production, I developed the passengers' activities as well as their lines through improvisation with actors. In rehearsal, I took the actors to Wrocław Central Station, where they improvised the scene for the production in a real carriage that I rented for this purpose. The initial page-and-a-half scene became a 45-minute, multi-scene piece in performance.

Scene 3 (Essay), *Growing of the Factual Material.* In this scene, the growth embraces objects. The Author's material for his play has been growing, a collection of "clippings from newspapers . . . extracts from brochures and books . . . correspondence . . . heap of notes and news items . . . the journalistic and statistical manure." Later, the Author adds "quotations from the writings of Saint Jerome . . . popular pamphlets published by the Planned Parenthood Association . . . memoirs, marriage manuals, etc., etc." All this contributes to creating another variant of the action: the growth of notes, books, documents, and others. This mass of objects begins to suffocate the Author.

Scene 4 (Vision), *Mass Production of Babies.* In his poetic imagination, the Author sees the mass production of babies in a hospital room or perhaps a bakery, or—his imagination still in motion—a factory or a coal mine, with an assembly-line belt or a transporter. Nurses sort and move babies using small carts or, rather, a transporter. The Author sees nurses as angels and devils in a medieval painting, and babies as souls of the condemned or saved, transported to hell or to heaven—another vision of a "mass."

Scene 5 (Vision), *Researching Reproductiveness.* Starting with "another image that I wanted to include," Różewicz writes about a scholar-hermit in his study-cave who conducts research on the reproductivity of humans. His study is also a workshop for chastity belts. Perhaps the scholar is a devil. In this scene only, the Author introduces two short soliloquies in verse.

Scene 6 (Essay), *Writing Is Dying*. The Author, overwhelmed by somber news from the world, tries to inspire himself by reading Chekhov, in vain. He realizes that "writing is like a fact of dying deprived of any sense."

Scene 7 (Essay), *A Frenzy of Theories*. The Author, not being able "to work out anything new for this play," throws himself in a whirlpool of readings, intellectual speculations, historical associations, and structural theories. He allows his memory and imagination to call upon a multitude of events and scores of figures, such as scholars, playwrights, politicians, leaders, ministers, and great evildoers of the twentieth century. He speculates on the effectiveness of different dramatic structures and playwriting techniques, introducing a distinction between "the external theatre," a theater of intrigue, sharp denouement, linear action, crowd scenes, and spectacular stage effects, and "the internal theatre," a theater in which the action "disintegrates" and contains "the emptiness between events," considerable waiting, and long moments of motionlessness. He debates the problem of time in drama. He highlights and analyzes silence on stage.

Scene 8 (Vision), *Farewells and Welcomes*. The Author recalls the final scene of *The Cherry Orchard*. "Anya exclaims: 'Farewell, old life!' And Trofimov answers her: 'Welcome, new life!'" It is both a summary of the past and an opening of the future. Both are filled with love. The characters in this scene include Anya, Trofimov, and other characters from *The Cherry Orchard*. The action takes place in the Ranevsky family mansion in Russia at the beginning of the twentieth century. But Różewicz interprets this scene as a mythical and universal one, representing every departure with no return, every final farewell, and every irrevocable parting, as well as every hope for a new opening, new adventure, and new life.

Scene 9 (Vision), *In Search of the Heart of Tragedy*. The Author recalls a scene from *Lord Jim* in which he finds "the external theatre" and "the internal theatre." On the surface the action is banal, simple, loud, and clear—a wretched dog is "weaving himself in and out amongst people's legs" in a crowded hallway of a courthouse. Yet the most significant action takes place in Jim's heart and soul: he is devastated by his sense of guilt and oversensitive to any reference to his cowardly act (jumping off the ship and abandoning passengers). So when somebody says, "Look at that wretched cur," Jim takes these words as directed to him. As in the scene from *The Cherry Orchard*, an internal action has universal and timeless character; it is a conflict of conscience for every sensitive person who has a sense of good and evil, right and wrong, and is aware that he committed an awful deed. Everybody, at every time and in every place, can experience such a conflict.

Scene 10 (Essay), *A Ray of Hope*. Throughout the writing of *Birth Rate*, the Author struggled with himself, his concepts and imagination, and with the material he has collected. Now he seems to announce—without fanfare, though—his victory. After a long journey in darkness, he has found the heart, the principle, and the essence of his "internal theatre." The Author is the only character in this scene.

Scenario of *Birth Rate*

This analysis of *Birth Rate* prepared me for the next stage of work: to construct the scenario (or script) for production. I knew I had to do three things: (1) "translate" Różewicz's visions, actions, ideas, thoughts, and remarks from the language of literature into that of theater; (2) leave room for actors to improvise during rehearsal, in particular the scene of the growth of the human mass in a train compartment; and (3) include Różewicz during my preparations and rehearsals and encourage him to provide the additional material necessary to build the production. I visited Różewicz frequently to inform him about the progress of this work. I showed him my graphic, analytic drafts. I invited him to rehearsals to talk to the actors. I discussed every step of the process with him.

The basic action of the literary text does not have a traditional linear character. It is fragmented and compartmentalized, composed of scenes, activities, images, and thoughts that flow into each other and remain open-ended. For his reason, the structure of the production, I thought, must also be fragmented, floating, dreamy, and imaginative; it should allow actors to improvise during rehearsals and performances. I sought a structure that would echo Różewicz's original literary text, yet I knew that I had to develop a new performance structure, ruled by its own logic. I also believed that the structure should include the spectators' participation; the emotional, intellectual, and physical involvement of the audience should be based on direct contact with the actors.

As a starting point, I needed to make fundamental decisions about the central action of the production. The action of *Birth Rate* (as literary text) focuses on the Author's writing a play and imagining a production. It shows the human race experiencing runaway population growth. People are trying to remedy this situation by conducting scholarly research on human reproduction; by controlling the sexual behavior of individuals and social groups; by using contraceptives; by influencing the fabric of the population through means such as the widespread but illegal practice of killing female fetuses in India or laws limiting birth, such as the Chinese law prohibiting parents from having more than two children. None of these solve the crisis. The growth of "the human mass," as the poet imagines and interprets it, leads to the escalation of conflicts and the degradation of culture. Eventually, some universal catastrophe will result, yet the Author remains hopeful. He suggests that a profound moral renewal can save the world.

Birth Rate's action embodies the growth of human mass, an image that would be repeated several times in the production. The growth takes place on a global scale, and the amount of territory, ozone, and food that Mother Earth can provide is limited. Therefore, some barriers or restrictions must be established, and somes structures or characters controlling the population must be imposed; yet the original literary text did not specify these controls or suggest a theatrical mechanism for bringing them to the stage. But Różewicz had written an experimental play about total control, *The Guards*, which had never been staged in the theater, and I proposed to him that we use this text and its characters. In the production, the Guards would be present all the time. They would control both the characters and the spectators. They would become a symbol of murky, controlling forces—a symbol clearly readable in a country ruled by a totalitarian system. In this way *Birth Rate* acquired a political dimension in Poland under the Communist regime.

These decisions about action led me to start the production with a meeting of the director and spectators in which the growth of the human mass was dramatized several times: by actors performing characters, by actors interacting with spectators, and by spectators themselves. I introduced the Author as a character performed by an actor, a character who appears in many scenes as a participant or an observer. All the other characters listed in *Birth Rate* belong to "the human mass"—in almost all scenes, fragments, and images of the text, there is a crowd. They are people in transit. They go somewhere, they arrive from somewhere. They are passengers. They will perform the "mass" in many group scenes. But from this mass, individual characters will emerge from time to time, as needed in different scenes

The text indicates that the action takes place in the Author's study, the space in which he wrote the text, yet later the action spans the globe. But where do the rehearsals and the subsequent performances usually take place? In the theater, of course. Consequently, I made the space of the production the theater—indeed, the whole theater building—as well as the space surrounding it. In Wrocław, near the Contemporary Theatre, we had a second stage, called "The Prop Room" ("Rekwizytornia") that we used as one of the venues for the production.

Although the text of *Birth Rate* does not contain traditional dialogues and soliloquies, words will be needed, even if many of the play's core actions might be performed with minimal or no use of words. I needed a source for these words and for any dialogue for the characters. To stay true to the author's intentions, I stuck closely to his writings and suggested sources, including texts "borrowed" from Różewicz's other plays, prose, and poems; texts from *The Cherry Orchard* and *Lord Jim*; and texts developed by the actors through improvisation in rehearsal and performance. Based on these fundamental decisions, I constructed the scenario, which became, through rehearsal, the form of the production. The scenario contained descriptions of actions and images as well as spaces, lighting, and music/sound; dialogues and monologues of the characters; and "blank spots"—scenes described vaguely and left for improvisation.

The scenario and, consequently, the production were broken into five major parts: (1) the Prologue, performed in the rehearsal room and based on the interaction between director and spectators; (2) an interaction among the spectators, followed by their interaction with the actors on the street in front of the theater; (3) an interaction between actors and spectators in the "Prop Room"; (4) a performance on a proscenium stage; and (5) a performance in theater in the round, arranged on the stage with the spectators standing.

During tours of Poland and abroad, and in my production at Chicago Actors Ensemble, the production always had these five parts, yet I adapted the staging to various venues: in a theater, in an adjacent building, or in open air. For example, the second part in Sitges, Spain, took place on a beach and then at a railway station, and the third part in Dublin[v] was done in the Ambassador Theatre (in ruins at the time) next to the Gate Theatre, where the other parts were performed. In Hamburg, Germany, the first part took place in the press club near the theater.[vi]

Each of the five parts included several short scenes. Generally, every scene discerned during the analysis, every smallest incentive found in the text, every bit of action, every image and every vision were used in the production and put together like pieces of a puzzle. The production demonstrated that Różewicz's text could be realized as a complex and dynamic interaction between actors and spectators, developed through the collaboration of writer, director, and acting ensemble. The performance brought to life Różewicz's prophetic visions and the multiple meanings in the original text. It also revealed a layer of the text waiting to be discovered: a glimmer of hope shining within a looming global catastrophe.

[v] See Eric Shorter, "Slow Train to Dramatic Revelation." *Daily Telegraph*, Dublin, October 8, 1981. B.A. Young, "Enter the Poles." *Financial Times*, London, October 12, 1981

[vi] Visits in England and America were canceled because Communist authorities fired the director of the production and Artistic and Managing Director of the Contemporary Theatre, Kazimierz Braun, for his opposition political activities on July 5, 1984. The company disbanded and the theater was closed temporarily.

With The Bread and Puppet Theatre

An Interview with Peter Schumann

Helen Brown and Jane Seitz

TDR: What are you trying to do?

SCHUMANN: We want to work directly into and out of the interior of people. A demonic thing.

TDR: Why use masks and puppets whose expressions can't change?

SCHUMANN: Oh, they change greatly. Puppets have tremendous possibilities in their faces and bodies and hands. I build them not as sculpture but as actors. I experiment with movement—with their stiffness or floppiness. I moved from small puppets to the huge ones after I visited a Sicilian theatre in which large puppets were used. I saw here a pure and strong line. I only saw a short excerpt from a play that lasts one year—it is performed two hours every night with big, heavy wooden puppets. They play it only for male audiences. When they performed they wore mikes around their necks—so close that I could hear every intake of breath. The puppets were made from solid wood and metal—they made the whole stage shake. There were fighting scenes in which ten puppets would jump in the air and clash together. Every puppet must have weighed eighty or ninety pounds. They were held by heavy iron rods and they would move roughly to the center of the stage. It was the greatest theatre I have ever seen.

By the way, those guys live in Coney Island now—working as mechanics. They don't make theatre anymore. They used to perform on Mulberry Street in Little Italy. But no more.

TDR: What was so good about the Sicilian theatre?

SCHUMANN: It was great because the artists invented a way of telling, a way of translating and creating a reality, that first of all defines reality. Even

Reprinted from *TDR*, vol. 12, no. 2 (1968): 62– 73. Reprinted by permission of MIT Press and TDR.

though I didn't understand a word of the Sicilian dialect I could sense the purity of this theatre. It was necessary. I feel that art in the modern world is generally superfluous. Either we should find a true need for it, or give it up. We named our theatre the Bread & Puppet because we felt that the theatre should be as basic as bread.

TDR: Do you still believe that?

SCHUMANN: I used to hope, and I don't hope any more. But, sure, I still believe it. I've seen a lot of protests, but few movements. Castro in Cuba: that was a movement. But most of the Vietnam War protests? The hippies? The New Left? And I am disturbed at having the Bread & Puppet called a protest theatre. We are all sick of the Vietnam War. But the theatre must do more than protest.

TDR: But your theatre is associated with the politics of protest.

SCHUMANN: Once we were invited to play by the Communist Party. We did. We thought the play was good and had a basic thing to say—but it didn't come across. Later we did the same play for a very square audience and it went beautifully. Our only specific protest material is about the War. We do one play over and over again: *A Man Says Goodbye to His Mother*. But most of our stuff is more general. We are not very interested in ideology.

TDR: Do you use much satire?

SCHUMANN: I dislike satire—it's too easy. When I use a Johnson speech, I use it for documentation, not satire. I like documented dialogue and narration; it has a substance that invented stuff can't have. I like to write with the help of a tape recorder—to hear what people really say.

TDR: I think political satire has been outmoded because the politicians are so much in the public eye they become parodies of themselves.

SCHUMANN: No, that's not so. Our "leaders" have not been shown up as fools yet. In this society they are still the movie star figures that they pretend to be. Their power is pathetic, but real.

TDR: I've noticed that the radical theatre—at least in New York—substitutes commitment for craft. So much of the new theatre is worse than the old bourgeois stuff.

SCHUMANN: I think you have it wrong. I believe that if their commitment were sensitive enough, the craft would come up to it. I've seen a number of groups who seemed more interested in insulting people than in getting to them. You can't simply try to shock an audience. That will only disgust them. And it is cheap: If you reach out to an audience with what you want to get from them you're hung up.

We don't necessarily have to revolutionize theatre. It may be that the best theatre—if it comes—will develop from the most traditional forms. A theatre is good when it makes sense to people. A small theatre that tries simply to do that does not exist in this country. We do not yet have our own version of the *commedia dell'arte*.

TDR: I heard recently that you were thinking of leaving New York and going into a rural area. Why?

SCHUMANN: The stink. The thick column that you see when you come into NY, and the dirt under your fingernails.

TDR: Who would be your audience out there?

SCHUMANN: Trees. Farmers. We're not leaving the city so that we can do social action theatre in new environments. We simply want to get out of NY because it's too stinky and dirty. We'll live out in the country and return to the cities when we have to. Also this business of being a "professional protest theatre" doesn't seem good enough. I don't think our business is to protest but to say what needs to be said or what feels good to say.

TDR: But don't the protests work?

SCHUMANN: Usually not. A person protests because he feels bad about something and he gets up and shouts. It has to be as genuinely spontaneous as that. When it becomes a profession it feels wrong. A good protest show makes people laugh. And that's a lousy result. For example, when the Teatro Campesino (T36) played Newport they put on a big show about farm workers' troubles—and people stood there and clapped and went crazy with fun. That's the best professional protest can hope for.

TDR: What you're saying seems to negate the role of the Bread & Puppet Theatre.

SCHUMANN: That's right. It's no good as a profession.

TDR: The heart of your theatre is performances in the streets?

SCHUMANN: Yes. But we don't always get a chance—we need permits.

TDR: Does the audience react differently in the street than they do indoors?

SCHUMANN: We've had our best—and sometimes our most stupid—performances in the streets. Sometimes you make your point because your point is simply to be there in the street. It stops people in their tracks—to see those large puppets, to see something theatrical outside of a theatre. They can't take the attitude that they've paid money to go into a theatre to "see something." Suddenly there is this thing in front of them, confronting them.

TDR: Does this confrontation translate itself into action?

SCHUMANN: No one who does a play, or plays music, or gives a speech, has any specific idea of what he wants to achieve with his audience. You say what you want to say and hope you're being understood. The consequences of your activities are pretty much out of your control.

TDR: How do street performances influence your aesthetics?

SCHUMANN: You don't make your point unless a five-year-old girl can understand it. If she gets it, the grownups will too. The show almost has to be stupid. It has to be tremendously concentrated. You need that intensity on the street much more than in a theatre. Indoors you can get by with technique, by sticking to your dialogue, but on the street you come across only if you have your mind on What Has To Be Done. Everything should be focused, and everything will become awkward and lame if your guts aren't in what you're saying. Just look at the Peace Marches. Hippies happily singing while carrying photos of burnt children. People running around with coffee and sandwiches. But carrying pictures of burnt children is something very hard to do, something very heavy. And unless you know that you don't get your message across. Most of our street performances taught us how to concentrate, how to get across. We learned how to make large crowds stop drinking cokes and start to listen.

TDR: And the public reacts differently outside than in a theatre?

SCHUMANN: Look at Uncle Fatso. He is a big puppet with a ring on his finger, he looks like Johnson. He looks like everyone's uncle that no one likes. During the Peace March most of the right wing groups were peaceful. But when they saw Uncle Fatso they jumped at him. They went crazy.

TDR: Why do you think the public reacts to sharply?

SCHUMANN: When you walk a white elephant through the streets of NY it has a different effect than when you drive a taxi.

TDR: Why are you in theatre, and not some other art form?

SCHUMANN: The other forms seem very hung up in specific materials. In music there's sound and in painting it's the role of the museum and the paint. In theatre you're involved in a political context. You can say what Humphrey said, but say it more efficiently—you can expose and probe. You can say what you want to say so that it gets to the brains and feelings of people.

But we don't take a problem-solving attitude. We just try, with each show, to be a little real.

We want to evoke a direct emotional response to what is happening—like protesting the War or urban society, or telling kids about violence in our children's plays. We have a show—*The Dead Man Rises*—which doesn't prescribe a thing. It's much stronger than protest. It's a clear expression of outrage and disgust with city life. It's an answer to living in the city. It's a celebration of something else, maybe love.

TDR: How do you develop a show?

SCHUMANN: We have many ways of beginning. Sometimes we just play around with the puppets, trying out different movements. Sometimes we begin with music and end up with politics. A lot depends on the space, and on whether we decide to use the little hand puppets or the bigger-than-life things.

TDR: Do you use dialogue?

SCHUMANN: Yes. But we don't use scripts as such. We play with the puppets and improvise with the characters. Each of us ties to feel what the genuine speech of our character would be like. We leave the exact words open. Sometimes we use narration accompanied by mute action. Dialogue depends a lot on the size of the puppets. Hand puppets are very good for dialogue. Huge puppets aren't so good—they never look like they are talking. With the large puppets we almost always use a single narrator who is obviously talking for the characters.

TDR: What is the relation between the size of the puppets and the aesthetics of the theatre?

SCHUMANN: The very small puppets are best in comedy. The really large ones—the eighteen foot ones—are also at their best when they are buffoons. The medium sized puppets are very good for drama.

TDR: How did you arrive at the size of your puppets?

SCHUMANN: The eighteen foot ones are the largest we ever built. I just wanted big ones. Once we had that set we played around to see what they could do. Puppets have terrific intrinsic power. They can be funny—or scary. They can say things that actors and dramatics can't say—just by their size. I mentioned the Sicilian puppets. Well, they were five feet high—and they looked larger than life.

TDR: Why?

SCHUMANN: Because the movements of the human body are so intricate —the harmonious details of a live body make a smooth totality. But in a puppet there is movement that is simple and uncomplicated—there isn't so much detail, and so there seems to be increased size and power.

TDR: It sounds Brechtian.

SCHUMANN: Yes. Alienation is automatic with puppets. It is not that our characters are less complex. They are just more explicit.

TDR: Is your use of space different from that of the traditional theatre?

SCHUMANN: The biggest difference is that we don't pay attention to space. Professional theatres care a great deal for space and design. They do something new for every play they put on. There are hundreds of designs for *Hamlet* and in *Marat/Sade* they talked about something fancy called "space explosion." We do a show for a particular space—the space we happen to be in. The one space we reject is that of the traditional theatre.

TDR: Why?

SCHUMANN: It's too comfortable, too well known. Its traditions upset us. People are numbed by sitting in the same chairs in the same way. It conditions their reactions. But when you use the space you happen to be in you use it all—the stairs, the windows, the streets, the doors. We'll do any play anywhere—provided we can fit the puppets in. And in each space it will be different.

TDR: Why do your shows work in so many different kinds of spaces?

SCHUMANN: Because the plays themselves are so rough, raw. We don't go in for stylish events that depend on scenic subtlety. Whether an actor walks a short distance or a long distance in this space or that one—that is what makes a play. It is one kind of play on a small platform and another kind on a huge lawn. We've performed in the streets, indoors, on the back of a truck, in the woods, on lawns, in a convent. When we played for the nuns at Manhattan-ville College we were on a huge lawn. The nuns walked around and looked at the puppets before we began. Then we came right out into the middle of them and they made a space for us. When the action permitted they closed in and came up close to listen. And after the play they followed us and picked up our props and we turned it into a procession.

TDR: Do you think puppetry is more valid than the theatre of live actors?

SCHUMANN: I really don't like the regular theatre much. But there have been theatres that made sense—news reports, religious services: these things communicate. And the Greek theatre, the Egyptian theatre, the Chinese theatre.

TDR: In modern times? The thirties?

SCHUMANN: Our theatre is still in the thirties. We still hang onto that little cultural revolution.

TDR: In modern times? The thirties?

SCHUMANN: Our theatre is still in the thirties. We still hand onto that little cultural revolution.

TDR: The Teatro Campesino?

SCHUMANN: Their big hangup is doing their thing Monday through Sunday. They have become too smooth, too professionally arranged. I suspect they are very good in their own environment playing for farm workers. But in a theatre—no.

TDR: Who are your best audiences?

SCHUMANN: Kids. And the people that are just usually in a place. At Montreal the best audiences were the people who worked at Expo—the people who swept up, the cops. The audience which doesn't go to the theatre is always the best audience.

TDR: How large is your company?

SCHUMANN: I wouldn't really consider us a company. There's a large turnover—and the size of each production is different. Last year we did *Bach Cantata* with more than 100 people. And each of the parades was very large. But sometimes we use only 15 people. There's no trouble finding people. On *Bach Cantata* we had 20 people making puppets for three weeks. Very often we are like a carpentry, furniture making, and moving company. There's so much involved!

TDR: How do you make money?

SCHUMANN: No one gets paid. We charge $1.00 for performances indoors. Nothing on the street. We accept contributions. And if we take a commission we get paid. I tried foundations earlier. They didn't give us money—for political reasons.

TDR: Why did you name your theatre Bread & Puppet?

SCHUMANN: Bread means bread. Something basic. We give it out during or after the show.

TDR: Why?

SCHUMANN: We would like to be able to fed people.

Edited by Kelly Morris *and* Richard Schechner

part four

Camp

even though camp has always been on the margins of the avant-garde, its anarchic humor, inversion of prescribed roles (of gender and sexuality in particular), and parody of social norms are consistent with the aims and strategies of the avant-garde. The works in this section—Charles Ludlam and Bill Vehr's *Turds in Hell* and Copi's *Loretta Strong*, with essays by Ludlam and Susan Sontag—invite the reader to reassess camp's avant-garde potential.

Scholars have used "camp" to embrace a wide range of artistic styles and concepts, ranging from oppositional, marginal subculture to the commercial mainstream, from an aesthetic category to an ideological strategy. It has been linked to the mass culture of pop art and kitsch as well as to the avant-garde. But before its entrée into cultural studies in the 1960s, camp was first associated with the development and establishment of gay social identity, beginning with Oscar Wilde's promotion of dandyism at the end of the nineteenth century. (The etymology of the term can be traced to sixteenth-century England, where "camping" referred to young men wearing women's clothes "in play."[1]) Originally considered "homosexual lingo" in the early twentieth century, the word "camp" entered "the sanctioned space of 'the language' in a dictionary of late-Victorian slang, meaning 'actions and gestures of exaggerated emphasis,'" wrote Fabio Cleto, editor of the comprehensive collection *Camp: Queer Aesthetics and the Performing Subject* (2002).[2] The word gained popularity in various circles of society ranging from British high culture to the city's underground life, and it referred to the aspects of "aestheticism, aristocratic detachment, irony, theatrical frivolity, parody, effeminacy and sexual transgression—traced in the drag urban scene."[3]

In "Notes on 'Camp'" (1964), Sontag first assigned a critical meaning to camp by defining it as a sensibility, rather than an idea, that "converts the serious into the frivolous," further characterized by its "love of the unnatural: of artifice and exaggeration."[4] Although she emphasized camp's marginality and attraction to duplicity, Sontag argued that it has a "disengaged [and] depoliticized"[5] nature, taking it out of the exclusively gay subculture. She maintained that camp's flamboyancy, theatricality, exaggerated mannerism, desire to convert one thing into its opposite, and assertion of the "good taste of bad taste" reveal its deeply ironic attitude.

As the scope and application of camp expanded critically, so did its audience. But the appropriation of camp by mass culture in the late 1960s and 1970s sacrificed some of its unique qualities, most significant among them its ability to challenge accepted standards, Ludlam wrote in his essay "Camp." By "admiring what people hold in contempt" and "holding in contempt things other people think are so valuable,"[6] camp revalues mainstream culture; tied to the more "acceptable" forms of pop art and kitsch, however, camp loses its subversive potential and its marginal, oppositional character. Because of the fluidity of its boundaries and its resistance to any stable and sustained definition,[7] camp maintains a complex identity, part aesthetic category and part sociopolitical discourse. As queer theorists in the past two decades have reclaimed camp as an essential component of queer discourse, its avant-garde undercurrents have become more evident, yet tension remains between camp's artistic sensibility and ideological strategy.

Ludlam's theatrical explorations exemplify some of camp's major contradictions, specifically the cross-over(s) between its marginal and mainstream tendencies as well as the tensions between camp as a style and camp as an ideology. He first established himself in the 1960s as an avant-garde artist whose farcical, highly self-conscious provocations were reminiscent of those of Alfred Jarry and whose radical approaches to performing gender challenged the dominant ideology of the time. By the 1980s, though, Ludlam was on the verge of mainstream acceptance and commercial success, winning major fellowships and Obie awards and performing in sitcoms. His insistence on the importance of fusing "high art" with popular entertainment was most evident in his later productions of *Camille* (1973) and *The Mystery of Irma Vep* (1984), both staged at the Ridiculous Theatrical Company, which he founded in 1967.

Ludlam conflated camp's marginality and commercialism, highlighting the century-long tension between the avant-garde and popular art, in his aesthetic of the "ridiculous," a style that Gautam Dasgupta defined as "an anarchic undermining of political, sexual, psychological, and cultural categories, frequently in dramatic structures that parody classical literary forms or re-function American popular entertainments, and always allude to themselves as 'performances.' "[8] Although his plays and performances embrace camp's "anarchic undermining," Ludlam's fascinations with lighthearted comedy, burlesque, and sensational, sometimes melodramatic plots and his overall emphasis on the humorous and jovial in his works help make camp's sensibility accessible to mainstream audiences. Moreover, Ludlam himself argued that his portrayal of women continues the classical theater's tradition of transvestism and should be seen as a theatrical device rather than an expression of his homosexuality, an argument that perhaps undercuts the subversive effect of his work.[9] Still, through blatant satire of cultural, religious, and political icons, he continued to employ camp—if unintentionally—as a critique of the dominant ideology of gender and sexuality, particularly in *Turds in Hell*. Ludlam's complex negotiations with camp's aesthetic and ideological indicators thus mark his career as both an experimental and commercial artist.

Written in collaboration with Bill Vehr, *Turds in Hell* (1968) reveals Ludlam's early iconoclastic style. Loosely drawn upon the Latin *Satyricon*, this work uses principles of collage to juxtapose various religious figures and mythological motifs. The main character's quest to discover his lost mother is infused with phantasmagorical imagery, Rabelaisian bawdy humor, obscene sexual transformations, and post-Jarry savagery. Orgone, an abandoned child raised by a gypsy, is a hunchback, pinhead, and sexual maniac with Satyr-like goat legs and enormous genitals. Dressed as Santa Claus and carrying a Christmas tree, he enters the convent to fornicate with nuns. He then attacks and rapes Sister Vera, who, according to Orgone, is nothing more than a filthy prostitute. Fornication, rape, and sexual orgies drive the play's narrative. Religious figures are parodied and sacred references are inverted; the convent and the brothel are both sanctuaries for lust and sexual perversion. The Devil, disguised as a newscaster, invites his audience to "choose heaven for climate but hell for company"[10]; the Pope recites the litany of Satan. Permeated with sexual perversions and scatological images, the play is an overt parody of the church and its religious symbolism.

Turds in Hell is a theatrical triumph of chaos and anarchy, in which various disconnected locations are strewn together; sacrilegious text, drag, and simulated sex are pushed to the extreme; and any concerns for dramatic structure and psychological characterization are abandoned. Although it contains homosexual references in text and performance, *Turds in Hell* celebrates and satirizes all forms of sexual intercourse. "You're a pervert?" Sister Vera asks Orgone after he rapes her. Orgone responds, "I'm trisexual. I'll try anything!"[11] Reviews of Ludlam's productions describe sexual escapades reaching into the audience, as performers invited spectators to join the orgies on stage. Ludlam and his cast did not intend to offend the audience; they aimed to entertain and engage spectators visually and sometimes physically. Nevertheless, in its use of exaggerated social stereotypes and its parody of moral conventions, the Ridiculous Theatrical Company pushed the boundaries of public acceptance.

The Argentina-born French designer, cartoonist, playwright, and performer Copi [Raul Damonte Bontana] shared Ludlam's interest in working on the edge between mainstream culture and the subversive.[12] Although he, like Ludlam, loved cross-dressing and self-parody, Copi's artistic choices and allegiances reflected his experience as an artist in exile under Argentina's political dictatorship. Furthermore, whereas Ludlam drew his iconography and parodic references primarily from American popular culture, Copi's theater is more directly in dialogue with the European avant-garde, particularly its poetics and politics of alienation. Indeed, Copi's marginality as an outsider—émigré and homosexual— is translated in the ambiguity and loneliness of his heroes, reminiscent of existentialist and absurdist characters.

Borrowing directly from the early European avant-garde, Copi includes in his theater aspects of exaggerated mannerism, overt theatricality, and "un-closeted" male homosexuality that link his aesthetic to camp's sensibility and ideology. Imbuing incongruous plots and bizarre characters with camp's outrageous anarchy and gender inversion, he also draws upon the type of surrealist and absurdist imagery exemplified in plays by Fernando Arrabal, Jean Genet, and Eugène Ionesco. For instance, a character from his play *The Fridge* (1983), "a homicidal maid armed with a cleaver, in a ballooning black hoop-skirt with leg-of-mutton sleeves, a frilled apron and eyebrows like a caterpillar," is a direct descendant of Claire and Solange in Genet's *The Maids*.[13] His use of language and silence to invoke a feeling of isolation and destruction bears resemblance to Beckett's writing style.

In *Loretta Strong* (1974), a dramatic monologue, Copi fashions a blend of the farcical and the nightmarish, the grotesque and the terrifying, suggestive of the tragic-grotesque vision of the earlier avant-garde. Heading to Betelgeuse to plant gold, an astronaut is stuck in the spaceship with her colleague's corpse, whom she killed at the outset of the play. On her fantastically absurd journey, she is attacked by Monkey-Men from the Polar Star, plays imaginary sex games over the phone, battles a multitude of rats that invade her internal organs, partakes in cannibalism, and gives birth to a variety of monstrous creatures. The fluidity of images and the instability of identities, sexual and otherwise, characterize Copi's work.[14] Too, an abundance of poetic metamorphoses in both the text and Copi's own performance marks this rather sophisticated, extravagant, and refined form of camp.[15] Copi is not attracted to the crude and vulgar humor that camp often embraces, and in most of his plays, the ridiculousness is married to despair and the anarchic irony transforms into metaphysical chaos.

Camp operates on many levels and permits a broad array of artistic approaches. A wide range of artists with drastically different writing and performance styles, such as Jack Smith, Holly Hughes, Lindsay Kemp, Tim Miller, Lois Weaver, Peggy Shaw, and Kate Bornstein, have been associated with camp. In fact, Sontag and Ludlam note the difficulty—perhaps even the impossibility—of defining camp, whose essential qualities continue to elude critics. "If camp 'is' something," Cleto posited, "it is the crisis of identity, of depth, and of gravity. Not a stable code, but rather a discourse produced by the friction with and among other discourses."[16] Camp lives on the edges of these discourses. In its most subversive instances, it keeps one foot in the avant-garde.

Notes

1. See Vincent Brook, "Puce Modern Moment: Camp, Postmodernism, and the Films of Kenneth Anger," *Journal of Film and Video* 58.4 (2006): 4.
2. Fabio Cleto, ed., *Camp: Queer Aesthetics and the Performing Subject: A Reader* (Ann Arbor: University of Michigan Press, 2002), 9.
3. Ibid.
4. Susan Sontag, "Notes on 'Camp'" in *Against Interpretation*, 312 below in this volume.
5. Ibid., 313.
6. Charles Ludlam, "Camp," in *Ridiculous Theatre: Scourge of Human Folly*, 326 in this volume.
7. See Cleto, who wrote that camp "tentatively approached as sensibility, taste, or style, reconceptualised as aesthetic or cultural economy, and later asserted/reclaimed as (queer) dis-

course . . . hasn't lost its relentless power to frustrate all efforts to pinpoint it down to stability" (*Camp: Queer Aesthetics and the Performing Subject*, 2–3).

8. Bonnie Marranca and Gautam Dasgupta, eds., *Theatre of the Ridiculous*. Rev. ed. (Baltimore: Johns Hopkins University Press, 1998), xiv. Dasgupta's introduction was reprinted in the 1998 revised edition.

9. See Kate Davy, "Fe/Male Impersonation: The Discourse of Camp" in Moe Meyer, ed., *Politics and Poetics of Camp* (London: Routledge, 1994), 140.

10. Ludlam and Vehr, *Turds in Hell*, 263 below in this volume.

11. Ludlam and Vehr, *Turds of Hell*, 266. Incidentally, an actor playing Orgone added this line during the performance.

12. It is noteworthy that Copi's last play, *The Grand Finale* (1988), was performed at the Théâtre National de la Colline with great success and was awarded the best production of the year by the French Critics Guild.

13. Laurence Senelick, *The Changing Room: Sex, Drag and Theatre* (New York: Routledge, 2000), 413.

14. See Jason Weiss, *The Lights of Home: A Century of Latin American Writers in Paris* (New York: Routledge, 2003) for a more detailed description of Copi's work.

15. Senelick (in *The Changing Room*) describes the play's narrative and refers to the play's infusion of the "spaceship kitsch" (in the manner of another camp artist, Charles Busch) with a "poetic sense of transmutation and mystical possession" (413). This poetic sensibility was particularly manifest in Copi's own performance: "Copi walks in a curtain of fog. He sees men who are women, who are animals, who are objects, who are toys, of children born of a rat, or a tortoise, or of a man who is a woman, etc. And he relates it with gestures which are a dance, with silences, with his smile" (Senelick, 413. Senelick is quoting Collette Godard in Jorge Damonte, ed., *Copi* [Paris: Christian Bourgeois, 1990], 42).

16. Cleto, *Camp: Queer Aesthetics and the Performing Subject*, 34.

Turds in Hell

Charles Ludlam and Bill Vehr

CAST OF CHARACTERS

THE DEVIL

TURZAHNELLE

ORGONE, *the Hunchback, Pinhead, Sex Maniac*

THE ANGEL

CARLA, *the Gypsy Wildcat*

THE SOLDIER

CROUPIER

BARON BUBBLES IN THE BATHTUB, *the Brazilian Brassiere Buster*

MADAME TRYPHOENA

TURTLE WOMAN

VERA, *Madame Tryphoena's ward*

SAINT OBNOXIOUS

SAINT FRIGID

THE PIMP

THE POPE

DEVILS

GYPSY VIOLINIST

WEDDING GUESTS

GAMBLERS

MUSICIANS

SAINTS

MONKS

NUNS

WHORES

Reprinted from *The Complete Plays of Charles Ludlam* (New York: Harper and Row, 1989), 49–81. Copyright © 1970 by Charles Ludlam and Bill Vehr.

(Enter the DEVIL*)*

DEVIL: The play you are about to see is a mortal sin. Any person witnessing this play takes part in that sin and thereby risks his immortal soul.

The Mountaintop

(The bell in the watchtower strikes twelve. The curtains open revealing TUR-ZAHNELLE *on a mountaintop, pushing a shopping cart in which, swathed in swaddling clothes, lies her newborn son,* ORGONE, *the Baby Hunchback, Pinhead, Sex Maniac.* TURZAHNELLE *sings a lullaby to her son before she abandons him on the mountaintop. The* ANGEL *appears above and scatters snow on the scene below.)*

TURZAHNELLE:

> Little lamb, child of mine,
> Let's go to the shores of the sea;
> The tiny ant will be at his doorway;
> I'll nurse you and give you your bread.
>
> *(Refrain)*
> Orgone, baby hunchback,
> Orgone, baby pinhead,
> Orgone, baby sex maniac,
> Little lamb . . .
> Rock, rockaby,
> Let's go to the palms at Bethlehem's Gate.
> *(She laughs.)*
>
> Neither you nor I would want to sleep.
> The door will open itself,
> And on the beach we'll go and hide
> In a little coral cabin.
> *(Repeat refrain.)*

ANGEL: Grandmother, where are you going?

TURZAHNELLE: Are you going to part the clouds for me? Who are you?

ANGEL: How did you get out here?

TURZAHNELLE: I escaped.

ORGONE: From Creedmore.

TURZAHNELLE: You, who are you? And when are you going to have a baby? I've had this one.

ANGEL: Where did you get that lamb?

ORGONE: Bamberger's, Newark!

TURZAHNELLE: I know it's a lamb. But can't a lamb be a baby? Besides, children born know nothing of life, not even its greatness. *(She repeats her song, putting a purse full of money in the shopping cart. Speaking like a somnambulist)*

One nonday I sleep.
I dreamt of a someday.
Of a wonday I shall wake.
Ah! May he have now of here fearfilled me!
Sinflowed, O sin flowed!

(*She exits, abandoning the baby in the shopping cart*)

(*Enter* CARLA, *the Gypsy Wildcat. She discovers the Baby Hunchback, Pinhead, Sex Maniac and wheels him off.*)

The Gypsy Encampment

(*Several years later.* CARLA *dances in singing, accompanied by an orchestra of* DEVILS.)

CARLA:
A Gypsy wasn't born to live in slavery
He wasn't born to bow or bend on knees.
So raise your voices, and let them hear you.

A Gypsy's life is like the wind, it must be free.
Shout it from your wagons, sing it at your campfire.
Who makes the Gypsy's life of toil a life of pleasure?
She whom he takes to wife and loves beyond all measure.

She makes each day more lovely seem.
She is his treasure, his only treasure.
Satan! My fiery Gypsy music, if you please.

(*She goes into a wild Gypsy dance. A* SOLDIER *ambles on during the dance and leans against the wagon.*)

SOLDIER:
Her cheeks are red, her eyes are bright.
Her hair is black as wing of night.
Let no blond man in her sight,
For she will bewitch his baby blue eyes.

(*Speaking to her*) Are you leaving this camp?

CARLA: We Gypsies never linger.

SOLDIER: Your voice was talking to me while you were dancing.

CARLA: Did you listen to it?

SOLDIER: I had to, you were singing so loudly.

CARLA: Over the music?

SOLDIER: Over everything. You smiled at me while you were dancing.

CARLA: You dropped a coin in my tambourine.

SOLDIER: You sell your smiles. Your kisses too. (CARLA *slaps him*) Ha! Ha! Ha! I deserved that. Listen.

CARLA: The Baron's men?

SOLDIER: No, our inner voices are talking to us.

CARLA: What is your saying?

SOLDIER: A beautiful Gypsy girl smiled and danced her way into my heart.

CARLA: And mine is saying, "Keep me there and never let me go."

(*The* SOLDIER *kisses* CARLA. *Enter* ORGONE, *the Teenage Hunchback, Pinhead, Sex Maniac.*)

ORGONE: (*Calling*) Mother! Mother!

CARLA: You are a most unruly one: you are still up while you should be sleeping.

ORGONE: How can I sleep with you making all this racket?

SOLDIER: Is he in love with you?

CARLA: All Gypsies are in love.

(*Enter* GYPSY VIOLINIST, *playing.*)

CARLA: Listen! The Gypsy song of freedom.

SOLDIER: I heard it yesterday in the wagon.

CARLA: Yes, we always sing it when we are in trouble.

SOLDIER: Why, is the Brazilian Brassiere Buster, Baron Bubbles in the Bathtub, bugging you, baby?

CARLA: Last week the madly chic Turzahnelle broke the bank at his casino. And now he's taxing the Gypsies to death to recover the loss.

SOLDIER: Couldn't you refuse to pay?

CARLA: Any Gypsy refusing to pay the taxes is turned into a galley slave and lashed a hundred times to make him row.

SOLDIER: What makes the Baron so cruel?

CARLA: When greed takes hold of a man, he will stop at nothing.

SOLDIER: I'm going. I'll stop the Baron's men!

(*He exists marching.* CARLA *goes to kiss him, but he only salutes her.*)

ORGONE: He's left us. Come tell me that tale of which you sang today.

CARLA: To think that you don't know it. (*Aside*) How could he know that other footsteps guided him far from his country? (*To* ORGONE) I sang the gruesome tale of a mother who bore a son, wrapped him in swaddling clothes, and brought him to a mountaintop. I followed her sad procession. In vain I tried to reach her. She left him there in the snow, and in failing accents, "Sinflowed, O sin flowed," she wailed. Those bitter words of anguish on this, my heart, are nailed.

ORGONE: O tale of horror!

CARLA: I stole the child from that wicked mother and brought him hither with me.

ORGONE: I am not your son? Then who am I? Who the hell am I?

CARLA: (*Tenderly*) Of course you are my son.

ORGONE: But just now you told me . . .

CARLA: I told you? I told you? Forget it! When it comes back to me, that dreadful vision, my mind becomes overclouded and the words that I speak are often foolish. There is a voice within all of us that never lies. But appearances often do.

ORGONE: I know, I know. But tell me, whose son am I?

CARLA: When I found you on the mountaintop, did I not find you living still? Was it not my skill in leechcraft that healed the wounds of which you were bleeding?

ORGONE: (*Aside*) I used to have the syph! (*To* CARLA) Who is this woman? I must find her and avenge my childhood.

CARLA: That is not for me to say. But I'll help you. Out there beyond this forest lies the world.

ORGONE: Forty-second Street!

CARLA: Go. And when you find your mother, give her this seat. (*She produces a toilet seat which she plays to the rhythm of her words like a giant castanet, as she utters this incantation*) Whoever sits on this seat, sits on this seat forever! Till tree from tree, tree among trees, tree over tree become stone to stone, stone between stones, stone under stone forever!

ORGONE: (*Exultant*) The silent cock crows at last. The West shall shake the East awake!

CARLA: Go while ye have the night for morn.

ORGONE: Bye-bye, Mother.

CARLA: Good-bye, Son. (*She blows him a kiss and exits*)

On the Road

ORGONE: Ah, if only I had a crust of dry bread to eat and a faggot to keep me warm in the winter.

(*The* ANGEL *appears.*)

ANGEL: Let me be your faggot, sir.

ORGONE: Are you an angel?

ANGEL: No, Orgone, I'm a fairy. Do you want to see how many angels can fit on the head of a pin?

(*The* ANGEL *lifts his skirt and bends over.* ORGONE *shoves his pinhead up the* ANGEL's *ass.*)

ORGONE: Oh, I must stop whatever it is we're doing because the windmills of your asshole are fucking with my mind.

ANGEL: Do you mind if we go a little way on foot?

ORGONE: Do you want to talk to me about something?

ANGEL: I ask myself whether you are worth all the pains that I should have to take with you. We trim yews, as a last resort, because yews and begonias submit to treatment. But we should like to give our time to a plant of human growth. In the heart of our tub, like Diogenes, we cry out for a man. (*They stroll out.*)

The Gambling Casino

(*There is a change of lighting.* MUSICIANS *dressed as Devils enter and play the theme of* Turds in Hell. *Flames are projected behind them. Money begins to fall as the snow fell in the first episode.*
In the gambling casino, the wheel of fortune spins. The GAMBLERS, *in formal evening dress, place bets, win and lose money. There is the constant murmur of the words* "rouge," "noir," "baccarat," *etc. The stage if flooded with money and poker chips.* ORGONE *slips into the casino unnoticed by the* GUESTS, *in spite of his goat legs, hunchback, pinhead, and enormous cock and balls. Although he wears no complete human clothing, he wears a tuxedo jacket with tails and a black tie. The* DEVIL *acts as Butler and announces the* GUESTS *as they arrive.*)

DEVIL-AS-BUTLER: Your host, the Brazilian Brassiere Buster, Baron Bubbles in the Bathtub.

(*Enter the* BARON, *a man of enormous girth who sounds exactly like Arthur Godfrey with a French accent.*)

BARON: How ay ya? Howaaiya? Hawaii ya? (*Belly laugh*)

ORGONE: He is a voluptuary. He knows all the toilets in Paris that have seats.

BARON: To do a good job, I've got to be sitting down.

ORGONE: He walks for miles preciously carrying in his bowels the desire to shit, which he will then gravely deposit in the mauve, tiled toilets of the Café Terminus at the Saint Lazare Station, Gai Paris!

BARON: (*Announcing to all his* GUESTS) My friends, do not be envious of this wealth of mine you see before your eyeballs. For remember in this one thing we are all created equal. (*The* DEVIL *plays a fanfare of farts*) When nature calls, we must all take down our pants, or, with deference to the ladies present, lift up our skirts, and unload. (*Belly laugh*)

ORGONE: He needs a hearing aid for his asshole.

BARON: My chamber pot! (*The* DEVIL-AS-BUTLER *brings his chamber pot.* BUBBLES *drops his pants and squats on the pot*) You see, ladies and gentlemen, lacquered ladies and gentle gentlemen, all men are created equal! (*He shits a torrent of gold coins into the chamber pot. The* DEVIL-AS-BUTLER *wipes the* BARON's *ass with a twenty-dollar bill. To the* DEVIL-AS-BUTLER) Keep the change!

(*The* DEVIL-AS-BUTLER *kisses the twenty-dollar bill and pockets it. All the* GUESTS *applaud except* ORGONE.)

ORGONE: (*Aside*) It's a shame to see so much money go to waste in other people's pockets. This is my big chance to turn the numbers racket into a legal lottery.

DEVIL-AS-BUTLER: Enter Madame Tryphoena.

(MADAME TRYPHOENA *enters, dressed like Elizabeth I.*)

BARON: (*to the* DEVIL-AS-BUTLER) Would you mind helping me off with my leg? (*He has a wooden leg which fastens to the stump, below the knee, by a system of straps and buckles*) Sometimes I feel like beating it for Brazil. But with my trick paw, it's not so easy.

DEVIL-AS-BUTLER: (*Back at his post by the door*) Enter Turtle Woman. She is like a turtle in every way, except that she is rich.

TURTLE WOMAN: I like to take my time.

ORGONE: (*Aside*) You see what two million dollars can buy?

DEVIL-AS-BUTLER: Enter Vera.

(VERA *enters wearing a gown and hat made out of dollar bills. Her jewelry is made of mint-condition Kennedy half-dollars. She wears a dollar-bill mask and peers through the eyes of George Washington. The* BARON *rushes up to her, ecstatically hopping on one foot.*)

BARON: Believe me, Vera, I have never admired your acting as I do tonight. How brilliantly you understand your role!

TURTLE WOMAN: What great interpretation, and how forceful!

MME. TRYPHOENA: What artistry!

VERA: Yes, every word and gesture comes down to me on wings of inspiration; the words flow forth, as if not learned by rote but like the beatings of my heart itself.

BARON: How true! And even now your eyes are gleaming, your cheeks aflame, your passion not extinguished. And since it glows, don't let the embers die. Sing us a song. Oh, Vera, sing for us. Sing anything you like.

(TURTLE WOMAN *loses all her clothing except her merry widow at baccarat.*)

DEVIL: (*To the audience*) O credulous mankind, is there one error that has woo'd and lost you? Now listen and strike error from your mind: The King, whose perfect wisdom transcends all, made the heavens and posted angels on them to guide the eternal light that it might fall from every sphere to every sphere the same. He made earth's splendors by a like degree and posted as their minister this dame, the Lady of Permutations. All earth's gears she changes from nation to nation, from house to house, in changeless change through every turning year. No mortal power can stay her spinning wheel. The nations rise and fall by her decree. None may foresee where she may set her heel. She pauses and things pass. Man's mortal reason cannot encompass her. She rules her sphere as other gods rules theirs. Season by season, her changes change her changes endlessly. Those whose time has come press her so, she must be swift by hard necessity. For this is she so railed at and reviled that even her debtors in the joys of time blaspheme her name. Their oaths are bitter and wild. But she in her beatitude does not hear. Among the primal beings of God's joy, she breathes her blessedness and wheels her sphere. (*He spins the wheel of fortune*)

VERA *sings Kay Starr's 1956 hit "The Wheel of Fortune" and the Crowd cheers.*)

ALL: Brava, brava! Sublime! Superb! Divine! (*They resume gambling*)

BARON: Enchantress, thank you. You have reached our hearts. Of all life's pleasures, music is surpassed only by love, itself a melody.

(*A flagellant procession of* SAINTS, MONKS, NUNS, *etc., and the* ANGEL *enter the casino, heralding the entrance of* TURZAHNELLE. SAINT OBNOXIOUS *carries a cross.* SAINT FRIGID *crawls on her knees, crowned with thorns. The* ANGEL *scourges* SAINT OBNOXIOUS. *The* DEVIL-AS-BUTLER *and* ORGONE *attempts to crack the casino safe.*)

FLAGELLANTS: (*In chorus, speaking in a round*) Enter Turzahnelle! How serene does she now arise, a queen among the Pleiades, in the penultimate antilucan hour, shod in sandals of bright gold, coiffed with a veil of . . . what do you call it?

TURZAHNELLE: Gossamer!

FLAGELLANTS: Gossamer. It flows, it floats about her starborn flesh and loose it streams emerald, sapphire, mauve, and heliotrope, sustained on currents of cold interstellar wind, winding, coiling, simply swirling, writhing in the skies a mysterious writing, till, after myriad metamorphoses of symbol, it blazes, alpha, a ruby, and triangled sign, upon the forehead of Taurus.

TURZAHNELLE: How humiliating! Life has but one true charm: the charm of gambling. Spin the wheels! Break the bank!

(*In the following speeches, each company may insert names of critics who have given them bad reviews.*)

TURTLE WOMAN: My dear, speaking of Madame de L. reminds me of Y. She came to me yesterday evening and if I had known that you weren't engaged, I'd have sent round to ask you to come. Madame M. turned up quite by chance, and recited some poems by Queen Ronald Tavel in the author's presence. It was too beautiful.

MME. TRYPHOENA: (*Aside*) What treachery! Of course. That was what she was whispering about to Madame B. and Madame de C. the other day. (*Aloud*) I had no engagement. But I should not have come. I heard M. in her great days, she's a mere wreck now. Besides I detest Ronald Tavel's poetry.

TURTLE WOMAN: Didn't Ronnie write *The Anus of Leukorrhea*?

MME. TRYPHOENA: M. came here once—the Duchess of A. brought her—to recite a canto of the *Inferno*, by Dante. In that sort of thing she's incomparable.

CROUPIER: Madame, your beauty is exceeded only by your towering wisdom.

MME. TRYPHOENA: Thank you. Now, sir, if you are fond of painting, look at the portrait of Madame de M. It's one of the finest examples of porno-graphic art. (*She shows the portrait*)

ORGONE: Oooh! If I had a face like that I'd have it lanced!

MME. TRYPHOENA: (*Murmuring*) *There's* Monsieur L. He had a sister, Ma-dame A. D. Coleman, not that that conveys any more to you than it does to me.

TURTLE WOMAN: (*Exclaiming*) What! Oh, but I know her quite well! (*Putting her hand over her lips*) That is to say, I don't know her! But, for some reason or other, Wynn Chamberpot, who meets her husband at the St. Mark's Baths, took it into his head to tell the wretched woman she might call on me. And she did. I can't tell you what it was like. She informed me that she had been to London, and gave me a complete catalog of all the things in the British Museum. And this very day, the moment I leave your house, I'm going, just as you see me now, to drop a card on the monster. And don't for a moment suppose that it's an easy thing to do. On the pretense that she's dying of some disease or anther she's always at home, it doesn't matter whether you arrive at seven at night or nine in the morning, she's always ready for you with a dish of strawberry tarts.

DEVIL-AS-BUTLER: I've got everything, but I can't get into the safe. They must have changed the combination.

ORGONE: This is a seaman's hook. It will sink eleven inches into wood. I wonder how far it will penetrate human flesh.

DEVIL-AS-BUTLER: Don't you trust me?

ORGONE: (*Sinisterly*) Of course I trust you. I just want you to see how worried I am.

TURTLE WOMAN: No, but seriously, you know, she is a monstrosity. (MADAME TRYPHOENA *questioningly glances*) She's an impossible person, she talks about plumitives and things like that.

MME. TRYPHOENA: What does "plumitive" mean?

TURTLE WOMAN: (*With mock indignation*) I haven't the slightest idea! I don't want to know. I don't speak that sort of language. (*Then, to show she is a scholar as well as a purist*) Why, of course. (*With a half-laugh that the traces of her pretended ill humor keep in check*) Everybody knows what it means: a plumitive is a writer, a person who holds a pen. But it's a dreadful word. It's enough to make your wisdom teeth drop out. Nothing will ever make me use a word like that. So that's the brother, is it? But, after all, it's not inconceivable. She has the same doormat docility and the same mass of information, like a circulating library. She's just as much of a flatterer as he is, and just as boring. Yes, I'm beginning to see the family likeness now quite plainly.

MME. TRYPHOENA: (*to the* BARON) Sit down, we're just going to take a dish of tea. Help yourself. You don't want to look at the pictures of your great-grandmothers. You know them as well as I do.

BARON: Don't shrug your shoulders as me, my friends. (*He shits*) I'm not crazy. All men are created equal.

DEVIL-AS-BUTLER: That old guy is washed-up. He can't even get a hard-on.

ORGONE: His father and mother were in the iron and steel business—his mother used to iron and his father used to steal.

DEVIL-AS-BUTLER: Hellstones and flamballs, it's hot down here.

(ORGONE *cracks the safe. The safe cracks. Explosion.*)

DEVIL-AS-BUTLER: You broke the bank!

(*Money falls like snow as the cast sings "We're In the Money."*)

ST. OBNOXIOUS: What do I behold? Shall my Father's house be thus dishonored? Is this the house of God or is it a marketplace? Shall strangers, who come from heathen lands to worship God, perform their devotions amidst this tumult of usury? Woe unto you! He who searcheth the heart knows wherefore ye permit this wrong.

ANGEL: It is the great prophet of Nazareth in Galilee.

ST. OBNOXIOUS: Go hence, ye servants of Mammon! I command it. Take that which is yours and depart from this holy place.

TURTLE WOMAN: Are men no longer to offer sacrifices?

ST. OBNOXIOUS: Without the temple are places sufficient for your business. My house, saith the Lord, shall be called a house of prayer for all people! But ye have made it a den of thieves. (*Overturning the tables*) Take all this hence!

BARON: Who will make good the loss to me?

ST. OBNOXIOUS: (*With a scourge of cords*) Go hence! I will that this consecrated place be given back to the worship of the Father.

BARON: What signs showest thou that thou hast power to do these things?

ST. OBNOXIOUS: Ye seek after signs! Yea, a sign shall be given unto you: Destroy this temple and in three days I will raise it up.

MME. TRYPHOENA: Rebuke thy disciples!

ST. OBNOXIOUS: I say unto you, if these should hold their peace the stones would cry out.

ANGEL: Grind them to a powder!

ST. OBNOXIOUS: Come, my disciples! I have done as the Father gave me commandment, I have vindicated the honor of His house. The darkness remains darkness; but in many hearts the day star will soon arise. Let us go into the sanctuary and take the Last Supper. I'll pick up the tab.

(*Exit all but the* BARON *and* TURZAHNELLE.)

The Marriage Proposal

TURZAHNELLE: Baron!

BARON: Will you be mine?

(TURZAHNELLE *hesitates. The* BARON *shits money.*)

TURZAHNELLE: (*Seeing the money*) Yes!

BARON: Congratulations, my dear.

TURZAHNELLE: Thank you, darling.

BARON: You have a national responsibility, I hope you understand.

TURZAHNELLE: You mean the money.

BARON: Shh! Let's not speak of those profane things at such a tender moment!

TURZAHNELLE: Baron, I do admire your candor.

BARON: It is such a lovely night and a happy occasion—isn't it wonderful?

TURZAHNELLE: Wonderful. (*Aside*) Charming man, really. The nuts! (*She laughs*)

BARON: Too much excitement?

TURZAHNELLE: I can hardly wait.

BARON: Come dear, let's drink to this!

TURZAHNELLE: Oooh, Bubbles!

(*They exit.*)

Marriage Television Style

(*The* DEVIL *is seen on a television screen as a Newcaster. He is reading the news of the day.*)

DEVIL-AS-NEWSCASTER: (*In conclusion*) . . . Turzahnelle will be a miniskirted bride wearing an ivory own by Valentino with a hemline four inches above her crack for her marriage to the Brazilian Brassiere Buster, Baron Bubbles in the Bathtub. She will also be wearing a crown of orange blossoms as will her sixty-two-year-old bridegroom, if they are married in the Greek Orthodox tradition as is expected. The last-minute arrangements for the wedding were made by Turzahnelle, on Bubbles in the Bathtub's yacht, which is docked in the brilliant blue waters of the Ionian Sea. The gleaming white yacht has been there for two months. The wedding guests, numbering between twelve and fifteen, are *living* on the yacht. It has many more luxuries than the living quarters on the island where the Baron is building his villa.

(MADAME TRYPHOENA *enters, calling for her ward,* VERA.)

MME. TRYPHOENA: Vera! Vera! VE-RA!

(VERA *enters, skipping rope.*)

VERA: (*Timidly*) You wanted me, Tryphoena?

MME. TRYPHOENA: (*Looking around quickly*) Ah, Vera! Yes, I want talk you.

VERA: You all right?

MME. TRYPHOENA: Yes, why ask?

VERA: Look spent.

MME. TRYPHOENA: Oh, no, hot, that's all.

DEVIL-AS-NEWSCASTER: Choose heaven for climate but hell for company.

MME. TRYPHOENA: Sit down. (VERA *sits down*) You busy?

VERA: Busy? No.

DEVIL-AS-NEWSCASTER: Women are like money: keep them busy or they lose interest.

MME TRYPHOENA: Vera, want to talk serious.

VERA: What? Serious?

MME. TRYPHOENA: You smart girl. Time to think about your future.

VERA: What?

MME. TRYPHOENA: Future.

VERA: Future.

MME. TRYPHOENA: You like daughter, house for you.

VERA: Oh.

MME. TRYPHOENA: You orphan. You not rich.

VERA: Poor?

MME. TRYPHOENA: Time you come to dislike live permanently other people.

VERA: Who?

MME. TRYPHOENA: Me.

VERA: Oh.

MME. TRYPHOENA: You like own house?

VERA: (*Slowly*) I don't understand.

MME. TRYPHOENA: You. (*After a pause*) Men ask hand.

VERA: Huh?

DEVIL-AS-NEWSCASTER: Women would be more charming if one could fall immediately into their arms without falling into their hands.

VERA: Hands?

MME. TRYPHOENA: Yes!

VERA: No.

MMC. TRYPHOENA: You didn't expect. Me, too. You young. I don't push you. Soon for marriage.

(VERA *buries her face in her hands.*)

MME. TRYPHOENA: (*Coming on dyky*) Vera crying? (*Taking her hand*) Vera trembling! Vera afraid?

VERA: (*Tonelessly*) I'm in your hands, Madame Tryphoena.

MME. TRYPHOENA: Vera, shame crying. My hands? My daughter, you thought . . .

(MADAME TRYPHOENA *turns, lifting her dress.* VERA, *smiling through her tears, kisses* MADAME TRYPHOENA'S *ass.* TRYPHOENA *puts an arm around her and draws her toward herself.*)

VERA: All right.

MME. TRYPHOENA: Vera, you not emotional, you not sincere.

VERA: I *am* emotional! I *am* sincere!

MME. TRYPHOENA: Better! Laugh! (VERA *laughs*) Command.

DEVIL-AS-NEWSCASTER: He who laughs last, laughs best, may laugh best but soon gets a reputation for being dumb.

MME. TRYPHOENA: Vera, pretend me your mother.

VERA: What?

MME. TRYPHOENA: Mother.

VERA: Mother.

MME TRYPHOENA: No, better sister. Have good talk. Wonderful.

VERA: You mean there's a language of the senses too?

MME. TRYPHOENA: Vera, if you had known this perhaps you would have been less bored.

VERA: Perhaps I would have been more bored.

(ORGONE *enters.*)

MME. TRYPHOENA: Orgone! Orgone, Vera. Vera, Orgone.

ORGONE: (*Presenting a box of candy and a bouquet*) How's tricks?

VERA: (*Screaming in horror*) Hie me to a nunnery! (*She exits*)

MME. TRYPHOENA: I can't understand it. I thought for sure she'd love you.

ORGONE: Maybe she had the rag on today. (*Exiting with* MADAME TRYPHOENA) I used to subscribe to *Mother's Monthly*—it's a periodical. You write to the Department of Labor Pains, Washington D and C.

En Una Noche Oscuro

ST. OBNOXIOUS: Harélo aunque fuera justo poner mi enojo en efecto.

ANGEL: Vienes ya desenojado.

ST. OBNOXIOUS: Por los que me han pedido.

ANGEL: Perdon mil veces te pido.

ST. OBNOXIOUS: ¿Y Turzahnelle?

ANGEL: Aqui ha jurado. No entra en la corte más.

ST. OBNOXIOUS: ¿A donde se fué?

ANGEL: A Toledo.

ST. OBNOXIOUS: Bien hizo.

ANGEL: ¡No tenga mierda que vuelva in Madrid jamás!

ST. OBNOXIOUS: Hijo, pues simple nasciste. Y por milagro de amor dejaste el pasado error como el ingenio perdiste.

ANGEL: ¿Que quieres, hermano? A la fe de bobos, no hay que fiar.

ST. OBNOXIOUS: Yo lo pienso remediar.

ANGEL: Como si el otro se fué?

ST. OBNOXIOUS: Pues te engañan facilmente los hombres.

ANGEL: Pues, ¿donde?

ST. OBNOXIOUS: In parte secreta.

ANGEL: Será bien en un desván, donde los gatos están. ¿Quieres tú que alli me meta?

ST. OBNOXIOUS: Hay que tomar la muerte como si fuera aspirina.

ANGEL: En el desván sea. Tú lo mandas su justo y advierte que lo has mandado.

ST. OBNOXIOUS: Una y mil veces.

The Convent

("O Holy Night" begins playing as SAINT OBNOXIOUS, the ANGEL, and SAINT FRIGID pose as statues in the convent. ORGONE, the Hunchback, Pinhead, Sex Maniac, sneaks into the convent disguised as Santa Claus, carrying a Christmas tree. VERA, dressed as a nun or roller skates, skates in.)

VERA: I open the window and influenza like the autumn wind which turns the leaves to yellow.

ORGONE: So here you are, transformed into a woman! And I a man!

VERA: No! Orgone, no. I am going to take the veil.

ORGONE: I can't believe it! Is this you?

VERA: Yes! Oh, it is—I have renounced the world. However, before I leave it, I should like to have your opinion—do you think I'm right to become a nun?

ORGONE: Don't ask me about that. I could never get into the habit, myself.

VERA: Orgone, answer my question. Am I right to stay in the convent?

ORGONE: No.

VERA: Then should I do better to marry you?

ORGONE: Yes. (He laughs)

VERA: If your village priest breathed on a glass of water and told you it was a glass of wine, would you drink it as if it were?

ORGONE: No.

VERA: If your village priest breathed on you and told me you'd love me all your life, would I be right to believe him?

ORGONE: Yes and no. Because I'm AC and DC.

VERA: What would you advise me to do the day I saw you didn't love me anymore?

ORGONE: Take a lover.

VERA: Then what shall I do the day my lover doesn't love me anymore?

ORGONE: You'll take another.

VERA: How long will that last?

ORGONE: Till your hair is gray and then mine will be white.

VERA: Do you know what the cloister is, Orgone?

ORGONE: Oh, sure. You take the A Train and get off at Two-hundredth Street.

VERA: Have you ever sat there for a whole day?

ORGONE: Oh, God, no! I had to stand—it was rush hour! (*He leaps up insanely, shouting*) You're nothing but a filthy prostitute!

VERA: (*Enraged*) What did you say?

ORGONE: (*More viciously*) You're nothing but a filthy prostitute.

VERA: (*Relieved*) Oh, I thought you said Protestant.

ORGONE: Are you a nun or are you straight?

(ORGONE *attacks and rapes* SISTER VERA.)

VERA: You're a pervert?

ORGONE: I'm trisexual. I'll try anything.

VERA; (*Screaming*) Saint Frigid! Protect me!

(VERA *and* ORGONE *disappear behind the statue of Saint Frigid.*)

ST. OBNOXIOUS: Nuns should never have intimate friends.

ST. FRIDIG: (*Showing her grill*) I am the Holy Frigid, flogged with rods day after day for seven days and then roasted alive on this grill over a slow fire. No other being has suffered as frightfully as I!

ST. OBNOXIOUS: Is that anything to speak of! I am the Holy Obnoxious with the skin, who, at the command of Emperor Pamphilius, was flayed alive all the way down to my knees. And all the miracles that took place after my death! And haven't you heard of the many mysterious happenings— or about the devil appearing in the shape of a woman—or the presaging of the erupting of the volcano? No mortal man has ever suffered as I have.

ANGEL: Obnoxious? Obnoxious! Is that you?

ST. OBNOXIOUS: Gaybriel!

ANGEL: How many years has it been, Obnoxious?

ST. OBNOXIOUS: Five or six years, I'd say.

ANGEL: Five or six years! There's something different about you—you've changed. What is it?

ST. OBNOXIOUS: You haven't changed a bit, Gaybriel—just a bit holier, I expect.

ANGEL: Yes, Obnoxius, you have changed! What is it? What is it?

ST. OBNOXIOUS: (*In a panic*) Have I lost my looks?

ANGEL: No, you're lovelier than ever—it's something else. What have you been doing these five or six years?

ST. OBNOXIOUS: Praying, Gaybriel.

ANGEL: Hah!

ST. OBNOXIOUS: Fasting and penance, solitude—the hard road.

ANGEL: The hard road?

ST. OBNOXIOUS: Oh, Gaybriel, no mortal man has ever suffered as I have. I was forced to carry a heavy cross up a steep hill and I was crucified upside down.

ANGEL: Oh, pshaw!

ST. OBNOXIOUS: On the third day after my death my flesh was boiled in oil and fed to the lions.

ANGEL: You talk to me of suffering? I, who've walked through hell and purgatory and seen the eyes and faces of the many suffering, you talk to me of suffering?

ST. OBNOXIOUS: But Gaybriel, what of the dead body of the nun?

(VERA *screams and reappears with* ORGONE, *who is now dressed in Vera's habit.* VERA *is naked except for crucifix pasties on her tits, a rosary G-string, and a pig mask. Kneeling in front of* SAINT FRIGID, *she says the "Hail Mary" in pig latin.*)

ST. FRIGID: (*To* VERA) And you, you little tramp! Where did you get your morals? In some gutter?

ORGONE: (*Remorsefully, as his good side shows through*) Oh Sister, oh God, I'm sorry. . . . (*Pause*) What will you do now?

VERA: I'll return to the Convent, make a good confession, and tell the priest that as I was walking home, you grabbed me, dragged me into the bushes, and raped me . . . *twice,* if you're up to it!

ORGONE: Don't worry, baby, they call me "woman of mystery"—the Mona Lisa in drag. But don't worry. Mother's got a box in heaven. (*He exits, singing*) "Sunrise, sunset . . ."

The Monastery

ST. OBNOXIOUS: (*Speaking off*) Laurent, put away my hair shirt and my scourge and continue to pray heaven to send you grace. If anyone asks for me I'll be with the prisoners distributing alms.

DEVIL: (*Aside*) The impudent hypocrite!

ST. OBNOXIOUS: Where have you been?

DEVIL: Going to and fro on the earth and walking up and down on it.

ST. OBNOXIOUS: You're a devil.

DEVIL: In little hell. Yes, look at me, I am worse than a heretic—I am a pagan.

ST. OBNOXIOUS: You were an evangelist once too, but you tired of that.

DEVIL: I did not tire, but when I found I could not live what I taught, I stopped teaching in order not to be called a hypocrite. And when I discovered that nowhere was there any putting into practice of those beautiful doctrines, I left their realization for the land of fulfilled desires.

ST. OBNOXIOUS: (*Beside himself*) Yes, I want to bite your throat and suck your blood like a lynx. You have roused the wild beast in me which for years I've been trying to kill by self-denial and penance. I came here thinking myself rather better than you . . . but it is I who am vile. Now that I have seen you . . . in the full horror of your nakedness—now that passion has distorted my vision, I know the full force of evil. Ugliness has become beauty and goodness is growing ugly and feeble. . . . Come to me! I will suffocate you . . . with a kiss! (*He embraces the* DEVIL *and kisses him on the mouth*)

DEVIL: (*Breaking loose*) You're mighty susceptible to temptation, then! The flesh must make a great impression on you! I really don't know why you should get so excited. I can't say that I'm so easily aroused. I could see you naked from head to foot and your whole carcass wouldn't tempt me in the least.

ST. OBNOXIOUS: Peel off my skin. I won't cry, but you will. What am I?

DEVIL: (*Crying*) An onion! (*He exits*)

The Woodland Shrine of Saint Obnoxious

(SAINT OBNOXIOUS *friezes in a niche, as a statue,* CARLA *enters and places a bouquet of lilies of the valley at his feet. Muguel du Bois cologne is sprayed on the audience. The* BARON *and his men [including the* DEVIL] *enter. The* BARON *spots* SAINT OBNOXIOUS *and mistakes him for* CARLA.)

BARON: Seize her! Seize her!

ST. OBNOXIOUS: (*Struggling to get away*) No, no, not me! You have the wrong person! I haven't done anything—I'll give you indulgences—anything!

(*The* BARON *and his men brand* SAINT OBNOXIOUS *on his ass*)

ST. OBNOXIOUS: Ahhgh aghh!! (*Weeping*) I'll urn the other cheek.

(*They brand his other buttock.*)

BARON: I could have sworn I saw Carla, the Gypsy Wildcat, placing a bouquet of lilies of the valley next to the statue of Saint Obnoxious.

ST. OBNOXIOUS: Even through the scent of one kosher grilled bun . . . (*He points to his branded ass*) . . . I can still smell the scent of lilies of the valley. Carla must be close at hand.

BARON: Ah! That can mean only one thing. That Carla is very near to us and all we have to do is to sniff our way through the trail scent of the lilies of the valley. Allons!

(*The* BARON *and his men begin sniffing.* OBNOXIOUS *sniffs also. Sniff! Sniff! Sniff! They reach* CARLA.)

BARON: Ohio, just as I thought! Seize her!

(CARLA *screams and a wild chase ensues.*)

BARON: Allons! Allons!

(*The* DEVIL *seizes* CARLA.)

CARLA: Take your filthy hands off me, you dirty old man. (*She stamps on the* DEVIL's *foot.*)

DEVIL: Oooh!

ST. OBNOXIOUS: Why, Carla, the Gypsy Wildcat, has stepped on his open-toed wedgies with her high-heeled, red vinyl boot trimmed in red marabou.

CARLA: That just goes to show you that these boots were not just made for walking. Go ahead, Baron, brand me if you like. (*The* BARON *hesitates*) Well, why did you not brand me?

BARON: It's your combination of that Latin intense look mixed with courage. Oh, Carla, would I like to brown you now!

CARLA: I don't quite understand it, Baron—first you wanted to brand me, now you want to brown me.

BARON: Her breath takes my beauty away.

ST. OBNOXIOUS: (*In an* ENGLISH *accent*) Which do you prefer, my deah, Kipling or Browning?

CARLA: Oh, Browning, definitely!

ST. OBNOXIOUS: Why's that?

CARLA: Well you see, I have never been kippled, so I really cannot say.

BARON: We could make a deal, Carla. I'll take you to my pavillion so you can tell my fortune.

(*The* BARON *throws* CARLA *over his shoulder and carries her off.*)

CARLA: (*Singing*) A Gypsy wasn't born to live in slavery. . . . (*Etc.*)

The Pavillion

(*The* BARON *and* CARLA *reenter at the other side of the stage. The* BARON *is still carrying* CARLA—*she is still singing. They sit at a table. The* BARON *pours some wine.*)

BARON: Carla, we're together at last. Can you tell my fortune in my hand, Carla?

CARLA: (*Looking at the palm of his hand*) Of course, Baron, that's right up my alley, nothing easier. Everybody's future is in their face. Nothing easier.

BARON: But what about my past—my youth, where did it go?

CARLA: I'm sorry about that, but I cannot undo what you have done already. It slipped away while you weren't looking. While you were asleep. While you were drunk? Think! Think!

BARON: What good are you Gypsies?

CARLA: I can't tell the past and neither can you, but I *can* tell you about tomorrow.

BARON: You say "tomorrow," but tomorrow never comes.

CARLA: That's what's so intriguing about tomorrow.

BARON: Carla, tell me, whom will I marry?

CARLA: I can tell you without looking at my cards, Baron, that it is not a Gypsy you will marry.

BARON: Then who is it?

CARLA: You will find a clue in your toilet.

BARON: What do you mean, in my toilet?

CARLA: That's exactly what I mean: Turds in Hell! (*She spits*)

BARON: Turds in Hell? Turds in Hell? Merde en enfer? What can you mean? How can you know so much?

CARLA: You seem to forget, Baron, that I am a *gitana*—Gypsy to you.

BARON: A Gypsy yes, but . . .

CARLA: And because of you, I long for a man who has left me; because of Turds in Hell . . . (*She spits*) . . . I weep for a child.

BARON: You speak rashly, my dear. Watch your language.

CARLA: There's more things in Turds in Hell . . . (*She spits* . . . than are dreamed of in your philosophies, Baron. (*She turns to leave*)

BARON: Wait, Carla! Where are you going?

CARLA: I am going back to my people. Hasta la vista. (*She starts off*)

BARON: (*Following her*) Wait! I have another question to ask.

(*He whispers in* CARLA's *ear. She slaps him. They exit.*)

The Brothel

(*Enter* VERA, *wearily.*)

PIMP:
There was a woman, and she was wise, woefully wise was she;
She was old, so old, yet her years all told were but a score and three;
And she knew by heart, from finish to start, the Book of Iniquity.

VERA:
There is no hope for such as I on earth, nor yet in Heaven;
Unloved I live, unloved I die, unpitied, unforgiven;
A loathéd jade, I ply my trade, unhallowed and unshriven.

I paint my cheeks, for they are white, and cheeks of chalk men hate;
Mine eyes with wine I make to shine, that man may seek and sate;
With overhead a lamp of red I sit me down and wait.

Until they come, the nightly scum, with drunken eyes aflame;
Your sweethearts, sons, ye scornful ones—'tis I who know their shame.
The gods, ye see, are brutes to me—and so I play my game.

For life is not the thing we thought, and not the thing we plan;
And Woman in a bitter world must do the best she can—
Must yield the stroke, and bear the yoke, and serve the will of man;

Must serve his need and ever feed the flame of his desire,
Though be she loved for love alone, or be she loved for hire;
For every man since life began is tainted with the mire.

And though you know he loves you so and sets you on love's throne;
Yet let your eyes but mock his sighs, and let your heart be stone,
Lest you be left (as I was left) attainted and alone.

PIMP:

Fate has written a tragedy; its name is *The Human Heart*.
The theatre is the House of Life, Woman the mummer's part;
The Devil enters the prompter's box and the play is ready to start.

(*The* PIMP *them introduces the* WHORES *as they enter*.)

PIMP: The charming whores, those in which beauty consists, are: the Tyrannical . . .

TYRANNICAL WHORE: Anyone for a little rubber and discipline?

PIMP: . . . the Too Too Mahooch, the Compulsive, the Tarantula . . .

DEVIL-AS-TARANTULA: (*Holding a set of chattering teeth between his legs, in a German accent*) I was featured in *Beavers on Parade*—I was the famous snapping pussy.

PIMP: . . . the Scarcely Credible, the Blasé, and, last but not least, the Empty-Headed . . .

VERA-AS-EMPTY-HEADED-WHORE: I may be dumb, but you didn't come here for any conversation, either!

(ORGONE *enters in the nun disguise, and looks the* WHORES *over*.)

ORGONE: Proud fondling whores, in spite of talc and rouge and all the gaudy lipstick, you smell of death.

PIMP: Are you the gentleman from Shirley?

ORGONE: Yeah!

PIMP: I have important news for you: you are afflicted with a grave sickness.

ORGONE: What kind of sickness it? And how have you come by this information?

PIMP: It is an inner sickness. Your body has been filled with a most dangerous poison. I learned this from revelations by the gods.

ORGONE: What would you have me do?

PIMP: The only way to cure the sickness is to draw the venom out of you.

ORGONE: Oh.

PIMP: You are fortunate in that we are equipped with tools which are capable of extracting the venom quite painlessly. In fact, it is certain that you will find the extraction enjoyable. (*Yells*) Yab Yum!

(*Displaying the Whores' extractors, the* PIMP *removes* ORGONE's *clothes and takes hold of his dick. The* WHORES *scream in ecstasy when they see* ORGONE's *giant cock and balls and dive on him. An orgy ensues.*)

BLASÉ WHORE: Holy Toledo, you must have been born in a barn or something—why, you're hung like a horse.

DEVIL-AS-TARANTULA: Looks more like an elephant's trunk to me. I don't think I can take it.

ORGONE: What do you think this is, a fucking mike? C'mon, spread your cheeks a little wider, baby—it'll fit in there like a glove.

TYRANNICAL WHORE: I think by the size of that salami we are going to have to spread ourselves out just a little bit more, girls.

BLASÉ WHORE: I'm sick and tired of working like a horse. Why can't we get those nice guys—just a mere four-and-a-half inches?

VERA-AS-EMPTY-HEADED-WHORE: I know what you mean. You're referring to the ones that just barely tickle your ovaries.

COMPULSIVE WHORE: I don't know about you girls, but I ain't chicken—I can take it. (*She begins to blow* ORGONE's *giant cock*)

TOO TOO MAHOOCH: Honey, you ain't chicken, you're a gobbler.

BLASÉ WHORE: With a tool like that one, you certainly don't have to have your box scraped.

DEVIL-AS-TARANTULA: If I continue, he will rise up, become erect, and penetrate me so deeply that I shall be marked with stigmata.

VERA-AS-EMPTY-HEADED-WHORE: Dreamin' again, huh?

DEVIL-AS-TARANTULA: Listen, honey, I ain't never met a man yet who could take care of all this sauerkraut, but I worship him. When I see him lying naked, I feel like saying Mass on his chest

TYRANNICAL WHORE: To the heart, to the hilt, right to the balls, right in the throat.

ORGONE: Suck it yourself, sugarstick!

VERA-AS-EMPTY-HEADED-WHORE: The nights are mad about me! Oh, the sultanas! My God, they're making eyes at me! Oh, they're curling my hair around their fingers—the fingers of the nights, men's cocks! They're patting my cheek—stroking my butt!

TYRANNICAL WHORE: I'm not in the business for love, you know. I was in love once and I got the business.

PIMP: Time wounds all heels. I remember that some ten years ago, a beautifully plump, fresh young girl, the personal chambermaid of the queen, was found guilty of high treason for trying to poison the king, and consequently was condemned to suffer the cruelest death that could be devised for her. It was decreed that, after she had been crucified, she should be kept alive for as long as possible. The sentence was scrupulously carried out; when she fainted from the pain, the executioner gave her a little glass of liquor to revive her. She only died six days later. Her long suffering, her young age, and her robust constitution had made her flesh so tender, so savory, and so sought after that the executioner was able to sell it for more than eight sequins.

WHORES: Eight sequins! Get *her!*

PIMP: (*Shouting them down*) This inhuman market was so thronged with customers that persons of quality esteemed themselves happy if they could buy a couple of pounds.

WHORES: Fleshmongers—all of them!

TYRANNICAL WHORE: Thinness is more naked, more indecent than corpulence.

DEVIL-AS-TARANTULA: (*Singing*) Such a dick a day or die!

WHORES: (*Singing*)
> Spermatozoa,
> I love you so-a
> I want to know-a
> When you will come.

> You are so tasty
> I want to taste ye
> I will not waste ye
> Please give me some.

> Yum yum yum yum.

ORGONE: I saw something horrible last night as I was going home.

TYRANNICAL WHORE: You astonish me; what was it startled you?

ORGONE: It was terrible—it made my blood stand still to behold what I beheld.

TYRANNICAL WHORE: What was it met your gaze?

ORGONE: I saw a young man and a young lady swinging on a gate in the moonlight, biting each other.

VERA-AS-EMPTY-HEADED-WHORE: The impulse to bite is the origin of the kiss.

TYRANNICAL WHORE: To kiss means the act of biting rather than that of sucking.

ORGONE: Suck it yourself, sugarstick!

VERA-AS-EMPTY-HEADED-WHORE: Not only is he strange and queer, but he's got a one-track mind as well.

DEVIL-AS-TARANTULA: We always need to make a certain effort to understand the loves of others, and their way of making love. If it were possible to watch, the practices of our nearest neighbor would seem as strange, and even as extravagant—and, let us say, as monstrous—as the couplings of reptiles, insects, dogs, and prehistoric monsters.

PIMP: There is no exalted pleasure which cannot be related to prostitution. At the theatre, in the ballroom, each one enjoys possession of all. God is the most prostituted of all beings, because He is the closest friend of every individual, because He is the common inexhaustible reservoir of love.

ORGONE: Oh, hideous Jewess, lay with me for hire one night: two corpses side by side.

(ORGONE *and the* DEVIL-AS-TARANTULA *begin to fuck.*)

COMPULSIVE WHORE: What are you so smug about, you doxy trollop?

VERA-AS-EMPTY-HEADED-WHORE: Nothing—only this invitation to the biggest party of the year.

TYRANNICAL WHORE: Not Turzahnelle's!

VERA-AS-EMPTY-HEADED-WHORE: The one and only.

TYRANNICAL WHORE: Yeah, well she sure thinks her shit don't stink, huh, but she's no better'n the rest of us—I hear she murdered her child.

COMPULSIVE WHORE: She didn't murder him, just left him on a mountain-top—he had two heads or something.

(ORGONE *is listening intently while fucking the* DEVIL-AS-TARANTULA. *The more he realizes it's his mother they're talking about, the closer he gets to his orgasm. When he reaches it, he lets out a joyous yell, a scream.*)

DEVIL-AS-TARANTULA: (*Aside*) The devil's semen is as cold as ice. (*To* OR-GONE) Auf Wiedersehen. I must return to the dead. As thou hast bragged of having fucked my body, so also canst thou boast of having fucked my soul.

ORGONE: And she fucks like she's got a newspaper asshole.

(*The* PIMP *and the* WHORES *exit, talking.*)

COMPULSIVE WHORE: What is the greatest pleasure in love?

BLASÉ WHORE: To receive.

TYRANNICAL WHORE: To give oneself.

VERA-AS-EMPTY-HEADED-WHORE: The pleasure of pride.

COMPULSIVE WHORE: The voluptuousness of humility.

TYRANNICAL WHORE: To beget citizens for the State.

PIMP: For my part, I say the sole and supreme pleasure in love lies in the absolute knowledge of doing evil. And man and woman know from birth that in evil is to be found all voluptuousness.

(ORGONE, *left alone, finds the invitation* VERA *dropped—the invitation to his mother's wedding.*)

ORGONE: Thou, nature, art my goddess. To thy law my services are bound. Why should I stand in the plague of customs and submit for the curiosity of nations to deprive me? Just because my mother dumped me? Why hunchback? Wherefore pinhead? How come sex maniac? When my form is as well compact, my mind as sharp . . . (*He lights his pinhead*) . . . and my shape as true as any honest madam's issue. Why brand they us with base? with baseness? with bastardy? Why base? Why basement? Why not try the roof? Well, Orgone, if this invitation gets you on the yacht, Orgone the Base shall grow and prosper. Now, gods! Stand up for hunchbacks, pinheads, and sex maniacs! (*He exits doing the shuffle-off-to-Buffalo*)

The Yacht on the River Styx

(*The wedding party yacht begins to float onstage, headed by* VERA *who, as the masthead of the ship, has turned into a harpy with a bird's head and claws for hands. The other* GUESTS *float in. The* DEVIL-AS-CHARON *steers the ship. In the background is heard "The People Who Walked in Darkness" from Handel's* Messiah. *All wear sporty nautical costumes and sway with the roll of the boat.*)

DEVIL-AS-CHARON:
>Woe unto you, depraved souls!
>Bury here and forever all hope of paradise:
>I come to lead you to the other shore,
>Into eternal dark, into fire and ice.
>And you who are living yet, I say,
>Begone from these who are dead.
>By other windings and by other steerage
>Shall you cross to that other shore.
>Not here! Not here!
>A lighter craft than mine must give you passage.

(*The* ANGEL *and a procession of* SAINTS, *led by* ORGONE, *brandishing his invitation, approach the ship.*)

ST. OBNOXIOUS: How melodorous is thy bel chant, O songbird, and how exqueezit thine afterdraught!

(*A masked ball is in full swing on the yacht.*)

ORGONE: (*to the* DEVIL-AS-CHARON, *showing his stolen invitation*) Charon, bite back your spleen: this has been willed where what is willed must be and is not yours to ask what it may mean.

GUEST 1: Do you see clearly what is going on?

GUEST 2: I don't see clearly, but I hear well.

GUEST 1: Plenty to see and hear and feel and yet . . .

GUEST 3: I don't mind the heat, but the humidity.

GUEST 2: Feel live warm beings near you.

GUEST 1: Let them sleep in their maggoty beds. Thy are not going to get me this inning.

GUEST 2: Oh heaven, who can sufer this?

GUEST 1: I CAN.

(*The* ANGEL *and the* SAINTS *begin to row the ship like galley slaves.*)

ANGEL: The summer evening had begun to fold the world in its mysterious embrace. Far away in the west the sun was setting and the last glow of all too fleeting day lingered lovingly on sea and strand, on the proud promontory of the dear old mountain guarding as ever the waters of the bay, on the weed-grown rocks along the shore and, last but not least, on the quiet church whence there streamed forth at times upon the stillness the voice of prayer to her who is in her pure radiance a beacon ever to the storm-tossed heart of man, Mary, star of the sea.

ST. OBNOXIOUS: And still a light moves long the river. And stiller the mermen ply their king. Its pith is full. The way is free—their lot is cast.

TURZAHNELLE: I don't think the Baron exactly likes me—between ourselves, of course.

GUEST 2: You're wrong. I promise you. He's often told me he thinks you're one of the prettiest women on earth.

TURZAHNELLE: Really? That's very charming. But I deserve it, as I've a very high opinion of him too.

GUEST 1: The dresses that Palmira woman makes. You can never feel the shoulders and you think the whole time that everything's going to fall down. Did she make those sleeves of yours?

GUEST 2: Yes.

GUEST 1: Very pretty, very pretty indeed! Definitely there's nothing like straight sleeves, but it's taken me a long time to come round to them. Besides you mustn't be too fat to wear them or you look like a grasshopper with an enormous body and tiny feet and hands.

GUEST 2: What a charming thought.

GUEST 1: But isn't it true? Look at Madame Tryphoena. But of course you mustn't be too thin either or there's nothing left at all. Everybody's talking about the Turtle Woman. But to me she looks like a gallows. She has a lovely face, I agree, but she's just a Madonna on the end of a flagstaff.

TURZAHNELLE: Can I get you something to drink, dear?

GUEST 1: Nothing but hot water, with a dash of tea and a wisp of milk. (*Raucous laugh*) Now, look, there's another of them! With all those curls and lanky legs, she looks to me like one of those long-handled brooms you use for dusting picture rails.

TURZAHNELLE: She really is a little odd. (*She sees* VERA) Oh, Vera, come here.

VERA: Why?

TURZAHNELLE: Look me straight in the face.

VERA: What's so extraordinary about me? Into every life a little rain must fall.

TURZAHNELLE: Yes, I was right, your eyes are red; you've just been crying, it's as clear as daylight. Why, what's happened, Vera?

DEVIL-AS-CHARON: Man has no Body distinct from his Soul; for that call'd Body is a portion of Soul discerned by the five Senses, the chief inlets of Soul in his age. Energy is the only life, and is from the Body. Reason is the bound or outward circumstance of Energy. Energy is Eternal Delight!

ANGEL: How do you know but every bird that cuts the airy way is an immense world of delight, clos'd by your senses five?

(VERA *is shot—a shot in the dark. She crows as she falls.*)

ST. OBNOXIOUS: An albatross! The ship is doomed!

(*All rush to* VERA's *side.*)

BARON: Water, water everywhere, and not a drop to drink. I know what will revive her. My specialty de la maison.

(*He dons goggles and a raincoat, pops the cork of a bottle of champagne, and lies flat on his back. The women straddle him one at a time, lifting their skirts. He spits a stream between the legs of each in turn, douching their cunts with champagne.*)

MME. TRYPHOENA: (*Singing*)
>I was a virtuoso virgin.
>Avoided upper crust lust.
>Befuddled studs kept urgin' for a mergin'
>With my size forty bust.

>Liberalism led me astray,
>Fell in a rebel's hotbed.
>You know the type, a pothead,
>Anyway, I thought he was gay.
>(I'm not that type of girl.)

>Some girls pray for a rape.
>Not me, I'm no torrid tease.
>I fell prey to rape because
>I just wanted to please.

>(A likely story.
>No, really, it's on the up and up.)

>I was caught in a rampage,
>He had a masculine scent,
>I was the torrid target of
>A sex quest hard to assuage.

>So here's a tip for you lonesome gals—
>Don't give your heart to no stuck-up studs
>Because manipulators you think are your pals
>May be dykes in some stud's duds.

>I was lost in the shuffle,
>Thought it was true love but then

I found myself alone with a lezzie,
In her dyky den.

I know where I went wrong
So I'm singing this song.
So I'm singing this song.

VERA: Do you mean to say there's a language of the senses, too?

TURZAHNELLE: Yes, Vera, if you had known this, perhaps you would have been less bored.

VERA: Perhaps, perhaps . . .

ANGEL: (*Appearing to* VERA) Perhaps? O maid, I tell thee, when I pass away it is to tenfold life, to love, to peace, and raptures holy: we're all skating on thin ice.

VERA: (*Crossing herself in awe*) If I've only one life to live, let me live it as a blonde.

ANGEL: So you have only one life to live, eh?

VERA: I meant no offense, sir.

ANGEL: You didn't give any. But you know yourself you could live a devil of a long life if you really wanted to.

VERA: Oh, don't say that sir. It's so unsettling.

ANGEL: Well, what do you think of living for several hundred years? Are you going to have a try at it?

VERA: Oh, I tell you straight out, sir, I'd never promise to live with the same man as long as that. I wouldn't put up with my own children as long as that. Why, sir, when you were only two hundred, you might marry your own great-great-great-great-great-great-grandson and not even know who he was.

ANGEL: Well, why not? For all you know, the man you've married may be your great-great-great-great-great-great-grandmother's great-great-great-great-great-great-grandson.

VERA: But do you think it would ever be thought respectable, sir?

ANGEL: My good girl, all biological necessities have to be made respectable whether we like it or not, so you needn't worry your head about that.

VERA: There is nothing like biology.

ANGEL: "The cloud-capped towers, the solemn pinnacles, the gorgeous temples, the great globe itself: yea, all that it inherit shall dissolve, and, like this influential pageant faded, leave not a rack behind." That's biology for you: good sound biology.

VERA: Measured by that yardstick, we all stand condemned.

ANGEL: It is not enough to bathe in the sweat of anguish; you must pass through the fire of torture. That you *cannot* will be forgiven; that you *will* not, never.

VERA: Yes, it must be so. Oh, lift me, lift me to where you climb. Lead me towards your high heaven. My longing is great, my courage weak. I grow dizzy, my feet are tired and clogged with earth.

ANGEL: Listen, Vera. There is but one law for all men: no cowardly compromise! If a man does his work by halves, he stands condemned.

VERA: (*Bowing her head*) Lead and I shall follow. (*She raises her head. The* ANGEL *is gone*)
Did you see the apparition, Turzahnelle?
Was he from heaven or was he from hell?

TURZAHNELLE: What did he look like? Did he sing?

VERA: Yes, he sang.

TURZAHNELLE: I didn't hear him, but he sang. Did he speak?

VERA: Well, he spoke to me in a well-articulated warble. I couldn't understand what he said, but the syntax was so pure that I could guess which were verbs and which were pronouns.

TURZAHNELLE: Is it true that the joints of his wings creaked harmoniously?

VERA: Perfectly true, like a grasshopper's only less metallic. With my fingers I touched the roots of his wings. It was like a harp of feathers!

TURZAHNELLE: Oh why are you so mad? You've a pound of rouge on your cheeks. Where did you get this costume? And aren't you ashamed?

GUEST 1: (*In alarm*) Turzahnelle. They say it's going to rain—shouldn't we turn back?

TURZAHNELLE: Never! Drink! Dance! I want to be happy—happier than I've ever been.

ST. OBNOXIOUS: Warmest climes but nurse the cruelest fangs; the tiger of Bengal crouches in spaced groves of ceaseless verdure. Skies the most effulgent but basket the deadliest thunders; gorgeous Cuba knows tornadoes that never swept tame northern lands. So, too, it is, that in these resplendent Japanese seas the mariner encounters the direst of all storms, the typhoon. It will sometimes burst from out that cloudless sky, like an exploding bomb upon a dazed and sleepy town.

GUEST 2: It never rains but it pours.

ST. OBNOXIOUS: Nor seldom in this life, when, on the right side, fortune's favorites sail close by us, we, though all adroop before, catch somewhat of the rushing breeze, and joyfully feel our bagging sails fill out.

TURZAHNELLE: I've planned this party for months and I'm not going to let a little rain stop me now.

GUEST 1: I've always admired people who make plans—I often change mine at the last moment. There is a question of a summer frock which may alter everything. I shall act upon the inspiration of the moment.

TURZAHNBELLE: Charon, what time is it?

DEVIL-AS-CHARON: Why, my watch has stopped. Say, Vera, what time is it?

VERA: I don't know. My clock's stopped. Hello, Tryphoena, what time is it? (*Etc.*)

TURZAHNELLE: No matter the time! Keep rowing! Keep rowing! The night is young.

(*Sound of thunder. Lightning.*)

ORGONE: No doubt, this is a Ship of Fools!

DEVIL-AS-CHARON: What do you want of me! Do you want minstrel songs? The dance of the hours? Do you want me to vanish, to dive after the ring? Is that what you want? I will make gold; remedies . . . anything—but don't make me row! I am bound on a wheel of fire and my very tears do scald!

TURZAHNELLE: Row on, Charon! For all we know—it's all a dream. The greatest crime of man is having been born.

(*The ship lunges. Thunder, lightning.*)

ST. OBNOXIOUS: We dream much of paradise, or rather of a number of successive paradises, but each of them is, long before we die, a paradise lost, in which we should feel ourselves lost also. Full in this rapid wake, and many fathoms in the rear, swam a huge, humped old bull, which by his comparatively slow progress, as well as by the unusual yellowish incrustations overgrowing him, seemed afflicted with the jaundice, or some other infirmity.

(*The ship lurches and all the passengers are thrown overboard. A scrim falls over the stage and only* SAINT OBNOXIOUS *and the* ANGEL *are left.*)

ST. OBNOXIOUS: (*Singing*)
Full fathom five thy father lies;
Of his bones are coral made;
Those are pearls that were his eyes:
Nothing of him doth fade,
But doth suffer a sea-change
Into something rich and strange.

(*Music for an underwater ballet comes up and the drowned passengers, changed into sea creatures, reappear and dance.*)

The Desert Island

(BARON BUBBLES IN THE BATHTUB *is now called* CHARLIE THE CANNIBAL.)

CHARLIE: Tryphoena the Cannibal, I heard a funny thing about you today.

MME. TRYPHOENA: Well, Charlie the Cannibal, where'd you hear it?

CHARLIE: The other part of this desert island—Coconut Grove?

MME. TRYPHOENA: What was it?

CHARLIE: They say that when your stomach is empty and your pocket also, you sit down near a hot fire and read a cookbook.

MME. TRYPHOENA: Funny you should bring that up, Charlie, for just the other day I came across a recipe for cookin' human balls.

CHARLIE: Balls?

MME. TRYPHOENA: Yeah, it goes like this: Sprinkle balls with a small amount of toasted sesame seeds. Place a small amount of Japanese salted plum in the center of each ball. Place Taduku mash in one hand and roll on balls. Deep-fry balls in hot corn oil until golden. To ½ cup brown rice flour and ½ tablespoon salt, add enough water to form firm balls. Deep-fry. Test center to see if they are done. Toast sheets of Nori Seaweed by passing them gently over burner on stove until the color changes. Use amount needed to wrap each ball, dipping fingers in water and patting Nori at the edges, until it adheres to balls.

CHARLIES: Hm . . . hmmmm! Does that sound scrumptious!

MME. TRYPHOENA: Well, all we need are some ingredients . . . if you know what I mean. Quick, here comes some now. . . Let's ambush 'em.

(*They go off to hide, as* TURZAHNELLE *and* ORGONE, *the sole survivors of the shipwreck, enter.*)

TURZAHNELLE: Careful, fellows, I think these guys are cannibals, and if there's one thing I hate it's cannibals. We better get out of here.

ORGONE: What you mean, "we," dark meat?

TURZAHNELLE: I said "be careful" for it's true that religion can't explain what happens when a missionary on his way to heaven is eaten by a cannibal on his way to hell.

(SAINT OBNOXIOUS *and the* DEVIL *appear.*)

MME. TRYPHOENA: I'll grill her until she's well done.

ST. OBNOXIOUS: I remember the night we met, I drank a quart of champagne from your slipper. It would have held more but you were wearing inner-soles.

MME. TRYPHOENA: When we go in to dinner you will sit on my right hand, and . . . (*To the* DEVIL) . . . you will sit on my left hand.

CHARLIE: How will you eat . . . through a tube?

TURZAHNELLE: I'm very drunk and in a few minutes with any luck I'm gonna be a whole lot drunker.

ST. OBNOXIOUS: If you wake up the next morning with your hat on, it's a sure sign you've had a touch too much the night before.

ORGONE: You must have been blind drunk last night, too.

TURZAHNELLE: Why so?

ORGONE: Why, Vera said she saw you on the starboard deck, arguing with your shadow.

DEVIL: Why is dancing like new milk?

ST. OBNOXIOUS: Because it strengthens the calves.

DEVIL: Dat is to say dat an indulgence in terpsichorean pleasure is calculated to enlarge and strengthen de calf.

ST. OBNOXIOUS: If dancing is good for the calf I would recommend the exercise to you.

DEVIL: You're a cowherd to offer such an insult.

MME. TRYPHOENA: I'll offer her another drink while you get the pot started. Have another drink, madame.

TURZAHNELLE: Don't mind if I do. (*Drinking up, dreamily*) There's an odor of lovers around my house. No one passes naturally before my door. It rains guitars and secret messages.

DEVIL: Does ye know why dar am no more cream in de cities now?

ST. OBNOXIOUS: Can't say as I does. Can you 'splain de cause?

DEVIL: Well, y' see, milk has raised so high dat de cream can't reach de top.

ST. OBNOXIOUS: Dar's a peeler comin', we'd better cheese it.

(CHARLIE and TRYPHOENA jump TURZAHNELLE.)

TURZAHNELLE: (*Resisting*) A very simple calculation shows the impossibility of any species living off its own kind. Let us take man, for example. It takes about twenty years to raise a man, while an adult man will eat, though not exclusively, at least one man (average weight about 120 pounds) every sixty days (at the rate, therefore, of two pounds a day), thus eating six men in a year. This means that while one man is growing up (in twenty years), he will have to eat 120 men. As can be seen, in a short time this would mean the destruction of the entire species, especially as men would not be caught for eating without fights and there would be a wastage of life sometimes resulting in a supply of dead men exceeding the demand. It will therefore only be possible for a man to eat other men at long intervals of several months.

(*By now she's in the pot and stirring. The* CANNIBALS *dance around her, singing.*)

TRYPHOENA AND CHARLIE:
> A negress with a margaret once,
> Lolled frousting in the sun,
> Thinking of all the little things
> That she had left undone.
> With a hey, hey, hey, hi hey ho . . .

TURZAHNELLE: Eternity's a great nest and every creature flies away from it one after the other like young eagles, to cross the sky and vanish.

(ORGONE *comes to the edge of the pot.*)

TURZAHNELLE: He's here: my blood retreats towards my heart, and I forgot what I had meant to say.

ANGEL: Think of a son whose sole hope lies in you.

TURZAHNELLE: (*To* ORGONE) I come to wed my tears unto your griefs; and to explain my anxious fears to you. My son is now without a father; and the day is near which of my death will make him witness too. His youth is threatened by a thousand foes, and you alone can arm against them—but secret remorse is fretting in my soul. I fear you're deaf to his cries, and that you'll break on him your wrath against an odious mother.

ORGONE: Madame, I do not harbor such base feelings. It is not time to grieve. Perhaps your husband is alive.

TURZAHNELLE: He is not dead since he still lives in you. Ever before my eyes I see my husband. I see him, speak with him, and my heart still . . .

ORGONE: I see Love's wonderful effects. Dead though he is, he is always present to your eyes; your soul is burning with your love.

TURZAHNELLE: Yes, Orgone, I pine and burn for him. I love him. He had your bearing, your eyes, your speech. Why were you too young to sail with him unto our shores? For then you would have slain the Minotaur. And, yes, it would have been me, Orgone; by timely aid, I would have led you through the labyrinth. How many cares that charming head of yours would then have cost me! I would not have trusted to that weak thread alone, but walked before you, companion in the peril which you chose: and going down into the labyrinth, Turzahnelle would have returned with you, or else been lost with you.

ORGONE: O gods! What do I hear? Do you forget that this man you speak of is my father and you his wife?

TURZAHNELLE: Oh, cruel! You've understood too well. I've said enough to save you from mistaking. Know Turzahnelle then, and all her madness. Yes, I love; but do not think that I condone it, or think it innocent; nor that I ever with base complaisance added to the poison of my mad passion. Hapless victim of celestial vengeance, I abhor myself more than you can. The gods are witnesses—those gods who kindled in my breast the flame fatal to all my blood, whose cruel boast was to seduce a weak and mortal heart. Recall what's past. I did not flee from you, Orgone; no, I drove you away. I wished to seem to you both hateful and inhuman. To resist you better I aroused your hatred. But what have profited my useless pains? You loathed me more, I did not love you less; I've languished, shriveled in the flames, in tears. Your eyes will tell you so—if for a moment your eyes could look at me. What am I saying? Think you that this confession I have made was voluntary? I trembled for a son I did not dare betray—futile schemes devised by a heart too full of what it loves. Alas! I could only speak to you about yourself. Avenge yourself; punish an odious love; free the universe of a monster who offends you. Excuse me, son, I must take a piss. (*She begins to spread her legs*)

CANNIBALS: Not in the pot! Not in the pot!

(TRYPHOENA *bends over the pot.* CHARLIE *gooses her. She screams.*)

TURZAHNELLE: My cook is goosed.

MME. TRYPHOENA: Let her boil in her own stew.

(*The* CANNIBALS *help* TURZAHNELLE *out of the pot, while* ORGONE *arranges an electric chair as a toilet, religiously placing the seat—the one on which* CARLA *cast a spell.*)

ORGONE: Well, here we are, now, try this on for size.

TURZAHNELLE: (*Sitting down on the toilet*) There is my heart: there you should aim your blow. I feel it now, eager to expiate its sins.

ANGEL:
>One nonday I sleep.
>I dreamt of a someday
>Of a wonday I shall wake.
>Ah! May he have now of here fearfilled me!
>Sinflowed, O sin flowed!

TURZAHNELLE: Advance towards me, Orgone. Strike. Or if you think it unworthy of your blows, your hatred envying me a death so sweet, or if you think your hand with blood too vile would be imbued, lend me your sword instead.

(*She flushes the toilet-electric chair!!!*)

ORGONE: The douche of death!

(*The flagellant procession enters with trumpets, banners, candles, swords, icons, palms, incense, etc.*)

ST. OBNOXIOUS: Turzahnelle will be no more—a cruel flame will leave all her glory but a name.

DEVIL: Founded upon His everlasting word, Turzahnelle will be protected by the Lord.

ST. OBNOXIOUS: My eyes behold her glory disappear.

DEVIL: I see her brightness spreading everywhere.

ST. OBNOXIOUS: Turzahnelle has fallen into the abyss.

DEVIL: Aspiring Turzahnelle and heaven's kiss.

ST. OBNOXIOUS: What sad abasement!

DEVIL: What immortal glory!

ST. OBNOXIOUS: How many cries of sorrow!

DEVIL: What songs of triumph!

TURZAHNELLE: Peace! Trouble not yourselves; someday the mystery will be revealed.

ORGONE: (*Beginning to weep*) The throne of grace is a spiritual toilet.

TURZAHNELLE: Do you see him? He is crying, the baby hunchback, pinhead, sex maniac—all the hoarfrosts of the world have passed through his lips. He is the god of volcanoes and the king of winters! (*Looking up, she sighs*

a long moan) The eagle has already passed by, the new spirit calls me. . . .
I have put on for him the dress of Jezebel—he is the beloved child of
Turzahnelle.

DEVIL: Do you recognize the temple with the vast peristyle, and the bitter
lemons which were marked by your teeth, and the grotto, fatal to impudent guests, where the old seed of the anguished dragon sleeps? He will
return—the dragon for whom you still weep! Time will bring back the
order of the former days: the earth has trembled with a prophetic breath.

*(Enter the Dragon from the Book of Revelation, with seven heads and seven
crowns on each head, followed by the* POPE, *who recites the litany of Satan, as
money and white roses [snow?] fall profusely over all the living and the
dead. . . .)*

POPE:

O grandest of the Angels, and most wise,
O fallen God, fate-driven from the skies,

CHORUS:

Satan, at last take pity on our pain.

POPE:

O subterranean king, omniscient,
Healer of man's immortal discontent,

CHORUS:

Satan, at last take pity on our pain.

POPE:

To lepers and to outcasts thou dost show
That passion is the paradise below.

CHORUS:

Satan, at last take pity on our pain.

POPE:

Thou, by thy mistress Death, hast given men
Hope, the imperishable courtesan.

CHORUS:

Satan, at last take pity on our pain.

POPE:

Thou knowest the corners of the jealous Earth
Where God has hidden jewels of great worth.

CHORUS:

Satan, at last take pity on our pain.

POPE:

Thy awful name is written as with pitch
On the unrelenting foreheads of the rich.

CHORUS:

Satan, at last take pity on our pain.

POPE:
> In strange and hidden places thou dost move
> Where women cry for torture in their love.

CHORUS:
> Satan, at last take pity on our pain.

POPE:
> Father of those whom God's tempestuous ire
> Has flung from paradise with sword and fire,

CHORUS:
> Satan, at last take pity on our pain.

(VERA, *looking younger and more innocent than ever before, delicately approaches* TURZAHNELLE *on her throne.*)

VERA: Turzahnelle, with your hands full of fires, rose with the purple heart . . . did you find your cross in the desert of the skies? White roses, fall! Fall, white phantoms, from your burning skies: the saint of the abyss is more saintly in my eyes!

(*Choirs of angels sing joyously as the curtain falls.*)

Loretta Strong

Copi

First performed 30th May 1974 at the Théâtre de la Gaite-Montaparnasse. Direction, sets and costumes by Javier Botana. Loretta Strong played by Copi.

CHARACTERS

LORETTA STRONG
STEVE MORTON
> (LORETTA STRONG *and* STEVE MORTON.
> LORETTA STRONG *kills* STEVE MORTON.)

LORETTA STRONG. Hello, John?
> Just my luck, Steve's dead!
> Is everything O.K. with you, John?
> That's good, give my love to Linda!
> Hello, earth?
> You forgot to plug in Steve Morton's oxygen supply, Mr. Drake!
> It's all very well apologizing, but it's not you who's going to impregnate me on the Milky Way!
> I'm all alone again with the rats!
> Hello, Linda?
> Did you hear what I just threw at him?
> What's that? John's dead?

Reprinted from *Plays of Copi* [Raul Damonte], trans. Anni Lee Taylor (London: Calder, 1976), 97–128. Republished by permission of Calder Publications Ltd.

We've had it!

Hello, earth?

What shit!

Hello, earth?

John Balling died of a heart attack!

What did you say?

You're mad!

Hello, Linda?

They want the rats to make us pregnant!

No way! Not me!

Well, you can do what you like!

I'll find someone or other out in space!

Hello? Hello? Hello?

An earthwoman speaking!

Hello? Hello? Hello?

Who are you?

A Monkey-Man from the Polar Star?

Who the fuck do you think you're talking to?

Is that you, Mr. Drake?

You've been invaded by the Monkey-Men from the Polar Star?

Hello, Linda?

Did you hear that?

There's nothing else we can do!

Let's get on with it!

Come on, come here!

Are you a little boy?

Ow, stop biting, you nasty thing!

I'm not going to hurt you!

You want to get down on me?

Oh, that's horrible!

Take it easy down there!

Yuk!

Get back in your cage!

Hello, Linda?

Is your fridge big enough to take John?

We're not very well equipped, are we?

Besides, it's not all that easy to cut up such a big man!

What if we ate him, Linda?

We're not cannibals but after all we do need our calories!

I'll try a toe.

Well, it's not fantastic, but it is meat after all.

What if we tried a haunch?

Oh, I'm really hungry!

We're not going to give all this meat away to the worms of Betelgeuse!

Isn't your oven big enough?

Bend the knee!

Just minute, there's someone on my line.

Hello? Hello?

It's nothing, it's just my own voice echoing off the rings of Saturn!

Linda, Linda . . . it's not just because we're alone that we'll become lesbians. Listen to me!

Listen, Linda, you're making me laugh!

I've never done that with a woman!

Linda, we're not even on the same satellite!

We can't screw over the telephone, silly!

Listen, is the leg simmering yet?

We can give the bones to the rats!

That way we'll save on cereals, one never knows!

Good, hey?

It tastes like turtle.

Yes, overhung turtle.

Can't you feel the rats moving inside you?

They grow very quickly!

Look, that hurts.

Are you sure they're born without teeth?

Oh, shit, here it comes!

Ouch . . . here's another one!

Aaah, it's disgusting!

Three!

Aaaah, another one!

Four rats!

They do have funny looking heads for rats!

Oh no, they're bats, they've got little wings!

Are yours about to arrive?

Well, make an effort!

Yes?

A child?

But then you were pregnant by John!

Eight kilos?

You're kidding!

It's eating John's haunch?

And biting you as well?

It's a monster!

Get rid of it!

Throw it out into space!

Have you got it tied up then?

Oh listen . . . it's crying!

No, no, Linda, don't kill it just like that. Push it out into space, then it'll have a chance of surviving.

Linda? Linda?

Hello, Linda?

Can you hear me?

Dr. Drake?

Are you the only one left?

Give me your last instructions, Mr. Drake!

Hello? Hello? Hello?

Hello, Linda?

Did you see the latest?

The earth has blown up!

Mr. Drake?

Where are you?

Here?

Oh, no! Don't touch me, you're freezing cold!

Eat something, Mr. Drake!

They're bats!

They're quite fresh!

They're not bad!

Don't touch me, Mr. Drake!

Hello, Linda, I'm talking very low because I've got the astral body of Mr. Drake in the satellite!

We've got to work out what we're going to do with all this gold. We don't have to explain ourselves to anyone now!

Don't touch me, Mr. Drake!

Stop it!

Oh no, that's revolting, stop it!

Go on, push him in the fridge!

It's a good job he's not very heavy!

Heave ho!

Lool, Linda, what are we going to do with all this gold?

What do you mean, what gold?

But we're carrying gold!

We're going to plant it on Betelgeuse, that's our mission!

Don't you remember anything?

I can always tell you about your past but I don't see the point if you've lost your memory!

Get back in the fridge, Mr. Drake!

Hello? Hello? Hello? Hello?

Venus?

This is an earthwoman speaking! A terrestienne!

No, I didn't say a turreen—An Argentine!

Fuck, I've got the Venusian cock-eaters at my heels!

They're in cahoots with the Monkey-Men!

Linda, listen to me, we've got to get organised!

That's all you ever think about, Linda!

The main thing is to grow some gold on Betelgeuse!

One thing's got nothing to do with the other, but we haven't got the time!

It's a long business this gold planting, you know.

Quite apart from it being heavy.

Oh, he's pissing all over me, the dirty thing!

Get back in the fridge!

Get back in the fridge!

I've had quite enough of Mr. Drake!

I don't know what he wants but he won't leave me alone!

Ah yes, when it comes to eating, he certainly knows how to eat!

Three bats and a rat in less than three minutes!

Right now here's there, gnawing at Steve's tibia!

Get back in the fridge!

Hello, Linda?

The tele?

But there's no more programmes, there's no earth anymore!

You can see me, can't you?

I must have a funny looking face!

Oh, d'you think so?

Listen, Linda, don't start that again. How can we possibly screw each other?

Are you masturbating right now?

But I'm not beautiful at all, I'm well built but I'm not beautiful!

Let's talk about something else, Linda!

You're beginning to get on my nerves!

Are you coming?

Don't moan like that, you'd think your throat was being cut!

Your throat is being cut?

The Venusians?

Linda, hello, Linda?

Shit, it's going to be my turn next!

Who's speaking?

Is it a bat speaking?

Mummy?

It wants to suck my breast?

After all, they should be able to learn to grow gold, these animals, they don't look that stupid!

It's a shame Mr. Drake ate the rest!

I'll just have to conceive a few more!

I'm sorry, chum, but I don't have any milk!

Oh, no! Don't bite me!

Eat a bit of Steve, go on!

Come, ratty darling, come!

Linda, I'm going to conceive again!

There's a rat up my vagina but he's taking a long time to come!

Did the Venusians eat you?

Did they, the shits?

Are you stuck, where? Between my lights and my liver?

Ow, fuck, he bit me!

Oh, he's gone right up inside me, I can't catch him!

Ow!

Nasty thing!

I've got hold of his tail!

It's impossible, it's slippery!

Ah, there you are, you naughty rat!

Get back in your cage!

Get back in your cage!

Hello? Hello?

Loretta Strong speaking!

You're from Pluto?

The earth has blown up!

It blew up, just like that!

The Monkey-Men from the Polar Star couldn't blow up such a big planet. Are you mad?

It's not the first planet that's blown up!

Oh, they do go on, these plutonians!

No, it's not true!

Don't hang up; Linda, I've got a plutonian on the line.

Listen, let me get a word in!

Can you hear me?

Let me get a word in!

I'm not looking for a male, and in any case we're a million light years apart, you and I!

I'm just looking for someone to plant my gold on Betelgeuse, even if it takes an eternity!

Do you understand my problem?

Hello? Hello?

Oh, that little slut of a bat has gobbled down Steve's prick!

Oh, the little shit!

I'll shove you in the fridge!

Disgusting animal!

That's what I get for having it off with the rats!

Hello, Linda?

We've got to get organized!

We can't rely on these plutonians, they're absolutely stupid!

Anyway, I don't think they exist, it's one of those answer-phones!

Hello? Hello? Hello? Hello? Hello?

Linda, aren't you hungry?

What about the sweetbreads?

But you can open the skull!

The heart's quite good too, but it's not so tender!

Sweetbreads just melt on your tongue!

It makes you fat?

You're floating over there, are you?

Whatever happens don't explode, Linda, don't leave me alone!

Hello, Linda?

Hello?

That's all I needed, Linda has exploded!

Hello?

Who is it, me?

You again!

My line is always engaged, and you're not the one who pays the telephone bill, are you?

Listen!

Will you let me get a word in?

Pregnant?

By whom would I be pregnant?

By you?

But who are you?

Aura what?

Aura? *Kia-Ora?* [What-a-for-a?]*

He's stuttering!

This guy stutters!

Aura what?

Aura Borealis! My name's not Alice! . . . But I have an aura!

Hello Linda?

I'm leaking *Kia-Ora!* [da-gold, what-a for-a!]

Speak up a bit, I can't hear you!

Where are you?

In the fridge?

I thought you were on the end of the line!

You're completely frozen!

Listen, don't start again! I don't want a bottle of Kia-Ora up my vagina!

Are you mad?

Perhaps you're right as it grows on Betelgeuse!

But gently, hey!

I've already had two rats in less than a quarter of an hour and one of them but my uterus!

Oh, it's so cold!

I said gently!

Don't move! There we are!

Hello? Hello?

Don't move!

*American alternatives are given in square brackets after the italicized English word or phrase.

Hello? Hello?

Who?

We've got the Monkey-Men from the Polar Star after us, impregnate me quickly!

No, you can't have my *Kia-Ora!* [gold-a, what-a-fora!]

And don't forget I've got an Interplanetary machine-gun!

Now that we know what you use it for, *your Kia-Ora!*[What-a-for-a!]

Have you come yet, down there?

You can't stay in there for ever!

Go on, get out!

Don't suck me, I hate that!

Don't cry like that!

Hello? Hello? Hello? Hello?

Is that you, the plutonian?

He's incapable!

He's clapped out with the clap!

What did you say?

Laura what?

Loretta?

I'm Loretta! What about it?

Linda, wake up!

Have a chewing gum, we're coming down!

Get yourself dressed! Come on!

Oh dear, can't she do anything right!

Fasten your seat belt, stupid!

We're going backwards!

We're going to crash into what's left of the earth!

Ow, fuck it! The Himalayas just hit me on the head!

Hello? Hello? Hello? Hello, Linda?

Oh, no! Not now, it's not the time for that!

Get back in the fridge!

Hello? Hello?

Oh, damn, I'm giving birth!

One . . . two . . three . . . four!

They're little golden bats!

Ah, look! The eyes are little rubies!

I'm hugging them to my breast!

They don't even have a mirror on these satellites!

I'm going to look at myself in the water in the *loo!* [John!]

A rat!

He was waiting there to bite me!

I'm going to cut its throat!

They've gobbled down all my gold while I wasn't looking!

Look, there's another one!

He's full of gold, the beast!

There's another!

Three ingots in his belly, the swine!

Get out of it!

I'll pull the chain!

Go on, float off into space!

Hello? Hello? Hello? Hello?

The plutonian?

You're in the oven?

Wait, I'll open it for you!

He's burned to a frazzle!

I'm not going to get pregnant with a black pudding, it looks like shit!

Eat that, Mr. Drake!

The Monkey-Men from the Polar Star!

They want to come up through the *loo!* [John!]

I'll throw in a hand-grenade!

There we go!

Good riddance!

Ow, I'm burning!

Make room for me in the fridge!

Move over, Mr. Drake!

Move over!

No, no, Linda! It's not the right moment to have me!

No, Linda, stop it!

Oh, the slut, she's gone inside me!

Hello, Linda, get out this minute!

I told you to get out!

She's going higher!

She's crushing my stomach!

Ow, my lungs!

Get out, Linda, get out this minute!

Linda, my anorak!

What the fuck's she done with my anorak?

What's she saying?

I can hardly hear you!

I didn't say anything about my rats, I said my anorak!

I'm not going to wear a rat-skin to go down to Betelgeuse!

What? What?

Speak up a bit!

You're hungry?

You're a bloody nuisance!

There's some black pudding in the fridge!

Eat that!

She's choked herself with the black pudding, the cunt!

Aaah . . . get out, Linda! Aaah . . . get out!

I know perfectly well you're there, I can see you reflected in the *loo!* [John!]

I'm not going down to Betelgeuse with you inside me!

I'm cutting my throat open!

Don't scream like that!

Come on out! Into the oven! Look what you've done to me, you bitch!

I've no vocal chords left!

Hello? Hello? Hello?

Oh, the plutonian! I'm on my way!

I've no more gold, the rats ate it all. I've only got little nuggets, but we can always plant those!

Can't you hear me?

I don't believe it, he's deaf!

Oh, la, la!

What's that beating? This is no time for playing the bongos!

The oven?

The oven's exploded!

Linda, where are you?

There are bits of her all over the place!

Bits of you?

Bits of metal, but not bits of her!

Shut up!

That's a bit of her!

And that too!

One golden randy. . . ! I mean a golden Rand. Is that all that's left of her?

There! I'll put it in my porcelain rat-bank!

Hello? Hello? Hello? Hello? Hello? Hello?

What did he say?

I don't believe it!

The plutonian was a parrot, that's the best yet!

It's a survivor from the satellite of animals that was lost on Jupiter last year!

I'm coming down! I'm on my way!

Hello? Hello? Linda, can you hear me?

I'm on Betelgeuse!

Wow! it's not a planet, it's a comet!

Can you hear me?

Where are you, Linda?

There are little bits of gold flying around all over the place!

Hello, Linda?

Hello? Hello?

Aura what?

Loretta what?

In what?

Out of the question?

Will you let me get a word in?

Oh, I hate her!

Get back in your cage!

Get back in your cage!

You are talking about a fellow crew member of mine!

Hello? Hello?

I've lost the controls!

Linda? Linda?

Linda, I'm blowing up!

Oh shit, I'll have to put all the pieces of me back together myself!

That's going to be nice, sticking all these fingers back on!

There's hair stuck all over the walls!

I'd better do it quick before the blood clots!

Ow, what's she shouting about?

You're breaking my eardrums!

This girl-rat isn't mine, it must be Linda's!

She just has to put herself together!

Shut up!

Shut up!

Hello? Hello?

I can hardly hear myself, I'm being strangled by Linda's intestines!

There's no way out except through the *loo!* [john!]

It's a good job I'm not fat, isn't it!

So, I'll pull the chain!

Glug . . . glug . . . glug . . . Linda, I'm stuck in the U-bend!

Can you hear me?

Do something!

Glug!

Hello?

Glug! Glug!

Push me!

Hello? Linda?

Push me!

Someone's pushing me from below!

It's the Monkey-Men!

Let me go, I want to get out of here!

Glug!

Oh shit, here I am again!

Let go of my feet, you pigs!

Linda, where are you?

We've got to get organized!

They're coming up through the *loo!* [john!]

We can block it with the fridge!

There, like that!

Hello? Hello?

I'm not going to be sucked off by a porcelaine rat, even if it is you!

You mean the money inside will breed!

Come here!

Don't bite me, stupid!

Hello? Hello? Hello? Hello?

They're speaking to me from all over, how annoying!

Valparaiso?

Hong Kong?

It's what's left of the earth!

Is somebody there?

It's my own voice bouncing back off the remains of the earth!

Timbuctoo?

Rio?

The Alps?

The Danube?

Moscow?

Dallas?

Cordoba?

Lausanne?

Linda, shut up!

It's not the moment to start crying! Don't bite me!

Oh, I've broken it!

It's only gold dust!

Atchoo!

Hello? Hello?

Hello, Linda?

Hello? Hello?

Where's my anorak?

Atchoo!

Everywhere the rocks are melting, but I'm freezing!

Hello, Linda?

Where are you?

We're going to blow up!

We're exploding!

I'm going to go down!

Where's my anorak?

Hello, Linda, come here right away!

Hello? Hello?

Hello, hello?

She's outside!

How did she get out?

Hello, Linda?

How?

Oh, not that way!

It would put at least a thousand years on me!

On top of which it takes for ever to digest the metal!

I swallowed a screw but it hurt me!

I'm eating a handle!

Give me a chance to breathe!

I'll get an ulcer?
The fridge door?
I've broken all my teeth, it's just not possible!
Can you hear me?
Hello, Linda?
There's nothing but blood on Betelgeuse?
Hello, Linda?
Have you drowned?
Wait for me, Linda, I'm going out!
Hello? Hello?
I'm here!
Speak up, I can't hear a thing!
Hello? Hello? Hello? Hello?
Linda's been shipwrecked!
Hello? Hello?
I can't see you any more!
Hello?
Swim, Linda!
There's an island!
There's the sand!
Watch out for the crabs!
Hello, Linda?
And the cockatoos?
Hello, Linda?
Oh, shit!
The island's sinking!
Hello, Linda?
Let me go!
I'm sinking!
Hello?
Glug! Glug! Glug! Glug! Glug! Glug!
Glug!
A cockatoo fish!
I'm being eaten up!
Crunch!
I'm right at the centre of Betelgeuse!
It's boiling gold.
Betelgeuse is blowing up, that's really a laugh!

Where are you, Linda?
You've been thrown up by a volcano?
You're covered in gold and it's getting hard, just like a sarcophagus?
Speak up, I can hardly hear you!
Hello, Hello, Hello, Linda?
But that's awful, how can we ever fuck?
I'm not having a fridge shoved up my vagina, you're crazy!
The handle alright, but not the rest!
Ow, it's freezing cold!
The deep freeze might just go in, but that's all!
Ow, I can't take any more, I'm giving birth!
Ouch! Ouch!
Only one, but it's enormous!
I don't know!
It's not a rat, it's made of metal!
It's alive, it's flying about!
It's bumping into the walls!
It's screaming!
Ow!
Stop it!
Ow!
It's pinched my nose!
It's exploding!
Hello? Hello?
I've got bits of it stuck all over me!
Hello, hello, can you hear me?
Not me, my eardrums have burst!
You're sitting on a scythe?
It's a new moon?
Watch out, it's sharp!
Ow, Linda!
You've spurted all over!
Keep your head up!
Breathe deeply!
There's someone on my line!
It's a parrot!
Get out! Get out!
Get back in your cage!

In your cage!
Hello, hello, hello, hello?
It was a cockatoo! They're all over the place!
Will you let me get a word in?
Will you let me get a word in?
It has a receding head! It looks like a midget!
You can't see it any more!
I'm changing the programme!
Hello, hello, hello, Linda?
What did you say?
She's mad!
What intermission?
There isn't an intermission!
She wants to sell me an anorak?
But it belongs to me!
Give me back that anorak!
Where is she?
Hello, hello, hello, hello?
She's stolen my anorak!
What? What?
What did she say?
An egg?
There's a cockatoo on my line!
I don't give a fuck about your hardboiled eggs!
Get back in your cage!
Get back in your cage!
Hello, Linda?
I'm germinating!
I've got blisters under my skin!
Can you hear me?
They're coming out on the walls, too but not as many!
Wait while I spray them!
They're roses!
Golden roses!
The cockatoos are all white and so cute!
They're singing!
Hello, Linda?
We've got to get organized!

Can you hear me?
You've lost everything, but I've still got the gold!
Wait for me and we'll arrive together!
What's your position!
Kia-Ora Orangina?
It's not detailed in my space cards!
Not at all!
I've got to collect up my souvenirs!
Where's my pocket dictionary?
I know very well you're a red-head, if you think that excites me!
Kit-Ora Orangina?
Is that where they do the tango?
You're out of your mind!
But where are you, anyway?
Where is here?
In the gold?
No, you can't, the gold's mine!
Oh, the little thief!
Where is she?
Hello? Hello?
She's got to be somewhere!
Where are you?
Hello, Linda?
Hello, Linda?
Hello, Linda?
You're floating about?
In a sewer?
That's nothing to be proud of!
Wait a minute!
I'm cracking up!
I'm losing the marrow in my bones!
I'm melting!
Hello, hello, hello, Linda?
I'm floating!
Wait for me!
Hello, Linda?
Hello, Linda?
There's no Betelgeuse any more!

Where are you?

Speak a bit louder!

Yes, I can see you!

How elegant, Linda!

What? You've lost your head?

Wait for me, I'm giving birth again!

Ow! Ow!

It's enormous! It's coming!

Wait for me!

Hello? Hello?

It's a golden ball!

It's got little eyes like pins!

Wait for me, it's not over!

Ow!

Hello, Linda?

It's even got some bones!

Can you hear me?

Hello, Linda?

Should I stick it together?

It looks like a puppet!

Hello, Linda?

It's sucking my breast!

It's cutting me!

It's torn off one of my breasts with its beak!

I'll have to crush it to death!

Hello, Linda?

It's pissing blood!

I'm drowning in it!

Hello, Linda?

Glug, glug!

Flying cockatoo fish!

I'll catch some!

Hello, hello, hello, hello?

Where are you?

I'm flying!

I'm there!

Wait for me!

Hello, Linda?

I'm squashed against the wall!
Ow, the chandelier!
Ow, that bastard cockatoo has slashed my clitoris with its beak!
I'll strangle it!
I'm falling over!
Don't scream!
I've cut its head off!
One, two, down the loo! [Down you go, you little bastard!]
Glug, glug, my arse!
It's floating?
What did it say?
Rat-a-tat-tat!
It doesn't even know how to talk!
What did it say?
Go and waltz with the stars, you swine!
I'm pulling the chain!
Hello, Linda?
Oh shit, it's overflowing!
Are you there, Linda?
Wait till I catch you up!
A rat!
A squirrel!
It's full of dead animals!
Is that you?
It's a page of the telephone book!
A quail?
Doesn't it stick!
Hello? Hello?
What shit!
A lynx!
Oh, my! Oh, my!
Wait, I'm coming!
It's alive!
It's you!
Wait
I've got hold of your head, look!
I'm pulling, now you make an effort!
It's slipping!

One, two, three! There!

It's a snake!

Linda, you're covered in muck!

You're cold?

Come and wrap yourself round me!

Don't suck my breast, I hate that!

Eat this hand-grenade, that'll warm you up!

Let me go!

Not in my mouth!

Oh, glug, not in my mouth!

Ow, no, Linda!

Ooow!

Oh, the bitch!

Hello? Hello?

Get out, Linda!

Can you hear me?

Oh shit, I'm blowing up!

Hello, Linda?

Hello, Linda?

Get out! Get out!

She's taking so long to get out!

And you, get in your cage!

Hello, hello?

Oh no! It's impossible, she's gobbling up the cage!

Wait, I'm opening it!

Don't scream like that!

Don't scream like that!

She's full of nuggets!

Will you let me get a word in?

Will you let me get a word in?

Will you let me get a word in?

Hello, Linda?

Listen to me!

Listen to me!

Are you listening?

Are you listening?

Listen to me!

Can you hear me?

Hello, hello?
Hello, hello?
Hello, hello?
Hello, hello?
No, I don't believe it!
You're nothing but a boa skin, how could we possibly fuck?
Just a minute, there's someone on my line!
The fridge is talking, is there someone inside?
Oh no, that's disgusting, not that!
I don't know but it's horrible!
I'll shut it again!
It's exploding!
It's spurting out blood!
It's flooding everything!
Where are you, Linda?
I'm swimming!
My head's jammed against the chandelier!
Glug, glug!
I'm drowning!
It's freezing!
Glug! Glug!
Where's my anorak?
Is that you, Linda?
Wrap yourself round me, it's freezing!
If we could just pull the chain!
Glug! Glug!
I'm in a vortex!
Can you hear me?
Can you hear me?
Glug, glug!
Can you hear me?
The pipes are frozen and the lavatory's cracking!
I've got porcelaine forming over my eyes!
Hello, Linda?
I'm outside!
Can you hear me?
There's nothing left of the Monkey-Men but their arses hung on the tip of the moon!

But that's waning!

Hello, Linda?

Hello, Linda?

What did she say?

What about my anorak?

Take the nuggets and go and buy yourself a choc ice! I'll stay here and read the programme!

Oh, shut up, and go by yourself!

One choc ice, please, Miss!

Where is she?

Miss?

She's deaf!

Can you hear me?

Don't shout like that!

One choc ice, please, Miss!

Hello, hello, hello, hello?

I don't know, Linda, I don't know!

I'm turning, but my head's still at the bottom!

My skull's being squeezed!

Hello? Hello?

I'm coming back!

Where are you?

Hello, Linda?

I'm exploding!

Pick up my pieces!

I'm still turning!

I have no more air!

He-lo-lo-lo-lo-lo-li-li-li-li-li-li-li-n-n-n-da-da-da-da-da-li-li-li-li-il-il-il-il-a-a-a-o-o-o-o-ad-ad-ad-ad-n-n-n-n-

Where are you?

What's she saying?

Hello, hello?

Hello, Linda?

My memory, my memory, what's she talking about?

Cockatoos?

They're laying what?

Beating what?

Flakes of what?

Where's my anorak?
I'm going down!
I'm freezing!
Wrap yourself round me!
Not so rough, Linda. Let go!
You're asphyxiating me!
I can't breathe!
I'm being squeezed to death!
I'm exploding!
But you're in streamers!
Come here and let me pick up the bits!
I'll sew you together, Linda!
You're no very pretty to look at!
You look like a patchwork quilt!
And get back in your cage!
And stop complaining!
I've just got worms crawling through me!
What a fuck up!
They're frozen!
Get out! Get out! Get out! Get out!
Oh, the shits, my lips are riddled with them!
Get out! Get out!
They're crawling through me!
Get out! Get out! Get out! Get out!
Hello, Linda?
Where do you want me to look at you?
She's cracking up!
Where is she?
It smells like burning!
Oh, fuck, I put her in the toaster!
Look how she's shrunk, she's just dried skin!
Wait for me!
Hello, hello? Hello?
Wait for me, I'm eating Linda!
Crunch, crunch!
It's good but it's too hot!
It's hardening inside me, it feels like hail!
I'm exploding!

I've got nuggets coming out of all my pores.
They'll make holes in the walls of the satellite!
Are you outside?
Can you hear me?
Shout louder!
I'm shouting!
It's me, Linda!
Can you hear me?
It's me!
Hello, hello, hello, hello?
It's raining here, the roof's leaking!
There's blood pouring in from all sides!
I haven't got any sacking, I've only got your skin!
Oh la, la!
Wait for me!
I'm coming out.

CURTAIN

Notes on "Camp"

Susan Sontag

Many things in the world have not been named; and many things, even if they have been named, have never been described. One of these is the sensibility—unmistakably modern, a variant of sophistication but hardly identical with it—that goes by the cult name of "Camp."

A sensibility (as distinct from an idea) is one of the hardest things to talk about; but there are special reasons why Camp, in particular, has never been discussed. It is not a natural mode of sensibility, if there be any such. Indeed the essence of Camp is its love of the unnatural: of artifice and exaggeration. And Camp is esoteric—something of a private code, a badge of identity even, among small urban cliques. Apart from a lazy two-page sketch in Christopher Isherwood's novel *The World in the Evening* (1954), it has hardly broken into print. To talk about Camp is therefore to betray it. If the betrayal can be defended, it will be for the edification it provides, or the dignity of the conflict it resolves. For myself, I plead the goal of self-edification, and the goad of a sharp conflict in my own sensibility. I am strongly drawn to Camp, and almost as strongly offended by it. That is why I want to talk about it, and why I can. For no one who wholeheartedly shares in a given sensibility to analyze it; he can only, whatever his intention, exhibit it. To name a sensibility, to draw its contours and to recount its history, requires a deep sympathy modified by revulsion.

Though I am speaking about sensibility only—and about a sensibility that, among other things, converts the serious into the frivolous—these are grave matters. Most people think of sensibility or taste as the realm of purely subjective preferences, those mysterious attractions, mainly sensual, that have not been brought under the sovereignty of reason. They *allow* that considerations of taste play a part in their reactions to people and to works of art. But this attitude is naïve. And even worse. To patronize the faculty of taste is to patronize oneself. For taste governs every free—as opposed to rote— human response. For state governs every free—as opposed to rote—human response. Nothing is more decisive. There is taste in people, visual taste, taste in emotion—and there is taste in acts, taste in morality. Intelligence, as well, is really a kind of taste: taste in ideas. (One of the facts to be reckoned with is that taste tends to develop very unevenly. It's rare that the same person has good visual taste *and* good taste in people *and* taste in ideas.)

Taste has no system and no proofs. But there is something like a logic of taste: the consistent sensibility which underlies and gives rise to a certain taste. A sensibility is almost, but not quite, ineffable. Any sensibility which can be crammed into the mold of a system, or handled with the rough tools of proof, is no longer a sensibility at all. It was hardened into an idea. . . .

To snare a sensibility in words, especially one that is alive and powerful,* one must be tentative and nimble. The form of jottings, rather than an essay (with its claim to a linear, consecutive argument), seemed more appropriate for getting down something of this particular fugitive sensibility. It's embarrassing to be solemn and treatise-like about Camp. One runs the risk of having, oneself, produced a very inferior piece of Camp.

These notes are for Oscar Wilde.

> One should either be a work of art, or wear a work of art.
> —*Phrases & Philosophies for the Use of the Young*

1. To start very generally: Camp is a certain mode of aestheticism. It is *one* way of seeing the world as an aesthetic phenomenon. That way, the way of Camp, is not in terms of beauty, but in terms of the degree of artifice, of stylization.

2. To emphasize style is to slight content, or to introduce an attitude which is neutral with respect to content. It goes without saying that the Camp sensibility is disengaged, depoliticized—or at least apolitical.

3. Not only is there a Camp vision, a Camp way of looking at things. Camp is as well a quality discoverable in objects and the behavior of persons. There are "campy" movies, clothes, furniture, popular songs, novels, people, buildings. . . . This distinction is important. True, the Camp eye has the power to transform experience. But not everything can be seen as Camp. It's not *all* in the eye of the beholder.

---

*The sensibility of an era is not only its most decisive, but also its most perishable, aspect. One may capture the ideas (intellectual history) and the behavior (social history) of an epoch without ever touching upon the sensibility or taste which informed those ideas, that behavior. Rare are those historical studies—like Huizinga on the late Middle Ages, Febvre on 16th century France—which do tell us something about the sensibility of the period.

4. Random examples of items which are part of the canon of Camp:
   Zuleika Dobson
   Tiffany lamps
   Scopitone films
   The Brown Derby restaurant on Sunset Boulevard in LA
   The Enquirer, headlines and stories
   Aubrey Beardsley drawings
   Swan Lake
   Bellini's operas
   Visconti's direction of *Salome* and *'Tis Pity She's a Whore*
   certain turn-of-the-century picture postcards
   Schoedsack's *King Kong*
   the Cuban pop singer La Lupe
   Lynn Ward's novel in woodcuts, *God's Man*
   the old Flash Gordon comics
   women's clothes of the twenties (feather boas, fringed and beaded
       dresses, etc.)
   the novels of Ronald Firbank and Ivy Compton-Burnett
   stag movies seen without lust

5. Camp taste has an affinity for certain arts rather than others. Clothes, furniture, all the elements of visual décor, for instance, make up a large part of Camp. For Camp art is often decorative art, emphasizing texture, sensuous surface, and style at the expense of content. Concert music, though, because it is contentless, is rarely Camp. It offers no opportunity, say, for a contrast between silly or extravagant content and rich form. . . . Sometimes whole art forms become saturated with Camp. Classical ballet, opera, movies have seemed so for a long time. In the last two years, popular music (post rock-'n'-roll, what the French call *yé yé*) has been annexed. And movie criticism (like lists of "The 10 Best Bad Movies I Have Seen") is probably the greatest popularizer of Camp taste today, because most people still go to the movies in a high-spirited and unpretentious way.

6. There is a sense in which it is correct to say: "It's too good to be Camp." Or "too important," not marginal enough. (More on this later.) Thus, the personality and many of the works of Jean Cocteau are Camp, but not those of André Gide; the operas of Richard Strauss, but not those of Wagner; concoctions of Tin Pan Alley and Liverpool, but not jazz. Many examples of Camp are things which, from a "serious" point of view, are either bad art or kitsch. Not all, though. Not only is Camp not necessarily bad art, but some art which can be approached as Camp (example: the major films of Louis Feuillade) merits the most serious admiration and study.

7. All Camp objects, and persons, contain a large element of artifice. Nothing in nature can be campy. . . . Rural Camp is still man-made, and most campy objects are urban. (Yet, they often have a serenity—or a naïveté—which is the equivalent of pastoral. A great deal of Camp suggests Empson's phrase, "urban pastoral.")

8. Camp is a vision of the world in terms of style—but a particular kind of style. It is the love of the exaggerated, the "off," of things-being-what-they-are-not. The best example is in Art Nouveau, the most typical and fully developed Camp style. Art Nouveau objects, typically, convert one thing into something else: the lighting fixtures in the form of flowering plants, the living room which is really a grotto. A remarkable example: The Paris Métro entrances designed by Hector Guimard in the late 1890s in the shape of cast-iron orchid stalks.

9. As a taste in persons, Camp responds particularly to the markedly attenuated and to the strongly exaggerated. The androgyne is certainly one of the great images of Camp sensibility. Examples: the swooning, slim, sinuous figures of pre-Raphaelite painting and poetry; the thin, flowing, sexless bodies in Art Nouveau prints and posters, presented in relief on lamps and ashtrays; the haunting androgynous vacancy behind the perfect beauty of Greta Garbo. Here, Camp taste draws on a mostly unacknowledged truth of taste: the most refined form of sexual attractiveness (as well as the most refined form of sexual pleasure) consists in going against the grain of one's sex. What is most beautiful in virile men is something feminine; what is most beautiful in feminine women is something masculine. . . . Allied to the Camp taste for the androgynous is something that seems quite different but isn't: a relish for the exaggeration of sexual characteristics and personality mannerisms. For obvious reasons, the best examples that can be cited are movie stars. The corny flamboyant femaleness of Jayne Mansfield, Gina Lollobrigida, Jane Russell, Virginia Mayo; the exaggerated he-man-ness of Steve Reeves, Victor Mature. The great stylists of temperament and mannerism, like Bette Davis, Barbara Stanwyck, Tallulah Bankhead, Edwige Feuillière.

10. Camp sees everything in quotation marks. It's not a lamp, but a "lamp"; not a woman, but a "woman." To perceive Camp in objects and persons is to understand Being-as-Playing-a-Role. It is the farthest extension, in sensibility, of the metaphor of life as theater.

11. Camp is the triumph of the epicene style. (The convertibility of "man" and "woman," "person" and "thing.") But all style, that is, artifice, is, ultimately, epicene. Life is not stylish. Neither is nature.

12 The question isn't, "Why travesty, impersonation, theatricality?" The question is, rather, "When does travesty, impersonation, theatricality acquire the special flavor of Camp?" Why is the atmosphere of Shakespeare's comedies (*As You Like It*, etc.) not epicene, while that of *Der Rosenkavalier* is?

13. The dividing line seems to fall in the 18th century; there the origins of Camp taste are to be found (Gothic novels, Chinoiserie, caricature, artificial ruins, and so forth.) But the relation to nature was quite different then. In the 18th century, people of taste either patronized nature (Strawberry Hill) or attempted to remake it into something artificial (Versailles). They also indefatigably patronized the past. Today's Camp tastes effaces nature, or else contradicts it outright. And the relation of Camp taste to the past is extremely sentimental.

14. A pocket history of Camp might, of course, begin farther back—with the mannerist artists like Pontormo, Rosso, and Caravaggio, or the extraordinarily theatrical painting of Georges de La Tour, or Euphuism (Lyly, etc.) in literature. Still, the soundest starting point seems to be the late 17th and early 18th century, because of that period's extraordinary feeling for artifice, for surface, for symmetry; its taste for the picturesque and the thrilling, its elegant conventions for representing instant feeling and the total presence of character—the epigram and the rhymed couplet (in words), the flourish (in gesture and in music). The late 17th and early 18th century is the great period of Camp: Pope, Congreve, Walpole, etc., but not Swift; *les précieux* in France; the rococo churches of Munich; Pergolesi. Somewhat later: much of Mozart. But in the 19th century, what had been distributed throughout all of high culture now becomes a special taste; it takes on overtones of the acute, the esoteric, the perverse. Confining the story to England alone, we see Camp continuing wanly through 19th century aestheticism (Burne-Jones, Pater, Ruskin, Tennyson), emerging full-blown with the Art Nouveau movement in the visual and decorative arts, and finding its conscious ideologists in such "wits" as Wilde and Firbank.

15. Of course, to say all these things are Camp is not to argue they are simply that. A full analysis of Art Nouveau, for instance, would scarcely equate it with Camp. But such an analysis cannot ignore what in Art Nouveau allows it to be experienced as Camp. Art Nouveau is full of "content," even of a political-moral sort; it was a revolutionary movement in the arts, spurred on by a utopian vision (somewhere between William Morris and the Bauhaus group) of an organic politics and taste. Yet there is also a feature of the Art Nouveau objects which suggests a disengaged, unserious, "aesthete's" vision. This tells us something important about Art Nouveau—and about what the lens of Camp, which blocks out content, is.

16. Thus, the Camp sensibility is one that is alive to a double sense in which some things can be taken. But this is not the familiar split-level construction of a literal meaning, on the one hand, and a symbolic meaning, on the other. It is the difference, rather, between the thing as meaning something, anything, and the thing as pure artifice.

17. This comes out clearly in the vulgar use of the word Camp as a verb, "to camp," something that people do. To camp is a mode of seduction—one which employs flamboyant mannerisms susceptible of a double interpreta-

tion; gestures full of duplicity, with a witty meaning for cognoscenti and another, more impersonal, for outsiders. Equally and by extension, when the word becomes a noun, when a person or a thing is "a camp," a duplicity is involved. Behind the "straight" public sense in which something can be taken, one has found a private zany experience of the thing.

To be natural is such a very difficult pose to keep up.

—An Ideal Husband

18. One must distinguish between naïve and deliberate Camp. Pure Camp is always naïve. Camp which knows itself to be Camp ("camping") is usually less satisfying.

19. The pure examples of Camp are unintentional; they are dead serious. The Art Nouveau craftsman who makes a lamp with a snake coiled around it is not kidding, nor is he trying to be charming. He is saying, in all earnestness: Voilà! the Orient! Genuine Camp—for instance, the numbers devised for the Warner Brothers musicals of the early thirties (*42nd Street; The Golddiggers of 1933; . . . of 1935; . . . of 1937*; etc.) by Busby Berkeley—does not *mean* to be funny. Camping—say, the plays of Noel Coward—does. It seems unlikely that much of the traditional opera repertoire could be such satisfying Camp if the melodramatic absurdities of most opera plots had not been taken serious by their composers. One doesn't need to know the artist's private intentions. The work tells all. (Compare a typical 19th century opera with Samuel Barber's *Vanessa*, a piece of manufactured, calculated Camp, and the difference is clear.)

20. Probably, intending to be campy is always harmful. The perfection of *Trouble in Paradise* and *The Maltese Falcon*, among the greatest Camp movies ever made, comes from the effortless smooth way in which tone is maintained. This is not so with such famous would-be Camp films of the fifties as *All About Eve* and *Beat the Devil*. These more recent movies have their fine moments, but the first is so slick and the second so hysterical; they want so badly to be campy that they're continually losing the beat. . . . Perhaps, though, it is not so much a question of the unintended effect versus the conscious intention, as of the delicate relation between parody and self-parody in Camp. The films of Hitchcock are a showcase for this problem. When self-parody lacks ebullience but instead reveals (even sporadically) a contempt for one's themes and one's materials—as in *To Catch a Thief, Rear Window, North by Northwest*—the results are forced and heavy-handed, rarely Camp. Successful Camp—a movie like Carné's *Drôle de Drame*; the film performances of Mae West and Edward Everett Horton; portions of the Goon Show—even when it reveals self-parody, reeks of self-love.

21. So, again, Camp rests on innocence. That means Camp discloses innocence, but also, when it can, corrupts it. Objects, being objects, don't change when they are singled out by the Camp vision. Persons, however,

respond to their audiences. Persons begin "camping": Mae West, Bea Lillie, La Lupe, Tallulah Bankhead in *Lifeboat,* Bette Davis in *All About Eve.* (Persons can even be induced to camp without their knowing it. Consider the way Fellini got Anita Ekberg to parody herself in *La Dolce Vita.*)

22. Considered a little less strictly, Camp is either completely naïve or else wholly conscious (when one plays at being campy). An example of the latter: Wilde's epigrams themselves.

> It's absurd to divide people into good and bad. People are either charming or tedious.
> —*Lady Windemere's Fan*

23. In Naïve, or pure, Camp, the essential element is seriousness, a seriousness that fails. Of course, not all seriousness that fails can be redeemed as Camp. Only that which has the proper mixture of the exaggerated, the fantastic, the passionate, and the naïve.

24. When something is just bad (rather than Camp), it's often because it is too mediocre in its ambition. The artist hasn't attempted to do anything really outlandish. ("It's too much," "It's too fantastic," "It's not to be believed," are standard phrases of Camp enthusiasm.)

25. The hallmark of Camp is the spirit of extravagance. Camp is a woman walking around in a dress made of three million feathers. Camp is the paintings of Carlo Crivelli, with their real jewels and *trompe-l'oeil* insects and cracks in the masonry. Camp is the outrageous aestheticism of Sternberg's six American movies with Dietrich, all six, but especially the last, *The Devil Is a Woman.* . . . In Camp there is often something *démesuré* in the quality of the ambition, not only in the style of the work itself. Gaudí's lurid and beautiful buildings in Barcelona are Camp not only because of their style but because they reveal—most notably in the Cathedral of the Sagrada Familia—the ambition on the part of one man to do what it takes a generation, a whole culture to accomplish.

26. Camp is art that proposes itself seriously, but cannot be taken altogether seriously because it is "too much." *Titus Andronicus* and *Strange Interlude* are almost Camp, or could be played as Camp. The public manner and rhetoric of de Gaulle, often, are pure Camp.

27. A work can come close to Camp, but not make it, because it succeeds. Eisenstein's films are seldom Camp because, despite all exaggeration, they do succeed (dramatically) without surplus. If they were a little more "off," they could be great Camp—particularly *Ivan the Terrible I & II.* The same for Blake's drawings and paintings, weird and mannered as they are. They aren't Camp; though Art Nouveau, influenced by Blake, is.

What is extravagant in an inconsistent or an unpassionate way is not Camp. Neither can anything be Camp that does not seem to spring from an irrepressible, a virtually uncontrolled sensibility. Without passion, one gets pseudo-Camp—what is merely decorative, safe, in a word, chic. On the barren edge of Camp lie a number of attractive things: the sleek fantasies of

Dali, the haute couture preciosity of Albicocco's *The Girl with the Golden Eyes*. But the two things—Camp and preciosity—must not be confused.

28. Again, Camp is the attempt to do something extraordinary. But extraordinary in the sense, often, of being special, glamorous. (The curved line, the extravagant gesture.) Not extraordinary merely in the sense of effort. Ripley's Believe-It-Or-Not items are rarely campy. These items, either natural oddities (the two-headed rooster, the eggplant in the shape of a cross) or else the products of immense labor (the man who walked from here to China on his hands, the woman who engraved the New Testament on the head of a pin), lack the visual reward—the glamour, the theatricality—that marks off certain extravagances as Camp.

29. The reason a movie like *On the Beach*, books like *Winesburg, Ohio* and *For Whom the Bell Tolls* are bad to the point of being laughable, but not bad to the point of being enjoyable, is that they are too dogged and pretentious. They lack fantasy. There is Camp in such bad movies as *The Prodigal* and *Samson and Delilah*, the series of Italian color spectacles featuring the super-hero Maciste, numerous Japanese science fiction films (*Rodan, The Mysterians, The H-Man*) because, in their relative unpretentiousness and vulgarity, they are more extreme and irresponsible in their fantasy—and therefore touching and quite enjoyable.

30. Of course, the canon of Camp can change. Time has a great deal to do with it. Time may enhance what seems simply dogged or lacking in fantasy now because we are too close to it, because it resembles too closely our own everyday fantasies, the fantastic nature of which we don't perceive. We are better able to enjoy a fantasy as fantasy when it is not our own.

31. This is why so many of the objects prized by Camp taste are old-fashioned, out-of-date, démodé. It's not a love of the old as such. It's simply that the process of aging or deterioration provides the necessary detachment —or arouses a necessary sympathy. When the theme is important, and contemporary, the failure of a work of art may make us indignant. Time can change that. Time liberates the work of art from moral relevance, delivering it over to the Camp sensibility. . . . Another effect: time contracts the sphere of banality. (Banality is, strictly speaking, always a category of the contemporary.) What was banal can, with the passage of time, become fantastic. Many people who listen with delight to the style of Rudy Vallee revived by the English pop group, The Temperance Seven, would have been driven up the wall by Rudy Vallee in his heyday.

Thus, things are campy, not when they become old—but when we become less involved in them, and can enjoy, instead of be frustrated by, the failure of the attempt. But the effect of time is unpredictable. Maybe Method Acting (James Dean, Rod Steiger, Warren Beatty) will seem as Camp some day as Ruby Keeler's does now—or as Sarah Bernhardt's does, in the films she made at the end of her career. And maybe not.

32. Camp is the glorification of "character." The statement is of no importance—except, of course, to the person (Loie Fuller, Gaudí, Cecil B.

De Mille, Crivelli, de Gaulle, etc.) who makes it. What the Camp eye appreciates is the unity, the force of the person. In every move the aging Martha Graham makes she's being Martha Graham, etc., etc. . . . This is clear in the case of the great serious idol of Camp taste, Greta Garbo. Garbo's incompetence (at the least, lack of depth) as an actress enhances her beauty. She's always herself.

33. What Camp taste responds to is "instant character" (this is, of course, very 18th century); and, conversely, what it is not stirred by is the sense of the development of character. Character is understood as a state of continual incandescence—a person being one, very intense thing. This attitude toward character is a key element of the theatricalization of experience embodied in the Camp sensibility. And it helps account for the fact that opera and ballet are experienced as such rich treasures of Camp, for neither of these forms can easily do justice to the complexity of human nature. Wherever there is development of character, Camp is reduced. Among operas, for example, *La Traviata* (which has some small development of character) is less campy than *Il Trovatore* (which has none).

Life is too important a thing ever to talk seriously about it.

—Vera, or The Nihilists

34. Camp taste turns its back on the good-bad axis of ordinary aesthetic judgment. Camp doesn't reverse things. It doesn't argue that the good is bad, or the bad is good. What it does is to offer for art (and life) a different—a supplementary—set of standards.

35. Ordinarily we value a work of art because of the seriousness and dignity of what it achieves. We value it because it succeeds—in being what it is and, presumably, in fulfilling the intention that lies behind it. We assume a proper, that is to say, straightforward relation between intention and performance. By such standards, we appraise *The Iliad*, Aristophanes' plays, The Art of the Fugue, *Middlemarch*, the paintings of Rembrandt, Chartres, the poetry of Donne, *The Divine Comedy*, Beethoven's quartets, and—among people—Socrates, Jesus, St. Francis, Napoleon, Savonarola. In short, the pantheon of high culture: truth, beauty, and seriousness.

36. But there are other creative sensibilities besides the seriousness (both tragic and comic) of high culture and of the high style of evaluating people. And one cheats oneself, as a human being, if one has *respect* only for the style of high culture, whatever else one may do or feel on the sly.

For instance, there is the kind of seriousness whose trademark is anguish, cruelty, derangement. Here we do accept a disparity between intention and result. I am speaking, obviously, of a style of personal existence as well as of a style in art; but the examples had best come from art. Think of Bosch, Sade, Rimbaud, Jarry, Kafka, Artaud, think of most of the important works of art of the 20th century, that is, art whose goal is not that of creating harmonies but of overstraining the medium and introducing more and more violent, and unresolvable, subject-matter. This sensibility also insists on the principle that an *oeuvre* in the old sense (again, in art, but also in life) is not possible. Only "fragments" are possible. . . . Clearly, different standards apply here than to traditional high culture. Something is good not because it is achieved, but because another kind of truth about the human situation, another experience of what it is to be human—in short, another valid sensibility—is being revealed.

And third among the great creative sensibilities is Camp: the sensibility of failed seriousness, of the theatricalization of experience. Camp refuses both the harmonies of traditional seriousness, and the risks of fully identifying with extreme states of feeling.

37. The first sensibility, that of high culture, is basically moralistic. The second sensibility, that of extreme states of feeling, represented in much contemporary "avant-garde" art, gains power by a tension between moral and aesthetic passion. The third, Camp, is wholly aesthetic.

38. Camp is the consistently aesthetic experience in the world. It incarnates a victory of "style" over "content," "aesthetics" over "morality," of irony over tragedy.

39. Camp and tragedy are antitheses. There is seriousness in Camp (seriousness in the degree of the artist's involvement) and, often, pathos. The excruciating is also one of the tonalities of Camp; it is the quality of excruciation in much of Henry James (for instance, *The Europeans, The Awkward Age, The Wings of the Dove*) that is responsible for the large element of Camp in his writings. But there is never, never tragedy.

40. Style is everything. Genet's ideas, for instance, are very Camp. ✔ Genet's statement that "the only criterion of an act is its elegance"* is virtually interchangeable, as a statement, with Wilde's "in matters of great importance, the vital element is not sincerity, but style." But what counts, finally, is the style in which ideas are held. The ideas about morality and politics in, say, *Lady Windemere's Fan* and in *Major Barbara* are Camp, but not just because of the nature of the ideas themselves. It is those ideas, held in a special playful way. The Camp ideas in *Our Lady of the Flowers* are maintained too grimly, and the writing itself is too successfully elevated and serious, for Genet's books to be Camp.

41. The whole point of Camp is to dethrone the serious. Camp is playful, anti-serious. More precisely, Camp involves a new, more complex relation to "the serious." One can be serious about the frivolous, frivolous about the serious.

42. One is drawn to Camp when one realizes that "sincerity" is not ✔ enough. Sincerity can be simple philistinism, intellectual narrowness.

43. The traditional means for going beyond straight seriousness—irony, satire—seem feeble today, inadequate to the culturally oversaturated me-

---

*Sartre's gloss on this in *Saint Genet* is: "Elegance is the quality of conduct which transforms the greatest amount of being into appearing."

dium in which contemporary sensibility is schooled. Camp introduces a new standard: artifice as an ideal, theatricality.

44. Camp proposes a comic vision of the world. But not a bitter or polemical comedy. If tragedy is an experience of hyperinvolvement, comedy is an experience of underinvolvement, of detachment.

I adore simple pleasures, they are the last refuge of the complex.
—*A Woman of No Importance*

45. Detachment is the prerogative of an elite; and as the dandy is the 19th century's surrogate for the aristocrat in matters of culture, so Camp is the modern dandyism. Camp is the answer to the problem: how to be a dandy in the age of mass culture.

46. The dandy was overbred. His posture was disdain, or else *ennui*. He sought rare sensations, undefiled by mass appreciation. (Models: Des Esseintes in Huysmans' *A Rebours, Marius the Epicurean,* Valéry's *Monsieur Teste.*) He was dedicated to "good taste."

The connoisseur of Camp has found more ingenious pleasures. Not in Latin poetry and rare wines and velvet jackets, but in the coarsest, commonest pleasures, in the arts of the masses. Mere use does not defile the objects of his pleasure, since he learns to possess them in rare way. Camp—Dandyism in the age of mass culture—makes no distinction between the unique object and the mass-produced object. Camp taste transcends the nausea of the replica.

47. Wilde himself is a transitional figure. The man who, when he first came to London, sported a velvet beret, lace shirts, velveteen knee-breeches and black silk stockings, could never depart too far in his life from the pleasures of the old-style dandy; this conservatism is reflected in *The Picture of Dorian Gray.* But many of his attitudes suggest something more modern. It was Wilde who formulated an important element of the Camp sensibility—the equivalence of all objects—when he announced his intention of "living up" to his blue-and-white china, or declared that a doorknob could be as admirable as a painting. When he proclaimed the importance of the necktie, the boutonniere, the chair, Wilde was anticipating the democratic *esprit* of Camp.

48. The old-style dandy hated vulgarity. The new-style dandy, the lover of Camp, appreciates vulgarity. Where the dancy would be continually offended or bored, the connoisseur of Camp is continually amused, delighted. The dandy held a perfumed handkerchief to his nostrils and was liable to swoon; the connoisseur of Camp sniffs the stink and prides himself on his strong nerves.

49. It is a feat, of course. A feat goaded on, in the last analysis, by the threat of boredom. The relation between boredom and Camp taste cannot

be overestimated. Camp taste is by its nature possible only in affluent societies, in societies or circles capable of experiencing the psychopathology of affluence.

What is abnormal in Life stands in normal relations to Art. It is the only thing in Life that stands in normal relations to Art.
—*A Few Maxims for the Instruction of the Over-Educated*

50. Aristocracy is a position vis-à-vis culture (as well as vis-à-vis power), and the history of Camp taste is part of the history of snob taste. But since no authentic aristocrats in the old sense exist today to sponsor special tastes, who is the bearer of this taste? Answer: an improvised self-elected class, mainly homosexuals, who constitute themselves as aristocrats of taste.

51. The peculiar relation between Camp taste and homosexuality has to be explained. While it's not true that Camp taste is homosexual taste, there is no doubt a peculiar affinity and overlap. Not all liberals are Jews, but Jews have shown a peculiar affinity for liberal and reformist causes. So, not all homosexuals have Camp taste. But homosexuals, by and large, constitute the vanguard—and the most articulate audience—of Camp. (The analogy is not frivolously chosen. Jews and homosexuals are the outstanding creative minorities in contemporary urban culture. Creative, that is, in the truest sense: they are creators of sensibilities. The two pioneering forces of modern sensibility are Jewish moral seriousness and homosexual aestheticism and irony.)

52. The reason for the flourishing of the aristocratic posture among homosexuals also seems to parallel the Jewish case. For every sensibility is self-serving to the group that promotes it. Jewish liberalism is a gesture of self-legitimization. So is Camp taste, which definitely has something propagandistic about it. Needless to say, the propaganda operates in exactly the opposite direction. The Jews pinned their hopes for integrating into modern society on promoting the moral sense. Homosexuals have pinned their integration into society on promoting the aesthetic sense. Camp is a solvent of morality. It neutralizes moral indignation, sponsors playfulness.

53. Nevertheless, even though homosexuals have been its vanguard, Camp taste is much more than homosexual taste. Obviously, its metaphor of life as theater is peculiarly suited as a justification and projection of a certain aspect of the situation of homosexuals. (The Camp insistence on not being "serious," on playing, also connects with the homosexual's desire to remain youthful.) Yet one feels that if homosexuals hadn't more or less invented Camp, someone else would. For the aristocratic posture with relation to culture cannot die, though it may persist only in increasingly arbitrary and ingenious ways. Camp is (to repeat) the relation to style in a time in which the adoption of style—as such—has become altogether questionable. (In the modern era, each new style, unless frankly anachronistic, has come on the scene as an anti-style.)

One must have a heart of stone to read the death of Little Nell without laughing.
—*In conversation*

54. The experiences of Camp are based on the great discovery that the sensibility of high culture has no monopoly upon refinement. Camp asserts that good taste is not simply good taste; that there exists, indeed, a good taste of bad taste. (Genet talks about this in *Our Lady of the Flowers.*) The discovery of the good taste of bad taste can be very liberating. The man who insists on high and serious pleasures is depriving himself of pleasure; he continually restricts what he can enjoy; in the constant exercise of his good taste he will eventually price himself out of the market, so to speak. Here Camp taste supervenes upon good taste as a daring and witty hedonism. It makes the man of good taste cheerful, where before he ran the risk of being chronically frustrated. It is good for the digestion.

55. Camp taste is, above all, a mode of enjoyment, of appreciation—not judgment. Camp is generous. It wants to enjoy. It only seems like malice, cynicism. (Or, if it is cynicism, it's not a ruthless but a sweet cynicism.) Camp taste doesn't propose that it is in bad taste to be serious; it doesn't sneer at someone who succeeds in being seriously dramatic. What it does is to find the success in certain passionate failures.

56. Camp taste is a kind of love, love for human nature. It relishes, rather than judges, the little triumphs and awkward intensities of "character." . . . Camp taste identifies with what it is enjoying. People who share this sensibility are not laughing at the thing they label as "a camp," they're enjoying it. Camp is a tender feeling.

(Here, one may compare Camp with much of Pop Art, which—when it is not just Camp—embodies an attitude that is related, but still very different. Pop Art is more flat and more dry, more serious, more detached, ultimately nihilistic.)

57. Camp taste nourishes itself on the love that has gone into certain objects and personal styles. The absence of this love is the reason why such kitsch items as *Peyton Place* (the book) and the Tishman Building aren't Camp.

58. The ultimate Camp statement: it's good because it's awful. . . . Of course, one can't always say that. Only under certain conditions, those which I've tried to sketch in these notes.

Camp

Charles Ludlam

Camp has a number of different origins. It's a slang term. I think it originated in the theatre as an actor's word for another actor who was carrying on in excess of a role or who may have been overdoing it just enough to make a sly comment. Sometimes camping is just taking a hopeless piece of drivel, something terribly serious, and playing it for laughs to save it.

Camp had a homosexual usage that came from a special view of things. Proust explains it very clearly. In the C. K. Scott-Moncrieff translation [of] *Remembrance of Things Past*, there's a long section where Proust describes camp as an outsider's view of things other people take totally for granted. Because of the inversion, everything that everyone else has taken for granted isn't true for you. Suddenly things become funny because you're seeing it as through a mirror, a reverse image. Camp became a sly or secret sense of humor that could only exist to a group that had been through something together; in this case, the gay world.

Then it became popularly known as a word and, as it left the theatre and the homosexual underground, it started to take on a popular meaning. It gained a bad reputation, mainly because it had been hanging out with all those homosexuals, who had a bad reputation anyway.

In the hands of the critics who wanted to define it and tie it down, it started to become very special things. Susan Sontag really did a number on camp by saying it was specific things—a Tiffany lampshade is camp, a

Reprinted from Charles Ludlam, *Ridiculous Theatre, Scourge of Human Folly*, ed. Steven Samuels (New York: Theatre Communications Group, 1992), 225–27. Copyright © 1992 by the Estate of Charles Ludlam. Published by and used by permission of the Theatre Communications Group.

Ronald Firbank novel is camp, a Hollywood movie with a Busby Berkeley number in it is camp.

What's wrong with that is camp ceases to be an attitude toward something and loses all of its relativity. It nails it to the wall and makes it very literal. Therefore something becomes definitely camp, which is absurd. Values change. The value of camp, the ability to perceive things in this unique way, is that it turns values upside down.

I think the whole keynote of the Ridiculous and camp is a rigorous revaluing of everything. What people think is valuable ain't valuable. Admiring what people hold in contempt, holding in contempt things other people think are so valuable—it's a fantastic standard.

For one thing, you can get a great art collection going, because you buy the paintings at the time when people won't sniff at the artist, and they become worth a million dollars in a few years. A Tiffany lampshade in the fifties couldn't be given away, now they're $25,000 minimum.

Most people will only value what is obviously already valued. If you were going to start an art collection, you wouldn't go out and try to buy a Picasso. You couldn't. It's museum quality. It's not for us anymore. It's too late.

The same with stocks and bonds. If you use the rule of camp and Theatre of the Ridiculous in the stock market, you could make a fortune. You buy when it's low and nobody wants it, and then it goes up. If you buy it when it's high, you know it's only going to go down.

❖ ❖ ❖

The worst thing that happened to camp was that the straight world took this cult word and decided they were going to do camp. Then you get something that has nothing to do with camp. There's no vision. The perfect example— let's say I was going to camp on Hitchcock. I would get some editors— everything about Hitchcock is the way the movie looks, the incredible editing; the juxtaposition is highly synthetic and artificial, yet it's so compelling. That should've been the look of *High Anxiety*. Instead, *High Anxiety* was a totally flaccid movie. Everything that's so great about Hitchcock was not there, except that it made reference to one of his movies occasionally. There was no essence in it.

The thing that's really horrible is heterosexual camp, a kind of winking at you saying, "I don't really mean it."

❖ ❖ ❖

I don't think camp can be defined. The word had a value once, in that private language a group enjoys among themselves—doctors; lawyers; theatre people above all, I suppose. Now it has been taken over by everyone, gotten lost in the world, become a meaningless cliché. Anything different these days is "camp." It's as bad as all those great old films and "nostalgia."

❖　❖　❖

Camp is all about something in the action or the dialogue or the dress—even in the sets—which in itself is not necessarily unbelonging, but which in relationship to everything else is out of line, on its own. Camp is a way of looking at things, never what's looked at.

I think camp is great. The more people have told me that I had to get away from the word "camp," that it's terrible that people would call my work "camp," the more I decided to embrace it. If nobody wants it, come to me! Bring me your poor, your tired, your yearning to be free! Let my theatre be the repository of all forbidden theatrical conventions!

part five

Landscape

The stage is not ~~~~~, ~~~~~ of ~~~~~
of a ~~~~~

t he works selected for this section cover a range of applications
and notions of "landscape" to the theater of the second half of the
twentieth century, transcending disciplinary lines and highlighting
the relationships between the artist's imagination and its visualization on
stage. The landscapes suggested by the texts and the mindscapes they
reflect take shape in the space between text and performance, coalesc-
ing in the eyes and minds of the audience.

Gertrude Stein first applied the term "landscape" to theater in a
series of lectures written for her 1934 tour of the United States, maintaining that landscape drama lives in a continuous present in which
events from different temporal zones exist in the same space without relative
weight or focus. The notion of theater as landscape resists the traditional use of
time and space in realistic narrative structure. Events are no longer structured
by linear chronology; actions accumulate vertically through accretion and juxtaposition. Story and character slip from the foreground. Causal narrative and
realistic, representational space are sacrificed in favor of the simultaneous depic-
tion of events from more than one time in a single space—the landscape.

Although Stein was the first to apply the term to theater, the concept of
theatrical landscape can be seen in the turn-of-the-twentieth-century Symbolists' fascination with "internal" or "psychic" landscapes, which Daniel Gerould
sees as a "magical space":

> An extension of the human mind, such invented space was fluid and multilayered,
> existing along shifting planes and given to undulation and pulsation. In apparent
> violation of the law of theater that mandates only one unchanging point of
> observation between spectator and represented reality, magical space could
> accommodate close-ups and long shots at one and the same time, as well as two
> or more simultaneous actions, as in film or medieval mystery plays.[1]

Maurice Maeterlinck's static drama, in which mood dominates and the slender narrative line slips into the background, is therefore one of the earliest examples of landscape drama. In plays such as *Interior* (see *Theater of the Avant-Garde, 1890–1950*) and *The Blind*, his landscapes "carry a freight of meaning exceeding that borne by the characters."[2]

Elinor Fuchs reinvigorated the term "landscape" as a theoretical and critical lens for viewing the works of several theater artists in this anthology, including Richard Foreman, Heiner Müller, Reza Abdoh, and Suzan Lori-Parks. "We are interested in the entire *field*, the whole *terrain*, the total *environment* of the performance, as performance, and as imaginative construct,"[3] wrote Fuchs, who distinguishes between two aspects of landscape on stage: representational and perceptual. Representational landscape refers to productions in which the spatial elements of a performance use simultaneous actions but deliberately avoid a single focal point. By using multiple focal points and weighting them equally, the performances encourage the audience to view the entire stage at once. Objects from different places and temporal zones occupy the stage at the same time, forcing the audience to absorb juxtapositions and inconsistencies into a new vision of the theatrical world. Perceptual landscapes, however, form in the spectator's mind rather than eye. The landscape is not visible at any one moment but is created over the course of the performance. By layering repeated and revised actions rather than forwarding a plot, the performance allows spectators to accumulate similar events and images in their minds. Whereas in representational landscape the audience sees a variety of times and places compressed into one stage space and time, in perceptual landscape spectators apprehend a similar multilayered image as it builds in their minds over time. The two aspects of landscape sometimes overlap, reinforcing Fuchs's claim that "each approach— whether representational or perceptual, in the eye or in the mind—appears somehow embedded in the other."[4]

Viewing theater as landscape also focuses on the "interplay between the land and human adaptations to and indeed *of* it."[5] In this way, landscape foregrounds the points of view of the artists who created it. The arrangement of key elements on stage communicates a point of view through contrasts and juxtapositions, though the central elements will vary depending upon the formal concerns of the artist. Stein discovered in such works a new dramaturgy, in which "the stage itself [was] the ground on which landscapes of words could be arranged and put in motion."[6] These arrangements communicate ideas in a nonlinear way, allowing audience members to experience the totality of a theatrical event, rather than to follow a plot through time.

John Cage, whose contributions to the post-1950 avant-garde are described in Michael Kirby's essay "The New Theatre," included in this section, might be the most significant influence on the growth of this type of landscape-driven theatrical event, as a result of his mid-twentieth-century performances and teaching. In his "Experimental Composition" classes at the New School for Social Research in New York, Cage taught many of the artists who went on to develop and create "Happenings"; he therefore can be viewed as the progenitor of Happenings in all their forms, including Fluxus's "Events." Cage advocated the use of chance as an aesthetic element, an approach that the Surrealists and Marcel Duchamp had explored earlier, though Duchamp focused on the use of chance in visual art and the Surrealists applied it to verbal and visual games such as "exquisite corpse." One of Cage's early students, Allan Kaprow, coined the term "Happenings" to describe theatrical events that "provide participants with an immediate, sensual experience of reality,"[7] though Cage's 1952 works *4'33"* and *Theater Piece No. 1* predate the term and yet are often cited as the first Happenings. With their focus on the audience's experience, Happenings extend the operations of chance to the immediacy of performance.

In 1960, shortly after studying with Cage, Kaprow and fellow visual artists Robert Whitman, Jim Dine, and Claes Oldenburg began to create multimedia pieces for the theater, the first wave of Happenings after Cage's initial experiments. Blending actors, film, slides, sound, and props to create non-narrative theatrical events, which were performed in galleries and, eventually, found spaces, they initiated a move from visual arts to live performance, laying the foundation for modern and contemporary performance art.

By definition, Happenings take place only once; if repeated, each performance should take on a wholly different character through the use of improvisation, the purposeful influence of chance, and the ways in which the audience interacts with and shapes the action. As one-time events, Happenings avoid becoming commodities in the art market, their ephemeral nature serving as a resistance to mainstream culture and capitalism. Happenings might also include simultaneous action, as in Kaprow's *Eighteen Happenings in Six Parts*, in which six artists contributed actions that occur at the same time within the larger work, each one created with deliberate ignorance of what the others would present. More organically connected to their found settings, Whitman's works produced expressive nonverbal images; he favored the representative over the perceptual and relied heavily upon the absence of language to focus spectators' attention on the visual, creating a landscape for the audience to dwell in and experience. Whitman's Happenings often place the audience within a created space, yet his stage landscape, created primarily by objects, usually corresponds to a real space, as in *The Night Time Sky*, in which the audience sits beneath a giant white dome of cloth meant to represent the sky.

In another growing influence, many avant-garde artists have moved away from scripted texts to constructed and collaborative scripts and performances. The strong voices of several types of collaborative teams—choreographer and writer (Martha Clarke and Charles Mee in *Vienna: Lusthaus*), writer and director (Heiner Müller and Robert Wilson in *Explosion of a Memory*), auteur and ensemble (Tadeusz Kantor and the original cast of *The Dead Class*)—add to the layers of competing production elements that create the landscape effect. [Landscape plays require spectators to absorb and process a great deal of complex and often contradictory information, much of which can be fully realized only in rehearsal and some of which cannot come to life completely until performed before a live audience; thus, landscape lives on the border of text and performance.] In this respect, Foreman's work, though central to the understanding of language and silence explored in this book, is relevant to landscape as well. To create a

surrealistic pillows

performance, Foreman selects text from his daily notebooks and crafts it into a script on the basis of thematic resonance, with little or no narrative line. Once he completes his text, he begins to work on a model of his set, upon which he expands throughout his lengthy rehearsal period, layering visual elements to [create a landscape not seen in nature]—indeed, one removed from nature, a landscape of cryptic but evocative objects, signs, and symbols.

Other landscapes not seen in nature also link the works of Hélène Cixous, Heiner Müller, Tadeusz Kantor, and Charles Mee and Martha Clarke, included in this section. They share an impulse to explore, through writing and staging, dream sequences, memory processes, and webs of associations and fantasies. These landscapes of the mind, to use Gerould's term, capture free-flowing associative process of the human mind and [reflect the effect of fragmented and "traumatized" memory on perceptions]

The focus on memory and human mind in Cixous's *Portrait of Dora* (1976) is closely linked with the author's explorations of the roles of gender and femininity through writing. A literary critic and writer born in Algeria, Cixous was educated in France and co-founded the experimental University of Paris VIII, where she has been a leading force at the Center for Feminine Studies (*Centre d'Études Féminines*) for more than three decades. She based *Portrait of Dora* on Sigmund Freud's famous case study of female hysteria in his patient Dora. Influenced by [the principles of collage,] the play is a labyrinth of memories, dreams, and fantasies of Freud's Dora. By making the convoluted mind of Dora the engine of the play, Cixious undermines Freud's rational attempts to analyze and contain her. By strengthening Dora's feminine voice in the play, she diminishes Freud's authoritative power as interpreter and removes his voice as narrator of her story.

Throughout the play, time compresses, collides, and overlaps, existing simultaneously on multiple levels. The voices of characters from Dora's memories and dreams unexpectedly intrude on the action and then disappear; events are interwoven illogically; narrative is disrupted; and truths are conflated. The fragmentation and selectivity of Dora's memory [preclude interpretation] through repetition and tangled narrative patterns. Time is circular, as Cixous rejects a clear sense of linearity or chronology in favor of a continuous present. Voices from Dora's past, real and imagined, interrupt the dialogue between Dora and Freud; characters from Dora's childhood and adult years intermingle and merge, and distinctions between the remembered "past" and stage "present" blur.

The theatrical experiments of Kantor, a Polish director and the founder of the Krakow theater company Cricot 2, focus on the dynamics of memory. Kantor's theater aesthetic, influenced by his early career as a visual artist, embraces and expands Dadaist characteristics by integrating the use of found, discarded objects with principles of Happenings, such as indeterminacy and chance. Kantor's interest in collage and assemblage inevitably led him to his experimentation with constructed texts such as *The Dead Class* (1975), in which he draws from the writings of Stanisław Witkiewicz, Witold Gombrowicz, and Bruno Schultz. Michal Kobialka, the primary translator of Kantor's works in English, refers to the included text of *The Dead Class* as a "partytura"—a "collage of various texts, notes, and descriptions of terms and concepts that were used [by the director] during a process of putting on a production."[8] Yet such a text only suggests the qualities of the play in performance. In *The Dead Class*, text loses its primary literary value and becomes one of many components of the theatrical experience created by actors.

The Dead Class explores memory through the interplay between the living and the dead: the Old People in black, carrying life-size, wax figures of children, embody an image of the dead carrying "the memory of their childhood."[9] As the journey into the world of the dead continues, the line between life and death becomes less discernible. In constructing a series of fascinating interactions between humans and objects in performance, Kantor, inspired by Edward Gordon Craig's theory of the Über-marionette, created a paradox: human characters (the Old People) appear to inhabit the world of the dead, but inanimate objects (life-size mannequins) embrace the world of the living, if only in Kantor's staged memory. Both worlds, the living and the dead, make up a landscape of his memory, as well as the representational landscape on the stage.

By employing objects such as wax figures of children and schoolroom benches as tools to retrieve memory, Kantor transforms "a flat, still memory into a multidimensional spatial fold."[10] In his landscape theater, memory functions as "a poor and forgotten storage-room where dry and forgotten people, faces, objects, clothes, adventures, emotions, and images are thrown."[11] When the theatrical act of retrieving and reliving the past breaks down, the memories of the Old People turn into dreams and nightmares or disappear. As Kantor inhabits the theatrical space of the production, the audience feels his palpable role as author and director, a theater "conductor" conceiving and guiding the characters' journeys through the labyrinths of memory. His presence highlights his place in constructing this theatrical experiment in memory retrieval, leading his audience through the spaces of his characters' journey to the past.

Whereas Kantor's productions map a personal landscape of his memory, Müller's texts evoke post-apocalyptic images drawn from individual and collective memory and reflect multiple, sometimes parallel, states of consciousness. Echoing Samuel Beckett's timeless, indeterminate imagery (especially in his later prose), Müller creates in *Explosion of a Memory/Description of a Picture* (1984) "a landscape neither quite steppe nor savannah," in which "animals appear only as clouds," "the bird in the tree is the last of its kind," "a multitude of Suns" will scorch the remaining grass, and "the throng of graves [will] turn into the tempest of resurrection."[12] Fuchs linked Müller's imaginative landscapes, which offer no solace or reconciliation to the viewer, to the post-Beckett consciousness with its "collapse of boundaries between human and world, inside and outside, foreground and background."[13]

Müller's most influential work was directed by Robert Wilson, including *Explosion of a Memory*, which was staged as a prologue to Wilson's production of *Alcestis* in 1986 at the American Repertory Theater (Cambridge, Massachusetts). Mutually influential artists, Müller and Wilson repeatedly collaborated on the conception and creation of composite mindscapes—still, multilayered visual compositions permeated by dreams, nightmares, and hallucinations.

Bonnie Marranca refers to Wilson as a "symbolist, a seeker of truth and arche-types" whose visual "dramaturgy of the dispersed texts of different cultures and continents dwells in the realm of allegory."[14] Müller, in his short prose text "Dove and Samurai," calls Wilson's theater a "theatre of resurrection," through which the director "articulates the theme of our age: war of classes and races, species and genders, civil war in every sense of the term."[15] In *Explosion of a Memory*, Müller, too, embraces the imagery of civil war among various species ("man against bird and woman, woman against bird and man, bird against woman and man")[16] and explores the regions of traumatized imagination in hopes for resurrection. Through their collaborations, Wilson visualizes Muller's percep-tual landscapes in his complex stage compositions, which affect the mind and the eye of the spectator profoundly.

Müller's aesthetic defies any dramatic and/or theatrical principles that are even remotely plot-based and character-centered. *Explosion of a Memory* is a "scenic poem," in Hans-Thies Lehmann's term, whose poetic quality is em-bedded in a flow of associative spaces that make up a complex and somewhat incongruous picture.[17] In Müller's plays, "the speaker is the picture": the col-lapse of the temporal structure, the erasure of borders between the humans and inanimate objects, and the dissolution-cum-unification of multiple iden-tities result in a vivid picture of indeterminate meaning.[18] Spectators must perceive and interpret the images for themselves; by accepting the disso-lution of characters and the absence of relationships among time, logic, and space, audience members create landscapes in their minds. Each spectator, no longer a simple viewer, must accept responsibility as co-author of this theatri-cal journey.

Like *The Dead Class*, Mee's *Vienna: Lusthaus* (1986) is a constructed theatrical collage or pastiche. Whereas *The Dead Class* is the product of a single auteur—a writer and director, but also a persistent stage presence—*Vienna: Lusthaus* was conceived and choreographed by Martha Clarke and written by Mee. A member of Pilobolus Dance Theatre and a founder of the chamber dance group Crows-nest, Clarke creates original works in which she integrates elements of dance, theater, and opera. In synthesizing various artistic forms and breaking down traditional generic boundaries, her aesthetic interests coincide with those of contemporary avant-garde artists such as Wilson, Pina Bausch, and William Forsythe.

Clarke began to develop *Vienna: Lusthaus* at the Joseph Papp Public Theater in New York after visiting an art exhibition of late nineteenth-century Vienna. Discussing her conception of *Vienna: Lusthaus*, she refers to the paintings of the early twentieth century Viennese artists Egon Schiele and Gustav Klimt as cata-lysts for the eroticism and sexual fantasies that her dancers strove to create. "My work deals with sensuality, eroticism, repression, sexual fantasy, and obsession," which might be best expressed on stage through dancers because "dancers are boundary-free" when it comes to transforming "physical impulses" into dance, Clarke writes.[19] Mee observed one of her rehearsals, then offered to write a text for the production. The collaboration evokes a late nineteenth–century

Vienna permeated with intoxication, disease, hallucinations, and sexual fantasies. This world is a multilayered dreamscape, a compilation of dreams woven together and influenced by different sources, including Freud's *Five Lectures on Psycho-Analysis* and Mee's dreams about late nineteenth- to early twentieth-century Vienna. In this terrain of subconscious, surrealist imagery, the connection to Freud is inevitable, but the play repeatedly undermines Freud's authority as an interpreter of dreams, just as Cixous did in *Portrait of Dora*.

Mee's constructed text consists of short, seemingly unrelated fragments unified by recurrent perceptions and dream states: a woman carrying "an armful of tulips" lets her mind wander and, as a result, walks through an open window, falling to her death;[20] a plume of fountain water drenches a daughter; a white-and-black butterfly thinks it is camouflaged on a green leaf; a dead soldier inquires about the signs of death and the meaning of *rigor mortis*. Layering fantasies and dreams, Mee's text opens a myriad of interpretive possibilities for visual representation in Clarke's choreography, thus fusing perceptual and representational landscapes. The incomplete and fragmentary nature of Mee's spoken text, along with Richard Peaslee's music, corresponds to the boundless web of visual compositions created by the dancers' bodies on the bare white setting that Robert Israel designed for the original production: an old woman in a chair watches the passionate embrace of two lovers rolling on the floor; when the couple stand up, the woman, lost in the memory about her youth, steps between the lovers to share their world of ecstasy and desire. Also noteworthy, as Carol Martin comments in her production review, is the interplay between appearance and disappearance, between inner and outer space, in which scenes sometimes begin offstage and then continue, even if outside the lighting focus, until they disappear from the audience's view, thus expanding the limits of the visible theatrical space.[21] A scrim on stage intensifies the imaginary realm of the stories; memories overlap as scenes cross-fade and dancers transgress temporal and geographical boundaries.

The fluidity and permeability of disciplinary boundaries characterize the works in this section, from the collage-inspired approach in Cixous's dramatic writing to the influence of Happenings on Kantor's "theatre of death," from the "imagistic" theater of Müller as interpreted by Wilson to the dance-theater aesthetic of Martha Clarke and Charles Mee. This cross-pollination of artistic forms in the later decades of the twentieth century has its antecedents in the mid-century experimental performances of Cage, Merce Cunningham, and the Judson Dance Theater, among others, which aimed to reduce traditional divisions among disciplines. Moreover, in their focus on memory and dreams, many of these works refer to the historical avant-garde—the mystical worlds of the Symbolists and the dreamlike realities of the Surrealists. By redefining memory and calling attention to multiple states of consciousness, these works push spectators' boundaries of perception and imagination, asking them to engage their associative thinking. Each viewer must weave together disparate images in his or her mind, comprehend action in multiple times, and discover relationships between seemingly disconnected text and staging.

Notes

1. Quoted in Elinor Fuchs and Una Chaudhuri, eds., *Land/Scape/Theater* (Ann Arbor: University of Michigan Press, 2002), 318.

2. Elinor Fuchs, *The Death of Character* (Bloomington: Indiana University Press, 1996), 96.

3. Ibid., 106.

4. Ibid., 96.

5. Fuchs and Chaudhuri, *Land/Scape/Theater*, 2 (italics in original).

6. Ibid., 5.

7. Günter Berghaus, "Happening and Fluxus," in *Avant-Garde Performance: Live Events and Electronic Technologies* (New York: Palgrave Macmillan, 2005), 86.

8. Michal Kobialka, ed. *A Journey Through Other Spaces: Essays and Manifestos, 1944–1990* (Berkeley: University of California Press, 1993), 390.

9. Ibid., 318.

10. Ibid., 326.

11. Kantor, quoted in Kobialka, *Journey Through Other Spaces*, 318.

12. Heiner Müller, *Explosion of a Memory/Description of a Picture*, 413 and 415 below in this volume.

13. Fuchs, *The Death of Character*, 92.

14. Bonnie Marranca, *Performance Histories* (New York: PAJ, 2008), 59.

15. Heiner Müller, "Dove and Samurai," 457 in this volume.

16. Heiner Müller, *Explosion of a Memory/Description of a Picture*, 417 below in this volume.

17. Hans-Thies Lehmann, *Postdramatic Theatre*, trans. Karen Jürs-Munby (London: Routledge, 2006), 110.

18. Jonathan Kalb, *The Theater of Heiner Müller* (Cambridge: Cambridge University Press, 1998), 170.

19. Martha Clarke, "Body Heat: Five American Director Choreographers Break Down the Steps that Lead to Sex, Intimacy, and Erotic Tension," in *American Theatre* 20:4 (2003): 32.

20. Charles L. Mee, *Vienna: Lusthaus* in *History Plays*, 420 below in this volume.

21. Carol Martin, review of *Vienna: Lusthaus*, in *Performing Arts Journal*, 10:2 (1986): 88–90.

The Night Time Sky

Robert Whitman

I began with an idea about a piece that had to do with the making of a theatre work, with itself as its own subject. It seemed to me that one of the first theatrical things is when the sun goes down, night falls, the stars come out, and people imagine what the constellations are.

Out of this came *The Night Time Sky*, performed in May 1965.

The audience arrive a few at a time and walk down a tunnel toward the place. They hear steel drum band music, crowd noises, and steamship whistles: boat-leaving sounds. At the end of the tunnel is a movie, projected on a white cloth, of passenger liners leaving. As an audience member approaches this, his shadow is cast on the screen. His shadow is momentarily in the movie, participating in the boat leaving. All this is seen on both sides of the screen.

One enters the space by pushing this cloth aside. Inside there are mats on the floor to sit on. The people walk around to find a place and then sit. Floor and mats are lighted so that they are green. This green light and the boat movie provide all the light. Other people's shadows join the movie as they come down the tunnel. If a person came right on time and went right into the place he might see seven or eight minutes of this. Then it is over and the green lights go out too.

The space into which the people have come is a billowy dome shape fifty feet in diameter and sixteen or seventeen feet high. The enclosure is of cloth and the billowy shapes are soft and cloudlike. In the center of the space is a cloth-covered thing about six feet high. It is rather squared off but was meant

Reprinted from *TDR*, Vol. 10, no. 2 (1965): 101– 106. Reprinted by permission of MIT Press and *TDR*.

to be mound or haystack shaped. The set-up time didn't allow some things to be done as perfectly as one would have liked.

Very, very slowly the space is lit a red-orange sunset color, from lights on the outside. This holds for a while, then it goes out even more slowly and blue comes up; the interior space is now the night time sky.

Up in the dome, spaced fairly evenly around, are four holes. Three are about ten feet long, rounded at the corners and top, and about five feet high. The fourth is about five feet wide and a little more squared off. All of these holes are about ten feet off the floor.

There is quiet for a while, then one of the holes lights up slowly. There is a man in a white lab coat, a clipboard in hand, at an instrument panel. He reads the meters, adjusts dials with knobs, switches switches. He is at work running some kind of industrial process, and checking it.

Another film starts up, close to this stage. It is below and to the right. It is of a steel mill. The men move about in slow motion; there are glowing things and sparks flying. The image is about six feet high and rectangular. (It was meant to have been circular, about the same size.) At a certain time the man in the lab coat switches on the light behind a foot-square panel of translucent plastic which is on his control panel. For the rest of the performance the plastic panel glows with shifting colors and lights.

A light comes up in another hole. There is a pretty, thin, dark girl in black tights. The light in the other hole fades out very slowly. The girl takes dirt and marbles (which we can't see) and puts them into an opaque projector at one side of the platform. The projector projects them at an angle onto the ceiling, so that we see her fingers moving the three or four many-colored marbles about in the dirt on the roof of the space. They might be like stars in the sky. Then the girl sits and smokes a cigarette. Her light slowly goes out.

The haystack thing in the middle begins to glow a red-orange. This comes up so slowly that it is not noticed until it is really glowing. As this is happening the sound of wind is coming up too. The wind shrieks and the haystack glows, then both suddenly subside and there is silence and darkness.

The light on the man in the lab coat comes up again. He is still at the same kind of business. Sometimes only sitting there. A light on the smaller hole comes up slowly. It is a blue light. There is a girl in a raincoat behind a cheesecloth curtain that is hanging in front of the hole. The girl walks to a chair, sits down, and puts a record on a record player which is on a table next to the chair. The record is of rainfall. The girl listens to the record and when it is over she takes it off as the light slowly dims and goes out. The light on the man in the lab coat has slowly gone out during the beginning of this.

Now the light on the girl in black comes up. She is suspended and flying. She flies slowly across her little area and the lights go slowly out again.

The lights come up on the second girl again. Now the light is red and her coat is off. She is dressed in a dress of aluminium foil and plastic pieces, the average size of which is about six by eight inches. These parts shine and reflect the light. The curtain is gone now. This time she plays and listens to a sound-effects record of fire. When the record is over her light goes out slowly and comes up on the man in the lab coat. He is at the same business, it never changes. Marking down figures, sitting at a table, walking around, reading dials, turning knobs, switching switches.

The light on the flying girl comes up and she makes another slow flight. This time a different kind. The light fades out again.

There is darkness and three lights come on, spotting three areas on the floor in which six people appear in three groups. They are grouped together as: a man and a man, a woman and a woman, and a man and a woman. They are standing. The three groups are spaced out in the area so that each part of the audience can see two of the groups, or if some in the audience are standing they'll be able to see at least one of the couples. Each performer has a razor blade with which he cuts down the middle of his partner's chest. Then, with the other hand, he smears black or white pasty paint around on the shirt. The paint has bled from the wound. Half the people have black or dark shirts or blouses, the other half have white. The white-shirted people bleed black, the dark-shirted people bleed white. During the smearing part all the lights go out at once. In the darkness the performers leave the area.

The light on the girl in aluminium foil comes up and this time it is green. The record that the girl plays now is of waterfront sounds. When the record is over the girl gets up, turns off the record player, and goes about doing things that we can't identify. She may reach out of the area that we can see and do something with her hands, or to one side or the other, or above or below out of our sight. She does a few different things this way. Then she begins to take her costume apart one piece at a time. As she takes off these pieces she piles them up on top of one another, making a wall between herself and the audience.

Then the light comes up in the fourth hole. This is an amber spotlight on a girl who looks as though she has nothing on. Very slowly she peels off her skin and she becomes a blue person. The light on the other hole has dimmed and gone out now and this is all that is visible. The girl continues and peels off the blue skin, to become a yellow person with silver hair. This whole series of actions takes a lot longer to do than to describe.

As the girl is finishing, a film appears projected on the top of the space. We also begin to hear a watery sound with rattling, bubbling, and drips. The film starts out as a vague kind of abstract film of watery patterns with something happening that is hard to see or identify. The movie goes on and it becomes impossible not to understand what its subject mater is. It is a movie of what the toilet sees. The sounds are also clear now. They are the toilet flushing, and bubbling sounds. The toilet sees a cigarette being tossed into it, then the reverse with the rushing water bringing the cigarette back, then throwing it out of the toilet. Then a man urinates into the toilet. The more reverse vague stuff until at the end of the shot a lady gets off the toilet. Then the reverse of a man urinating. Then the reverse of a man defecating. It is possible to avoid the subject of the film until about halfway through this shot. People begin to react now and there's a lot of giggling and comment from the audience. The last shot is a straight shot of a man defecating and the toilet being flushed. The movie ends, the sound ends, and lights come on coloring the floor blue. Then a light is on in the entrance/exit tunnel and the cheering crowd, steel drum band, steamship boat leaving sound comes on loud and it is clear that the piece is over. The sound continues until all the people are gone.

Now I will just mention some of the things that I was concerned with when I made certain images, to make as obvious as possible one context in which the images are presented. I have already mentioned that in a way it is about itself. This was a night shadow voyage. The self-cast shadows of entering the movies-fantasy. Projections of fantasy in the dark sky. Making them from constellations. The shape and nature of the tent suggest all kinds of things and among them I thought especially of a few. In the circus the acts are spaced out and presented so as to accent their fantastic and superhuman qualities, attributes, and functions. It is another entrance into fantasy land, the land of make-believe, the land of death. We also see living images. Exaggerations and celebrations of life and weird dreams. Entrance and exit to and from the worlds of real and strange. The people appearing and cutting each other are real people on the same level as the audience. Something violent and surprising like the wound of finding something out or understanding. I also thought of people thinking things, digesting them, defecating them, a work fertilizing something. The audience, fertilized by the experience, leaving. People-boat-turds leaving the pier, shat out into the streets as they leave the performance. In spite of my ponderous description I also thought it was funny.

Anyway, these things are like the plot of a story, the framework. The real context is the time the piece takes and how it is composed. The mages make real the experience of the time. Things like comment, acting, exposition, in the terms of conventional theatre are extraneous and lessen the depth of the experience of the real time of the piece. The direct presentation of the images and the character of the time are the most important things.

Portrait of Dora

Hélène Cixous

Translated by Ann Liddle

CHARACTERS (IN ORDER OF APPEARANCE)

VOICE OF THE PLAY
DORA
FREUD
MR K.
MRS K.
MR B., DORA'S FATHER

VOICE OF THE PLAY " . . . *These events declare themselves, like shadows, in dreams, they often become so clear that we feel we can reach out and grasp them, but, in spite of this, they elude any final clarification, and if we proceed without skill or particular caution, we find ourselves unable to determine whether or not such a scene ever really took place.*"

DORA [*in a voice that shatters a silence—with a tone between a request and a threat*] If you dare to kiss me, I'll slap you! [*With a cajoling inflection*]

DORA [*suddenly in his ear*] Just dare to kiss me, I'll slap you!

FREUD Yes, you will tell me about it. In every detail.

DORA [*in a faraway voice*] "If you like." [*In an awakened voice*] If you wish. And then?

Reprinted from *Selected Plays of Hélène Cixous*, ed. Eric Prenowitz (London: Routledge, 2004), 35–59. Reprinted by permission of Taylor and Francis. Translated by Ann Liddle.

[Translator's note] This translation is based on the 1976 edition which differs slightly from the 1986 edition.

FREUD You will tell me about the scene by the lake, in every detail.

DORA Why did I keep silent for the first few days after the scene by the lake?

FREUD To whom do you think you should address that question?

DORA And then why did I suddenly tell my parents about it?

FREUD Why do you think?

DORA [*doesn't reply but relates in a dream voice*] When Papa was getting ready to leave, I said that I wouldn't stay there without him. Why did I tell my mother about the scene so that she would repeat it to my father?

MR B. Mr K. has always been very kind to my daughter, ever since our two families became such close friends several years ago. When he was there, Mr K. would go for walks with her. With an almost paternal affection. Although she was only a child. He gave her little presents and looked after her with an almost paternal affection. And Dora, for her part, took marvellous care of my friend's two little children. She was like a mother to them. Two years ago, my daughter and I joined the K.'s who were vacationing at one of our mountain lakes. Dora was to stay with them for several weeks.

DORA I'm not staying, I'm leaving with my father.

MR B. But the lake and mountain air would be so good for your nerves. I'm sure that in a few days.

DORA I'm leaving with you. [*Then abruptly threatening*] I'll never forgive you!

MR B. I don't understand you!

DORA You understand me, but you're not sincere. You have a strain of falseness in your character. You only think of your own satisfaction. You don't understand. I'm not sincere. I reproach myself for being unfair to you. Give me a bracelet.

[*A pause*]

My father is very generous. He enjoys doing things to please poor Mrs K. At the same time, he is generous with his wife and his daughter. My father never buys a piece of jewellery for me without buying one for my mother and one for Mrs K.

MR B. Dora is still a child and Mr K. treats her like a child. He sent her flowers, he gave her little presents. She was like a mother to the children, she gave them lessons, took them for walks. Gave them the same tender care that their own mother would have shown them.

DORA I have never loved Mr K. I was never mad about him. I could have loved him, but ever since the scene by the lake, it's altogether impossible. There had been talk of divorce between Mr and Mrs K. I took care of the children. When my father visited Mrs K. I knew that the children would not be at home, I liked to turn my steps in a direction where I would be sure to meet them and then I would go for a walk with them.

MR K. Dora is no longer a child.

MRS K. Dora *is* a child, who is only interested in sexual matters. When she was staying at our house on the lake, she used to slip off and read *The Psychology of Love* by Montegazza and other such books, which excited her. She adores me. She trusts me. She is a child who arouses mixed feelings; you can't give credence to all that she says, this reading material goes to her head.

MR B. She probably "imagined" the entire scene by the lake.

DORA Do you hear him?

FREUD Yes.

DORA There's a door in Vienna through which everyone may pass except me. I often dream that I arrive in front of this door, it opens, I could go in. Young men and women are streaming through it, I could slip in among them, but I don't, yet I can't walk away from this door forever, I go past it, I linger but I don't do it, I am unable to, I am full of recollections and despair, what is strange is that I could go through but I am held back, I fear, I am beyond all fear, but I don't go in, if I don't go in I die, if I went in, if I wanted to see Mr K. but if Papa saw me, but I don't want to see him, but if Papa saw me see him he would kill me, I could see him just once. It would be the last time. Then

MRS K. [*in a laughing, mocking voice*] I've always said that the key is in the lake! . . .

DORA Then . . . nothing. Nothing to be done.

As soon as I understood Mr K.'s intention I cut him off, I slapped him and I ran away. I ran away I slapped him, I cut short his intent. I understood his words.

VOICE OF THE PLAY "*This initial account may be compared to an unnavigable stream, a stream whose bed is sometimes obstructed by rocks, sometimes divided by sandbanks.*"

FREUD I happen to know Mr K. He is still a young man, with a pleasing appearance. The father, Mr B., was a man of means, mild-mannered, an affectionate father and a patient husband. I never I knew Dora's mother.

    The father was very attached to his daughter. Every time he was questioned about her health, tears came to his eyes.

DORA My mother means nothing to him.

MR B. You must have imagined it! A man like Mr K. is incapable of such intentions!

DORA [*beside herself*] I must have "imagined" it! He said: "You know that my wife means nothing to me." As soon as I understood his intention, I slapped him and ran away.

                        [*On the side stage*]
As soon as Mrs K. understood Papa's intention, she cut him off, slapped him and ran away. She slapped him. And you, *you* say that I "imagined" it! Now "choose"! *Choose!* [*Shouts*]

MR B. *Don't shout!*

DORA Her or me!

MR K. I never made the slightest move that could have been open to such an interpretation. I sent her flowers for a whole year, I treated her like my own daughter. Mr B., who is known for his delicacy with the ladies, is aware of how disinterested my attentions were.

DORA Answer. Well, answer!

DORA It wasn't exactly at the edge of the lake. It was in the forest. I had understood Mr K.'s intention long before. During the walk, he rolled a cigarette.

[*A silence, during which, in another time* (DORA *at age fourteen*) *the scene by the door near the staircase is performed*]

Every morning when I wake up, I smell smoke. It's always the same. I don't open my eyes. I sniff, and it's him.

DORA When I entered the store, there was a faint smell of smoke. Mr K. was alone. Mrs K. and my mother were late. The time for the procession was drawing near.

FREUD Where there's smoke, there's fire.

DORA Mr K. and my father were like you, passionate smokers. I myself smoked at the edge of the lake. He had rolled me a cigarette. He smelled of smoke. I loathe the smell of smoke.

I remember that the door that led from the store to the apartment was open, and I noticed the smell of smoke, Mrs K.'s perfume, mixed together. When the time for the procession drew near, he asked me to wait for him . . . to wait for him.

FREUD Go on. Go on. Go on.

DORA He asked me . . .
To wait for him, when the time drew near.

[*Silence*]

FREUD Yes. And then?

DORA There is a door. Which opens onto the staircase, leading to the upper storey; there. While he lowered the blinds. I waited for him. There was a smell . . . that was . . . familiar.

FREUD And then?

DORA

He came back and next and then, instead of going out through the open door, he clasped me to him, he held me tightly against him, and he kissed me on the mouth. I felt such intense disgust then, I hated him with all my soul, I was disgusted, I tore myself free from him violently.
I can still feel it today, at this moment, I feel it, so intensely.

I can still feel that kiss, and the pressure of that embrace; his lips were very wet. Here, on my chest, and right through to my back. I ran past him, past that man.

I tore myself free, I hurried away, I gave him a look, I hurried to the staircase, past that man (I thought: I'm going past "that man") to the staircase, and, from there, to the street door.

FREUD And then?

DORA And then . . . Nothing. Only that. The door.

DORA I loathe tête-à-têtes.

MR B. She has suffered from a respiratory disturbance ever since the age of eight. My daughter has always been very nervous, very fragile. At one time her health caused me a good deal of concern.

FREUD And her mother?

MR B. The relations between my wife and my daughter are not very affectionate. My wife doesn't mean much to me. Unfortunately. She is not a very well-educated woman. She has no understanding of her children's aspirations. Dora naturally favoured me. I myself was seriously ill: I have no doubt that her tenderness was heightened by what I went through.

DORA During his illness, Mrs K. apparently saved him. She has an eternal right to his gratitude. When I was ten years old, my father had to go through a course of treatment in a darkened room on account of a detached retina. I liked to keep him company in the dark. He would take me in his arms and kiss me.

I myself saw to it that the blinds were always lowered.

MR B. The migraines and the attacks of nervous coughing appeared when she was about twelve. (I remember, because it was at that time that my friend K. persuaded me to consult you.) The coughing fits sometimes last for three or four weeks. But what worries me most are these spells of aphonia.

DORA But the relationship didn't become intimate until Mrs K. took over as sick nurse.

My mother kept away from the room, because she doesn't love my father. She is a stupid woman.

MR B. I am bound to Mrs K. by ties of sincere friendship. Dora, who is very close to me, felt a kind of adoration for her.

DORA Adoration.

I had never seen such a beautiful, elegant woman. How I loved to look at her! I drank in her every movement. I thought that she knew how to do everything that women should know how to do. I loved to bring flowers into her bedroom. When she and my father changed rooms and they both moved into the end rooms, I understood everything. [*Shout directed as* MR B.] Everything. Do you hear me?

MR B. [*very aggressively, defending himself*] An extremely nervous woman herself, Mrs K. has in me her only friend. With my state of health and her fragile nature, I don't need to tell you that we are united by nothing more than an exchange of friendly sympathy. Dora's animosity is unjust. Her irritability, her thoughts of suicide! All of this obviously comes from her mother.

DORA Why haven't I ever confessed this story to anyone?

FREUD Except me.

[DORA *exits. Footsteps on the staircase, running footsteps, she stops on the staircase*]

DORA It's dark here . . .

MR K. [*whispering*] Wait for me, I'll lower the blinds and then I'm all yours.

DORA [*whispers, all in a rush. What is unsaid, lost, in the body, between the bodies*] No need to open it. It's always open. I can open up. Not open up. *That man had beautiful teeth, like the pearls of a bracelet. I can open a little. And why shouldn't you open up?* What is open might not be open. What has happened might not have happened.

MR K. Nothing is irremediable. Why not?

DORA [*whispering*] I can still feel it. *I can hardly breathe. I've already felt someone behind the door. Pushing with his whole body. It was a new sensation* . . . But, what about what didn't happen?

[*Abrupt return to her normal voice*]

FREUD How did you know that it was a man? Since he was behind the door.

DORA [*whispering*] *Pressing against the door with all of his weight. I felt his member stiffen. Who told you that?*

[*Pause*]

It was Mrs K. who told me.

She used to read me books that no one has ever read before, when I was doing her hair.

[*Silence*]

DORA [*she performs this on a side stage, in a voice that is at once clear and lethargic*] *It would have been pointless to wait for him.* One could wait, if one liked. *I had seen him in a dream.* He was a gentle, prepossessing man, who never took his eyes off of me. *But it wasn't him. Is that him, now, behind the door? One never knows.* I open up a crack. There's a man in the shadows. I can't see his face. He stoops down. I understand his intention. I push *it back.* I have no doubt that he intends to force the door open. And he presses against it. *I feel his erection. He leans forward. Too late. He's going to force the door open.* His decision is already forcing it open and keeping me from closing it. The door weights heavily and I weigh heavily against the door. I squeeze myself behind it, on the left. I smell smoke. *How simple and deadly everything is! It's Him or Me.* In the obscurity I am obscure. The fictional flesh that fills the door disgusts me. *There will have to be a killing. It's a law.* It's a key. One has to kill the other who kills the one who wants to kill who wants to be killed? *I want to kill him. He knows it. He wants to kill me. I know it.*

A little while later I would like him to kill me. Who will kill me? The one who kills me is the one I want. That's what I want. One can go on for a long time without making a move, then one has to. *Kill me! Kill me! Kill me! It's taking so long. That man* who's behind the door, *I can't see him. He's a tall man. He's still young. Because I want him like that.* He has a familiar look about him: a lady's man. *There's something false in his expression.* His eyes are a little murky, they don't go at all with his mouth. *And now for the throat.* This action requires the utmost concentration of energy. It may kill me, but I put all of my strength into it. *I clasp him, I take him in my arms, I lean forward.* His face seen up close isn't familiar; it isn't terrifying, as if I knew it well. The thing is that we know and there where our knowledge intersects we touch secret places which escape neither him nor me. I'm anxious to get on with it. I'm not sure of success, despite the division and the multiplication of my strength. While I clasp him in front, *I turn him over* halfway and hold his head from behind, my arm encircles his forehead and his skull weighs on my chest, *I hold him tightly and I slit his throat.* The knife has become one with my hand.

How hard it is to cut his throat. I
don't make a big stab because
I'm holding him tightly, I cut all
the way across his neck, but not
through it. Long afterward I still
feel the resistance of the throat.
As though I were still doing it I
feel the specificity of that resistance. I used my left hand,
and I drew a straight line from
left to right. I was holding his
head with my right arm. *It takes
a lot of pressure, it's like opening
a tin can. His pain makes me
sick. I had a very sore throat. It's
hard for me to speak.*

FREUD Mr K. travelled a good deal, no doubt?

DORA I don't know. I'm not interested in what Mr K. does.

FREUD Do you like to write? Yes.

DORA No.

FREUD You sent me a very pretty postcard. Do you like receiving postcards?

DORA I don't much care. Mr K. spent part of the year travelling. Like Papa.
Journeys have their uses. Whenever my father feels his health failing, he
leaves for Berg.

FREUD Does he stay long in Berg?

DORA [*following up immediately in a very low but abrupt tone of voice, with
violent outbursts on the words in quotes*] I'll write a letter. It will be
hesitant. It will start with these words: "You have killed me." And I'll
write: "You, dear, have killed me." Then I'll write another letter on paper
as fine as onion skin, that will start with these words: "That's what you
wanted . . . " I'll leave it ambiguous, for him to complete "himself."
Because I don't know what he wanted. Yet "it's me" who is dead. My
body is buried. In the forest. It's dark there. I am voiceless.

FREUD Tell me about the letter.

DORA [*almost inaudible*] What letter?

MR B. I found a letter on the desk. It was inside her desk. She said that she
could no longer endure life. "This is what you all wanted," she said, she
was bidding us farewell. I didn't think she was really determined to
commit suicide, but I was shaken; a few days later, after an insignificant
argument, she had a fainting spell, for the first time. That really did
frighten me.

DORA How did they find that letter? It was locked up in my desk.

FREUD Is your desk locked?

DORA I don't know. Does anyone else have the keys?

FREUD Who has the keys?

MR B. On her desk. It was a first draft. I worried about it especially when she had her fainting spell.

DORA [*in a painful, staccato voice*] You don't love me!
You think I don't see the two of you? You're abandoning me!
You love her more than me! I don't want anything, do you hear? *Nothing.*
You disgust me!
You think you can buy me? You think you can sell me?
[*She is yelling,* MR B. *is frightened, and tries to make her be quiet*]

MR B. [*in a hurried voice*] Dora, Dora, Dora, my darling, my little one, my little child . . .
Come, come now.

DORA You can't imagine how I detest that woman! When she is dead, I will marry you.

FREUD What were you arguing about?

MR B. I don't remember anymore. I had just returned from a journey. She looked tired. I remember I had given her a pearl bracelet.

DORA I used to be very fond of jewellery, but I don't wear it anymore. When I was living at the K.'s she used to like to show me her jewels. She would loan them to me. She told me the pearls would be even more becoming to me than to her.

FREUD What was your attitude toward Mrs K. before the incident?

DORA I don't know. Normal.
I'm sure that the jewellery my father gave me was chosen by her. I recognize her taste. My father used to give me jewellery, especially pearls. Like the ones I had seen at Mrs K's.
[*A pause*]
She used to tell me . . . when I was doing her hair. Me. Standing behind her. The whiteness . . . of her body.
[*The characters change places, as in a ballet*]

MR K. [*voice on telephone*] I am prepared to come and meet with you, to clear up all of these misunderstandings. Dora is a mere child to me. You know what respect I have for you and your daughter. Didn't she live in our house? And on the most intimate terms with my wife?

MRS K. You haven't the right to criticize your father's behaviour, my little darling; he's a generous man. You know how much your father cares for you. He can't even speak to me about you without tears coming into his eyes.

MR B . . . every reason in the world, rather, to be grateful to Mrs K.

MR K. . . . always absolute confidence in her.

MR B. A man like Mr K. could not have presented any threat to her.

MRS K. He's a man with coarse appetites; he doesn't know what a real woman is. Men are often like that: they only think of their own satisfaction. Not your poor papa . . . He was so unhappy at that time that he wanted to commit suicide. I was seized with a premonition, without a moment's hesitation, I headed toward the forest, I found him. I pleaded with him and managed to persuade him to go back on this terrible decision. To preserve his life for the sake of his family.

DORA Always in white. Milky white veils. Crêpe de chine. I saw HER.
The whiteness of her body, especially her back. A very soft lustre; pearly.

MR K. I am prepared to come and meet with you immediately to clear up this misunderstanding. No girl who reads such books should have any title to a man's respect. When she was staying with us, my wife went so far as to let Dora share her room. And I kept my distance quite willingly, because we thought Dora was in need of affection. My wife was astonished at such curiosity in a young girl.

MRS K. You know that you can tell me everything and ask me anything. There is nothing I need to hide from you. The brutality of certain practices has totally alienated me from men.

DORA You are absolutely everything. And I am nothing, nothing. No one.
Listen! I love you as if you were God. Someone.
For whom I do not exist.
For whom I live. For no one.
[*In adoration, before* MRS K. *who, seated in front of her mirror, looks at her*
without turning around, with a long, serene, terribly calm and
uninterpretable smile]

MR B. There had often been talk of divorce between Mr and Mrs K. It never took place, because Mr K., who was an affectionate father, would not give up either of the two children.

MR K. Neither of my two children!

DORA I went to Dresden. My cousin wanted to take me around the gallery. I refused. I ran to the door. I went out. I wandered about in the strange town. I went to the gallery alone. There is a painting, that I cannot look at—without . . . I stood for a long time. In front of that painting. It was the "Sistine Madonna," I stood there, alone, immersed. In that painting. For two hours. In the aura. A very gentle smile. You couldn't see the teeth. But a pearly glimmer, between the lips.

FREUD What was it about this painting that held you there?

DORA The . . . Her . . .

[*Suddenly, something obvious, which may go unnoticed by everyone: the infant Jesus held by the Madonna is none other than a little* DORA]

[*Filmed sequence, in three scenes. The Sistine Madonna, substitution of the Madonna, and* MRS K. DORA *behind the Madonna, seen in a mirror. The audience won't know who is speaking, Mary or* MRS K.]

MRS K. [*with infinite tenderness*] You, too, must live.

DORA [*to* FREUD] I shared her room, I was her confidante and even her counsellor. She told me about all the difficulties of married life. There was nothing we couldn't talk about . . .

MRS K. [*laughing gently*] I call a spade a spade.
There is more than one way. A body has many resources.
You'll see.

DORA Let me kiss you!
[MRS K. *smiling, more and more gentle, more and more distant, ephemeral, infinite, very near, inaccessible, says no with her gestures, with her body, resists* DORA's *embrace. Calmly*]

DORA Let me take you in my arms! Just once!

DORA [*to* FREUD] I don't know. That's just it. She showed herself to me. Her smile. As if she were smiling to herself . . .

FREUD Two hours? What was it that touched you?

DORA [*after a long silence*] Her.

DORA [*to* MRS K.] I am standing here! Before you. I'm waiting. If only! If only you would tell me!

MRS K. But I have nothing to tell you.

DORA Everything you know. Everything I don't know. Let me give you this love.
Her body, its ravishing whiteness. Her tiny breasts, the smooth skin of her belly.

MRS K. [*her hand over* DORA's *mouth*] Oh! Impossible, impossible, my mad little child.

DORA I ache, I never stop aching, put your hands on my head, hold me.

MRS K. My God. What am I going to do with you?

DORA Look at me. I wish I could step into your eyes. I wish you would close your eyes.

DORA Her way of looking at herself. Of loving herself. Of not suffering. Of not looking at me. Of looking at me, so calmly. With that smile.

DORA I owe her everything. I cherished her.

FREUD How could you be attracted to the man about whom your cherished friend had so many bad things to say?

DORA [*replies off to one side to* MRS K.] She is an intelligent woman, superior to the men who surround her, and adorably beautiful! . . . how white your back is! like your skin! How I love you!

[*Murmuring, and the very faint sound of a kiss*]

May I? . . . and here too, just above.

You cannot imagine how much I love you: if I were a man, I would marry you, I would carry you off and marry you, I would know how to please you.

MRS K. Dora!

DORA [*To* FREUD] They were not made for each other.

MR B. I'm waiting for an explanation.

MR K. No girl who is interested in such things should have any title to a man's respect. She has read Montegazza. She knows more than you know. My wife was so surprised that she had a word with me about it.

DORA Tell me more, tell me everything, everything.

[*With, against* MRS K.]

All the things that women know how to do: make jam, make love, make up their faces, make pastry, adopt little babies, cook meat, dress fowl. I watched my grandmothers do those things when I was small. But me, do I know how to do them? I should find out. When she told me that if she had to choose between coming back to earth as a man or a woman, she had given a lot of thought to it, she wouldn't hesitate, it's definitely women who run things, I told myself that I wouldn't know, I've given a lot of thought to it, but I don't know. Which side. But if I were a man I'd know. But I would be a quick-tempered man. But what else? I'd be too gentle, I might be brutal, I'd be restless, I'd be shifty.

MRS K. Patience, patience! It takes a lot of work. Patience, my darling, it comes with time. With a bit of cunning as well. Our sex has to learn its lesson. Draw the curtains.

[*Sound of curtains being drawn; then murmuring,* DORA's *voice fades away*]

DORA It's like a cave. Where are you? It's like a cave; it's me! Me inside of myself, in the shadows. Inside of you.

[DORA's *faraway voice*] Sometimes full, sometimes empty, and always dark. One might understand everything. Then one might change the world. This time opens and closes like hesitant eyes. Don't tell anyone what I know. Swear you won't tell.

MRS K. It's a promise.

DORA [*sharply, hissing*] You have killed me! You have betrayed me. You have deceived me!

"Who" is abandoning me

Didn't I write you innumerable letters?

Didn't I worship the ground you walked on?

Didn't I open my doors?

Didn't I break down my heart for you?

There's nothing I didn't do to please you. I followed you.

I stroked, I polished; I put my right hand at your service. I spoke to you when you listened to me, and when you didn't listen to me, I told you, I surrendered, I smashed myself up against your law, I made your bed, I turned the shadow away from your bed, who are you, who is abandoning me?

And now, to whom shall I address this letter?

To whom shall I address my silence? My suicide?

And you? Who are you jealous of, how, why "are" you jealous. Tell me? Well, answer! Do you want me to tell you? Draw the curtains! Draw the curtains! I'm going to show you everything you want. That's the way *you* are, too.

FREUD No, if that's how it is, then leave . . .

DORA Is that all?

[*Door. Opened. Closed. Footsteps*]

MR K.'S VOICE But what did she want after all?

DORA Nothing, now. Nothing ever again.

[A *still shot, on film, of the Madonna. Before which, in a sad voice*]

DORA I beg of you, give me something. Do something for me. Tell me the words that give birth. Nourish me. I am dead, dead! I am even unable to want anymore. Make something happen to me!

MR K. Don't be afraid. You know me. Can't you trust me a little?

DORA Yesterday you called me—"darling."

MR K. Come, dear, don't be afraid.

DORA He said to me: "Come. I'll tell you your real name." I wanted so much for him to tell me.

MR K. Come now, come, take my hand—What's stopping you?

DORA He was calling me. I had trouble moving. As if the world were going to open up. He had to pull me. I wanted him to carry me away.

MR K. You know me. Don't close yourself up. Trust me.

Don't you know you can trust me?

DORA I would like t. I don't understand myself. I was so heavy. I want so much to believe you, Mr K.

MR K. Yesterday you called me by my first name. You know we don't have much time . . . Dora. That doesn't mean that nothing is possible. I'm a man of my word.

DORA Don't say a word. Whatever you do, don't say a word. There's something in your voice . .

MR K. What should I do? What haven't I done?

DORA You talk too much. It's in your silences that I'd like to touch you.

FREUD And you thought: "I know who the other is"?

DORA I don't know.

MR K.'S VOICE As if she feared the best. As if she arranged to be alone, because she didn't want to be alone. On the contrary.

DORA [*to* FREUD] I dreamed that he was rejecting me and that I was seeing him for the last time. He was saying to me: "I don't hold anything against you. I don't take back anything that I said; I'm a man of my word, didn't I keep my word, yes." And he was saying: "I hold nothing against you, you know me a little"—and it's true—yes—I know him better than anyone—and: "I've made everything as bright as day, and I'm making my decision as clear to you as I always have, and this is the way it is." And the tears were rolling down my cheeks, but I was saying yes, yes, it's true, then he said these words: "I'm taking back my pearls!" And it was indeed he who said that, and also: "I gave you the key to the box; I'm taking it back." What was the use of crying? In the midst of all those strange words? And I was saying: yes, yes—as if I wanted to die. But what key?

MR K. What key?

FREUD What box?

DORA Some time before, Mr K. had given me a very precious little jewellery box. For my birthday.

FREUD Fine. And the key?

MR K.'S VOICE And if I had asked her to wait for me?

DORA In the afternoon following the excursion to the lake, from which Mr K. and I had returned home separately, I lay down on the lounge chair in the bedroom, to sleep for a while. Suddenly, I woke up.

[*Sudden noise*]

What are you doing here!

MR K. This is my room, no one is going to keep me from coming in when I like.

Besides, I came in here to get something!

DORA [*breathless and painful recital*] I got up in a hurry to run away. I was running away. Then *I dreamed that I was running away. I saw myself running away on a beach. The sand was so hard that it wore my foot raw. I was accompanied by a woman who was bigger and stronger than me and who was my opposite in every way. I called her dear Mrs K. She made me feel ashamed of myself. She was what I might have been, in every way. I*

355 ◆◆◆ *Portrait of Dora*

didn't have to explain to her. She was sublimely indifferent to my failures. On the way down, I felt that I was moving away from myself. I, too, was abandoning myself.

FREUD'S VOICE As if she were running away from herself. In order to keep from getting there. In order to keep from dying, too.

DORA That's when I saw him again. There! It was Him! So far way! Yet just a few metres away from me. But too far away. So far away. I knew very well that one day.

FREUD'S VOICE Searching for Him everywhere, from the beginning of time. As if He existed. As if He were waiting only for her. For her arrival, to disappear.

DORA There was no reason to hope. Everything separates us. He said to me: "Thus, nothing changes." And I couldn't reach him. Because where I am, nothing is living. I was in the past.

FREUD'S VOICE Everything that happened to her, only happened to her in the past. She lived on memories. A prey to the past. Without any hope of ever reaching anything like the present.

DORA She urged me to live. Unaware of the enormity of my suffering. Which doesn't even reach me. I couldn't even cry out.

FREUD Completely lost, between love and desire.

DORA In the afternoon, when I wanted to lock myself in to take a rest, the key was gone! I am sure that Mr K. had removed it.

FREUD The question whether a girl is "open" or "shut" can naturally not be a matter of indifference. It is well known what sort of key effects the opening in such a case.

DORA I was "sure" you would say that!

FREUD Didn't you ever feel like giving Mr K. a present in return? That wouldn't have been out of place.

DORA Absolutely not. I never thought of it. I was on my guard. I was afraid that he would come into my room while I was dressing.

FREUD Into "his" room?

DORA Mrs K. always went out very early to take a walk with him. But he didn't bother me any more.

FREUD You regretted it perhaps?

DORA Absolutely not. It was then that I made up my mind not to stay at the K.'s without Papa. Because Papa was living at the hotel and he always went out early. I used to dress myself quickly to run and meet him!

MR K. This is my house. You don't belong here.

DORA There is some mistake.

MR K. There is no mistake. You are in my house.

DORA I'm taking my pearls, and I'm throwing them away.

[*Sound of pearls rolling across the floor*]

MR K. [*a cry of anger*] I'm taking back my key. Give me back my keys.

DORA [*childishly*] No.

[*from far away*] Where are we going. Where are we going? Where are we going! And if something goes wrong, it will be Papa's fault, Mr K. gave me a jewellery box. So. I give Mr K. my jewellery box. Or rather, no.

FREUD Let's go on.

[DORA *is looking about*]

FREUD If it's your little purse you're looking for, it's there on your knees. You haven't stopped fingering it for the past hour. It's very pretty, by the way.

DORA [*suspiciously*] This is the first time you've noticed it?

FREUD This is the first time I've seen you with it. Here, in any case.

DORA I always have my little purse with me wherever I go.

[*anxiously*] It gets stuck, you see, I was fingering it because I couldn't get it open. Here: see for yourself how hard it is. It just won't open.

FREUD Don't you think that your words might apply to another meaning for that little purse?

DORA [SCORNFULLY] Yes, if you like. That's what men think.

FREUD He whose lips are silent chatters with his fingertips.

In the train of associations, equivocal words are like switch-points.

DORA Cross stitch, railway stitch, needle point, petit point. That's women's work.

DORA I have a dream.

FREUD Go on.

DORA I know how to . . .

FREUD What do you know how to do?

DORA How to make dreams rise, puff them up, bake them, roll them, put them into my mouth. I sit down at the table next to my grandmothers. They're joyfully eating little cakes. The sounds in the distance announce the arrival of the matrimonial procession. I am shocked by it; sad and ashamed; I realize that there aren't enough cakes left. I myself have eaten several of them, I've gorged myself out of nervousness, violent embarrassment at the thought that I've eaten the others' portions, enter Mr and Mrs K. holding hands, then my father and his wife, holding hands. I don't know what they're thinking. They are all beautiful, and gracious and familiar. As this is the first time I've seen them all together, I don't know whom to serve first. I go to ask my three grandmothers how to divide the cakes equally. They nearly choke laughing, their mouths are full, they've gobbled up everything.

Mr K. turns to me and says quite naturally: "Can you, no matter when, at a moment's notice, be ready to set aside two hours of your time?" Shaken by the simplicity of another time, bewildered. What does Papa think about this?

I can't bring myself to answer. For what? Ready for what? I put it off, I apologize for not answering. I ask them if they want to play cards, which I don't know how to play, but maybe checkers . . . There are five of them for with against me.

And if one of them killed me, ah, if one of them killed me right before my very eyes what revenge. My body in pieces on the table to replace the cake.

DORA I smell smoke.

FREUD Tell me about the smoke.

DORA The smell of smoke, came to me, in the last dream. And in the other dreams.

FREUD Yes? And?

DORA There was always the smell of smoke. Like a sudden blow. I would wake up with a start. And I had this dream three times: my father is standing beside my bed and wakes me up. I'm asleep, but I see him. There must be a fire in the house. I dress myself quickly. Mama wants to save her jewellery box, but Papa says: "I refuse to let my two children and myself be burned for the sake of your jewellery box." We hurry downstairs and as soon as I'm outside, I wake up.

FREUD Did you have the dream during your first nights at Linz or during your last ones before your departure?

DORA I don't know. I think it was afterward.

FREUD How long did you stay on at Linz after the scene?

DORA Four more days.

The afternoon following the excursion to the lake, I lay down, as usual, on the lounge chair in his bedroom to sleep for awhile. I woke up with a start and saw Mr K. standing beside me . . .

FREUD Was it Mr K.? Are you sure?

DORA What's the matter?

MR B. Quick, get dressed, quick, go downstairs.

[MR B. *cries out violently*]

I refuse to let my two children be burned because of you!

DORA As soon as I am outside, I wake up. I wonder why Mama is in this dream? She wasn't with us at Linz.

FREUD'S VOICE But it was to her, or to another, that her father brought back jewellery. And Mr K. gave her a jewellery box.

DORA [*To whom? To Papa? To* MR K.?] I am ready. I would have given you what your wife refuses you. It will be her fault.

FREUD The secret lies with your mama. What role does your mother play here? She was once your rival for your father's affections.

DORA I "knew" that "you" were going to say that!

FREUD So you know who replaces whom.

DORA [wearily] Know. Know. But no one knows anything. What does it mean: to know? Do I know what I know, how do I know? Nothing means anything. If there were a god . . .

FREUD Who stood beside your bed when you were small?

DORA I don't know. My father. . . ?

FREUD I don't know. Someone stood beside you and woke you up. Why?

DORA Tell me what you know.

FREUD I don't "know" anything.

DORA What's the point of this? What are you trying to make me say?

FREUD . . . To make you see.

DORA I forgot. Yes, I don't see.

FREUD Where there's smoke, there's fire.

DORA [ironically] And where there's fire, there's water?

FREUD Exactly. [He smiles] Fire is the opposite of water: in the dream where there is fire, there is water. You surely "needed to go out" because of the fire. But also in order that some little mishap might not occur . . . On the other hand, fire enflames, it can directly represent love. So that from fire, one set of rails leads . . .

DORA I see you coming!

FREUD You don't know how well chosen your words are. You see me coming. To where another came before, a long time ago, a very long time ago.

DORA Don't you think you're interpreting all of this a little too personally?

FREUD That's possible. However, all I'm doing is pointing out to you what the dreams are saying. I see that the contrast between fire and water has been extremely useful to you in the dream. What does one do to prevent children from wetting their beds? One awakens them. Your father awakens you in the dream. Mr K. awakens you.

DORA Tell me, Doctor, why exactly did this disease strike me, why me in particular?

FREUD What disease? You're not . . .

DORA [cutting him off] It comes from my father. He had already been ill before his marriage. It's a poison that gets passed on. He fell ill because of his dissolute life. He passed his disease on to Mama. And I have the disease as well.

FREUD What disease?

DORA Like Mama, when we had to go to Franzensbad for her cure. She had abdominal pains and a discharge.

FREUD Do you think you have a venereal disease? Since when?

[*Silence*]

Since when?

[*Silence*]

Do you know why you cough?

DORA My father coughs too.

FREUD You see, the "disease" comes from your father, but it is displaced from above downwards or from below upwards, depending on whether it's you or your mama. With the symptom of the cough, you are proclaiming your father's responsibility for what you call "your disease."

DORA But I really do cough!

FREUD Yes.

DORA I was getting dressed quickly. I was afraid he would surprise me while I was dressing. So I was getting dressed very quickly.
[*murmuring*] I get dressed quickly.
[*panting*] As soon as I'm outside I wake up, I'm wet with perspiration. The smell of smoke wakes me up.

FREUD You get dressed quickly: to keep the secret.

DORA But I never said anything of the kind.

FREUD He whose lips are silent . . .

DORA Yes, yes, I know. And he whose fingertips chatter? Why do you turn your pen over in your hands seven times before speaking to me? Why?

FREUD We must respect the rules!

DORA [*she mimics him*] "We must respect the rules."

[*She paces back and forth across the room*]

Where are your cigarettes?

FREUD [*sound of a lighter*] All right. That's it. See you on Tuesday, right?

DORA Right?

[*She bursts out laughing*]

VOICE OF THE PLAY Doctor Freud might have had this dream, at the end of December, 1899. Dora is by then a blossoming girl, of eighteen or nineteen. There is something contradictory and strange about her, which makes her quite charming. Ripe-looking flesh but a hard mouth, the forehead of a girl, a fixed icy stare. She resembles hidden, vindictive, dangerous loves. Doctor Freud cannot take his eyes off of her. Dora, who is holding him by the hand with the firm and irritated grip of a governess, has led him to the shores of the mountain lake which she points out to him. She does not throw him into the water; but she insists that he go and pick her a bouquet of those shimmering white flowers that grow on the other side of the lake, and whose perfume he can smell in spite of the distance. Although his hesitation is natural, Freud is anxious, for he senses that this is some sort of test or maybe a trap. He wonders why they didn't get off the train at the previous station which was precisely on the other side of the lake. But not for long, for Dora suddenly looks him up and down, throws him a glance full of scorn and then turns her back on him with a movement of her neck that stuns him: unrestrained, superb and implacable. Then, without a moment's hesitation, she lifts her dress in a willfully seductive way, allowing her ankles to show a bit, and she crosses the lake, walking over hundreds of bones. Something keeps Freud from doing the same.

[*Then a canon of voices:* MR B., MR K., MRS K., FREUD *and* DORA, *successively*]

MR B. The girl insisted that he go and pick her a bouquet of those white flowers that grow on the other side of the lake.

MR K. She loathed those white flowers that grew on the other side of the lake: the perfume they gave off was surely too bitter.

MRS K. She agrees with him that it would be better not to touch them.

MR B. With an awkward white hand she fingered the pearls around her neck. Without thinking about it. Her eyes were elsewhere.

FREUD Irritated, Freud suddenly gives her a slap to stop her.

DORA Sometimes she wondered if she herself were not Mr K. In his place, how she would have loved her!

FREUD She said that she would have liked to sleep on the grass of his chest.

DORA Whose? You know that you mean everything to me. To whom? Do I mean nothing to you?

FREUD The worst of it was that he felt like a fool when deep down inside the greatest dream was just beginning.

———————————

MR B. Then my fear was perfectly natural.

FREUD Naturally.

MR B. That can't be right! One can have the need to go out at night.

FREUD And if someone awakened her?

DORA Papa came over to my bed. He awoke me with a kiss; he protected me. How beautiful everything was when he loved no one more than me and when he would awaken me!

FREUD Go on.

DORA And now . . .

Mr K. smokes. I smoke. Passionately. Papa too is a passionate smoker.

FREUD Given that I too am a smoker.

DORA I have to go. I have to run away. I can't stay any longer.

FREUD But who takes whose place in this story?

DORA Yes. Everyone. Except me.
[*sudden outburst*] How I adored him! My God! How he loved me, then.

FREUD Yes, who takes whose place? At one time, he stood beside your bed. He used to wake you up with a kiss. And what if it were your father who was standing beside your bed? Instead of Mr K.

DORA And now, what am I to him?

FREUD And Mr K.?

DORA [*looking at* MRS K.] I feel absolutely nothing for that man. Papa takes advantage of the opportunities that Mr K. allows him. Mr K. takes advantage of the opportunities that Papa allows him. Everyone knows how to manage.

FREUD And Dora?

DORA He didn't want to look too closely into Mr K.'s behaviour, that would have disturbed him in his relations with her.

FREUD And you?

DORA I never went to see her when Papa was there. It was only natural. I was glad that he had found a woman that he could get attached to. What my father does is none of my business.

FREUD And what Dora does?

DORA I don't blame anyone. How could I blame him? My reproaches were unfair. He sacrificed me to that woman. She took him away from me. But how could I blame her?

FREUD Who is to blame then?

DORA Who betrays whom in this story? No one. There are no reproaches? . . . Give me my coat. I'm leaving.
[*As she leaves* FREUD, *she is repeating all her departures, she is already gone, she doesn't look at him: she sees herself, moving away again, being abandoned*]

DORA Alone again. Everyone else stays behind. You let me go. I was the first to hang up my coat on the coat rack. And you all hung your coats on top of mine. That was a way of saying: You're not wanted here.

DORA [*in a slow, sleepy voice*] I'm taking back this coat. Too beautiful for me. It was a coat that wasn't familiar to me, the skin of an animal that I don't know, extraordinarily fine and supple, light-coloured, with an orangey tint to it.
Is it mine? I went through the pockets to make sure. He had warned me so many times. I might have left something in the pockets: some letters?

MR K.'S VOICE What carelessness! I warned you a thousand times!

DORA It didn't matter any more.

[*Sound of paper being slipped into a pocket*]

FREUD What are you crumpling up in your pocket?

DORA Nothing. Good-bye.

[*She exits noisily*]

FREUD'S VOICE In a dazzling silence, she walks back along the burning streets of Linz, moving slowly, stiffened with deadly mourning. She says nothing. She feels minuscule. A convulsed speck of dust. She knows the horror of regret, far more powerful than desire.

DORA Nearly dead from exhaustion. All that might have been. Exhausts me.

MR K.'S VOICE Where are you going?

DORA To a place where I, too, may sleep.

As far as going ahead is concerned, I am ready to give that up.

FREUD She felt used. Ridiculed.

DORA I could have said Yes. Just once! His mouth would have smelled of smoke. You haven't understood anything! You've never understood anything then?

FREUD If only she had been able to speak . . .

DORA It isn't my fault. When one can no longer speak, one is dead. If I wrote him a superhuman letter, with my blood, if I explained to him who I could have been if I could have if he looked at me if I showed him, my hands in my pockets, the letters rolled up in my hands, if I proved to him my strength my life my worth right here where I'm burning if I caught his eye just long enough to set the sea on fire, and cast the sun into a cage, if I stung him with this regret if I excited him. And then if I brought him down, if I crushed him . . .

[*silence*]

FREUD It remains to be seen why you felt to offended by Mr K.'s advances?

DORA [*in a voice that descends upon* FREUD *from far above from far away*] Good-bye.

[*Blackout*]
[*then she murmurs*]
[*chanting*] *One never knows who the killer is, dying can kill. Who wants to kill who wants to die who wants to make someone die I don't know who any more,* did I know it before, I know that I did, I knew it before I wanted to, but as soon as I wanted to, what? What's holding me back, if I am held back but I'm not, is the other. But is it, and the other if it is the other is it him or her or? One can kill by putting oneself to death.

MR K. I'm taking the keys and I'm going to shoot.

[*A pistol shot*]

And I'm taking back my keys.

DORA How can I forgive you?

MR K. You know me. I would have given everything.
What I have given I'm taking back.

DORA Give me back the keys. Such tiny little keys.

MR K. I'm taking them back.

DORA This isn't the first time. Is this all that it's come to?

FREUD On the threshold.

––––––––––––––––

DORA Aren't I on time? Why are you looking at me that way? So insistently?

FREUD I'm not looking at you insistently.

DORA Why not?

FREUD No, no. None of that. You know very well that I'm an institution.

DORA Do you mind if I take off my shoe?

[FREUD *is silent. He sighs*]
My foot hurts. Does my foot bother you? Is it deformed in some way?
[*she laughs*] All right, tell me something, and I'll do it, just to please you.

FREUD Put your shoe back on and tell me a dream.

DORA Who was that?

FREUD Who?

DORA You know very well. That woman. This isn't the first time I've seen her leaving here. I see everything. You, too, like playing secrets.

FREUD No, she's a former patient; she kept up relations with my family after her recovery.

DORA Relations with my fa-mi-ly.

FREUD Come now, don't act like a child. Believe me. And tell me your dream.

DORA Don't act like a child.

MRS K. Come here. Tell me what's new with you.

DORA I have nothing to tell. There's never anything new.

MRS K. Tell me a little about yourself.

DORA Can't you love me a little? Just a little bit?

MRS K. Why yes, I can love you a little. But what does that mean? To love?

DORA You don't love me at all then? I don't appeal to you at all?

MRS K. Why I don't even think about it! You *are* lovable.
Someone will love you. I love everything about you.

DORA There's nothing I can give you? Is it out of the question that you might need me?

MRS K. I need nothing, no one. That doesn't mean that you are nothing.

DORA Will you see me again?

MRS K. Why not?

DORA One day, I would like to be lying against you. Not sitting—Lying against you. I close my eyes, and I see. There would be blood all over. I would have blood on my face.

MRS K. How gory! Me, I see you standing up, very much alive, getting ready for a journey . . .

DORA And me, I see you dead. I would like to see you dead. So that no one could touch you. Or see you.

MR K. That's what one thinks when one's ten years old.

DORA When one has too much love.

MRS K. The most desirable the most dreadful.

[*Silence*]

DORA I had a dream.

FREUD Tell me your dream.

DORA I dreamed about you . . .

[*she stops short*]

FREUD Tell me your dream.

DORA What will you give me?

FREUD [*smiling*] Not a jewellery box. But all of my attention.

DORA It's curious, I see myself climbing *the stairs that lead to your apartment. I ring the bell. Your former patient opens the door and says to me: "You may come in, he's already dead."* I look at her face. Although she's at least ten years older than me, her skin is fresh, her features are full-blown and natural-looking. I don't realize until later that she is abnormally tall. *After she tells me this, I don't feel the least bit sad. I notice that there are a lot of women waiting in a parlour; to become household employees.*

Just then I hear a dance melody. The young woman comes over and asks me to dance. She puts her arm around my waist. A little surprised as I was expecting a male partner instead, I accept. Who am I? Who am I following? *I don't know how to dance;* but I let myself be led. I feel awkward. I propose, or she proposes, a third person, a man or a woman, I don't know which.

[DORA *murmurs*] *I wonder who I am to her. We dance our way downstairs; I dance badly.*

Then I realize that I feel awkward too because my knickers have fallen down to my knees.

[*She leans her head on her partner's shoulder and sighs*] I lift my dress and pull them up right in front of my partners. I realize that all three of us have been your patients and I wonder if you had a preference. *What do you think about it?*

FREUD And you?

DORA I didn't feel the least bit sad. I felt an unspeakable tenderness for my companion, but my awkwardness kept me from feeling it. It was only when I woke up that I felt overwhelmed with sorrow, as if I had really loved her, and then lost her.

FREUD Didn't it ever occur to you that something stood in the way of your wish to have your father rescue you from some danger: the thought that it was your father himself who had exposed you to this danger?

DORA What does that have to do with anything? Is that all that you can come up with?

FREUD That thought doesn't appeal to you

DORA [*exasperated*] What's the connection? Good God! What's the connection?

During the dance, I felt very awkward, but very mellow, as if I were overflowing with tenderness. At one point it's strange, she tells me that she has to carry this heavy bag around with her, every day. I offer to replace her, to relieve her for a while. But instead of carrying it by the handle as she was doing, I sling it over my shoulder bandoleer-style, and I tell her that my arms are too weak and limp, but that my shoulders are strong. In fact, this bag was so extraordinarily heavy that, staggering under the weight of it, I had to go and crouch down at the edge of space, at the edge of the road so as not to be carried away by my own burden. Impossible to go a step further.

FREUD And the dead man?

DORA I knew that you were dead. That was understood between us. I wasn't coming to see you in fact, because that's just it, we had this understanding between us. So I was coming to hear or to share the news.

FREUD Do you know why you wanted to kill me?

DORA No, do you?

FREUD And with the young woman, you didn't feel threatened?

DORA No, not really. It was more a feeling of awkwardness. As though I were backward, mentally. In one sense, I was flattered that she had confidence in me, but I realized that I was disappointing her: I was dancing badly, I was caught up in my knickers. I no longer thought about you being dead. It was as if you always had been. Or as if it were normal for you to have always been dead.

FREUD That's not untrue. But perhaps I'm not. For you.

DORA Perhaps. Yes. It doesn't matter.

FREUD We'll speak about this again. See you on Tuesday?

DORA Perhaps.

FREUD You'll let me know . . . I'll accompany you.

DORA No.

DORA [*sharp outbursts in a staccato voice*] This-treatment-is-taking-too-long. How much longer?

FREUD I told you: one year. So there are still six more months to go.

DORA One year, why? Why not two years? or two days?

FREUD You still need some help for a few more months.

DORA I don't need a governess.

FREUD Did you ever have a governess?

DORA Oh, yes! She was an unmarried woman, no longer young, who was well read and very liberal-minded.

FREUD Was she pretty? Seductive?

DORA No. She was flabby.

MR B. That woman is constantly trying to turn my daughter against Mrs K.

DORA I got on rather well with her.
She didn't like Mrs K. She explained to my mother that it was incompatible with her dignity, to tolerate such an intimacy between her husband and another woman.

FREUD Did she have any influence on you?

DORA She was in love with Papa. But I didn't hold it against her. For that matter, my father never paid any attention to her.

MR B. She quarreled with her all of a sudden and insisted upon her dismissal.

FREUD And what ever became of her?

DORA She was dismissed. And two hours later, she was gone, without saying a word.

DORA How would they be able to walk, were I not there to fall?

MR B. You are stronger than all of us put together.

VOICE OF THE PLAY They all pick up their guns. They spray Dora with thousands of pearls to prove that she is stronger than all of them put together. They prove it, in a cloud of smoke.
When the smoke clears, one sees Dora's ghost, stronger than all of them, gathering thousands of these little pearls into the lap of her apron, and then releasing the corners of the apron over an open attaché case. This is in case they should run out of ammunition.

DORA There was also a governess who did that at the K.'s.

FREUD Really! You have never told me about her before.

DORA She behaved in the strangest way to Mr K. She never greeted him, never answered him, never passed him anything at the table; in short, she treated him as if he didn't exist. For that mater, he was hardly any politer to her. A day or two before the scene by the lake, she told me that Mr K. had begged her not to refuse him anything; he had told her that his wife meant nothing to him, etc. . . .

FREUD Why, those are the words . . .

DORA Yes. She gave in. Afterward, he stopped caring for her; from that time on, she hated him.

FREUD And what became of this girl?

DORA I only know that she went away.

FREUD If he has persisted anyway, if he had continued to woo her with a passion capable of winning her over, perhaps love would have triumphed over all of the difficulties? Incidentally, this scheme would by no means have been so impracticable. Mrs K. would consent to a divorce, and, as for your father, you can get whatever you want out of him.

DORA What I wanted? And you, what do you want?

———————————

DORA Mr K. was serious when he spoke to me I think.

FREUD Yes.

DORA But I didn't let him finish.

FREUD What were his actual words?

DORA I don't remember anymore. He said to me: you know that my wife means nothing to me. And I cut him off immediately.

MR K. You know that my wife means nothing to me.

DORA In order to avoid meeting him again, I decided to get back to Linz on foot, by walking around the lake, and I asked a passer-by how long it would take me. He said: two and a half hours. I remember another detail: in my dream I saw the "inside" of the forest, as though I could penetrate it with my vision. From far away, I saw flowers . . . Beds of flowers. They were white. Suddenly, a young-looking woman appeared.

MRS K. What are you looking for?

DORA I saw a big bed of white flowers in the distance. Are they forbidden? No.

MRS K. Those plants grow naturally, and abundantly.

DORA How long does it take?

MRS K. They're quite far away. The flower-bed must be about two kilometres from here overland.

DORA That's too far. I give up.
I went back to the boat after all. Mr K. was on board.

MR K. And I beg you to forgive me, and to say nothing about what happened.

DORA And what if I told your wife?
You offer me a cigarette. And I agree to postpone my departure for twenty-four hours because you assure me that you will help me tomorrow. Out of weariness, I agree to spend the night with you. You smoke two cigarettes. You have one in your mouth and one in your hand. You never stop talking.

This can't go on any longer. Besides, the cigarette is burning out.

FREUD [*insinuating voice*] Just one more puff!

DORA Well, let's hurry up and get it over with then!

FREUD [*insinuating voice*] And what if we went on a journey somewhere?

DORA I don't have the strength to start all over again. I accepted the cigarette out of weariness. But it's impossible for me to desire. I can no longer smoke or travel. Adieu, adieu! Where is the station?

FREUD Were those lilies-of-the-valley that were growing in big white patches next to the forest, just a kilometre or two away from your hand?

DORA And if the white flowers had been blue, would I have given up? [*Imitating her mother's voice*] I am told: Shame on you! Dora, what are you doing? That's poison. It makes people stupid.

DORA Where! is! the! station! [*She shouts*]

VOICE OF THE PLAY What lilies-of-the-valley say in a dream
Mr K. said with a jewellery box.
What one says with flowers
Papa said with pearls.
What Dora did not say
The Doctor said with smoke.

DORA At last, at last, I arrive at the station.

MR K. There's no train. The rails have been cut.

Are you annoyed at seeing me?

DORA Frankly—Yes.

MR K. Is this the last time I'll see you?

DORA [*a furtive silence—that's like a look*]

MR K. Such silence! You, who were usually so talkative.

FREUD [*in a normal voice*] You knew there would be no train? No flowers for the forest; no train for the station. This is no accident. There is something you don't want to touch or catch.

DORA I arrive at the station. I am alone. You had insisted that I come.

FREUD This journey to Vienna would last six months, perhaps. Or rather nine.

MR K. Dora, my little darling. You know how much I care for you.

DORA You treated me like a servant. I'm abandoning you. No one will accompany me. I am alone in a strange city. I am looking at a painting of the Madonna. No one touches me. I will never marry.

MRS K. You are a virgin, my little pal!

FREUD And you spent hours gazing at this portrait?

DORA Her whiteness was so soothing.

FREUD That's what you thought about Mrs K.

DORA No, it's me!

[*A dance melody*]

MRS K. Why don't you dance?

DORA She was a mature woman by then. But age had not touched her. She spent most of her life in bed, for that matter.

MRS K. Wouldn't you like to have children? You have such a motherly way with my children! Why don't you dance? There, that's what I like. One must be gay, active, live life to the fullest. You, you're always so serious.

DORA That's true. No. Yes.

MRS K. You're so serious! You're too serious, my little pal.

DORA She lectured me gaily. It's true that I was serious and reserved. She said to me: you're always so serious, my little pal. My little pal! It's strange, isn't it? I asked her questions about being pregnant and giving birth. And she liked to satisfy my curiosity. To talk to me about virginity and child-birth, things of that sort.

MRS K. You're always so serious, my little pal: too serious. Be careful. One must know where to draw the line. Do you know where to draw the line? You can't be a Madonna. You are too handsome, my little pal.

DORA Too handsome! That's strange.

MRS K. It's so easy to make a false step. Listen.
[*Whispering*] You don't know how to live.
It is rather sweet, though. I could be your mother. Listen . . .

DORA What if I pounced on her? Pushed her around? Gave her a spanking? She doesn't love me. If she could see herself. I'm too headstrong to let my head be turned by her. I could take my revenge.

FREUD Yet how do you explain the fact that you've always so generously spared Mrs K., your slanderer, while you persecute the others with an almost sly vindictiveness. . . ?

DORA She had slow and gentle movements, which I loved. One day, a long time ago, I had twisted my right foot slipping on the stairs. My foot swelled up. She had to bandage it for me. I had to lie up for several weeks. She kept me company and spoke to me as if I were her girlfriend. She confided in me. She told me that her husband didn't want a divorce because of the children.

FREUD Didn't you think a divorce would have been the best thing for every-one?

DORA I had the strangest dream. I was running. I had a bad pain in my right foot. I had to sit down. My ankle had swollen up. I couldn't move any-more. I wanted to talk to Dr K. At the same time, I knew that he wasn't a real doctor. I wanted to ask his advice. I ask for him on the 'phone. Finally I get him. And it isn't him, it's his wife. I feel her presence over the 'phone, obscure, white, insinuating.

MRS K. [*on the 'phone*] Who is calling?

DORA She says to me.
It's Mrs K. . . . I say.

DORA Strange situation!

MRS K. [*on the 'phone*] What nerve!

DORA [*in a hushed voice, without any embarrassment*] I know. Put him on.

MRS K. [*on the 'phone*] Very well.

DORA She puts him on. He tells me that there isn't much he can do: that I'll have to wait until next year. I laugh. He says: "You know that . . ." But I don't let him finish. I cut him off.

FREUD Exactly, you don't let things finish. Your ankle swells up. You give birth. Nine months after the scene by the lake. So, in spite of everything, you manage to have a "child" by Mr K. Something happened during the scene by the lake.

DORA Nothing happened!

FREUD Precisely. That's where you made that false step whose consequences, even today, are still affecting you. You regretted it. You still regret the outcome of that scene. It's not the Madonna that you wanted to be. Your love for Mr K. doesn't end there.

[DORA is silent]

FREUD Why did you keep him from going on?

DORA Is that all?

FREUD I'm not dissatisfied with the results.

DORA You're giving birth to a mouse.

DORA Do you know, Doctor, that I am here for the last time?

FREUD Is that so!

DORA Yes, I told myself that I'd try to be patient, but I don't want to wait any longer to be "cured."

FREUD You know that you are free to stop the treatment at any time. When did you come to this decision?

DORA Two weeks ago, I think.

FREUD Two weeks? That's the notice a governess gives before leaving.

DORA Are you alone? Where is your wife?

[The tempo in this last part should be extremely violent]

FREUD'S VOICE Did he or did he not want to cure her, in his own time, or did he want to only on that 1st of January 1900, he will never know and neither will I and neither will she.

DORA If only I simply knew where I am now, in what country. I could begin to believe.

FREUD You didn't give me a chance to finish expressing myself! Your tendency toward self-injury profited there. Never before have I felt such violence.

DORA I am here for the last time today.

FREUD [*doesn't conceal his panic*] You're taking your revenge on me as you would have liked to take your revenge on Mr K. And you are abandoning me as he abandoned you.

DORA You don't understand anything. That won't prevent you from existing! Here is my revenge: I'll go on "alone." I'll get well "alone." And I've decided to abandon you on a day determined by me. It will be the 1st of January 1900.

FREUD Listen . . . Your decision . . . We had decided . . .

DORA No.

FREUD You know . . .

I admit . . .

I am stupefied. But I was expecting it. I'd never really thought about it. I could have sworn it. How well I understand her! Too well!

MR K. I found her beautiful. She seemed taller to me, too.

DORA This desire still this desire. Yes.

FREUD This is a murder that you're committing here. Of someone else whom I rep . . .

[DORA's *calm smile cuts him off*]

Why didn't you tell me sooner?

[*She listens to him in a deafening silence*]

DORA Should I have chosen another day? Yes . . . You could have gotten your wife to stay here?

FREUD [*bitterly*] You are trying to hurt someone else through me . . .

DORA Dear Doctor, you are an institution. So, respect the will and the point of view of a patient who wishes you well.

MR B. *I assure you, Doctor, that my daughter will come back again.*

FREUD *She will not come back again.*

DORA Act as if I had never come. As if I were dead.

Do you deny having kissed me?

MR K. No.

DORA [*to* MRS K.] I know that you're having an affair with Papa.

FREUD Maybe you know too much? Or, in a way, not enough?

DORA [*mockingly*] And what if that were true? What if I did know too much. Always too much? A little bit more than all of you?

FREUD No. Rather not enough.

DORA Or maybe you love yourself a little too much?

FREUD Stop and think. Don't hurt yourself.

DORA You could make me laugh. But I don't want to hurt you. Because you, Doctor, I would never have loved.

FREUD I could have succeeded. What stops me short, is the date, the 1st of January, there's still this one drop of time that resists, that holds my breath in my chest. I would need another lifetime. I could . . .

DORA [*cutting in and lashing out*] You could—push me, knock me down the stairs? Propose one last session.

Well thought out? Look relieved that I'm leaving, while at the same time letting me see that you're hiding your satisfaction?

Tell me that you're delighted with my decision. That you were hoping for it? Counting on it? That you'd foreseen it. That I'm thus fulfilling your fondest desire?

You could—you couldn't—give me a beating. I wouldn't defend myself. If you could slap me.

We would both take a certain pleasure in it.

FREUD I would have taught you what I have learned from you. [*With effort*] I would really have liked to do something for you.

DORA No one can do anything.

FREUD Do let me hear from me [*he makes a slip of the tongue in such a way that it might go unnoticed*]. Write to me.

DORA Write? . . . That's not my affair.

VOICE OF THE PLAY In May of 1900. In Vienna, at a crossroads where there was a great deal of traffic, Dora saw Mr K. get knocked down by a carriage. She saw him fall. It was the most horrible day of her life. It was the happiest day of her life. She walked across the avenue dry-shod, lifting her elegant dress with her fingertips, barely allowing her ankles to show. It was only a minor accident. The inside of Mr K. was in hell, his outward appearance was still prepossessing. He had seen Dora pass. There is no greater sorrow than the memory of love.

And that, Freud knew.

THE END

The Dead Class
Selections from the Partytura

Tadeusz Kantor

Translated by Michal Kobialka

FROM THE DIRECTOR'S NOTEBOOK—1974

FOREIGNNESS. This is a very important and essential characteristic of the actor. From the "Theatre of Death Manifesto:" "it is necessary to recover the essential meaning of the relationship: spectator and actor. It is necessary to recover the primeval force of the shock taking place at the moment when, opposite a human (a spectator), there stood for the first time a human (an actor), deceptively similar to us, yet at the same time infinitely foreign, beyond the impassable barrier."

Foreign . . . the impassable barrier—and deceptively similar to us, the spectators.

One day, or one night, I found a model for the actor which would fit ideally into these conditions: the dead—I felt afraid and ashamed. . . . It was difficult for me to accept this model. . . . But this difficulty also meant that I was onto something. . . .

I continued to write: "if we agree that one of the traits of living people is their ability and the ease with which they enter into various relationships, it is only when encountering the body of a dead person that we realize that this essential trait of the living is possible because of the lack of differentiation between them, because of the sameness and . . . the 'invisibility.' It is only the DEAD who become visible to the living at the price of acquiring their individuality, difference, and their IMAGE. . . ."

The DEAD and the ACTOR, these two notions started to overlap in my thoughts. More and more, I started to accept these two conditions. Multiple ideas were

Reprinted by permission of University of Minnesota Press and Michal Kobialka born in my head. Finally, they all became part of my thinking about theatre. . . . The wax figure became an entity touched by death, fake, existing between a dead person and a living actor. . . .

I want to achieve a degree of foreignness which would be painfully noticeable by the audience.

Maybe this condition will establish the necessary [impassable] barrier.

For example: a group of people is sitting in a room. They know each other well. The room creates the condition of total isolation and safety. Suddenly the doors are opened and there appears an unknown person, a stranger, someone dressed differently, or someone who does no belong here.

Such a sudden appearance of a STRANGER is always accompanied by a sensation which feels like fear or trepidation.

In Wyspiański's play, *Warszawianka*, a soldier covered in blood and mud—a messenger of woeful tidings—enters a room where high society women in evening gowns and generals in full regalia are gathered. In Wyspiański's *The Wedding*, ghosts are having conversations with cheerful guests attending the wedding party.

In 1967 [translator's correction: 1968], in my Happening, *Hommage a Maria Jarema*, into a gallery filled with opening night guests, I brought a real homeless person in soiled clothing, sticky with sweat, dirty and unshaven, who earned his living on the streets carrying packages and bundles and here was calmly sawing a piece of wood. . . .

Yet another possibility, as if from the regions of deep dreams. In our dreams, we often meet people, who were close to us, but now, without reason, behave towards us as if they had never met or known us. They behave like STRANGERS! The STRENGTH of the feeling of foreignness is very powerful in such a case. Only dead people generate such a feeling in our dreams.

These two examples were for me steeped too much in narrative and psychology, however. I wanted to stay with the real—in the sphere of material things and space.

I discovered a simple method, which had not been used before, to accomplish this.

In 1963, when I was working on the idea of the Zero Theatre, I played with the idea of acting "on the sly," as if "in spite" or "on the side." Indeed: on the side!

IN THE CORNER! . . .

From the people gathered in a room, let us try to make one of them behave "abnormally" in the middle of that room. Everyone around will see this "abnormal" behavior as performance. Imagine the same action taking place in the corner of the room, on the side. It will be perceived with embarrassment, maybe even with fear. The same action, which in the middle, was a performance, a make-believe, a safe event—now, in the corner, was true and real. There appeared a barrier and the condition of being estranged!

The stage has always been and is placed "in the middle"; an extension of the audience's viewing axis; to be seen; to watch a performance!
It is enough to shift the PLACE of the so-called PERFORMANCE to the side, to the corner, skew its axis in order for a strange thing to happen. From the audience's "natural" field of vision, there disappears that which they have been used to—"a performance." Let us state this clearly: a false-pretence and the idea of showing.
In a corner, it will be seen as an embarrassing exhibitionism, a shameful act, an event which is not for viewing, completely isolated but autonomous and independent; an event which does not rely on the audience's presence. . . .

Kraków 1974

FROM THE DIRECTOR'S NOTEBOOK—1974

[These are the notes following the Grand Parade of the Circus of Death—i.e., the Old People walking around the school desks.]
This is the MAIN IDEA of the piece.
This is the spine of the piece.
At one stage of the production's development, I have an idea of merging the actors, the Old People, who are returning to their classroom of yesteryear in order to reclaim their childhood, with the wax figures representing children in school uniforms. To integrate them once and for all. I begin to make the first drawings, where the figures of the children "grow out" from (or "grow into") the costumes of the old people.
It looks as if they share the same costume.
Later, I come to the conclusion that the Wax Figures of the children had to be autonomous, because, otherwise the actors could not move freely. Thus, these wax figures are the mannequins of the boys and girls wearing fresh school uniforms—the boys are wearing long pants; the girls long skirts. They are all in black.
The difference is in how the Wax Figures are carried by the Old People.
The Wax Figures are carried on their back, in their hands, across, dragged behind, etc.
. . . as if these were corpses of the children. . . .
. . . The Old People, carry them—their own childhood. . . .
. . . the dead carcasses of children are hanging over or trying to cling to the Old People not to fall off; others are dragged behind, as if they were heavy

burdens, bad consciences, "chains around their necks," as if they "crawled"
over those who got old, and who killed this childhood of theirs with their
sanctioned and "socialized" maturity. . . .

. . . There emerge human CREATURES
with the carcasses of the children grown into them.
In the production notes, it was possible to accurately describe
this ANTHROPOLOGICAL SPECIMEN,
which continues to develop and grow,
beyond the stage of adolescence
as if against all biological laws,
giving birth to new organs,
parasitic "tumors."
On stage, these are humans
who have reached their old age. . . .

Because all of this takes place on stage
(and therefore the costumes should be of interest),
I want to emphasize that the Old People are dressed
in funeral clothing,
as demanded by the old tradition, which still exists in the Polish countryside,
made ready for them long before their hour of death.

These "tumors" are THEY THEMSELVES, Old People's "LARVAE"
containing inside them the entire memory of their CHILDHOOD,
which was killed by their ADOLESCENCE,
its rationality,
its severe and unforgiving, delinquent laws. . . .

The past of the childhood has become a desolate and forgotten storage-room,
where the memories *of forgotten* people, faces, objects, pieces of clothing,
feelings, and images were laid to rest. . . .
. . . This is not being sentimental about getting old;
a desire to bring the childhood back to life in one's memory.
This is the condition of complete and TOTAL life,
which cannot continue along the narrow narrative of
the time present!

These CREATURES walk onto the stage
annoyed, irate, ruthless, indifferent, full of themselves. . . .
ANIMAL BEASTS,
with the carcasses of the children.
They walk like the condemned,

stranglers,
child murderers . . .
as if trying to run away from their bad consciences,
enlivened by their long-lost desire . . .
the last waltz—one more time . . .
they jiggle and jerk like mannequins . . .
they shuffle their feet, move their arms, stretch out their heads, put out their chests with pride . . .
ostentatiously, as if to prove that they are still alive!
tragic automatons. . . .

Kraków 1974

FROM THE DIRECTOR'S NOTEBOOK—1972–75

GRAMMAR

I have always been interested in grammar. At the beginning it was its rules of ordering and construction that fascinated me. Later, I discovered its other possibilities, which I found helpful in my artistic practices.

One of them was a critical analysis of a sentence structure.

A sentence, having an assigned meaning in daily life, is the core of a plot, a narration, which, as it is well known, in a traditional theatre, constitutes the very fabric of a presentational and representational theatre. It was this very life-affirming structure that I blamed for everything that was wrong with theatre and tried to destroy it as often as I could.
This is why I thought that critical sentence structure analysis was an excellent means to destroy life-affirming meaning, life-affirming relations and their consequences.
I found an effective, artistic measure in GRAMMAR. A phrase sentence structure analysis I could easily replace with the notion of deconstruction or decomposition.
I thought about the GRAMMAR LESSON already in 1972, when I was working on the idea of the Impossible Theatre and when I had selected Witkiewicz's *Dainty Shapes and Hairy Apes* for the next production. I tried to break down the plot, a literary reality of the dramatic text with this OTHER, SECOND, OR FOREIGN REALITY!
It was supposed to be a school, a class room.
And GRAMMAR!
The mechanism which would accelerate the decomposition of the plot, narration, and the production. I ordered that school desks be built. I placed the actors in them. A strict and terrifying teacher wreaked havoc among

those who had been told to be school children despite the fact that they had other plans and intentions.

In *Dainty Shapes and Hairy Apes*, there are 40 Mandelbaums, the essence of manhood, as stipulated by Witkiewicz.

I wanted to title the scene: GRAMMAR LESSON AND 40 MANDELBAUMS. Later I decided against this merger because this particular arrangement did not provide me with a sufficient degree of contradiction.

A cloakroom became a substitute for a classroom.

A school and GRAMMAR returned only in 1975 in *The Dead Class*.

GRAMMAR and its principal function proved to be an effective means of destroying the life-affirming condition of stage action, plot, narration, and production. That is, of ILLUSION! And this is exactly what I am after.

The imperative is to bring down sentences, statements, actor's parts to
different tenses,
modes of declension,
ways of conjugation,
to obliterate their life-affirming meanings and functionality,
to reduce them to etymology,
to phonemes,
morphemes,
verbally,
chorally,
in a linguistic orgy
in a gibberish sing-song
until they become one long groan!

Expose stage actions
situations,
gestures
to similar procedures.
Obliterate their life-affirming meanings,
reduce them to morphemes.
This is difficult and almost impossible.
It requires both theatrical imagination
and the lack of respect for life-affirming processes and procedures.
As a consequence, autonomous forms will emerge—
rather than abstract forms, because they still have the traces of their life-affirming functions.
For example, someone is leaving; but this is a futile act.
That is, s/he will continuously be trying to leave
but shall never leave. . . .

MAKING FACES

Centuries old schoolboy's pranks: making faces, twisting one's body, contorting one's face. Making faces is a strikingly effective weapon of immaturity against the "seriousness" of adulthood, which often does nothing more than mask its lack of sensitivity, feelings, imagination, or its ruthlessness, duplicity, emptiness. . . .

Making faces, twisting one's body, strips off this official mask of indifference, penetrates into the deep—into the interior, which is guarded cautiously. . . . None can escape the power of a contorted face. . . .

Making faces contradicts the so-called natural condition and trust-inspiring "truthfulness" of a well-composed face; it deprives it of the exclusive right to represent human kind; it proves beyond any doubt, that this part of a human body believed to express the soul and spirituality, is also that face, which is malleable enough so that it can adapt and adjust to any situation.

These are just its formal attributes.

Contorting one's face is an equivalent here to shattering the academic, indifferent, monotonous, conformist FAÇADE; to preventing the common desire of keeping one's "FACE" at all costs.

MAKING FACES—CONTORTING ONE'S FACE is a mirror held up to the adversary, in which s/he needs to see her/his own reflection. Making faces is an expression of all human monstrosities, deviations of nature, brutality, bestiality, debauchery, madness; of all desires and wickedness.

It is enough to look at them closely.

There is one more aspect of MAKING FACES—CONTORTING ONE'S FACE worth considering:
while making them—and who does not—
we cast aside or cleanse ourselves—
in a witty and clever way—
of all the above-mentioned, none too flattering, characteristics.

MAKING FACES must pierce the audience like an arrow.

It is necessary first to compose the face; only then one can "make" the face, blasphemously, obscenely, cruelly, loathingly. . . .

THE WORLD OF IMMATURITY

Through the lessons and school incidents, it is necessary to expose and disclose this reality, to which ADULTS want to introduce children in school. It is necessary to place this world, believed to be mature and responsible, in contrast to the un-reality, not yet deformed by life's practices, to this "MATIÈRE PREMIÈRE," "RAW MATERIAL" of life.

In this mature world, there are:
History, wars, never-ending wars, battlefields—battlefields of courage and victory, and their equivalents on the other side: infamy, genocides, historical necessity, monuments of glory and death, grand ideologies, pantheons, mausoleums, nightmarish ceremonies, civilizations built on armies, police, prisons, and the laws.
In that other world, there are:
the regions pushed aside by sanctioned consciousness,
ignored with embarrassment,
deeply hidden in bourgeois interiors,
banned, marked by the original sin, fined, constrained and restricted by law and court verdicts as a menace to and an enemy of the people—if truth be told, exposing only conformism and a hidden secret of the OLD PEOPLE . . .
the regions, which are
poor,
forlorn,
naked,
defenseless,
marked by spots,
snot-nosed,
driven by hormones,
pitiable and indecently clothed,
not-yet-fully-developed . . .

ideas-not-fully-flashed-out,
underdeveloped intentions,
impaired. . . .

This is not a happy, sentimental childhood,
but the dark regions, full of fear, anxiety, gone astray,
that is, according to the opinions of the adults,
rather useless
and to be discarded. . . .

The impossibility of linking itself to the world of the ADULTS,
the impossibility of communicating with it. . . .
The awareness that it will always remain on the other side, lonely, and
locked upon itself. . . .
What it contains are solidarity, secret initiations, a feeling of belonging to a
different species,
like in a reserve. . . .

All these comments can be read easily and without doubt as a literary text.
Our goal however is theatre, not literature.
It is necessary to find a theatrical equivalent for these literary investigations.
Theatrical and autonomous. In this literary text, children are the *dramatis
personae*. It is necessary to get rid of the presentational style, which would
show them literally the way it would surely be done in a traditional theatre.
It is necessary to do the opposite—use a method which yields excellent
results in art. The actors must not play the parts of the children. They have to
be either old people themselves or play the parts of the old people, who
return perversely to their childhood.

The solution to this problem was found in my unrealized projects, which I
had created a few years earlier at the time when Poland was dominated by student and youth theatres—when the admiration for the human body reached
the zenith of ritual, initiation, celebration, and, in the end, of counterfeit.
It was at that time that I decided unashamedly to found a group that com-
prised the old people. Today, this decision naturally coincides with the above-
mentioned issues. It became clear to me that the old people must play the
parts of children.
Earlier, I wrote the first draft of my "Theatre of Death Manifesto."
The Old People almost dead, standing by their own graves.

The Old People slip into the bodies of the boys (1974).
This "slipping into" is a rather awkward metamorphosis. The Old People
slip into the bodies of children as if this metamorphosis was the only (though
forbidden) sexual pleasure left to them.
They slip into the bodies of the boys; they brown-nose them. . . . To express
this in acting demands a high degree of subtlety and sophistication.
This is one of the ways of imagining oneself experiencing adolescence as if
in a dream (and thus also in art). All those symptoms of adolescence or the
condition of being an adolescent—clumsy way of expressing oneself, schoolboy's pranks, throwing tantrums, the exhibitionism of basic instincts—
should be "shown" as if "on the sly," awkwardly, clumsily, with a painful
seriousness of children, as if wallowing in the inner belaborings of trivial
problems. . . .

One always needs to remember, to emphasize this condition of the "low rank," embarrassingly naïve, "snotty," bashful (the only concrete reality!).
The Old People, individuals already withdrawn from life,
because of the way they behave now,
because of the shameless return of those "serious and mature" adults to their days of "knee-pants,"
as if they got stuck in their adolescence
and time, without their participation, carved out the faces of the old people,
an embarrassment to their own age
though, this embarrassment and suffering,
return to it human dignity.

and one more encounter:
the world of the childhood and the world of the old people.
Neither of them can really adapt to the accepted, dominant condition, the officially-sanctioned reality and its pragmatism.
Both are on the margins, like human reserves.
Both touch upon the condition of nothingness and death.
The return of the OLD PEOPLE—at the threshold of death—to the classroom.
Birth and death—two extremes which explain each other.

A WAR LESSON.
NAME CALLING.

The entire class goes through the process of making faces, contorting their bodies, making grimaces to A FIST FIGHT.

FROM THE DIRECTOR'S NOTEBOOKS—1974

Every so often, there come to life actions and pranks, which are scandalous, embarrassing, and cheap, without any logic or explanation, selfless.
Let us put together a list, which will help us in rehearsals and actors' improvisations: a brawl . . .
pushing,
crowding,
getting squashed,
knocking down,
convulsive motion,
spastic motion,
a group jerk-off,
a crawl around the schooldesks,
through the schooldesks,
dispersed motion,
an embrace,

full of suffering,
painfully serious,
with an obsessive/annoying thought on their faces,
engaged in a fist fight,
kicking and screaming.

"THE LOWER FORMS OF LIFE"
"THE FAMILY SCENE"

FROM THE DIRECTOR'S NOTEBOOK—1974

From this moment on, the imagined, "fictitious" sphere of Witkiewicz's play, *Tumor Brainowicz*, slips into the reality of the classroom, which has already been clearly defined. From the very beginning, it must be obvious that this particular strategy has nothing to do with a representation of or finding a stage equivalent to convey the meaning and content of the play, the way traditional theatres would do.

I want to create the impression that the OLD PEOPLE, characters from the "Dead Class," defined clearly and unequivocally by their past and destiny, were as if "programmed" by the content of *Tumor Brainowicz*. This might have happened by accident, or maybe it was Fate which wanted to make the end of their lives a little bit more exciting. It is possible that this maneuver (a kind of transplant) could have been made successfully and that, under favorable circumstances, all the stage action and the events in the play could have been faithfully and logically repeated—thus represented.

But this would have been a simulacrum bereft of any reality; it would have been nothing more than a stylistic gesture—an improvisation of sorts or just a "dressing-up."
More important, this would have been against my ideas of theatre.

We have to agree that the reality of the classroom—which is concrete and not ephemeral or illusionary (a playtext)—by absorbing the imaginary, fictitious content and sphere of the play, must, to say it carefully, be altered.
Of course it is the question of the degree.
One must proceed very carefully (a necessary action even in the most radical transformations), conscious of the hierarchy among the objects: the reality of the classroom is the primary matter, an autonomous reality.

I would like to emphasize the unusual nature of the maneuver, which we will be engaged in during the rehearsal process. This must be described with precision, because it is very easy to drift ashore, run aground, go to extremes, and destroy a thin layer of humor and relativism, perversion, disdain and mystification with pedantry and literalness.

It is those features only that can save us from false seriousness and logic.

This maneuver is unusual because the rehearsals are not a part of putting a production together. At no stage in the process is one given the impression that there will ever be an opening night.

The rehearsal process is a battlefield where two indifferent realities will clash, have a fight, whose rules and regulations will make it impossible for either of the two sides to be victorious.

It is openly stated that a failed scene and defeat may bring about a positive solution to the problem; that one of the conditions which can lead to success is a careless offensive and throwing down of the weapons; that one calls for an interruption of a solid line of attack, for sudden breaks in a front line—all of this looks like a battle fought by children or by a madman.

Observe the encounter between the two realities—one, which is autonomous, free, and concrete ("The Dead Class"), and the other one, which is imagined and a stylistically fictitious literary structure (a play).

During those sinful and shady maneuvers; during those crossings over and slippages; during those attempts at creating new characters, often the members of "The Dead Class" would be bigger than life, puff up dangerously, or would become nuanced and more complex.

A reverse could also happen: the events, the play's dramatic personae lose their literary details and circumstances; they become more abstract, general; are filled with disreputable symbolism. . . .

The reality of "The Dead Class" is constantly intertwined with or slips into the sphere of the play and vice versa.

Because the reality of the classroom has already been painted with the broad brush strokes of "hope" and delimited with the horizon of further development (of that I am sure), let us now focus on the dramatic action of *Tumor Brainowicz*.

We will try not to be seduced by the stage action, but to see in it conditions, emotions, and the essence of reality.

"THE MEETINGS BETWEEN THE CHARACTERS"
"TUMOR BRAINOWICZ"

"THE DEAD CLASS"

Tumor Brainowicz, a mathematical genius, the head of a horrid family, a vital force, in a state of exceptional psychological commotion, inner pandemonium, exhibitionism mixing shamelessly knowledge, sex, poetry, and morality or to be more precise the lack thereof.

The Old Man in the WC, an Old Jew, the head of the family, continuously engaged in buying and selling, always counting his profits and losses, quarrelling with his debtors, for sure he is a usurer, bargaining with Jehovah, too; from the time when he was in school, he has indulged in the unhealthy custom of spending long hours in the WC; secretly a sex maniac and exhibitionist.

Caution: it is possible that a schoolboy is modeled after Tumor Brainowicz. But there are sufficient differences between them as well as their respective professions separating them that an interesting individual can be born out of this cross-breeding of characters.

The Old Man in the WC definitely belongs to the world of the "Reality of the Lowest Rank." It is only appropriate that this shabby character play the part of the "genius." This will help us to avoid a literary representation of the Fiction of drama.

Jósef
Tumor's father, an old scatterbrain, who understands nothing about the decadent life style of the genius, embarrasses Tumor with his peasant dialect.

The Old Man with a Bicycle
for whom the memory of nighttime bicycle escapades is the only emotion and meaning of life left. . . .
The precision with which he moves this strange-looking and non-functional vehicle can be equated with dysfunctional behavior. . . .

Note well: the bigger the "class" and professional differences, the better results can be achieved. The more scandalous the behavior, the closer it gets to being real.

Gamboline Basilius
from the princely house, wishing she could breed like a rabbit (in her own words) giving birth to Tumor's children, pregnant with a baby already named Ibisa (Iza). Giving birth is the highest sexual pleasure for her.

The Woman with a Mechanical Cradle
A cruel joke played on her by the whole class is imprinted in her memory of schooldays—when caught after a chase, she recalls being forced onto this strange gym equipment, which forced her to spread and close her legs mechanically.
This is how she learned about giving birth.
Now, in this "Dead Class," the Old People bring back this cruel memory using the Family Machine, which could only been dreamed up and executed in a nightmare. . . .
The Somnambulistic Whore's pregnancy is "brought to its logical conclusion" in this nightmare with a precise recitation of the elementary school ABC's.

Ibisa (Iza)
In Witkiewicz's "list of characters," she is the daughter of Gamboline Basilius from her first, aristocratic marriage [to Roman Kretchborski], Tumor's step daughter, "wildly exciting," demonic, and cynical young girl, who torments even the biggest brains with her almost metaphysical organ, in which her intellect and sex were mixed together to create an unpredictably explosive concoction.

Because it is already in the first family quarrel that the family secrets are revealed, we find out that Tumor has betrayed Gamboline with none other than his stepdaughter Iza.

The Somnambulistic Whore
Following the rules of Theatre Cricot 2, she is placed much lower than Witkiewicz's women's intellectual and erotic perversion.
Her exhibitionism revealed itself already when she was at school.
Nobody knows what happened to her later.
She came back unexpectedly for this last lesson of the Dead—now, she plays the part of the Somnambulistic Whore. Tonight she walks around the schooldesks, rather than the streets, and, with an obscene gesture, shows her breast to the passers-by.

There are also two sons of Tumor:
Alfred and Maurice,
two exemplars well fitting to this dysfunctional family.
They function as foils to other characters.
They are like "exclamation" marks completing the scandalous undertakings of the main characters.

They can be found in the auras of two Old People:
The Old Man with his Double and The Double.
Sometimes, The Pedophile Old Man speaks their lines referring to some family secrets

A FAMILY SCENE

That which is just about to begin is no longer a school lesson, but a strange game played by the children, which is cruel, full of incomprehensible shortcuts, references, and secret codes. . . .
The Old People—The Pedophile Old Man, The Deaf Old Man, The Absent-Minded Old Man from the Last Row—pull unceremoniously, rather drag, The Old Man in the WC to the place, which figures prominently in his name—that is, to the poor, country, school outhouse—WC. It is only this vulgar name, an outhouse, which can fully express the function of this embarrassing object of the lowest rank.
Nobody really knows what is going to happen to the Old Man in the WC.

He is kept there by force. He is standing upright on the toilet, his hair disheveled, screaming his outrageous views.

This is his moment, which resembles an epilepsy attack, when an "ALIEN" force "slips into" a human and begins to speak through him.

Here this "alien" is Tumor Brainowicz.

The Old Man in the WC is still the same old Jew, a usurer, part-time Prophet, sitting at the top of the infamous Mount Sinai.

The Old People, whose advanced age adds a touch of madness to this schoolboy's prank, torture and torment the Old Man in the WC without purpose.

The Old Man in the WC complies and utters Tumor's lines scattered throughout the play; he puts them together in a meaningless way; regurgitates them, possibly not fully understanding their meaning; he abandons them easily and without scruples; he declaims them with artificial pathos and euphoria in his voice. . . .

FROM THE DIRECTOR'S NOTEBOOKS—1974

CHILDREN'S LANGUAGE—INFORMEL

In Witkiewicz's play, there are digressions which are of a completely different genre and nature.

These texts are poems, lacking any artistic value, kitschy, cabaret-style, pompous, which are a mockery of the so-called "legitimate" writing.

Written and read, the way one reads any book, they can, when perceived as a deliberate travesty, indirectly contribute to generating positive aesthetic responses.

This form of indirect action on stage—and to be more precise, in the autonomous theatre, which operates according to its own "direct" language not making a reference to any other language, and thus loses the quotation marks around the phrase, direct, and acts upon us directly without being screened by the mind—becomes kitsch. More important, it loses the element of mockery, especially in a situation when everything else is almost complete mockery and derision.

A proper declamatory style used to recite these poems, whose punch line is linguistically refined as well as its literary quality, would limit their reception to their linguistic nature, thus, a very particular domain of reception, and would be against my artistic convictions. I am always interested in assigning a universal character to all forms and objects.

For a long time, in my artistic practice, I have been interested in exploring the language used by children; the forms they use when they begin to talk, at the time when a very limited vocabulary can no longer satisfy the newly-born and quickly developing consciousness, the expanding emotional sphere or the realm of inner feelings and perceptions, which is still in the subconscious but already demanding a way of verbalizing its presence.

This type of language does not yet have a grammar, pauses, commas, periods, question marks—which demarcate, classify, or determine the linguistic structure.

It lacks connecting phrases, prepositions, conjunctions of any kind, which give a sentence meaning, direction, rationale. . . .

These overflowing and pouring-in-meanings crowd together, push, press, and bubble—and then stopped with a barrier or a levy constituted by the lack of "legitimate" means of expression, they express themselves spontaneously in a way which, as one may argue, is natural, original, and true!

This is "informel" matter, which acts and moves unfiltered. . . .

Its natural means of expression is a repetition of the same word or cluster of words. This act of repetition contains in itself the whole spectrum of emotion from hope to regret to despair to stubbornness—it is an act of "clamoring" to the outside world. . . .

The lack of connecting phrases is a sign of another condition of the children's language: the ability to quickly jump into a different and remote sphere of meanings and surprising, strange associations. . . .

What is created is a forlorn lament,
litany,
full of sighs, invocations, pleas,
sounding like a prayer. . . .

There exists one more way to recite lessons or poems: school-like, nonsensical, emotional, dull, monotonous, memorized, mechanical. . . .

There is a good word describing this: regurgitation; for example, one regurgitates a prayer or a poem. In this process, there are places where one "stumbles," forgets, a desperate quest for the forgotten fragment, hesitates, encounters empty places, which one wants to fill in. . . .

Again, repetition is the best solution is these situations. . . .

Following these rules, The Somnabulistic Whore recites a poem, which Iza wrote.

Iza, as it should be recalled, is a poetess in this horrendous household.

This is Iza's poem in Witkiezicz's play:

Once there was a little fetus in the dusky by-and-by's,
Someone gave a shove by chance, someone stole a secret glance
And out came pretty toes.
First of all they had to christen, find the name and then to baptize,
Then baptize it Moogle-wise.
Once there was a little kitten, once there was a soft green mitten,
Ate its breakfast in the by-and-by's.

Someone gave a secret glance, someone stole a shove by chance,
They all cried out their eyes.

In the production
THE SOMNABULISTIC WHORE recites the poem:
there was a little fetus in the du . . .
there was a little fe . . .
there was, there was,
there was a little fetus,
was, was, was
in the dusky. . . .
Someone gave a shove, someone gave a shove, someone, someone. . . .

Once there was a little fetus in the dusky by-and-by's . . .
Someone gave a shove by chance, by chance,
someone, someone, and out came pretty . . .
and pretty, someone, someone, someone stole a secret glance . . .
a secret glance and pretty . . .
and, pretty, and pretty. . . .
and out came pretty toes,
and pretty, first, first, first
they had to christen, find the name and then to baptize,
christen, then, then, then to baptize,
then baptize,
then baptize it Moogle-wise
Moogle-wise!!!!!

FROM THE DIRECTOR'S NOTEBOOK—

Different kinds of elocution appropriate for different situations must be used here.
God forbid: one must not assemble well-known and poor attempts at offering parody used as a method in bad political cabarets.
One must begin elsewhere.
One must begin with the reality of the classroom;
with the recitation of the poem by a lazy student, who is paralyzed by dreadful fear.
A great challenge for an actor.
A complete amnesia and paralysis of memory.
Stutter.
A hasty quest for the forgotten fragment in memory.
Repetition to gain time.
Exhausting repetition reaching the limits of abstraction.
A desperate desire to cling to the remnants of meaning.

Simultaneous confirmation and contradiction.
Reaching pure abstraction.
Then, we slowly leave the place of the classroom.
What follows is the process of finding "aesthetic" pleasure and delight in this
condition of absurdity.

FROM THE DIRECTOR'S NOTEBOOK—1974

From this moment, a total and complete DEBAUCHERY takes over—the
pieces of clothing are stripped off from the bodies—similar to the disrobing
of the dead bodies; a blasphemous robbery of the dead; a shameless practice
of necrophiliacs; an illicit procedure of exhumation of bodies;
from the cemetery to the orgy,
from the grave to the brothel,
"FOREFATHER'S EVE"—a night of touching the dead and death
followed by some kind of ghoulish secretion.
The OLD PEOPLE as if taken down from the catafalques,
exposed to the public view,
Death . . . a cheap shot . . . ersatz . . . shame . . . a rotten smell of the graves . . .
naked bodies . . . not bodies, but their individual parts; individual, shameless,
and into-your-face parts, which are separated and ostentatiously out in the
open—thighs . . . buttocks . . . calves . . . feet . . . breast . . . groins . . .
penises . . . stomachs . . . underbellies . . .
putrefaction and sex . . . faces painfully serious . . . the eyes attentively
following those ceremonies of nothingness, these celebrations and labori-
ous, pedantic, and meticulous practices leading NOWHERE, happening here
in the ruins of the school days, among the piles of molding books, at the heap
of scattered death announcements. . . .

Remember the faces . . . notes to the actors: our faces do not belong to us, the
face belongs to the audience . . . a defenseless face, exposed to insults and all
other invectives . . . empty and bare, defiant . . .
existing only for itself and in itself—like a sex organ. . . .

Invigorated by the tropics,
the "colonial" luxury of the European
conquistadors,
a decadent and perverse love exchange
between Tumor and his stepdaughter
IZA ends in an uncontrolled outburst of
jealousy and a complete
laxity of moral laws.
This is the apex of surrealist
freedom of expression and action.

Already earlier the waves of the "EVENTS," which seemed to be endless, began to lose their clarity, their ritual soothing monotony, and began to swirl up as if a different, new element wanted to come to life—a woeful resignation changed into a passionate calling, sudden spasmodic cries of thunderous passions and animal desires. . . .

It was as if DEATH, called for, has finally arrived with her Circus Troupe of nightmarish carnival revelers wearing contorted masks of Pain, Evil, Desire, and Sin. . . .

Two Old People—THE WOMAN BEHIND THE WINDOW and THE SOMNABULISTIC WHORE—throw themselves with fury at THE PEDOPHILE OLD MAN; they undress him piece by piece.

THE OLD MAN FROM THE LAST ROW meets the same fate—he is undressed by the Old People next to him.

Now, both are naked.

According to my belief that life in art manifests itself in the lack of life (the way it is defined in life) and this is why the dead façade is an equivalent of proper reality in art—the genitals of the two naked men are replaced with their exact, artificial, and, of course, dead replicas.

They are standing upright with their new appendages, helpless, not knowing what will happen to them next.

There are already two characters from Witkiewicz's play, Tumor and Iza, in the classroom.

In the above-mentioned love-dialogue, TUMOR—THE OLD MAN IN THE WC, made furious by a cynical IZA-WHORE, cries out:

THE OLD MAN IN THE WC—TUMOR

Now, I am really mad!
I feel such monstrous insatiability
that my brain is turning to hot mush.
Send for Anak Agong!

FROM THE DIRECTOR'S NOTEBOOK—

. . . Two Malays enter the stage.

The action of the play takes place in the island of Timor ruled by a deity-volcano, Ganong Malapa. In a moment, the rightful ruler of the Island, Patakulo Senor, will die. Iza will cause the death of his son, Patakulo Junior, with her cynicism. In this caricature of Colonial Robinson Crusoe, any desire for a "proper" costume design would be naïve and stupid.

We abandon any idea of having exotic costumes or make-up.

Instead, we have two naked men—relics and victims of a ghoulish and orgiastic ritual. This pair of naked men in a classroom of Old People dressed in black creates a sharp contrast between the two groups. This contrast is equally drastic and comical as the contrast between the Europeans dressed in tropical outfits and naked Malays wearing their exotic costumes.

FROM THE DIRECTOR'S NOTEBOOK—

In this production, where the action takes place at the threshold between life and death and where we are exploring matters far more important than the fictitious adventures of the play's characters—it would be stupid and naïve to pay attention to such unimportant questions, as for example, why did Professor Green come to the Island, or, for this matter, to the sensational episode of arresting Professor Tumor for the second time. Not to mention that paying attention to the happy ending, that is, the fact that, having removed his rival, Professor Green is finally free to conquer debauched Iza, would be nothing more than the stuff of Harlequin romance novels.
Let us then allow Professor Green to be that secretive and ambiguous character; that STRANGER, that NEW ARRIVAL, that political, government FUNCTIONARY. We had already met him once before.
Now, he is arriving with a black, pirate flag.
The augur of death, terror, and theatrical finale.
In order for the final, closing victory not belong to him, he is turned into an operatic Don Juan. This victory, in its much simplified version, is brought instead by A SOLDIER FROM WORLD WAR I.

A SOLDIER FROM WORLD WAR I

He is the same one who suddenly appeared during the Night Lesson—an uninvited guest, who came to the last meeting of the class before death; a ghost from the trenches or from the common grave, his tattered uniform splattered with mud, still moving forward in an attack formation. All signs indicate that these are his final moments. The hour of the empty victory. And of the empty parade. Just for show.
He leads this platoon in funeral suits for the last parade.
He raises his black standard high in the air in front of the school benches; in front of his class.

A SOLDIER FROM WORLD WAR I

Hip! Hip! Hurrah!
We are taking possession
of this country!

HISTORICAL DAGUERREOTYPE

Everybody spontaneously takes their place for a commemorative photograph. The dead, too. As if in the old photographs, their placement is

393 ◆•◆ *The Dead Class*

arranged; they are ready to "enter into history." Above them, there is a black flag.

All of this, like the sepia photographs in the family albums, looks too straight, too conventional, and . . . too banal.

To complete this picture all one needs is an old camera.

THE OLD MAN WITH A BICYCLE is the one who has one.

He places it in front.

The sounds of the waltz, "François Waltz," as always in important moments, accompanies this historical scene.

But the camera is not the usual camera.

It reveals surprising possibilities in its black box. The eye of the camera can be extended into infinity. It moves like a snake and grows like some kind of a mechanical, phallic organ.

The operating secrets of this mysterious box are shamefully simple. Technology should not obscure the allure of Mr. Daguerre's happy times.

At the end of the camera's bellows, there is a sufficiently long rope which runs behind the stage—its length is the length of the stage. The rope is in the hand of a helper who is waiting for the sign from the photographer.

When the sign is given, the rope is pulled, thus, causing camera's eye to telescope, which will be extended three times.

The bellows are getting longer and longer.

Once the photograph is taken, the rope is released.

The rest will be done by the photographer.

The helper is THE CLEANING-WOMAN/DEATH. She must be strangely attracted to this box; feel kinship; perceive common destiny of serving the same purpose.

THE OLD MAN WITH A BICYCLE—

a photographer—

places the camera, corrects its location; he is very precise and demanding; pulls out an old gun and cries out excited:

"Attention!"

and shoots.

At the same time the bellows of the camera are extended forward.

The Old People posing for the photograph, deafened by the scream and the shot, step back.

The photographer shoots again.

He cries out:

"Attention!"

With visible trepidation, with the faces obediently turned towards the camera and the demonic photographer, hypnotized by the attack of the "organ" from the magic box, the Old People posing for the photograph run into the school benches, fall down, stumble.

The Photographer shoots one more time. His triumphant scream: "Attention!"

If one is to abandon the phallic metaphor, the bellows of the camera can be compared to an elephant's trunk, used to attack its victims.

In panic and fear, the "models" of the victorious photographer withdraw into the back of the classroom, behind the school benches.

FROM THE DIRECTOR'S NOTEBOOK—1974

That which moved me the most and excited me about working on the production—beyond and above the idea of "The Dead Class"—was the need to move forward; to go beyond the existing experiences; to find a new structure for a theatre; in which the relationship between a preexisting playtext and the content of the production would enhance the notion of the autonomous art work.

I have to admit that my attachment to a literary text and to my recognition of its existence in a production were very strong.

The method of parallel actions—the playtext and the stage action—used by me until now was no longer sufficiently productive. It was no longer good enough, even though it eliminated well-known and approved methods of professional theatre practice, starting with the lowest degree of being "faithful" to the text, via the process of "decoding" the playtext, and finishing with the loftiest realm of "interpreting" the playtext.

I viewed these actions as the pretentious posturing of professional con-artists and the main reason why the theatre was in crisis.

Even though—let me repeat this—I thought that I had exposed those emptied out methods in my theatre practice (unfortunately, or maybe fortunately, this was rarely noticed), *The Dead Class* was to be a more radical step towards achieving a complete autonomy of theatre.

Let me elaborate here on my definition of the above-mentioned methods of parallel action: the playtext and the stage action.

This method is deeply grounded in my desire to fulfill my own creative process without looking for supporting a text, which has already been formed by someone else.

The idea of fulfilling my own creative process means an act of expressing the ideas, which were born or are still being born in the realm of visual arts; my poetic musings; philosophical or aesthetic!

I want to express these ideas in theatre, in the stage action.

When asked why I do not write a play myself, I respond:

(And this is the second point I would like to make.) One should not write plays. For me, this is an outmoded literary genre, which hinders the theatre's potential for attaining its autonomy. And it is this autonomy that I have been interested in from the very beginning. A written play must be repeated on stage with the help of theatrical means. This justifies the employment of the idea of reproduction, illustration, and even worse, of interpretation. I say, even worse, because every second-rate theatre director claims rights to offer an interpretation when his/her knowledge is not sufficient to faithfully realize a playtext.

I create the stage action out of events, activities, situations, accidents, characters.

The stage action consists of a chain of sequences, which do not form a logical plot, are not logically connected; each one of them is its own beginning; from the beginning, they are isolated and exist for themselves.

Moreover, the fact that they are "close to each other" is shocking and absurd. These are the activities, situations, objects, which are separated from life and no longer in relation to its other elements.

Bereft of life's use-value and service-value, they become autonomous, real, and, more important, they are freed from the tired desire to use them to illustrate and symbolize something else

They are REAL. This word expresses their radical status.

What joins them is the common idea. For example, in the production of *The Water-Hen* the common idea was the idea of a journey.

As mentioned above—this chain of sequences is outside of the logic of life.

The strategy of generating provocative and surprising (this is very important!) encounters is the expression of FREEDOM!

The sequence of events in a production is an equivalent of the drama's plot, but it does not illustrate or symbolize it.

The sequence of events of the free and autonomous realm of the stage action is born (this is a correct phrase here) in the process of distancing and alienating itself from the plot; by rejecting and setting up contradictions, which are an insult to all legitimate customs; which are the threshold of the "impossible;" which are shameless and shocking.

That which conjoins them is TENSION.

The power and strength of this tention is a barometer of success for this creative act; the creative act, when it is impossible to define which was first: the chicken or the egg.

This suggests that the attempt to find an equivalent of the autonomous stage action for the drama's plot is nothing more than a naïve and academic investigation. Such an investigation would only reduce the process to interpreting or illustrating—the idea of autonomy would thus be lost.

This is simply an act of creation which is impossible to define—it can only be described by phrases such as a flash of inspiration, a fluke, a coincidence. . . .

1974

A small digression and explanation: I have mentioned that we should stop writing plays and, at the same time, I indicated that I am very much attached to this literary genre. I would like to explain these two conflicting statements.

I believe that a dramatic text is a very significant element of theatre. I am far from restructuring the literary genre called theatre. I am fully convinced that it will exist for a long time. This is beyond the point, however.

I do believe that drama should exist as one of the possibilities in theatre, which could be as revolutionary as the idea of the autonomous theatre, rather than only as a text "to be performed."

There are also other possibilities. When I am faced with my favorite plays by Maeterlinck, Wyspiański, or Ibsen, I am very much aware of the importance of this literary genre. It may be so, because we were brought up respecting centuries-long tradition of drama. Their theatre is a grand theatre of imagination. It does not require a material form. I am convinced of this!

There is one more thing that needs to be mentioned—the choice of a playwright. (In Cricot 2 Theatre, Witkiewicz is the author of choice.) This is an important consideration. By choosing only one playwright, I negated the idea of a professed "formal richness" which is revealed in a vast selection of playwrights.

Such a phrase only covers up the poverty of ideas, or even lack of them, and the possibility for a development.

The choice of one playwright in Cricot 2 Theatre created a unity; a necessity of a singular solution—these are the most profound characteristics of an autonomous and authentically creative process.

The discovery of the idea of the parallel action (1961), which I described above, was my argument for coining the phrase that "we do not play Witkiewicz's texts, but we play with Witkiewicz."

This is the end of this much too long, though necessary, digression.

1974

When I started to work [on *The Dead Class*], I felt that I was losing my fascination with the method of parallel actions and that I would have to go beyond it.

The materials gathered for the production were becoming more substantial . . . the atmosphere of the classroom, attempts to bring back memories, childhood, victories and defeats, more and more clearly defined the idea of the theatre of death, new territories and horizons . . . all of this pointed to the possibility of creating an autonomous production without the need to fall back on drama.

In the process of building and multiplying new images, situations, and characters, there emerges a real threat that this new and original matter of the production, just emerging, which is becoming more dense, may unwittingly become a self-enclosed production, which folds back upon itself, points to its own content—thus, that it can become a plot, which will demand that it be presented according to the rules that I had banned.

I am fully aware that a uniform, logical expansion of the matter of the production will give birth to the elements of the plot.

I return to the idea of parallel action. This time, however, its meaning is different. This time, I made use of Witkiewicz's *Tumor Brainowicz*, a creation of pure imagination which, as in Witkiewicz, was grounded in the sphere of our lives. My fondness for literature returned again. This will explain why my conflicts and doubts, at one moment, lean towards drama and, at another moment, towards theatre.

The Dead Class emerges at the threshold of these indecisions.

The characters from *Tumor Brainowicz*, who enter the stage, which is the classroom, or the classroom, which is the stage, bring with them their fate and destiny. Since they contain in themselves the content of the play, the real action of "The Dead Class" is freed from the play's potent thought. They merge with the figures from the classroom, who also exist at the borderline between life and death. All hell breaks loose. We enter the world of dreams and nightmares. The characters from *Tumor Brainowicz* leave the stage. They disappear. The reality of the classroom begins to exist on its own. After some time they return, but different, as if changed by events about which the audience knows nothing and which must have happened behind the doors. They return in a different moment of the plot. This is how the plot functions in this poetic rendering; at the same time, because of the lack of logical explanation for the gaps in its unfolding, the plot itself is invalidated and not taken too seriously.

Above all, these gaps play yet another function, which was already described.

This programmatic ignoring of the plot; the act of diminishing its value and significance—that significance, which is used to help carry the burden of the idea—is partially justified by the fact that it was Witkiewicz himself who placed this lofty idea in the fabric of the plot, which had a dubious rank and status, almost equal to that of kitsch, of Harlequin romance novels, lacking any artistic value, an operetta.

By so doing, he successfully avoided falling into the trap of pathos, thoughtless procreation, or other plagues.

In my vocabulary, I use the term:

REALITY OF THE LOWEST RANK

to describe similar practices.

FROM THE DIRECTOR'S NOTEBOOK—1974

In Witkiewicz's play, it is already the third act. The plot is becoming more and more complex and difficult to decipher. From this moment on, everything is rushing helter-skelter towards the end. The pace accelerates like a film in fast-forward. The author does not hide the fact that he must bring all the conflict to swift resolution. He is doing this hurriedly and—it must be noted—carelessly pays little or no attention to verisimilitude or psychological motivations. The feeling of an impending catastrophe and panic drives these actions. Everything rushes headlong recklessly. It is only natural that little attention is paid to the aesthetic values and the logic of the plot, both of which are closer to glitziness of operetta than to those of legitimate drama. The cause-and-effect logic of hope and the unfolding of plot, which have existed until now, disappears. It seems that a new kind of plot is constructed, as if, in this rush of insanity, we were to start again from the beginning. Even the most diligent and patient audience member hastily gives up on the idea of following events and moods, which change with a maddening speed, and surrenders to the power of the whirlwind within the four walls of this HORRENDOUS BOURGEOIS ROOM.

On stage, all of this matters very little.
In this poor classroom, DEATH takes its heavy toll.
No one even attempts to consider a proper denouement.
The characters of *Tumor Brainowicz* will drop dead one by one and their bodies will be massed with other nameless bodies!

Continued:

A DIALOGUE—EMPTY SHELL

Tumor is at home again.
It seems that everything is back to normal. There is no trace of the past adventures and escapades.
As if they had never taken place.
Isidore, with whom Gamboline was pregnant
during the first two acts, was finally born.
A tempestuous and, as always, shocking
dialogue between Tumor and Gamboline.
Tumor announces that he is definitely
leaving Gamboline and
getting a divorce.

FROM THE DIRECTOR'S NOTEBOOK—

It would be simply naïve to partake in this bourgeois conflict. There are more important things that we need to attend to.
We will focus on the intensity of this marital scene. A comic aspect of this affair, which is always lurking at the bottom of such a quarrel, will control the increasingly tragic sentiment and will make it seem starker without the pathos, which also accompanies such events and makes the sense lose its sharpness and realness.

In order to remove the narrative [plot] structure from this quarrel, let us reduce its "semantic" layer to a pattern, which is almost abstract and which does not lead to any resolution, but which retains the "thickness" of its language—its everyday expressions bordering on mental decrepitude bereft of any logic or sense Circumventing all analytical speculations, let us say that it resembles an endless chatter.

In my vocabulary, such a dialogue will be called "a dialogue—empty shell." Bereft of real aim and left without knowing what a resolution might be, THE OLD MAN IN THE WC—TUMOR, who is its receiver, responds making races and with meaningless murmurs under his breath.

A Dialogue—Empty Shell.

A string of words and phrases, whose intonation only is heard and which help decipher the meanings.

Someone is quarreling; someone is being chastized; someone is bitterly complaining, etc.

Each phrase and each line end categorically and unquestionably,

that is, it is directed towards some kind of a definitive conclusion,

which closes the matter once and for all.

On stage, there is no sign of reaching a conclusion, an end, or a goal.

Intonation, which, full of meaning and determinate sonic value,

hovers over the complete nothingness.

Each phrase and line must have its clear sonorous meaning:

reproach, rebuke, admonishment, complaint;

excuses, threats, curses,

persistent questioning, boring enumerations. . . .

. . . Actually, we should forget about the plays' plot which is becoming more and more complex.

However, this mutual interplay

between the dramatic plot and the fate

of the Dead Class—becomes as equally fascinating a game as the dramatic plot proper.

I call it: NEGOTIATIONS WITH DEATH.

This is why we will follow Tumor's fate a bit longer.

THE WASHING OF THE CORPSES

FROM THE DIRECTOR'S NOTES—

In their childhood, THE CLASSROOM and THE SCHOOL DESKS brought them [the Old People] together. Then, they all went their separate and individual ways. And now, when they come back for their last performance at the end of their lives, they have nothing in common,

they are STRANGERS to each other.

The tiny bodies of children—their childhood—which they carry with them, the only thing that could awaken their memories . . . are lifeless. They, too, are almost dead, touched by death; by a deadly malaise. For the price of being STRANGERS to each other and of DEATH, they win a chance of being art OBJECTS.

This very feeling of ESTRANGEMENT, which brings them closer to the condition of the object, eradicates their biological, organic, and naturalistic liveness which has no meaning in art.

They become the elements of the work for having "sacrificed" it.

For having "sacrificed" [live-ness], they became the elements of the work of art.

THE PERFORMANCE gave them their lives.

However, during the performance, new relationships, differences and attachments were created among them.

There began to emerge, like nebulous specters, new figures to be formed by this new life, whose shape and not always noble character are well-known to them.

Slowly, everything started to find its justification in the logic of the unfolding plot, the life's cause-and-effect patterns; to leave that place where a perfect, absolute, autonomous and self-contained work of art was to be made—that place, where a godless and lawless creation, rather than god-like reproduction of nature, was to be made.

It is imperative that they be turned into STRANGERS again. It is necessary to take away from them those appearances of normality rationalized by a plot and life itself. It is necessary to expose them to the effects of shame. To strip them bare. To make them all equal as if for the Last Judgment. Worse than that. To bring them to the most discreditable and shameful condition—that of a dead corpse in a mortuary.

It is only THE CLEANING WOMAN—DEATH who can perform this ruthless, but indispensable, maneuver.

THE CLEANING WOMAN—DEATH performs her duties professionally and ruthlessly. She enters the stage with a bucket of water and a dirty rag. She washes the corpses, wrings the rag; dirty water drops onto the ground.

Stripping the bodies bare, washing their intimate parts, thighs, stomachs, buttocks, feet, faces, fingers; cleaning their noses, ears, groins; a vicious and unceremonious throwing and turning of the bodies.

A continuous and rhythmic rattle of the wooden balls in a cradle.

A poorly-made CRADLE, looking like a tiny coffin, tilts monotonously back and forth; the mechanical movement of the gears of this grim box is completely bereft of tender motherly care; the sounds of a baby are replaced with the rattle of two wooden balls, hitting the walls of the coffin.

A mortuary.

THE CLEANING-WOMAN performs the ritual of scrubbing the corpses with appalling disinterest, with precision, and systematically.

in the play:
a family disagreement
ends up with Tumor's
final decision
and also with curses:

in the performance:
At the end of the DIALOGUE—EMPTY SHELL, THE CLEANING-WOMAN forces
THE OLD MAN IN THE WC-TUMOR to lay down on the school desks and pulls off
his pants, socks, and shoes. She lifts his legs one by one and wipes them with a
dirty rag.
While stretched out like a dead corpse, THE OLD MAN IN THE WC-TUMOR
listens to the arguments of the dejected WOMAN WITH A MECHANICAL CRADLE-
GAMBOLINE.
Driven to the limits by her endless and tedious litany, he sits enraged on the
top of the school desk with his feet dangling; he straightens his glasses and, at
the very moment when the unhappy madwoman finally stops a long list of
her accusations, he screams at her:

THE OLD MAN IN THE WC-TUMOR

Today, I am divorcing you!
Out of my sight, you damned slut!
I am the lord of the world!

These are the same lines which Tumor speaks in the play.
They have a clear meaning now in the context of the earlier explanations. . . .

FROM THE DIRECTOR'S NOTEBOOK—

At this moment, in Witkacy's play, an extremely dramatic and shocking
event takes place: Gamboline, with a look of total madness and despair,
dashes to the window and throws the still-diapered baby out of it. In a
reading, this action may impress a poorly-educated reader. When presented
on stage of the most traditional theatre, this action will be nothing more than
a pitiful trick.
This is why, as well as because I reject the idea of the presentational or representational aspect of drama, we will pay no attention to this action in the play.

Using this as an example, my very basic conviction can be explained: no
stage action, which is to illustrate the text, can equal the power contained in
a given action expressed through the dramatic structure of the play.
The idea of stage acting based on this old convention and belief is today
naïve and simplistic.

Let us return to the incident with the still-diapered baby, who was thrown out the window by his own mother.

Let me emphasize that we respect all life categories and conditions, since the dramatic text makes direct references to life's experiences. This it the law of the dramatic structure of the play. The shock caused by this monstrous act cannot be adequately expressed by any presentational or representational (most *trompe-l'oeil*) strategy or technique.

This is why I abandon this naïve practice.

A MAD ACTION OF THE WOMAN WITH A MECHANICAL CRADLE

in the play:
Gamboline
responds to
Tumor's insults:

in the performance:
THE WOMAN WITH A MECHANICAL CRADLE-GAMBOLINE reaches an inner decision in response to the insults of THE OLD MAN IN THE WC-TUMOR. She says:

THE WOMAN WITH A MECHANICAL CRADLE-GAMBOLINE

So, this is it?
Everything I have done for you means nothing to you now?
I am to be treated like a dog for my attachment to you?
You dare to insult
what is most precious and holy in me?
Deal with this you double-trickster?

Gamboline throws the baby out the window.
Everyone freezes; and full of expectations, stares at the mad woman.
She walks steadily, as if on stilts, toward the cradle.
At this tense moment, the rattle of the wooden balls becomes impossible to bear. The barefoot mad woman, wearing her torn and dirty night-shirt, bends over the cradle and wraps the wooden balls in dirty rags. She holds them in stretched-out hands; and, holding them as if something precious and holy, she slowly approaches THE OLD MAN-TUMOR.

FROM THE DIRECTOR'S NOTEBOOK—

It all should have the atmosphere of a dream.
The wooden dry balls, which during the course of the performance, became a sign of a mystical image or a symbol of a child—because of their low and shameful object-ness or condition of being an object—somehow reduce this child into being a dead object; they deaden and lessen him.

The wooden balls became holy and,
at the same time, sacrilegious;
this which is untouchable and,
at the same time, cursed.
Invisible inside of the CRADLE-COFFIN, they seemed to be
intimately connected with it.
Taking them out became an act which was forbidden and prohibited.

in the performance:
THE OLD MAN-TUMOR, in the grip of fear, stares wide-eyed at the cradle and at that something that THE WOMAN-GAMBOLINE carries in her hands while she approaches him; he covers his face with hands in a defensive gesture.
THE WOMAN-GAMBOLINE stands in front of him; throws the bundle at him; he tries to catch it; the rest makes a loud groan.
Suddenly, OLD MAN-TUMOR, as it nothing has happened, takes the bundle and puts it into his pocket.

in the play:
Green is appalled by
Gamboline's crime:

At this moment, THE OLD MAN WITH HIS DOUBLE-GREEN comes up and horror-struck shouts:

THE OLD MAN-GREEN

But Mrs. Tumor Brainowicz!
People do not do things like that!
This is sheer barbarity!

A SCANDALOUS BEHAVIOR OF THE OLD MAN COMING OUT FROM THE WC

in the performance:
THE OLD MAN WITH A BICYCLE-JÓZEF comes out at the most inopportune moment.
The old scatterbrain has no idea what is going on around him. While pushing his bicycle, he is reading a newspaper; he is pointing at something in it; but nobody pays any attention to him.

in the play:
Józef, Tumor's father,
as Pilot unwittingly "falls" into the "Crucifixion-story":

shoves the newspaper in THE OLD MAN-TUMOR's face, his son, and speaks through clenched teeth:
Begging your humble pardon. But they have
written up my boy here in the paper!
A hero! A thinker! A genius at ideas!
But where is that island? And is it true that
he claimed to be the son of a fiery mountain?
Oh, my boy, that was not nice of you to disown
your legitimate father and you will be punished. . . .

Tumor
at the brink of exploding:
    THE OLD MAN-TUMOR stammers; irritated, he grabs the newspaper from THE OLD MAN WITH A BICYCLE-JÓZEF and flings it to the floor. . . .

THE OLD MAN-TUMOR
Damn it all to hell,
get rid of that trashpaper.

He stares at the old man, his father, no matter what; pulls out two wooden balls from his pocket and gives them to him as a "gratuity" [*pour-boire*].
He corrects his glasses. Despite the fact that he is still without his pants and his feet are dangling, he is sitting aloof.

The porters carry in
a "dead corpse"
of the child.

The Old Józef takes the two wooden balls into his hands with tenderness and very carefully.

THE OLD MAN WITH A BICYCLE-JÓZEF

They did not even spare the child, sons and daughters of a bitch!

Holding the wooden balls in his hands, as if they are relics, he marches forward towards the cradle; he stops in front of it; with all his focus directed at them, he raises them up, as if wanting everybody to see them; then, suddenly and unceremoniously, he drops them into the cradle, as if into an open grave. He stares at them a bit longer. . . .
Then, resolutely, he returns to where he left his BICYCLE and embarks on his last journey.

However, before he departs forever, he turns towards the audience, smiles, and, with a solemn gesture, pulls a big folded handkerchief out of his pocket; he unfolds it very carefully and in stages; he grabs one of its corners and waves it as if saying good-bye. He must be saying farewell to the audience and everyone else.

Then, he folds the handkerchief equally carefully—first into halves; then, into quarters—and puts it back into his pocket.

And so, he will keep repeating this sequence of folding and unfolding until the very end.

This sequence is called:

THE DUMBSTRUCK OLD MAN WITH A BICYCLE LEAVES SAYING GOOD-BYE TO THOSE PRESENT

From this moment on, he will endlessly be leaving and saying good-bye.

THE WASHING OF THE CORPSES—CONTINUED

During these events, THE CLEANING-WOMAN continues "washing the corpses." THE WOMAN WITH A MECHANICAL CRADLE-GAMBOLINE is the next one in line for this cruel and shameless ritual. After her tumultuous row and her horrendous action, she is sitting, completely exhausted, barefoot and almost naked in her dirty nightgown shirt, on a pile of dirt and garbage. She does not resist.

THE CLEANING-WOMAN begins to hurry. With a basket and a dirty rag, she rushes towards THE SOMNABULISTIC WHORE-IZA. She pulls off her high-laced shoes; she knocks her over and pulls up her dress; she takes her time to wash her carefully: the thighs, the knees, the calves, and the feet; unceremoniously, she pulls out her breast—the one that THE SOMNABULISTIC WHORE shamelessly exposed—and washes it with zeal.

This is too close to necrophilia.

GREEN AGAIN. DISGUSTING BROWN-NOSING

in the performance:

Having seen THE OLD MAN WITH A BICYCLE-JÓZEF, who is saying good-bye to everyone waving his big, white handerchief, THE WOMAN WITH A MECHANICAL CRADLE-GAMBOLINE says:

Your own Papa-Anthropoid
has evaporated into thin air!

Having said this, she sits on the toilet of the already well-known outhouse and gets ready for her last appearance in this show.

Even though nothing should surprise us in this apocalyptic circus, something unexpected and embarrassing happens, however.

in the play:
Green, who is cunning and obsequious,
flatters
Tumor:

THE OLD MAN WITH HIS DOUBLE-GREEN, this despicable and sleazy character, runs up to Tumor and lies down at the bare feet of THE OLD MAN IN THE WC-TUMOR. He begins to feel them up, lick them, and almost makes love to them as if to satisfy his perverted, erotic fetish. . . .

THE OLD MAN-GREEN

I am still here,
I will stay with him.

This disgusting moment is compounded by THE CLEANING WOMAN, who, with passion and fierceness pulls down the pervert's pants, strips him naked, knocks him down and begins to scrub one by one: his legs, thighs, buttocks; ruthlessly, not paying any attention to the screams and shouts coming from every corner, she whips his body with a dirty rag.

Tumor
calls him unspeakable
names:

THE OLD MAN IN THE WC-TUMOR

indifferent to THE OLD MAN-GREEN's flattery, calls him names:
You miserable crab, you eavesdropper on
unthinkable thoughts,
you psychic kept-man of a degenerate adolescent,
you blockheaded intellectual rag-picker,
you birdcage for colored feathers,
you powderpuff, you lackey of
strumpeted infinity. . . .

THE DEAF OLD MAN BRINGS AN AWFUL PIECE OF NEWS. ETERNITY OR CLEANING OF THE EARS

in the play:
Tumor's son brings

an awful piece of news, spread around
by his enemies—
Professor Brainowicz,
in his new theory, has renounced
the concept of infinity. . . .

in the performance:
THE CLEANING WOMAN enters trotting. She carries THE DEAF OLD MAN on
her back. THE DEAF OLD MAN, a newspaper crier, announces the sensational
news:
THE DEAF OLD MAN (Tumor's son)
Listen to me! Listen to me!
Only I beg you, be brave,
do not let this news upset you!
Tumor Brainowicz has fallen victim
to his own weakness. . . .
(he repeats this news endlessly. . . .)

The entire class is getting ready for the last adolescent prank, whose victim is
of course a stone deaf OLD MAN, as if brought in for that purpose by THE
CLEANING WOMAN.
This circus-like trick requires a special mechanism.
THE OLD MAN WITH HIS DOUBLE and THE DOUBLE drag THE DEAF OLD MAN
away from THE CLEANING WOMAN. They stand him upright and pull a long
rope through a tube attached to the back of THE OLD MAN's old-fashioned hat.
The tube's ends are just above the ears. From a distance, one has an impres-
sion that a rope was threaded trough the ears and head of THE DEAF OLD MAN.
Now, all that needs to be done is to pull the rope.
And, indeed, the two doubles, who positioned themselves on either side,
pull the rope in one direction and next in the opposite one.
THE DEAF OLD MAN, standing in the middle, seems to be strung on a thread.
And this is how the cleaning of his ears is done.
The old man never stops repeating the news.

INEXCUSABLE RUN OF THE DEAF OLD MAN

And he, too, from now on, will run endlessly in circles without purpose.

It is quite possible that THE DEAF OLD MAN, on his own initiative, became
eager to continue with his circus-like exercise.
He pulls the rope right and left with both of his hands.
His movements are mechanical.
He rushes forward. Stops. Cleans his ears.
Cries out: Tumor Brainowicz has fallen victim. . . .
Freezes, as if the mechanism stops operating.

Pause. The mechanism is in motion again. Its springs must be working The old man, as if unexpectedly, reaches a decision. He rushes forward. Stops. Cleans his ears by pulling the rope right and left. Cries out: Tumor Brainowicz has fallen victim. . . . Freezes.

Pause.

And so this will endlessly continue.

TWO NAKED CORPSES—THE VICTIMS OF THE OLD MAN IN THE WC—
    DRIVE HIM TO DESTRUCTION.
THE OLD MAN IN THE WC DROPS DEAD TOGETHER WITH HIS TWO CORPSES.

And so, this is how they will endlessly continue dropping dead and getting up, one by one.

THE OLD MAN IN THE WC-TUMOR continues with a strange activity, which he began some time ago, of standing at the top of the desk and of washing the WINDOW, mechanically, monotonously, and tirelessly as if he were in a dream. THE WOMAN BEHIND THE WINDOW stands on her toes in order to better observe the final death throes of the entire CLASS.

THE SOLDIER FROM WORLD WAR I must have some devilish plan for one more and last prank. He drags THE ABSENT-MINDED OLD MAN FROM THE LAST ROW-PATAKULO SENIOR, who was inexcusably shot dead by THE OLD MAN-TUMOR and is now laying in the CORNER. THE SOLDIER FROM WORLD WAR I places him next to THE OLD MAN-TUMOR, who keeps washing the dirty WINDOW; and on the other side, he places THE PEDOPHILE OLD MAN-PATAKULO JUNIOR. He whispers something to the two of them and leaves.

Both Patakulo Senior and Junior are stark naked as at the Last Judgment. Both, as dead corpses should, stand stiff upright, facing the audience.

Now, THE DEAD-JUNIOR slowly turns his naked upper body around, as if on an axis, towards THE OLD MAN-TUMOR. He lifts his face up towards him and makes a face of a "dead person." Then, he drops dead. THE OLD MAN-TUMOR screams in panic and turns his face away from this dreadful DEAD mask.

An even more terrifying image is he going to see on the other side. THE DEAD-SENIOR, old Patakulo exactly repeats his "unhappy" son's mask of a "dead person." He regains composure (still as if on an axis) facing the audience. He drops dead with his face down.

Only the naked back and the back of his head are visible.

(It is necessary to keep the precision and mechanical nature of the movements, which are to imitate the mechanism of a clock.)

THE OLD MAN-TUMOR, the way it happens in the play, suddenly clutches at his heart in pain and cries out: . . . Patakulo! . . . and, as if thunderstruck, falls onto the bodies of his victims.

And so they will endlessly continue to drop dead and get up until boredom strikes. . . .

PEDEL'S PARTICIPATION

When "Patakulo!" is heard, Pedel, as if on somebody's command, gets up, salutes, and sings a servile Austrio-Hungarian anthem:
Gott erhalte,
Gott beschütze,
Unsern Kaiser,
Unser Land. . . .

A WOEFUL COURTSHIP OF THE SOLDIER FROM WORLD WAR I
HESITATION OF THE WOMAN WITH A MECHANICAL CRADLE

THE SOLDIER FROM WORLD WAR I takes upon himself the responsibility of completing the play's plot, even though he is not mentioned among the dramatic personae.
He adds this duty to the responsibilities of a soldier in the trenches, getting ready for the attack. In order to stay close to the atmosphere of the Dead Class, he holds a black, funeral banner in his hand. He leaps forward to attack bearing the funeral banner; falls down in front of THE WOMAN WITH A MECHANICAL CRADLE-GAMBOLINE, as if mortally wounded, and cries out, while raising a banner in the well-known gesture of the soldiers who had died in the battle of Verdun, which can be seen on a post-card:
"Will you, Madam,
become the fifth marquise of Nevermoore?"

Attacked in such a prosaic manner, THE WOMAN WITH A MECHANICAL CRADLE-GAMBOLINE, answers coyly:
"But, Mr. Alfred
it is much too early!"

And they, too, will endlessly continue repeating their gestures and words, which become more and more empty and meaningless. . . .

THE PUPILS PLAY A CARDGAME WITH DEATH ANNOUNCEMENTS

THE ABSENT-MINDED OLD MAN FROM THE FIRST ROW, THE OLD MAN WITH THE DOUBLE, THE DOUBLE, THE SOMNABULISTIC WHORE, AND THE WOMAN BEHIND THE WINDOW sit down in the first row and begin to do that which is always done when there is nothing else to do, that is play cards.
Moreover, this activity is banned at school and, therefore, is inseparably connected with the atmosphere of the classroom.
And because this is the Dead Class, the pupils play with DEATH ANNOUNCEMENTS.
They become more and more involved, taking many risks. THE DEATH ANNOUNCEMENTS are passed back and forth from one person to another, are

thrown down and trumped; the clatter of the wooden balls in the cradle-coffin is mixed with the sounds of the "François" waltz.

The players chant a well-known choosing game:

EENIE, MEENIE, MINEY MO.

CATCH A MONKEY BY THE TOE.

IF HE HOLLERS, LET HIM GO.

EENIE, MEENIE, MINEY, MO!

and so they will eternally play this game.

THE CLEANING WOMAN-DEATH ACTS OUT HER NEW PART SHAMELESSLY

THE CLEANING WOMAN, who, at one moment, disappeared unnoticed, returns to play her new part.

The successive stages of the metamorphoses of this class janitor from an odious and menacing CLEANING WOMAN, progressively revealing the sharp traits of DEATH, lead to the only possible final metamorphosis in this threatre of death—to a vulgar OWNER OF THE BROTHEL.

Now, with her arse and huge breast protruding provocatively and her lips painted with a perverse lipstick, she is smoking a cigarette—

a vulgar and sensuous face;

an arrogant, but confident, walk;

her entire figure makes one forget

about nostalgia and a woeful mourning for this performance. . . .

There is no more time to contemplate this character

because the wild and mad

THEATRE OF THE AUTOMATONS CONTINUES—

everyone keeps repeating their halting gestures and words, which will never be completed, as if shackled and imprisoned by them forever. . . .

Explosion of a Memory / Description of a Picture

Heiner Müller

Translator's Note

Explosion of a Memory/Description of a Picture (*Bildbeschreibung*) was written in 1984 and first published in Rotbuch # 290, *Shakespeare Factory 1,* volume 8 of *Heiner Müller Texte,* West Berlin, 1985, and also by Droschl Verlag, Graz, 1985, on the occasion of its first performance during the Austrian theatre festival "Steirischer Herbst," at Vereinigte Bühnen, Graz, October 6, 1985, in a production directed by Gina Cholakova. Müller had earlier offered the text to Robert Wilson when the director asked him for a prologue to his *Alcestis* project, to be staged first at American Repertory Theater in Cambridge, Massachusetts, and later at Staatstheater, Stuttgart. These productions occurred in 1986 and 1987. A first version of this translation for the Cambridge performance was published in *Performing Arts Journal* 28, New York, 1986.

The piece had been evoked in Müller's mind by the drawing of a young Bulgarian student which he was given in the late sixties. In an interview, published in *PAJ* 28, Müller stated: "She had a dream and she was drawing the dream. I was interested in this drawing because it was not a work of art. She never read one line of Freud and doesn't know anything about it, but it had a very clear and very compelling psychoanalytic surface." He began to jot down notes about the drawing in the early seventies, but actually wrote the piece nearly fifteen years later. Such long germination of an idea is quite usual for Müller's work. In this context, it is interesting that he eventually wrote portions of the text in an act of "automatic writing," very much like the process the surrealists proposed. Quite logically, he wanted a quote from his end note, "Explosion of a Memory," to be used for the English title.

Müller claims this note, with its citing of Hitchcock's *The Birds,* was mainly written to mislead future directors: "I like to confuse them. A danger . . . is that the director has a clear concept and then he breaks the text . . . and kills the play with his concept." However that may be, the sources mentioned in the note can clearly be traced in the text; in particular, Homer's Eleventh Canto of the *Odyssey* provided themes and imagery to it. The piece continues Müller's thirty-five-year-long revisioning of the classic Greco-Roman tradition of Western culture. . . .

The translation's use of punctuation may at times differ from familiar usage to the same extent as the German original does. Michael Roloff collaborated on this second English version.

C.W.

A landscape neither quite steppe nor savannah, the sky a Prussian blue, two colossal clouds float in it as though held together by wires, or some other structure that can't be determined, the larger one on the left might be an inflated rubber animal from an amusement park that has broken away from its mooring, or a chunk of Antarctica flying home, at the horizon a low mountain range, to the right—in the landscape—a tree, upon closer inspection there are three trees, each a different size, mushroom shaped, trunk next to trunk, perhaps with the same root, the house in the foreground a prefab rather than the work of craftsmen, probably of concrete: a window, a door, the roof hidden by the leaves of the tree that stands in front of the house, overgrowing it, a tree of a different species than the clump in the background, its fruits apparently edible, or fit for poisoning guests, a glass bowl on a garden table, still partially shaded by the treetop, contains six or seven available specimens of the citrus-like fruit, from the position of the table, a crude handhewn piece, the crosslegs made of unfinished young birch trunks, one may conclude that the sun or whatever it is that sheds light on this place stands at its Zenith at this instant of the picture, perhaps THE SUN is always there and TO ETERNITY: that it moves can't be verified from the picture, the clouds too, if clouds they are, are floating perhaps at one and the same spot, the wiring their attachment to a blotchy blue board with the whimsical designation SKY, a bird on a branch, the leaves concealing its identity, a vulture or a peacock or a vulture with a peacock's head, gaze and beak pointed at a woman whose image rules the right half of the picture, her head splitting the mountain range in two, the face is gentle, very young, the nose too long, with a swelling at its root, perhaps a fist hit her, her gaze directed on the ground as though there were an image she cannot forget and/or another one she refuses to see, her hair long and wispy, blond or whitish-gray, the harsh light makes no distinction, her clothing a moth-eaten fur coat, tailored for broader shoulders, flung over a threadbare flimsy shirt, likely of linen, from whose right sleeve, too wide and badly frayed at one spot, a fragile forearm lifts a hand to heart level, i.e., the left breast, a defensive gesture or from the language of deaf-mutes, the defense is meant against a familiar terror, the blow shove stab has happened, the shot has been fired, the wound no longer bleeds, the repetition hits a void where there is no room left for fear, the woman's face becomes readable if the second assumption is right, a rat's face, an angel of the rodents, the jaws grinding word carcasses and language debris, the left coat sleeve hanging in tatters as after an accident or an assault by some fanged beast or machine, peculiar that the arm isn't injured, or are the brown stains on the sleeve dried blood, the gesture of the long-fingered right hand, is it meant for a pain in the left shoulder, is the arm hanging limply in its sleeve broken or disabled by a flesh wound, the arm is cropped at the wrist by the picture's edge, the hand might be a claw, a stump (encrusted with blood perhaps) or a hook, up to even above her knees the woman stands in a void, amputated by the picture's edge, or is she growing from the ground as the man steps from the house and will disappear into the ground again as the man into the house, until one unending movement sets in which bursts the frame, the flight, the tree root engine pouring lumps of earth and ground water, visible only between one glimpse and the next when the eye HAVING SEEN IT ALL squinting closes over the picture, between tree and woman wide open the large solitary window, the curtain billows out, the storm appears to issue from inside the house, no hint of wind in the tree, or is the woman attracting the storm, or does her appearance evoke it in the ashes of the fireplace where the storm has been waiting for her, what or who has been burned, a child, another woman, a lover, or are the ashes her actual remains, her body on loan from the graveyard's stockpile, the man in the doorway, his right foot on the brown patchy grass that is parched by an unknown sun, holds in his right hand, arm extended, with a hunter's grip a bird at the spot where you tear off the wing, the left hand, equipped with overlong curved fluttering fingers, caresses its feathers, ruffled by deathly fear, the bird's beak wide open to emit a shriek inaudible to the viewer, as it is dumb to the bird in the tree which isn't interested in birds, the skeleton of his kin, visible through the window rectangle at the black-veined interior wall which he cannot see from his place in the tree, would have no message for him, the man is smiling, his step is winged, a dance step, no way of telling if he's already seen the woman, perhaps he has lost his sight, his smile the blindman's precaution, he is seeing with his feet, every stone his foot stumbles on is laughing at him, or it's the smile of the murderer on his way to work, what is going to happen at the crosslegged table with the bowl full of fruit and the overturned shattered wine glass with the remains of a black liquid still swirling that spilled on the table top and is dripping down at the edge spreading in ever wider puddles on the ground under the table, the high-backed chair in front of which has its peculiarity: halfway up its four legs are tied by wire as if to keep the chair from collapsing, a second chair lies discarded behind a tree on the right, its back broken, the protective wiring merely a Z, not a rectangle, perhaps an early attempt at fastening, which strain broke the chair, made the other unstable, a murder perhaps, or violent copulation, or both at once, the man on the chair, the woman on top of him, his member in her vagina, the woman still heavy from the grave soil out of which she worked her way to visit the man, from the ground water with which her furcoat is dripping, her movement first a gentle rocking, then an increasingly vehement riding, until the orgasm thrusts the man's back against the back of the chair that gives way with a crack, the woman's back against the edge of the table top upsetting the wine glass, the bowl loaded with fruit starts to slide and when the woman throws herself forward, her arms clutching the man, his arms under the furcoat clutching her, he biting her neck, she biting his, it comes to a stop with the table just by its edge, or the woman on the chair, the man standing behind her, his hands placed around her neck, thumb to thumb, first like in a game, only the middle fingers touching, then, as the woman rears against the back of the chair, her fingernails clawing the muscles of his arms, the veins in her neck and her forehead protruding, her head filling with blood coloring the face a bluish red, her legs knock twitching against the table top, the wine glass topples, the bowl starts to slide, the strangler closes the circle, thumb to thumb, finger to finger, till the woman's hands drop off his arms and the soft cracking of the larynx or the vertebrae indicates the work's finish, perhaps the back of the chair gives way again now under her weight as the man withdraws his hands, or the woman slumps forward with her bluish red face falling against the wine glass from which the dark liquid, wine or blood, seeks its way to the ground, or is the streaky shadow at the woman's neck beneath her chin a knife incision, the streaks dried blood from a wound as wide as the neck, black with clotted blood also the strands of hair to the right of her face, trace of the lefthanded murderer on the threshold, his knife writes from right to left, he'll need it again, it bulges under the cloth of his jacket, when the broken glass reassembles its shards and the woman steps to the table, no scar on her throat, or it will be the woman, the thirsty angel, who bites the bird's throat and pours its blood into the glass from the open neck, the food of the dead, the knife isn't meant for the bird, up to eye level the man's face is earthcolored, forehead and visible hand, the other hidden by the plumage of the bird he holds, is as white as paper, he seems to wear gloves when working outside, why not at the moment of the picture, and something like a hat against the hot star that shines down on the landscape bleaching its colors, what might his work be, apart from the perhaps daily murder of the perhaps daily resurrected woman, in this landscape, animals appear only as clouds, no hand can catch them, the bird in the tree is the last of its kind, one call and he is snared, no need to pull up the grass, the SUN, maybe a multi-tude of SUNS, will scorch it, the fruits of the bird-tree are quickly plucked, have the fluttering fingers of the strangler knitted the steel mesh around the low mountain range from which only one paper-white peak protrudes, still unprotected, the mesh protection against rock slides triggered by the wanderings of the dead, underground, the secret pulse of the planet which the picture is meant to represent, protection offering some prospect of permanence perhaps when the growth of the graveyards will have reached its limit with the small weight of the presumed murderer on the threshold, of the swiftly digested bird in the tree, there's space on the wall for its skeleton, or will the movement go into reverse when the number of the dead is complete, will the throng of graves turn into the tempest of resurrection that will drive the snakes out of the mountain, is the woman with the furtive gaze and the mouth like a suction cup a MATA HARI of the netherworld, reconnoiterer exploring the terrain where the Grand Maneuver shall be held that will wrap the starved bones in flesh, the flesh in skin, shot through with veins that drink blood from the ground, homecoming of the viscera from nothingness, or is it a hollow angel under her dress because the dwindling meat pit beneath the ground refuses to yield further bodies, an EVIL FINGER held up in the wind by the dead against the police of the heavens, harbinger and BRIDE OF THE WIND who steals the wind from the natural foes of the resurrection in the flesh, the wind which they inhabit, it blows, a storm, into the trap, the curtain's arrow points at the woman, the murderer, too, perhaps merely a corpse-on-duty, his (secret) mission the extermination of birds, the relaxed dance step signifying the imminent completion of his work, perhaps the woman already is on her way back into the ground, pregnant by the storm, seed of the rebirth from an explosion of corpses, bones, splinters, and marrow, the wind supply marking the distance between the parts, the parts which perhaps once, when after the resettlement of the air for breathing an earthquake blasts them through the planet's skin, THE WHOLE will reassemble, the star's insemination by its own dead, first signal the clouds with their wiring which actually is made of nerve fibers that precede the bones, i.e., of spiderwebs from the bone marrow, like the vine's tendrils without visible roots that are climbing the walls of the bungalow, already covering the inside as far as the ceiling, or the wire tangle of the chairs, or the steel mesh that nails the mountain range to the ground, or it's all different: the mesh the whim of a careless crayon that refused to provide plasticity to the mountains with its botched hatching, perhaps the composition's capriciousness adheres to a plan, the tree standing on a tray, its roots cut off, the oddly shaped trees in the background especially long stemmed mushrooms, plants of a climate that doesn't know trees, how did the slab of concrete appear in the landscape, no trace of transportation or vehicle, I TOLD YOU YOU SHOULDN'T COME BACK DEAD IS DEAD, no tracks of dragging or hauling, was it forced out of the round, dropped from the SKY, or did the arm of a crane controlled from a fixed point in the above called SKY lower it out of air only the dead can breathe, is the mountain range a museum piece, on loan from a subterranean showroom where the mountains are stored because at their natural habitat they obstruct the low flights of angels, the "whole" picture an experimental set-up, its crude design an expression of contempt for the experimental animals man, bird, woman, the blood pump of the daily murder, man against bird and woman, woman against bird and man, bird against woman and man, provides fuel for the planet, blood the ink that inscribes its paper life with colors, even its sky threatened with anemia by the resurrection of the flesh, wanted: the gap in the process, the Other in the recurrence of the Same, the stammer in the speechless text, the hole in eternity, the possibly redeeming ERROR: the distracted gaze of the killer while he probes the throat of his victim on the chair with his hands, with the edge of the knife, at the bird in the tree, into the emptiness of the landscape, hesitating before the incision, a closing of the eyes before the gush of blood, the woman's laughter, one glimpse long loosening the stranglehold, making tremble the hand with the knife, the bird dive-bombing at the blade's gleam, the landing on the man's skull, the beak's slashes, one right, one left, reeling and roaring of the blinded, blood spraying in the tempest's whirl, who gropes for the woman, fear that the blunder will be made while he's squinting, that the peephole into Time will open between one glimpse and the next, hope lives on the edge of the knife that rotates ever faster, with increasing attention that equals fatigue, insecurity lightening the certainty of the ultimate horror: MURDER is an exchange of sexes, ALIEN IN YOUR OWN BODY, the knife is the wound, the neck is the axe, is the fallible surveillance part of the plan, to which instrument is the lens attached that leeches all color from the view, in which socket is the retina stretched, who OR WHAT inquires about the picture, TO LIVE IN A MIRROR, is the man doing the dance step: I, my grave his face, I: the woman with the wound at her throat, right and left in her hands the split bird, blood on the mouth, I: the bird who with the script of his beak shows the murderer the way into the night, I: the frozen storm.

Description of a Picture may be read as an overpainting of Euripides' *Alcestis* which quotes the Noh play *Kumasaka*, the Eleventh Canto of the *Odyssey*, and Hitchcock's *The Birds*. The text describes a landscape beyond death. The action is optional since its consequences are past, explosion of a memory in an extinct dramatic structure.

H.M., 1985

Vienna: Lusthaus

Charles L. Mee

Vienna: Lusthaus was conceived and directed by Martha Clarke, created with the company of performers, and composed by Richard Peaslee. It had its New York premiere in April 1986, at St. Clement's Episcopal Church and was performed subsequently at the New York Shakespeare Festival, at the Kennedy Center, and in Venice, Vienna, Paris, and elsewhere. It won the Obie for best play in 1986. The text for this piece is taken in part from, or inspired by, Freud, Musil, letters of the Austro-Hungarian imperial family, principles of Viennese architecture, and Diane Wolkstein, among other sources.

At the Cafe

HUGO: I was at a performance of *Fidelio* last night.

MAGDA: At the Hofoper.

HUGO: Yes. I was sitting in the stalls next to Leonard.

MAGDA: Leonard?

HUGO: Kraus's nephew, you know, a man who is, in fact, quite congenial to me.

MAGDA: I'm not sure.

HUGO: A man with whom, in fact, I have long felt I should like to make friends.

MAGDA: Leonard, of course. I understand.

Reprinted from Charles L. Mee, *History Plays* (Baltimore: Johns Hopkins University Press, 1998), 1–10. © 1998 Charles L. Mee. Reprinted with permission of the Johns Hopkins University Press.

HUGO: At any rate, I was sitting there, quietly enough, inoffensive really, looking at my program, and all of a sudden, without any warning at all, Leonard flew through the air across the seats, put his hand in my mouth, and pulled out two of my teeth.

Aunt Cissi

At night Aunt Cissi wore a face mask lined with raw veal.

In strawberry season, she covered her face with crushed fruit.

Always, in every season, she took baths of warm oil to preserve the suppleness of her skin—though once the oil was nearly boiling, and she nearly suffered the fate of a Christian martyr.

She slept on an iron bedstead. She took it with her wherever she went. She slept absolutely flat. She scorned pillows.

Sometimes she slept with wet towels around her waist to keep her figure.

And in the morning she would drink a decoction of egg whites and salt.

Once a month, she had her hair washed with raw egg and brandy. And then she put on a long waterproof silk wrap and walked up and down to dry her hair.

She wore tight-fitting little chemises. And satin and moire corsets made in Paris. She never wore a corset for more than a few weeks before she threw it away.

She wore silk stockings attached to her corset by silk ribbons.

She never wore petticoats. In truth, in the summer, when she took her early morning walks, she would slip her feet into her boots without stockings on, and she wore nothing at all beneath her bodice and skirt, and she would walk forever. She would walk for four or five hours, every day.

She would walk forever and ever.

She could never get enough of walking.

India

I was in India several thousand years ago fondling a horse.

[*Silence. She checks to see if this is going to be believed. Proceeds.*]

A blond-haired boy was on the horse. We were strangers. I was touching the horse, and then I was touching him, and others were watching us. And then he came down from the horse and kissed my quim.

Oh . . .

I thought . . .

Oh . . .

He is French, because . . .

because he . . .

because he knew how much I loved to have him . . .
kiss my quim.
And I was very glad. And so we danced.
And I saw that he was very strong, and hard as a rock.
His penis was small, but very firm and round and powerful, and I loved it.
And I was ready to have him come inside me.
But he didn't.
I thought: perhaps this is the way it is in India.
Penetration is not important.
And I felt like a barbarian,
expecting entry
when he had something
more civilized in mind.

Mother's Speech

My mother and I were in a white, sun-filled summer house together, and my mother was at the top of the stairs, and I was at the bottom looking up at her, and she said to me all of a sudden: "Do you remember always to hold on to the bannister when you go up and down stairs?" And I reassured her that I did, even though I didn't. "Good," she said, and yet, she didn't remember herself, because one day she was carrying an armful of tulips in the upstairs hallway, and, even though she had lived in the house for thirty-five years, she forgot to pay attention, she let her mind wander for a moment, and she walked right out through an open window and fell to her death.

The Fountain

My daughter and I were standing on a balcony in an interior courtyard looking down at the fountain. She was just about to turn around and go back in to dance when I said, "No, wait a moment," because I wanted her to see the fountain. It's beautiful. From the very center comes a great gush of water. Just at that moment the central plume of water started to rise. It grew higher and higher and I said to Marie, "Perhaps they haven't quite got it under control." And then it inclined slightly toward us so that suddenly the plume of water rose up directly into Marie's face and positively drenched her. And she laughed. I put out my hand to deflect the water so it wouldn't continue to shoot right into her face. And just then a woman's voice called to me from inside the ballroom: "Let her get wet!" "What's that," I said. "Let her get wet," the woman called, "let her get drenched. Otherwise what's the point of life." And so, of course, I did.

Orchard Speech

I was descending from a great height . . . not the sort of place meant for climbing. I was holding a large branch in my hand that was covered with red blossoms. By the time I got to the bottom the lower blossoms were already a good deal faded. I saw . . . a manservant there. Yes . . . using a piece of wood to comb thick tufts of hair that were hanging from the tree like moss. I asked how I might transplant this beautiful tree into my garden. And this young man put his arm around me and embraced me. I was shocked of course. I pushed him away and asked whether he thought people could just embrace me like that . . . and he said it was allowed.

River Speech

I was standing once on the bank of the Danube near a small bridge with several students from the university. We had gone down to the river with the idea of rowing, and all of us, not just I alone, were struck suddenly by the unexpected beauty of the water, which looked almost silky. We longed to have it run through our fingers, to swim in it, to taste it.

The stream swelled up over the bank, over the wet grass that was a shade of emerald green almost painful in its brilliance and depth. It seemed that the stream overflowed with the very essence of life itself. And then it started to rain. A great, heavy, drenching rain, clear raindrops as large as crystal prisms.

But this was what was most extraordinary of all—it rained on only one half of the river, leaving the other half and its bank in brilliant sunlight. I stood back from it and looked. I couldn't move at all. I understood that I might have stood on this river bank all my life waiting for this to happen—but this would be the only moment that I would be in the midst of such a miracle.

Hugo/Magada [*speaking both parts together, out of sync*]

I was at a performance of *Fidelio* last night
At the Hofoper.
Yes. I was sitting in the stalls next to Leonard.
Leonard?
Kraus's nephew, you know, a man who is, in fact, quite congenial to me.
I'm not sure.
A man with whom, in fact, I have long felt I should like to make friends.
Leonard, of course. I understand.
At any rate, I was sitting there, quietly enough, inoffensive really, looking at
    my program, and all of a sudden, without any warning at all, Leonard
    flew through the air across the seats, put his hand in my mouth, and
    pulled out two of my teeth.
Why would he want to do that?

I'm sure I wouldn't know.

Is he a Jew?

No.

So much of life is unaccountable these days.

The other night I was running down the staircase in pursuit of a little girl who had made some taunting remark to me . . .

Yes.

When, part way down the stairs, an older woman stopped the girl for me so that I was able to catch up with her.

The little girl.

Yes. Exactly. I can't tell you whether or not I hit her, although I certainly meant to.

We all have these feelings.

But the most extraordinary thing did happen: the next thing I knew I found myself copulating with her there in the middle of the staircase, in the middle of the air as it seemed.

Copulating.

Well, not copulating really; in fact, I was only rubbing my genitals against her genitals.

This is the little girl still.

Yes, and while I was copulating with her, or, as I said, rubbing my genitals against her genitals, at the very time I was copulating with her, I saw her genitals extremely distinctly, as well as her head, which was turned upwards and sideways, if you can imagine just how we were at the time, on the staircase.

No.

Never mind then, but here's the point: while we were copulating like that I noticed hanging above me, to my left, two small paintings—and at the bottom of the smaller of these two paintings, instead of the painter's signature, I saw my own first name. Don't you find that extraordinary?

No.

I Don't Like [*spoken to music*]

I don't like Johann Strauss.

I don't like tropical flowers.

I don't like mother of pearl.

I don't like ivory tortoise shell.

I don't like green silk.

I don't like Venetian glass.

I don't like to have my initials embroidered on the edge of my underwear. All those little songs about love, loneliness, woodland whispers, and twinkling trout.

I don't like crochet
I don't like tatting.
I don't like antimacassars.
I don't like a house that looks like a pawn shop.
I don't like flower paintings done by archduchesses.
I don't like peacock feathers.
I don't like tarot cards.
I don't like cinnamon in my coffee.
I don't like women who wear a lot of underwear.
I don't like buildings decorated like bits of frosted pastry.
I like my windows without eyebrows.
A man is born in a hospital, dies in a hospital, he ought to live in a place that
    looks like a hospital.

Sweetgirls: Klara

Klara, a seamstress. Once.
Elke, a shopkeeper's daughter. Twice.
Christine, daughter of a Bohemian weaver. Once. After an evening in the
    Prater.
Alma, dressmaker. Three times.
Mitzi, an actress. Daughter of a bargeman. Three times.
Lina, a music student. Jew. Once. In the private room at Felix's cafe.
Jeanette, milliner. From Moravia. Five times.
Her friend Elizabeth, a laceworker. Three times.
Grisette, domestic, from the Sudetenland. Once.

Mother's Speech

My mother was sick and she woke up very early one morning in pain. And
she asked the nurse to get her a cup of tea. And as soon as the nurse left the
room, she said: "I'm going to jump out the window with Paulie. Come jump
with us." I said: "Why?" She said: "Because we don't want to live anymore."

Aunt Alexandra

My Aunt Alexandra, you know, was always convinced that she was covered
with dust, and no one could persuade her otherwise, and so she and her
clothes had always to be brushed by relays of maids and even her food and
drink had to be dusted before her eyes. She believed, too, that a sofa had
become lodged in her head so that she felt it was dangerous for her to try to
go through a door in case she knocked the ends of the sofa.

Black-and-White Butterfly

This morning, I saw a black-and-white butterfly on a green leaf, and I waved my hand toward it, and it didn't move. I thought, well, it doesn't notice me. And then I thought, no; it thinks it is camouflaged. It doesn't realize that its black-and-white color is the wrong camouflage for a green leaf. It is sitting there thinking "I am safe," when it is completely exposed. And then I thought, no; it isn't even thinking whether it is safe or exposed. That whole issue has been left to natural selection.

The Rat

The other night I returned to the one-room place where I was staying. I opened the door and saw a gigantic rat.

I clapped my hands to frighten it away but it didn't flinch.

It looked me right in the eye.

So I lunged for it and got it by the neck and started to choke it, gripping tighter and tighter, twisting its neck, but the little bastard wouldn't die . . .

And I thought—This is some kind of Greek Fate, isn't it, to be left forever trying to choke a rat.

The Dead Soldier

SOLDIER: How can you tell when a person's been shot?

SPEAKER: At what hour, you mean?

SOLDIER: No. I mean if they were shot before or after they died. What does *rigor mortis* actually mean?

SPEAKER: That cellular death is complete.

SOLDIER: What does one do to support the lips if the teeth are missing?

SPEAKER: A strip of stiff cardboard, a strip of sandpaper, cotton.

SOLDIER: How does a drowned body look?

SPEAKER: Discoloration over the face, neck, upper chest. Because the body floats downward in the water, usually.

SOLDIER: What colors does a body pass through after death?

SPEAKER: Light pink, red, light blue, dark blue, purple-red.

THE END

The New Theatre

Michael Kirby

In his music [John] Cage abandoned harmony, the traditional means of structuring a composition, and replaced it with duration. This was logically consistent, since duration was the only dimension of music which applied to silence as well as to sounds. Duration could also be used to structure spoken material, and Cage built lectures with these same techniques. Indeed, duration is the one dimension which exists in *all* performance, and in the summer of 1952, stimulated no doubt by his awareness of the performance aspects of music and by his programmatic refusal to place limits upon the sounds used or the manner in which they were produced. Cage presented a work at Black Mountain College which combined dance, motion pictures, poetry and prose readings, and recorded music. These materials were handled exactly as if they had been sounds. The musical and nonmusical elements were all precisely scored for points of entry into the piece and duration—a wide variety of performance materials was "orchestrated."

Theatre as we have generally known it is based primarily upon *information structure*. Not only do the individual elements of a presentation generate meaning, but each conveys meaning to and receives it from the other elements. This was not true of the piece which Cage presented at Black Mountain College. Although some of the elements contained information, the performance units did not pass information back and forth or "explain" each other. The film, for example, which was of the cook at the school and later of a sunset, did not help the spectator to "understand" the dance any more clearly than if the dance had been presented by itself. The ideas

Excerpted from *TDR*, vol. 10, no. 2 (1965): 154– 71. Reprinted by permission of MIT Press and *TDR*.

expressed in the poetry had no intentional relationship to the ideas contained in the prose. The elements remained intellectually discrete. Each was a separate compartment. The structure was *alogical*.

The information structure of traditional theatre is not alogical but either logical or illogical. Information is built and interrelated in both the logical well-made play and the "illogical" dream, surreal, or absurd play. Illogic depends upon an awareness of what is logical. Alogical structure stands completely outside of these relationships.

Of course the structure of all music (overlooking the "waterfalls" and "twittering birds" of program music and the written program itself, which adds its own information structure to the composition) and of abstract or nonobjective painting and sculpture is alogical. It depends upon sensory rather than intellectual relationships. Literature, on the other hand, depends primarily upon information structure. It is this fact rather than a reliance upon written script material or the use of words which makes it so easy and so correct to call traditional theatre "*literary* theatre." As Cage's piece demonstrated, "verbal" should not be confused with "literary." Nor is the nonverbal necessarily alogical. Information is conveyed by movement, setting, and lighting as well as by words, and a mime play, although more limited in its technical means, constructs the same web of information that a dialog play does. Both are literary. The spectator "reads" the performance.*

A performance using a variety of materials (films, dance, readings, music, etc.) in a compartmented structure, and making use of essentially non-matrixed performance, is a Happening. Thus the distinction between Happenings and Events can be made on the basis of compartments or logically discrete elements. The Event is limited to one compartment, while the Happening contains several, most often sequential, compartments, and a variety of primary materials.

The name "Happening" was taken by the public from *18 Happenings in 6 Parts* by Allan Kaprow (who had studied with Cage), which was presented in 1959. Since then it has been applied indiscriminately to many performances ranging from plays to parlor games. It has been a fad word, although the small attendance at presentations prevents Happenings themselves from being called a fad. Nobody seems to like the word except the public. Since the name was first applied to a piece by Kaprow, it tends to be his word, and some other artists, not caring for the slightest implication that their work is not at least 100 percent original, do not publicly apply the name "Happen-

*Thus it is not essentially the degree of correlation between the written script and the performance which makes a theatre piece "literary." Whether or not it began from written material, any production, no matter how alogical, may be described in words, and the description could then be used as the literary basis for another production. On the other hand, there is the additional question of the latitude of interpretation allowed by a printed script—e.g., George Brecht's *Exit*, the "score" of which consists in its entirety of the single word with no directions or suggestions for interpretation and realization. *Any* written material, and even nonverbal material, may serve as the "script" for a performance.

ing" to their productions. (I am reminded of the person who said he did not want to go to a particular Happening because he had seen a Happening already. It was as if he were saying that he did not want to read a particular novel because he had read a novel once.) Names are beginning to proliferate: Theatre Piece (Robert Whitman), Action Theatre (Ken Dewey), Ray Gun Theatre (Claes Oldenburg), Kinetic Theatre (Carolee Schneemann), etc. The ONCE group and Ann Halprin perform works which I would call Happenings, but they refer to them as "music," "dance," or by no generic name. Because nothing better has been coined to replace it, I will use the term "Happening."

A dominant aspect of Cage's thought has been his concern with the environmental or directional aspects of performance. In addition to the frequent use of extremely loud sounds which have a high density and fill the space, he often distributes the sound sources or loudspeakers around the spectators so that the music comes to them from various angles and distances. In his presentation at Black Mountain College, the audience sat in the center of the space while some performers stood up among them to read, other readings were done from ladders at either end, Merce Cunningham danced around the outer space, and a film was projected on the ceiling and walls.

This manipulation and creative use of the relationship between the presented performance material and the spectator has been developed extensively in Happenings. Spectators are frequently placed in unconventional seating arrangements so that a performance element which is close to some is far from others and stimuli reach the observer from many different directions. In some arrangements the spectators are free to move and, in selecting their own vantage points, control the spatial relationship themselves. At other times they are led through or past spatially separated performance units much as medieval audiences passed from one station to another.

A major aspect of directional and environmental manipulations is not merely that different spectators experience stimuli at different intensities but that they may not experience some of the material at all. This is intentional, and unavoidable in a situation that is much like a three-ring circus.

If a circus were a work of art, it would be an excellent example of a Happening. Except for the clowns (and perhaps the man with the lions who pretends that they are vicious), the performances are nonmatrixed. The acrobats, jugglers, and animal trainers are "merely" carrying out their activities. The grips or stagehands become performers, too, as they dismantle and rig the equipment—demonstrating that nonmatrixed performing exists at all levels of difficulty. The structure of a three-ring circus makes use of simultaneous as well as sequential compartments. There is no information structure: the acts do not add meaning to one another, and one can be fully "understood" without any of the others. At the same time the circus is a total performance and not just the sum of its parts. The flow of processions alternates with focused activity in the rings. Animal acts or acrobatic acts are presented at the same time. Sometimes all but one of the simultaneous acts end at the same moment, concentrating the spectators' previously scattered attention on a single image. Perhaps tumblers and riders are presented early in the program, and a spatial progression is achieved by ending the program with the high wire and trapeze artists. And the circus, even without its traditional tent, has strong environmental aspects. The exhibits of the side show, the menagerie, and the uniformed vendors in the aisles are all part of the show. Sometimes small flashlights with cords attached are hawked to the children: whenever the lights are dimmed, the whole space is filled with hundreds of tiny lights being swung in circles.

But although the acrobat may be seen as an archetypal example of non-matrixed performing, he can be something else. In Vsevolod Meyerhold's biomechanics, actors were trained as acrobats and gymnasts. The actor functioned as a machine, and the constructivist set was merely an arrangement of platforms, ramps, swings, ladders, and other nonrepresentational elements that the performer could use. But the performers were still matrixed by place and character. Although the set did not indicate a particular place, the dialog and situations made it clear. Biomechanics was used merely as a way of projecting the characters of the story. An actor turned a somersault to express rage or performed a salto-mortale to show exaltation. Calm and unrest could both be signified on the high wire rather than in the usual ways. Determination could be projected from a trapeze. Although biomechanics used movements which, out of context, were nonmatrixed acrobatics, it used them within place and character matrices created by an information structure.

The nonmatrixed performing in Happenings is of several types. Occasionally people are used somewhat as inanimate objects. In *Washes* by Claes Oldenburg (1965), for example, a motionless girl covered with balloons floated on her back in the swimming pool where the piece was being presented while a man bit the balloons and exploded them. At other times the simple operation of theatrical machinery becomes part of the performance: in *Washes* a record player and a motion-picture projector were turned on and off in plain view of the audience; the "lifeguard" merely walked around the pool and helped with certain props. Most nonmatrixed performing is more complicated, however. It might be thought of as combining the image quality of the first type with the purposeful functioning of the second. At one point in *Washes*, for example, four men dove into the pool and pushed sections of silver flue pipe back and forth along a red clothesline. There was no practical purpose in shoving and twisting the pipes, but it was real activity. Manufactured character or situation had nothing to do with it. The men did not pretend to be anyone other than themselves, nor did they pretend—unlike the swimmers in *Dead End* or *Wish You Were Here*—that the water they were in was anything other than what it actually was: in this case a health-club pool with spectators standing around the edge.

When acting is called for in a Happening, it almost always exists in a rudimentary form. Because of the absence of an information structure, the job of acting tends to fall into its basic elements. Perhaps an emotion is created and projected as it was by the exaggerated frenzy with which the man in *Washes* bit the balloons attached to the floating girl. Although the rate or tempo of this action had no necessary connection with character, and the activity could have been carried out in a nonmatrixed manner, it could not be denied that the agitated and mock-ferocious quality that was dominant was acting. The acted qualities stood out and remained isolated because they did not fit into a character matrix or into a larger situation. Other facets of acting—"playing an attitude," place, details of characterization, etc.—are also found in Happenings, but they are usually isolated and function as a very weak matrix.

This is not to say that emotion of any sort during a performance is necessarily acted. Although much nonmatrixed performance is comparatively expressionless, it would be erroneous to think that this type of performing is without emotion. Certainly feelings are expressed in the "nonmatrixed performing" of everyday life: in the runner's face as he breaks the tape, in the professor's intonation and stress during his lecture, in the owner's attitude as he handles his dog in a dog show. The important point is that emotions apparent during a nonmatrixed performance as those of the performer himself. They are not intentionally created, and they are the natural result of the individual's attitude toward the piece, of the particular task being performed, or of the particular situation of being in front of an audience. Without acted emotions to mask their own feelings, the performers' own attitudes are more apt to become manifest than they are in traditional theatre.

Of course acting and nonmatrixed performing have certain elements in common. When the production of various kinds of information is eliminated from the actor's task, certain requirements still remain. They are the same requirements which exist for performers of any kind. Concentration, for example, is as important to athletes and Happeners as it is to actors, and stage-presence—the degree to which a person can mask or control feelings of nervousness, shyness, uncertainty, etc.—is equally useful to actors, public speakers, and musicians.*

One final point about performance in the new theatre concerns the question of improvisation and indeterminacy. Indeterminacy means that limits within which the performers are free to make choices are provided by the creator of the piece: a range of alternatives is made available from which the performer may select. Thus in a musical composition the number of notes to be played within a given time period may be given but not the notes themselves; the pitch ranges may be indicated for given durations but specific

*The *use* of stage presence is an aesthetic question. Some performances place a high degree of emphasis upon it, while in others it is intentionally excluded or performers are employed *because* they are somewhat ill at ease.

notes not required. Indeterminacy is used in the new theatre when, for example, the number of steps a performer should take is limited but the direction is option; when the type of action is designated but no specific action is given; etc. The choices involved in indeterminacy may be made before the actual performance, but they are most frequently left until the moment of presentation in an attempt to insure spontaneity.

Indeterminacy is not the same as improvisation. Although spontaneity may be a goal of both, it is also the goal of much precisely detailed acting. The primary difference between indeterminacy and improvisation is the amount of momentary, on-the-spot creativity which is involved. Not only is the detail —the apt comment, the *bon mot*, the unexpected or unusual reaction— central to improvisation, but the form and structure of a scene may also be changed. Even when, as was common in commedia dell'arte, the general outline of the scene is set, the performer is responding to unfamiliar material and providing in return his inventions, which require a response. As evidenced by the so-called "improvisational theatres" such as Second City, an improvisation loses these values once it has been repeated a few times. It no longer is an improvisation, and most of these groups make no pretense among themselves that it is. In indeterminacy the alternatives are quite clear, although the exact choice may not be made until performance. And the alternatives *do not matter:* one is as good as another: Since the performers usually function independently and do not respond to the choices made by the other performers, no give-and-take is involved. The situation is not "open-ended" as it is in improvisation.

Thus the four men who manipulated the sections of pipe in *Washes,* for example, did no creative work although the details of their actions and procedure were different during each performance. They merely embodied the image of man-and-pipe which Oldenburg had created. They were not, in the true sense, improvising. Only the type of behavior mattered and not the details. Whether they swam for a while rather than "working," whether they twisted this length of pipe rather than that one, whether they worked together or individually, did not matter provided they kept within the directed limits. The image was the same each night.

A somewhat related attitude is the acceptance of incidental aspects of audience reaction and environmental occurrences as *part* of the production. One of Cage's most notorious musical compositions is 4' 33" (1952)—four minutes and thirty-three seconds of silence by the musician or musicians performing it. The nonplaying (in addition to focusing the "performer" aspects of the piece) allows any "incidental" sounds—perhaps traffic noises or crickets outside the auditorium, the creak of seats, coughing and whispering in the audience—to become "music." This exploitation and integration of happenstance occurrences unique to each performance into the performance itself is another common, but not universal, trait of the new theatre.

On Theatre
An Interview with Hélène Cixous

Eric Prenowitz

PRENOWITZ The plays included here were written between 1974 and 1998. At the beginning of the 1980s, when Ariane Mnouchkine asked you to write for the Théâtre du Soleil, you were already a playwright (*The Pupil, Portrait of Dora, The Name of Oedipus, The Conquest of the School at Madhubaï* . . .): what changed then in your relationship to theatre writing?

CIXOUS In the first place, the feeling that I was beginning to do theatre. Which is to say that what I wrote before embarking on the theatrical adventure and alliance with Ariane Mnouchkine and the Théâtre du Soleil can be thought of as pre-theatrical. As the prehistory of an engagement or an event. A veritable event: the day when *Ariane asked me* to try to write for the Théâtre du Soleil. Because I had a very strong, disturbing, alarming feeling that I was being called, that I was being summoned to respond by the theatre in person, if you will. I do not mean Ariane herself, who was its representative, but the theatre in its eternal figure. I was summoned to answer to the call of an ancient and ever-present world, a quasi-divine world: whether or not I really wanted to do theatre. Why? Because I must say in all humility that I had not considered what had preceded that moment to be theatre, but rather an allusion, a childish game. It was as if I had been going on excursions, practically tourism, on a continent or in a universe, a cosmos which I never thought I would ever really come to inhabit. For many reasons. In some cases, as for *The Pupil*, it consisted in theatralizing a kind of vision of the world which was at once political and rather abstract, as if in an attempt

Excerpted from *Selected Plays of Hélène Cixous*, ed. Eric Prenowitz (London: Routledge, 2004), 1–24.

to make it concrete, but this theatralization remained intra-literary. Which is to say that I did not think that *The Pupil* had a properly theatrical destiny, that it would ever be produced. It was an extremely experimental text.

The Accident

CIXOUS The adventures which preceded my entry into the universe of the Soleil were always kinds of accidents for me. I was not looking for the theatre universe, but it was as if without my knowing it "theatricality," more than the theatre, crossed my path and was pointed out to me by others. The case of *Portrait of Dora* is exemplary. In fact *Dora* even made me think that I would never write theatre. It is paradoxical, but here's why: one day Simone Benmussa, who was the assistant, playwright and administrator for Jean-Louis Barrault at the Théâtre d'Orsay, and who read my books, told me that in one of my books of fiction called *Portrait du soleil*, she saw a play. I saw nothing at all. I saw a fiction. And she literally told me "But look hard," as if I had to lean over a river, "and you will see there is a play in there." What Simone Benmussa had sensed was a diffuse theatricality in my texts which is certainly related to the presence of voices in what I write. She must have heard voices which were there, because I have the habit of lending an ear to them. But I did not think they were emanations of what is called the theatre. Yet I obeyed Simone Benmussa's injunction and I cut and pasted the text. I considered that act to be an artifice, which is to say not at all like a creation but what would now be called an adaptation, for example, a kind of handiwork, a montage. I did not take the act at all seriously, I thought of it as a form of literary tinkering. To my great surprise this little mock-up, which was directed by Simone Benmussa, was an enormous success. I concluded that the audience considered it to be theatre. So if the audience considers it to be theatre, including Lacan himself, who was an enthusiastic spectator, then perhaps I was doing theatre without knowing it, as Mr Jourdain did prose without knowing it. But I was not convinced. I did not think of myself as a theatre writer. I thought of myself as a *theatrical accident*.

I also considered *The Name of Oedipus* not to be theatre. Because there too I had responded to a call: the composer André Bouckereshliev had been commissioned to write an opera, which was later to be performed in the Cour d'Honneur of the Palais des Papes in Avignon (Claude Régy was the director), and he asked me to write the libretto. But here too I felt I was writing poetry, for example, and for me this poetry, which was incantation and which staged characters, was not the work of theatre. I think I also had a memory of what is called "theatre" which led me not to consider these acts which I committed with caution, or on the contrary with recklessness, to be "theatre." This memory was that of my book-knowledge of Shakespeare. I thought that theatre is what Shakespeare did, i.e. to create the universe: it is not only that "All the world's a stage," but his stage was truly the entire world. I felt I was extremely far from this. What I learned later—

THESSIE Mieaoo!

CIXOUS Now the cat has spoken, for example, as I was speaking to you. This intrusion of the cat, who enters into the scene where we are, is precisely a theatrical act. Which is to say that the theatre is itself an action, a drama, and one of the marks of the theatre is the *unexpected intervention*. The fact that at any moment characters enter or events take place which are completely uncalculated. It seems to me that in my first plays I had not opened the door to the *event*. If only in so far as there were no events in *Portrait of Dora* because it was already there. I lifted *Portrait of Dora* from *Portrait du soleil*, and I myself had no surprises, there was no surprise; there was sculpting. For *The Name of Oedipus* it was quite similar, because it involved reanimating our resuscitating the legend of Jocasta and Oedipus, which I did in my own way, but here too I think the element of surprise was textual, aesthetic, and not dramatic

The Event

CIXOUS It was only later that I had the first moment of temptation, or the first attempt at what I continue to consider to be the theatre, which is to say the great machine of events. It can be said that *the god of theatre is the event*: an event that happens on the stage, but that *happens to the author*. The first time I let events come to me, which is to say the first time I myself engaged in a voluntary exercise in which I said to myself "This time I am going to open my interior space, my interior theatre, to events," was with *The Conquest of the School at Madhubaï*. It was certainly the first time I lent myself to the theatre or that I gave myself over to the theatre (I prefer "lent" because it is more modest). So what is the event? To *create emptiness* in oneself. An emptiness that is not an abyss. It is the *plateau* (in English: stage, platter, plateau). And the *plateau* is not a particular, concrete, referential object. Every time I say *plateau*, and I like this word in French, I am reminded of the plateaux, the high plateaux, for example, what were called the high plateaux in Algeria. Immense, telluric geographic zones, flat like a stage, where storms can erupt, or all of a sudden a nomad can appear, one never knows. At first there is nothing, it is barren, it is deserted, and all of a sudden a camel or a bird arrives, some animate being arrives and becomes the character of this *plateau*. But it is unforeseeable. I had never experienced this unforeseeability, this desertedness which is suddenly animated, which receives the soul of a being. Quite simply because on the contrary I had always been preceded, all the texts I had previously written were preceded and occupied.

The Desert

CIXOUS The non-occupation which is indispensable to what I now consider to be the theatre constitutes the first moment of my practice with the Théâtre du Soleil. Which is to say that everything I do with the Théâtre du Soleil begins with this non-occupation and this desert. But I had never practised it, I had never even thought of thinking of it, and I had never had the thinking and imagining experience of this inaugural state, which is indeed a state. With *The Conquest of the School at Madhubaï* I did it on purpose for the first time. It started with something that was very interesting and entirely new and revolutionary for me—an attempt to answer the question: Is it possible today to imagine or identify in the world someone who has the dimensions, the stature, the mystery of what is called a theatrical character? Because characters and not human beings are what inhabit the theatre. But there are also characters in the world's theatre. And I thought: But are there any today? Is there someone on the earth today like Oedipus? Is there a king who is at once innocent and guilty? Is there a woman who takes up arms to restore justice, or to attack injustice or to make war—is it possible that there exist today heroes or heroines like those we know from the archives of memory and legend? And I thought not, that there are none. Or at least I imagined it would not be easy to find them. And in the end they did exist. I searched, I looked, it was as if I had climbed up a tree or a tower and I was scrutinizing the horizon, I saw nothing, I saw nothing, and then all of a sudden I saw someone, and it was none other than Phoolan Devi, called the Queen of the Bandits. An incredible contemporary Indian character, but whose history and whose every gesture was worthy of the legends, of the Mahabharata. She was a sort of untouchable Joan of Arc, and I realized that she indeed had all the traits of a character, someone who resists the ready-made, or what has already been done, who resists the attribution of a form of life or of destiny that leaves no freedom of invention to the human being. I thought: Here is someone who invents. And from the moment she invents new situations, she also encounters new situations. I found her in a newspaper. And I decided I would see if I could make her live, if I could make her arrive in my desert and have her invent a play—it no longer had to do with me or what I thought or my double, because she became the author—in which fictive events would happen to her. To tell the truth, this was a great shock for me . . .

So I entered into a passiveness, which ought to be comparable to a trance, a passivity, an emptiness, an evacuation of myself, in which I let this character I did not know enter. I had only read a few references in a newspaper and I let entirely fictive events take place as if I were an observer or a witness of events I knew nothing about ahead of time. For example, with *Oedipus*, I knew. For her, I knew nothing. And because I had to be in a state of trance I wrote it without stopping, I think in a single day, and at the end I passed out. I had to undergo such a tension of substitution—in order to let myself be replaced, since I was not there, by someone entirely foreign—that at the end of this experience of trance, of possession, I fainted, I had a terrible and frightening feeling of faintness. I lost myself. At the same time this play was very small. There were only three characters and I lacked the strength, and the *connaissance*—I do not mean the knowledge: the consciousness—

necessary to pursue the experience any further. What's more it was quite brief. But I thought: Ah, the theatre must be something like that. And shortly thereafter, a year later perhaps, Ariane asked me: "Would you like to work for the Théâtre du Soleil?"

PRENOWITZ But you already had some sense of the emptiness of the interior *plateau* and this relationship with history, the search for a character in the world who could become an event on your stage?

CIXOUS Yes, of course. But this could have been an isolated experience. What happened next was that Ariane asked me—which was another event because it was totally unexpected, this request that was turned towards me at a time when I had known her for nearly ten years, and we were friends. But I had never had either the idea or the desire to write a play for the Théâtre du Soleil. In fact it was out of the question. For two reasons. A writing reason: my writing, which had nothing to do with Ariane's theatrical practice. And a theatre reason: what Ariane did seemed to me to participate in the great theatrical tradition I believed in—I had faith—but in which I did not at all see myself as a participant. If only because of the immense dimensions of the ambition and the scope of her enterprises. Ariane belonged to that epic dimension of the theatre that is found in the Greeks, in Shakespeare, etc., but at the time I did not feel I was concerned. I watched as a spectator but absolutely not as an agent. I did not at all think I could ever in any way be called by or respond to that space. And so when Ariane proposed that I try, she was very prudent, very just, very wise, she asked me to try and she did not guarantee either that I would succeed or that what I would do would be received by her troupe. And this was very good because it gave both of us great freedom. I did not commit myself, I could not promise, I did not believe in it, and neither did she. It was a possibility. And quite honestly I did not succeed right away. I wandered as I always wander. Which is to say that each time I start off again on a trail with Ariane I go through a period of wandering, of erring and of error before glimpsing in the distance the light of a theatre. Always. It remains for me the *foreign country*. Each time I start off again I go towards a foreign country and don't even know what this country is. All I know is that I'm off. Which is to say that I move away from myself. I move away from the interior in the interior, I move away from my limits, and I take to the open sea.

The Foreign Country

CIXOUS I think that for me, although this is also part of its essence and its mystery, the theatre remains, the theatre will always remain the place of two types of laying bare: the change of country, the un-country, it is an un-country, another country, another world, it is the world but a world that is other, or it is the world that can tear itself away from the world as it is by becoming the sublime form of the world as it is. It is no longer the world as it is; it is the world's world, it is the world par excellence. And it is a world that is a figure. It is entirely transfigured. It is true that in a certain way the theatre as world, the theatre-world exists virtually in the great epics. This is why it was not absolutely impossible for me, because I am someone who has always frequented the epic, it is my childhood imagination, my place of childhood. The Bible is extremely theatrical; nearly all the great stories of the Bible could be staged. All the adventures that are related in the Bible as being historical—whereas they are not at all historical, they are fantastical—have a partner who is none other than God. From time to time the Devil, but rarely, and in fact God. Which is to say the gods. There is no theatre without gods. It is the first thing that becomes clear when you turn to the theatre: there are god(s). In the singular and in the plural. God in all forms, at times the lowly forms, or else sublime forms. They are superior forces. God is what I would call all the superior forces with which we negotiate or which treat us or mistreat us, which we imagine at times to be interior but which we experience as exterior, against which we fight. Sometimes they have names of powerful abstraction like King or Justice or State or Honour, all those sorts of values that precipitate the great theatrical actions, even War, Hate. At the theatre, God or the gods are always blowing, as if in the sails of the theatre, in the theatre's invisible sails; they give to the theatre, they take the theatre, they lift it above the earth, up to the *plateau*, higher still. This is what we see in the Bible: everything is lifted, one is always setting off towards the mountains, further along, higher up, stronger, more terrible. It is more. The theatre is more, always more. It is what the Greeks called enthusiasm, possession by the gods.

PRENOWITZ It is bigger-than-we-are. . . .

The fact that you write for a real theatre company or troupe, the Théâtre du Soleil, is in itself very important it seems to me, and your relationship with it, the singularity of the theatrical project of this troupe which devotes all its many lives (including yours) to an amazing adventure in "creation," is at once rare and I would think decisive for the theatre it produces. This is what Shakespeare and a certain number of others no doubt did, but there are very few real troupes left today. What is the importance of this relation to a theatre company in the history of your writing, in your plays and for the theatre in general?

CIXOUS It is indeed decisive. I think the word "adventure" is very important. It is decisive in the first place with regard to the dream. If there is an art that has a structural complicity with the dream, it is the theatre. I mean the dream in the sense that children have grand dreams. Where they dream that they will be a king, or a bandit or a corsair. The theatre company dreams that it will play all the roles and that it is going on an adventure like the great heroes in the epics, or like those who went in search of the golden fleece. It is a treasure hunt. And the treasure is the theatre. It is simultaneously a dream that has an absolutely magnificent goal, which is to do theatre together; and at the same time something very dangerous because to do theatre together is like going in search of India, which became America. The spices, the gold are this art which can only be done together, it is a collective art; and on the other hand no one knows where the country is. Just as they went in the wrong direction, they went to the East in order to find what later turned out to be to the West. It is the same thing with the theatre: you go in one direction and you arrive at another. At the same time what is shared is the sense of adventure without any certainty that the goal will be reached, for it is entirely possible that the company will fail, that it will not find what it is searching for. The adventure is very dangerous because the collection of sixty dreams is always dangerous: it is never sure that all the dreams will hold together in the same boat. What is more, the adventure is heroic in the sense that it is very costly. It comes at a very high social, mental and economic price.

No One Knows

CIXOUS Doing theatre is a question of passion: the reward is not assured at any level. So it involves consciously putting oneself in danger, and by the way one never knows what the extent of the danger is, without a guarantee of any benefit or that anything will be found. What animates the members of a theatre company is also the capacity to take this risk. The people who come to the Théâtre du Soleil are very diverse: there are the actors, the technicians, the painters, the sculptor, the musician, the silk painters . . . Each one goes there in the hopes of satisfying at least his or her artistic taste. And I think that this satisfaction exists. But it must be said that they pay for it "economically," because the salaries are very modest. Everyone earns the same thing. Each of the people engaged in this adventure is paid exactly the same sum; the actors, the technicians, Ariane the director, myself, the musician-composer, we all earn the same thing. The salaries are modest relative to the salaries that are current in the institutional theatres, not to mention in the film industry. All of these people could in fact go in other directions and earn money. But what they want here is not money (*argent*) but art (*art*) and people (*gens*).

At the same time it is fragile: from time to time the company must rely on unemployment benefits, so they earn even less and find themselves in a holding pattern that would be difficult to put up with and even intolerable, impossible, if they thought of themselves as workers. But they are dreamers. Dreamers who have a profession. Professional dreamers. Whose profession is dreaming. But again, it is very dangerous. People's destinies, their lives, their material conditions of existence are all at stake. On the other hand, working together is a pleasure. But it is a trembling happiness. And then there is the moment the play is presented to the audience, and it's double or nothing. Which is to say it will either be a triumph or a failure. Thank God it is generally a triumph. But it is a triumph because everyone has worked for it, with sweat and tears. Has struggled to get to this point. Without any stability ever setting in: one never settles down. No one is a functionary. The reward, when it is achieved, is the relation to the audience, the happiness of sharing an experience with the audience which, at the Théâtre du Soleil, is very large: 600 people a day, and when we give 100 or 150 performances that makes 100,000 people who come. That is a lot of people. This means that we speak the same language, 100,000 people speak the same language for at least a few hours, and share the same dream. This is ethically and politically powerful. This is of course the reward, when there is one. In addition, as with *Drums on the Dam*, when the production ends up going beyond our theatre, when it travels, goes out into the world, to Japan, to Korea, to Canada, to Australia, we have the sense of an extraordinary vision of humanity. The feeling that in the world, in the universe, there are no borders, because of course art passes across everything, that the desire for dreams is shared by a great number of very diverse populations, and that they communicate through a common language which is the language of theatre. This clearly gives immense happiness, but it is a fragile happiness: for *Drums* it will have lasted two or three years, and now we are going to find ourselves once again before the unknown. It means starting off again on an adventure, towards another imaginary country without knowing where we are going, if we will arrive, and who will arrive. Because I must also say that exactly as Ulysses lost men along the way in the *Odyssey*, along the way we also lose members of the crew. For many reasons: since these are very long voyages people can fall ill, and all sorts of accidents can occur. On these magnificent long voyages there is also mourning—and one has to be aware of this.

So it is very important for me to work inside this troupe, in community, in communion. With human beings I know and love, and with whom we all share. Just as people share bread and wine, here we share bread and wine that are sublime, symbolic. My desire, my appetite for sharing and love and friendship and beauty are fulfilled. On the other hand I also pay in my way, which is to say that I am in a dependent relationship to the group. Inside the troupe one does not have the freedom one has alone. There are immense human benefits and they are paid for in restrictions, because there are common laws, common rules, obligations. The other thing that should be noted is that what I do in this case is to adopt the direction of the dreamer which is a direction that I do not command alone. I respond to an order. This order is formulated by Ariane, who must be thought of as herself-plus-the-troupe. The Soleil has its own aesthetics, there are aesthetic and political choices, and if I did not share them, quite simply I could not be the troupe's author. But it happens that we have common visions, we have a relationship to society, to political commitments, to art that is shareable and that has been in place for a long time. We have been in agreement for nearly thirty years. We are in tune, we are musically harmonized.

There is an order. Which is to say that I have never made a proposition to Ariane saying "This is what we must do." She proposes a direction to me, but she proposes it after long discussions between us. We discuss different possible projects. And what orients the choice of a subject—because in the end what we agree on is an initial subject—is in the first place that it must of course correspond to the history of the art of the Théâtre du Soleil, but even more that it should inspire Ariane. She must be able to see, even before I write, she must have the possibility of having a vision in the fullest sense of the word: to have visions, which are visions in space. This has to do with her own art. Her art must be nourished, set ablaze, or else she cannot create. There is a sort of order: when we talk, when we have our discussions, as we always do in these situations, we cannot take an orientation if she has no visions, even for example if I say: Ah! I'd like to go in that direction! Her workshop must be illuminated. This suits me, I can function in a certain number of directions because my functioning is not based on visions but on voices. My visions are auditory, if I can put it that way. I simply have to be able to hear voices.

To Hear Voices

CIXOUS That is what it is to be in a troupe. It is an experience which is not only of being on stage, but one of sharing a certain time which is out of the ordinary. And it is a time that goes on. Twenty years of creation with Ariane. But with the company it is a human time, a prolonged time that overflows the simple stage to go into the kitchen, into the workshops and very often into the particular, intense and subjective moments of each actor. But I would say that it succeeds rather well, because after all it has been twenty years that Ariane and I have been working together unfailingly. It is the same thing with the composer of the company, Jean-Jacques Lemêtre, whom I consider to be absolutely brilliant and with whom from time to time we take little excursions. For example, he recently did the music for another of my plays in a reading directed by Daniel Mesguich, and I know that he has a project for an opera whose libretto he wants me to write. In the end we weave together living and continuous affinities: there are no divisions among us. It is very well orchestrated. It is clearly quite miraculous. And this leaves a mark, this marks everything I write for the Théâtre du Soleil.

PRENOWITZ Is there a chronology, a history, an evolution from play to play in your work with the Théâtre du Soleil? If so, to what extent is it due to the history of this theatre and to what extent does it have to do with an evolution in your works or life as a writer?

CIXOUS It is possible now, twenty years later, to talk in terms of a history. Because there has been a history, there has been time. When you begin, the first play has no history. It is an event, and you do not know what it will lead to. But after twenty years, like all stories that go on for a certain time, if you look back, yes, you can imagine or make out a shape that has emerged, but which was not anticipated. When we began this was not our goal. Each time we have proceeded as if from play to play it was the first time we were working on something. This is not true, because from one play to the next something gains in depth, or appears in a slightly more familiar way. For example, I realized after a few plays that there were elements that returned, types of characters, but this was never planned in advance. It is only with experience that you recognize signs and accents. Going from play to play I noticed that there were recurrent characters. Characters from my own unconscious who come onto the stage. If I had not written a series of plays, in the first place they simply would not have returned, nor would I have noticed them. I spoke of this in "Enter the Theatre": the character who is constantly returning and who is therefore in some sense my signature in the play, is the character of the border-crosser. The one who goes between the living and the dead, between eras, between different circles, between the different "houses." When I was working on *Sihanouk*, we used this word "house," which came from Shakespeare's theatre. In Shakespeare you have this royal house and that royal house, and with *Sihanouk* there were the house of the king, the house of the Americans, the house of the people. These are groups, sorts of microcosms that form a macrocosm. These houses are closed in, they are enclosures, and then there is a character who can pass from one to the other, and who, in this first play, can even go from the house of the dead to the house of the Khmer people, and all the way to Chou En Lai's house in Peking—and the whole way on a bicycle. He is a magic character who crosses through everything. This magic character was Sihanouk's father, who was dead, a dead king who can pass from one house to the other; it is the magic of theatre. At the time I did that, for me it was necessary for the play, I needed someone who could go from one place to another, and it is only very recently that I realized there was always such a character in my plays. That there was always someone who could give passage, like the needle that takes the thread through the tapestry. I did not recognize it myself because the play was what required it. The theatre required it. It was not some recipe I had. Suddenly I noticed that in *The Perjured City* the person who passed from the scene of the Cemetery to the scene of the City, which do not communicate otherwise, or between the living and the dead, was Aeschylus, the guardian of the Cemetery. This little character was also present in *The Indiad*: it was the Baul woman who could cross India on foot, or the bear tamer. These are characters who do not belong to any house, who precisely do not belong, who are not identified with houses and who are the messengers the envoys the border-crossers of theatre, of the spirit of the theatre, of the spirit of humanity, from one place to another. Because there is a path and along this path from one play to the next something is communicated: the spirit, memory. It was not a decision or a calculation, it was not a kind of speculation. It was necessity.

CIXOUS So from play to play: there is certainly something even if, once again, for each play we go back to zero, we start from nothing. We are on the beach, on a sandbank, and we do not know what is before us. Once the work is underway and has developed, in looking back we can say that each play was engendered by the previous one. That *The Indiad* is in a certain sense the child of *Sihanouk*. And one could continue and say that from play to play there is engendering and causality, which we are not able to see when we begin. When we begin, it is really in a state of innocence. We start the world over. The feeling of genesis, of creation *ex nihilo*, is always there, otherwise we would do nothing. But after all we are ourselves human beings with memories. I think that if we were to analyse the question, which I don't wish to do or don't have the time to do here, we would see the lineage, where elements of *The Perjured City* come from *Sihanouk* by way of *The Indiad* . . . At times it disturbs me, for example when I was writing *Drums*, at a certain point I said to myself "But there are elements of *The Perjured City* here: the tidal wave." But then I forget. I do not want to know. If we feel we are repeating ourselves or doing something over again then we have to stop.

But these elements that travel in a subterranean fashion and which reappear differently—because when they reappear it is in an altogether different way—probably come from the fact that when I write for the Théâtre du Soleil, I always place things at the root, at the *causes*, what causes the behaviours, the catastrophes, the wars, the destructions in humanity. And here we are in a space that is continuous with the space of engendering, thus of mythologies, of all that caused the first literary works: the epics, etc. There are fundamental structures. In the same way that one talks of the fundamental elements of genealogical ties, there are fundamental elements in the history of humanity, and each time we ask how things happened, where they came from, we find driving elements that are universal. This is why the theatre can travel from continent to continent.

Causes

CIXOUS The one which functioned explicitly in *Drums on the Dam* is auto-immunity. This is a force of self-destruction that is at work in humanity. Take what is going on at this moment, the great drama that is occupying the entire world and which began on 11 September, 2001. We can see it as a play, and who could imagine more of a play: the most symbolic, the most beautiful, the most triumphant place in the universe, the World Trade Center, disappears. It is an extremely spectacular event. Scene 1. And then we discover in Scene 2 that this was done by a character who is the opposite: the towers are as visible, obvious and ostentatious as he is hidden. The metaphors are incredibly powerful. He is in a cave. They are as naked as he is hidden. And the entire world is at the theatre, the tragic theatre. The auto-immunity factor, the self-destruction, is everywhere. Some people have asked: "Is it not the United States that caused this?" which is a perverse question. However, there is auto-immunity in that Bin Laden will come to a bad end. He has already lost the war, he is destroying what he wants to save, he has already lost his power, he risks losing his freedom and his life. We can ask what principle guided him: it was the certainty that he would triumph, that his power would grow enormously. The fantasy that this character could have is to crush the most powerful country in the world, to have his God rule over the earth, his God being the partial god (in both senses of the word) that is the Islamist God. Afterwards we can transport ourselves a bit later in time: if we look at this story we see that he set everything up for his own destruction. Why is it that he brings about his own destruction?

Drums on the Dam is set in an absolutely magnificent kingdom which has always been prosperous and which in the excesses of the exercise of power—it is always the same thing—overturns itself. It turns its power, its beauty, its riches, into absolute destruction. We wonder: Why do people do what will produce their own ruin? But this question exists in Shakespeare. It is a question that is being increasingly described, thought about, philosophized today. It is like the question of globalization: the Americans have refused to sign the Kyoto accords. They ought to protect human life on earth, but they do not want to put a limit on the exercise of their industrial and capitalistic power. They are heading quite simply towards their own suicide. It is at a great distance, it is always the question of the great distance: I am not the one who is going to die, it is my children. This is an enormous question. We think: How can human beings think such a thing? How can human beings say to themselves "I don't care"? In France there is a phrase for this, Louis XV's phrase: "Après moi le déluge," "After me the flood." A king who is the successor to Louis XIV, the greatest king of the French monarchy, who little by little causes the catastrophes of his kingdom, and who, when reprimanded and told that this is not a good policy, says "Après moi le déluge." And the deluge arrives: the death of Louis XVI, the French Revolution . . . We look at this each time and wonder: But what is it that motivates these people? The phrase says that after all I will have lived well and if the deluge comes after me I don't care. It is incredible, and yet this is what rules power. Power thinks it rules, yet it is ruled. And it is ruled over by death.

PRENOWITZ So there are elements that return, continuities such as the border-crosser, the tidal wave, the "causes," the fundamental structures. But you said that on the one hand you have to begin each time at zero and on the other hand that you must not repeat yourself. So what changes? How would you describe the evolution? Where are you going?

CIXOUS First remark: if I look retrospectively—because clearly only retrospectively can one begin to recount the history of a collaboration or of series of works—looking backwards from *Drums* successively to *The Perjured City,*

The Eumenides, The Indiad, Sihanouk, I see an evolution I find very interesting, though it was not planned out, towards less and less realism, or fewer and fewer references to existing facts, and more and more inventions. Less and less reliance on immediately readable current affairs, to the point of attaining pure fiction with *Drums on the Dam*. Once again this was not planned by us; it is like a telluric, organic evolution, the natural maturation of a working engagement over time. In the first place because in an obvious way, it is not simply an arbitrary succession: each of the plays can be seen to come out of the previous one. They cause each other, they engender each other, they suggest each other but without there ever being an omniscient project. It is a process.

Less and Less Realism

CIXOUS I think I have already told the story of *Sihanouk*. The first play I wrote for the Théâtre du Soleil was *Sihanouk*, a play of enormous dimensions. Here is what I could say about the prologue to the story of the creation of the play: when Ariane asked me if I wanted to write for the Théâtre du Soleil, although I had known her for a long time by then and had never thought of writing for the Théâtre du Soleil, she asked me very directly to write on India. That was her dream. And I was struck with terror. I was emerging from a chamber; and in this little room or in this little office I had convoked characters like Freud. My dimensions and my imaginary horizon were no greater than that. The most I had done, and it was already in the direction of India, was the little play *The Conquest of the School at Madhubaï*. But even if it took place in India and even if the character was Indian, India was only in the atmosphere, which is to say the rain, the monsoon: everything took place in a cabin, the equivalent of a plain little room. It could be performed in a small theatre, there were no more than three or five characters. I had not gone beyond the dimensions of what I have always called "chamber theatre." When Ariane said India I knew that for her it was the Indian continent. And I truly panicked. I ruled it out right away, I immediately said no, I cannot do it. I saw that I was a little ant before the Himalayas, and I thought: What is she talking about" An ant cannot write the Himalayas. It's impossible. It will take me centuries to climb the Himalayas. I was incapable of *envisaging* India, in the proper meaning of the word. I understood Ariane's desire, but for me it was out of the question. It was a question of proportion, of capacity—and this is very important because it is a question of theatrical art—which is to say that my capacity, what I could contain, was very small. It could not be anything so gigantic. So Ariane conceded to my concerns and we started looking for something else, but in Asia none the less. This is where the Théâtre du Soleil's Asia comes from: Ariane needs to be Asian, and what she wanted was an author who could write something Asian for her, because Asia has always been the cradle of all her images, of all her references.

In the first place *Asia*; in the second place *today*. A today that has never been rigidly tied to current events, but a present—the present being in any case the time of the theatre—making reference to something very close, contemporary, because what she wanted was something contemporary, but which would be valid for all times. I could understand a present that would apply to all times, but not a universal Asia. So I began to look around in the twentieth century which is relatively easy to explore mentally from a historical, political point of view. It is clear that the great events of the twentieth century can be seen in the light of their universal implications: for example the chaos produced by the Vietnam war which affects Asia. I saw all of this. And while searching I read a great deal—I have always done this for the Théâtre du Soleil—I read everything that could be seen to interweave the political and the mythological, the theatrical and the ethnological. All the books that are archives relating to structures of the imagination or of a culture, as well as the narratives of the tragedies of our times. I even think that Ariane must have told me she was looking for the story of a people—the theatre is itself a people—whose tragic destiny could be the image of other tragedies, of other contemporary stories. In this research I was attracted by the tragic history of a little people named the Jarai, a tiny ethnic group between Cambodia and Vietnam that simply disappeared during the Vietnam war because they were bombed, massacred, and nothing was left. A people that has disappeared. I had begun working on this, I began writing a few scenes and when I showed them to Ariane she cried: "What is this? It's much too small. This is the story of a village!" And indeed it took place in a village. "This is not for us. We are a kingdom, you have got the wrong dimensions." I had gone from too big to too small. This woke me up. It was as if I had forgotten the dimensions of the Théâtre du Soleil, which are royal dimensions. So I looked for a kingdom with Ariane, and very quickly, because we only had to take a step to the side, we were either in Vietnam or in Cambodia. So we were in Cambodia, and we found a lot of very good books. The one that acted as a trigger for us was a remarkable book by an American journalist (*Sideshow* by W. Shawcross). The epic dimensions of this universe became clear to me in reading this book. At the same time, and in a way that was enlightening for me, what carried me was the fact that Cambodia resembled Shakespeare's England. Like two peas in a pod. England saw itself as a large kingdom, but it was small, three million inhabitants. The exact dimensions of Cambodia.

The Theatre of Death

Tadeusz Kantor

Translated by Michal Kobialka

1

Craig's postulate: bring back a marionette. Eliminate a live actor.
A human being—nature's creation—is a foreign intrusion into the abstract structure of a work of art.

According to Gordon Craig, somewhere on the banks of the Ganges River two women forced their way into the temple of the Divine Marionette, which was jealously hiding the secrets of the true THEATRE. They envied this Perfect Being its ROLE of illuminating human minds with the sacred feeling of the existence of God; its FAME and GLORY; they secretly watched and copied its Movements and Gestures, its sumptuous dress; and began to satisfy the vulgar taste of the mob by offering them their cheap parody. At the moment when they finally ordered that a similar monument be built for them, the modern theatre, as we know it only too well today and as it has lasted to this day, was born. A noisy Public Service Institution. Together with it, there appeared the ACTOR. In defense of his theory, Craig quotes the opinion of Eleanora Duse, who, as he claims, said, "To save the theatre, it must be destroyed; it is necessary that all actors and actresses die of plague . . . for it is they who render art impossible."

Reprinted from "The Theatre of Death" in Michal Kobialka, *Further on, Nothing: Tadeusz Kantor's Theatre* (Minneapolis: University of Minnesota Press, 2009), 230–39. Reprinted by permission of University of Minnesota Press and Michal Kobialka.

Craig's version: A Human being-actor eliminates a marionette, takes its place, thereby causing the demise of the theatre.

There is something very impressive in the stand taken by this Grand Utopian when he says, "I demand in all seriousness the return of the image of a supermarionette to the theatre, . . . and when it appears, people will again, as was the case in the past, be able to worship the happiness of Existence, and render DEATH its due divine and euphoric homage." Craig, following the Symbolist aesthetics, considered a human being, driven by unpredictable emotions, passion, and, consequently, by coincidence, as an element which is completely foreign to the homogeneous nature and structure of a work of art and which destroys its principal trait: cohesion.

Not only Craig's idea but also the well-developed program of Symbolism, impressive in its own time and its own way, had, in the nineteenth century, the support of isolated and unique phenomena heralding a new era and new art: Heinrich von Kleist, Ernst Theodore Amadeus Hoffman, Edgar Allan Poe. . . . One hundred years earlier, Kleist, for the same reasons as Craig, demanded that a marionette be substituted for an actor, regarded the human organism, which was subject to the laws of NATURE, as a foreign intrusion into Artistic Fiction built according to the principles of Construction and Intellect. He added to this his indictment of the limited physical capabilities of a human being and the charges against consciousness, incessantly controlling and excluding the concepts of refinement and beauty.

3

From the romantic mysticism of mannequins and the artificial creation of a human being in the nineteenth century to the rationalism of abstraction in the twentieth century.

On what seemed to be a safe road traveled by the man of the Enlightenment and Rationalism there appeared out of darkness, suddenly and in increasingly greater number, DOUBLES, MANNEQUINS, AUTOMATONS, HOMUNCULI. Artificial creations, mocking NATURE's creations, bearers of absolute degradation, ALL human dreams, DEATH, Horror and Terror. A faith is born in the unknown powers of MECHANICAL MOVEMENT, a maniacal passion for the invention of a MECHANISM surpassing in perfection and ruthlessness the human organism susceptible to all its weaknesses.

All of this is veiled in the mist of demonism, on the brink of charlatanism, illegal practices, white magic, crime, and nightmares.

This was the SCIENCE FICTION of those days, in which the demonic human brain created an ARTIFICIAL MAN.

All of this together signified both an abrupt loss of faith in NATURE and in that realm of human activity which was closely connected with nature. Paradoxically, from these extreme romantic and diabolical efforts to take away nature's right of creation there evolved more and more independent from and more and more dangerously distant from NATURE a RATIONALISTIC, and even MATERIALISTIC MOVEMENT of an "OBJECTLESS WORLD," CONSTRUCTIVISM, FUNCTIONALISM, MACHINISM, ABSTRACTION, and finally, PURIST VISUALISM, recognising only the "physical presence" of a work of art.

This risky hypothesis, whose provenance is none too attractive for the age of technology and science, I take on my conscience and for my personal satisfaction.

4

Dadaism, introducing "ready-made reality," elements of life, destroys the concept of homogeneity and cohesion in a work of art as postulated by symbolism, Art Nouveau, and Craig.

Let us return to Craig's marionette. Craig's idea of replacing a live actor with a mannequin, an artificial and mechanical creation—for the sake of preserving perfect cohesion in a work of art—is today invalid.

Later experiences of destroying the unity of structure in a work of art, introducing "FOREIGN" elements in collages and assemblages, the acceptance of "ready-made reality," full recognition of CHANCE and COINCIDENCE, the placement of a work of art at the sharp edge between REALITY OF LIFE AND ARTISTIC FICTION, made irrelevant those scruples from the beginning of the twentieth century, from the period of Symbolism and Art Nouveau. The two possible solutions—either autonomous art and intellectual structure or naturalism—ceased to be the ONLY ones.

When the theatre, in its moments of weakness, submitted itself to the laws of the human being's live organism, it automatically and logically agreed to follow the laws of imitation of life, its representation and recreation. Under different circumstances, when the theatre was strong and autonomous enough to free itself from the pressure of life and human beings, it created artificial equivalents to life, which turned out to be more alive because they submitted easily to abstraction of time and space and were capable of achieving absolute unity.

Today both of these possibilities have lost their right to exist and their validity as viable alternatives. This is due to the fact that there emerged new situations and new conditions in art. The concept of the "READY-MADE REALITY," wrenched away from life—and the possibility of ANNEXING it, INTEGRATING it into a work of art through DECISION, GESTURE, or RITUAL—has replaced a fascination with (artificially) CONSTRUCTED reality, ABSTRACTION, and a surrealist world, Bréton's "MARVEILLEUX." The Happenings, Events, and Environments with their colossal impetus have achieved the rehabilitation of whole regions of REALITY, disdained until this time, cleansing it of the ballast of life's intentions.

This "DÉCALAGE" of life's reality, its derailment from the tracks of life's practices, moved the human imagination more strongly than the surrealistic reality of dreams. As a result, fears of direct intervention by life and by human beings into the realm of art became irrelevant.

5

From the "Ready-Made Reality" of the Happenings to the dematerialization of the elements of a work of art.

But as with all fascination, so, too, this one after a time became a convention practiced universally, senselessly and in a vulgar manner. These almost ritualistic manipulations of Reality, connected with the contestation of the ARTISTIC CONDITION and the PLACE reserved for art, gradually started to acquire a different sense and meaning. The material, physical PRESENCE of an object and the PRESENT TENSE, in which the activity and action can only happen, turned out to be too burdensome, had reached their limit. SURPASSING it meant depriving these conditions of their material and functional IMPORTANCE, that is, their ability to COMMUNICATE. Because this is the most recent period, still open and in flux, the following observations derive from and refer to my own artistic practice.

The object (*The Chair*, Oslo, 1970) became e m p t y, bereft of
e x p r e s s i o n,
c o n n e c t i o n s, r e f e r e n c e s, characteristics of programmed
c o m m u n i c a t i o n, its "m e s s a g e," directed towards
"n o w h e r e," it changed into an empty f a ç a d e.
Situations and activities were enclosed in their own CIRCUMFERENCE; ENIGMATIC (The Impossible Theatre, 1973); in my own piece, *Cambriolage*, an unlawful and illegal BREAK-IN into the place where tactile reality was extended into its INVISIBLE REALM. The role of THOUGHT, memory, and TIME becomes increasingly more visible.

6

The rejection of the orthodoxy of conceptual art and the mass "Official Avant-garde."

The certitude impressed itself on me more and more strongly, that the concept of LIFE can be vindicated in art only through the ABSENCE OF LIFE in its conventional sense (again Craig and the Symbolists!); this process of DEMATERIALIZATION was found on a path, which circumvented the whole orthodoxy of linguistics (semantics) and conceptual art. This was partially due to the colossal stampede which took place on this already official path and which will be remembered as the last stage of the DADA and its slogans of TOTAL ART, EVERYTHING IS ART, ALL ARE ARTISTS, and ART IS IN THE MIND.
I hate crowds. In 1973, I wrote a draft of a new manifeseto, which dealt with this false situation. This is its beginning:

From the time of Verdun, Cabaret Voltaire, Marcel Duchamp's urinal, when the "artistic conditions" were drowned out by the roar of Fat Bertha, DECISION became the only remaining human chance; an act of reliance on something that was or is unthinkable; it functioned as the first stimulant of a creative act as well as conditioned and defined art. Lately, thousands of mediocre artists have been making decisions without scruples or any hesitation whatsoever. We are witnesses of the banalization and conventionalization of decision. This once dangerous path was transformed into a comfortable freeway with improved safety measures and information. Guides, maps, orientation tables, directional signs, signals, Art Centers, Art Co-operatives guarantee the excellence of the functioning of creativity. We are witnesses of the MASS MOVEMENT of artists-commandos, street fighters, artists-mediators, artists-mailmen, epistologs, peddlers, street magicians, proprietors of Offices and Agencies. Movement of this official freeway, which threatens with a deluge of graphomania, and deeds of minimal significance, increases with each passing day. It is necessary to exit it as quickly as possible. This is not easily done. Particularly, at the apogee of the UNIVERSAL AVANT-GARDE, blind and favored with the highest prestige of the INTELLECT, which protects both the wise and the stupid.

7

On the side streets of the official avant-garde. MANNEQUINS appear.

My deliberate rejection of the solutions of the conceptual art, despite the fact that they seemed to be the only way off the path upon which I found myself, led me to place on the side streets the abovementioned facts about the most recent stage in my artistic practice and the attempts to describe them, which provided me with a better chance to encounter the UNKNOWN! I have more confidence in such a solution. Any new era always begins with its actions of little or no importance; actions which happen as if on the sly; which have little in common with the recognized trend; actions which are private, intimate, I could even say, shameful.
Vague. And difficult! These are the most fascinating and essential moments of a creative act.

All of a sudden, I became interested in the nature of MANNEQUINS.
The mannequin in my production of "THE WATER-HEN" (1967) and the mannequins in "THE SHOEMAKERS" (1970 [1972–MK]) had a very specific role: they were as if immaterial extensions, a kind of ADDITIONAL ORGAN of an actor, who was their "proprietor." The mannequins, already widely used in my production of Słowacki's *Balladyna,* were DOUBLES of live characters, endowed as if with a higher CONSCIOUSNESS, attained "after the completion of their lives."
These mannequins were already clearly marked with the sign of DEATH.

8

The mannequin as manifestation of the "REALITY OF THE LOWEST RANK."
The MANNEQUIN as procedure of TRANSGRESSION.
The MANNEQUIN as an EMPTY object. A FAÇADE. Message of DEATH. A model for an actor.

The mannequin which I used in 1967 in Cricot 2 Theatre (*The Water-Hen*) was a successor to *The Eternal Wanderer* and *Human Emballages*; a figure which appeared naturally in my *Collection* as yet another phenomenon, which was consistent with a long-held conviction that it was only the reality of the lowest rank and the poorest and least prestigious objects which are capable of revealing their full objectlessness in a work of art.
Mannequins and Wax Figures have always existed on the periphery of sanctioned Culture. They were not admitted any further; they occupied places in FAIR BOOTHS, suspicious MAGIC CABINETS, far from the splendid temples of art, treated condescendingly as CURIOSITIES destined for the tastes of the masses. For precisely this reason, it was they, and not academic, museum creations that caused the curtain to rise for the blink of an eye.
Mannequins have also their TRANSGRESSIONS. The existence of these creatures, created in the image of a human being, almost "godlessly," illegally, is the result of heretical activities, a manifestation of the Dark, Nocturnal, Rebellious human side. Of Crime and a Trace of Death as the source of cognition. This vague and inexplicable feeling that through this entity, looking almost like a human being but deprived of consciousness and human destiny, a terrifying message of Death and Nothingness is transmitted to us. It is precisely this feeling that is the cause simultaneously of transgression, rejection, and attraction. Of indictment and fascination.
All arguments have been exhausted in indictment. They were all absorbed by the very mechanism of action, which if thoughtlessly defined as the very purpose of action, could easily be relegated to the l o w e r   f o r m s   o f   c r e-a t i v i t y. *Imitation and deceptive similarity*, which serve the conjurer in setting his TRAPS and deceiving the spectator, the use of "unsophisticated" means, slipping away from the realm of aesthetics, the abuse and fraudulent deception of APPEARANCES, practices from the chest of con-artists!
This indictment completed the accusations directed against a philosophical worldview, which, from the time of Plato to this day, considers the process of revealing Being and a Spiritual Sense of Existence as the purpose of art, rather than the involvement in the Material Shell of the world or in that deception of appearances, which are the lowest stage of existence.
I do not believe that a MANNEQUIN (or a WAX FIGURE) could replace a LIVE ACTOR, as Kleist and Craig wanted. This would be too simple and too naïve. I am trying to describe the motives and the uses of this unusual creature which suddenly appeared in my thoughts and idea. Its appearance complies with my ever-stronger conviction that l i f e can only be expressed in art through

the a b s e n c e o f l i f e, through an appeal to DEATH, through APPEARANCES, through EMPTINESS, and the lack of MESSAGE.

The MANNEQUIN in my theatre will be a MEDIUM through which passes a strong feeling of DEATH and the condition of the Dead. A model for the Live ACTOR.

9

My elucidation of the situation described by Craig. The appearance of the LIVE ACTOR as a revolutionary moment. The discovery of a HUMAN BEING'S IMAGE.

I derive my observations from the domain of the theatre, but they are relevant to all current art. We can take Craig's suggestively depicted and disastrously incriminating picture of the circumstances surrounding the appearance of the Actor, which he had composed for his own use, a starting point for his idea of the "SUPER-MARIONETTE." Even though I continue to admire Craig's magnificent contempt and passionate accusations (especially since I see before me an absolute demise of today's theatre) and fully accept the first part of his Credo, in which he denies the institution of theatre its reason for artistic existence, I dissociate myself from his well-known conclusions about the fate of the ACTOR. For the moment of the ACTOR's first appearance before the HOUSE (to use current terminology) seems to me, on the contrary, r e v o l u t i o n a r y and a v a n t - g a r d e. I will even try to construct and "ascribe to History" a completely different picture, in which the course of events will have quite the opposite meaning! The shared circle of tradition and religious rituals, shared ceremonies and shared ludic activities was left by SOMEONE who made a risky decision to BREAK away from the ritualistic Community. He was not driven by pride (as in Craig) to become an object of universal attention. This would have been too simplistic. Rather it must have been a rebellious mind, defiant, skeptical, free, and tragic, daring enough to remain alone with Fate and Destiny. If we also add "with his ROLE," we will have before us the ACTOR. This revolt took place in the realm of art. This described event, or rather manifestation, probably caused much confusion in the minds of others and clashing opinions. This ACT must undoubtedly have been seen as a betrayal of the old ritualistic traditions and practices, as secular arrogance, as atheism, as dangerous subversive tendencies, as scandalous, as amoral, as indecent; it must have been seen as clownery, buffoonery, exhibitionism, and deviation. The actor himself, standing apart from society made not only fierce enemies, but also fanatical admirers. Simultaneously, condemnation and fame.

It would require ludicrous and shallow formalism to explain this act of BREAKING-AWAY (RUPTURING) as egotism, as a lust for fame, or as a manifestation of latent inclinations towards acting. Something much greater must have been at stake—a MESSAGE of extraordinary importance.

Let us try to imagine once again this fascinating situation: OPPOSITE those who remained on this side, there stood a HUMAN DECEPTIVELY SIMILAR to them, yet (by some secret and ingenious "operation") infinitely DISTANT, shockingly FOREIGN, as if DEAD, cut off by an invisible BARRIER—no less horrible and inconceivable, whose real meaning and THREAT appear to us only in DREAMS. As if in the blinding flash of lightning, they suddenly perceived a glaring, tragically circus-like IMAGE OF A HUMAN, as if they had seen him FOR THE FIRST TIME, as if they had seen THEIR VERY SELVES. This must have been a SHOCK—a metaphysical shock. The life image of a HUMAN emerging out of the shadows, as if constantly walking forward—was a moving MESSAGE of its new HUMAN CONDITION, only HUMAN, with its RESPONSIBILITY, with its tragic CONSCIOUSNESS, measuring its FATE on an inexorable and final scale, *the scale of DEATH*. This revelatory MESSAGE, which was transmitted from the realm of DEATH, evoked in the SPECTATORS (let us use our term here) a metaphysical shock. And the craft and the art of this ACTOR (also according to our terminology) revealed that realm of DEATH and its tragic and full-of-DREAD beauty.

It is necessary to redefine the essential meaning of the relationship: SPECTATOR and ACTOR.

IT IS NECESSARY TO RECOVER THE PRIMEVAL FORCE OF THE SHOCK TAKING PLACE AT THE MOMENT WHEN, OPPOSITE A HUMAN (A SPECTATOR), THERE STOOD FOR THE FIRST TIME A HUMAN (AN ACTOR), DECEPTIVELY SIMILAR TO US, YET AT THE SAME TIME INFINITELY FOREIGN, BEYOND THE IMPASSABLE BARRIER.

10

RECAPITULATION:

Despite the fact that we may be suspected and even accused
of scrupulousness, inappropriate under these circumstances,
conquering my own inborn prejudices and fears,
for the sake of a more precise picture
and possible conclusions,
let us establish then the limits of that boundary, which has the name of
THE CONDITION OF DEATH,
for it represents the most extreme point of reference
no longer threatened by the conformity of
the CONDITION OF AN ARTIST AND ART.

. . . this specific relationship,
which is terrifying
and at the same time compelling,
this relationship of the l i v i n g to the d e a d,
the dead, who not so long ago, while still alive, gave not the slightest
reason for this unforeseen spectacle,

for creating unnecessary separation and confusion;
they were not d i f f e r e n t,
did not place themselves above others,
and as a result of this seemingly banal
but, as it would later become evident, rather essential
and valuable characteristic,
they were simply, normally,
in no way transgressing the universal laws,
u n n o t i c e d;
and now suddenly
on the other side,
opposite
they shock us
as if we
were seeing them for the first time
placed on display
in an ambigous ceremony:
venerated
and, at the same time, rejected;
irrevocably different
and infinitely foreign;
and more: somehow deprived of all meaning,
inconsequential,
without the any hope of occupying some position
in our "full" life relationships,
which are only accessible to us, familiar
and comprehensible,
but for them meaningless.

If we agree that a trait of
living people
is their ease and ability
with which they enter into mutual and manifold
life relationships,
it is only
in the presence of the dead
that there is born in us a sudden and startling
realization of the fact that
this basic trait of the living
is brought forth and made possible by
a complete
lack of difference
between them;
by their
i n d i s t i n g u i s h a b i l i t y,

by their universal s a m e n e s s,
mercilessly abolishing all other and opposing delusions,
which is common,
consistent,
all-binding.
Only then when they are d e a d
that they become
n o t i c e a b l e (to the living);
having paid the highest price,
they gain
their individuality,
distinction,
their IMAGE,
glaring
and almost
c i r c u s - l i k e.

"Dove and Samurai" and "A Letter to Robert Wilson"
Two Prose Texts

Heiner Müller

Translator's Note

"Dove and Samurai" (*Taube und Samurai*) and "A Letter to Robert Wilson" (*Brief an Robert Wilson*) were written in the 1980s. Heiner Müller first observed Wilson's work when the latter rehearsed his *Death, Destruction & Detroit* at the Schaubühne in what was then West Berlin in 1978. The same year, Müller wrote a text, *Terror Is the First Appearance of the New,* in which he stated, "The theater of Robert Wilson, as naïve as it is elitist, infantile toe dance and mathematical child's play, doesn't make any difference between amateur and professional actors. Prospect of an Epic Theater as Brecht conceived it yet never realized it, with a minimum of dramaturgic labor and beyond the perversity that makes out of luxury an occupation."

Müller and Wilson then met briefly in Cologne, in 1981, and became friends in 1983 when the latter was directing the German segment of his project *CIVIL warS,* to be shown at the 1984 Olympic Arts Festival in Los Angeles. It was planned to consist of several parts that were to be staged in Germany, Holland, Italy, Japan, and other places. Due to financial reasons, the project was eventually canceled. When Wilson desired a text for the German segment, Müller was recommended to him as a feasible author. They discovered they had much in common in spite of their vastly different backgrounds. Müller: "The beginning of our relation was his remark, 'We are so different.'" Wilson used in his production texts by Müller about Frederick II and Prussian-German history and also other authors' texts which Müller had selected. The production was presented

Reprinted from *A Heiner Müller Reader: Plays, Poetry, Prose,* ed. and trans. by Carl Weber (Baltimore: Johns Hopkins University Press, 2001), 112–17. © Suhrkamp Verlag Frankfurt am Main 2005. All rights reserved.

in Cologne, in 1984, and at the American Repertory Theater in Cambridge, Massachusetts, in an American version, in 1985. It was the beginning of their intensive collaboration and close friendship, Wilson went on to employ Müller's text *Explosion of a Memory* in his staging of *Alcestis*, at Cambridge (1986) and Stuttgart (1987). He then directed Müller's *Hamletmachine* in New York and Hamburg (1986), as well as *Quartet* in Stuttgart (1987) and Cambridge (1988). In 1987, when Wilson staged *Death, Destruction, & Detroit 2* at the Schaubühne, he wanted a text from Müller, who instead wrote his "Letter to Robert Wilson;" and in 1988 Müller contributed texts to Wilson's version of the Gilgamesh epic, *The Forest*, produced at the Freie Volksbühne Theater in West Berlin. Their last collaboration was the first European high-definition video-film, *The Death of Molière*, which Wilson produced for the French Institut de L'Audovisuel in 1994. At his friend's funeral, 16 January 1996, Wilson gave a eulogy, and he recently included Müller's *Landscape with Argonauts* in his staging of Brecht's *The Ocean Flight* at the Berliner Ensemble, 1998.

"Dove and Samurai" was first published in *ERSTE, Magazin für das Deutsche Schauspielhaus Hamburg*, May–June 1986. (The German title, *Taube und Samurai*, is difficult to translate since it conveys more than one meaning: *Taube* translates as *dove* but also as *deaf woman* and *deaf persons*, the plural. *Dove* appeared to be the most appropriate English title in view of the text's topic.) A slightly different version was originally sent by Müller as a telegram to Wilson, in 1984, after the planned production of *CIVIL warS* at Los Angeles had been canceled.

"Letter to Robert Wilson" appeared first in the program brochure for *Death, Destruction & Detroit 2*, at the Berlin Schaubühne, 1987. Wilson had asked Müller to contribute text to the production, based on writings by Kafka, and later, the mentioned text by Tshingis Aitmatov. The result of his efforts, as Müller explains it, was the "Letter." Wilson used it eventually in the production, along with other texts.

Müller once pointed out, "The essential aspect of Wilson's theater is the separation of the elements, a dream of Brecht."

"Dove and Samurai"

Robert Wilson comes from a space Ambrose Bierce disappeared into after he had seen the horrors of civil war. The one who returns carries the horror under the skin, his theater is the resurrection. The dead are liberated in slow motion. On this stage Kleist's marionette theater has a playroom, Brecht's epic dramaturgy a dance floor. An art without exertion, the step is planting its path. The dancing god is the marionette. His/her dance designs humans of a different flesh that is born from the wedding of fire and water of which Rimbaud was dreaming. Just as the apple from the tree of knowledge has to be eaten once again so that humans may return to the state of innocence, the tower of Babel has to be built anew so that the confusion of languages will come to an end. With the fairy tales' wisdom that the history of humans cannot be separated from the history of animals (plants, stones, machines) but for the price of extinction, Robert Wilson articulates the theme of our age: war of classes and races, species and genders, civil war in every sense of the term. When the eagles come gliding down and tear the banners of separation asunder and panthers walk about between the counters of the World Bank, the theater of resurrection will have found its stage.

Its reality is the union of humans and machines, the next step of evolution.

"A Letter to Robert Wilson"

For one week I have been trying to produce a text which could serve as a gravitational center to your production of *DD&D II*, a creation that more than any of your earlier works consists of its own explosion. My efforts have failed. Maybe, the explosion already had progressed too far, the degree of its acceleration (I'm not talking of Greenwich time) was already too high, that a text which willy-nilly means something could still inscribe itself in the vortex of the detonation. To speak of progress in context with an explosion seems paradoxical, but maybe for a long while now the liberation of the dead hasn't been happening in slow motion anymore but in quick motion. What remains to be done is the effort of describing my failure so that it will at least become an experience. The starting point was a text by Tshingis Aitmatov that describes a Mongolian torture which served to turn captives into slaves, tools without a memory. The technology was simple: the captive, who had been sentenced to survival and not designated for the slave trade but for domestic use by the conquerors, had his head shaved and covered with a helmet made from the skin of a freshly slaughtered camel's neck. Arms and legs shackled, his neck in the stocks so that he couldn't move his head, exposed on the steppe to the sun which dried the helmet and contracted it around his skull so that the regrowing hair was forced to grow backward into the scalp, the tortured prisoner lost his memory within five days—if he survived them—and was, after this operation, a laborer who didn't cause trouble, a Mankurt. There is no revolution without a memory. An early design of total utilization of labor, until its transformation into raw material in the concentration camps. I couldn't represent this event—the disintegration of thinking, the extinction of memory—only describe it, and any description is silenced, as our experiment with Kafka texts already was, when confronted with the centrifugal force of your images: Literature is experience congealed. The dead are writing with us on the paper of the Future at which flames are licking already from all sides. (Technology merely trains reflexes, it prevents experience. Our camel's skin, the computer, it is nothing but the present.) Yesterday I dreamed the end of libraries: next to workmen's barracks and engine rooms where geometrical modules were manufactured —I couldn't figure out their function or intended use—stacks, heaps of books, books in the grass, books in the mud, in the excavated building sites, putrid paper, decomposed letters. On his way to the toilet a worker with an empty face. Another dream of the same night: we were eating, tightly packed at narrow tables, in the spacious inner court of a castle in Switzerland, beneath helicopter flights. Sirens interrupted the meal: air raid warning. A waiter or the castellan in his armor informed us what had triggered it. Seventeen coaches of the Federal Soccer League had run over two children while driving in France. When I tried to translate the news for you, hoping for your coyote-like laughter, I discovered you weren't sitting at the table anymore but standing on the castle's ramparts, harnessed in a spacious steel construction, nearly grown together with it, because of your headphones not reachable by my voice, unreachable also for the sirens of the Swiss air raid warning. Next to my typewriter on the desk, which is full of burn marks and hasn't been cleaned up in years, there lies a reproduction, a picture postcard, of Tintoretto's *Miracle of Marcus*. Perhaps you have seen the painting in Milan, at the Pinacoteca Brera. I haven't seen it there, maybe it was just being restored, or I cannot remember it and have to be content with the postcard. That offers the advantage of the imprecise view, like at times a bad seat during a performance of yours. (The ideal audience of *DD&D II* would be one single spectator, enormously stretched between the four playgrounds of the dead in the vault of the stage space, crucified by geometry as in Leonardo's drawing after Vitruvius's text about *homo circularis* and *homo quadratus*: "If a man lies on his back, his arms and legs stretched out, and you place your drawing compass's needle at the point of his navel and draw a circle, such a circle will touch the fingertips of both hands and the tips of the toes. As there is a circle to be found at the body, there also will be the figure of the square. Namely, if you take measure from the soles of the feet to the crown of the head and then apply such measure to the stretched out hands, it will result in equal width and height as with surfaces that are laid out in a square by means of T-square." This One-Person-Audience should have one eye that is attached to a pillar rising from the naval, circular and catholic, or turning with great speed as the eye of a certain reptile whose name I have forgotten. (Maybe, it only exists in my dreams.) Back to the Tintoretto: What I'm seeing is a church nave, vaulted by Roman arches, diagonally tapered toward the back, the right wall with its moldings and balconies is fully visible. Two men standing on ladders, the one with his right, the other one with his left hand holding on to the parapet, lower from the foremost balcony a naked old man, maybe a corpse, head first towards the ground. A white cloth with which he probably was clothed serves as a rope; his sex isn't important anymore. A third helper reaches from below for his right arm that is hanging down. He is the only one in the room who is wearing a turban. Behind him a man with arms spread out, expectation or salutation, how does one salute a dead man whose resurrection still is in the future. The left foreground is dominated by the Saint himself. With stretched out left arm he directs—like a foreman the crane—the labor at the balcony that is a deposition from the cross. The right hand holds the tablet or the book with Future's diagram. Before the Saint's feet a gray-white corpse. The skin color of the muscular body is meant to indicate that the soul has already left it: it belongs to art and putrefaction. On the right behind the corpse, a mourning father figure. The dead's head is twisted, as if to avoid the father's blessing hand. And so forth the personnel of the legend. The picture's secret is the trap door in the background, held open by two men. From the depths light emanates: the heavens are below. Hit by the light from the depths, the group of figures in the right foreground reels: Two men on their knees, the upper trunks thrown backwards, the faces turned away from each other. The stronger one of the two, head and breast in a different light which emanates from the Saint and the dead man, tries with both his arms to prevent the fall of the second man who, falling, clutches the knees of a woman. The woman is the counterpart of the Saint, one hand in front of her eyes, protection against the imperious gesture of Future's architect or against the light from the underground. The light is a hurricane. Written as the crow flies between the two German capitals Berlin, separated by the chasm of their shared and not shared history, piled up by the latest earthquake as a borderline between two continents. Accept this letter as an expression of my desire to be present in your work.

Heiner Müller
23 February, 1987

part six

Terror

Over the past century, theater has periodically examined and dramatized political terror characterized by mass arrests and executions. From Georg Büchner's *Danton's Death* (1835) to Harold Pinter's *The Birthday Party* (1958), theater artists have investigated the impact of terror on the human psyche. Stylistic continuity spans the historical avant-garde, tying the surrealist, nightmarish images in Roger Vitrac's *Mysteries of Love* to the irrational violence alluding to the horrors of totalitarianism in the plays of the Soviet Oberiuty Daniil Kharms and Aleksandr Vvedensky (see *Theater of the Avant-Garde, 1890–1950*). Antonin Artaud's Theatre of Cruelty, to which this section refers through Charles Marowitz's "Notes on the Theatre of Cruelty," reveals another common link among various periods of avant-garde experimentation with theatrical "terrorism."

Yet in the wake of the unavoidable association between the concept of "terror" and global terrorism after September 11, 2001, a meta-narrative on the latter in the arts and society has blurred the borders between imagined and actual terror and heightened the sense of imminent danger (but obscured the source). The avant-garde shifted from the shocking, visceral experience proposed by Artaud and the dreamlike, nonsensical violence in surrealist and absurdist plays to an overwhelming sense of paranoia and loss of control and a pervasive feeling of indeterminate danger. The plays featured in this section, although created before 9/11, capture and, to some extent, foreshadow post–9/11 conceptions of terror. The work of Iranian-American theater artist Reza Abdoh, Argentinean dissident writer Griselda Gambaro, and British political dramatist Caryl Churchill offers a global perspective on terror that might serve as the basis for theater artists' examination of later responses to the complex interplay of terror and terrorism in contemporary politics. These stylistically and geographically diverse artists investigate the impact of terror on humanity in the context of nuclear threats, religious wars, and desensitized consumer culture, seemingly foreshadowing the terror to come.

An actor, playwright, and director born in Iran, Abdoh spent his youth in London and Los Angeles; he then directed his own plays in Los Angeles and New York until his death at age 32 from AIDS. He founded Dar a Luz, a theater company whose work assaulted audiences with brazen images of violence and sex in a constant interplay of irony and cruelty. From his perspective as a queer, HIV-positive immigrant artist crossing between Eastern and Western cultures, Abdoh influenced the aesthetics and helped broaden the politics of the avant-garde in the last two decades of the twentieth century.[2]

Abdoh expressed both admiration and anger toward American mass-media culture by embracing and parodying popular iconography and cultural stereotypes. His theater, although it was passionately engaged in the postmodern dialogue with popular culture, demonstrated the influence of earlier avant-garde experiments: Artaud's Theatre of Cruelty; Brecht's distancing effects; jarring, surrealist juxtapositions; expressionist agony and distortion; symbolist poetic images; and the principles of montage and collage of multimedia and found materials explored by Richard Foreman and the Wooster Group. Intrinsically connected to American popular culture and the urbanism of Los Angeles and New York, Abdoh's work confronts society's glorification of violence as well as its ambiguous moral standards toward aggression and destruction; his plays question America's political stand on sanctioning violence "in the name of progress" and democracy.[3]

In *The Hip-Hop Waltz of Eurydice*, selected for this collection, Abdoh transforms the myth of Orpheus and Eurydice into an unspecified realm of sexual politics, physical oppression, and gender/identity reversal, heightening the fusion of absurdity, irony, and sadism. He couples fragmentation of the narrative with a barrage of visual and auditory stimuli: video images colliding with stage action, repeated buzzing sounds, periodic pantomime and dance scenes subverting and punctuating the cruelty of preceding episodes. The moments of interrogation and torture, which the Captain administers, morph into sequences of paranoia and sexual brutality peppered with obscenities and pseudo-ideological slogans such as "We will cure you of your perversions."[4] Abdoh's graphic, multimedia-driven, collage-based theater assaults the audience's senses, shaking spectators out of the numbed acceptance of fixed dogmas and violence, but by employing direct political messages, it combines Artaud's cruelty with scathing satirical commentary on a deepening social crisis. Working during the first wave of American awareness of the AIDS crisis, Abdoh viewed the epidemic as a symbol of society's incurable disease. His work theatricalizes the large-scale devastation of cultures and environments and the inconceivable cruelty inflicted on the human body and psyche during this era.[5]

In *Stripped*, Gambaro explores terror as a state of mind that government imposes on the individual. Having lived in self-imposed exile during Argentina's military dictatorship of the 1970s and early 1980s, she created her works in the context of political oppression, examining the psychological effects of power and violence that lead to subjugation and complicity. Emerging from the Argentinean theatrical tradition of *el grotesco criollo*, Gambaro interweaves absurd, exaggerated, and grotesquely distorted elements of plot, characterization, and dialogue with politically and socially committed theater. She emphasizes the conspicuous presence of political and social content in her plays, setting them apart from the works of Eugène Ionesco and Samuel Beckett and bringing them closer to the political theater of Brecht.

Stripped is a one-act allegory about authority and submission written during a period of extreme social and political disruption in Argentina, when the government staged "spectacular acts" of "torture and abduction," to terrorize and silence civilians, as Diana Taylor described it.[6] The play, a monodrama of sorts, depicts a moment in a woman's life during which she allows a silent, unremarkable young man to establish full control over her mind and body. In a small, impersonal room, an aging actress desperate to be cast awaits her appointment with a director; the man, indifferent to her frantic pleas, enters the room at regular intervals, only to take away a piece of her clothes, rip off an earring, or remove a piece of furniture. The absurdity and indeterminacy of the offense increase the terror the woman experiences. Her psychological paralysis in the face of this repeated physical assault can be seen as emblematic of Argentina's passive acceptance of dictatorship.

Through the central metaphor of "theater," *Stripped* alludes to the theatrical nature of publicly staged acts of terror and torture by oppressive political regimes.[7] The woman is both a victim of terror and a passive spectator unable to stand up to the violent acts staged by an absent director. Gambaro's appropriation and subversion of the "nation-as-woman metaphor," which the Argentinean military typically used,[8] broadens the implications of the play beyond a single case of torture to implicate the nation's subjugation to authority and complicity with fascist practices. As passive observers of the woman's abuse, the first audience members to see *Stripped* (Argentina, 1983) were forced to relive recent experiences of witnessing terrorist acts when they became complicit with terrorists by accepting the "theatrical conventions" of terror.

In her 2000 play *Far Away*, Churchill erases the borders between the imagined and the real, a child's nightmarish vision and actual violence, comic absurdity, and inhumane brutality. Drawing upon a technique used in many fairy tales, she creates a world in which the failure to distinguish between seeing and imagining results in a complete devastation of humanity. An act of violence, witnessed by a little girl named Joan, is first dismissed by her aunt as a fantasy. As Joan's questions persist and she vividly recalls and describes the horrors she witnessed, her aunt reveals the family secret: the abused people in a nearby shed are being saved from persecution by Joan's uncle. Joan must never talk about these people, and the witnessed brutality must remain a mystery. But what could indeed be perceived as an imagined nightmare reappears as a macabre reality of mass execution in the second act. Now a young woman, Joan has learned to remain silent in fear of persecution; the "enormous and preposterous" hats[9] she designs to make her living are worn by prisoners on their marches to death, alluding to mass killings during World War II, as well as more recent political atrocities in the former Yugoslavia and Rwanda. By the third act, the child's nightmare has become an all-encompassing war of nations, animals, and plants, in which cats have been "killing babies" and "crocodiles invade villages at night and take children out of their beds."[10]

Churchill compels the audience to accept the coexistence of the ordinary and the bizarre, the mundane and the preposterous. Like Gambaro, she shows the consequences of silence, denial, and complicity in a society that uses terror to oppress and alienate its citizens. In this political parable, she invites viewers to reevaluate the false safety of "far away" in an era when borders are erased and catastrophic events have far-reaching consequences. Stephen Daldry's production of *Far Away* at the New York Theatre Workshop commemorated the first anniversary of 9/11 by exploring the tension between audience perceptions of "far away" and "nearby" which brought "the chilling images of Churchill's parable close to home."[11]

All three plays capture the political dimensions and global implications of terror: violence is glamorized; acts of terror become public spectacles; lies and denials lead to worldwide catastrophes. "We are born in terror and trembling," director Anne Bogart writes, and "the artist's responsibility is to bring the . . . mystery and terror, the trembling, back."[12] Abdoh, Gambaro, and Churchill achieve that, creating theatrical experiences that embody the human experience of terror, evoke the spectacular nature of terrorist acts, and trigger the feelings of disorientation and paranoia that have become all too familiar to us.

Notes

1. The history of terror in the second half of the twentieth-century theater encompasses the works of Harold Pinter, Edward Bond, Howard Baker, Sarah Kane, and Martin McDonagh, among others, but it is also connected to the modernist sensibilities of alienation, anxiety, and negation exemplified in the tortured vision of Franz Kafka or the philosophies of Martin Heidegger and Søren Kierkegaard.

2. Abdoh's major works include *The Hip-Hop Waltz of Eurydice* (1991), *Bogeyman* (1991), *The Law of Remains* (1992), *Tight Right White* (1993), and *Quotations from a Ruined City* (1994).

3. See Daniel Mufson, *Reza Abdoh* (Baltimore: Johns Hopkins University Press, 1999), 24.

4. Abdoh, *The Hip-Hop Waltz of Eurydice*, 474 below in this volume.

5. In characterizing Abdoh's theater practice as "a culmination of modernist and postmodernist" aesthetics, John Bell argues that Abdoh's rejection of postmodern cultural complacency and political disengagement places his theatrical works in contrast to the "disconnected neutrality [of] postmodernist theatre" and closer to the American counterculture of the 1960s (i.e., Living Theatre, Open Theatre, Happenings, etc.). See John Bell, "AIDS and Avantgarde Classicism: Reza Abdoh's *Quotations from a Ruined City*," *TDR* 39.4 (1995): 21. As Bell posits, "working confidently within the established theatre language of the twentieth-century avant-garde, Abdoh freed himself to return to the political, social, and spiritual content in a way normally unavailable to high post-modern performance" (41).

6. Diana Taylor, "Theater and Terrorism: Griselda Gambaro's *Information for Foreigners*," *Theatre Journal* 42.2 (1990): 165–82.

7. "Terror," Taylor writes, "draws on the theatrical propensity to bind the audience to paralyze it" ("Theater and Terrorism," 166).

8. See Ana Elena Puga, "The Abstract Allegory of Griselda Gambaro's *Stripped*" (El Despojamiento), *Theatre Journal* 56.3 (2004): 420.

9. Caryl Churchill, *Far Away*, 504 in this volume.

10. Churchill, *Far Away*, 507, 508.

11. See Una Chaudhuri's production review, "Different Hats," *Theater* 33.3 (2003): 132–34.

12. Anne Bogart, "Terror, Disorientation, and Difficulty," 000 in this volume.

Stripped
(El Despojamiento, 1974)

Griselda Gambaro

Translated by Ana Puga

CHARACTERS

WOMAN
YOUNG MAN

(*A small table with magazines, a chair, a small sofa. The woman enters. She is dressed with a pretense of elegance, a mid-length skirt, blouse, and a short cape. She wears dangling earrings and high-heeled shoes, twisted and worn. She carries an ordinary purse and a big envelope, with photos, and speaks with a smile out toward the audience.*)

WOMAN: Yes, yes, I know I got here early. I'm not in a hurry, I'll wait. Thanks! (*To herself*) Cretins! Why even make an appointment? They waste your time like it was theirs. (*She looks around*) They could have a nicer waiting room with what they earn. Cheapskates.

(*She leaves the purse and the envelope on top of the table. She takes off the cape. She hesitates. She puts it on again. She takes a few steps, thinks, she takes off the cape. She folds it and puts it on top of the sofa. She hesitates. She puts it on the back of the chair. She opens the purse, takes out a mirror, looks at herself*)

Reprinted from *Women and Performance: A Journal of Feminist Theory*, 2000, Issue 22, 11.2, 97–106. Reprinted by permission of Taylor and Francis Ltd (http://www.informaworld.com) and Ana Elena Puga.

What eyes! One look and they fall at my feet. (*She thinks, sighs*) Well, not everyone now . . . (*She puts away the mirror*) Anyway, in photos you can't see the wrinkles, you can't see the pain . . . Bull. The photos this jerk took of me! He hated me. (*She laughs softly*) I didn't pay him. He deserved it. He didn't just get my crows' feet, he got the whole crow. (*She looks from the sofa to the chair, uncertain about which to sit in. She chooses the sofa*) But if I don't bring photos they'll think I'm a . . . one of the crowd that doesn't even . . . They're terrible, but they'll do: I'm the original. They'll look at me, and I'll come out on top. (*She is subtly disconcerted*) Or not? "Ah, are you the one from the photos? They don't do you justice, ma'am! No one would say that you're that girl there (*She sinks*), that woman . . . How you've changed!" (*She remains preoccupied for a moment. Abruptly, she recovers*) I hope Pepe doesn't get home early. I didn't leave him his dinner, and he's so fussy! Everything ready, everything on the dot. You would think I was his maid! I don't know why I put up with it. (*Sad*) I love him, that must be it . . .

(*The young man enters. His manner is depersonalized, as if he were dealing only with objects, including the woman, to whom he is indifferent. Without noticing her smile, which carries a pretense of seduction, he nears the table. After finding the envelope, he takes it and exits*)

How rude! He could have asked for it! I hope they notice the ones where I look good. In which ones do I look good? In almost all, I think. I was thinner then, without a belly. (*She sucks in her stomach, laughs bitterly*) Without a belly. But with crow's feet! And why did I bring the girl ones? Yellowing . . . the urge to show how I was then, without wrinkles, innocent. They'll see . . . how I've aged. I'm nervous, how stupid. Everything turned out badly for me. Even Pepe. Just a poor guy. (*The young man enters. She smiles instantly*) How about it? How did they seem to you? Lovely, no? (*With a gesture that she doesn't finish*) Did you notice the one where I'm by the sea, my hand extend . . . (*The young man stops for a second, walks past her, and exits on the opposite side. She is left with her mouth hanging open in surprise. She composes herself*) Hired help. I always make these mistakes. I think any nobody is worthwhile. I think being decently dressed is enough, and that's that. I'll never learn! Too anxious . . . And what I need is . . . (*She can't find the word*) condescension.

(*She smiles, sits, crosses her legs, with effort adopts an attitude that she supposes attractive. She stiffens in the pose. She abandons it. She opens her purse, looks.*)

I didn't bring cigarettes. What a shame! If I go buy some . . . No, better not move. Someone might come and take my turn. Who do I complain to? Screw yourself, they'll tell me. I could call an office boy and send him . . . (*She shrinks*) But how to tell him that I smoke the cheapest ones? And . . . and I'd have to give him a tip.

(*The young man enters. She notices him a second later. Quickly, she puts together her smile and her elegant pose. The young man ignores her, searches for something. He finds the cape, takes it and leaves. She looks surprised and moves forward*)

What are you doing? How dare you? (*She follows him anxiously*) Do you need it? Don't ruin it, please! It's not mine! (*The young man stops and looks at her*) Of course it is, it is mine. I said that so you would be careful. Fold it well. (*Timidly, she takes it out of the young man's hands, she folds it and hands it to him*) It looks very good, very elegant. It wears well. My friend always lends it to me. (*She corrects herself*) I lend it to her. As if it were mine. Elegant, no? What do you need it for?

(*The young man doesn't answer and exits*)

Idiot, why did I apologize? Why did I explain? I'll never learn to be quiet! I could cut out my tongue! And I put it in his hands myself! It's all right, calm down, a courtesy can't hurt me. On the contrary. The director must have asked for it. He must want to know how I'm dressed. A cape, not just anybody wears a cape.

(*She sings softly, very badly, happy:*)

I'll be loving you eternally.
There'll be no one new, my dear, for me
Though the sky should fall, remember I shall always be
Forever true and loving you, eternally.

How badly I sing. It's a shame. That would be another possibility. Everyone pays with pleasure to have their ears caressed. (*She hums briefly*) Pepe never let me sing. "Shut up, foghorn!" He's frustrated, that's Pepe. He's a sad sack and won't let anyone else be happy. Wonder if he's home yet? When are these people going to take care of me? You would think they had all day! What time could it be? If I asked? What could I lose? (*Dignified*) "Please, the time." (*She answers herself*) "Don't you have a watch?" (*Insecure*) I don't know what sort of impression that would make, not having a watch. They might think I'm penniless. Like Pepe, you look at him and your heart aches. What a guy! He doesn't make a good impression at all. I didn't iron his shirt, I didn't leave him his meal. He'll raise hell. "What good are you if I can't have a clean shirt?" As if that were my mission in life, when I'm here to . . . (*She gets tired. Suddenly, she opens her purse, takes out a mirror, looks at herself, touches her cheek*) No, you can't see it. What a punch he gave me, the bastard. He tried to ruin me. It's black.

(*She sits. Nervously, she pats a large amount of face powder on the cheekbone. She moves the mirror back and looks at herself*)

They'll think I made myself up badly. (*She rubs it in. She looks at herself, desolate*) What a wreck! But people don't look at your face hunting for bruises, they look into your eyes, they search for what you are and then, with these eyes . . . (*Laughs*) I've got the battle won! I still have a pair of eyes in my tool kit that. . . . When that jerk comes back, I'll look at him like this (*With pathetic coquetry*), seductively, and I'll leave him stiff. "Boy, have you ever seen a look like this?" No, I'd better not speak. No familiarity. I won't risk it!

(*The young man enters*) But I can ask him if he liked the photos, and . . . (*She crosses her legs, smiles. She hikes up her skirt a bit, swinging her leg. She tries to look at him intensely. In spite of herself*) And the cape? (*He doesn't answer*) Bring me the cape, please.

(*He draws closer, takes off the shoe she is swinging in the air and takes it away. After a moment of complete confusion, she recovers quickly and follows him*)

Impertinent! Come here! How dare you! (*He exits, as if he hadn't heard her, leaving her totally perplexed*) And if they call me now? What will I tell them? That I was swinging my leg, and he took it away from me? And if he's not there? If he went to the bathroom? "I let him take my shoe, sir." What a ridiculous situation! What does he take me for? No, I'm going to go and ask him for it.

(*She goes limping toward the door. She stops, fixes her blouse. She turns, takes the purse, goes again toward the door and runs into the young man*)

Give me the shoe! I'm talking to you! They're new. I bought them to come here. They cost me enough! No. It doesn't matter. I have others, but they're at home. Is it that . . . the director wants to know what shoes I'm wearing? They're not very elegant, but . . . I liked them. I took a fancy to them. I don't usually use them. I have better ones: of leather, suede, clogs, sandals. I can give you these. They aren't worth anything. Not now, naturally. But tomorrow I'll bring them to you. (*Without conviction, sadly*) You must have a little friend and want to . . . make an impression. I understand. You understand that I can't go around barefoot, or half-barefoot, no? Unless you have other shoes in the dressing room and you want me to change these for those because they go better with . . . (*The boy looks at her, immobile*) Well, you decide! That's what I'm here for. (*Humble*) Tell the director to see me.

(*Suddenly, but without brusqueness, the boy extends his hand toward her, as if he were going to caress her, though the gesture is without emotional charge. She looks at him in suspense, as if in the face of an unexpected friendly gesture. The young man holds his hand still and then, with a rough gesture, he rips off her earring. She screams*)

Watch what you're doing! You hurt me! (*The young man exits*)

If Pepe were here! Pepe! No, why do I scream? Relax. He could have ripped my ear off. And if they were gold? Huh? If they were gold? They'll realize they're junk. When they're on, they pass, they seem elegant. At least I should have told him that the real ones are at home, or in the bank, or in a safe. But why don't they come here and see me in one piece? When it's my turn, the first thing I'm going to say is: This employee you have is a brute, a brute with no manners. In my day . . . we worked differently. You'd tell him what to do and he'd do it. No, he does whatever he wants! Goes up to people and treats them like garbage! With me he's sunk, he's met . . . his match. Relax, honey. They're testing to see how much I can . . . Ma'am, they'll come to tell me, you have an amazing serenity. We congratulate you. (Puzzled) But why do they need serenity? I can manage myself well, I know how to move, no role is too large or too small for me.

And how I photograph! Even if they don't know how to set lights, my face is naturally luminous, because of my skin. (*She takes out the other earring, goes to put it in her purse. She hesitates, puts it on again*) They don't know what they'll be losing if they don't take me! And I have so many ideas! When he comes back, I'll tell him, ideas are born in me, kicking, like flowers. "Honey, what an imagination you have!" Pepe marvels. That's another advantage in this business: They give me a script and I enrich it. Most people think like slaves! I, on the other hand, I fly. That story, do you remember, Honey? The girl was going to marry her boyfriend, because they thought, the idiots,that love always triumphs. With money it triumphs better. So, I went like a shot to the director. I know so much about life! And I said to him: No, let the poor boyfriend be a millionaire, he abandons everything for her: home, family, status, everything, except the millions. And afterwards they forgive her, his mother forgives her, she calls her "daughter dear," and then the grandchildren come! (*She sighs sweetly*) What a hit I was! The director gave me a kiss and said, "Honey, you are a gem!" The last time I was a gem for someone. I remember how it was before. It just so happens that I didn't get to be in films, bad luck. I played ingenues, girls in love. Until my face got full of lead. The neighborhood girls would look at me with their magazines open and they'd die laughing. Sluts! And from ingenues to now . . . nothing. Except Pepe's blows . . . and Pepe's love.

(*The young man enters, looks at her*) You've turned up! And? I'm waiting. Give me back what you took! Everything! And you almost . . . ripped off my ear! If you ruin the cape or you lose it on me . . . You'll see what I'm made of! It's a cape that costs a lot, that . . . it's not even mine! Bring it in now, right now! What are you here? Thieves? Where did I end up? In a den of outlaws? (*The young man turns away to go*) Come here, you crook! Answer me! (*The young man stops and looks at her. A pause. She is disarmed*) I didn't mean to say that. I . . . I lost my head. You could be more courteous. I'm not uppity with you, so why take advantage? And I wait patiently, as you can see. When it comes to work, I can wait all the time you want, time means nothing to me, I'll lend you the cape, yes, I'll lend it to you! But . . . when the director calls, I want to be . . . (*She ends with a gesture. The young man indicates the skirt, impassive. She looks at herself, she looks at him*) What do you want? You're crazy! I'll scream. Go! (*The young man turns and exits*)

What . . . ! (*She reconsiders*) Oh, my God! What did I do? I threw him out. And now? What a stupid way of losing my head! Always the same. This stubbornness that gets the better of me and . . . Everything goes like this for me! But why didn't they tell me that they need a . . . I don't know . . . a show girl. It's all right. I'm not against that! Work is . . . work, one has to be willing to be . . . flexible. It's all right. Not nude! Show girl, well, I still know how to kick up my little leg. (*She does so*) If Pepe could see me. "Careful what you do. Bring me the photos, Honey." It's easy for him to ask. A doormat, that's what you are. Not that much, not me. At least I still demand respect. I was right to tell him off. What do they think? That I don't have any backbone, that they can walk all over me? (*Smiles*) I remember that time, when Pepe beat me until I was out flat and the neighbors called the police, and I said, "Nothing happened here, I fell from the ladder." (*Laughs*) They got their comeuppance! And Pepe came and kissed me. On the other hand, if I had accused him, poor Pepe! What a humiliation! For him, for me.

(*She remains lost in thought for a second*)

For me, already humiliated because I let him hit me. (*Pause. She hums*) A show girl in photos, I could do. It's classier. They'll pay me more, surely. (*She sings and dances awkwardly*) If Pepe sees me, he'll strangle me! (*Laughs*) I give him the name of another magazine, he buys it and nothing! I'm not there. But if they're postcards . . . not in the nude! He'll kill me. He expects wives, housewives, mothers of youngsters. Grandmothers! He never wanted me to pose nude, he checked my necklines, and now he'll have a good excuse. (*Laughs acidly*) "You're too wrinkled to pose naked." Cretin! And why does he have to know? I can lie to him, protect him . . . (*She opens her purse brusquely*) I'll put on more makeup. This makeup is very subtle and my skin now . . . I'll come out too pale, anemic.(*She makes herself up crudely*) How do I get rid of these dark circles? These spots? They could audition me and get it over with! What do they want? How should I behave? (*She sinks*) Where does it say how I should behave? Where?

(*The boy enters. Quickly, she puts away the powder case in her purse and shuts it. She straightens up, smiles*)

I'm sorry. I was nervous. What time is it? No, the time isn't important, I told you. I can do any work. I thought it was something more serious, no, not more serious. More in keeping with my age, not with my age, with my experience of . . . I know how to dance, too! Not sing! (*Laughs*) Well, one doesn't sing in photos, no . . . (*The young man draws near to her, tries to rip off her skirt*) What are you doing? Get away! (*She resists*) What are you doing? Let go! Let go, I tell you! (*She moves away. The young man gestures toward her skirt, impassive*) Stop ripping things off me! Weren't you taught any manners? Ask me for what you need! Who do you think I am? You could be more pleasant! . . . You could be more . . . delicate . . . What does it cost? It doesn't cost anything . . . you tell me . . . the director is busy, he needs to see how you're dressed to decide if . . . you'll work out, if you can stay . . . now. And I'll give it to you! We all have our own style. I don't know anything about technique. I suppose that this is . . . faster, more effective. Take it! I'll give it to you. (*She unfastens the skirt and hands it to him*) See? Such friends.

Why infuriate me when with a little bit of delicacy, we can understand each other and work better together? (*The young man exits*) We're happy. On the other hand, if you have the gall to rip things from me by force, I get mad. I don't know what I'm saying. I'm liable to . . . leave. You won't get anything that way. Believe you me! And I won't get . . . anything either. (*Low*) It takes so much . . . (*She looks at herself, buttons her blouse. Trying to be humorous*) What a look! Like . . . a little too much. I'm out of shape, that's what's happened. (*She looks at her legs*) Stay in shape, that's the bottom line. Be docile. If I had cigarettes. (*She stands up straight*) It looks good, chic. I'll have to send the cape to the dry cleaners after so much handling. If I return it stained, she won't lend it to me again. (*She takes off her shoe, rubs her foot, puts it on again*) It's so tight! (*Laughs, acidly*) I'm a size larger! Let's see if they lose the other one on me. No, they're sure to bring me some more elegant ones from the dressing room . . . I'll show them that there is no role I can't face with . . . talent. I have more than enough of that. When I act for Pepe, he's captivated. "Honey, do the ingenue for me . . . "

(*She lowers her eyes, acts*) "No, sir, no sir! Mama won't let me talk to strangers. What are your intentions? (*Laughs prudishly. She balances pathetically. She stiffens*) They want a show girl. Too bad. With the experience I have in ingenues! I should have studied dance. If I'd known about this opportunity, I'd have made the effort. I'm always late. I'm going to be on time for my burial, that's for sure! (*Laughs bitterly*) Who knows! One of these days, maybe I'll be lucky. They'll wait for me with the grave ready but I don't show up. And Pepe will be angry. "Honey, you're always the same! Why did I cry so much? Drop dead!" (*Laughs*) And that would be even better. To be timely, not to fail . . . there. What did he expect? An ingenue? Not even if I were born again could I do it, because . . . all things come to an end, no? Pepe will come home hungry. I should have left him an omelet . . . I shouldn't be frightened of the work, they'll put on music, they'll be nice. Will there be others, or will it be me . . . alone? But there are younger, prettier girls (*She smiles sadly*) The competition. Why would they choose me? Why . . . me? An . . . old hag who isn't even in shape? Wrinkled and . . . bow-legged. And I threw him out! He shouldn't have been offended, if people talk, dialogue, they understand each other. Could he have understood? Was I clear? He was so impertinent.

Too bad that I didn't tell him I have some ideas about acting on the spur of the moment. A show girl dances, winks, wiggles her bottom. I'll come up with some brilliant idea! I'll leave them with their mouths open. And after all, why would he complain about me? I myself put the cape in his hands, the skirt. And if he had told me that he wanted the earrings, well the earrings, too! A savage. I'm used to good manners. I yelled at him. Why is he taking so long? A flunkey, that's what he is. Not too nice, but nice doesn't put food on the table. That must be his way, insolence. Of course, they think they walk on water and that they're not going to sink. They don't want a show girl, maybe they want a slu . . . a prostitute. And well, in photos! It doesn't mean I am one! They put, "a woman of questionable virtue." And if it's not that . . . they might have some other idea. They'll tell me. What do I care? They contract, they shoot, they make sure the work comes across. They give me my cues, the script, and I'm off! With my talent, my flexibility, I can act all sorts of mothers, crazy women, caring ones, distinguished ones. Pepe will be waiting, I should have left him the omelet . . . I'll do moms and later grandmothers, and afterwards they'll realize that I'm young and I'll be able to be the girl in love or the ingenue . . . (*She takes off her shoe, slowly takes off her stockings*) And later . . . later . . .

(*The young man enters and takes away the little table*)

When he comes back, I'll look at him with these eyes . . He still hasn't noticed my eyes, but when he looks at them he'll be stunned. And I'll tell him that my imagination is boundless. I enrich a script, if they let me, I . . . I round it out. In this scene, I can kiss father, and later, in this one, I disrobe . . . and it will come out tender . . . moving. I have to act naturally, as if I were an ingenue. (*Tries to laugh*) Innocence is the last thing you lose! When you have it, and I've already . . . No work is beneath you. Work is what's visible, it's outside; and inside, how do you have to be inside for certain jobs? You have to be broken or dead. Not me! Me: daisies inside! And a girl who swings on a hammock like it's the gallows, because I am . . . happy. They'll have a good time with me, and that's something, no? Poor guys . . . alone. They don't touch you. . . . it's a job that humiliates . . . no one. I don't even think they get excited. They're so . . . used to it. They . . . take pictures of you, alone or . . . with others, with children or old people. I'll be the madam, or they'll put a beautiful girl in bed and I'll . . . I'll be the mirror where everything ends. No. I'm still good, my beauty still . . . (*Laughs. She covers her mouth*) Come on, I shouldn't fall apart.

What's wrong, Honey? Get up on the wrong side of the bed? What energy you have for work! I can still . . . attract . . . They can still . . . go crazy for me. They'll pay me well. In poses that are . . . pleasant. And there will be a heater, so that I don't feel the cold . . . (*Sitting, she unbuttons her blouse, she reveals her cleavage in a pathetically provocative gesture, her legs open. The young man comes in and takes away the sofa. She doesn't move, she follows him with her eyes wide open and an artificial smile. Jovial*) I'm waiting here! (*The smile freezes on her, she lowers her head, bursts out crying*) Pepe!

THE END

The Hip-Hop Waltz of Eurydice

Reza Abdoh

At *five minutes to curtain,* JULIANA *enters, dressed as Orpheus/Tommy, and sits in chair. She chooses a woman to be the "blue lady," giving her the "blue lady ribbon." Then she returns to her chair and sits. At curtain,* TOM, *dressed as Eurydice/Dora Lee, enters with a towel. He crosses to the chair, takes out a straight razor, and begins to sharpen it on a leather strop. He strops faster and faster, until the bell sounds, at about thirty seconds after curtain.* TOM *puts shaving foam from a mug onto* JULIANA's *face, then shaves her. As* TOM *does a final stroke, removing a hair from her upper lip, a bell sounds.*

JULIANA *crosses to bed, pulls out a manual typewriter, places it on the bed, and begins to type. The keys jam occasionally, and she pulls them back.* TOM *strikes chair off stage right. Crosses to shelf, and begins filling the kettle and pot with water. He places the bucket under the faucet and begins cross down center to table, carrying a basket of vegetables.*

TOM *begins to chop vegetables. The faucet drips very loudly. He goes to the faucet, turns it tight, watches it for a second. Satisfied, he returns to his chopping board. The dripping resumes. He goes to the faucet again, turns it, then takes out a metal pail. He sits on it and pees. Goes to the faucet, wets his hand and cleans under his slip, then dries with a hair dryer. He goes back to the table, the drip resumes, and* TOM *begins savagely chopping a zucchini.*

JULIANA *takes a big pipe wrench from under the bed, crosses to the faucet, and pounds on it with the wrench. There is a moment's peace, but then the dripping resumes.*

TOM *hurls eggs into a mixing bowl, still in their shells. A stagehand wearing a black welder's helmet enters* stage right, *carrying a stool with a kitchen blender.* TOM *crosses, pours the eggs into the blender and whips them.* JULIANA *crosses with the wrench and hammers on the faucet again.* TOM *put the eggs in a bowl, then takes the table off. He pours contents of bowls into a pot and stirs.*

JULIANA *tears the paper from the typewriter. She puts the typewriter away under the bed, and takes out an old vacuum tube radio. She pushes the radio along the floor for a few feet, then switches it on. We hear the sounds of a horse race. Suddenly, a man's voice breaks in. They listen for a moment, then static overwhelms the voice.* JULIANA *quickly shuts off the radio.*

A video image of BORRACHA *knocking at the window appears.*

TOM: Go away, I told you before, we don't want any cookies.

TOM *puts food into the dishes, then takes the buckets, utensils, etc., offstage.* JULIANA *sits* downstage, *takes out a pitch pipe. She plays a note on it, then sings part of an unrelated scale. Repeat. In the video image,* BORRACHA *bangs on the window again.*

TOM: GO AWAY!

TOM *serves the food. He blows on his bowl then begins to eat.* JULIANA *sees that there is nothing in the bowls, pours her "food" on the ground, and bangs on her bowl with the spoon.* TOM *grabs her bowl, crosses* upstage right, *and hurls the bowl out the door. We hear a loud crash as the bowl breaks.* TOM *crosses* upstage right, *to the faucet. The kettle boils,* TOM *grabs it and burns his hand.* JULIANA *rushes over, takes his hand, kisses it, and lays her face on it.* TOM *raises her face to his, but as they are about to kiss, they hear loud sounds next door. Through the following, to* ALAN's *voice breaking in,* TOM *and* JULIANA *listen, he with growing interest, and* JULIANA *with alarm. At the sound of* ALAN's *voice, they both become fearful and bewildered.*

WOMAN: Fuck me.

MAN: No, I can't do that.

WOMAN: Fuck me now.

MAN: What do you want to do, get me in trouble?

WOMAN: Fuck me now.

Orgasmic noises

ALAN: From the egg laid by night, say the birds, came Eros. We will cure you of your perversions. You return to your dung as a dog to its vomit. Come on, boys, throw her out the window.

A crash. A scream

Lights out!

The lights bump out.

JULIANA *snores.* BORRACHA *on video opens window, looks through, then disappears.*

TOM: Tommy, Tommy! (*Throws a glass of water in* JULIANA's *face. Sound of splash.*) Are you in pain?

JULIANA: Are you in pain?

TOM: What's the matter with you?

JULIANA: What's the matter with you?

TOM: Stop repeating everything I say like a parrot. Why do you repeat everything?

JULIANA: You just said that.

TOM: I know I did.

JULIANA: Well, why do you repeat everything? You are repeating like a parrot.

TOM: Very funny. I bet you're a riot with those broken down friends of yours. I never want to see them or your boss in this house again.

JULIANA: None of my friends have ever been in this house.

TOM: Why are you ashamed of me?

JULIANA: I'm not ashamed of you.

TOM: Then why don't you invite them here. Because they're a bunch of bums.

JULIANA: THEY'RE NOT BUMS! (*Knocks* TOM *out of bed.*)

BORRACHA *enters and begins to sing.*

TOM: Oh I just love that Xavier Cougat.

JULIANA: BUZZ-Z-Z-Z

TOM: Don't do that! When we got married I gave up all my girlfriends. Why don't you do it?

JULIANA: All right I'll give up all your girlfriends.

TOM: Oh very funny. Oh I wish we could meet some nice people. Why don't you join the Elks Club?

AMEN *enters, starts saying "stop singing" in Portuguese.*

JULIANA: I will next week.

TOM: You say it but you don't do it. Why don't you join now? Go on get up and join the Elks Club.

JULIANA: Are you out of your mind? It's three o'clock in the morning.

TOM: It's only half past two.

JULIANA: Oh, why don't you let me sleep? You know I have to get up early.

TOM: I won't let you sleep because if you sleep you'll snore then you'll wake me and I'll wake you and we'll argue and I won't get any sleep.

JULIANA: I PROMISE I WON'T SNORE. (*Falls asleep and snores.*)

AMEN *and* BORRACHA *exit.*

TOM: You always snore, week in week out. On Monday you snore, on Tuesday you snore, on Wednesday you snore, on Thursday you snore . . . oh, what's the use. (JULIANA *begins to have convulsions.*) He's having that dream again. Tommy, Tommy. (*Throws a glass of water in his face.*)

JULIANA: Yes, dear?

TOM: You said you wouldn't snore.

JULIANA: What did you say, Dora Lee?

TOM: I didn't say (*A bell rings. The dripping resumes.*) anything.

JULIANA: Put a pan under it. I'll have a plumber in the morning.

TOM: I have indigestion. I've never been so sick in all my life.

JULIANA: I'm awake now. What's the matter.

TOM: I don't feel well, Tommy. Call the doctor.

JULIANA: You don't need the doctor. I'll handle it. Where does it hurt you?

TOM: Right here in the pit of my stomach, it's a shooting pain. (BORRACHA *enters wearing dog collar and chain; starts singing.*) Oh I just love that Xavier Cougat.

JULIANA: BUZZ-Z-Z-Z

TOM: Don't do that. It's a shooting pain, it comes about every five minutes.

JULIANA: How long does it last?

TOM: At least a quarter of an hour.

JULIANA: How can it last a quarter of an hour if it comes every five minutes. Huh? Huh? Huh?

AMEN *enters wearing same, speaks.*

TOM: Don't yell at me; I'm sick. If I say the pain lasts a quarter of an hour then that's how long it lasts.

JULIANA: Okay.

TOM: Ow! I think it's that meal we ate at the Captain's. The fish disagreed with me.

JULIANA: IT WOULDN'T DARE DARE DARE DARE DARE.

TOM I never want to eat there again. Every mouthful was poison. And the portions were so small.

JULIANA: Well you ate like you were condemned. (*The last word reverberates and echoes.*)

AMEN *and* BORRACHA *exit.*

TOM: Well you have to be polite when you go out to dinner. I wish we hadn't eaten anything at all. Oh, my God, I'm suffering so terrible. C-c-c-c-c-call the doctor.

JULIANA: Oh, you don't need a doctor! It's just indigestion. I know how to handle it. I'll fix you some h-h-h-hot ginger ale and oatmeal.

TOM: Hot ginger ale!

JULIANA: Make a new man out of you.

TOM: You treat me for indigestion and I'll probably die of liver trouble.

JULIANA: Listen, if I treat you for indigestion you'll die of indigestion. Now you want me to help you or not, hey? Hey? Hey?

TOM: Not if you are going to yell at me. (*Weeps.*) You wouldn't yell at Gloria Goosby if she got sick.

JULIANA: Now don't start with Gloria Goosby.

TOM: I saw the two of you at the dinner table playing footsie.

BORRACHA *enters, pantomimes singing.*

JULIANA: Footsies.

TOM: You were so flustered when she smirked at you, you couldn't eat.

JULIANA: I wasn't flustered.

TOM: Then why did you put gravy on your ice cream?

AMEN *enters, speaks.*

JULIANA: I always put gravy on my ice cream. I put gravy on anything and you know it.

AMEN *enters, speaks.*

TOM: A likely story. And the gown that woman was wearing. She ought to be arrested. I think she purposely swallowed that fish bone so you could stroke her back.

JULIANA: I didn't stroke her back, and I'd done that even if she hadn't swallowed the fish bone.

All laugh.

TOM: I don't know how Leo stands for it. Leo honey, how do you stand for it? He is such a wonderful man and Gloria is always playing sick around him just to get sympathy. (JULIANA *grunts.*) A lot you care what happens to me. Every time Gloria gets a headache Leo hugs and kisses her and fawns over her. Why don't you do that for me?

JULIANA: I'm never there when you have a headache.

TOM: Why don't you make a fuss over me?

JULIANA: Now listen, Dora Lee. You are not sick and you know it, know it . . . know it.

TOM: If you cared for me, if you cared for me, if you cared for me, you wouldn't leave me.

JULIANA: I'm not leaving you. I'm going out on business. I'll only be gone twenty-four hours.

TOM: Suppose a burglar breaks in the house and fuh-fuh-fuh-finds me?

JULIANA: It'll serve him right.

BORRACHA *sings and* AMEN *plays tambourine.* JULIANA *does a frenetic dance. Black out.*

Lights up *as* TOM *whistles "My Buddy."* JULIANA *lip-synchs his whistling.* TOM *crosses* downstage, *lies down, and goes into a yoga position with legs over his head and buttocks in the air. Sound of wolves howling.*

TOM: (*Fondling himself*) Fuck me.

JULIANA: Shh. I can't do that.

TOM: Fuck me now.

JULIANA: Shh. What do you want to do, get me in trouble?

TOM: Fuck me now.

JULIANA: Shut up! Shut up now!

TOM: Fuck me now.

JULIANA: (*Sings.*) I do not know with whom Aiden will sleep, but I do know
    that Fair Aiden will not sleep alone.

JULIANA *begins to cross* down *to* TOM. *There is a loud buzzing sound, then big band music under* ALAN'S VOICE.

ALAN: (*Voice over*) From the egg laid by night, say the birds, came Eros. We
    will cure you of your perversions. You return to your dung as a dog to its
    vomit. Come on boys, throw her out the window.

ALAN *and* BORRACHA *and* AMEN *enter.*

TOM: Oh my God, I just pissed myself.

TOM *and* JULIANA *struggle but are caught by* BORRACHA *and* AMEN.

TOM: He's feeling feisty.

ALAN: Get the bitch out of here.

9 TO 5: PART ONE

ALAN: Hey, hot stuff, grab your pad and pencil and get your buns in here.

JULIANA: Yes sir. Good morning.

ALAN: Hold it. Just hold it right there.

JULIANA: Something wrong?

ALAN: No, no nothing is wrong. I just want to check your bod. Turn around
    for a second. (*He whistles.*) Boy you have a nice ass frame. But you ought
    to get your pants cut a little tighter. You need to bring them up just a little
    in the crotch. I mean you got a nice package you might as well show it off.

JULIANA: Oh, Captain.

ALAN: Come over here I want you to take a memo. To all personnel . . . Boy
    that's a great cologne you're wearing Tommy.

JULIANA: Oh,thank you.

ALAN: Stuff's turning me on. What's it called?

JULIANA: Stud.

ALAN: STUD! (*Laughs.*) Well, it's very sexy. Only I don't like that tie you're wearing. What happened to the ones I gave you?

JULIANA: Well, nothing . . . I just . . .

ALAN: Take it off.

JULIANA: Excuse me?

ALAN: Take it off. I can't work with those stripes glaring out at me like that. And how about unbuttoning that shirt and coat. You need to loosen up. That's better. Now where were we?

JULIANA: Your memo.

ALAN: Oh yes . . . by the way I have a surprise for you here. (*Pulls out a huge strap-on dildo.*)

JULIANA: Aah! Captain. I'm a married man.

ALAN: Forget about your wife, Tommy. I mean you may be hers in the evening but you are my boy from 9 to 5. Have a look now. Isn't this pretty?

JULIANA: Yes, it's pretty. But you shouldn't be buying gifts for me, boss man.

ALAN: Captain. Call me Captain. Let me put it on you. (*Puts the dildo on JULIANA.*) Don't worry, it won't bite. If it bites we'll sue. Now that wasn't so bad was it?

JULIANA: No.

ALAN: I love your hair. It's so sexy. (*Stroking her bald head.*) Why don't we go over on the couch and I'll lock the door.

JULIANA: No.

ALAN: Oh, let's be friendly Tommy. You'll have to be a little more cooperative if you want to keep this job.

JULIANA: I'm not that kind of boy.

ALAN: Oh get off it. One little kiss.

JULIANA: No!

ALAN: What's it gonna hurt?

JULIANA: No! I won't.

ALAN: Tommy, you get back here. Tommy, I'm warning you, get back here.

JULIANA: No I won't.

ALAN: And he's out the shoot, ladies and gentlemen. He's out the shoot. Look at him. Now the Captain is gonna try and rope this one up (ALAN *lassos* JULIANA.) and he's already got him down. Ladies and gentlemen, let's see how long it takes to hog-tie this disobedient imp. (*Sounds of a stopwatch ticking*) Five seconds, ladies and gentlemen, . . . just five seconds.

(*Verdi's* Requiem *plays.* ALAN *pulls* JULIANA *over to the bed and pushes her onto it. A statue with* TOM's *face is brought on* down right.)

> Slide onto the table. A twilight sleep. We can cure you. Incisions are made in the hairline, tucking sutures down the crease at the ear to the upper neck. Using a crowbar, he breaks a bone in her leg and embuggers her. We're going to bore desire right out of you.

ALAN *exits.* TOM *appears in a doorway, whistles "My Buddy." The head of the statue is sliced off with a swinging blade.* JULIANA *stands up on the bed, and* AMEN *sticks his head through the bed and makes a birdlike cry.*

RONALD REAGAN AND THE CONCEPTUAL AUTO DISASTER

JULIANA: Today was like an old, worn out film being run off. Dim, jerky, flickering, full of cuts, with a plot I couldn't seize. (*A trumpet appears in the bed.*) Incidence of orgasms in fantasies of sexual intercourse with Ronald Reagan. Patients are provided with assembly kit photographs of sexual partners during intercourse. In each case, Reagan's face is super-imposed upon the original partner. You want me to fuck him? Vaginal intercourse with Reagan proves uniformly disappointing, producing orgasm in two percent of subjects. I can't fuck him! The preferred mode of entry overwhelmingly proves to be rectal. Forgotten voices wait for the rain. Empty condom waits for the rain. A knife blade and silence. (*Falls asleep . . . trumpet disappears . . . bell rings.*) Where am I?

ALAN: Twelve. (ALAN *keeps repeating "Faster" under* JULIANA's *speech until he exits on the line "steals his insulin."*)

JULIANA: In an extreme twelve percent of cases, the simulated anus of post-colostomy surgery generated spontaneous orgasm in ninety-eight per-cent of penetrations. (*Harp appears from under bed.*) I can't pay my bills. Better to die. I close my eyes. The archangels applaud. Multiple-track cine films were constructed of Reagan in intercourse during: A) Cam-paign speeches. Shut up. B) Rear end auto collisions with one- and three-year-old model changes. Shut up. C) With rear end assemblies. Shut up. D) With Vietnamese child atrocity victims. Shut up. (*Falls asleep.*) Where am I? (*Harp disappears.*)

ALAN: For the price of a movie ticket . . .

JULIANA: You can spend a couple of hours with a sociopathic madman with a Robin Hood complex. Watch him order the killing of oh maybe seventy or eighty guys and rub out a few himself. Then finance a hospital for the poor in his neighborhood and show his affectionate side by fondling his lawyer's breasts in a subway train. Or meet a hollowed ex-boxer who, despite having the shuffle, stubble, and odor of someone living in a storm drain, manages an affair with a gorgeous widow who cuts him in on a lucrative kidnapping scheme. He's not such a bad guy, though. When the k-k-k-kid falls into a diabetic coma, he kills the doctor who once supported him and steals his insulin.

TOM: Am I neurotic because I want a nose job?

JULIANA: Yes, yes, yes.

TOM: Will it change my personality?

JULIANA: I don't know.

TOM: What if the surgeon removes too much?

JULIANA: Was your father an overbearing ass?

TOM: I have bags under my eyes. I'm forty years old. I'm married to a man twenty years younger than me. Tell me, am I neurotic for wanting a face lift?

JULIANA: Do you have dimmed vision?

TOM: No.

JULIANA: Do you have gastric distress?

TOM: Stop asking me questions.

JULIANA: Take me with you.

TOM: I can't.

JULIANA: BUZZ-Z-Z-Z

TOM: Don't do that. Where's my head?

JULIANA: There. Sound. (*She motions "cut" and crosses* downstage.) She's bi, I've got coke, you want to party? And you going to answer me or not? Mr. Martin, I gather that your plan to remove the show to planet Venus has miscarried. Is that correct?

TOM: (*As Mr. Martin, on video*) Yeah, it looks that way. The entire film is clogged.

JULIANA: In that case, where will you go, when you go, if you go?

TOM: That's quite a problem. You see I'm on the undesirable list with every immigration department in the galaxy.

JULIANA: Use Tom Metzger's Nova number, 567–68–0515. (*Sound of police.*) Disrupt. Attack. Disappear.

TOM: (*Simultaneous with above*) Look away. Ignore. Forget.

ALAN *enters.*

JULIANA: (*To* ALAN) What do I do?

ALAN: Push. Push. Push. Push (JULIANA *climbs on the bed and pushes* AMEN's *head down till it disappears.*) Good. Sing.

BORRACHA *and* AMEN *enter and do capoeira.* JULIANA *hides behind the bed, then bangs the bed against the floor.*

JULIANA: (*Sings.*) "I am sixteen going on seventeen / innocent as a rose. / Fellows I meet will tell me I'm sweet / and willingly I believe. / I need someone older and wiser / telling me what to do."

JULIANA *pulls bed offstage.* BORRACHA, AMEN, TOM *and* JULIANA *dance the* Metropolis Dance *as skyscrapers rolled* onstage. *Stagehand appears in doorway with small coffin, which* AMEN *carries* downstage.

JULIANA: (*To audience*) Tinkerbell, Tinkerbell, you're blushing, Tinkerbell, you're blushing . . .

ALAN *enters.*

ALAN: Forget that Tinkerbell crap and get over here. (*Places the torture helmet on* JULIANA's *head.*)

9 TO 5: PART TWO

ALAN: (*To* BORRACHA) Play! (BORRACHA *begins playing conga drums as* AMEN *pounds on coffin with hammer. To* TOM) Hold it right there.

TOM: What?

ALAN: Turn around for a second.

TOM: Is something wrong—do I have something on my skirt?

ALAN: Nothing is wrong. As a matter of fact everything is very ripe.

TOM: So what do you want?

ALAN: Take a letter to Vernon Henshaw over at Metropolitan Mutual. Dear Vern, as you know, the chairman of the board of Consolidating Companies, Mr. Russell Timsworthy, spends most of his time in Brazil working on the jungle-clearing operation. My contact here . . . Dora Lee, yesterday I'm afraid I got a little carried away. I—I would just like to apologize to you.

TOM: Oh, don't you worry, Boss man.

ALAN: Captain . . . call me Captain.

TOM: I've been chased by swifter men than you and I ain't been caught yet, Captain. Shall we get back to the letter now?

ALAN: Yeah—um—well—um—could you just come over here for a minute. I have a little something for you. You know ever since I made that stupid mistake about the convention in San Francisco I . . .

TOM: Oh you didn't make a mistake, boss man. You see I'll just have to make sure the next time that I'm asked to go to work at a convention that there is a convention going on.

ALAN: And nothing happened anyway, so why don't we just forget the whole thing?

TOM: Fine.

ALAN: Dora Lee, you know you mean so much more to me than just a dumb secretary. So I bought you something. I picked it out myself. (*Pulls out a pair of fake, strap-on tits.*)

TOM: Well thank you. You didn't have to do that.

ALAN: I know I didn't have to do it. I couldn't resist. I took one look and it had

Dora Lee written all over it. (*Puts the fake tits on* TOM.) I mean it was you. Well, what do you think?

TOM: Oh, thank you sir, they're very nice.

ALAN: It's really nothing. Dora Lee, I'm a very rich man. I've got a checkbook here in my pocket—you just say the word and you can write your own figure.

TOM: Oh, I could do that now, Boss—Captain. I can write your name better than you do.

ALAN: No, Dora Lee, I'm serious. Don't you understand I'm crazy about you. You're all I ever think about.

TOM: Captain, I've told you before, I am a married woman.

ALAN: And I'm a married man. That's what makes it so tasty. Let me sit on your face. Let me sit on your face. Let me sit on your face.

TOM: Oh, go sit on your own face. The exercise will do you good.

ALAN: You dried up old whore; we're going to set your clit on fire.

I Don't Need God

TOM: I don't need God. I don't need God. (*Repeats this until he is shot.* BORRACHA *stands on* AMEN's *shoulders.* ALAN *gets a gun from an opening in the wall and hands it to* TOM. TOM *shoots himself.* TOM, BORRACHA, *and* AMEN *fall down.*)

ALAN: *Raus!*

JULIANA: Where are you going? Where are you going? (*She repeats this throughout the following.* BORRACHA *and* AMEN *place* TOM *in an incinerator.* TOM *climbs out the other side of the incinerator and begins painting himself white.* AMEN *opens the incinerator and pulls out a charred skeleton.* BORRACHA *breaks off a bone of the skeleton and brings it to* ALAN.)

ALAN: (*Holding up the bone*) The fuel! (*He places the bone inside a blender and turns it on.* BORRACHA *brings him an oil can.* ALAN *pours the contents of the blender into the can.*)

JULIANA: Eurydice! (*Word reverberates.*)

TOM: What?

JULIANA: I'm scared.

TOM: No you're not.

JULIANA: What do I do?

TOM: The place that you rip open again and again, that heals, is God. I'll be waiting for you.

JULIANA: I love you. I love you. I love—

She is cut off by ALAN *to dance the* Heaven Dance. AMEN *cries.* BORRACHA *makes fun of him. The dance ends when* ALAN *drops* JULIANA *and exits. Wolves howl.* JULIANA *stands up slowly and sings the* Lament. BORRACHA *and* AMEN *do slow capoeira. The song ends.* TOM *enters dressed as the travel agent lady and screams. A motorcycle is brought on* center stage. BORRACHA *puts a motorcycle jacket on* JULIANA *and lies on the floor with his head on her feet.*

TOM: Going to hell, dear? Looking for the perfect travel package? At the tip of the Baja Peninsula lies a land of beginnings. Horseback riding over the desert bluffs or relaxing under a palaba. Windsurfing across the sea or scuba diving under it. Things go better with Coke, dear, right? Or so they say. Just try asking Roscoe "Fatty" Arbuckle and Virginia "Boom Boom" Rappe, the best-dressed girl in the movies, 1918. When driving in a strange city remember this: discourtesy to pedestrians can turn out to be manslaughter. First advice, that'll be a dime. (*To the audience*) That'll be a dime. Are we dealing with the English as a Second Language class here? That'll be a dime, one-tenth of a dollar. Fork it over. You—front row center—I saw you put that booger under your seat before the show. Booger, booger, booger, booger, right down front, I said it and I'm glad. Well, if your conscience gets the better of you, lay that dime right down on the edge of the stage—I'll be looking for it. If you dream of dying beneath the midnight sun, take only a few intimate, personal items with you as luggage, dear. Why load yourself down? Second advice, that will be a quarter.

JULIANA and TOM: Like the pig who lay on a barrow dead, eyes closed, pink, white eyelashes, trotters stuck straight out behind.

TOM: Move him out boys. (BORRACHA *and* AMEN *pick* JULIANA *up on their shoulders, run a full circle of the stage then seat her on the motorcycle.*) Frankly I don't care if you threw this puppy out the window. Move—move—move—move. Here's a bonus travel tip, my dears. When traveling in strange lands, you should always carry a few assorted sweets about your person to distribute amongst the native youngsters. (*He throws candies into the audience.*) Otherwise there's no guarantee the little fuckers won't get you flat on your ass in some historic plaza and commence to rend and eat your flesh. Katharine Hepburn, *Suddenly Last Summer.* Now look here. Where you're going there's no tourist information, no American Express, no currency exchange, no post office, no telephone, no trains, no embassy, no budget travel, no medical assistance, no habla ingles, no kissing madam, no pissing sir, and for God's sake, no fucking in public. Twenty minutes of silence followed from Fatty's bedroom, broken by a piercing scream. (*Video image of a woman screaming.*)

ALAN: (*Appearing in doorway*) If you lose all your money, don't fret. The pay phones don't work! (*Exits.*)

TOM: Also, don't take all of the family jewels with you. Other than the ones you . . . carry between your legs! (*He grabs* JULIANA's *crotch. She yells.*) Say, that's quite a cucumber you got there. Well! That still leaves Fatty Arbuckle in his hotel room, with Virginia "Boom Boom" Rappe in his room, Best-Dressed Girl in the Movies, 1918, who may, or may not, have a Coke bottle rammed up her twat. P-p-p-p-p-poor Fatty! He really got fucked! But not, as it turned out, by Virginia! Now remember. If you make every game a life and death proposition, you're gonna have problems. For one thing, you'll be dead a lot. (*To* AMEN, *who's been drumming*) Why don't you shitcan the jungle atmosphere, honey, I can't hear myself think. (AMEN *stops. To* BORRACHA, *who's been doing capoeira and yelling in Portuguese*) Take a break, José.

BORRACHA: (*To* TOM) Puta!

TOM: (*To* JULIANA) Time to go, Sport. Will you write? Don't worry, I will never be far from the telephone. Here's your fuel. (*Pours fuel from can into motorcycle.*) Where's my dough? (*Pulls a wad of bills out of* JULIANA's *pocket.*) Just remember. We're making a movie here, and you're . . the star. (*Pause*) Where you're headed, there's a clock that never strikes. There's a hollow with a nest of white beasts. The paths are rough. The hillocks are covered with broom. This can only be the end of the world. (*Takes out ignition key.*) And I alone have the key to this savage sideshow. (TOM *turns on the motorcycle, exits laughing.*)

Music. BORRACHA *and* AMEN *enter and dance.* JULIANA *rides the motorcycle with a video image of the road behind her. The dance ends with a video image of a crash.* BORRACHA *and* AMEN *push* JULIANA *and the motorcycle off* left *as* ALAN *and* TOM *enter* right. ALAN *places torture helmet on* TOM. BORRACHA *reenters, stands and pants like a dog.* ALAN *pats* BORRACHA's *head.*

OVERTURE TO FOREST

As BORRACHA *and* AMEN *push* JULIANA *and the motorcycle offstage left,* TOM *and* ALAN *enter from stage right and cross to their positions.* BORRACHA *runs back to* TOM *and attaches the helmet to his head, then crosses on his hands and feet to* ALAN *and pants like a dog under dialogue. Trees flown in; image of forest on screen.*

ALAN: You're deaf. You're dumb. You're deaf. You're dumb.

ALAN, TOM, *and* JULIANA's *next lines are said at the same time.*

ALAN: You're deaf. You're dumb. You're deaf. You're dumb. You're deaf. You're dumb. You're deaf. You're dumb. You're blind. You're deaf. You're dumb. You're blind. You're deaf. You're dumb. You're blind. You're deaf. You're dumb. You're blind. You're deaf. You're dumb. You're blind. I'll release black widows in your granny's outhouse. What will you do?

TOM: I'm deaf. I'm dumb. I'm deaf. I'm dumb. I'm deaf. I'm dumb. I'm deaf. I'm dumb. I'm deaf. I'm dumb. I'm deaf. I'm dumb. I'm blind. I'm deaf. I'm dumb. I'm blind. I'm deaf. I'm dumb. I'm blind. I'm deaf. I'm dumb. I'm blind. I'm deaf. I'm dumb. I'm blind. I will, I will, I will.

JULIANA: (*From offstage*) No you're not. (*Repeated at five-second intervals*)

ALAN: I'll release black widows in your granny's outhouse. What will you do?

TOM: I will—I will—

ALAN: I'll put sulfuric acid in your Listerine. What will you do?

TOM: I will—I will—I will—

ALAN: You are safe here. No one can touch you. But safety is the most dangerous of all conditions. Yes?

TOM: He's coming for me. I feel it in the pit of my stomach.

ALAN: He won't get anywhere. Let the dead bury the dead.

TOM: But mother, how the fuck is that possible?

ALAN: Don't be coarse. It's just a figure of speech.

JULIANA: (*Appearing half-dressed in armor at doorway*) Where was I?

TOM *and* ALAN'S *next lines are said at the same time.*

TOM: He's coming. He's coming.

ALAN: Dahling, you look like a bit of ancient Egyptian kitsch. Just say no.

JULIANA and TOM: No?

JULIANA: BUZZZZZZZ

TOM: Don't do that! My mother tried to kill me by poisoning me with arsenic because she wanted to collect the life insurance money.

ALAN: You're joking.

TOM: No I'm not. Vampires only come out at night. But she didn't succeed. The doctors at the hospital discovered it and then I testified against her. That's the way it goes with evil and crime. You do it and then it comes back to you.

ALAN: Wo er sich versteckt?

TOM: I don't know.

ALAN: Wo er sich versteckt?

TOM: I don't KNOW!

ALAN *burns* TOM *with his cigar.*

ALAN: We're making a movie and you're the star!

TOM: You think you can buy talent and then throw it out when you've wrung it dry?

ALAN: It's important to make up for the things you fuck up.

TOM: He's coming for me, my studpuppy.

ALAN: Liebst du ihn noch?

TOM: I don't know.

ALAN: Liebst du ihn noch?

TOM: I don't know.

ALAN *burns* TOM *with his cigar.*

ALAN: (*Removes helmet from* TOM'S *head.*) *Raus!* (*Sings.*) "Nights are long since you went away. I think about you all through the day, my buddy, my buddy. Nobody quite so true. Miss your voice, the touch of your hand.

Just long to know that you understand, my buddy, my buddy. Your buddy misses you."

ALAN *and* TOM *dance the* Heaven Dance. *Trees flown offstage.* ALAN *drops* TOM *and exits.* TOM *drags himself off.* JULIANA, *wearing full armor, is pushed in on a wooden boat. A huge blue cloth is stretched across the stage, then disappears as* BORRACHA *enters as the dragon.* JULIANA *slays* BORRACHA *the dragon.*

INTERROGATION

Rockets rolled onstage. One is rotated to reveal torture unit. TOM *climbs onto it.* JULIANA *removes her armor. Video of* JULIANA *undressing with cast members watching.* ALAN *enters and sits in a chair.* BORRACHA *and* AMEN, *wearing medieval dresses, play capoeira instruments.*

TOM: Ladies, are you fed up with salads instead of meals? Now you can find a heaven no man can touch. Tonight's my night for a miracle. Don't count your calories a moment longer, ladies, count your happinesses instead. He's coming for me, my studpuppy. Now you can twirl up a plateful of pasta, bury your mug in a bowl full of Häagen Dazs, or just tap into what makes you high—high—high—hiya kids, hiya, hiya! Introducing the amazing new weight-loss program from Phyllis Schlafly. No lies, ladies. With Phyllis's amazing new program, you can consume, dine, feast, feed, graze, nibble, snack, chomp, ingest, inhale, absorb, chew, nosh, gnaw, guzzle, masticate, pig out, gorge, gobble, and stuff your face. Tonight's my night for a miracle. Under the guidance of one of Phyllis's trained technicians, make a small incision in the soft part of your upper arm. Hiya kids, hiya, hiya! Let the blood and the fat flow. He's coming for me, my studpuppy. Under the guidance of one of Phyllis's trained technicians, make a small incision in the soft part of your inner upper thigh. Tonight's my night for a miracle. Now you'll be waist deep in pools of liquid flesh. Yuck. Step out, shower off, for the next step is to eat.

AMEN *speaks a line in Portuguese.* BORRACHA *answers in Portuguese.*

ALAN: Is that what they call a Mona Lisa smile?

JULIANA: I can't make decisions at all anymore.

ALAN: Is London Bridge falling down?

JULIANA: There will be no more war, there will only be weapons.

ALAN: What do you want?

JULIANA: My wife.

TOM: He's come.

ALAN: Do you love your country?

JULIANA: Is my ass worth that much to you?

ALAN: Fucking should be devoted to the business of procreation.

The Hip-Hop Waltz of Eurydice ◆◆ 487

JULIANA: On the rack, pregnant, the woman, the hangman binds. Heart would fain, he racks her till break.

ALAN: Have you ever stolen any material—books, magazines, small amounts of cash, office supplies, etc. from your place of employment or college library? Explain.

JULIANA: I don't know how many people were in the bathroom with me.

ALAN: How about the other guy that was in there with him? Do you know him? Do you know your condition is pretty serious, Martin? Can you hear me, Martin?

BORRACHA and AMEN: Yes.

ALAN: Can you hear me?

BORRACHA and AMEN: Yes.

TOM: The question of a fatally wounded man.

JULIANA: The dog soldiers are on line to assassinate the governor of South Dakota.

ALAN: Shut up.

JULIANA: Head it burned, over oil it poured, not confess.

ALAN: Shut up.

JULIANA: Sulfur, armpit burned, placed in her . . .

ALAN: How would you feel in an area that had no running water, toilet facilities, or where you would be forced to spend extended periods of time in a tent? Don't respond. Sit down.

JULIANA: Of course I do. That's why I'm here.

ALAN: Sit down. Take a load off your feet as they say . . . and unless my eyes deceive me you have quite a load.

JULIANA: Did you fart?

ALAN: Why of course, dahling. Do you think I always smell like this?

JULIANA: Never mind. I give up. . . . I'll do the dishes.

ALAN: I got up from the chair to greet Suzette.

JULIANA: Set up! (ALAN *fires rifle*.)

ALAN: I couldn't conceal my anxious expectancy.

JULIANA: Set up! (ALAN *fires rifle*.)

ALAN: It had been days since I'd seen her.

JULIANA: Set up! (ALAN *fires rifle*.)

ALAN: And my heart was conscious of the absence.

JULIANA: Set up! (ALAN *fires rifle*.)

ALAN: I waited at the door.

JULIANA: Set up! (ALAN *fires rifle*.)

ALAN: Did you say Egyptian gods?

BORRACHA and JULIANA and AMEN: Yes.

ALAN: Did she say Egyptian gods? What a coincidence.

JULIANA: What kind of coincidence?

ALAN: Oh, there's the nicest little man.

JULIANA and TOM: Where?

ALAN: Call me when you're ready to come home. I don't want you out in the junkyard tonight.

JULIANA: Don't worry, mother. Peter will be with me.

ALAN: The door opened and then Suzette appeared, radiant in her skin tight klemperer . . . whatever that means.

JULIANA: I blame myself all the time for my faults.

ALAN: Would you rather serve in the overt or covert capacity?

JULIANA: I blame myself for everything bad that happens.

ALAN: Did you ever lose your luggage?

JULIANA: I don't have any thoughts of killing myself.

ALAN: Do you want a shave and a haircut?

JULIANA: I have thoughts of killing myself, but I would not carry them out.

ALAN: Would you betray the trust of someone who has supplied you with valuable information?

JULIANA: I would like to kill myself.

ALAN: We're making a movie and you're the star!

JULIANA: I would like to kill myself if I had the chance.

ALAN: The police are with us. Are you thirsty?

JULIANA and TOM speak at the same time.

TOM: Yes I am. Yes I am. Yes I am.

JULIANA: Give this man a dozen. Overseer, overseer, give this man a dozen.

ALAN: Are you thirsty?

JULIANA: Tied, dropped suddenly from the ceiling, hands, hauled up . . . the hangman and his helpers went to lunch.

ALAN: Are you thirsty?

JULIANA: Mother told us not to play in the woods for the next few days and we obeyed her.

ALAN: Well, she was a foolish woman. A good quality water pistol filled with freshly squeezed lemon juice is the ticket. You shoot the felonious fur ball right in the eyes and it will soon stop the canine harassment.

JULIANA: Soft white male, age thirty-five, wants to play with black lady with large buttocks. Bi couples welcomed for Greek and French culture.

ALAN: There was a bit of nastiness last night, yes? I once shot a big nasty cur with the juice and he never bothered me again. Dead animals are so useful, don't you agree?

JULIANA: Why should fucking be devoted to the business of procreation?

ALAN: I've never believed in getting too intimate with the help.

JULIANA: But you have. But you have. But you have.

ALAN: What is the best type of agent? A) An adventurer (ALAN *lowers screw into* TOM—TOM *screams.*) B) A pacifist. (ALAN *raises screw—*TOM *screams.*) C) A combination of the adventurer-pacifist. (ALAN *lowers screw—*TOM *screams.*)

JULIANA: (*Pants for 20 seconds.*) What's an adventurer?

ALAN: The adventurer does it for thrills. Set up! (ALAN *places a pomegranate on* JULIANA's *head, then shoots it off.*)

JULIANA: Imagine for a minute, Billy, that you're one of my toes.

ALAN: Do you take orders well?

JULIANA: That you're a part of me. That you're unhappy.

ALAN: Can you carry out a direct personal command from your superior if you disagree with it?

JULIANA: The place that you rip open again and again, that heals, is God.

ALAN: Have you ever lied about your name, occupation, salary, or place of residence?

JULIANA: The place that you rip open again and again, that heals, is God.

ALAN: Shut up.

JULIANA: The place that you rip open again and again, that heals, is God.

ALAN: Shut up.

JULIANA: It's okay to show a man getting his balls kicked on TV, but not okay to show him getting his balls stroked. What do you want from me?

ALAN: I want your snails, your snakes, your groundhogs, your weasels, your Japanese beetles. You can't desire her.

JULIANA: Many Englishmen feel that flogging is the only answer to the growing problem of the "teddyboys." Do you?

ALAN: I don't know. I'll think about that.

All laugh.

JULIANA: I'll take her.

ALAN: You can take her, but you can't fuck her, or else I'll leave you with a mess of pet maggots to raise.

JULIANA: I'll take her.

ALAN: You'll take her, but you can't desire to fuck her.

JULIANA: It's okay to show a man getting his balls kicked on TV, but not okay to show him getting his balls stroked.

ALAN: Right. Don't touch.

JULIANA: I will. The agency does not believe in letting you stagnate in one position throughout your Agency career. Your upward mobility in the Agency is limited only by your own ambitions. Over and out.

TOM: Tonight is my night for a miracle. He's coming for me, my studpuppy.

ALAN: Have a pomegranate. (*Tosses a pomegranate to* JULIANA.)

TOM: DON'T.

ALAN: EAT.

TOM: DON'T.

ALAN: EAT.

TOM: DON'T.

ALAN: EAT.

TOM: DON'T.

ALAN: EAT.

TOM: DON'T.

ALAN: EAT.

JULIANA: I'm thirsty. (*Eats.*)

TOM: Don't swallow the seeds!

ALAN *exits.* JULIANA *sees* TOM, *crosses to him. They embrace and lie down.* BORRACHA *and* AMEN *sing. End of song.* TOM *gets up off floor.* BORRACHA *and* AMEN *exit. A twelve-foot penis comes up out of floor.* TOM *turns and reaches for it.* ALAN *shoots it down.* JULIANA *sits up and screams.*

ALAN'S FINAL SOLUTION

ALAN: One God. One Party.

TOM: I'm queer. I'm queer. I'm queer. What's it to you, you fat PIG! Hey. Hey. Hey. Ha. Ha.

JULIANA *staggers toward* ALAN, *pulls gun away from him, and exits.*

ALAN: Anyone want a shave and a haircut? A close shave. Anyone want a haircut? You! (*Crosses down* into the house.) Do you believe God will touch you? I want to avoid a face-lift. Does it make sense for me to do facial exercises like clenching my teeth and so on? One of the things about male Oriental whores—when you buy them, their body is yours to do whatever you want.

TOM: Tonight's my night for miracle . . (*Continues under* ALAN's *monologue.*)

ALAN: Roger, she died three months ago. You showed me a copy of the death certificate. Don't you remember? This one was old enough to know the score and had been to the bar before. So we go in, we go in and have another beer. Where's my Blue Lady? Where's my Blue Lady? (*Goes to Blue Lady.*) Blue Lady, love's going to get you. Love's going to get you. Love's going to get you. Always be as well dressed as your circumstances will permit. THESE ARE THE ANSWERS. Remember these answers. Number 1) Mazda. Number 2) Citizen Kane. Number 3) Quantum mechanics. Number 4) Forty-eight pounds. Remember. I slip this guy another five and he's all smiles. Well I wasn't going to stand around looking like a freak. So I started undressing and ordered the kid—his name was Safi—to do the same. (*To* TOM, *who has stopped his ad-libs*) Why are you stopping? Don't stop. Don't stop. Go. Go. Go. Tonight you will be robbed of your Rolex. You will crash your car. Your house has burned down. Your baby suffocates in its crib. The babysitter gets stoned. There will be an earthquake. Iraq has the atom bomb. The ceiling above you will collapse. The man next to you is going crazy. Your wife wishes to murder you.

JULIANA: Liar, liar, liar.

ALAN: You'll lose your job. Number 5) Islam. Number 6) The fatal flaw. Number 7) Wise Man. Number 8) Après moi le déluge. Remember. (*To Blue Lady*) I have a card in my pocket with something written on it, and I would like you to read it to me in a low, clear voice. (*He hands the Blue Lady the card.*)

AUDIENCE MEMBER: I'm a self-starter. I enjoy and am excited by producing.

ALAN: (*To Blue Lady*) We're making a movie and you're the star! You believe that? Busy young creatures, you don't have a chance. So we all get up and I order beers for me and my whore. I got my drink and took Safi over to a small table by the wall and had him start sucking. Judas is posing with the Bee Gees in a white leisure suit. No one could replace Andy Gibb. Ashes, whiskey, and tears.

TOM: Do you know "Mrs. Miller's Greatest Hits"? I miss you. Come and get me.

ALAN: I don't want him to go. My memory is failing. My bladder is weak. My arches are falling. My tonsils and adenoids are gone. My jawbone is rotting, and now my little boy wants to cast me away and leave me behind. I'll end up in a geriatric ward. I'll have to have enemas. I will be incontinent. There's a heart miracle taking place! You! Stand up, put your hand over your heart and call that a miracle. You! Lift up your head and call that a miracle. Tonight's my night for a miracle. . . .

TOM: Do your flower beds have barren or weed-choked areas? Do they lack color?

ALAN: Shut up. Chico, you're so groovy. About this same time a marine busted his nuts in this guy's ass. And one of the sailors got up on a table and told a kid to suck his cock. You! With the glasses . . . am I neurotic for wanting a face-lift? Remember these. Number 9) The Tower of London. Number 10) You could have had a V-8. Number 11) Dietrich Bonhoeffer. What if Noah had failed? (*Wolves howl.*) A lady may remove her gloves or not when partaking of supper. Guests do not bid their hostess good-bye; they quietly withdraw.

TOM: As you examine your personal landscape do you see anything else you don't like or would like improved?

ALAN: Shut up. Boy, I couldn't take no more. I started busting my nuts and

Safi started sucking cum from my cock till I was weak. (*He sings.*) "Love, your magic spell is everywhere. Love, I saw you and I knew . . ."

They had this rice wine and I started drinking it. I got drunker than a coot. We are as driven to kill as we are to live and let live. Isn't that so? I heard that. I picked up the bottle and I smashed it on his face, he dropped to the floor. Everyone turned. No one said a word. Round and firm and fully packed, I crowned the Shenandoah Apple Queen. Men don't get smarter as they get older. They just lose their hair. Isn't that so? I heard that. (*To* TOM) Why are you stopping? Don't stop. Don't stop. Go. Go. Go. Healing is like ringing the dinner bell to lure sinners to salvation. Isn't that so. I heard that. Before you kill somebody, make sure he isn't well connected. Here lies old Fred. It's a pity he's dead . . . I am obsessed with the little toe on my left foot. It is turning into a claw. A species that is going nowhere. And I'm having to do this alone. Not like Cousteau with his assiduous team aboard the sun-flooded schooner but here. Alone. Alone. Alone.

Question number 1) What is the name shared by the Zoroastrian Creator God of Light and a popular car? Question number 2) What film was consistently booed at the 1940 Academy Awards? Question number 3) What does the Heisenberg Uncertainty Principle apply to? Question number 4) What did Oprah Winfrey Lose? Question number 5) What is Arabic for submission to God's will? Question number 6) What did Louis XV never really say? Question number 7) Where were the little princes kept? Question number 8) Who said religion should take place in the marketplace of life? Question number 9) What is the phrase which illustrates the economic principle of opportunity cost?

You could have had a V-8. You fucked up. (*He chops off his finger. Scream begins and continues under* Ballroom Dance.) I'd like to cut off a dead man's member and have it sewn onto me. I should like to be a man. I should like to rob a dead man's soul before it went to heaven and turn myself into a man. I would then seduce all women. I want to taste every man and every girl. I believe you are too good for this calling. I'd like to wallow in something, just so that I can say I've wallowed in it. I know it now. I'd like to wallow in corpses. I want to be stronger and stronger. I have never had a facial injury. I think I'd go mad if I ever did. Is my body now obsolete? Is my body now obsolete? (*A tiny casket is lowered.* ALAN *opens the casket and the sound of the scream moves into it. He turns and throws the casket towards the video screen. Video Image of a casket crashing through a window.* Blackout.)

BORRACHA *and* AMEN *dance with machetes in semi-darkness.* JULIANA *opens upstage door and leans through.*

JULIANA (*Whispering at door*) Go and wash yourself, I'm coming to get you. (*Repeats until stage* lights *are brought up, then closes door.* ALAN *crosses upstage* to door and bangs on it.)

ALAN: Öffnen die Tür. (*He repeats this ten times.*)

The entire back wall collapses. JULIANA *is revealed as the Blue Angel carrying a sword.* ALAN *and* JULIANA *walk slowly* downstage. JULIANA *stabs* ALAN. BORRACHA *and* AMEN *embrace.* TOM *crawls out of a trap door.* ALAN *dies. A blue curtain slowly closes.*

While the blue curtain remains closed, a Wonder Woman radio show is played. BORRACHA *comes through the curtain carrying a tray of cookies and condoms. He throws cookies and condoms into the audience, then exits through the curtain. The curtain is drawn revealing* TOM *and* JULIANA *posed in a pastoral scene.*

TOM: Darling, I thought that fat slob would never shut up.

JULIANA: I want to be alone with you forever. My application to enter the United States has arrived.

TOM: Wonderful! Hurry and fill it out. I'll help you.

They dance downstage *saying "Am I right?" "You are wrong." "Are you wrong?" "Right I am." etc., until they reach their next position.*

TOM: Oh, if I had to sail for home without you, I'd just shoot myself.

JULIANA: No, you wouldn't.

TOM: You're right, I probably wouldn't.

They dance across right, *again alternating the lines "Am I right?" "You are wrong," etc., until they reach the next position.*

TOM: Darling, was it bad?

JULIANA: I'd rather not talk about that.

TOM: Whatever you say.

They dance to center *repeating "Am I right," "Am I wrong" sequence.*

JULIANA: You're a trusting soul, aren't you?

TOM: You didn't kiss me good night.

JULIANA: I am you.

TOM: You I am.

JULIANA: Wanderers cling to their fading homes.

TOM: (*As they break away and move* downstage *doing a chorus line kick step*) You didn't kiss me good night!

JULIANA: What's red and sits in the corner?

TOM: What darling?

JULIANA: What's red and sits in the corner?

TOM: What darling.

JULIANA: (*As they meet in the middle*) A baby chewing on a razor blade.

An upside down tree flies in with a baby in its branches: Sound of a baby crying. TOM *walks towards it, sits down in lotus position.* JULIANA *falls asleep on the floor. Sound of snoring.*

TOM: Oh please, not that again, quit it!

JULIANA: (*Waking up, rising to her feet*) What is it?

TOM: There must be something that will put an end to that hideous snoring. Why do you do it?

JULIANA: Do what?

TOM: Snore. (JULIANA *turns and crosses to* TOM, *grabs his wrists.*) I'm going out of my mind (JULIANA *pulls* TOM *around;* BORRACHA *appears behind the window upstage.*) For years you've been telling people you have insomnia. Not only do you sleep like a log, but you sound like you're sawing it! The house could fall down and you'd never know it!

JULIANA: (*As she and* TOM *slide step away from each other*) Very funny.

TOM: It's not funny, it's tragic.

JULIANA: Say something nice.

TOM: I love you.

They run and embrace center.

JULIANA: The secret of flesh is in the lost Mayan books. All the forces of suppression have now converged on Mexico to find these books and prevent a new race of beings on this planet.

TOM: Darling, Ornament Magazine is here to take our picture. Smile. (*They smile. A flash. They press their heads together and turn left, right, and then a full circle. Sound of conga drums. They sink to the floor. Sound of knocking.* JULIANA *stands up and drags* TOM *slowly across the floor.*) Oh there's that boy again. I told him before we didn't want any cookies. (*To* BORRACHA *in the window*) Please go away. We don't want any cookies. (TOM *and* JULIANA *freeze for a moment. Then* JULIANA *crosses to the tree, detaches baby, and carries it* upstage, *reciting a Danish children's rhyme.* TOM *mimes rocking the baby.*)

TOM: Oh, the baby. Oh, the baby. Oh, the pretty baby. (TOM *crosses up to* JULIANA *and the baby, then goes offstage and returns with a papier-mâché turkey.*)

AMEN *enters dressed as a milkman, carrying bottles. Sound of Nat King Cole singing Christmas carols.*

TOM: (*To* AMEN) Merry Christmas, Mr. Howard.

AMEN: Thank you. (*Picks up empty bottles and leaves full ones*). Merry Christmas, Ma'am. (*Turns to leave but doesn't.*)

JULIANA *hands the baby to* TOM *and crosses to get the milk. She comes back to the table, pours a glass of milk, and pulls a leg off the turkey and puts it on a plate. She takes the plate and glass to* BORRACHA, *who is still standing behind the window.* ALAN *shuffles on* stage left, *out of fatsuit and wearing dingy longjohns.* JULIANA *crosses to the lawnmower and begins to mow.*

ALAN: 1) At night I am woken up, bathed in sweat, by a cough which strangles me. My room is too small. It is full of archangels. 2) I know I have loved too much. I have stuffed too many bodies, used up too many orange skies. I ought to be stamped out. 3) The thin white bodies, the softest of them, have stolen my warmth, they went away from me fat. Now I'm thin and freezing. Many blankets are piled on top of me. I'm suffocating. 4) I suspect they will want to fumigate me with incense. My room is flooded with holy water. They say I have got Holy Water Dropsy. And that's fatal. 5) My sweethearts bring a bit of quicklime with them in hands which I have kissed. The bill comes for the orange skies, the bodies, and the rest. I cannot pay it. 6) Better to die. I lean back. I close my eyes. The arch-angels applaud.

During ALAN's *monologue,* JULIANA *stops mowing, crosses to the sink and washes compulsively. The faucet begins to drip.* TOM *and* JULIANA *kiss.* JULIANA *takes the baby from* TOM.

JULIANA: (*Singing to the baby*) Tinkerbell, Tinkerbell, back from hell, we wish you well. (*Spoken*) Little fat man, lick the pot man, tallest man, gilded man, little St. Peter the actor man. (*Wolves howl.* JULIANA *sings.*) "Children of the Heavenly Father / safely in His bosom gather / nestling bird or star in Heaven / ne'er a refuge e'er was given.

Lights slowly fade.

THE END

Far Away

Caryl Churchill

CHARACTERS

JOAN, *a girl*
HARPER, *her aunt*
TODD, *a young man*

The Parade (Scene 2.5): five is too few and twenty better than ten. A hundred?

1.

HARPER's *house. Night.*
JOAN: I can't sleep.
HARPER: It's the strange bed.
JOAN: No, I like different places.
HARPER: Are you cold?
JOAN: No.
HARPER: Do you want a drink?
JOAN: I think I am cold.
HARPER: That's easy enough then. There's extra blankets in the cupboard.
JOAN: Is it late?

Reprinted from Caryl Churchill, *Far Away* (New York: Theater Communications Group, 2001). Reprinted by permission of Nick Hern Books.

HARPER: Two.

JOAN: Are you going to bed?

HARPER: Do you want a hot drink?

JOAN: No thank you.

HARPER: I should go to bed then.

JOAN: Yes.

HARPER: It's always odd in a new place. When you've been here a week you'll look back at tonight and it won't seem the same at all.

JOAN: I've been to a lot of places. I've stayed with friends at their houses. I don't miss my parents if you think that.

HARPER: Do you miss your dog?

JOAN: I miss the cat I think.

HARPER: Does it sleep on your bed?

JOAN: No because I chase it off. But it gets in if the door's not properly shut. You think you've shut the door but it hasn't caught and she pushes it open in the night.

HARPER: Come here a minute. You're shivering. Are you hot?

JOAN: No, I'm all right.

HARPER: You're over-tired. Go to bed. I'm going to bed myself.

JOAN: I went out.

HARPER: When? just now?

JOAN: Just now.

HARPER: No wonder you're cold. It's hot in the daytime here but it's cold at night.

JOAN: The stars are brighter here than at home.

HARPER: It's because there's no street lights.

JOAN: I couldn't see much.

HARPER: I don't expect you could. How did you get out? I didn't hear the door.

JOAN: I went out the window.

HARPER: I'm not sure I like that.

JOAN: No it's quite safe, there's a roof and a tree.

HARPER: When people go to bed they should stay in bed. Do you climb out of the window at home?

JOAN: I can't at home because—No I don't.

HARPER: I'm responsible for you.

JOAN: Yes, I'm sorry.

HARPER: Well that's enough adventures for one night. You'll sleep now. Off you go. Look at you, you're asleep on your feet.

JOAN: There was a reason.

HARPER: For going out?

JOAN: I heard a noise.

HARPER: An owl?

JOAN: A shriek.

HARPER: An owl then. There are all sorts of birds here, you might see a golden oriole. People come here specially to watch birds and we sometimes make tea or coffee or sell bottles of water because there's no café and people don't expect that and they get thirsty. You'll see in the morning what a beautiful place it is.

JOAN: It was more like a person screaming.

HARPER: It is like a person screaming when you hear an owl.

JOAN: It was a person screaming.

HARPER: Poor girl, what a fright you must have had imagining you heard somebody screaming. You should have come straight down here to me.

JOAN: I wanted to see.

HARPER: It was dark.

JOAN: Yes but I did see.

HARPER: Now what did you imagine you saw in the dark?

JOAN: I saw my uncle.

HARPER: Yes I expect you did. He likes a breath of air. He wasn't screaming I hope?

JOAN: No.

HARPER: That's all right then. Did you talk to him? I'll expect you were frightened he'd say what are you doing out of your bed so late.

JOAN: I stayed in the tree.

HARPER: He didn't see you?

JOAN: No.

HARPER: He'll be surprised won't he, he'll laugh when he hears you were up in the tree. He'll be cross but he doesn't mean it, he'll think it's a good joke, it's the sort of thing he did when he was a boy. So bed now. I'll go up too.

JOAN: He was pushing someone. He was bundling someone into a shed.

HARPER: He must have been putting a big sack in the shed. He works too late.

JOAN: I'm not sure if it was a woman. It could have been a young man.

HARPER: Well I have to tell you, when you've been married as long as I have. There are things people get up to, it's natural, it's nothing bad, that's just friends of his your uncle was having a little party with.

JOAN: Was it a party?

HARPER: Just a little party.

JOAN: Yes because there wasn't just that one person.

HARPER: No, there'd be a few of his friends.

JOAN: There was a lorry.

HARPER: Yes, I expect there was.

JOAN: When I put my ear against the side of the lorry I heard crying inside.

HARPER: How could you do that from up in the tree?

JOAN: I got down from tree. I went to the lorry after I looked in the window of the shed.

HARPER: There might be things that are not your business when you're a visitor in someone else's house.

JOAN: Yes, I'd rather not have seen. I'm sorry.

HARPER: Nobody saw you?

JOAN: They were thinking about themselves.

HARPER: I think it's lucky nobody saw you.

JOAN: If it's a party, why was there so much blood?

HARPER: There isn't any blood.

JOAN: Yes.

HARPER: Where?

JOAN: On the ground.

HARPER: In the dark? how would you see that in the dark?

JOAN: I slipped in it.

She holds up her bare foot.

I mostly wiped it off.

HARPER: That's where the dog got run over this afternoon.

JOAN: Wouldn't it have dried up?

HARPER: Not if the ground was muddy.

JOAN: What sort of dog?

HARPER: A big dog, a big mongrel.

JOAN: That's awful, you must be very sad, had you had him long?

HARPER: No, he was young, he ran out, he was never very obedient, a lorry was backing up.

JOAN: What was his name?

HARPER: Flash.

JOAN: What colour was he?

HARPER: Black with a bit of white.

JOAN: Why were the children in the shed?

HARPER: What children?

JOAN: Don't you know what children?

HARPER: How could you see there were children?

JOAN: There was a light on. That's how I could see the blood inside the shed. I could see the faces and which ones had blood on.

HARPER: You've found out something secret. You know that don't you?

JOAN: Yes.

HARPER: Something you shouldn't know.

JOAN: Yes I'm sorry.

HARPER: Something you must never talk about. Because if you do you could put people's lives in danger.

JOAN: Why? who from? from my uncle?

HARPER: Of course not from your uncle.

JOAN: From you?

HARPER: Of course not from me, are you mad? I'm going to tell you what's going on. Your uncle is helping these people. He's helping them escape. He's giving them shelter. Some of them were still in the lorry, that's why they were crying. Your uncle's going to take them all into the shed and then they'll be all right.

JOAN: They had blood on their faces.

HARPER: That's from before. That's because they were attacked by the people your uncle's saving them from.

JOAN: There was blood on the ground.

HARPER: One of them was injured very badly but your uncle bandaged him up.

JOAN: He's helping them.

HARPER: That's right.

JOAN: There wasn't a dog. There wasn't a party.

HARPER: No, I'm trusting you with the truth now. You must never talk about it or you'll put your uncle's life in danger and mine and even your own. You won't even say anything to your parents.

JOAN: Why did you have me to stay if you've got this secret going on?

HARPER: The lorry should have come yesterday. It won't happen again while you're here.

JOAN: It can now because I know. You don't have to stop for me. I could help uncle in the shed and look after them.

HARPER: No, he has to do it himself. But thank you for offering, that's very kind. So after all that excitement do you think you could go back to bed?

JOAN: Why was uncle hitting them?

HARPER: Hitting who?

JOAN: He was hitting a man with a stick. I think the stick was metal. He hit one of the children.

HARPER: One of the people in the lorry was a traitor. He wasn't really one of them, he was pretending, he was going to betray them, they found out and told your uncle. Then he attacked your uncle, he attacked the other people, your uncle had to fight him.

JOAN: That's why there was so much blood.

HARPER: Yes, it had to be done to save the others.

JOAN: He hit one of the children.

HARPER: That would have been the child of the traitor. Or sometimes you get bad children who even betray their parents.

JOAN: What's going to happen?

HARPER: They'll go off in the lorry very early in the morning.

JOAN: Where to?

HARPER: Where they're escaping to. You don't want to have to keep any more secrets.

JOAN: He only hit the traitors.

HARPER: Of course. I'm not surprised you can't sleep, what an upsetting thing to see. But now you understand, it's not so bad. You're part of a big movement now to make things better. You can be proud of that. You can look at the stars and think here we are in our little bit of space, and I'm on the side of the people who are putting things right, and your soul will expand right into the sky.

JOAN: Can't I help?

HARPER: You can help me clean up in the morning. Will you do that?

JOAN: Yes.

HARPER: So you'd better get some sleep.

2.

Several years later. A hat maker's.

1.

JOAN *and* TODD *are sitting at a workbench. They have each just started making a hat.*

TODD: There's plenty of blue.

JOAN: I think I'm starting with black.

TODD: Colour always wins.

JOAN: I will have colour, I'm starting with black to set the colour off.

TODD: I did one last week that was an abstract picture of the street, blue for the buses, yellow for the flats, red for the leaves, grey for the sky. Nobody got it but I knew what it was. There's little satisfactions to be had.

JOAN: Don't you enjoy it?

TODD: You're new aren't you?

JOAN: This is my first hat. My first professional hat.

TODD: Did you do hat at college?

JOAN: My degree hat was a giraffe six feet tall.

TODD: You won't have time to do something like that in the week.

JOAN: I know.

TODD: We used to get two weeks before a parade and then they took it down to one and now they're talking about cutting a day.

JOAN: So we'd get an extra day off?

TODD: We'd get a day's less money. We wouldn't make such good hats.

JOAN: Can they do that?

TODD: You'd oppose it would you?

JOAN: I've only just started.

TODD: You'll find there's a lot wrong with this place.

JOAN: I thought it was one of the best jobs.

TODD: It is. Do you know where to go for lunch?

JOAN: I think there's a canteen isn't there?

TODD: Yes but we don't go there. I'll show you where to go.

2.

Next day. They are working on the hats, which are by now far more brightly decorated i.e. the ones they were working on have been replaced by ones nearer completion.

JOAN: Your turn.

TODD: I go for a swim in the river before work.

JOAN: Isn't it dangerous?

TODD: Your turn.

JOAN: I've got a pilot's licence.

TODD: I stay up till four every morning watching the trials.

JOAN: I'm getting a room in a subway.

TODD: I've got my own place.

JOAN: Have you?

TODD: Do you want to see it? That's coming on.

JOAN: I don't understand yours but I like the feather.

TODD: I'm not trying. I've been here too long.

JOAN: Will you leave?

TODD: My turn. There's something wrong with how we get the contracts.

JOAN: But we want the contracts.

TODD: What if we don't deserve them? What if our work isn't really the best?

JOAN: So what's going on?

TODD: I'll just say a certain person's brother-in-law. Where does he work do you think?

JOAN: Where does he work?

TODD: I'm not talking about it in here. Tell me something else.

JOAN: I don't like staying in in the evenings and watching trials.

TODD: I watch them at night after I come back.

JOAN: Back from where?

TODD: Where do you like?

3.

Next day. They're working on the hats, which are getting very big and extravagant.

TODD: I don't enjoy animal hats myself.

JOAN: I was a student.

TODD: Abstract hats are back in a big way.

JOAN: I've always liked abstract hats.

TODD: You must have not noticed when everyone hated them.

JOAN: It was probably before my time.

Silence. They go on working.

JOAN: It's just if you're going on about it all the time I don't know why you don't do something about it.

TODD: This is your third day.

JOAN: The management's corrupt—you've told me. We're too low paid—you've told me.

Silence. They go on working.

TODD: Too much green.

JOAN: It's meant to be too much.

Silence. They go on working.

TODD: I noticed you looking at that fair boy's hat. I hope you told him it was derivative.

Silence. They go on working.

TODD: I'm the only person in this place who's got any principles, don't tell me I should do something, I spend my days wondering what to do.

JOAN: So you'll probably come up with something.

Silence. They go on working.

4.

Next day. They are working on the hats, which are now enormous and proposterous.

TODD: That's beautiful.

JOAN: You like it?

TODD: I do.

JOAN: I like yours too.

TODD: You don't have to say that. It's not one of my best.

JOAN: No it's got—I don't know, it's a confident hat.

TODD: I have been doing parades for six years. So I'm a valued old hand. So when I go and speak to a certain person he might pay attention.

JOAN: You're going to speak to him?

TODD: I've an appointment after work.

JOAN: You might lose your job.

TODD: I might.

JOAN: I'm impressed.

TODD: That was the idea.

JOAN: Will you mention the brother-in-law?

TODD: First I'll talk about the money. Then I'll just touch in the brother-in-law. I've a friend who's a journalist.

JOAN: Will you touch in the journalist?

TODD: I might imply something without giving the journalist away. It might be better if he can't trace the journalist back to me.

JOAN: Though he will suspect.

TODD: However much he suspects. One thing if I lost my job.

JOAN: What's that?

TODD: I'd miss you.

JOAN: Already?

5.

Next day. A procession of ragged, beaten, chained prisoners, each wearing a hat, on their way to execution. The finished hats are even more enormous and preposterous than in the previous scene.

6.

A new week. JOAN *and* TODD *are starting work on new hats.*

JOAN: I still can't believe it.

TODD: No one's ever won in their first week before.

JOAN: It's all going to be downhill from now on.

TODD: You can't win every week.

JOAN: That's what I mean.

TODD: No but you'll do a fantastic body of work while you're here.

JOAN: Sometimes I think it's a pity that more aren't kept.

TODD: There'd be too many, what would they do with them?

JOAN: They could reuse them.

TODD: Exactly and then we'd be out of work.

JOAN: It seems so sad to burn them with the bodies.

TODD: No I think that's the joy of it. The hats are ephemeral. It's like a metaphor for something or other.

JOAN: Well, life.

TODD: Well, life, there you are. Out of nearly three hundred hats I've made here I've only had three win and go in the museum. But that's never bothered me. You make beauty and it disappears, I love that.

JOAN: You're so . . .

TODD: What?

JOAN: You make me think in different ways. Like I'd never have thought about how this place is run and now I see how important it is.

TODD: I think it did impress a certain person that I was speaking from the high moral ground.

JOAN: So tell me again exactly what he said at the end.

TODD: "These things must be thought about."

JOAN: I think that's encouraging.

TODD: It could mean he'll think how to get rid of me.

JOAN: That's a fantastic shape to start from.

TODD: It's a new one for me. I'm getting inspired by you.

JOAN: There's still the journalist. If he looks into it a bit more we could expose the corrupt financial basis of how the whole hat industry is run, not just this place, I bet the whole industry is dodgy.

TODD: Do you think so?

JOAN: I think we should find out.

TODD: You've changed my life, do you know that?

JOAN: If you lose your job I'll resign.

TODD: We might not get jobs in hats again.

JOAN: There's other parades.

TODD: But I think you're a hat genius.

JOAN: Unless all the parades are corrupt.

TODD: I love these beads. Use these beads.

JOAN: No, you have them.

TODD: No, you.

3.

Several years later. HARPER's *house, daytime.*

HARPER: You were right to poison the wasps.

TODD: Yes, I think all the wasps have got to go.

HARPER: I was outside yesterday on the edge of the wood when a shadow came over and it was a cloud of butterflies, and they came down just beyond me and the trees and bushes were red with them. Two of them clung to my arm, I was terrified, one of them got in my hair, I managed to squash them.

TODD: I haven't had a problem with butterflies.

HARPER: They can cover your face. The Romans used to commit suicide with gold leaf, just flip it down their throat and it covered their windpipe, I think of that with butterflies.

TODD: I was passing an orchard, there were horses standing under the trees, and suddenly wasps attacked them out of the plums. There were the horses galloping by screaming with their heads made of wasp. I wish she'd wake up.

HARPER: We don't know how long she'd been walking.

TODD: She was right to come.

HARPER: You don't go walking off in the middle of a war.

TODD: You do if you're escaping.

HARPER: We don't know that she was escaping.

TODD: She was getting to a place of safety to regroup.

HARPER: Is this a place of safety?

TODD: Relatively, yes of course it is. Everyone thinks it's just a house.

HARPER: The cats have come in on the side of the French.

TODD: I never liked cats, they smell, they scratch, they only like you because you feed them, they bite, I used to have a cat that would suddenly just take some bit of you in its mouth.

HARPER: Did you know they've been killing babies?

TODD: Where's that?

HARPER: In China. They jump in the cots when nobody's looking.

TODD: But some cats are still ok.

HARPER: I don't think so.

TODD: I know a cat up the road.

HARPER: No, you must be careful of that.

TODD: But we're not exactly on the other side from the French. It's not as if they're the Moroccans and the ants.

HARPER: It's not as if they're the Canadians, the Venezuelans and the mosquitoes.

TODD: It's not as if they're the engineers, the chefs, the children under five, the musicians.

HARPER: The car salesman.

TODD: Portuguese car salesman.

HARPER: Russian swimmers.

TODD: Thai butchers.

HARPER: Latvian dentists.

TODD: No, the Latvian dentists have been doing good work in Cuba. They've a house outside Havana.

HARPER: But Latvia has been sending pigs to Sweden. The dentists are linked to international dentistry and that's where their loyalty lies, with dentists in Dar-es-Salaam.

TODD: We don't argue about Dar-es-Salaam.

HARPER: You would attempt to justify the massacre in Dar-es-Salaam? She's come here because you're here on leave and if anyone finds out I'll be held responsible.

TODD: It's only till tomorrow. I'll wake her up. I'll give her a few more minutes.

HARPER: Did you see the programme about crocodiles?

TODD: Yes but crocodiles, the way they look after the baby crocodiles and carry them down to the water in their mouths.

HARPER: Don't you think everyone helps their own children?

TODD: I'm just saying I wouldn't be sorry if the crocodiles were on one of the sides we have alliances with. They're unstoppable, come on.

HARPER: Crocodiles are evil and it is always right to be opposed to crocodiles. Their skin, their teeth, the foul smell of their mouths from the dead meat. Crocodiles wait till zebras are crossing the river and bite the weak ones with those jaws and pull them down. Crocodiles invade villages at night and take children out of their beds. A crocodile will carry a dozen heads back to the river, tenderly like it carries its young, and put them in the water where they bob about as trophies till they rot.

TODD: I'm just saying we could use that.

HARPER: And the fluffy little darling waterbirds, the smallest one left behind squeaking wait for me, wait for me. And their mother who would give her life to save them.

TODD: Do we include mallards in this?

HARPER: Mallards are not a good waterbird. They commit rape, and they're on the side of the elephants and the Koreans. But crocodiles are always in the wrong.

TODD: Do you think I should wake her up or let her sleep? We won't get any time together.

HARPER: You agree with me about the crocodiles?

TODD: What's the matter? you don't know whose side I'm on?

HARPER: I don't know what you think.

TODD: I think what we all think.

HARPER: Take deer.

TODD: You mean sweet little bambis?

HARPER: You mean that ironically?

TODD: I mean it sarcastically.

HARPER: Because they burst out of parks and storm down from mountains and terrorise shopping malls. If the does run away when you shoot they run into somebody else and trample them with their vicious little shining hooves, the fawns get under the feet of shoppers and send them crashing down escalators, the young bucks charge the plate glass windows—

TODD: I know to hate deer.

HARPER: and the old ones, do you know how heavy their antlers are or how sharp the prongs are when they twist into teenagers running down the street?

TODD: Yes I do know that.

He lifts his shirt and shows a scar.

HARPER: Was that a deer?

TODD: In fact it was a bear. I don't like being doubted.

HARPER: It was when the elephants went over to the Dutch, I'd always trusted elephants.

TODD: I've shot cattle and children in Ethiopia. I've gassed mixed troops of Spanish, computer programmers and dogs. I've torn starlings apart with my bare hands. And I liked doing it with my bare hands. So don't suggest I'm not reliable.

HARPER: I'm not saying you can't kill.

TODD: And I know it's not all about excitement. I've done boring jobs. I've worked in abattoirs stunning pigs and musicians and by the end of the day your back aches and all you can see when you shut your eyes is people hanging upside down by their feet.

HARPER: So you'd say the deer are vicious?

TODD: We've been over that.

HARPER: If a hungry deer came into the yard you wouldn't feed it?

TODD: Of course not.

HARPER: I don't understand that because the deer are with us. They have been for three weeks.

TODD: I didn't know. You said yourself.

HARPER: Their natural goodness has come through. You can see it in their soft brown eyes.

TODD: That's good news.

HARPER: You hate the deer. You admire the crocodiles.

TODD: I've lost touch because I'm tired.

HARPER: You must leave.

TODD: I'm your family.

HARPER: Do you think I sleep?

JOAN *comes in and walks into* TODD's *arms.*

HARPER: You can't stay here, they'll be after you. What are you going to say when you go back, you ran off to spend a day with your husband? Everyone has people they love they'd like to see or anyway people they'd rather see than lie in a hollow waiting to be bitten by ants. Are you not going back at all because if you're not you might as well shoot me now. Did anyone see you leave? which way did you come? were you followed? There are ospreys here who will have seen you arrive. And you're risking your life for you don't know what because he says things that aren't right. Don't you care? Maybe you don't know right from wrong yourself, what do I know about you after two years, I'd like to be glad to see you but how can I?

JOAN: Of course birds saw me, everyone saw me walking along but nobody knew why, I could have been on a mission, everyone's moving about and no one knows why, and in fact I killed two cats and a child under five so it wasn't that different from a mission, and I don't see why I can't have one day and then go back, I'll go on to the end after this. It wasn't so much the birds I was frightened of, it was the weather, the weather here's on the side of the Japanese. There were thunderstorms all through the mountains, I went through towns I hadn't been before. The rats are bleeding out of their mouths and ears, which is good, and so were the girls by the side of the road. It was tiring there because everything's been recruited, there were piles of bodies and if you stopped to find out there was one killed by coffee or one killed by pins, they were killed by heroin, petrol, chainsaws, hairspray, bleach, foxgloves, the smell of smoke was where we were burning the grass that wouldn't serve. The Bolivians are working with gravity, that's a secret so as not to spread alarm. But we're getting further with noise and there's thousands dead of light in Madagascar. Who's going to mobilise darkness and silence? that's what I wondered in the night. By the third day I could hardly walk but I got down to the river. There was a camp of Chilean soldiers upstream but they hadn't seen me and fourteen black and white cows downstream having a drink so I knew I'd have to go straight across. But I didn't know whose side the river was on, it might help me swim or it might drown me. In the middle the current was running much faster, the water was brown, I didn't know if that meant anything. I stood on the bank a long time. But I knew it was my only way of getting here so at last I put one foot in the river. It was very cold but so far that was all. When you've just stepped in you can't tell what's going to happen. The water laps round your ankles in any case.

Notes on the Theatre of Cruelty

Charles Marowitz

In the fall of 1963, Peter Brook and Charles Marowitz formed an experimental group affiliated with the Royal Shakespeare Company. The intention was to explore certain problems of acting and stagecraft in laboratory conditions, without the commercial pressures of public performance. The following account is based on notes and jottings from that period, as well as reflections after the event.

The First Company

Out of about fifty actors, a dozen were selected, and then presented to Brook for approval. (Ironically, there was a slight hassle only in the case of Glenda Jackson, over whom Brook took some convincing. She turned out to be— along with Alexis Kanner—one of the two most resourceful members of the group.)

The average age of the group was twenty-four. Only one member was over thirty, and most were just over twenty. The backgrounds were television, drama-school, a minimal amount of repertory, no West End experience to speak of. The general formation was naturalistic—a grounding in Stanislavski techniques as attenuated and distorted by English drama schools. I felt the need to start from scratch, to plunge the whole company into elementary Method exercises before totally demolishing the Stanislavski ethic. Brook disagreed. He felt the level of proficiency was high enough to tackle the new work directly. I thought this a mistake because Stanislavski was the grammar out of which we were going to build a completely different syntax

Excerpted from "Notes on the Theatre of Cruelty," *TDR*, vol. 11, no. 2 (1966): 154–71. Reprinted by permission of MIT Press and *TDR*.

and I wanted the basis to be sound before shifting it. It is difficult to say, in retrospect, whether we were right or wrong in plunging a group of twelve young actors and actresses into the swirling waters of Artaudian theory, but, of course, there was the time-factor. We had only twelve weeks for training and a preliminary workshop performance. We worked in a small church hall behind the Royal Court Theatre in Sloane Square; a bare, wooden room littered with Brownie posters and the relics of ancient whist-drives. It was a long day, beginning at 10 a.m. and ending at 6 p.m. Each night Brook and I consulted by phone about the objectives of the next day's session, then I sat down and devised the exercises which made up the next day's work. My notes of these sessions are not chronological, and so what follows is in no particular order.

Introduction to Sounds

On the very first day of work, before the actors had properly met each other and without Brook or me delivering any orientation-lectures, the actors were handed objects: boxes, bangers, scrapers, vessels, sticks, etc. Each actor had something or other to bang with, and something or other to bang on. They were then asked to explore the range of their *instrument* (the sound the thin end of a ladle made on a tin can; the sound the tin can made against the floor, muted with one palm, held suspended, in two hands, tucked inside a sweater, rapped with the knuckle instead of the ladle, with the forehead instead of the knuckle, the elbow instead of the forehead . . .) Once the range of the instrument had been explored, a series of rhythms were rapped out. Some of these were then varied while others remained the same; some were accelerated while other were slowed down; there were combinations of twos and threes; dialogues between broomhandles and empty crates; scenes from *Romeo and Juliet* played out between metallic tinkles and bass percussions; mob violence with soapcrates and pitched battles with tennis rackets.

Eventually *rhythm*, a generalized and over-used word in the theatre, got re-defined in exact, physical terms. Not only did actors experience the basic changes of rhythm—slow, fast, moderate—but the endless combinations and counterpoints that rhythms were capable of. Shortly, the same attitude the actors had taken to their objects was applied to their voices and bodies. This was a tortuous adjustment, and one was always fighting the primordial instinct in English actors that believes the voice is the medium for *good speech*, *projection*, and *resonance*, the carrier of the theatrical "message," and the body a useful but secondary adjunct. Little by little, we insinuated the idea that the voice could produce sounds other than grammatical combinations of the alphabet, and that the body, set free, could begin to enunciate a language which went beyond text, beyond sub-text, beyond psychological implication and beyond monkey-see-monkey-do facsimiles of social behav-

decenter the voice as the actor's tool.

iorism. And most important of all, that these sounds and moves could communicate feelings and ideas.

Sound and Movement Similes

Exercise: You come back to your apartment after a hard day's work. Enter, take off your coat, hang it up, pour yourself a drink and sit down at the table. On the table is a letter which you suddenly notice. You put down the drink, open the letter and begin to read. The contents of the letter are entirely up to you; the only condition is that it contains news which puts you into a highly emotional state of one sort or another. Express this state using only a sound and a movement.

The moments in the exercise leading up to the final beat are entirely naturalistic, but the final beat is an externalized expression of the character's inner state and totally non-naturalistic. At first, all the choices were commonplace. People jumped for joy, fell into weeping, bolted upwards with surprise, stamped with rage. When none of these simple expressions was acceptable, the actors began to realize the nature of the exercise. With all their naturalistic choices dismissed out of hand, they had to go in search of a more stylized means of communication. Eventually, the choices became more imaginative. Sounds were created which had the resonance of wounded animals; of pre-historic creatures being slain by atomic weapons. Movements became stark and unpredictable. Actors began to use the chairs and tables as sculptural objects instead of functional furniture. Facial expressions, under the pressure of extended sounds, began to resemble Javanese masks and Zen sculpture. But once the actors realized what we were after, some of them began to select an arbitrary sound or movement, effective in itself but unrelated to the emotional state growing out of the exercise. Very quickly, frighteningly quickly, actors became as glib with non-naturalistic sounds and movements as they were with stock, dramatic clichés. One wondered if Artaud's idealized theatre ever were established whether, in five or ten years, it too would not become as practiced and cliché-ridden as the present-day Comédie Française, or the West End.

Discontinuity

One of the main objects behind the work was to create a discontinuous style of acting; that is, a style which corresponded to the broken and fragmentary way in which most people experience contemporary reality. Life today (I am not philosophizing, merely trying to illustrate) is very much like the front page of a daily newspaper. The eye jumps from one story to another; from one geographical location to another; from one mood to another. A fire in Hoboken; an election in Paris; a coronation in Sweden; a rape in London;

comedy, passion, ceremony, trivia—all flooding one's consciousness almost simultaneously. The actor, however, through years of training and centuries of tradition, moves stolidly from point A to point B to point C. His character is *established*, his relationships *develop*; his plot thickens and his conflicts resolve. In short, he plods on in his Aristotelian way, perpetuating the stock jargon of drama and the arbitrary time-system of the conventional theatre.

To break the progressive-logical-beginning-middle-and-end syndrome, one uses improvisation (personal and organic material rather than theatrical *données*) and uses it simply as rhythmic matter.

Exercise: The life of a character is briefly built up. X is an out-of-work writer.

Scene 1: His landlady asks him for rent which is months in arrears.
Scene 2: His girlfriend wants to know when they're going to get married.
Scene 3: His father urges him to give up writing and take a job with the firm.
Scene 4: His pub-crony exhorts him to come out, have a drink, and forget his troubles.
Scene 5: His schoolfriend drops in and wants to re-live old times.
Scene 6: An insurance salesman persistently tries to push an unwanted policy on him.

Each scene is built up independently for five or ten minutes; just long enough for it to have a little meat, but not long enough to develop any real sinew. Then X is placed in the center of the room and each character—on cue—resumes his scene with him. The scenes, all unrelated except that they all center around the same main character, follow hard upon each other. With the addition of each new scene, X quickly adapts to the changed situation, the different relationship. Eventually, three and four scenes are being played at once. Soon all are being played simultaneously. At a point, the exercise becomes unbearable and impossible, but before that point, X and his fellow-actors have experienced a frantic sense of discontinuity that just begins to convey the complexities to which any, even the simplest, sensibility is prone. . . .

Stanislavski and Artaud

Having been brought up on Stanislavski and the idea of inner truth, it was a major adjustment to discover there was also *surface truth*, and that in certain contexts, the latter was more persuasive than the former. An even more difficult adjustment was to realize that artifice and downright artistic fraud could create a plenitude of truth for an audience and was therefore, according to the pragmatic laws that govern acting, legitimate. The Method argument for inner truth holds water only if its main contention is true: that is, that the spectator experiences feeling to the same degree the actor does. But we all know this is not always the case; that there are hundreds of instances of turned-on actors splitting themselves with inner intensity communicating nothing to an audience but effort and tension. It is equally true that an actor who is almost totally turned-off but going through the right motions in the right context can powerfully affect an audience—almost involuntarily.

The Method actor's test for truthfulness is the intensity and authenticity of his personal feeling. The Artaudian actor knows that unless that feeling has been shaped into a communicative image, it is a passionate letter without postage. Whereas pure feeling can be mawkish or leaden, a pertinent stage-image—a gesture, a movement, a sequence of actions—is a statement in itself which doesn't require the motor-power of feeling in order to register, but when emotionally charged is many times more potent.

There is no fundamental disagreement between the Method actor and the Artaudian actor. Both rely on consciousness to release the unconscious, but whereas the Method actor is chained to rational motivation, the Artaudian actor realizes the highest artistic truth is unprovable. Like certain rare natural phenomena that defy scientific analysis, they *can* exist—and the actor's task is to conjure them into being.

The Artaudian actor needs Stanislavski in order to verify the nature of the feelings he is releasing—otherwise he becomes merely a victim of feeling. Even Artaud's celebrated actor-in-trance is responsible to the spirit that is speaking through him. A seance where nothing is communicated but atmosphere is not half as rewarding as one in which messages are received loud and clear. The very state of trance itself is arrived at methodically. The medium's secret is knowing when to let go of the mechanisms that have produced it, in order to transcend them; the same is true for the actor—any actor—who uses either intellect or instinct to bring him to an important jumping-off point.

Changing Gears

Three actors, A, B, and C, are given cue-sounds (a bell for one, a buzzer for the second, a gong for the third). When A hears his cue, he initiates a scene, and B & C, adapting themselves to A's choice, enter into the situation as quickly as possible. After two or three minutes, when the scene is either approaching a highpoint or running down because of lack of invention, B is given his cue. B suddenly leaps into a completely new situation, entirely unrelated to the one preceding; A & C adapt themselves immediately. Short development, then C is cued, another unrelated scene, the others adapt again, etc., etc., etc.

As important as the actual material thrown up by the scene is the moment chosen for breaking it and beginning another. There is a moment in almost every improvisation where things reach a head and are moving quickly towards a resolution. If one can trigger off the new scene just at that moment, the actor's emergency-equipment is instinctively brought into play.

Improvisations like these feed on (and sometimes are destroyed by) their sense of danger. There is an inescapable imperative forced on the actors. They must think and act with lightning speed. They know that within a seven or ten minute period, they have to devise as many as five or six different situations, and they soon discover they cannot cheat by planning ahead, because a pre-arranged choice is immediately apparent—as is the instinctively appropriate choice which could not have come from anywhere else but the given circumstances. It brings into play a quality that actors tend to think they do not possess: the ability to associate freely and without regard to fixed character or logical consistency. For me, the great eye-opener in this exercise was how, under the pressure of changing gears, actors who never heard of surrealism were able to make the most stunning surrealist choices; and actors who claimed to have no sense of humor suddenly found themselves dipping into deep wells of fantasy and absurdity that lay on the threshold of their consciousness. Choices which, if actors had time to deliberate over them, would never be made, or would be doctored or modified, leaped out with astonishing clarity and boldness. . . .

Theatre of Cruelty

The first showing of the group's work unfortunately was titled Theatre of Cruelty and ran a scheduled five weeks at the LAMDA Theatre Club in London. It was never intended as a *show*, but merely a demonstration of work-in-progress, of interest, we assumed, to the profession. The press was not invited in the usual way, but letters were sent explaining that if they felt like coming along, they were welcome, but that we were not particularly desirous of reviews, as this wasn't strictly speaking a show. All of which was a kind of self-delusion that both Brook and I swallowed whole. Only after the event did the obvious truth of the situation strike us. Any presentation, call it what you will, that is done before an audience, invited or otherwise, becomes a show and is judged according to traditional criteria. This is not a harangue against the critics. On the whole, we got interesting, up-beat notices, but the point was that we weren't really intending a theatrical performance, and the overriding point was that it seemed impossible, in London, to present anything short of one.

The program consisted of two short nonsense sketches by Paul Ableman, similar to our sound-exercises; a production of Artaud's three-minute *Spurt of Blood* (played through first in sounds, then as Artaud wrote it); a dramatization, in movement only, of a short story by Alain Robbe-Grillet; two collages by Brook, one (*The Public Bath*) a splicing-together of newspaper accounts of the Kennedy funeral and the Christine Keeler testimony; the other (*The Guillotine*) made up from original sources; three scenes from Genet's *The Screens*; an anti-Marceauvian mime-sketch called *The Analysis*;

a short play by John Arden, *Ars Longa, Vita Brevis* and the collage—*Hamlet*.

There were two sections in the evening which were deliberately marked out as "free." One, the improvisations, the forms of which changed every evening with the actors never being forewarned; and two, a section towards the close of the second half, into which we inserted whatever "specials" occurred to us. On the first night, Brook used this section to rehearse a scene from *Richard The Third*. Another night, the section was used for a spontaneous exchange between Brook and myself in which we questioned the audience's motives in coming to the theatre, and the whole point of what we were doing there. Early in the run, on the night John Arden was in the audience, without warning we asked him to come forward to justify his short play, and for the occasion we set against him one of the actors from *Ars Longa, Vita Brevis* who hated the play and what it was saying.

For the improvs, which I supervised from the stage, I tried to invent new and different challenges every night. On one occasion, we played the Changing Gears exercise entirely in sound; on another, entirely in music phrases; on another, using only animal-noises. The audience was incorporated every evening and, very much like The Premise, actors worked from suggestions thrown out to them on the floor. The random factors maintained a degree of freshness almost to the end of the run, but their main point was not simply to keep actors on their toes, but to break the hypnotic effect of continuous performance, and to un-settle the myth that grows up once a performance has begun a run. No two audiences saw the same show, and so no two people from different audiences could recount exactly the same memories. Towards this end, roles were swapped (frequently at the last moment); bits altered or dropped, and one piece (written by Paul Ableman) completely unstaged and unrehearsed, played out each evening as the spirit happened to move the actors. Some nights, this was disastrous; others, after it seemed that every possible interpretation had been tried, startlingly new moods would appear. The playing of this particular dialogue was greatly enhanced by the fact that the two players, who were sometimes required to play quite lyrically with one another, hated each other's guts. The tensions that charged, disfigured, and enlivened the piece prevented it from ever becoming dead material.

It is to the everlasting credit of Peter Hall and the Royal Shakespeare Company that it was understood from the start that this work required total subsidy. There was no question of making money or breaking even, for that matter, and it went without saying this was unrecoverable money (therefore, seats were deliberately cheap—five shillings each). There was no balking after the event, when accountants would solemnly point out £5000 had gone down the drain in a matter of twelve weeks. The drain, in this case, led to a very interesting cellar where certain rare wines were being culled, and even if it should turn out they had all gone sour and had to be dumped, no one was going to burst a blood vessel or demand an official investigation.

Phase Two

After the Theatre of Cruelty showing, the plan was to begin work on Genet's *The Screens*. The group was enlarged to seventeen and training was re-started. The newcomers, who had seen the LAMDA program and heard fanci-ful tales about the work, were wary and suspicious. The mother company was either distrustful or openly antagonistic towards the "mutation at Earl's Court," as one senior member described it. The original group of ten, al-though still committed to the work, was beginning to eye the mother com-pany covetously. They wondered what was going on at the Aldwych and where they would fit in. An inevitable concern and natural in the circum-stances: twelve young actors working for peanuts with the prospect of gradua-tion into a major London company. (An in-group definition of Theatre of Cruelty was twelve actors working for twelve pounds a week.) I mention this now, not to descend into theatre gossip, but to point out how even the best intentions can be subverted by an over-powering commercial atmosphere. Ostensibly, we had an experimental group concerning itself with craft-prob-lems and difficult stylistic pursuits, but in fact, we had a group of talented, underpaid actors who were wondering how long they would have to work for subsistence wages. I don't want to exaggerate this undercurrent It wasn't crippling or disastrous, but it did generate preoccupations that affected the work. Training and rehearsals became, in some instances, miniature audi-tions for the better-paid work, and because the group, or some of them, were going to be assimilated into the larger company, it became impossible to build a healthily incestuous group-feeling; the kind of group-feeling that companies like Grotowski's in Poland, or the Becks' Living Theatre, build automatically because a shared attitude and mutual allegiance bind the company together. Good work can be done without such an adhesive; but not exceptional work; not enduring, un-self-consciously creative work.

The Screens

The work on *The Screens* could be an essay in itself. The early exercises continued, and were gradually adapted to the specific needs of the play. The crucial production problem, apart from perfecting a style that would cope with such a monumental structure, was to communicate both the poetic and political tremors in the play without veering too far in one direction or the other. The Artaudian exercises had prepared us for Genet's metaphysic, and we now began to apply a Brechtian approach to get at the play's political bedrock, and also to define for ourselves precisely what each of those extrava-gant little scenes was about.

The early rehearsals were spend in reading, discussion, and translation amendments. After rehearsing each scene, key characters were asked to tell the story of what had just happened: 1. as a factual news report; 2. as a policeman summing up before a magistrate; 3. as a fairly tale ("once upon a time . . . "); 4. as a horror story; 5. from the Marxist point of view; 6. from a Freudian standpoint; 7. as it might be described by a highly poetic sensibility, etc.

Brechtian titles were employed as epigraphs for each scene.

SAÏD RELUCTANTLY GOES TO MEET HIS NEW WIFE

THE COLONISTS DISCUSS THEIR POSSESSIONS

SAÏD'S MOTHER INSISTS UPON BEING INCLUDED AT A FUNERAL

Sometimes the work-sessions threw up more material than we knew what to do with, and eventually the problem became one of discarding highly interesting but irrelevant insights. More and more, we concentrated on the text: its coloration, its timbre, its weight and feel. As with Shakespeare, one began to test the truthfulness of every moment in terms of the ring of the words in their context. We found that every moment of naturalism, even the most obvious and unquestionable, benefited by being knocked off balance; by being winged by a metaphor, or studded with a stylization. *Ritualistic* may be a critic's cliché when writing about Genet, but it becomes a directorial Rosetta Stone in rehearsal. Even the crudest situation, three soldiers farting a farewell to their dead Lieutenant (Scene 15), becomes both more comic and more understandable by being acted ceremoniously, instead of in a loose, naturalistic manner.

Like *The Blacks* or *The Balcony*, *The Screens* appears to be about some great social topic (the Algerian War) but is essentially a private fantasy couched in convenient social imagery. Saïd's salvation through progressive degradation is portrayed with all the relentlessness of a thesis-playwright laboriously proving his point. As a play, it proliferates incidents without opening up new ground, and keeps winding back on itself like a badly-wrapped package which becomes fussy without becoming any firmer. Which is not to belittle the genius of certain individual scenes; nor the breadth of the conception; nor the grandiose lunacy in the character of Saïd's mother; nor the hypnotic other-worldliness of the scene where Madani is transmuted into the Mouth of the murdered rebel-leader Si Slimane; nor the easy, unpretentious shuttling between the worlds of the rebellious living and the settled dead; nor the black, urinal comedy between the Arab hooligans and the Algerian Cadi; nor the stunning scene where Arab rebels paint their atrocities onto a series of ever-multiplying screens. But on studying the entire play Brook felt, and I concurred, that the first twelve scenes contained all the gnarled genius of the work, and the remaining two and a half hours held only endless out-riding variations.

One last observation on *The Screens*: in the work of no other writer is the external life of the play quite so essential. In the last weeks of rehearsal, *The Screens* looked murky and gauze-covered in spite of many weeks of trying to cut sense and meaning into the scenes. Then, using Genet's own color suggestions, Sally Jacobs' stark designs, and Brook's faultless eye for surface-effect, a great wave of color was spread over the entire play. In the space of four hours (the hours during which costumes and design were added), the play was transformed into something bold, brazen, aptly rhetorical and hieratic, as if the arrival of objects and color seemed to coincide with the arrival of Jean Genet. One part of me rebelled at what I took to be the spreading of dazzling camouflage, but another was entirely swept up by the camouflage itself. I am not simply describing the extra-dimensionalism dress rehearsals bring to a production. No amount of fancy surface can obliterate a faulty foundation, but in the case of *The Screens*, the costume and decor produced —in one day—two-thirds of the truth, only one-third of which had been evoked in six weeks of rehearsal.

Still, for me, *The Screens* was never an organic production, but a substructure and an overlay with a vital middle layer missing. The production made a kind of stark, physical sense in spite of, not because of, our work, and the intellectual uncertainty of cast and producers, the unresolved ambiguities in the text, left an inner fuzziness which a longer run would undoubtedly have revealed. . . .

Marat/Sade and Completion

When Peter Weiss's play *Marat/Sade* came along, it was the natural conclusion of the Group's work: a play which could not have been contemplated before the Group's existence and which now, after the work on Artaud and Genet, could not be ignored. The play even contained certain features from our first Theatre of Cruelty program: Marat's bath tub was mystically related to Christine Keeler's in *The Public Bath*, the guillotine imagery to Brook's collage-play. Weiss acknowledged Artaud as his mentor, Artaud had played Marat in a film for Abel Gance, sounds and "happenings" were embedded in the play in a way that had been integral to the group's thinking from the start.

Although I cannot be absolutely objective about the *Marat/Sade*, I can be somewhat detached as I wasn't directly involved in its production. That it is a spectacular and breathtaking production—perhaps the boldest we are to see this half-century—seems to me unquestionable. It restores something riotous and vital to the theatre, a kind of stylized mania which is closer to the personality of Antonin Artaud than any other single thing. But just as the Group's work itself had been diluted by being a demonstration of techniques, so the production of the *Marat/Sade* appeared the ultimate application of a theory which had been hatched before the egg of the play ever arrived. It seemed to say: this kind of theatrical expression is soul-stirring and mind-widening—if only there was a play to accommodate it. Weiss's play, at base, is a rather old-fashioned and long-winded polemical tract. In the original Swinarski production which I saw at the Schiller-Theater before the London production, it was an indictment of revolutionary fascism that set out to make a Marxist point. One either took the play or left it alone, but it was what it was, and there was no question about its point of view. In the London production, its ambiance was neither political nor (despite polemical longeurs) philosophical, but exclusively theatrical. All the time it was saying: an Artaudian-inspired theatre, strong on imagery, disrespectful of plot and suspicious of theses, can resuscitate something in our jaded senses and overhaul our aesthetic appreciation. That I happen to agree with that implication does not blind me to the fact that this is not what the play is about. One tends to appreciate the work in somewhat the same way one admires the resilience of a diving-board that allows a world-champion to perform a breathtaking triple somersault. Once the swimmer is in the water, that diving board looks mighty bare.

Excerpts from "Violence—Death—Theatre"
An Interview with Reza Abdoh

Hortensia Völckers and Martin Bergelt

HV, MB: In your piece *The Law of Remains* you combine very different elements: on the one hand the Egyptian *Books of Death,* on the other hand Andy Warhol, and both with the man-eating mass murderer Jeffrey Dahmer, whose crimes have only recently been cleared up. What is the connection between these subjects that seems to be so very different?

RA: In one word: death. A kind of obsessive yearning for bodily existence beyond Death. A problem that preoccupies our culture to a great extent, that torments the body and in doing so makes the problem evident. You can see that every day on TV: the usage of the body as a means of demonstrating eternal youth. I call it the excoriation of the body, a kind of release of the body from all defects, as it is shown to us for example by the cosmetics commercials. This is an obsession by which especially the American culture is affected. The culture seems to be addicted to death since it is always trying to somehow deny it.

HV, MB: So is there a kind of correspondence between the Egyptian mummies, the deep-frozen body of an American hoping to be revived in the future, the frozen time in the film, and on the other side a person like Jeffrey Dahmer confronting the parts of the body, the decomposing remains, in a shocking way?

Reprinted from Daniel Mufson, ed., *Reza Abdoh* (Baltimore: Johns Hopkins University Press, 1991), 23–26. © 1999 The Johns Hopkins University Press. Reprinted with permission of the Johns Hopkins University Press.

Originally published in *Theaterschrift,* no. 3 (1993): 48–65. Ellipsis points in square brackets here reflect excerpts from the original publication.

RA: Yes, that's right. With my theater I criticize the established culture models which deny death in its materiality by portraying, for example, one of those confused people whose actions do not fit into the sublimation model. But in addition to this cultural and socio-critical orientation, I am also looking for a philosophical path that is not prescribed, that in its openness might lead into darkness and destruction, too, but that in any case does not have a direction which is prescribed by means of cultural prohibition signs. In my opinion the important feature of my work is that it constantly questions the patriarchy, the patriarchal domination of any kind of discussion about religion, society, political structures, etc. The prescribed models can neither serve me as an artist nor the people being dominated. That is the political aspect.

HV, MB: And the philosophical one?

RA: Philosophically I am interested for example in the strange schizophrenia in the moral evaluation of violence and destruction. Both of them are wearing the sign "taboo." But that is completely untrustworthy, since the entire progress of our culture is based on violence and destruction.

HV, MB: You mean that evolution is understood too idealistically? Without violence and destruction, no history?

RA: Yes, because actually violence was and is still being used and glorified. None of us is completely innocent. When the U.S.A. starts the Gulf War, no matter for what reason, violence is legalized. And in political rhetoric all this is celebrated as a victory of good over evil. But how can one say that an act of violence which is committed in the street is less moral than the killing of hundreds of thousands of Arabs? That's schizophrenic. The whole sense of the moral argument seems to consist in disguising the act of violence or destruction. In our culture, violence is always sanctioned in the name of progress, which clearly demonstrates that it is not morality that counts but domination.

HV, MB: Let's talk about Jeffrey Dahmer. His acts of violence cannot be justified even if he is considered an aberrant terminator. Dahmer is homosexual, doing violence exclusively to colored people he had sexual contact with. The courts consider him sane. Where does this fatal chain of violence and sexuality stem from?

RA: Jeffrey Dahmer is a by-product of the stigmatization which is regarded as normal in this society. This man repressed his origin, his sexuality, his entire ego, thus obeying a ruling model of self-repression. Dahmer is an unskilled worker, he is a homosexual, he feels attracted to colored people—stigmas wherever you look. Between his ego and his superego a vehement tension came into existence to which Jeffrey Dahmer responded with destruction, because nobody who was taught to repress sexuality is able to love. After being arrested, it's not his murders that he denies but his homosexuality, which is typical. In prison he called the black people "niggers" and the Latinos "spics" and said that they deserved to die, although he felt sexually attracted to people of a different color. What becomes clear is that Dahmer cannot accept his own ego. In this case it is not a private demon but a product of the collective American superego that determines in its absolutism what's right and what's wrong. [. . .]

HV, MB: You are an advocate of the catharsis theory. Do you believe in the purifying force of the enacted shock?

RA: I believe in it not so much as a purifying of emotion, but as a celebration of it. I don't want to send the audience through purgatory but to create a solemn atmosphere of emotion. You know, the Tibetans take their dead to the mountain top, chop them up, and use them as feed. For a Westerner [. . .] that is unacceptable because it goes against every moral sense that you have. But to the Tibetans it is an act of redemption, of purity. They are perfectly aware that they are chopping up flesh. They are under no illusions that after death the body is anything more than just a piece of meat. Only when illusions take over—like in our body-fixated society that is not familiar with transcendence—the situation becomes problematic. In the Western world, death is not accepted as a condition of the body, but regarded as a defect, a construction fault.

HV, MB: Perhaps it might be said that Dahmer's sexually motivated cannibalism represents a—perversely heightened—expression of exactly that Western fixation on just the pure body? Where there is no spiritual dimension, love may be perverted to possession of the body and then literally to the consumption of it.

RA: Yes—and the macabre end is—as becomes clear at the end of my play— nothing more than a plate with bones. End of the illusions.

HV, MB: Your theater has a shocking effect. You work with the means of cruelty and pornography. Is shock a means of reaching the audience?

RA: [. . . S]hock for me is not a method but at best the result of a recognition. Theater has a lot more potential. I think theater is really a place to physicalize ideas, a kind of a forum to exchange ideas.

Terror, Disorientation and Difficulty

Anne Bogart

As a director making theatre at the cusp of the twenty-first century, I want to examine the role of certain personal aspects of the creative process, including the role of embarrassment, the role of violence, the role of stereotype, the role of humor, the role of doubt, the role of interest, and the role of cultural memory and tradition. I begin here with one of the most primal and basic human experiences: terror. What is the role of terror, of disorientation and of difficulty in my work and in the work of other theatre artists?

My first encounters with theatre were startling and exposed me to art alive with an unnamable mystery and danger. These early experiences have made it difficult for me to relate to art that is not rooted in some form of terror. The energy of individuals who face and incorporate their own terror is genuine, palpable and contagious. In combination with the artist's deep sense of play, terror makes for compelling theatre both in the creative process and in the experience of an audience.

I grew up in a Navy family and we moved every year or two to a new naval base in another part of the country or another part of the world. My cultural references were Disney movies, cocktail parties, and aircraft carriers. My first brush with terror in art happened in a park in Tokyo, Japan, when I was six years old. A huge white painted face leered down at me from an immense multicolored body. I hid, terrified, behind my mother's skirt. This horrendous and beautiful vision was my first exposure to an actor in costume

Reprinted from Anne Bogart, *Viewpoints*, ed. Michael Bigelow Dixon and Joel A. Smith (Lyme, N.H.: Smith and Kraus, 1995), 5–12. Reprinted by permission of Anne Bogart.

wearing a mask. A few months later in the same city, I watched, terrified, as huge wooden altars borne high by drunken Japanese men charged down the streets of Tokyo on a holy day. The drunken men and the altars sporadically smashed into shop windows. The men seemed out of control, out of their minds and utterly unforgettable.

At fifteen when my father was stationed in Newport, Rhode Island, I saw my first professional theatre production at Trinity Repertory Company in Providence, Rhode Island. The National Endowment for the Humanities had granted the company enough money to bring every high school student in the state into the theatre to see their plays. I was one of those students and traveled to Providence in a big yellow school bus to see *Macbeth*. The production terrified, disoriented and bewildered me. I couldn't figure out my orientation to the action. The witches dropped unexpectedly out of the ceiling, the action surrounded us on big runways and I didn't understand the words. The unfamiliar spoken language was Shakespeare and the fantastic visual language, also foreign to me, was my first encounter with the poetic language of the stage where size and scale were altered. The experience was frightening but compelling. I didn't understand the play, but I knew instantly that I would spend my life in pursuit of this remarkable universe. On that day in 1967, I received my first lesson as a director: Never talk down to the audience. It was immediately clear to me that the experience of theatre was not about us understanding the meaning of the play or the significance of the staging. We were invited into a unique world, an arena that changed everything previously defined. The Trinity Company could have easily used their big grant to present facile children's theatre and fulfill their requirements to the NEH. Instead, they presented a complex, highly personal vision in a compelling, rough fashion. The production and the artists involved spoke to me directly in a visceral and fantastic manner.

Most of the truly remarkable experiences I've had in the theatre have filled me with uncertainty and disorientation. I may suddenly not recognize a building that was once familiar or I cannot tell up from down, close from far, big from little. Actors I thought that I knew are entirely unrecognizable. I often don't know if I hate or love what I am experiencing. I notice that I am sitting forward, not leaning back. These milestone productions are often long and difficult; I feel disjointed and a little out of my element. And yet I am somehow changed when the journey is completed.

We are born in terror and trembling. In the face of our terror before the uncontrollable chaos of the universe, we label as much as we can with language in the hopes that once we name something we no longer fear it. This labeling enables us to feel safer but also kills the mystery in what has been labeled, removing the life and danger out of what's been defined. The artist's responsibility is to bring the potential, the mystery and terror, the trembling, back. James Baldwin wrote, "The purpose of art is to lay bare the questions which have been hidden by the answers." The artist attempts to undefine, to present the moment, the word, the gesture as new and full of uncontrolled potential.

I became a theatre director knowing unconsciously that I was going to have to use my own terror in my life as an artist. I had to learn to work in trust and not in fear of that terror. I was relieved to find that the theatre is a useful place to concentrate that energy. Out of the almost uncontrollable chaos of life, I could create a place of beauty and a sense of community. In the most terrible depths of doubt and difficulty, I have found encouragement and inspiration in my collaborations. We have been able to create an atmosphere of grace, intensity and love. I've created a refuge for myself, for actors and for audiences through the metaphor that is theatre.

I believe that theatre's function is to remind us of the big human issues, to remind us of our terror and our humanity. In our quotidian lives, we live in constant repetitions of habitual patterns. Many of us sleep through our lives. Art should offer experiences that alter these patterns, awaken what is asleep, and remind us of our original terror. Human beings first created theatre in response to the everyday terror of life. From cave drawings to ecstatic dances around numberless fires, from Hedda Gabler raising her pistol to the disintegration of Blanche Dubois, we create hopeful shapes for our distress. I have found that theatre that doesn't address terror has no energy. We create out of fear, not from a place of security and safety. According to the physicist Werner Heisenberg, artists and scientists share a common approach. They enter into their work with one hand firmly grasping the specific and the other hand on the unknown. We must trust ourselves to enter this abyss with openness, with trust in ourselves, despite the unbalance and vulnerability. How do we trust ourselves, our collaborators and our abilities enough to work within the terror we experience in the moment of entering?

William Hurt, the actor, recently interviewed in *The New York Times*, said, "Those who function out of fear, seek security, those who function out of trust, seek freedom." These two possible agendas dramatically influence the creative process. The atmosphere in the rehearsal hall, therefore, can be imbued with either fear or trust. Are the choices made in rehearsal based on a desire for security or a search for freedom? I am convinced that the most dynamic and thrilling choices are made when there is a trust in the process, in the artists and in the material. The saving grace in one's work is love, trust and a sense of humor; trust in collaborators and the creative act in rehearsal, love for the art and a sense of humor about the impossible task. These are the elements that bring grace into a rehearsal situation and onto the stage. In the face of terror, beauty is created and hence, grace.

I want to create theatre that is full of terror, beauty, love and belief in the innate human potential for change. In dreams begin responsibility. How can I begin to work with this spirit? How can I work, not to conquer, but to embrace terror, disorientation and difficulty?

Every time I begin work on a new production I feel as though I am out of my league; that I know nothing and have no notion how to begin and I'm sure that someone else should be doing my job, someone assured, who knows what to do, someone who is really a professional. I feel unbalanced, uncomfortable and out of place. I feel like a sham. I usually find a way to make it through the table work on the production, where the necessary discussions, analysis and readings happen, but then always the dreaded moment arrives when it is time to put something onto the stage. How can anything be right, true or appropriate? I desperately try to imagine some excuse for doing something else, for procrastinating further. And when we do begin work on the stage, everything we set out to do feels artificial, arbitrary and affected. I'm sure that the actors think that I am out of my mind. Every time the dramaturg steps into the rehearsal hall I feel that what I am doing with the actors reflects none of our dramaturgical discussions. I feel unsophisticated and superficial. Fortunately after a stint with this dance of the absurd, I start to notice that the actors are beginning to transform the idiotic staging into something I can get enthused about and respond to.

I have spoken with a number of theatre directors and found that I am not alone in this sensation of being out of my league at the beginning of rehearsals. We all tremble before the impossibility of beginning. It is important to remember that a director's work, as with any artist, is intuitive. Many young directors make the big mistake of assuming that directing is about being in control, telling others what to do, having ideas and getting what you ask for. I do not believe that these abilities are the qualities that make a good director or exciting theatre. Directing is about feeling, about being in the room with other people—with actors, with designers, with an audience—about having a feel for time and space, about breathing and responding fully to the situation at hand, being able to plunge and encourage a plunge into the unknown at the right moment. David Salle, the painter, said in an interview, "I feel that the only thing that really matters in art and life is to go against the tidal wave of literalism and literal-mindedness to insist on and *live* the life of the imagination. A painting has to be the experience instead of pointing to it. I want to have and give *access to feeling*. That is the riskiest and only important way to connect art to the world—to make it alive. The rest is just current events."

I know that I cannot sit down when work is happening on the stage. If I sit, a deadness sets in. I direct from impulses in my body responding to the stage, the actors' bodies, their inclinations. If I sit down I lose my spontaneity, my connection to myself and to the stage, to the actors. I try to soften my eyes, that is, not to look too hard or with too much desire, because vision is dominant and eviscerates the other senses.

When I am lost in rehearsal, when I am stymied and have no idea what to do next or how to solve a problem, I know that this is the moment to make a leap. Because directing is intuitive, it involves walking with trembling into the unknown. Right there, in that moment, in that rehearsal, I have to say, "I know!" and start walking toward the stage. During the crisis of the walk, something *must* happen: some insight, some idea. The sensation of this walk to the stage, to the actors, feels like falling into a treacherous abyss. The walk creates a crisis in which innovation must happen, invention must transpire. I create the crisis in rehearsal to get out of my own way. I create despite myself and my limitations and my hesitancy. In unbalance and falling lie the potential of creation. When things start to fall apart in rehearsal, the possibility of creation exists. What we have planned before, what we have in our mind in that moment is not interesting. Rollo May wrote that all artists and scientists, when they are doing their best work, feel as though they are not doing the creating, they feel as though they are being spoken through. How do we get out of our own way in rehearsal?

The vitality, or energy, in any given work is a reflection of the artist's courageousness in the light of her own terror. For me, the essential aspect of a work is its vitality. The creation of art is not an escape from life but a penetration into it. I recently saw a retrospective of Martha Graham's early dance works. I was astonished that pieces such as *Primitive Mysteries* are now fifty years old and *still* risky and exposed. Graham once wrote to Agnes DeMille:

> There is a vitality, a life-force, a quickening that is translated through you into action, and because there is only one of you in all time, this expression is unique. And if you block it, it will never exist through any other medium and be lost. The world will not have it. It is not your business to determine how good it is; nor how valuable it is; nor how it compares with other expressions. It is your business to keep it yours clearly and directly, to keep the channel open. You do not have to believe in yourself or your work. You have to keep open and aware directly to the urges that motivate you.

Vitality in art is a result of articulation, energy and differentiation. All great art is differentiated art. It is more comfortable to feel similarities, yet we need to accept the terror of differences in order to create vital art. The terrible truth is that no two people are alike, no two snowflakes are alike, no two moments are alike. Physicists now say that nothing touches, nothing in the universe has contact; there is only movement and change. This is a terrifying notion given our attempt to make contact with one another. The ability to see, experience and articulate the differences between things is differentiation. Great artworks incorporate this notion of differentiation in varying ways. An exceptional painting is one which, for example, one color is highly and visibly differentiated from another, in which we see the differences in textures, shapes, spatial relationships. What made Glenn Gould a brilliant musician was his openness to high differentiation in music, which created the ecstatic intensity of his playing. In the best theatre, moments are highly differentiated. An actor's craft lies in the differentiation of one moment from the next. A great actor seems dangerous, unpredictable, full of life and differentiation.

We not only need to use our terror of differentiation but also our terror of conflict. Americans are plagued with the disease of agreement. In the theatre, we often presume that collaboration means agreement. I believe that too much agreement creates productions with no vitality, no dialectic, no truth. Unreflected agreement deadens the energy in a rehearsal. I do not believe that collaboration means mechanically doing what the director dictates. Without resistance there is no fire. The Germans have a useful word that has no suitable English equivalent: *auseinandersetzung*. The word, literally "to set oneself apart from an another," is usually translated into English as "argument," a word with generally negative connotations. As much as I would be happier with a congenial and easygoing environment in rehearsal, my best work emanates from *auseinandersetzung*, which means to me that to create we must set oneself apart from each other. This does not mean, "No, I don't like your approach, or your ideas." It does not mean, "No, I won't do what you are asking me to do." It means, "Yes, I will include your suggestion, but I will come at it from another angle and add these new notions." It means that we attack one another, that we may collide; it means that we may argue, doubt each other, offer alternatives. It means that I may feel foolish or unprepared. It means that rather than blindly fulfilling instructions, we examine choices in the heat of rehearsal, through repetition and trial and error. I have found that German theatre artists tend to work with too much *auseinandersetzung*, which becomes debilitating and can create static, heady productions. Americans tend towards too much agreement, which can create superficial, unexamined, facile art.

The words in this essay are easier to write than to practice in rehearsal. In moments of confrontation with terror, disorientation and difficulty, most of us want to call it a night and go home. These thoughts are meant to be reflections and notions to help give us some perspective, to help us to work with more faith and courage. I'd like to close with a quote from Brian Swimme:

> How else can we express feelings but by entering deeply into them? How can we capture the mystery of anguish unless we become one with anguish? Shakespeare lived his life, stunned by its majesty, and in his writing attempted to seize what he felt, to capture this passion in symbolic form. Lured into the intensity of living, he presented this intensity in language. And why? Because beauty stunned him. Because the soul cannot confine such feelings.

bibliography

General Bibliography

The following covers articles and books relating to avant-garde theater written and originally performed between 1950 and 2000. We have excluded general theoretical works not focused primarily on theater. Instead, this bibliography focuses on sources that examine avant-garde theatrical movements or national traditions, comparative criticism of avant-garde theater artists, and contributions of particular theater artists to the development of avant-garde theater as a whole.

Adorno, Theodor. *The Culture Industry*. London: Routledge, 2001.

Ahrends, Günter. "The Nature and Function of Cruelty in the Theatre of Artaud and Foreman." *Forum Modernes Theater* 9.1 (1994): 3–12.

Aronson, Arnold. *American Avant-Garde Theatre: A History*. New York: Routledge, 2000.

——. *The History and Theory of Environmental Scenography*. Ann Arbor, Mich.: UMI Research Press, 1981.

Auslander, Philip. *Presence and Resistance: Postmodernism and Cultural Politics in Contemporary American Performance*. Ann Arbor: University of Michigan Press, 1993.

Aycock, Wendell M., ed. *Myths and Realities of Contemporary French Theater: Comparative Views*. Lubbock: Texas Tech University Press, 1985.

Banes, Sally. *Greenwich Village 1963: Avant-Garde Performance and the Effervescent Body*. Durham, N.C.: Duke University Press, 1993.

Barthes, Roland. "Whose Theater? Whose Avant-Garde?" *Critical Essays*. Trans. Richard Howard. Evanston, Ill.: Northwestern University Press, 1972.

Battcock, Gregory, and Robert Nickas, eds. *The Art of Performance: A Critical Anthology*. New York: Dutton, 1984.

Benamou, Michael, and Charles Carammello, eds. *Performance in Post Modern Culture*. Madison, Wisc.: Coda Press, 1977.

Benedikt, Michael, and George E. Wellwarth, eds. *Postwar German Theatre: An Anthology of Plays*. New York: Dutton, 1967.

Berghaus, Günter. *Avant-Garde Performance: Live Events and Electronic Technologies*. New York: Palgrave Macmillan, 2005.

——. *Theatre, Performance, and the Historical Avant-Garde*. New York: Palgrave Macmillan, 2006.

Berman, Marshall. *All That is Solid Melts into Air: The Experience of Modernity*. New York: Schuster and Schuster, 1982.

Bolton, Richard. "Enlightened Self-Interest: The Avant-garde in the 80s." *Afterimage* 16.7 (February 1989): 12–18.

Borradori, Giovanna. *Philosophy in a Time of Terror: Dialogues with Jürgen Habermas and Jacques Derrida*. Chicago: University of Chicago Press, 2003.

Bradby, David. *Modern French Drama, 1940–1990*. 2nd ed. Cambridge: Cambridge University Press, 1991.

Brater, Enoch, and Ruby Cohn, eds. *Around the Absurd: Essays on Modern and Postmodern Drama*. Ann Arbor: University of Michigan Press, 1990.

Braun, Edward. *The Director and the Stage: From Naturalism to Grotowski*. New York: Holmes and Meier, 1982.

Brockett, Oscar, and Robert R. Findlay. *Century of Innovation: A History of European Drama and Theatre Since the Late Nineteenth Century*. 1973. 2nd ed. Boston: Allyn and Bacon, 1991.

Brook, Peter. *The Empty Space*. New York: Touchstone, 1968.

Brook, Vincent. "Puce Modern Moment: Camp, Postmodernism, and the Films of Kenneth Anger." *Journal of Film and Video* 58.4 (2006): 3–15.

Brustein, Robert. *The Theatre of Revolt: An Approach to Modern Drama*. 1964. Chicago: Ivan R. Dee, 1991.

Bürger, Peter. "The Significance of the Avant-Garde for Contemporary Aesthetics: A Reply to Jürgen Habermas." *New German Critique* 8.1 (1981): 19–22.

——. *Theory of the Avant-Garde*. 1974. Trans. Michael Shaw. Minneapolis: University of Minnesota Press, 1984.

Calinescu, Matei. "Avant-garde, Neo-Avant-garde, Post Modernism: The Culture of Crisis." *CLIO* 4.3 (June 1975): 317–40.

——. *Five Faces of Modernity: Modernism, Avant-garde, Decadence, Kitsch, Postmodernism*. 1977. Rev. ed. London: Duke University Press, 1987.

Carr, C. *On Edge: Performance at the End of the Twentieth Century*. Hanover, N.H.: University Press of New England, 1993.

Carlson, Marvin. *The Haunted Stage: The Theatre as Memory Machine*. Ann Arbor: University of Michigan Press, 2003.

——. *Theories of the Theatre: A Historical and Critical Survey from the Greeks to the Present*. 1984. Rev. ed. Ithaca, N.Y.: Cornell University Press, 1993.

Case, Sue-Ellen. *Feminist and Queer Performance: Critical Strategies*. New York: Palgrave Macmillan, 2009.

Chase, Richard. "The Fate of the Avant-Garde." *Partisan Review* 24.3 (1957): 363–75.

Chin, Daryl. "The Avant-Garde Industry." *Performing Arts Journal* 9.2/3 (1985): 59–75.

Cleto, Fabio, ed. *Camp: Queer Aesthetics and the Performing Subject; A Reader*. Ann Arbor: University of Michigan Press, 2002.

Cohn, Ruby. *From Desire to Godot: Pocket Theatre of Postwar Paris*. Berkeley: University of California Press, 1987.

Cole, Susan Letzler. *Directors in Rehearsal: A Hidden World*. London: Routledge, 1992.

Creekmur, Corey, and Alexander Doty. *Out in Culture: Gay, Lesbian, and Queer Essays on Popular Culture*. Durham: Duke University Press, 1995.

Croyden, Margaret. *Lunatics, Lovers and Poets: The Contemporary Experimental Theater*. New York: Delta, 1972.

Deleuze, Gilles. *Essays: Critical and Clinical*. Trans. Daniel W. Smith and Michael A. Greco. Minneapolis: University of Minnesota Press, 1997.

Demastes, William W. *Theatre of Chaos: Beyond Absurdism, into Orderly Disorder*. Cambridge: Cambridge University Press, 1993.

Docherty, Brian, ed. *Twentieth-Century European Drama*. New York: St. Martin's, 1994.

Doorman, Maarten. *Art in Progress: A Philosophical Response to the End of the Avant-Garde*. Trans. Sherry Marx. Amsterdam: Amsterdam University Press, 2003.

Drain, Richard, ed. *Twentieth Century Theatre: A Sourcebook*. New York: Routledge, 1995.

Dukore, Bernard F., and Daniel C. Gerould, eds. *Avant-Garde Drama: A Casebook*. Originally published as *Avant-Garde Drama: Major Plays and Documents, Post World War I*, 1969. New York: Cromwell, 1976.

——, eds. *Dramatic Theory and Criticism: Greeks to Grotowski*. New York: Holt, Rinehart, and Winston, 1974.

Eagleton, Terry. "Capitalism, Modernism and Postmodernism." *New Left Review* 52 (1985): 60–73.

——. *The Ideology of the Aesthetic*. Oxford: Blackwell, 1990.

——. *Literary Theory*. Oxford: Blackwell, 1983.

Emigh, John. *Masked Performance: The Play of Self and Other in Ritual and Theatre*. Philadelphia: University of Pennsylvania Press, 1996.

Eng, Jan van der, ed. *Avant-Garde: Interdisciplinary and International Review*. Amsterdam: Rodopi, 1991.

Eskin, Stanley G. "Theatricality in the Avant-Garde Drama: A Reconsideration of a Theme in the Light of *The Balcony* and *The Connection*." *Modern Drama* 7 (1964): 213–22.

Esslin, Martin. *The Theatre of the Absurd*. 1961. Rev. ed. New York: Vintage, 2004.

Finter, Helga. "Antonin Artaud and the Impossible Theatre: The Legacy of the Theatre of Cruelty." Trans. Matthew Griffin. *TDR* 41 (Winter 1997): 15–40.

Fischer-Lichte, Erika. *The Show and the Gaze of Theatre: A European Perspective*. Iowa City: University of Iowa Press, 1997.

——. *Theatre, Sacrifice, Ritual*. New York: Routledge, 2005.

Fitch, Andrew. "A Fusion Avant-Garde." *Drama Survey* 5 (1966): 53–59.

Foster, Hal, ed. *The Anti-Aesthetic: Essays on Postmodern Culture*. Port Townsend, Wash.: Bay, 1983.

——. *The Return of the Real: Art and Theory at the End of the Century*. London: MIT Press, 1996.

Foster, Stephen C. *"Event" Arts and Arts Events*. Ann Arbor: University of Michigan Press, 1988.

Fuchs, Elinor. *The Death of Character: Perspectives on Theater After Modernism*. Bloomington: Indiana University Press, 1996.

Fuchs, Elinor, and Una Chaudhuri, eds. *Land/Scape/Theater*. Ann Arbor: University of Michigan Press, 2002.

Gaensbauer, Deborah B. *The French Theater of the Absurd*. Boston: Twayne, 1991.

Gaggi, Silvio. *Modern/Postmodern: A Study in Twentieth-Century Arts and Ideas*. Philadelphia: University of Pennsylvania Press, 1989.

Gerould, Daniel, ed. *Twentieth-Century Polish Avant-Garde Drama: Plays, Scenarios, Critical Documents*. Ithaca, N.Y.: Cornell University Press, 1977.

Giannachi, Gabriella, and Nick Kaye. *Staging the Post-Avant-Garde: Italian Experimental Performance After 1970*. New York: Peter Lang, 2002.

Gilman, Richard. *The Confusion of Realms*. New York: Vintage, 1970.

——. "The Idea of the Avant-Garde." *Partisan Review* 29.3 (1972): 382–96. York: Vintage, 1972.

——. *The Making of Modern Drama: A Study of Buchner, Ibsen, Strindberg, Chekhov, Pirandello, Brecht, Beckett, Handke*. 1974. New Haven: Yale University Press, 2000.

Goldberg, Roselee. *Performance Art: From Futurism to the Present*. Rev. ed. Originally published as *Performance: Live Art, 1909 to the Present*, 1979. New York: Abrams, 1988.

Gómez-Peña, Guillermo. *Dangerous Border Crossers: The Artist Talks Back*. New York: Routledge, 2000.

Graver, David. *The Aesthetics of Disturbance: Anti-Art in Avant-Garde Drama*. Ann Arbor: University of Michigan Press, 1995.

Grotowski, Jerzy. *Towards a Poor Theatre*. New York: Simon and Schuster, 1968.

Harding, James M. *Contours of the Theatrical Avant-Garde: Performance and Textuality*. Ann Arbor: University of Michigan Press, 2000.

Harding, James M. *Cutting Performances: Collage Events, Feminist Artists, and the American Avant-Garde*. Ann Arbor: University of Michigan Press, 2010.

Harding, James M., and John Rouse, eds. *Not the Other Avant-Garde: The Transnational Foundations of Avant-Garde Performance*. Ann Arbor: University of Michigan Press, 2006.

Harris, Geraldine. *Staging Femininities: Performance and Performativity*. Manchester: Manchester University Press, 1999.

Hassan, Ihab. *The Postmodern Turn: Essays in Postmodern Theory and Culture*. Columbus: Ohio State University, 1987.

Hayman, Ronald. *Artaud and After*. Oxford: Oxford University Press, 1977.

Higgings, Hannah. *Fluxus Experience*. Berkeley: University of California Press, 2002.

Hobbs, Stuart D. *The End of the American Avant-Garde*. New York: New York University Press, 1997.

Homan, Sydney. *The Audience as Actor and Character: The Modern Theater of Beckett, Brecht, Genet, Ionesco, Pinter, Stoppard, and Williams*. Lewisburg, Penn.: Bucknell University Press, 1989.

Hooker, Ward. "Irony and Absurdity in the Avant-Garde Theatre," in *Essays in the Modern Drama*, ed. Morris Freedman, 335–48. Boston: D.C. Heath, 1964.

Hopkins, David, ed. *Neo-Avant-Garde*. Amsterdam: Rodopi, 2006.

Howell, Anthony. *Analysis of Performance Art: A Guide to Its Theory and Practice*. New York: Routledge, 1999.

Hughes, Robert. "The Decline and Fall of the Avant-Garde," in *Idea Art: A Critical Anthology*, ed. Gregory Battcock. New York: Dutton, 1973, 184–94.

Hutcheon, Linda. *A Poetics of Postmodernism: History, Theory, Fiction*. New York: Routledge, 1988.

Huyssen, Andreas. *After the Great Divide: Modernism, Mass Culture, Postmodernism*. Bloomington: Indiana University Press, 1986.

Innes, Christopher. *Avant-Garde Theatre, 1892–1992*. Rev. ed. of *Holy Theatre: Ritual and the Avant-Garde*, 1981. New York: Routledge, 1993.

——. *Modern German Drama: A Study in Form*. Cambridge: Cambridge University Press, 1979.

Ionesco, Eugene. *Notes and Counter Notes*. Trans. Donald Watson. New York: Grove, 1964.

——. "Theaters of the Absurd." *Partisan Review* 56 (1989): 45–49.

Jameson, Fredric. *Postmodernism, or, The Cultural Logic of Late Capitalism*. Durham: Duke University Press, 1991.

Kaye, Nick. *Art into Theatre: Performance Interviews and Documents*. London: Harwood, 1996.

Kellner, Douglas. *Jean Baudrillard: From Marxism to Postmodernism and Beyond*. Stanford: Stanford University Press, 1989.

Kirby, Michael. *The Art of Time: Essays on the Avant-Garde*. New York: E.P. Dutton and Company, 1969.

Kirshner, Judith Russi. "The Possibility of an Avant-Garde." *Formations* 2.2 (Fall 1985): 81–103.

Kohler, Klaus. "The Establishment and the Absurd: Trends, Ideologies, and Techniques in Non-Realistic Drama from Beckett to Pinter." *Zeitschrift fur Angistik und Amerikanistik* 32 (1984): 140–52, 315–29.

Kott, Jan. "The Icon and the Absurd." *Drama Review* 14.1 (Fall 1969): 17–24.

Krauss, Rosalind E. *The Originality of the Avant-Garde and Other Modernist Myths*. Cambridge, Mass.: MIT, 1985.

Kubiak, Anthony James. *Agitated States: Performance in the American Theater of Cruelty*. Ann Arbor: University of Michigan Press, 2002.

Kuspit, Donald. *The Cult of the Avant-Garde Artist*. Cambridge: Cambridge University Press, 1993.

Lahr, John. *Up Against the Fourth Wall: Essays on the Modern Theatre*. New York: Grove, 1970.

Lehmann, Hans-Thies. *Postdramatic Theatre*. Trans. Karen Jürs-Munby. New York: Routledge, 2006.

Lyotard, Jean-Francois. *The Postmodern Condition: A Report on Knowledge*. Minneapolis: University of Minnesota Press, 1984.

——. *The Postmodern Explained*. Minneapolis: University of Minnesota Press, 1992.

Malkin, Jeanette R. *Memory-Theater and Postmodern Drama*. Ann Arbor: University of Michigan Press, 1999.

Mallan, Kerry, and Roderick McGillis. "Between a Frock and a Hard Place: Camp Aesthetics and Children's Culture." *Canadian Review of American Studies* 35.1 (2005): 1–19.

Mann, Paul. *Theory-Death of the Avant-Garde*. Bloomington: Indiana University Press, 1991.

Marranca, Bonnie. *Performance Histories*. New York: PAJ, 2008.

——. *The Theatre of Images*. New York: Drama Book Specialists, 1977.

McNamara, Brooks, and Jill Dolan, eds. *The Drama Review: Thirty Years of Commentary on the Avant-Garde*. Ann Arbor, Mich.: UMI Research, 1986.

Meyer, Moe, ed. *Politics and Poetics of Camp*. London: Routledge, 1994.

Murphy, Richard. *Theorizing the Avant-Garde: Modernism, Expressionism, and the Problem of Postmodernity*. New York: Cambridge University Press, 1999.

Orenstein, Gloria Fenman. *The Theater of the Marvelous: Surrealism and the Contemporary Stage*. New York: Peter Lang, 1995.

Plunka, Gene A., ed. *Antonin Artaud and the Modern Theater*. Rutherford, N.J.: Fairleigh Dickinson University Press, 1994.

Poague, Leland, ed. *Conversations with Susan Sontag*. Jackson, Miss.: University Press of Mississippi, 1995.

Poggioli, Renato. *The Theory of the Avant-Garde*. 1962. Trans. Gerald Fitzgerald. Cambridge, Mass.: Belknap Press of Harvard University Press, 2003.

Pronko, Leonard. *Avant-Garde: The Experimental Theatre in France*. 1962. Berkeley: University of California Press, 1966.

Puchner, Martin. "The Avant-Garde is Dead; Long Live the Avant-Garde!" *Avant Garde Critical Studies* 20 (2006): 351–68.

———. *Poetry of the Revolution: Marx, Manifestos, and the Avant-Gardes*. Princeton: Princeton University Press, 2006.

Raben, Estelle M. *Major Strategies in Twentieth Century Drama: Apocalyptic Vision, Allegory, and Open Form*. New York: Peter Lang, 1989.

Robinson, Marc. *The Other American Drama*. 1994. Baltimore: Johns Hopkins University Press, 2005.

Rogoff, Gordon. *Theatre Is Not Safe: Theatre Criticism 1962–1986*. Evanston, Ill.: Northwestern University Press, 1987.

Roose-Evans, James. *Experimental Theatre from Stanislavsky to Peter Brook*. London: Routledge, 1984.

Rorty, Richard. "Habermas and Lyotard on Postmodernity," in *Habermas and Modernity*, ed. Richard Bernstein, 161–75. Oxford: Polity, 1985.

Rose, Margaret. *The Symbolist Theatre Tradition from Maeterlinck and Yeats to Beckett and Pinter*. Milan: Edizioni Unicopli, 1989.

Roventa-Frumusami, Daniela. "The Articulation of the Semiotic Codes in the Theatre of the Absurd." *Kodikas/Code* 8 (suppl., 1982): 313–26.

Sainer, Arthur. *The New Radical Theater Notebook*. New York: Applause, 2000.

Savran, David. *Breaking the Rules: The Wooster Group*. New York: Theatre Communications Group, 1988.

Sayre, Henry M. *The Object of Performance: The American Avant-Garde since 1970*. Chicago: University of Chicago Press, 1992.

Schechner, Richard. "The Decline and Fall of the (American) Avant-Garde," in *The End of Humanism: Writings on Performance*, 13–76. New York: PAJ, 1982.

———. *Environmental Theater*. New York: Applause Books, 2000.

———. *The Future of Ritual: Writings on Culture and Performance*. New York: Routledge, 1993.

Schechner, Richard, and Willa Appel, eds. *By Means of Performance: Intercultural Studies of Theatre and Ritual*. Cambridge: Cambridge University Press, 1990.

Scheunemann, Dietrich. *Avant-Garde/Neo-Avant-Garde*. Amsterdam: Rodopi, 2004.

———, ed. *European Avant-Garde: New Perspectives. Avantgarde—Avantgardekritik—Avantgardeforschung*. Amsterdam: Rodopi, 2000.

Schneider, Rebecca. *The Explicit Body in Performance*. New York: Routledge, 1997.

Sell, Mike. *Avant-Garde Performance and the Limits of Criticism: Approaching the Living Theatre, Happenings/Fluxus, and the Black Arts Movement*. Ann Arbor: University of Michigan Press, 2008.

Shank, Theodore. *Beyond the Boundaries: American Alternative Theatre*. Enlarged edition of *American Alternative Theatre*. 1982. Ann Arbor: University of Michigan Press, 2002.

Shevtsova, Maria, and Christopher Innes. *Directors/Directing: Conversations on Theatre*. Cambridge: Cambridge University Press, 2009.

Solomon, Alisa. *Re-Dressing the Canon: Essays on Theater and Gender*. London: Routledge, 1997.

Solomon, Alisa, and Framji Minwalla. *The Queerest Art: Essays on Lesbian and Gay Theater*. New York: New York University Press, 2002.

States, Bert O. *Dreaming and Storytelling*. Ithaca: Cornell University Press, 1993.

Szabolcsi, Miklos. "Avant-garde, Neo-avant-garde, Modernism: Questions and Suggestions." *New Literary History* 3 (1971): 49–70.

Taxidou, Olga. "Actor or Puppet: The Body in the Theatres of the Avant-Garde." *Avant Garde Critical Studies* 17 (2005): 225–40.

Tharu, Susie. *The Sense of Performance: Post-Artaud Theater*. Atlantic Highlands, N.J.: Humanities, 1984.

Tomkins, Calvin. *The Bride and the Bachelors: Five Masters of the Avant-Garde*. 1968. London: Penguin Books, 1984.

Turner, Victor. *From Ritual to Theatre: The Human Seriousness of Play*. New York: PAJ, 1982.

Vanden Heuvel, Michael. *Performing Drama/Dramatizing Performance: Alternative Theater and the Dramatic Text*. 1991. Ann Arbor: University of Michigan Press, 1993.

Wolfram, Eddie. *History of Collage: An Anthology of Collage, Assemblage and Event Structures*. New York: Macmillan, 1975.

Select Bibliography

The following lists articles, book chapters, and books about the particular plays, dramatists, and theatre artists included in this anthology, organized by chapter. It is not intended to be comprehensive but rather to be a starting point for further study.

Language and Silence

Samuel Beckett

Albright, Daniel. *Beckett and Aesthetics*. Cambridge: Cambridge University Press, 2003.

Cohn, Ruby. *A Beckett Canon*. Ann Arbor: University of Michigan Press, 2001.

——. *Just Play: Beckett's Theater*. Princeton: Princeton University Press, 1980.

Essif, Les. *Empty Figure on an Empty Stage: The Theatre of Samuel Beckett and His Generation*. Bloomington: Indiana University Press, 2001.

Gontarski, S. E. "Reinventing Beckett." *Modern Drama* 49.4 (Winter 2006): 428–51.

Haynes, John, and James Knowlson. *Images of Beckett*. Cambridge: Cambridge University Press, 2003.

Kalb, Jonathan. *Beckett in Performance*. Cambridge: Cambridge University Press, 1989.

Lamont, Rosette C. "To Speak the Words of 'The Tribe': The Wordlessness of Samuel Beckett's Metaphysical Clowns," in *Myth and Ritual in the Plays of Samuel Beckett*, ed. Katherine H. Burkman, 56–72. Rutherford, N.J.: Fairleigh Dickinson University Press, 1987.

Levy, Shimon. *Samuel Beckett's Self-Referential Drama*. Brighton, U.K.: Sussex Academic Press, 2002.

Oppenheim, Lois. *Directing Beckett*. Ann Arbor: University of Michigan Press, 1994.

Richard Foreman

Richard Foreman papers, 1973–1987, Lincoln Center Library for the Performing Arts, Rose Collection.

Davy, Kate. *Richard Foreman and the Ontological-Hysteric Theatre*. Ann Arbor, Mich.: UMI Research Press, 1981.

Harries, Martin. "Richard Foreman and the Ends of an Avant-Garde." *Theatre Journal* 56 (2004): 83–96.

Sellar, Tom. "Magic Disappearances: Richard Foreman." *Theater* 32.2 (2005): 18–25.

Mac Wellman

Overmyer, Eric. "Mac Wellman's Horizontal Avalanches," *Theater* 21.3 (1990): 54–57.

Robinson, Marc. "Four Writers." *Theater* 24.1 (1993): 31–43.

Savran, David. "Interview" in *The Playwright's Voice*," 311–38. New York: Theatre Communications Group, 1999.

——. "The World According to Mac Wellman." *American Theatre* 16.2 (February 1999): 16–21.

Schacter, Beth, and Jay Plum, eds. *The Mac Wellman Journal*. New York: Sock Monkey Press, 1998.

Sellar, Tom. "Realms of the Unreal." *Theater* 32.1 (Spring 2002): 101–11.

Wegener, Amy. "Imagination that Beggars Description: Mac Wellman's Worlds." *Theatreforum* 20 (Winter/Spring 2002): 21–27.

The Ritualistic

Kenneth Brown and the Living Theatre

Beck, Julian. *The Life of the Theatre*. 1972. Pompton Plains, N.J.: Limelight Editions, 2004.

Bigsby, C. W. E. "The Violent Image: The Significance of Kenneth Brown's *The Brig*." *Wisconsin Studies in Contemporary Literature* 8.3 (1967): 421–30.

Callaghan, David. "At Home with the Living." *American Theatre* 25.3 (March 2008): 38–41.

Harding, James M., and Cindy Rosenthal, eds. *Restaging the Sixties: Radical Theaters and Their Legacies*. Essays by James M. Harding, Cindy Rosenthal, Erika Munk, and Alisa Solomon. Ann Arbor: University of Michigan Press, 2006, 27–74.

Tytell, John. *The Living Theatre: Art, Exile, and Outrage*. New York: Grove, 1997.

Suzan-Lori Parks

Brustein, Robert. "The Death of the Last Black Man in the Whole Entire World." *The New Republic* 206, no. 15 (April 13, 1992): 29–31.

Drukman, Steven. "Suzan-Lori Parks and Liz Diamond: An Interview by Steven Drukman." *TDR* 39.2 (1995): 56–75.

Rayner, Alice, and Harry J. Elam, Jr. "Unfinished Business: Reconfiguring History in Suzan-Lori Parks's *The Death of the Last Black Man in the Whole Entire World.*" *Theatre Journal* 46 (1994): 447–61.

Savran, David. "Suzan-Lori Parks," in *The Playwright's Voice*, 139–64. New York: Theatre Communications Group, 1999.

Whetmore, Kevin J., Jr., and Alycia Smith-Howard. *Suzan-Lori Parks: A Casebook.* New York: Routledge, 2007.

Disruption

Peter Handke

Barnett, David. "Dramaturgies of 'Sprachkritik': Rainer Werner Fassbinder's 'Blut am Hals der Katze' and Peter Handke's 'Kaspar.'" *The Modern Language Review* 95.4 (2000): 1053–63.

Defraeye, Piet. "You! Hypocrite Spectateur. A Short History of the Production and Reception of Peter Handke's Publikumsbeschimpfung." *A Journal of Germanic Studies* 42.2 (2006): 412–38.

Handke, Peter. *Collected Plays.* London: Methuen, 1997.

Klinkowitz, Jerome, and James Knowlton. *Peter Handke and the Postmodern Transformation.* Columbia: University of Missouri Press, 1983.

Marranca, Bonnie. "The Sprechstucke: Peter Handke's Universe of Words." *Performing Arts Journal* 1.2 (1976): 52–62.

Taubeneck, Steven A. "The Subversive Quotation as a Postmodernist Pattern." *Pacific Coast Philology* 22.1/2 (1987): 88–97.

Weber, Carl. "Handke's Stage Is a Laboratory: A Director's Notes at Lincoln Center." *TDR* 16.2 (1972): 55–62.

Tadeusz Różewicz

Baniewicz, Elzbieta. "Labyrinth of an Obscure Law: Różewicz Stirs Polish TV." *Performing Arts Journal* 13.2 (1991): 56–61.

Czerwinski, Edward J. "Tadeusz Różewicz and the Jester-Priest Metaphor." *The Slavic and East European Journal* 13.2 (1969): 217–28.

Gerould, Daniel C. "Tadeusz Różewicz: Playwriting as Collage." *Performing Arts Journal* 1.2 (1976): 63–66.

Filipowicz, Halina. *A Laboratory of Impure Forms: The Plays of Tadeusz Różewicz.* Westport, Conn.: Greenwood Press, 1991.

———. "Theatrical Reality in the Plays of Tadeusz Różewicz." *The Slavic and East European Journal* 26.4 (1982): 453.

Różewicz, Tadeusz. *New Poems.* New York: Archipelago, 2007.

———. *Reading the Apocalypse in Bed: Selected Plays and Short Pieces.* London: Marion Boyars Limited, 1999.

Różewicz, Tadeusz, and Adam Czerniawski. *They Came to See a Poet: Selected Poems.* London: Anvil Press Poetry, 2004.

Karen Finley

Carr, C. "The Fiery Furnace: Performance in the '80s, War in the '90s." *TDR* 49.1 (2005): 19–28.

Case, Sue-Ellen. "The Emperor's New Clothes: The Naked Body and Theories of Performance." *SubStance* 31.2 (2002): 186–200.

Epstein, Marcy J. "Consuming Performances: Eating Acts and Feminist Embodiment." *TDR* 40.4 (1996): 20–36.

Finley, Karen. *Aroused: A Collection of Erotic Writing*. Philadelphia: Running Press, 2001.

——. "Make Love: A Performance." *TDR* 47.4 (2003): 51–69.

——. *Pooh Unplugged: An Unauthorized Memoir*. Santa Monica: Smart Art Press, 1999.

——. *Shock Treatment*. San Francisco: City Lights, 1990.

Fuchs, Elinor. "Staging the Obscene Body." *TDR* 33.1 (1989): 33–58.

Hart, Lynda. "Motherhood according to Finley: 'The Theory of Total Blame.'" *TDR* 36.1 (1992): 124–34.

Kaye, Nick. "Telling Stories: Narrative Against Itself." *Postmodernism and Performance*. Basingstoke: Macmillan, 1994.

Lauter, Estella. "Feminist Activist Art: Losing the Edge?" *NWSA Journal* 19.1 (2007): 156–65.

Wheeler, Britta B. "The Institutionalization of an American Avant-Garde: Performance Art as Democratic Culture, 1970–2000." *Sociological Perspectives* 46.4 (2003): 491–512.

Camp

Charles Ludlam

Argelander, Ronald. "Charles Ludlam's Ridiculous Theatrical Co." *TDR* 18.2 (1974): 81–86.

Brecht, Stefan. "Family of the f.p.: Notes on the Theatre of the Ridiculous." *TDR* 13.1 (1968): 117–41.

Kaufman, David. *Ridiculous! The Theatrical Life and Times of Charles Ludlam*. New York: Applause, 2002.

Marranca, Bonnie, and Gautam Dasgupta, eds. *Theatre of the Ridiculous*. Rev. ed. Baltimore: Johns Hopkins University Press, 1998.

Roemer, Rick. *Charles Ludlam and the Ridiculous Theatrical Company*. Jefferson, N.C.: McFarland, 1998.

Copi

Senelick, Laurence. *The Changing Room: Sex, Drag and Theatre*. New York: Routledge, 2000.

Weiss, Jason. *The Lights of Home: A Century of Latin American Writers in Paris*. New York: Routledge, 2003.

Landscape

Happenings

Berghaus, Gunter. "Happening and Fluxus," in *Avant-Garde Performance: Live Events and Electronic Technologies*, 81–131. New York: Palgrave Macmillan, 2005.

Kaprow, Allan. *Assemblage, Environments & Happenings*. New York: Abrams, 1966.

——. *Essays on the Blurring of Art and Life*. Berkeley: University of California Press, 1993.

Kirby, Michael. *Happenings: An Illustrated Anthology*. New York: Dutton, 1965.

Kostelanetz, Richard. *The Theatre of Mixed Means: An Introduction to Happenings, Kinetic Environments and Other Mixed-Means Performances*. New York: Dial Press, 1968; London: Pitman, 1970.

Sandford, Mariellen R., ed. *Happenings and Other Acts*. London: Routledge, 1995.

Hélène Cixous

Cixous, Hélène. *Selected Plays of Hélène Cixous*. Ed. Eric Prenowitz. London: Routledge, 2004.

Diocaretz, Miriam, and Marta Segarra, eds. *Joyful Babel: Translating Hélène Cixous*. Amsterdam: Rodopi, 2004.

Sellers, Susan, ed. *The Hélène Cixous Reader*. London: Routledge, 1994.

Tadeusz Kantor

Kobialka, Michal. *Further on, Nothing: Tadeusz Kantor's Theatre*. Minneapolis: University of Minnesota Press, 2009.

——, ed. *A Journey Through Other Spaces: Essays and Manifestos, 1944–1990*. Berkeley: University of California Press, 1993.

Miklaszewski, Krzysztof. *Encounters with Tadeusz Kantor*. Polish and East European Theatre Archive 8. London: Routledge, 2002.

Heiner Müller

Holmberg, Arthur. *The Theatre of Robert Wilson*. Cambridge: Cambridge University Press, 1996.

Kalb, Jonathan. *The Theater of Heiner Müller*. Cambridge: Cambridge University Press, 1998.

Zurbrugg, Nicholas. "Post-Modernism and the Multi-Media Sensibility: Heiner Müller's *Hamletmachine* and the Art of Robert Wilson." *Modern Drama* 31.3 (1988): 439–53.

Martha Clarke and Charles Mee

Martin, Carol. Introduction to "Martha Clarke's *Vienna Lusthaus*: Play Text and Photo Essay." *TDR* 31: 3 (1987): 42–58.

——. Review of *Vienna: Lusthaus*. *Performing Arts Journal* 10: 2 (1986): 88–90.

Terror

Reza Abdoh

Bell, John. "AIDS and Avantgarde Classicism: Reza Abdoh's 'Quotations from a Ruined City.'" *The Drama Review* 39.4 (1995): 21–47.

——. "To Reach Divinity Through the Act of Performance: An Interview with Reza Abdoh." *The Drama Review* 39.4 (1995): 48–71.

Dasgupta, Gautam. "Body/Politic: The Ecstasies of Reza Abdoh." *Performing Arts Journal* 16.3 (1994): 19–27.

Finter, Helga, and Matthew Griffin. "Antonin Artaud and the Impossible Theatre: The Legacy of the Theatre of Cruelty." *The Drama Review* 41.4 (1997): 15–40.

Mufson, Daniel. *Reza Abdoh*. Baltimore: Johns Hopkins University Press, 1999.

Griselda Gambaro

Pottlitzer, Joanne. "Griselda Gambaro's Theatre of Violence." *Performing Arts Journal* 26.1 (2004): 103–105.

Puga, Ana Elena. "The Abstract Allegory of Griselda Gambaro's *Stripped*" (El Despojamiento). *Theatre Journal* 56.3 (2004): 415–28.

Taylor, Diana. *Disappearing Acts: Spectacles of Gender and Nationalism in Argentina's "Dirty War."* Durham, N.C.: Duke University Press, 1997.

——. Negotiating Performance: Gender, Sexuality, and Theatricality in Latin/o America. Durham: Duke University Press, 1994.

Taylor, Diana, and Roselyn Constantino, eds. *Holy Terrors: Latin American Women Perform*. Durham: Duke University Press, 2003.

Versényi, Adam. "Translation as an Epistemological Paradigm for Theatre in the Americas." *Theatre Journal* 59.3 (2007): 431–47.

Caryl Churchill

Amich, Candice. "Bridging the Global Home: The Commitment of Caryl Churchill's *The Skriker*." *Modern Drama* 50:3 (2007): 394–413.

Bahun-Rodunović, Sanja. "The History in Postmodern Theater: Heiner Müller, Caryl Churchill, and Suzan-Lori Parks." *Comparative Literature Studies* 45:4 (2008): 446–70.

Dymkowski, Christine. "Caryl Churchill: *Far Away* . . . but Close to Home." *European Journal of English Studies* 7:1 (2003): 55–69.

Holzapfel, Amy Strahler. "The Body in Pieces: Contemporary Anatomy Theatres." *Performing Arts Journal* 30:89 (2008): 1–16.

Randall, Phyllis R. *Caryl Churchill: A Casebook*. New York: Garland, 1988.

Reinelt, Janelle. "Caryl Churchill and the Politics of Style." *The Cambridge Companion to Modern British Women Playwrights*, ed. Elaine Aston and Janelle Reinelt. Cambridge: Cambridge University Press, 2000.

Select Media Bibliography

This section includes a selection of videos and DVDs by or about the work of the artists in this anthology, many of which are available for purchase from Facets or directly from distributors. The reader may also wish to check YouTube for clips from films and videos, but given the questionable copyright status of these clips, we have not referenced them below unless the original work is out of print.

Additional Film and Video

UbuWeb: Film & Video has videos available through online streaming video, with directions as to how to purchase higher quality video and DVD versions. The collection includes work by Samuel Beckett, George Brecht, John Cage, Richard Foreman, Jean Genet, Meredith

Monk, Claes Oldenburg, Robert Rauschenberg, and the Wooster Group, among others. http://www.ubu.com/film/index.html.

Reza Abdoh

The Blind Owl. Written and directed by Reza Abdoh. Glendale, Calif.: Collage Digital Video, 1996. VHS.

New York Public Library for the Performing Arts, Theatre on Film and Tape Archive has twenty-three videotapes documenting Abdoh's productions. Individual viewings may be reserved two to three weeks in advance (212-870-1642).

Cal Arts and the Walker Arts Center also have video collections of Abdoh's work.

Samuel Beckett

Beckett on Film. Produced by Blue Angel Films. New York: Ambrose Video, 2002. A 4-disc DVD set of nineteen Beckett plays turned into films by nineteen directors, including *Act Without Words*, directed by Enda Hughes. Directors include Atom Egoyan, Neil Jordan, David Mamet, Conor McPherson, Anthony Minghella, and Karel Reisz, and actors include Michael Gambon, Sir John Gielgud, John Hurt, Jeremy Irons, Julianne Moore, Harold Pinter, Alan Rickman, and Kristin Scott Thomas.

Bread and Puppet Theatre

Ah! The Hopeful Pageantry of Bread & Puppet. Directed by Tamar Schumann and DeeDee Halleck. Willow, N.Y.: Bread and Puppet Film Project, 2002. DVD.

Brother Bread, Sister Puppet. Directed by Jeff Farber. New York: Cinema Guild, 1993. VHS, DVD.

Recordings of several other performances are available on VHS from Green Valley Media <www.greenvalleymedia.com>.

John Cage

Cage Cunningham. Directed by Elliot Caplan. West Long Branch, N.J.: Kultur Video, 1991. DVD.

The Complete John Cage Edition, Volume 30: *From Zero*. Includes four films on John Cage directed by Frank Scheffer and Andrew Culver: *19 Questions, Fourteen, Paying Attention, Overpopulation and Art with Ryoanji*. New York: Mode, 2004. DVD.

John Cage: One11 with 103. Directed by John Cage. New York: Mode, 1992, 2006. DVD.

Variations VII by John Cage: E.A.T.–9 Evenings: Theatre & Engineering. Directed by Barbro Schultz Lundestam. San Francisco: Microcinema International, 1966. DVD. Includes work by Robert Whitman and Robert Rauschenberg.

Martha Clarke

Martha Clarke, Light and Dark (documentary). Directed by Joyce Chopra and Martha Clarke. PBS, 1981.

Karen Finley

A Certain Level of Denial. New York: Rykodisc, 1994. Audio CD.

East Village Compilation. Directed by Jim Covery, 1989. Includes footage of John Cage, Karen Finley, and others performing in the East Village during the 1980s.

Fear of Living. New York: Pow Wow, 1994. Audio CD. Includes her performance piece *A Constant State of Denial.*

Karen Finley Live. Directed by Timothy Greenfield-Sanders. Perfect Day Films, 2004. DVD. Includes *Shut Up and Love Me* and *Make Love.* http://KarenFinley.com.

Richard Foreman

City Archives. New York: Electronic Arts Intermix, 1978. VHS, DVD. http://www.eai.org.

Close Listening: Readings and Conversations at WPS1.Org. Three downloadable programs on MP3 with Richard Foreman, including an interview, readings from two prose works, and readings from four plays: *Bad Boy Nietzsche, Pearls for Pigs, Wake Up, Mr. Sleepy, Your Unconscious Mind Is Dead,* and *Permanent Brain Damage.* http://writing.upenn.edu/penn sound/x/Foreman.php.

The Missing Jewels of Benita Canova. Directed by Elka Krajewska. 1998, 2002. DVD. http:// www.foremanplays.com/MJ/MissingJewels.html.

Out of the Body Travel. Directed by Richard Foreman. New York: Electronic Arts Intermix, 1976. VHS, DVD. http://www.eai.org.

Richard Foreman: Sophia: The Cliffs/35+ Year Retrospective Compilation. New York: Tzadik, 2009. DVD. http://www.tzadik.com.

New York Public Library for the Performing Arts, Theatre on Film and Tape Archive has videotapes of a number of Foreman's productions: *Pandering to the Masses: A Misrepresentation* (1975); *Out of Body Travel* (1976); *Penguin Touquet* (1981); *Dr. Selavy's Magic Theatre* (1984); *Birth of a Poet* (1985); *Africanis Instructus* (1986); *Largo Desolato* (1986); *Lava* (1990); *Woyzeck* (1990); *Where's Dick?* (1990); *Eddie Goes to Poetry City* (excerpts, 1990); *Venus* (1996); *Pearls for Pigs* (1997); *Permanent Brain Damage* (1997). Individual viewings may be reserved two to three weeks in advance (212-870-1642).

Jerzy Grotowski

Grotowski's *Akropolis.* Out of print video, available from university libraries. Clips available on YouTube.

Jerzy Grotowski. The director of the Polish Lab Theater talks with theater critic Margaret Croyden (translated by Jacques Chwat, theater director). Grotowski discusses the relationship between director and actor, a playwright's function, and the idea of his "poor" theater that renounces everything not essential to the work. 1970.

Training at the "Teatr Laboratorium" in Wroclaw. Directed by Torgeir Wethal. Holstebro, Denmark: Odin Teatret Film, 1972. DVD. http://shop.odinteatret.dk.

Peter Handke

Wings of Desire. Directed by Wim Wenders. Co-written by Wim Wenders, Peter Handke, and Richard Reitinger. MGM, 1987. VHS, DVD.

Tadeusz Kantor

The Theatre of Tadeusz Kantor. Directed by Tadeusz Kantor and Denis Bablet. Chicago, Ill.: Facets, 1985. Includes extensive clips from *The Dead Class.*

Living Theatre

The Brig. Directed by Jonas Mekas. Williston, Vt.: Mystic Fire, 1964. http://www.mystic fire.com.

The Connection. Directed by Shirley Clarke. Jazz Movie Classics, 1961. VHS.

The Living Theatre Presents "Emergency." Directed by Gwen Brown. Mystic Fire, 1968. VHS. Includes scenes from Living Theatre productions of *Frankenstein*, *Mysteries*, and *Paradise Now.*

The Living Theatre: Signals Through the Flames. Directed by Sheldon Rochlin. Williston, Vt.: Mystic Fire, 1998. VHS.

Paradise Now: The Living Theatre in Amerika. Directed by Sheldon Rochlin. Williston, Vt.: Mystic Fire, 1970. VHS. Available for rental at http://www.otherfilm.org.

Resist: To Be with the Living. Directed by Dirk Szuszies and Karin Kaper. Belgium: Y.C. Aligator Film, 2003.

Robert Whitman

Robert Whitman: Performances from the 1960s. Microcinema International, 2003. DVD.

Robert Wilson

Absolute Wilson. Directed by Katharina Otto-Bernstein. New Yorker, 2006.

Deafman Glance. Byrd Hoffman Foundation, 1981. http://www.eai.org.

Einstein on the Beach: The Changing Image of Opera. Directed by Mark Obenhaus. 1986. DVD, 2007. http://www.directcinema.com.

The Making of a Monologue: Robert Wilson's "Hamlet." Directed by Marion Kessel. 1995.

Stations. Byrd Hoffman Foundation, 1982. http://www.eai.org.

Wooster Group

Electronic Arts Intermix has several videos of the Wooster Group, including *Flaubert Dreams of Travel But The Illness of His Mother Prevents It* (1986), *White Homeland Commando* (1992), *Rhyme 'Em To Death* (1993), *Where Where There There Where* (1998), *On Tour* (2001), and *The Emperor Jones* (2001). http://www.eai.org.

A DVD of House/Lights is available on the Wooster Group site: http://www.thewoostergroup .org.

index

Wilson, Robert, 2, 5, 8; *CIVIL warS*, 455, 456; collaboration with Müller, 16, 334, 455–56; collaborative projects of, 6; *Death, Destruction & Detroit*, 18, 455; *Death, Destruction, & Detroit 2*, 456, 458; design process of, 88; imagistic theater, 335; production of *Alcestis*, 333; use of simultaneous action by, 15

Wilson, Robert and Heiner Müller: *The Death of Molière*, 456

Witkiewicz, Stanislaw, 332: *The Shoemakers*, 449; *The Water Hen*, 449–50

Wooster Group, 9; collaborative projects of, 6; montage and multimedia, 462; use of technology, 4

The World in the Evening (Isherwood), 312

World Trade Center: September 11 attacks on, 441–42, 461